Praise for *The Encyclopedia of Positive Psychology*

"This wonderful encyclopedia – nearly 300 entries assembled from more than 300 contributors – is an unprecedented and valuable resource for today's (and tomorrow's) students and scholars of positive psychology."

David G. Myers, Hope College, author of The Pursuit of Happiness

"*The Encyclopedia of Positive Psychology* is the definitive source for understanding this exciting new field in its entirety. The entries cover the broad sweep of notable figures, important concepts, and curious ideas related to positive psychology. The list of contributors, too, is a vertible roll-call of insiders and experts."

Robert Biswas-Diener, Centre for Applied Positive Psychology

"A truly comprehensive overview of the dynamic field of positive psychology, written by a veritable 'Who's who' of the field. This will be an indispensable source for students of positive psychology, and a must-have for every university library."

Nicholas O. Haslam, University of Melbourne

"This is a welcome and timely compilation of the key concepts and personalities which form the new discipline of positive psychology. The entries are wide-ranging, authoritative, and accessible. *The Encyclopedia of Positive Psychology* is an invaluable resource for newcomers to the field and experts alike – informative, enjoyable, and engaging."

Felicia Huppert, University of Cambridge

"This encyclopedia is a strikingly comprehensive yet concise account of the breadth of positive psychology. It is skillfully compiled and an essential resource for those with an interest in positive psychology . . . the pages will not stay crisp for long!"

Dianne Vella-Brodrick, Monash University

"I wanted to read this one from cover to cover – not what I usually do with encyclopedias! History, personalities, organizations, concepts, theories, and controversies can all be found in this most comprehensive volume in the field to date. A must-have reference book for any positive psychology scholar, practitioner, or student."

Ilona Boniwell, University of East London

"This is a brilliant book that provides a rich picture of the field of positive psychology. The information in each entry provides a thoughtful and synthetic panorama of this emerging field. This is a book that should be on the shelves of any scholar or general reader interested in the area of well-being and positive psychology."

Carmelo Vázquez, Universidad Complutense

"We now live longer and more securely than earlier generations did. That allows us more opportunities to optimize our lives. Positive psychology helps to make the most of these chances. *The Encyclopedia of Positive Psychology* provides a comprehensive and accessible summary of this growing area of scholarship and practice."

Ruut Veenhoven, Erasmus University Rotterdam

The Encyclopedia of Positive Psychology

Edited by **Shane J. Lopez**, The Clifton Strengths Institute and Gallup

Managing Editors

Naif A-Mutawa, Kuwait University
Anne S. Beauchamp, University of Kansas
Lisa M. Edwards, Marquette University
Amy C. Fineburg, Spain Park High School / The University of Alabama
P. Alex Linley, Centre for Applied Positive Psychology, UK
Tom Rath, Gallup

The Encyclopedia of
Positive Psychology

Edited by
Shane J. Lopez

⊛WILEY-BLACKWELL

A John Wiley & Sons, Ltd., Publication

This edition first published 2009
© 2009 Blackwell Publishing Ltd

Blackwell Publishing was acquired by John Wiley & Sons in February 2007. Blackwell's
publishing program has been merged with Wiley's global Scientific, Technical, and Medical
business to form Wiley-Blackwell.

Registered Office
John Wiley & Sons Ltd, The Atrium, Southern Gate, Chichester, West Sussex, PO19 8SQ,
United Kingdom

Editorial Offices
350 Main Street, Malden, MA 02148-5020, USA
9600 Garsington Road, Oxford, OX4 2DQ, UK
The Atrium, Southern Gate, Chichester, West Sussex, PO19 8SQ, UK

For details of our global editorial offices, for customer services, and for information about how
to apply for permission to reuse the copyright material in this book please see our website at
www.wiley.com/wiley-blackwell.

The right of Shane J. Lopez to be identified as the author of the editorial material in this work
has been asserted in accordance with the Copyright, Designs and Patents Act 1988.

Wiley also publishes its books in a variety of electronic formats. Some content that appears in
print may not be available in electronic books.

Designations used by companies to distinguish their products are often claimed as trademarks.
All brand names and product names used in this book are trade names, service marks, trademarks
or registered trademarks of their respective owners. The publisher is not associated with any
product or vendor mentioned in this book. This publication is designed to provide accurate and
authoritative information in regard to the subject matter covered. It is sold on the understanding
that the publisher is not engaged in rendering professional services. If professional advice or
other expert assistance is required, the services of a competent professional should be sought.

Library of Congress Cataloging-in-Publication Data

Encyclopedia of positive psychology / edited by Shane J. Lopez.
    p.   cm.
    Includes bibliographical references and index.
    ISBN 978-1-4051-6125-1 (hardback : alk. paper)   1. Positive psychology–Encyclopedias.
I. Lopez, Shane J.
    BF204.6.E53 2009
    150.19′8–dc22   2008018464

A catalogue record for this book is available from the British Library.

Set in 11/13pt Dante by Graphicraft Limited, Hong Kong
Printed in Singapore by Markono Print Media Pte Ltd

1   2009

Contents

Labeling (Positive Effects)

Jeana L. Magyar-Moe
University of Wisconsin – Stevens Point

Labeling occurs when names are given to things categorized together based on shared characteristics. Labels can be useful in helping people to organize and simplify the world and they often serve as a shorthand method of conveying understanding. The process of labeling humans is full of inherent power as well as problems.

Negative Effects of Labeling People

Labels are very powerful, especially when applied to people. Within psychology, the most commonly used labels are diagnoses of pathology from the *Diagnostic and Statistical Manual of Mental Disorders* (DSM). Such diagnoses are considered by most to be negative, as they represent problems or deficits in functioning. Indeed, negative effects of labeling most often occur when the labels applied are negative or when they are inaccurate.

Miscommunication

Although labeling can promote discourse, it can also lead to miscommunication when the sender and receiver fail to hold the same definitions of the labels being applied. Unfortunately, most people assume that others share their meanings, thus, miscommunications go unnoticed. In addition, when labeling others, most people have the tendency to believe that the labeled person is now better understood by virtue of his or her label. In other words, the label is often erroneously seen as being very meaningful. In reality, the label is only a starting point for describing the person; full understanding of others cannot be achieved through the use of labels as verbal shortcuts.

Deindividuation

The application of labels to individuals results in the creation of ingroups and outgroups. Those who are labeled make up the *ingroup* whereas those who do not receive the label constitute the *outgroup*. When groups are labeled, most people fail to recognize the differences that exist among members within a group, and to overemphasize the differences between groups. Hence, deindividuation occurs whereby the behavior of a person who is perceived and labeled as a member of a group is overlooked or seen as less informative than if the same behavior were to be observed in that person in the absence of a label and group membership.

Prejudices may be developed through the process of labeling and creating ingroups, outgroups, and deindividuation. Indeed, prejudice occurs when people focus on one dimension of a person, label that person as part of a group based on that dimension, and then assign different, negative behaviors to people in that ingroup versus those who are part of the outgroup.

Miscommunication and Deindividuation in DSM Diagnostic Labels

The use of DSM diagnostic labels can result in unintentional error and bias on the part of clinicians, despite the popular notion that such labels serve to enhance therapist understanding of clients and to facilitate professional communications. These problems arise due to the fact that the DSM system is based on the assumption that all people who enter clinical settings are diagnosable and that there is a true dichotomy between normal and abnormal functioning. The criteria, however, for normality and abnormality are extremely vague. As such, the criteria for assigning distinct, categorical diagnostic labels are vague as well. For example, according to the DSM, fourth edition, text revision (DSM-IV-TR), one can be diagnosed with Borderline Personality Disorder if he or she meets criteria for five out of nine possible symptoms. Assume that two clients are assessed and one is found to meet the criteria for symptoms one to five and the other for symptoms five to nine. Both of these clients are labeled with Borderline Personality Disorder, yet they have only one overlapping symptom. As a result of deindividuation, most people will ignore the differences between these two people who are perceived to be members of the same ingroup while highlighting the differences between these individuals and those without the label that make up the outgroup. Indeed, the process of deindividuation may lead to dehumanization, whereby the person is seen as being equivalent to the disorder label. The conditions are ripe for prejudice and extreme biases at this point. In addition, members of the outgroup (i.e., clinicians) are more likely to pathologize the experiences of members of the ingroup (i.e., clients) and to ignore the role of environmental factors in contributing to the perceived problems of the ingroup. Such a system provides fertile ground for misunderstanding clients (research supports that people make poor decisions under conditions of uncertainty) and for transferring this potentially inaccurate client assessment to others through relying on the diagnostic label as a shortcut for communication. In addition, when psychodiagnostic labels are applied and used by those outside the psychology profession, the potential for misunderstanding and miscommunication becomes even greater.

Self-Fulfilling Prophecy

Labeling can shape the perceptions and beliefs of both those who assign labels to others, as well as those to whom the labels are assigned. In other words, labels influence how a person treats the labeled individual and even how the individual with the label comes to view him or herself. Through the self-fulfilling prophecy process, labels may be internalized and then affect behavior and motivation. This can be especially problematic when the labels applied are negative and/or inaccurate.

Self-Fulfilling Prophecy in DSM Diagnostic Labels

Diagnostic labels may skew the perception of the clinician, the client, and others who are informed about the diagnosis in such a way that all behaviors of the client are interpreted in light of the label. Information that is consistent with the deviant label (i.e., that which is negative) may be highlighted while that which is not consistent (i.e., that which is positive) is overlooked. It is possible, therefore, that a well-intentioned practitioner may develop a hypothesis about a client's functioning, gather and attend to information that supports this hypothesis, and to find support from the client who readily agrees with the assessment of the professional whom the client sees as an expert. Hence, a negative collaborative illusion is developed and internalized by both the clinician and the client which serves to effect how the clinician treats the client as well as how the client thinks about him or herself and subsequently his or her behaviors and motivations.

Positive Effects of Labeling People

Although there are many potential problems associated with labeling people, positive outcomes can be achieved through the labeling process as well. Labels can have positive effects and be very enabling when they are used to identify more than just problems or deficits in human functioning. Indeed, when strengths and resources are labeled in addition to weakness and deficits, even the labeling of psychological disorders can have positive effects. A balanced dimensioning model of labeling people has been proposed as an alternative to the traditional DSM diagnostic system.

Labeling Strengths

The application of a label to a person tends to bring with it the belief that one now better understands that person and that his or her label carries with it deep meaning. Such power is often detrimental when labeling weakness or deficits; however, when the valence of the label is changed and positive strengths and resources are being described, the power of the label is then strongly positive. Indeed, by explicitly naming human strengths, the person labeled as well as those who are informed of his or her label come to find merit in the label. Human strengths become salient when named.

Self-Fulfilling Prophecy

The self-fulfilling prophecy may come into play when people are labeled as having talents, strengths, abilities, and positive resources. Just as people who are labeled with disorders may come to internalize their negative labels, so too may people come to internalize positive labels. Just as clinicians may inadvertently change the way they treat a client based on the diagnostic label applied, so too may a clinician change the way the client is treated based on the positive label applied. Such a process may serve to further enhance the labeled strengths as the individual becomes more cognizant of his or her potential, more interested in nurturing these talents and strengths, and more confident in utilizing these skills and positive resources.

The Dimensioning Approach Alternative to the DSM Diagnostic System

In order to ensure that labels applied to people in psychological contexts result in positive effects, an alternative model to the current DSM diagnostic system has been proposed. The model consists of viewing clients as individuals whose behaviors and experiences can be charted at various places on a variety of continua. In other words, rather than determining whether the client meets inclusion/noninclusion criteria for a particular diagnostic category, practitioners assess the client on a variety of individual difference dimensions that will provide a thorough view of the specific person. Each dimension consists of a range of possible scores such that a client could fall anywhere along the continuum from maladaptive to adaptive. Clinicians are further urged to be sure that the dimensions of assessment represent the four major components of the four-front approach to assessment, namely exploration of both liabilities and assets within the person *and* his or her environment.

   The application of the balanced dimensioning approach to diagnostic assessment can counteract the many negative effects of negative labels as described previously. In addition, clinicians can capitalize on the positive effects of labeling, even when helping clients to overcome areas of problem and weakness. Indeed, the dimensioning approach provides a more balanced, well-rounded conceptualization of the client whose make-up had previously been closely linked by both the client and clinician to the presenting problem. Additionally, the labeling of assets and strengths may provide clinicians with a starting point from which to build a treatment plan and can serve as sources of motivation for clients to work from in the therapeutic treatment process.

SEE ALSO: ▶ *Diagnostic and Statistical Manual* ▶ Four-front assessment approach

Laughter

Rod A. Martin
University of Western Ontario

Laughter is a distinctive pattern of vocalization, respiration, and facial expression that accompanies the experience of humor and mirth. Many authors have commented on the oddity of this set of behaviors, noting the loud, barking noises that are emitted, the repetitive contractions of the diaphragm and associated changes in respiration, the open mouth and grimaces caused by contractions of facial muscles, the flushing of the skin, increased heart rate and general physiological arousal, production of tears in the eyes, and flailing body movements. Hearty laughter seems to take over the whole organism in an almost uncontrollable way, and is very contagious and difficult to fake. What a peculiar way for people to respond to the perception of humor!

Laughter is a universal aspect of human experience, occurring in all cultures and virtually all individuals, and the sounds of laughter are indistinguishable across cultures. Developmentally, it is one of the first social vocalizations emitted by infants, beginning at about four months of age. Cases of gelastic (i.e., laughter-producing) epilepsy in newborns indicate that the brain mechanisms for laughter are already present at birth. The innateness of laughter is further demonstrated by the fact that even children born deaf and blind laugh appropriately without ever having observed laughter in others.

Besides occurring in humans, a form of laughter is also seen in chimpanzees and other species of apes. Chimpanzee laughter has been described as a staccato, throaty, panting vocalization that accompanies the *relaxed open-mouth display* or "play face," and is emitted during playful rough-and-tumble social activities such as wrestling, tickling, and chasing games. These are very similar to the types of play activities that also accompany much of the laughter of human infants and young children. Although ape laughter sounds somewhat different from that of humans, it seems clearly to be a homologous behavior, suggesting that the evolutionary origins of laughter date at least to our common ancestor with chimpanzees, some 6 million years ago. Laughter therefore seems to have originated in social play and to be derived from primate play signals. With the evolution of greater intellectual and linguistic abilities, humans have adapted the laughter-generating play activities of their primate ancestors to the mental play with words and ideas that we now call humor.

Ethologists characterize laughter as a *fixed action pattern*, a type of ritualized and largely stereotyped behavior pattern that serves as a communication signal between members of a particular species. Charles Darwin noted that laughter is essentially an emotional display, a way of communicating to others that one is experiencing a particular emotion. Just as scowling, shouting, and clenching the fists form a set of behaviors that communicate the emotion of anger, laughter conveys the unique positive emotion associated with humor. Martin has proposed the word *mirth* as a technical term to denote this particular emotion. The more intense the emotion, the stronger the expressive display. At low levels of intensity, mirth is expressed by a faint smile, which turns into a broader smile and then audible chuckling and laughter as the emotional intensity increases. At very high intensity, it is communicated by loud guffaws accompanied by vigorous body movements, such as throwing back the head, rocking the body, slapping the thighs, and so on.

Functions of Laughter

The function of laughter seems to be primarily one of interpersonal communication. Most laughter occurs in the presence of other people rather than when alone. Many theorists have suggested that the main function of laughter, in humans as well as apes, is to signal to others that one is engaging in play, rather than being serious. When chimpanzees are playfully fighting and chasing each other, it is important for them to be able to let each other know that they are just having fun and not seriously intending to harm one another. Similarly in humans, laughter can be a signal of friendliness and playful intentions, indicating that one is in a nonserious and nonthreatening frame of mind. The laughter accompanying friendly teasing, for example, signals that a seemingly insulting message is not to be taken seriously.

More recently, researchers have suggested that the purpose of laughter is not just to communicate that one is experiencing a playful emotional state, but to actually induce this state in others as well. According to this view, the peculiar sounds of laughter have a direct effect on the listener, inducing positive emotional arousal that mirrors the emotional state of the laugher, perhaps by activating certain specialized brain circuits such as mirror neurons. Some recent brain imaging studies provide support for this view. In this way, laughter may serve an important biosocial function of coupling together the positive emotions of members of a group and thereby coordinating their activities. This would explain why laughter is so contagious.

Acoustics

The characteristic that most strikingly distinguishes laughter from other human activities is the loud and distinctive sounds that are emitted. Researchers have recently begun to study the acoustics of laughter using computer-based spectrographic procedures. The unit of analysis in these studies is the series of "ha-ha-ha" sounds that are made during a single exhalation. Such a laugh episode is referred to as a *laughter bout*, and the individual "ha" syllables are called *notes*. These studies reveal that the typical laughter bout averages between three and four notes, with a normal range of one to eight. Each note begins with a protracted voiceless aspirant (i.e., a hissing *h* sound not produced by vibration of the vocal chords), followed by a forcefully voiced vowel-like sound. Regardless of the number of notes in a bout, the duration of each note (onset-to-onset internote interval) tends to remain fairly constant, at about 200 milliseconds. The voiced segment of successive notes within an individual bout becomes progressively shorter, while the intervening unvoiced segment becomes correspondingly longer, thus maintaining the same overall duration for each note. The amplitude (loudness) of successive voiced note segments tends to decrease from the beginning to the end of a bout.

While these basic acoustic characteristics of laughter remain fairly constant, there is also a considerable amount of variability and complexity in other parameters, both within and between individuals. For example, several different types of individual laugh notes have been identified, including voiced "song-like" and unvoiced "grunt-like" and "snort-like" notes. Several of these different types of notes are often observed within a single bout of laughter, and there is little consistency within individuals in the types of notes they produce from one bout to another. In addition, the fundamental frequencies (corresponding to the perceived pitch) of laugh notes show a considerable amount of variability, both between and within individuals. Thus, while showing some degree of stereotypy, laughter may be characterized as a "repertoire of sounds" that may be combined in various ways to communicate subtle differences in emotional meanings.

Respiration and Phonation

Regardless of where the person happens to be in the normal breathing cycle when laughter begins (i.e., inspiration or expiration), it typically starts with an initial forced exhalation that brings the lung volume down to around functional residual capacity (i.e., the volume that remains after a normal expiration). This is followed by a sustained sequence of repeated, rapid, and shallow expirations which, when accompanied by phonation, produce the "ha-ha-ha" of laughter. By the end of this expiratory laugh bout, the lungs reach residual volume (i.e., the air volume remaining in the lungs after maximal expiration). Thus, laughter typically occurs at a low lung volume, forcing out more air from the lungs than normally occurs during breathing.

The predominantly expiratory respiration pattern during laughter is produced by saccadic contractions of muscles that are normally passive during expiration, including the diaphragm, abdominal (*rectus abdominus*), and rib cage (*triangularis sterni*) muscles. Respiration during laughter is also regulated by the larynx, which serves as a valve separating the trachea from the upper aerodigestive tract. In the larynx, the glottis (comprising the vocal folds) initially closes to prevent the air from being exhaled too quickly, causing a buildup of subglottal air pressure. The glottis then begins to open and close rhythmically, permitting short bursts of pressurized air to escape. Each time the glottis closes to a narrow slit, the vocal cords begin to vibrate, producing the "ha" sounds. Whenever the glottis opens more widely, it stops vibrating, and the escaping air produces the unvoiced *h* sound between each voiced note. The sound vibrations are carried through the vocal tract, whose shape amplifies or dampens various frequency characteristics of the sounds. The amount of tension on the vocal cords; position of the larynx, tongue, and jaw; shape of the mouth and lips; and even the degree of contraction of various facial muscles (all of which can be influenced by the person's current emotional state) further affect the sound quality of the laughter.

Facial Expressions

Studies of the facial expressions accompanying smiling and laughter have found only one pattern that is reliably associated with genuine enjoyment or amusement. This facial expression has been named the *Duchenne display*, after the French anatomist who first identified it in 1862. Other facial expressions are associated with feigned amusement or the presence of negative emotions such as embarrassment or anxiety mixed with the enjoyment. The Duchenne display involves symmetrical, synchronous, and smooth contractions of both the *zygomatic major* (the muscle in the cheeks that pulls the lip corners upwards) and the *obicularis oculi* (the muscle surrounding the eye socket that produces wrinkling of the skin at the outer edges of the eyes). Although most types of smiles involve contractions of the zygomatic major, only genuine enjoyment smiles and laughter also involve the obicularis oculi. Thus, the presence of "crow's feet" wrinkles along the outsides of the eyes is an indicator of genuine amusement.

Studies of individuals with damage to various parts of the brain indicate that Duchenne and non-Duchenne facial expressions are controlled by two different pathways in the brain. Non-Duchenne smiling and laughter are controlled by voluntary motor areas in the cortex, whereas the Duchenne display is controlled by subcortical emotion-related regions in the basal ganglia, limbic system, and brainstem. Thus, non-Duchenne laughter is subject to voluntary control, whereas Duchenne laughter is emotional, involuntary, and difficult to fake.

Autonomic and Visceral Concomitants

Like other emotions, the emotion of mirth that is expressed by laughter also produces changes in many parts of the body via the autonomic nervous system and endocrine (hormone) system. Studies of the bodily effects of mirth indicate activation of the sympathetic-adrenal-medullary (SAM) system, the well-known fight-or-flight response of adrenaline and noradrenaline secretion under the control of the hypothalamus and sympathetic nervous system. This system, which is also involved in stress-related emotional responses such as fear and anger, produces increases in heart rate, blood pressure, muscle tension, sweating, and so on. In addition, extended periods of mirth are associated with activation of the hypothalamic-pituitary-adrenocortical (HPA) system, the classic stress response that causes the adrenal cortex to release cortisol into the bloodstream.

It may seem puzzling that the positive emotion of mirth is accompanied by the same general pattern of physiological arousal as are stress-related negative emotions like fear and anger, which are known to be injurious to physical health. However, it should be noted that stress-related illnesses tend to result from chronic activation and inadequate recovery from sympathetic arousal. The more phasic, short-term arousal associated with mirth is therefore less likely to have such adverse consequences. In addition, some researchers have suggested that, although the peripheral somatovisceral changes accompanying mirth may be quite similar to those associated with negative emotions, there are likely to be important differences in the brain systems underlying these emotions, including the biochemical molecules (e.g., neuropeptides, neurotransmitters, opioids) that are produced. These in turn may have different implications for health, such as different effects on components of the immune system. The brain structures and biochemistry underlying mirth and laughter are not well understood, however, and further research is needed before we can say with confidence whether mirth and laughter have any beneficial health effects.

SEE ALSO: ▶ Evolutionary psychology ▶ Positive emotions ▶ Smiles

Leadership

Tiffany M. Greene-Shortridge and Thomas W. Britt
Clemson University

Leader emergence and effectiveness have long been of interest to researchers and practitioners alike. Research concerning leadership has concentrated on the trait characteristics that make effective leaders, the type of situation in which leaders emerge, and the importance of identifying a universal conceptualization of what leadership encompasses. As humans, we have a desire to understand why some leaders are more effective at leading teams, organizations, and countries than others who have attempted to do so and have failed. Interest in effective leader behaviors began in the 1950s and 1960s with the Ohio State University and Michigan University studies, with the focus on universal traits in leaders, and continues today with a heavier concentration on leader skills and development.

Theories of Leadership

Although there has been a vast amount of research in the leadership field, there tends to be little agreement on the definition of the construct. Indeed, leadership has been defined in terms of social exchange relationships, power and influence, personality characteristics, goals and purposes, and behavioral outcomes. Hence, our conceptualization of leadership may be confusing and somewhat perplexing. However, across most definitions of leadership, there tends to evolve a common theme that encompasses leaders as individuals who move a certain group toward a common goal or mission. The nature of this action though is rarely agreed upon by leadership researchers.

Generally speaking, there have been four major trends in leadership theory and research. Up to the late 1940s, the trait approach to leadership dominated the field. The trait approach claimed that leaders have an innate ability to lead; hence, leaders are born, they are not made. The style approach to leadership dominated the field from the late 1940s to the late 1960s, claiming that leader effectiveness depended upon leader behavior. From the late 1960s to the early 1980s however, the contingency approach took hold. The contingency approach claimed that leader effectiveness is contingent upon the situation or context that the leader is placed in. Since the early 1980s, leadership theory has focused on the "new look" of leadership, which claims that leaders inspire innovation, share and believe in a common vision, and have close social ties with others. Each of these trends is discussed in more detail below.

Trait Approach

The trait approach to leadership emphasized a search for the "great man." Leaders were believed to have specific innate traits that led them to be leaders over other individuals who may have lacked such characteristics. However, research utilizing the trait approach failed to yield any consistency among traits in individuals deemed to be effective leaders. Thus, trait theories of leaders tended to die out in the 1950s. Yet, with a renewed interest in examining leader traits, researchers in the mid 1970s began unveiling universal skills, such as persistence and vigor, which were found to be related to leadership. Today, traits predicting effective leadership include honesty, self-confidence, cognitive ability, high energy, and stress tolerance.

It is important to note that the way traits are conceptualized today may differ from the way that researchers have operationalized them in the past. In today's research, traits seem to encompass many more variables, such as behavioral patterns, than they have in the past. Thus, researchers today should be aware of the problems in treating 'trait' as an all-encompassing term, which may have negative consequences later.

Behavioral (Style) Approach

Around the late 1940s the shift in leadership theory moved from the trait approach to leadership style, which placed an emphasis on the type of behavior that leaders exhibited. With the emphasis on the behavior of leaders, the majority of research during this time concentrated on two primary concerns. The first concern was with identifying the dimensions of leadership styles, or behaviors. Second, researchers were concerned with distinguishing among these styles to identify the most important behaviors that would discriminate between effective and ineffective leaders. During this period that emphasized the behavioral approach, the Ohio State University and Michigan University studies were influential in their quest for behaviors emulated by effective leaders.

Many critics of the behavioral approach have pointed out problems with the theory, with the primary problem being the lack of situational analysis. Furthermore, measurement issues made interpretation of the findings problematic, such that results were often skewed due to leniency effects. However, the failure of the behavioral approach to acknowledge the influence of the situational context on leadership behavior and outcomes is the biggest omission of this theory. Thus, as will be discussed next, subsequent research began to take into account the importance of the environment or situation on leadership effectiveness.

Contingency Approach

Fiedler's contingency model was the first to articulate the interaction of leader traits and situational variables. More specifically, Fiedler divided the motivational structure of leaders into relationship and task-oriented groups based upon the leader's description of his/her least preferred coworker (LPC). Additionally, Fiedler examined these two types of leaders in eight different situational types. One of Fiedler's central arguments was that particular leadership styles worked best in particular situations. For example, a task-oriented leader is going to perform best in situations where subordinate ability and/or motivation is low, whereas a relationship oriented leader is likely to perform better under conditions of high subordinate motivation and ability. Fiedler's contingency model has attracted some criticism, primarily due to his utilization of the LPC scale in determining leadership style and the nature of the evidence Fiedler cites for supporting his framework.

The normative decision making model, proposed by Vroom and Yetton, is yet another contingency approach created to assist leaders in determining which type of decision procedure would be the most beneficial considering the situation at hand. The likelihood that subordinates will accept the decision, along with the quality of the decision to be made, is an important component of this model. Vroom and Yetton propose five decision procedures that could be used by leaders to ensure more effective decision making. These include two variations of autocratic decisions, two variations of consultative decisions, and one decision that is made jointly by the leader and the group. While this model is an improvement over Fiedler's contingency model and has received some empirical support, it is limited in its application to leadership.

Even though it has received mixed reviews, House's path-goal theory of leadership is likely to be the most influential contingency approach today. While Fiedler's model focused on the interaction of traits and situational variables, House's model focuses on the interaction of leader behaviors and the situational context. Although House initially proposed four separate forms of leader behavior (i.e., instrumental, supportive, participative, and achievement-oriented leadership), only the instrumental and supportive leadership behaviors have been tested. The lack of full examination of this model may be one reason for its mixed reviews. Yet, despite these mixed reviews, House is credited for the theory behind his framework, which assumes that leaders are effective when they use path-goal clarifying behavior with subordinates, and that subordinates are intrinsically and extrinsically rewarded for achieving their goals.

New Leadership

A new approach discriminating between transactional and transformational leaders arose in the early 1980s. This new framework approached leadership with an emphasis on inspiring, motivating, visionary, and innovative leaders. The theory behind this new approach attempts to explain how leaders gain the trust, dedication, respect and loyalty of their subordinates in order to increase performance. This "new" type of leader is often referred to as the *transformational* or *charismatic* leader.

Research has found that relationships between transformational leadership measures and performance measures are more positively correlated than transactional leadership measures and performance. Furthermore, additional research supports the notion that transformational leadership leads to unit and organizational effectiveness over and above transactional leadership. Yet, researchers warn of the possible negative effects that could be brought about by the "dark side of charisma." Negative effects such as these would include poor group decision making (i.e., groupthink), failure to plan for succession, impulsive behavior, and increased dependence upon a leader. Although some of these negative outcomes could result from transformational and charismatic leaders, it is believed that the positive effects of this new leadership will vastly outweigh the negative.

Measurement Issues in Leadership

The primary method for measuring leadership has been with survey methods that focus on leader behavior. Yet, these measures fail to take into account the situational context that is likely to moderate leader behavior and effectiveness. Furthermore, the construct of leadership has been argued to be directly unobservable.

In fact, observer ratings are often based in part on attributions, which inherently introduce error into any leader measure. However, recent work on implicit leadership theory (ILT) suggests that perceptions of leadership are based on prototypes formed from interactions and experiences with individuals. Because Lord and his colleagues have conceptualized leadership as being in the eyes of the beholder, ILT has implications for greater theory and measurement development in leadership.

In an effort to measure leadership in a quantifiable way, Bass developed the Multifactor Leadership Questionnaire (MLQ), which includes scales of transformational and transactional leadership. Concerning its factor structure, the MLQ has received both criticism and support. In response to these criticisms, the number of scales used in the MLQ has been modified. Avolio has found support for the original model proposed by Bass, as compared to eight other models that were tested. While efforts like this have made measuring leadership easier, critics still point out that leadership is often influenced by the context of the situation, which is nearly impossible to measure in a survey.

Antecedents of Effective Leadership and Leader Attributes

Research on personality characteristics of leaders grew out of a focus on charismatic leadership. Max Weber is often credited with the idea of charisma, which includes a situation that is most often a crisis, an exceptional leader with a solution to end or fix the crisis, and followers that believe in the leader's solution. Furthermore, charismatic leaders are often viewed as having high self-confidence, good communication skills, and a need for influence or power. It is also believed that effective leaders possess the ability to motivate or encourage people through the use of nonverbal gestures.

While it is important to study leader attributes, it is equally important to keep in mind that different contexts may require different traits to be portrayed by effective leaders. For example, stressful situations may demand a more charismatic leader, while situations that require creativity may demand a more innovative leader. However, with that being said, it has been speculated that there are a number of generic personality traits that differentiate effective leaders from the ineffective across most situations. Those leader attributes that have found to be effective across most situations include self-confidence and a tendency to be confident in others, optimism and determination, and the ability to be nurturant and offer developmental opportunities to others.

While counterintuitive to the stereotype of what characterizes a leader, most research findings conclude that effective leaders are nurturant and developmental, not forceful, assertive or aggressive, as most would assume. In fact, Bass contends that transformational leaders promote followers to think for themselves and question the decisions of their leaders. The main point behind transformational leadership is to mold and shape followers so that they are eventually able to think on their own and solve problems collaboratively with the leader. It is thought that by encouraging followers to challenge leader decisions, tackle opportunities on their own, and to be creative in decision making, they will one day be confident and independent enough to lead on their own.

In addition to leaders portraying certain attributes, leader effectiveness is also thought to arise out of a context that promotes leader emergence. For example, most researchers would argue that leaders are born out of stressful situations in which the leader challenges the status quo and gains follower support by campaigning for beliefs consistently held by the followers. In contrast, other researchers would argue that there need not be a stressful situation for leaders to arise. In fact, some would argue that the leader only needs to carry the same vision as his/her followers. Thus, while leader emergence may not be contingent upon purely stressful situations, a crisis situation may indeed allow for an effective leader to emerge more easily than would a noncrisis situation.

Outcomes of Effective Leadership

Past research has contended that the effects of charismatic leadership are more positive than that of transactional leadership. In fact, there seems to be agreement among leadership researchers that charismatic leaders induce group cohesion and a sense of empowerment, increase performance and motivation, and decrease intragroup conflict. Furthermore, effective leaders are likely to increase followers' commitment to shared goals and also enhance follower satisfaction. However, recent analyses of multiple studies of leadership also shows that both transformational and transactional leadership are frequently related to outcomes, and that the two forms of leadership can in fact work together to promote effective group functioning.

Similarly, recent research has highlighted the importance of gaining followers' social and personal identification. It has been argued that while leaders influence the attitudes and behaviors of their followers', leaders can have a more powerful influence through the identification of those that follow them. For example, research has found that one way leaders are able to influence their followers is through connecting with followers' self-concepts, such that the belief systems of the followers become more aligned with that of the leaders'. Furthermore, leaders can gain followers' social identification through encouraging others to identify with their group, and view membership as a privilege and important dimension of one's identity. Thus, effective leaders may be more likely to gain the personal and social identification of their followers.

Additionally, research has also examined the impact of transformational and transactional leader behaviors on organizational citizenship behaviors, or helping behaviors in the workplace. Findings suggest that transformational leadership behaviors directly influence employee trust and satisfaction, while indirectly influencing organizational citizenship behaviors, such that the relationship is mediated by followers' trust in the leader. However, transactional leader behaviors have found to directly influence organizational citizenship behaviors, rather than indirectly, like the transformational leadership behaviors. Researchers contend that the different findings between these two types of leader behaviors emphasize the importance of distinguishing transformational from transactional leadership.

Effective leadership has also been suggested to influence organizational and individual health, such that employees may be more happy and healthy when an effective leader is in charge. In alignment with the move towards positive psychology, research in positive organizational behavior suggests that leaders are now faced with the challenge of building employee strength and competence. Furthermore, it has been argued that similarly to the pursuit of the happy/productive worker, we should also be concentrating on the positive/authentic leader, which is likely to shed new light on strengths-based management.

Future Directions in Leadership

One of the most recent approaches to leadership that has garnered rapid attention among both practitioners and academics is authentic leadership. Avolio, Gardner, Walumbwa, Luthans, and May (2004) define *authentic leaders* as:

> those individuals who are deeply aware of how they think and behave and are perceived by others as being aware of their own and others' values/moral perspective, knowledge, and strengths; aware of the context in which they operate; and who are confident, hopeful, optimistic, resilient, and high on moral character. (pp. 802–804)

A key aspect of authentic leadership is leaders being "who they are" and being capable of harnessing the energy of followers by causing them to identify with the goals of the leader and group to which they belonged.

Research in this area is being guided by a model of authentic leadership illustrating how authentic behavior on the part of the leader results in followers being more likely personally to identify with the leader and collective (e.g., organization), which then leads the followers to experience hope, trust, and positive emotions. These positive emotional states then create the favorable work attitudes of commitment, job satisfaction, meaningfulness, and engagement, which result in the positive outcomes of performance, extra effort, and less withdrawal. The theory also represents the most direct attempt to apply basic principles of positive psychology to the area of leadership. Proponents of authentic leadership are concerned about more than followers improving the bottom line of material success. They emphasize the importance of leaders creating conditions under which followers can thrive and remain true to their underlying values, which should ultimately result in better performance and well-being among employees.

Leaders are in a unique position to influence the identities, well-being, and performance of those they supervise. Much prior research in the area of leadership has focused on ways in which leaders elicit optimal performance in followers as a function of particular traits or employing certain behaviors in different types of situations. The recent wave of interest in transformational and charismatic leadership emphasizes the importance of leaders being able to connect in important ways to the values of followers and instilling in them the motivation to persevere in the face of obstacles for the good of the group. However, authentic leadership really represents an approach to leadership that explicitly emphasizes the importance of moral character on the part of the leader in allowing employees to thrive at work. Future work along these lines will be necessary to completely utilize the principles of positive psychology in the field of leadership.

SEE ALSO: ▶ Authenticity   ▶ Organizational psychology
▶ Positive organizational behavior   ▶ Positive organizational scholarship
▶ Transformational leadership

Reference

Avolio, B. J., Gardner, W. L., Walumbwa, F. O., Luthans, F., & May, D. R. (2004). Unlocking the mask: A look at the process by which authentic leaders impact follower attitudes and behaviors. *The Leadership Quarterly, 15,* 801–823.

Learned Optimism

Amy C. Fineburg
Spain Park High School/The University of Alabama

Learned optimism is a phrase coined by Martin Seligman, to describe the process of adapting one's explanatory style toward a more optimistic orientation. An optimistic explanatory style is the opposite of a pessimistic explanatory style. A pessimistic explanatory style has been shown to predict depression in children and adults. Seligman, in his 1992 book entitled *Learned Optimism*, suggests that an optimistic explanatory style can be learned if one currently uses a pessimistic style. If pessimism can be altered by using strategies that promote an optimistic orientation, then the strategies for learning optimism can be a treatment for depression.

The concept of pessimistic explanatory style evolved from original research conducted by Seligman and Maier in which they explored the behavior of dogs who experienced uncontrollable situations and gave up avoiding aversive stimuli. Subsequent research demonstrated that dogs taught mastery over aversive stimuli did not later become passive when exposed to inescapable shock. As this research evolved, patterns of explanatory style in humans became evident based on the learned helplessness model of depression, reformulated by Abramson, Seligman, and Teasdale. The reformulated learned helplessness model of depression proposes that people will attribute helplessness in the face of uncontrollable circumstances to a particular cause. People then determine whether the cause will have a chronic, broad, detrimental impact to future self-esteem and agency. The explanatory style patterns of people in studies of learned helplessness fall along three dimensions – global/specific (projection of cause across different situations), stable/temporary (projection of cause across time), and internal/external (projection of cause to internal traits versus external factors). Researchers eventually categorized optimists and pessimists as having diametrically opposed explanatory styles of good and bad events. For example, if an optimistic student received a bad test grade, then the test grade is viewed as not reflective of her ability in other classes (specific), independent of future test opportunities (temporary), and likely to be caused by inefficient study habits (external). For a pessimistic student, the test score is explained as reflective of overall student ability (global), predictive of future test opportunities (stable), and due to personal flaws – inability to understand material, etc. (internal). Pessimistic explanatory style seems to have an impact on the incidence of depression, and by extension, lower academic achievement. Seligman proposes that the explanatory style theory of optimism provides pessimistic people with an avenue to alter their pessimistic thinking patterns to be more optimistic, thus fostering mastery and resilience. Studies with middle-school children seem to show that retraining pessimistic thinking into optimistic thinking can significantly reduce incidence of depression.

Explanatory style research is similar yet distinct from two other lines of research. The first is attribution theory, championed by Bernard Weiner. Weiner's attribution theory seeks to explain people's behavior in terms of how people attribute the cause of personal success and failure. Weiner has developed two strands of his theory, one intrapersonal and the other interpersonal. Intrapersonal motivations are mediated by several layers of causal attributions, beliefs, and consequences. People use specific information from the past along with their own personal points of view about a situation. People also assess their achievement and personal attributes to determine if the goal can be achieved. People then determine whether the cause of the event is internal, stable, or controllable. All of these factors combine to determine whether a goal will be achieved or even pursued. Weiner's model is predicated on whether the goal is unexpected, negative, or important. If a goal is achieved, people do not spend the time determining cause. They simply remain happy. Unexpected outcomes lead to contemplation, which then lead to developing alternative action plans when the situation returns. Interpersonal motivations hinge on the attribution of responsibility for an action. If a person attributes responsibility to another for a controllable negative outcome, he or she will become angry and seek retribution, retaliation, or condemnation or neglect the responsible party. If the person attributes a lack of responsibility for a controllable negative outcome, sympathy will be the predominate emotion leading to helping others. Weiner's theory closely ties to Seligman's explanatory style theory of learned optimism. While Weiner's theory activates only when a negative outcome is experienced, Seligman's theory explores how both good and bad outcomes are explained. Seligman's theory more directly follows a positive psychology paradigm since it focuses on both good and bad outcomes rather than just negative ones. Another area of departure between Weiner and Seligman involves the internal/external attribution of cause. Weiner discusses lack of effort as an internal, unstable dimension of behavior. Therefore, if a person attributes a failure to lack of effort, he or she will experience lowered self-esteem. The expectation of success in the future is not decreased, but feelings of guilt are increased. Seligman discusses lack of effort as an external, unstable component that shields the person from negative feelings about failure. Therefore, if a person explains failure due to lack of effort, he or she will not have a lowered self-esteem since future effort can be modified to ensure success. The feelings of guilt in Weiner's theory are contrasted by feelings of empowerment in Seligman's theory for the same outcome. The distinctions between these two theories are still being explored.

A second line of research related to learned optimism is *dispositional optimism*, coined by Scheier and Carver. Dispositional optimism is a trait referring to generalized expectancy outcomes that determine whether people will continue to work toward a goal or give up. Scheier and Carver's research focuses on general rather than specific expectations since people do not have advanced knowledge of specific stressors and experience general stress in life over time. Scheier and Carver study how an optimistic orientation, a belief that good things will happen in general, affects physical well-being. Their research has shown that people with dispositional optimism recover more quickly than those who expect bad things happen to them. This line of research is similar to Seligman's learned optimism in that both use similar terminology and explore the relationship between optimism and physical health. Seligman and Scheier and Carver deviate in their respective definitions of optimism and whether or not it can be adapted. Seligman proposes that explanatory style is learned and malleable, whereas Scheier and Carver advocate that optimism is dispositional and stable. The distinctions between these two uses of the term optimism need to be further explored. Both constructs reveal health and psychological benefits, but the mechanisms that lead to those benefits are quite distinct. Whether Seligman's learned optimism and Scheier and Carver's dispositional optimism are different concepts or different aspects of the same concept is still unclear.

Several studies show the impact of pessimistic explanatory style when people are presented with failure. Seligman and Schulman demonstrated that optimistic insurance salespeople were more likely to stay in the field longer than pessimistic ones. Seligman, Nolen-Hoeksema, Thornton, and Thornton gave varsity collegiate swimmers false failure feedback regarding their performance in practice races. Optimistic swimmers subsequently performed better (by swimming faster than expected) whereas pessimistic swimmers demonstrated decreased performance (by swimming slower than expected). Martin-Krumm, Sarrazin, and Peterson provided false failure feedback to middle-school students during a basketball dribbling activity. Optimistic students were less anxious, more confident, and performed better than their pessimistic counterparts. Optimists also view past failures differently than pessimists. Sanna and Chang found that optimists used retroactive pessimism to make past failures seem inevitable. While viewing failure as inevitable is an explanatory technique of pessimists, optimists used easily generated external reasons for past failure as a means to inoculate them from the sting of failure. Even though the failure was viewed as unavoidable, the reason for the inevitability was not due to internally controlled circumstances. Overall, optimists tend to regard failure as a challenge to overcome rather than an obstacle to crumble before.

Several lines of research reveal explanatory style's relationship with the diathesis-stress model of depression. In the diathesis-stress model, pessimistic explanatory style comes into play with depression only when people experience negative life events. Life stressors and pessimistic explanatory style interact to bring about the onset and maintenance of depressive symptoms. Research indicates that explanatory style may not play as significant a role in one's behavior without the presence of a stressor, such as failure.

Current emphasis on applying the benefits of learned optimism focuses on developing interventions that help those at risk for depression via a pessimistic explanatory style. The most extensive examination of the impact of learning an optimistic explanatory style is the Penn Resiliency Project (PRP), lead by Jane Gillham and Karen Reivich and detailed in the book *The Optimistic Child*. For more than a decade, the PRP has examined how certain cognitive-behavioral strategies affect school-aged children who are at risk of depression. Students were assigned to the PRP or a control intervention program typically offered by the school. PRP students were taught such strategies as identifying negative beliefs, using evidence to contradict pessimistic explanations, being more assertive, negotiating through conflict situations, and being more relaxed when anxious. Students in PRP were half as likely to report moderate to severe depressive symptoms after two years in the program. In recent years, the PRP program has expanded to include training parents to use optimistic explanations in their own lives, which will help their children continue with a learned optimism orientation after the school-based interventions end. Seligman contends that a child's explanatory style mirrors the mother's style, so parent-focused interventions should augment school-based interventions and further decrease depression in children.

Research into learned optimism faces methodological issues. The Attributional Style Questionnaire (ASQ) is the primary assessment tool to determine explanatory style. The ASQ is a self-report measure, which can fall victim to demand characteristics in which people do not respond truthfully for a variety of reasons. While the ASQ yields reasonably high internal reliability scores, separate scores for optimism and pessimism are not easily parsed from the single instrument, making it difficult to determine the relative importance of optimistic and pessimistic styles separate from each other. Peterson and Barrett developed an Academic ASQ (AASQ) that presents more academically based situations to be used with collegiate populations. Altering the original ASQ to fit particular domains of experience seems to yield more accurate assessments of explanatory style in different situations, although these claims need further validation. Finally, the role of an optimistic style in success needs to be clarified. Some studies seem to indicate that pessimistic students might actually perform better than their optimistic counterparts. This conundrum needs to be explored further to determine the exact role of optimism in a successful life.

SEE ALSO: ▶ Attribution theory   ▶ Optimism   ▶ Resilience
▶ Seligman, Martin

Life Coaching

Carol Kauffman[a] and Jordan Silberman[b]
[a]*Harvard Medical School;* [b]*Children's Hospital of Philadelphia*

Life coaching is a partnership through which coaches help clients to achieve goals, overcome challenges, and enhance well-being. While the purpose of therapy is to heal the patient, the purpose of coaching is to help the client design and live the best life possible. Coaches work with individuals, couples, or groups and interact with clients through face-to-face meetings, telephone conversations, or Internet discussions. The coaching field has been called a "natural home" for positive psychology (PP) because it provides an ideal medium for applying the principles of positive psychological science.

In recent years, coaching has changed both in its popularity and in the extent to which it is based on empirical evidence. The number of professional coaches and coaching clients has surged; tens of thousands of people now make their livings as coaches, or integrate coaching practices into their professions. Many of the early coaches began their work by using interventions that, although potentially effective, were not empirically tested. The life coaching field emerged from the human potential movement, and, when the field was younger, successes were often self-proclaimed or based on unrepresentative anecdotal accounts. As the profession moves from the first to the second generation of practitioners, it is outgrowing its dependence on gurus and focusing more on reliable, rigorous, scientific evidence. A recent definition of coaching psychology suggests that it is "grounded in established adult learning or psychological approaches," alluding to the scientific underpinnings that are becoming an increasingly integral part of coaching practice (Palmer & Whybrow, 2005, p. 7). The transition to a more evidence-based paradigm, in fact, has come to fruition in the newly-defined subfield of PP coaching. After providing an orientation to coaching, this article will discuss how the field can be enhanced by assessments, theories, and interventions that have been developed through the science of PP.

Life Coaching: A Brief Introduction

Life coaching involves more than just achieving goals. Clients develop awareness of their values and aspirations through coach-guided and self-directed learning processes, and strive to transform their lives such that their daily activities reflect these values and aspirations. The coaching process also involves overcoming challenges by applying strengths, improving work performance, and enhancing psychological well-being.

An effective coaching relationship is essential to achieving these aims. Gable and Haidt (2005) have defined PP as "the study of the conditions and processes that contribute to the flourishing or optimal functioning of people, groups, and institutions" (p. 104), and a solid coaching relationship is one example of a condition that helps people to flourish. While medicine and psychotherapy use a hierarchical "expert model," coaching utilizes an egalitarian, "coactive" model. Coach and client "design a relationship" that serves the client's ultimate agenda. Designing optimal coaching relationships, and using these relationships to provide outstanding coaching, requires that coaches develop competencies including: active listening, powerful questioning, creating awareness, designing actions, goal setting, and managing accountability.

A typical coaching session might include a lively dialogue designed to heighten awareness of core values, identify goals, assess how realistic those goals are, and explore gaps between who the client is and who he or she would like to become. The client-coach dyad (or group) might then develop multiple strategies for achieving goals and narrowing the aforementioned gaps. They would likely create specific learning or action plans, and then use mechanisms like cocreated accountability to ensure adherence to these plans.

Coaching sessions can be highly energizing, both for the client and for the coach. Although it has not demonstrated empirically, our experience suggests that the positive affect arising from coaching sessions often ignites an upward spiral. The increased positive affect that clients tend to experience often leads to a broadening and building of their thought-action repertoires, which may in turn help clients to achieve goals, overcome challenges, and perform more effectively. If achieving goals, overcoming challenges, and improving performance further increase positive affect, an upward spiral can ensue.

The processes of life coaching are highly concordant with the fundamentals of positive psychology. Both fields focus on core values, intrinsic motivations, and strengths. Interventions developed within positive psychology, like those developed within coaching, are intended to amplify self-efficacy, positive affect, hope, flow states, life satisfaction, and well-being. Both fields, of course, focus on more than just correcting deficiencies.

Positive Psychology Assessment, Theory, and Intervention

Incorporating PP into coaching involves thoughtful and ongoing assessment of clients, application of continually-evolving theory and research, and careful application of novel interventions. Scales developed within PP can be used to assess clients at baseline, and to monitor the effectiveness of the coaching process, as accurately as possible. Although psychological assessment might seem simple when first glancing at surveys, psychometrics is a complex science. Instruments that are applicable to coaching include the Steen Happiness Index, the General Happiness Scale, the Satisfaction with Life Scale, the Meaning in Life Questionnaire, the Positive and Negative Affect Schedule, and the Values in Action Institute Signature Strengths Questionnaire. A comprehensive catalogue and description of these assessments is outside the scope of this work, and more information on PP assessment is available elsewhere within this volume.

Many of the theories developed within PP – and the empirical findings associated with these theories – can also guide the coaching approach. Seligman's view of happiness, for example, may reveal which areas of life coaches should focus on to help clients achieve greater life satisfaction. Evidence suggests that satisfaction with life is associated more strongly with engagement and meaning than it is with positive emotion, so a coach seeking to increase a client's life satisfaction might focus on interventions that bolster engagement and meaning. C. R. Snyder's theory of hope suggests that, in order to increase clients' hopefulness, it may be useful to identify specific actions that can move clients closer to their goals, and to bolster clients' beliefs in their abilities to carry out those actions. Other theories that may inform and enhance coaching practice include Csikszentmihalyi's theory of flow experiences, Lyubomirsky's theories regarding the determinants of sustained happiness, Fredrickson's broaden and build theory of positive emotions, and numerous other PP theories.

Based on these theories, positive psychologists have developed interventions that can be invaluable for improving the coaching process. These interventions can be categorized into those that focus on increasing positive emotion regarding the past, present, and future; those designed to make individuals more engaged in their work and personal lives; and those that make life more meaningful. The *Gratitude Visit*, for example, involves connecting with positive emotions about the past (i.e., gratitude directed toward somebody who has helped you), by writing a letter of gratitude to a person who has made a difference in your life, and then reading the letter to the "gratitude recipient." Bryant and Veroff's *Savoring* interventions involve cultivating deliberate conscious attention to pleasant experiences in the present through techniques like sharing experiences with others and sensing without thinking. King, Lyubomirsky, and others use the *Best Possible Future Self* intervention that requires that people envision and write about their "ideal selves" in the future. In addition to increasing positive affect, this intervention may help to cultivate positive cognitions and optimism. Seligman has also developed numerous *learned optimism* techniques that help bolster positive emotion regarding the future. McDermott and Snyder's *Making Hope Happen* program is an intervention that helps people increase levels of hopefulness regarding future events.

Other interventions serve to enhance well-being by increasing the capacity to fully engage in activities. Creating the conditions that facilitate *flow* (e.g., a balance of challenge and skill, clear goals and feedback, etc.) in work can be harnessed to help people achieve greater engagement, and can also improve performance.

Identifying and applying signature strengths can also be used to recraft work in order to help people feel more engaged.

Finding meaning is highly associated with well-being, and involves activities that make the world a better place. Seligman (2002, p. 263) suggests that meaning is most likely to ensue from "using your signature strengths and virtues in the service of something much larger than you are." One might, for example, apply the strength of creativity to design interventions that help people lead happier lives. There are also more extensive systems that combine many PP interventions in organized and synergistic ways, such as Well-Being Therapy and Quality of Life Therapy. These are a few of the many empirically-validated PP interventions that are applicable to coaching.

The Future of Positive Psychology and Coaching

While positive psychology has elucidated many ways that coaches can work more effectively with clients, fundamental questions remain. How can clients best be matched with coaches? How can PP interventions be matched with unique clients under unique circumstances? When should clients seek psychotherapy rather than coaching, and when should psychotherapists refer their clients to a coach? How can scientist-coaches best be trained to apply the science of PP? Continued PP research will probably reveal some answers to these questions, and provide more assessments, theories, and interventions to apply within coaching contexts. As positive psychologists continue to broaden and improve the repertoire of tools that can be applied by coaches, the collaboration between PP and coaching will develop into a more mutually-beneficial partnership that will further enhance coaches' capacities to transform the lives of their clients.

SEE ALSO: ▶ Character strengths (VIA) ▶ Gratitude ▶ Hope ▶ Positive emotions

References

Gable, S. L., & Haidt, J. (2005). What (and why) is positive psychology? *Review of General Psychology, 9,* 103–110.

Palmer, S. & Whybrow, A. (2005). The proposal to establish a special group in coaching psychology. *The Coaching Psychologist, 1,* 5–12.

Seligman, M. E. P. (2002). *Authentic happiness.* New York: Free Press.

Life Satisfaction

Rich Gilman,[a] Scott Huebner[b] and Matt Buckman[a]
[a]*University of Kentucky* [b]*University of South Carolina*

Life satisfaction (i.e., cognitive evaluation of one's life based on self-selected standards) is one of the key components of happiness. The concept of happiness has shaped the thinking of some of the most influential writers. Philosophical, religious, and political treatises such as Aristotle's *Nichomachean Ethics*, Augustine's *The Happy Life*, and even the United States' *Declaration of Independence* contend that the pursuit of happiness is the ultimate goal of human existence, with the attainment of any other goal merely a means to this end. However, in spite of its prominence in the lay literature, scientific study of the nature and determinants of happiness has only recently begun.

Collectively, research indicates that happiness is not a unidimensional entity, but rather consists of frequent positive affect (emotions), infrequent negative affect and life satisfaction. Given that the affective and cognitive elements are related, albeit separable, researchers prefer the term *subjective well-being* rather than the more colloquially derived term "happiness" to reflect its multidimensional nature. It is also recommended that the components of subjective well-being be investigated separately because they have different correlates.

Life satisfaction reports incorporate objective standards such as relative income, employment status, and availability of environmental resources with more subjective impressions such as current mood states, attitudes, goals and expectations. Given the multiple standards that may be used by individuals, most studies have examined life satisfaction from a global perspective. This perspective assumes a "top-down" approach in which mean global scores presumably reflect individuals' perceptions of their life quality after taking all relevant life domains into account (e.g., relations with others, quality of living environment, etc.).

A number of important characteristics are related to life satisfaction. For example, life satisfaction judgments appear to be relatively stable, yet sensitive to change, thus facilitating researchers' abilities to monitor differences over time and in response to various life events. Further, and perhaps most important, life satisfaction is not simply a by-product of life events, but influences important life outcomes. For example, life satisfaction has been shown to predict interpersonal, educational, and vocational success as well as mental and physical health among adults. Life satisfaction has also been shown to be negatively associated with multiple risk behaviors in adolescence, including alcohol and drug use, sexual risk taking, aggressive behavior, victimization, and unhealthy eating and exercise behavior. Although differentiated from measures of psychopathology, levels of life satisfaction predict how some individuals respond to psychosocial interventions, suggesting that the construct, traditionally of interest primarily to basic science researchers, may be of import to clinical professionals (e.g., applied psychologists) as well.

Life satisfaction assessments have been used as part of the evaluation process across a variety of psychosocial, educational, and medical settings. Two of the most frequently administered measures in this regard are the *Satisfaction with Life Scale* (SWLS), which contains five items is appropriate for adults, and the *Students' Life Satisfaction Scale* (SSLS), which contains seven items and is appropriate for school-age children and adolescents. Both of these global measures yield strong psychometric properties, including high internal consistency and solid evidence of construct validity. However, global reports only partially explain variance within specific life domains. Thus, recent studies have incorporated domain-specific measures, which assume a "bottom-up" approach in which analyses of specific domains provide a differentiated analysis of factors that contribute to an individual's overall or general sense of satisfaction. Domains have been chosen based upon the age of the respondents, weightings of their importance, and the nature of the research questions. Examples of multidimensional life satisfaction measures for adults and youth can be found in works by Robert Cummins, Michael Frisch, and the current authors. As with global measures, multidimensional life satisfaction measures have demonstrated acceptable reliability and validity across a variety of ages and populations.

Correlates of Life Satisfaction

The origins of individual differences in life satisfaction have traditionally been studied by examining objective indicators such as income level, marriage status, gender, and nation of origin. Nevertheless, objective indicators together account for less than 20% of the variance attributed to life satisfaction. For example, level of income appears most strongly related to life satisfaction among countries suffering from exceedingly high rates of poverty and/or violence, but becomes less salient as per capita income increases. Based on Maslow's hierarchy of needs, it may be that once basic needs are met through stronger purchasing power and increased modernization, the effects of additional income become negligible, at least insofar as comparisons across nations are concerned. Nevertheless, within group analyses also reveals similar findings. Life satisfaction ratings also appear invariant as a function of gender and age, although the relative importance attributed to specific life domains differs depending on the age of the respondent.

Life satisfaction is less influenced by acquisition of material goods or social status (e.g., extremely wealthy or moderately comfortable, married vs. single); it is more influenced by persons' perceptions of their life circumstances. For example, it is not the amount of money that one makes but rather the perception of financial security or control that influences satisfaction; likewise, simply being married has less to do with one's satisfaction than the perceived quality of the marriage. Such cognitions are often related to dispositional characteristics, such as personality and temperament. For example, extroverted individuals who maintain positive self-efficacy beliefs report higher life satisfaction than individuals who are predisposed to emotional instability (neuroticism) and poor self-efficacy. Research with twins also reveals that a significant portion of life satisfaction may be genetically determined. The extant literature thus suggests that life satisfaction reports are determined by multiple factors, including individual (e.g., genetics, personality, cognitions) and environmental factors (interpersonal relationships, cultural differences).

Current Emphasis on Life Satisfaction: The Homeostatic Set Point

One of the more recent findings in life satisfaction research is that contrary to public opinions, most people report a moderately high level of satisfaction regardless of nationality, group membership, or life circumstance. These findings, taken together with the genetic studies, suggest evidence for a homeostatic "set point," which for most individuals is likely located at the positive end (i.e., above the neutral point) of the spectrum. Although much work remains in this area, a positive set point makes evolutionary sense given that it creates a background against which negative events are quickly perceived and addressed. Further, maintaining a positive set point allows the individual not only to be in a position to secure basic (food, shelter) and secondary needs (social support, relationships, etc), but also is fundamental to goal seeking, creativity, and adaptive coping behaviors, all of which are necessary for optimal functioning. Departures from the positive set point thus signal difficulties adapting to life experiences.

Although life satisfaction may in part be genetically determined, it can and does change in response to environmental context. Recent studies have shown that life satisfaction reports vary in response to significant fluctuations in perceived quality of marriage and employment, the amount of time spent in productive activities, and the types of goals that individuals choose to pursue. Should these perceptions or activities change, satisfaction reports change as well–at least in the short run. Indeed, studies of individuals experiencing many different types of negative life events show that life satisfaction reports plunge immediately following the event, but rebound for most individuals, often within a period of a few months. However, studies also show that life satisfaction can remain lower for years after some events, such as being laid off from work, experiencing the death of a spouse, or becoming disabled. Thus, the set point is sensitive to life circumstances rather than fixed, with various intrapersonal (e.g., coping styles, personality characteristics) and interpersonal (e.g., availability of social support) resources moderating the extent of change and time needed to return to baseline levels.

The existence of individual differences in life satisfaction and the variability of life satisfaction reports across time and circumstances suggest research and clinical implications. For example, Diener has argued persuasively for the development of national and international indexes of well-being (including life satisfaction) so that the effects of real time events occurring within and across nations and groups can be monitored. One such ongoing multinational database has provided a number of public policy implications, such as how a nation's fluctuations in economic, social, and political structures impact perceived livability and life quality among its residents. Life satisfaction research has also yielded promising clinical implications. Research with adults and youth indicates that individuals who maintain very high levels (upper 20% of the distribution of scores) of well-being (including life satisfaction) manifest a number of psychosocial benefits relative to individuals reporting average or low levels. These studies suggest that life satisfaction yields incremental advantages that may not be found even among individuals with average levels, thus serving as a key component of optimal functioning or "flourishing" among adults and youth. These studies also support calls for establishing interventions to enhance the life satisfaction of *all* individuals, not just those experiencing distress. Although clinical interventions specifically aimed at improving life satisfaction have been sparse, several interventions have yielded promising results. As the study of life satisfaction continues to be of interest to applied psychologists, it is anticipated that additional interventions will be formulated and empirically tested.

Given the wide range of correlates of life satisfaction, the usefulness of life satisfaction is apparent. Life satisfaction measures typically reflect the full range of subjective experiences, for example, from "terrible" through "delighted," allowing differentiations at the upper levels of the positive range. Researchers also have studied life satisfaction with respect to specific domains, especially satisfaction with work among adults and satisfaction with schooling among children and youth. Studies of the differential antecedents and consequences of life satisfaction differences in various domains are likely to reveal exciting new avenues for research and applications of life satisfaction research. Life satisfaction research thus promises to play an increasingly important role in the evaluation of planned and unplanned personal and environmental changes and their effects upon the quality of life of individuals and groups.

SEE ALSO: ▶ Diener, Ed   ▶ Positive emotions   ▶ Well-being

Locus of Control

Cecil Robinson[a] and Sage Rose[b]
[a]*University of Alabama;* [b]*Hofstra University*

Locus of control is a generalized expectancy about underlying causes of events in a person's life, specifically, whether causes of events are *internal* and influenced by personal action, or *external* and influenced by outside forces such as luck, fate or other people. Individuals with an internal locus of control tend to *take control* of their actions and make necessary changes to deal effectively with new life experiences. Several decades of research indicate internal control has positive benefits for many areas of one's life including increased physical and psychological health, achievement motivation, and subjective well-being. The research literature contributing to these findings is voluminous and spans many areas of psychology including clinical psychology, counseling psychology, educational psychology, health psychology, organizational psychology, psychology of religion and sports psychology. Further, the concept of control has formed the historical foundation for, or is related to, a number of many other well-known psychological constructs such as causal attribution, explanatory style, hope, learned helplessness, optimism, self-determination, self-efficacy, and self-handicapping.

The concept of locus of control has its roots in social learning theory and can be traced to research in the 1950s on typical and atypical expectancy shifts. It was made popular in 1966 by Julian Rotter through the publication of the classic locus of control scale in *Psychological Monographs*. Rotter posited that people with an internal locus are more likely to change their behavior after positive and negative reinforcement than individuals with external control perceptions because they believe they have control over the reinforcements and make the necessary changes in their behavior to affect the reinforcements. People with an external locus are less likely to change their behavior because they do not believe changes would affect the reinforcements, and instead attribute the reinforcements to chance, fate, God, or other people. Consider two students who do poorly on an exam. When asked how to improve performance on an upcoming exam, the first student responds, "I need to study harder." The second student responds, "I don't know. I was unlucky on a lot of questions." The first student demonstrated a response typical of people with an internal locus of control; their actions can influence future outcomes so they modify their actions (increase time studying) to achieve their desired outcome (better performance on an exam). The second student demonstrated a response typical of people with an external locus of control; forces outside of their control affect outcomes (luck, or lack thereof) so there is nothing to do but hope for better luck next time.

It is important to note that the concept of locus of control is also situated within expectancy-value theory. In order to increase the likelihood for reinforcements to result in behavior change, the reinforcement must be of value to the person. For example, if the first student from the previous example did not value academic success, then there is less likelihood that he or she will change behavior (e.g., study habits) to do better on future tests. Although the first student attributes poor grades to study habits (a behavior within one's control), he or she is not motivated to change study habits because grades are not of particular personal value.

Characteristics of Internal versus External Locus of Control

There is a large empirical research base about differences between individuals with internal and external locus of control. In general, research indicates that an internal locus of control is more desirable than an external locus of control. Individuals with internal control are more likely to have higher achievement motivation, tolerance for ambiguous situations, the ability to delay gratification, and the ability to resist coercion. Internal locus of control is also a buffer against self-handicapping, where individuals externalize failure by creating impediments that may explain or excuse the failure.

Internal locus of control is also positively related to subjective well-being (SWB). For example, college students with an external locus of control had lower levels of SWB than students with internal control. This relationship appears to continue across the lifespan, as additional research indicates that internal control is linked to increases in subjective well-being and positive affect throughout adulthood up to 90 years of age.

Internal control is also positively related to increased health. Examples of this relationship are evident when someone is trying to quit smoking, lose weight, is struggling with alcohol, or has arthritis, migraines, cancer, diabetes, and heart, kidney or lung disease. One example of this research examined the degree of perceived control that white male alcoholics and white male nonalcoholics had over future life events. Even though both groups had similar backgrounds and recent life experiences, alcoholics attributed less personal control over events than nonalcoholics. Alcoholics also attributed less control to themselves than to others, whereas nonalcoholics attributed more control to themselves than to others. Further, alcoholics who attributed less control to themselves than to others failed to complete treatment more frequently than alcoholics who attributed more control to themselves.

In business, leaders of companies (e.g., president, chief executive officer, chairperson of the board) tend to have greater internal locus of control. Within companies, workers with internal locus of control who are dissatisfied with their jobs are more likely to take action so that they can change jobs rather than talk about changing jobs.

Although much research demonstrates the benefits of internal control, research indicates that it is important that locus of control not be reduced to the simplistic model that internal is good and external is bad. There are instances when an internal sense of control may not be desirable. For example, individuals with internal locus of control can be less willing to take risks or work on self-improvement. Further, an individual with internal control who does not have the competence or opportunity to experience control needs to have a realistic sense of his or her influence or else can become neurotic, anxious and depressed.

Unidimensional versus Multidimensional Characteristics of Control

Rotter characterized locus of control as a unideminsional construct. That is, if a person has high internal control, then he or she by definition also has low external control. The notion that locus of control is a unidimensional construct has been challenged. Hanna Levenson proposed three independent dimensions: internality, chance and powerful others. Levenson treated chance and powerful others as separate external dimensions because external belief in more powerful others may reflect an accurate appraisal of a social or political situation, and highlights that external beliefs are not necessarily dysfunctional.

Attribution theory also challenges locus of control as a unidimensional construct. Attribution theory posits there are three causal properties to explanations of successes or failures: internal-external, stable-unstable, and controllable-uncontrollable. In attribution theory, locus and controllability are separate constructs because there are instances when an individual may attribute internal, but uncontrollable causes to events. For example, a student who thinks his or her ability affects school grades (internal), and that that ability is innate (uncontrollable) will likely not change his or her behavior to affect future outcomes. Innate ability is viewed as uncontrollable because a person cannot change genetics (it is stable). Attribution theory highlights the importance of control. Although an internal locus is still preferred, it is important to understand locus in relation to the stable-unstable dimension, and the effects of this relationship on the perceived controllability of the outcomes. Individuals who believe that they have *control* over aspects in their lives like academic achievement, physical illnesses, mental illnesses, and skill development, are more motivated and persistent, achieve at higher levels, and more likely to achieve goals than individuals with an internal locus without control.

Explanatory style, or attributional style, goes a step further than attribution theory by adding a global-specific dimension with the internal-external and stable-unstable dimensions. The global-specific dimension assesses whether an attribution affects all aspects of a person's life (global) or is limited to certain situations (specific). An example of a specific attribution is the student who attributes poor performance in math to math ability and has little control over future outcomes in math, but feels he or she has control over future outcomes in other subjects. An example of a global attribution is the student who attributes poor performance in math to an overall lack of academic ability. This student would not only feel he or she has no control in math classes, but in other academic areas as well.

Locus of Control and Other Psychological Constructs

The central role of locus of control within past psychological research is evident in the way that it has formed a basis for and has been absorbed into other psychological concepts. Locus of control explains the development of learned helplessness. It is also a historical foundation for self-determination, or the need to have a sense of autonomy to control one's life. Much like an internal locus of control, self-determination increases the likelihood that one will feel intrinsically motivated to engage in or complete a task. Research on students' perceptions of personal autonomy versus outside control has found that personal control predicted academic engagement. Internal feelings of control produce deeper engagement and higher persistence at learning activities.

Internal locus of control is related to hope, which explains individual goal attainment through perceptions of pathways and agency. Lower levels of hope are related to the perception that external factors control one's life. Research exploring health locus of control and levels of hope in Taiwanese cancer patients indicated that patients who were aware of their own diagnosis reported significantly higher levels of hope than those who were not informed of their own diagnosis. Patients who were aware of their diagnosis tended to have higher levels of internal locus of control than those who were not informed. Having an internal health locus of control was positively related to levels of hope. Other research examining outpatients with ocular melanoma and head and neck cancer emphasized the importance of locus of control as either a direct determinant of hope or a factor that buffers distress and supports coping.

An internal locus of control is also related to self-efficacy, which is the expectancy of success when completing a task. Research examining job interview performance of graduating seniors indicated that locus of causality attributions for interview outcomes moderated the relationship between interview success and interviewing self-efficacy. Other research has investigated new measurements of locus of control to incorporate self-efficacy and to investigate its relationship with motivation and academic achievement.

Current Issues and Research

An outstanding question for research, and largest methodological issue, is whether locus of control is best measured as a general or domain-specific expectancy. Research indicates that domain-specific measures of locus of control tend to be more predictive than domain-general measures, but it still remains an unresolved issue. Although research on the locus of control construct has waned since its heyday of the 1960s and 1970s, it is still a useful construct that is being used in conjunction with other constructs in research. Locus of control is being used in conjunction with constructs such as hope and self-efficacy to create models that better explain and predict behavior. Future research will likely continue the current trend and include locus of control with other constructs to examine ways to foster people's ability to take control of their lives and strive towards optimal physical and psychological well-being.

SEE ALSO: ▶ Attribution theory ▶ Learned helplessness

Longitudinal Studies

Anthony D. Ong and Thomas E. Fuller-Rowell
Cornell University

Longitudinal studies involve the collection and analysis of data over long periods of time. Unlike cross-sectional studies that only allow inferences about interindividual differences, the longitudinal approach offers information on intraindividual change. Longitudinal studies make use of prospective designs. The simplest prospective design involves panel data, in which the same individuals are interviewed repeatedly across time. In the typical longitudinal panel design: a) data are collected at two or more points in time; b) the same sample of people is interviewed at distinct points in time; and c) data from the respondents are compared across these time points to monitor patterns of change. Although longitudinal panel designs vary with respect to the composition of the sample, the number of follow-up assessments, and the intervals between assessments, such designs have two defining characteristics. First, the same research participants, who constitute the *panel*, are measured at two or more points in time (the measurement periods or *waves*). Second, at least one variable is measured at two or more waves. This is the longitudinal aspect of the data, which allows the measurement of qualitative or quantitative change within individuals from one wave to the next. In contrast to the longitudinal panel design, *cross-sectional* designs involve the assessment of research participants at only one measurement point.

Beyond the basic panel designs, other longitudinal designs that illustrate the breadth of longitudinal research include the *cohort study* and the *repeated cross-sectional* design. Cohorts consist of individuals who experience a common set of significant life events within a particular period. A birth cohort, for example, designates those who are born within a similar period. In comparison to panel studies, cohort studies follow the same individuals over two or more points in time. In addition, whereas panel studies allow the researcher to account for individual change, cohort studies aggregate data across all members of the cohort. In the repeated cross-sectional design, the data for each assessment period is regarded as a separate cross-section and the major goal is to make comparisons across periods. The major disadvantage of the repeated cross-sectional design is its inability to study developmental patterns within a cohort and to examine causal relationships. However, this design enables the researcher to examine aggregate trends during one period and to replicate cross-sectional results across periods.

The advantages of longitudinal studies are many. They allow researchers to measure change within individuals, to identify precursors of intraindividual change, and to establish causal relationships between variables. Additional advantages to the longitudinal design include the collection of prospective (rather than retrospective) data, the elimination of information duplication (background demographic data, in particular, need to be collected only once and can save interviewer time and cost), the flexibility of adding new variables after the first data collection, and the accumulation of a large number of variables, often not possible in cross-sectional designs. Finally, collection of data on individuals at three or more points enables powerful statistical modeling techniques.

One of the major goals of positive psychology is to determine factors that influence normal and optimal development. These factors may be fixed at a particular level (e.g., gender, ethnicity) or variable (e.g., physical health, emotions). Traditional statistical methods such as repeated measures analysis of variance cannot take into account the time-varying nature of covariates. The most commonly used approach to modeling change in continuous variables that allow for time-varying covariates is *growth curve models*. Growth curve models, such as hierarchical linear models, fit growth trajectories for individuals and relate characteristics of these individual growth trajectories (e.g., slope) to covariates. Because these models typically involve repeated-measures data, longitudinal designs are the design of choice when fitting growth curve models. The individual growth trajectory can be expressed as

$$Y_{ti} = \beta_{0i} + \beta_{1i} x_{ti} + e_{ti}$$

for a linear model of growth. Y_{ti} represents individual i's outcome score at time t, where $t = 1, \ldots T$; x_{ti} represents the measure of time for individual i; and β_{0i} and β_{1i} represent the intercept and slope, respectively, of linear growth for individual i. This is often referred to as the level-1 equation. The intercept and slope parameters are random effects; in other words, they may vary across individuals, as reflected in the need for the i subscript denoting individual. This leads to the level-2 equations:

$$\beta_{0i} = \gamma_{00} + u_{0i}$$

$$\beta_{1i} = \gamma_{10} + u_{1i}$$

Growth curve modeling is an appropriate technique for studying individual change because repeated measures can be considered as nested within individuals and can be represented as a two-level hierarchical model. At the within-person level, each individual's development is modeled as a unique growth trajectory. At the between-person level, the growth parameters of these trajectories become the outcome variables, which are then modeled as a function of person-level characteristics. Consider a growth trajectory of subjective well-being for individual A with intercept β_{0A} and slope β_{1A}. The level-2 equations state that individual A's intercept β_{0A} can be decomposed into two components: the grand mean of all the β_{0i}s for all individuals, γ_{00}, and β_{0A}s deviation from this grand mean, u_{0A}. Likewise, individual A's slope β_{1A} can be decomposed into two components: the grand mean of all the β_{1i}s for all individuals, γ_{10}, and β_{1A}s deviation from this grand mean, u_{1A}. Interindividual variability in intercepts is expressed in the variance of the u_{0i}s, and interindividual variability in slope is expressed in the variance of the u_{1i}s. It is possible to include predictors in addition to time (or even instead of time) in the level-1 equation, and to include time-invariant predictors in the level-2 equation.

Longitudinal studies are not without their methodological limitations, however. In addition to the time-consuming nature of longitudinal studies, the disadvantages of such designs include the possibility of selective sampling, participant survival and dropout, test-retest effects, and generation effects. These sources of error can affect the internal or external validity of the study. The first of these limitations is selective sampling. Because of the repeating nature of participation in a longitudinal study, cohort or panel studies often are not representative of the full population. In addition, selective drop-out refers to the fact that individuals who have poorer physical or mental health, or who are less motivated, will be more likely to discontinue in the study. Because the variables of interest to the investigator often involve physical and mental health, selective drop-out biases the remaining sample with respect to the variables of interest. A third problem faced by longitudinal studies involves testing effects. Participants learn from the experience of being assessed at the first wave of a study, and may perform better, for example on cognitive tests, on subsequent occasions, or answer questions differently simply because they are familiar with the issues being studied. Finally, concern about generation effects as a source of error can threaten the external validity of the longitudinal study. Because of the nature of the longitudinal design, the age effect of the study is generation specific. Findings from the longitudinal study represent results only for the age of individuals in the study and cannot be generalized to other age groups.

SEE ALSO: ▶ Change (stages of)   ▶ Successful aging

Lyubomirsky, Sonja

Ryan T. Howell
San Francisco State University

With publications focused on the topics of rumination, subjective happiness, and the mechanisms and benefits of positive emotions, Sonja Lyubomirsky's career substantially contributes to the growing science of happiness. Lyubomirsky began her academic career as an undergraduate at Harvard University (1989) where she received her AB *summa cum laude*. At Harvard, she was awarded the Faculty Prize for Outstanding Honors Thesis for the Department of Psychology (1989). She also received the prestigious National Science Foundation Graduate Fellowship (1989–92) to support her doctoral work in social psychology at Stanford University. After graduating from Stanford (1994), she began an appointment as Assistant Professor of Psychology at the University of California, Riverside, where she has continued to flourish a leader in the field of positive psychology. Currently, her research attempts to answer three questions: 1) What makes people happy? 2) Is happiness a good thing? and 3) How can we make people happier still?

What Makes People Happy?

To answer this question, Lyubomirsky has developed the influential construal theory of happiness. This proposes that to understand why some individuals are happier than others, we must understand the thoughts, goals, and behaviors that maintain happiness. For example, Lyubomirsky reports that chronically happy individuals construe life events and daily situations in ways that maintain their happiness, whereas the opposite is true of chronically unhappy individuals.

Is Happiness a Good Thing?

Lyubomirsky and colleagues recently published a comprehensive review of all studies that focused on the relation between positive affect and successful life outcomes. The review included 225 studies and comprised over 275,000 participants and confirmed that happiness appears to benefit individuals, families, communities, and societies. Specifically, the benefits of happiness include higher incomes, higher quality of work, more satisfying and longer marriages, stronger social support, better physical health, lower stress, and longer life.

How Can We Make People Happier Still?

Lyubomirsky is currently developing innovative interventions to aid individuals in sustaining and increasing happiness. The results of her most recent series of studies verified that three specific activities produced reliable happiness-boosting effects. Lyubomirsky and her colleagues found that expressing gratitude once a week, performing a wide variety of kind acts, and visualizing one's best possible self resulted in boosts in well-being for up to one month after the intervention.

Not surprisingly, Lyubomirsky's high-quality work has earned her several national awards and recognitions outside the academic community. In 2002, Lyubomirsky's research was recognized with a Templeton Positive Psychology Prize. Also, her research has been written up in dozens of magazines and newspapers. Further, she has appeared in multiple television shows, radio shows, and feature documentaries in North America and Europe. Her forthcoming trade book on happiness will be published in January 2008 by Penguin Press (North America) and by about a dozen foreign publishers.

SEE ALSO: ▶ Happiness ▶ Positive emotions ▶ Well-being

M

Marital Happiness

Frank D. Fincham
Florida State University

Marital happiness is a judgment made by a spouse that indicates the sense of well-being or satisfaction he or she experiences in the marital relationship. Ever since changing social and economic conditions at the end of the nineteenth century prompted concern about the breakdown of the family, social scientists have sought to understand marital functioning. The two earliest studies in this domain were on sexual behavior (predating Kinsey by a decade) and both examined its role in marital happiness. The central status accorded happiness in this nascent research area gained the attention of researchers from a variety of disciplines, including psychology, sociology, family studies and communications. To this day, what has been variously labelled marital happiness, satisfaction, adjustment, success, companionship or some synonym reflecting the quality of the marriage remains the most frequently studied aspect of marriage. This focus is perhaps not surprising because the protective effect of a happy marriage for the mental and physical health of spouses, as well as the healthy development of their children, is well-documented.

Initially researchers, mostly sociologists, paid greatest attention to identifying demographic correlates of marital happiness using large-scale surveys (the *sociological tradition*) and went on to complement this effort by examining individual differences associated with marital happiness. In reviewing 50 years of this research genre, Nye (1988, p. 315) concluded:

> early on [1939] . . . Burgess and Cottrell . . . took every individual characteristic they could think of and correlated it with marital success, producing an R of about .50. . . . Not a bad start, but we have not progressed much beyond that point in 50 years.

Not surprisingly, this approach was foregone when psychologists began to systematically study marriage in the late 1960s and 1970s. Efforts turned instead to
focus on identifying observable interaction behaviors that might underlie marital
happiness (the *behavioral tradition*). The findings of the extensive literature that
emerged on the behavioral correlates of marital happiness can be summarized in
terms of a simple ratio: the ratio of agreements to disagreements is greater than
1 for happy couples and less than 1 for unhappy couples. In addition, observational
research documented that the behavior of happily married couples is less predictable (structured) than that of unhappy spouses who tend to reciprocate one
another's (negative) behavior. Although seemingly obvious, such findings con-
tradicted the long-standing belief that happy couples are characterized by a quid
pro quo principle according to which they exchange positive behavior. Reliably
both observed and self-reported behavior account for approximately 25% of the
variance in marital happiness.

The limits of a behavioral account of marital happiness became apparent
by the 1980s at which time attention began to focus on processes that might mediate the behavioral exchanges associated with marital happiness (the *mediational
tradition*). One such process is affect and research on affect began to flourish (though
study of marital happiness as affect never took root). A simple index of affect, for
which considerable data already existed, was nonverbal behavior. For example, affect
codes are more powerful than verbal codes in discriminating happy from unhappy
couples and happy couples are distinguished from unhappy couples more by their
relatively fewer displays of negative affect, rather than by more displays of positive
affect. Other affect indices investigated include verbal reports and physiological
measures such as autonomic nervous system activity during couple interaction.
Happy couples score more highly on measures of affect-laden relationship beliefs,
such as love, affection, trustworthiness and honesty. As regards physiological
indices of affect, Gottman reports that greater correspondence in the physiological systems of spouses during interaction is inversely related to their marital
happiness. However, contradictory findings showing greater correspondence
among happy couples likely reflects the difficulty of obtaining reliable physiological data during spontaneous social interaction. Perhaps as a consequence promising hypotheses involving physiological data (e.g., that arousal prior to and during
marital interaction predict later marital happiness) have not been supported upon
further analysis.

Other potential mediators of behavior exchanges that underlie marital happiness are cognitive variables and they have also received considerable attention
from marital researchers. Most frequently investigated is the association between
attributions, or explanations for events, and relationship happiness, making it
possibly the most robust, replicable phenomenon in the study of marriage.
Happiness is associated with attributing negative relationship events (e.g., spouse
arrives home late from work) to impermanent, specific causes located outside of
the partner (e.g., s/he was delayed by traffic) and positive events to stable partner characteristics (e.g., personality traits). Alternative explanations for this

attribution–happiness association have been ruled out (e.g., depression) and these attribution patterns have been shown to not only predict responses to partner behaviors but also later levels of marital happiness as well as the trajectory of happiness over time. Marital happiness is also positively related to a number of other cognitive variables, including secure attachment models, smaller partner and ideal standards discrepancies, greater downward social comparison, memory biases that reflect negatively biased recall of the past (resulting in the belief that the marriage has improved), and self-evaluation maintenance processes that change the nature of couple communication and moderate responses to differences in decision making power.

The Need for Theory

As noted, interest in marital happiness was initiated and facilitated by practical concerns and this may be why research on marital happiness has never been heavily theoretical. As Glenn (1990) points out in his decade review, most research is justified on practical grounds "with elements of theory being brought in on an incidental, ad hoc basis" (p. 818). The relative absence of theory has had unfortunate consequences. For example, Spanier eliminated items from his influential measure when they were positively skewed thereby assuming that items reflective of marital quality approximate a normal distribution. But such items may be less critical indicators or even irrelevant to marital quality if marital quality inherently involves skewed data because spouses tend to report happy marriages. Moreover, if the outcome predicted by marital happiness is itself skewed (e.g., aggression), then a skewed predictor may be best.

The disjuncture between theory and measurement has had important consequences. First, it is not clear what most instruments used to index marital happiness actually measure. Most frequently, measures comprise a polyglot of items (e.g., subjective evaluations, behavioral reports) and responses to them are not conceptually equivalent. Typically, an overall score is computed by summing over the items but it is not clear how such a score should be interpreted. Although this problem was identified in the marital literature over 45 years ago, it remains an issue. As a result, knowledge of the determinants and correlates of marital happiness includes (an unknown number of) spurious findings that reflect overlapping item content in measures of marital happiness and measures of constructs examined in relation to it.

In response to these concerns several scholars have argued that marital happiness is best conceptualized as subjective, global evaluations of the relationship. The strength of this approach is its conceptual simplicity as it avoids the problem of interpretation that arises in many omnibus measures of marital happiness. Because it has a clear-cut interpretation, this approach allows the antecedents, correlates, and consequences of marital happiness to be examined in a straightforward manner.

Emerging Themes

One or Many Dimensions?

The above conceptualization of marital happiness has not changed the operational definition of the construct as a single, bipolar dimension. Thus, marital happiness reflects evaluation of the marriage in which positive features are salient and negative features are relatively absent whereas unhappiness reflects an evaluation in which negative features are salient and positive features are relatively absent. This view has been challenged on the grounds that positive and negative evaluations can be conceptualized and measured as separate, though related, dimensions. Data obtained with a simple measure used to capture this two-dimensional conception of marital happiness indicate that the dimensions have different correlates and account for unique variance in reported and observed behaviors and attributions independently of individual affect and omnibus measures of marital happiness. This stands in stark contrast to the widespread view, supported by factor analytic approaches, that standard measures of marital happiness reflect a single underlying dimension.

Continuum or Category?

A fundamental question that can be asked of many psychological constructs like marital happiness is whether they reflect underlying categories or an underlying continuum. Determining the underlying structure has important theoretical implications in pointing researchers towards linear vs. nonlinear models. Using recently developed taxonmetric procedures it has been shown that approximately 20% of recently married couples experience marriage in a way that may be qualitatively and not merely quantitatively different than their peers. Taxon and complement members also differed on a number of relationship variables and exhibited a different pattern of connections among marital variables.

Snapshot or Movie?

An important new development is the notion that marital happiness is appropriately conceptualized not as a judgment made at a single time point but as a trajectory that reflects fluctuations in happiness over time. Growth curve analysis that allows trajectories to be computed for individual spouses and their partners is being used increasingly in marital research and rate of change in marital happiness is being examined in relation to other variables of interest. From this perspective, marital happiness at one point in time cannot be fully understood without reference to earlier or later data points.

Context Independent or Context Specific?

The emergence of relationship science, that embraced the broader environmental context in which relationships exist, and an influential model of marriage, the vulnerability-stress-adaptation model, has focused attention on the milieus within which marriages operate, including microcontexts (e.g., the presence of children, life stressors and transitions) and macrocontexts (e.g., economic factors, perceived mate availability). Accordingly, marital processes (and by implication happiness) are thought to increase in importance to the extent that the couple experiences stress and research on contextual or ecological factors in marriage has expanded dramatically in recent years.

The Future: Consummating the Marriage with Positive Psychology

Concomitant with the rise of positive psychology as a new field of inquiry has been awareness that marital happiness is not simply the absence of unhappiness and an emphasis in public policy (at least in the USA) on "healthy" marriage. These developments have no doubt facilitated interest in larger meanings and deeper motivations about relationships, including a focus on constructs that are decidedly more positive. This has restimulated work on commitment in a marriage, a topic long emphasized but frequently overlooked in marital research. Equally important, it has introduced a number of constructs into marital research that are of particular interest to positive psychology.

A thriving literature on *forgiveness* in marriage shows that it is strongly related to marital happiness as well as several key constructs in the marital domain. Forgiveness can be seen conceptually as falling on a dimension of positive coping responses, like *social support*, another construct that is now receiving considerable attention. Not only is supportive spouse behavior related to current marital happiness, it also predicts less future marital stress, independently of conflict behavior.

In a related vein, *sacrifice* is beginning to emerge as a virtue in marriage. In the context of marriage, sacrifice refers to behavior in which one gives up some immediate personal desire to benefit the marriage or the partner, reflecting the transformation from self-focus to couple focus. Satisfaction with sacrificing for one's spouse is associated with both concurrent and later marital happiness, with attitudes about sacrifice predicting later happiness better than earlier marital happiness.

Viewing Marital Happiness through the Lens of Positive Psychology

It is apparent that a marriage has occurred recently between research on marital happiness and constructs central to positive psychology. Equally apparent is that the marriage with positive psychology has not been formally declared, let alone consummated. However, the case for consummating this marriage is strong.

Viewing marital happiness through the lens of positive psychology has implications for a more complete understanding not only of relationships but of the human condition. Marital happiness has the potential to enhance functioning and not simply protect against dysfunction. But like psychology itself, marital research has focused primarily on human dysfunction. What positive emotions, strengths and virtues correlate with marital happiness? As noted, the fledgling research relevant to this question is meagre indeed. Our inability to answer this question immediately points to the need to broaden the nomological network in which marital happiness is situated to include strengths and virtues.

Declaring and consummating the marriage with positive psychology has important practical implications and thus speaks to the motivating force that has propelled marital research. Specifically, programs designed to help couples should not be evaluated merely in terms of the prevention or amelioration of dysfunction (as is current practice) but also in terms of their ability to promote optimal functioning. How does the experience of marital happiness contribute to the good life? Indeed, the lens of positive psychology alerts us to an important but relatively unexplored issue pertaining to marital happiness, its meaning for the spouse. And, as Fincham, Stanley and Beach (2007, p. 276) point out, a focus on meaning sets the stage for "examination of transformative, rather than merely incremental, change in relationships."

Consummating this marriage is equally important for positive psychology. The individualistic bias in the broader discipline from which it sprung is also evident in positive psychology. It is hard to conceive of a fully actualized positive psychology that does not include a central focus on intimate relationships like marriage. Humans are nothing if not social animals. There is much for each party to gain from this marriage. Let the consummation begin.

SEE ALSO: ▶ Family functioning ▶ Family quality of life

References

Fincham, F. D., Stanley, S., & Beach, S. R. H. (2007). Transformative processes in marriage: An analysis of emerging trends. *Journal of Marriage and the Family, 69*, 275–292.

Glenn, N. D. (1990). Quantitative research on marital quality in the 1980s: A critical review. *Journal of Marriage and the Family, 52*, 818–831.

Nye, F. I. (1988). Fifty years of family research, 1937–1987. *Journal of Marriage and the Family, 50*, 305–316.

Maslow, Abraham

Sara K. Bridges[a] and Frederick J. Wertz[b]
[a]*The University of Memphis;* [b]*Fordham University*

Abraham Maslow (April 1, 1908–June 8, 1970) was one of the principal founders of Humanistic Psychology. He attended City College of New York and Cornell, before transferring to the University of Wisconsin where he earned his BA (1930), his MA (1931), and his PhD (1934) in psychology. While in Wisconsin he studied with Harry Harlow before being hired by E. L. Thorndike at Brooklyn College where he worked for 14 years. World War II convinced Maslow of the importance of psychology's confrontation with human problems such as the achievement of world peace. While in New York, Maslow formed relationships with Adler, Horney, Fromm and others and developed his theory of human motivation from the observation that studying healthy individuals was more logical than studying sick ones. This theory led to the third force in psychology: A psychology of health and growth which was more comprehensive than psychoanalysis and behaviorism (Humanistic Psychology). In 1951, Maslow became the Chair of Brandeis' Department of Psychology and founded the *Journal of Humanistic Psychology* (first editor Anthony Sutich) in 1961 and the Association for Humanistic Psychology (first president James Bugental) in 1963. Maslow was president of the American Psychological Association in 1968, and founded the *Journal of Transpersonal Psychology* (first editor Sutich) in 1969.

Maslow is best known for his hierarchy of needs – a theoretical/psychological approach to motivation in humans. Maslow asserted that the needs represented by each level of the hierarchy (i.e., physiological, safety, love, esteem, and self-actualization) motivate behavior when they are not met. The first four (i.e., hunger, thirst, safety, esteem) are referred to as *D* or *Deficiency needs*, meaning that one will more keenly notice when these needs are not met than when they are met. Once these prepotent, lower levels are satisfied, one can focus on higher level *B* or *Being needs* (i.e., ideals, beauty, wisdom, creativity, truth, etc). Maslow posited that partial fulfillment of one level is sufficient to allow room for growth at the next and subsequent levels. The highest level of the hierarchy is self-actualization, a termed first coined by Kurt Goldstein, that Maslow used to describe the desire to fulfill all that one has the potential to become. There are 15 characteristics of self-actualization, which requires both self-exploration and action. Maslow also studied the characteristics of "peak experiences," which are seen as momentary self-actualizing events. Maslow developed the concept of Eupsychia, the form of social organization that facilitates psychological health applied in industrial–organizational psychology. In Maslow's humanistic vision, psychological science serves the highest human values by fostering individual fulfillment and world peace.

SEE ALSO: ▶ Actualizing tendency   ▶ Humanistic psychology

Mature Defense Mechanisms

Ana C. DiRago[a] and George E. Vaillant[b]
[a]*University of Minnesota – Twin Cities;* [b]*Brigham & Women's Hospital, Harvard Medical School*

There are three broad classes of adaptive mental mechanisms. First, there are the ways in which an individual consciously elicits help from appropriate others:

namely *seeking social support*. Second, there are *conscious cognitive strategies* that we intentionally use to make the best of a bad situation. Third, there are *involuntary mental mechanisms* that distort our perception of internal and external reality in order to reduce subjective distress. For semantic consistency the *Diagnostic and Statistical Manual of Mental Disorders* (4th ed.) has labeled these mental mechanisms, *defenses*, and has organized them in a hierarchical Defensive Function Scale. Included within the "high adaptive level" of *DSM-IV* are the defenses: anticipation, altruism, humor, sublimation and suppression. These five adaptive mental mechanisms "maximize gratification and allow conscious awareness of feelings, ideas and their consequences" (APA, 2000, p. 752). They epitomize what is meant by positive transformations.

In many ways, the first two classes of coping are under volitional control, and therefore are of greater interest to psychology. In three ways, however, the involuntary defense or coping processes are superior to voluntary coping processes. First, they are independent of education and social privilege; second, they can regulate our perception of internal and external realities that we are powerless to change. Lastly, such processes can serve as transformative agents in the real world.

Adaptive involuntary coping mechanisms are essential to positive mental health. Defenses reduce conflict and cognitive dissonance during sudden *changes* in internal and external reality. If not modified, such sudden changes result in anxiety and/or depression. First, such mechanisms can restore psychological homeostasis by ignoring or deflecting sudden increases in affect. Second, such mechanisms can provide a mental time out to mitigate changes in reality and self-image, which cannot be immediately integrated – for example, after major surgery or promotion. Third, such mechanisms help cope with irresolvable conflict with important people, living or dead. Finally, these mechanisms soften conflicts of conscience – for example, after putting a parent in a nursing home. In short, defenses shield us from sudden changes in affect, reality, relationships or conscience.

For many years "defense mechanisms" have been deservedly unpopular in experimental psychology due to difficulty in empirical verification. Over the past 20 years, the idea of "involuntary" adaptation has reentered the literature of cognitive psychology under such rubrics as "hardiness," "self-deception," "emotional coping," and "illusion." Defense mechanisms are clearly as important in reducing anxiety from cognitive dissonance as they are in minimizing anxiety from conflict between conscience and impulse. In recent years experimental strategies for studying defense mechanisms have improved. Recently, the *DSM-IV* has offered a terminology, a glossary and a tentative diagnostic axis to provide a common language.

In order to overcome subjectivity, reliability of defense recognition requires objective longitudinal evidence. Using "triangulation" of real symptoms, autobiographical report and contemporaneously assessed biographical fact to measure invisible mental process is analogous to surveyors using triangulation to assess the height of mountains they cannot climb.

In nonconflictual situations, of course, the putative adaptive mechanisms of "sublimation," "humor," "anticipation," "altruism," and "suppression" seem quite conscious and voluntary. In highly emotionally charged situations, however, such deployment of these mechanisms can be transformative and surprisingly involuntary. A delinquent for the first time "counting to ten" (suppression) while consciously examining his anger rather than impulsively punching a policeman; a mother rehearsing affectively and realistically, rather than denying, the fact that her child is dying (anticipation); a survivor of child abuse rather than abusing her own children, working in a shelter for survivors of abuse (altruism) are such examples. Such behaviors emerge with maturation as delicate transformative mental balancing acts and not as a result of good advice and self-help cognitive strategies.

Adaptive or "mature" defenses (altruism, sublimation, suppression, humor, anticipation) are common among the mentally healthy and become more salient as individuals mature from adolescence to midlife. The association of mature defenses with mental health remains robust whether "health" is measured by subjective happiness, psychosocial maturity, occupational success, richness and stability of relationships or absence of psychopathology. Individuals with brain damage (e.g., alcohol dependence, schizophrenic relapse, multiple sclerosis) replace adaptive defenses with more maladaptive mechanisms most notably projection.

The prejudice of projection and tantrums of acting out appear to others as transgressions. In contrast, doing as one would be done by (altruism), a stiff upper lip (suppression), planning for the future (anticipation), the ability not to take one's self too seriously (humor), and "turning lemons into lemonade" (sublimation) are the very stuff of which a positive psychology should be concerned. However, although closer to consciousness than defense mechanisms like projection and repression, mature mechanisms cannot be voluntarily deployed.

The transformative nature of each of five "mature" mental mechanisms can be elaborated as follows.

Altruism

When used to transform conflict, altruism involves getting pleasure from giving to others what we ourselves would like to receive. For example, victims of childhood sexual abuse sometimes pathologically cut themselves (turn anger against the self), or abuse children (acting out) or use "neurotic" compromises such as becoming frigid (reaction formation). Alternatively, some victims work in shelters for battered women and in support groups or hotlines for abuse victims. Often, altruism is an adaptive outgrowth of the defense of reaction formation, a mechanism that can maladaptively make the subjects' desires all bad and the needs of others all good. Using reaction formation, an ex-drinker who suddenly declares drinking as a filthy habit annoys his friends. Using altruism, the ex-alcoholic who serves as a sponsor to a new AA member achieves a transformative process enjoyed by giver and receiver.

Sublimation

The sign of a successful defense is neither careful cost accounting nor shrewd compromise, but rather psychic alchemy. A member of a research study wrote, "I have twice the sex drive of my wife. We adjust ourselves by varying our sex play to suit each other. We believe that lovemaking should be practiced as an art!" Thus, sublimation allows an indirect resolution of conflict with neither adverse consequences nor marked loss of pleasure. Unlike the autistic fantasy of the child and schizophrenic, artists can peddle their most private dreams to others. In contrast, the mechanism of acting out – rape – dissipates the torrent of our unmodulated affect upon strangers, and reaction formation dams affect such expression completely.

Suppression

Suppression (stoicism) is not as elegant as sublimation; it has none of the humanity of altruism or humor; and is often regarded by psychotherapists as a vice, not a virtue. Suppression involves the semi-conscious decision to postpone paying attention to a conscious impulse and/or conflict. A critical difference between suppression and repression, between stoical suppression and Spartan reaction formation is the degree to which with suppression all the components of conflict are allowed to exist at least partially in consciousness. The distinction between suppression and Pollyanna's dissociation is more complex. Both the stoic and Pollyanna note that clouds have silver linings, but Pollyanna leaves her umbrella at home. Evidence that suppression is not a conscious "cognitive strategy" as many believe is provided by the fact that jails would empty if delinquents could learn to just say "No."

Anticipation

Like altruism, the use of anticipation is often voluntary and independent of conflict resolution. Rather, it is in cases of "hot cognition" that anticipation becomes an involuntary coping skill. If suppression reflects the capacity to keep a current impulse in mind and control it, anticipation is the capacity to keep affective response to an unbearable future in mind.

The defense of anticipation reflects the capacity to perceive future danger affectively as well as cognitively and by this means to master conflict in small steps. In the 1950s, as scientists began the deliberate study of healthy adaptation, Irving Janis discovered that moderate amounts of anxiety before surgery promoted adaptation. At the National Institute of Mental Health, David Hamburg and his colleagues noted the value of anticipatory mourning in parents of children with leukemia. Psychiatrists responsible for preparing Peace Corps volunteers noted capacity to anticipate affective future difficulty better predicted subsequent adaptation than by their apparent emotional stability on psychological tests.

Anticipation involves more than just the ideational work of cognitive planning. Anticipation involves both thinking and feeling about the future. For example, legendary aviators, like Charles Lindbergh and Chuck Yeager, dealt with stress as Mithradites did with poison – taking a little at a time. To have underestimated danger would have been fatal. To have exaggerated danger would have been emotionally incapacitating. Thus, they worried in advance; they made lists; and they practiced. Then, appreciating that they had prepared as well as they could, they relaxed. Like suppression and altruism, anticipation is so easy to prescribe but so difficult to do.

Humor

We all recognize that humor makes life easier. As Freud (1960) suggested, "Humor can be regarded as the highest of these defensive processes," for humor "scorns to withdraw the ideational content bearing the distressing affect from conscious attention, as repression does, and thus surmounts the automatism of defense" (p. 233). Humor permits the expression of emotion without individual discomfort and without unpleasant effects upon others. Humor, like anticipation and suppression, is such a sensible coping device that it ought to be conscious, but, almost by definition, humor always surprises us. Like the other mature defenses, humor requires the same delicacy as building a house of cards – "timing is everything." The safety of humor, like the safety of dreams during REM sleep, depends upon cataplexy. We see all, we feel much, but we do not act.

Humor keeps both idea and affect in mind. Mature humor allows us to look directly at what is painful, whereas dissociation and slapstick distracts us to look somewhere else. Much of humor is lost in the retelling and thus, it is difficult to illustrate.

Many questions remain unanswered in regard to defense mechanisms. It is unclear how mature defenses work to promote a positive psychology (enhanced ability to work, love and play) and at the same time reduce conflict and cognitive dissonance. It is yet to be determined whether adaptive defenses are inherited or whether they reflect traits that are acquired through education and maturation. Twin studies and f MRI could shed light on these unknowns. In addition, positive psychology needs to understand how best to facilitate the transmutation of less adaptive mechanisms into more adaptive ones. Existing methods include increasing social supports and interpersonal safety and facilitating the intactness of the central nervous system (e.g. rest, nutrition and sobriety). But the newer forms of integrative psychotherapies also can catalyze such change.

SEE ALSO: ▶ Altruism   ▶ Humor   ▶ Resilience

References

American Psychiatric Association. (2000). *Diagnostic and statistical manual of mental disorders* (4th ed., text revision). Washington, DC: American Psychiatric Association.

Freud, S. (1960). Jokes and their relation to the unconscious. In J. Strachey (Ed.), *The standard edition of the complete psychological works of Sigmund Freud* (Vol. 8, p. 233). London: Hogarth Press.

Meaning

Michael F. Steger
University of Louisville

Historically, one of humanity's prevailing concerns has been creating institutions, rituals, and beliefs that give life a sense of purpose, predictability, and comprehensibility. For example, religious beliefs express ideas of how and why the world came into being, cultural rituals lend predictability to the calendar year (a cultural notion itself), and the symbolism that drives language and human expression creates the disparate elements of life into an understandable whole. At a fundamental level, all of these processes can be considered efforts to identify meaning in the life around us. On an individual level, people are concerned with the purpose, predictability, and comprehensibility of each of their own lives. The psychological study of meaning in life is the study of the processes that lead to people's perceptions of purpose and comprehensibility in their lives.

Dimensions of Meaning in Life

The Presence of Meaning in Life

Meaning in life research has focused overwhelmingly on asking people whether their lives are meaningful or meaningless. This dimension of meaning in life is referred to as the presence of meaning in life, which has been defined as, "the extent to which people comprehend, make sense of, or see significance in their lives, accompanied by the degree to which they perceives themselves to have a purpose, mission, or over-arching aim in life" (Steger, in press). Those who report high levels of the presence of meaning in life are generally more satisfied with their lives and less distressed than those who report low levels.

Research also has illuminated the question of who has meaning, with highly religious people reporting the greatest presence of meaning in life. For example, nuns report higher levels of meaning in life than college students. In contrast, those who are struggling with psychological distress, such as psychiatric patients, and those who express a greater need for therapy report lower presence of meaning in life.

In addition to the presence of meaning, two other important dimensions of meaning in life exist, namely, the sources from which people say they draw meaning, and the degree to which people are engaged in the search for meaning.

Sources of Meaning in Life

Research has also progressed in identifying the sources from which people feel they derive their sense of meaning in life. Relationships with others have emerged as the most important sources of meaning, both when people are given a number of sources to rank order and when they are simply asked what gives their lives meaning.

The Search for Meaning in Life

Another dimension of meaning in life concerns people's search for meaning. Early theoretical work argued that people were endowed with an innate tendency to search for meaning in their lives, but empirical work generally failed to investigate these claims. The search for meaning in life refers to people's desire and efforts to establish and/or augment their understanding of the meaning, significance, and purpose of their lives. The presence of meaning and the search for meaning are empirically and theoretically distinct. As such, some people who are searching for meaning feel their lives are relatively meaningless, whereas others might consider the search for meaning to be a life-long devotion even though they feel their lives are relatively meaningful. Generally, those who are searching for meaning are a little more distressed than those who are not.

Historical Background

Early consideration of life's meaning emerged from the existential philosophers following the two World Wars of the twentieth century. The notion that there was a single, absolute nature to the universe had been challenged previously, but following these wars, the existentialists argued that life had no intrinsic meaning, but rather was open to each individual to interpret. Thus, in contrast to centuries of theological and philosophical teachings, the idea began to take hold that each person needed to discover life's meaning on his or her own. This idea was brought to psychology by Viktor Frankl, who argued that having a sense of purpose or mission in life was essential to healthy human functioning. He later argued that the principal cause of psychological maladies in the modern, post-World War II world was a loss of purpose, leading to people's experiences of life without meaning. Frankl became the figurehead of theoretical, therapeutic, and research efforts in psychology directed to understanding how psychotherapy affected people's sense of meaning and purpose (i.e., the presence of meaning in life). One of the most popular research topics in the early decades of meaning in life research was showing that some groups of people reported greater presence of meaning than others (e.g., nuns). This interest in group differences has persisted throughout the span of research on meaning, but over time, interest mounted in understanding the connections between meaning and other variables, such as religion, and the role of meaning-making processes in coping with stress and trauma.

Recent Work on Theory and Research

Currently, theoretical efforts attempting to place meaning in life within the broader context of human well-being have influenced researchers to examine the similarities and differences between meaning in life dimensions and other constructs such as life satisfaction, positive affect, and self-esteem. Other theoretical efforts have focused on explaining meaning in life in terms of cognitively based meaning systems, which consist of mental representations of one's self, the world, and the relationship between the two.

Recent research efforts have primarily focused on continuing to delineate the psychological nature of dimensions of meaning in life. For example, research has been conducted demonstrating that people report greater presence of meaning in life when they have been induced to feel positive mood. There is also heightened interest in using biological methods to look at the construct of meaning in life. For example, some research has examined whether the presence of meaning has unique biological markers.

Methodological Issues in the Study of Meaning in Life

Just as the preponderance of meaning research has focused on the presence of meaning, the methods used in meaning research show a similar imbalance. This is unfortunate, as a variety of methods have been used to understand meaning and meaning-related constructs, including the use of self-report surveys, informant reports, goals approaches, narrative approaches, daily diaries, longitudinal studies, quasi-experiments, and experiments.

Most of what we know about meaning in life is based on the use of self-report surveys. There are several merits to using such an approach, and the fact that findings have been very consistent across studies increases our confidence in survey-based reports. However, among the many, familiar limitations of survey methods, several in particular are relevant to this area of research. Methodological sources of error, including method variance and flawed measurement, have been a source of concern to meaning in life researchers for several decades. Studies that have used more psychometrically sound measures have generally replicated the findings obtained using potentially flawed measures, although the magnitude of relations observed has usually been lower. Thus, the concern here is not so much that we do not know what meaning in life is related to, rather that the exact magnitude of these relations might be obscured by shared method variance or flaws in the surveys used. The lack of precision associated with method variance and the use of flawed measures also can obscure multivariate relations between meaning in life and other variables. For example, a researcher might be interested in knowing whether therapy increases a sense of meaning in life, and whether such an increase in meaning is associated in turn with a decrease in depressive symptoms. The most commonly used meaning survey, the Purpose in Life Test contains items that are closely related to depressive symptoms (e.g., suicidal thoughts). If a researcher was using this survey, it would be impossible to identify the specific contribution of meaning in life to a reduction in depressive symptoms because the measures are conflated. An additional concern is the fact that survey methods cannot illuminate causal relationships to a satisfactory degree. Informant reports have been used to establish the convergent validity of some measures of meaning in life, and they, along with goals approaches (in which participants are asked to describe the goals they are typically trying to accomplish, and correlations are assessed between ratings along various dimensions and outcomes of interest), help reduce some of the concerns regarding methodological error sources. These methods are each fairly limited, however, in what they can tell us about how meaning in life is found or created.

One alternative approach focuses on the stories people develop about their lives or important life events. These narrative approaches have found that both the process of telling such stories, as well as the contents of the stories appear important. In regards to process, the act of writing about life events is associated with a range of positive outcomes, and is instrumental in finding meaning in it. It is thought that this is facilitated by the integration of the event in to a larger, overarching meaning system. In regards to the contents, researchers have found that who people tell a story in terms of their experience of an adverse event, and their eventual ability to overcome the event and find positive outcomes, showed improved adjustment (e.g., higher generativity). Narrative approaches are well-suited for understanding people's perceptions of how they came to feel their lives are meaningful, and are also less susceptible to shared method variance with meaning in life questionnaires.

Daily diary methods also serve to reduce concerns about shared method variance. In meaning in life research, diary methods have been used to demonstrate that meaning in life mediates the relation between religious experience and well-being. Diary methods are also longitudinal methods, and can be used to test hypotheses regarding the temporal sequence of meaning in life processes.

There have also been several studies that have examined meaning over longer periods of time. One important use of longitudinal methods has been to examine the role of meaning in successful aging. Findings from one study indicated that meaning in life was associated with successful aging 14 months later, controlling for demographic variables and traditional predictors, such as social and intellectual resources. Such encouraging work is integral to validating meaning as a key feature of optimal human development.

Quasi-experimental approaches have typically compared groups of individuals that differ on variables presumed to be influential to people's ability to find meaning in life. As noted previously, this research generally finds that normal populations report greater meaning than clinical populations, and that clergy report greater meaning than normal populations.

Finally, a limited number of experiments have been conducted looking at causal mechanisms underlying meaning in life. Most directly related is the research by King and colleagues, which used several experiments to demonstrate that inducing positive affect leads to higher assessments of meaning in life. Research associated with Terror Management Theory has demonstrated that following reminders of death, people feel their lives are more meaningful if they are given the opportunity to profess support for their culture's worldview, and less meaningful if they are not given that opportunity. The experimental investigations relevant to meaning have generally looked at meaning as an outcome, and as such this research helps illuminate some of the factors that influence people's perceptions that their lives are meaningful, implicating positive affect and adherence to cultural worldviews. More research of this type is needed to continue to make progress in understanding the consequences, as well as the precedents of meaning in life.

Future Directions

Several future directions have been suggested for meaning in life research. Among the most compelling are those that have the potential to demonstrate the relevance of meaning in life dimensions to psychological and physical health. As such, renewed interest in the role of meaning as a facilitator and an outcome of psychological treatment would be most welcome, particularly when included in well-designed, randomized clinical trials. Research on stress and coping should also help to solidify the importance of having a sense of meaning to people's ability to adjust to adverse life events. We should also endeavor to identify the neurological substrates, biological markers, and biometric features of meaning in life. As it becomes clear how meaning supports human functioning, it will become increasingly important to expand our understanding of the development and change in meaning over the lifespan.

As noted in the preceding sections, many questions remain about the fundamental nature of meaning in life dimensions, and their relations with other psychological variables. Thus, much basic research remains necessary. Cross-cultural research would enable us to understand the universality of experiences of meaning, as well as suggest some of the domains from which people draw meaning in life. For example, those from cultures that stress individual happiness (e.g., United States) report greater presence of meaning in life than those from cultures that stress collective harmony (e.g., Spain). Understanding the cultural mechanisms behind these differences would shed light on how people derive meaning from life. Another way to access this question is to use experimental methods that identify those factors that increase or decrease meaning (e.g., positive affect), as well as assessing the effects of temporary manipulations of meaning.

SEE ALSO: ▶ Eudaimonia   ▶ Frankl, Viktor

Reference

Steger, M. F. (in press). The pursuit of meaningfulness in life. In S. J. Lopez (Ed.), *Handbook of positive psychology* (2nd ed.). Oxford, UK: Oxford University Press.

Meditation

Shauna L. Shapiro
Santa Clara University

Meditation refers to a family of techniques used to consciously train attention in a nonanalytical, nondiscursive way. Meditation is independent of a religious orientation, although it can occur within religious or spiritual frameworks.

In the 1970s research on meditation began in earnest and has since increased significantly. The transplantation of meditation into Western study occurred, however, within a traditional behavioral framework emphasizing symptom reduction and alleviation with little attention to development, enhancement, growth and cultivation of positive psychological qualities and experiences. As a result, one of the principal original goals of meditation, to uncover the positive and to catalyze our internal potential for healing and development, has been largely ignored. Yet, a small number of researchers and theorists have and continue to explore the positive effects of meditation.

Meditation

Meditation originally was conceived within the religious/philosophical context of Eastern spiritual disciplines but is an essential element in nearly all contemplative religious and spiritual traditions, including Judaism, Christianity, and Islam. Various methods whose background and techniques are quite different from one another (for example, Transcendental Meditation [TM], Zen meditation, Vipassana meditation) are placed collectively under the umbrella term of *meditation*.

The family of techniques traditionally has been divided into concentrative meditation and mindfulness meditation. In all types of concentrative meditation, there is an attempt to restrict awareness by focusing attention on a single object. The practitioner attempts to ignore other stimuli in the environment and focus complete attention on the object of meditation. Attention is focused in a non-analytical, unemotional way, in order to directly experience the object of meditation, which can be located in either the external or internal environment. Examples of the object include the breath, a mantra, a single word (for example, "one") or specific sounds.

In mindfulness meditation, an attempt is made to attend nonjudgmentally to all stimuli in the internal and external environment, but not to get caught up in (ruminate on) any particular stimulus. Mindfulness meditation is referred to as an opening up meditation practice. Some meditation techniques involve integrated elements of both concentrative and opening types. For example, a person may focus on breathing (Zen and Vipassana meditation) or a mantra (e.g., TM), but be willing to allow attention to focus on other stimuli if they become predominant and then return to the breathing (or mantra).

Finally, in developing an understanding of meditation, it is crucial to note that meditation training differs both operationally and in its deep intentions from relaxation training. First, an emphasis of meditation is the development of greater understanding through the systematic cultivation of inquiry and insight, whereas the objective of relaxation training is to achieve a state of low autonomic arousal, with little or no emphasis on the cultivation of inquiry or insight. Relaxation is often a by-product of meditation, but it is not an objective of the process. Furthermore, relaxation is taught as a technique, to be used during stressful or anxiety provoking situations. Meditation, in contrast, is not a technique whose use is contingent upon stressful situations; rather, it is conceived as a "way of being" that is to be cultivated daily regardless of circumstances. The formal mediation practice seeps into daily life, bringing greater nonjudgmental consciousness to everything that an individual does, feels and experiences.

Original Intentions of Meditation

Abraham Maslow stated "what we call 'normal' in psychology is really a psychopathology of the average, so undramatic and so widely spread that we don't even notice it ordinarily" (1968, p. 16). Meditation disciplines have been suggesting this for over 2,500 years, teaching that individual "normal" minds are untrained and often unconscious, which inhibits them from reaching their fullest potential. The intention behind meditation is to "wake up" from a suboptimal state of consciousness; wake up to a person's true nature.

Walsh (1983), a pioneer in the field of meditation research, identified the ultimate aims of meditation practice as "the development of deep insight into the nature of mental processes, consciousness, identity, and reality, and the development of optimal states of psychological well-being and consciousness" (p. 19). Meditation provides roadmaps to help recognize and let go of old structures and evolve toward new ways of seeing and being as individuals experience deep insights into the nature of mind and the path toward optimal health (Walsh, 1983).

The intention behind meditation practice is to help develop and train the mind toward optimal states of empathy, joy, compassion, awareness and insight, with the ultimate intention of total liberation. And yet, research exploring the effects of meditation to attain these goals has been scarce. With few exceptions, research has not measured the deeper levels of meditation's original intent, but instead has focused on traditional psychological variables (e.g. reducing anxiety, depression).

Meditation Research

Over the past three decades, there has been considerable research examining the psychological and physiological effects of meditation. Moreover, meditative practices are being utilized in a variety of health care settings. Research demonstrates that meditation is an effective intervention for cardiovascular disease; chronic pain; anxiety and panic disorder; substance abuse; dermatological disorders; prevention of relapse of MDD and, reduction of anxiety and depressive symptoms in non-clinical populations.

As noted, few researchers have examined meditation's original purpose as a self-liberation strategy to enhance positive psychological qualities. Despite this, a small number of pioneering studies have addressed the effects of meditation on positive psychological health.

Meditation appears to result in improvements in intelligence, school grades, learning ability, and short- and long-term recall. There also is evidence that these improvements in memory and academic performance associated with meditation apply across the lifespan. Preliminary research confirms that meditation can cultivate creativity. Further, meditation has been shown to increase concentration and attention as well as relationship satisfaction in couples. In individuals, meditation has been shown to increase happiness and positive affect, optimism, self-compassion and empathy, and moral maturity and spirituality.

Meditation may help human beings identify and actualize their potential strengths. The field of positive psychology offers new opportunities and methodologies to examine the original intentions of meditation. In fact, meditation can be considered an applied positive psychology practice that has wide application for promoting positive health in medicine, business, and education. Meditation offers paths to exceptional states of mental well-being and attentional control that have been systematically developed and practiced for 2,500 years. In this way, meditation may help positive psychology examine and reevaluate the current definition of "normal" and expand Western psychology's concept of mental health. Exploration of meditation requires great sensitivity and a range of methodological glasses. Future research into the positive effects of meditation will help illuminate the richness and complexity of this age-old practice.

SEE ALSO:　▶ Buddhism　▶ Consciousness　▶ Mindfulness　▶ Religiousness
▶ Spirituality

References

Maslow, A. H. (1968). *Toward a psychology of being* (2nd ed.). New York: Van Nostrand Reinhold.
Walsh, R. N. (1983). Meditation practice and research. *Journal of Humanistic Psychology*, *23*(1), 18–50.

Menninger, Karl

Lisa Lewis and Roger Verdon
The Menninger Clinic

Karl Menninger, MD, one of the most influential figures in American psychiatry, cofounded The Menninger Clinic in Topeka, Kansas, in 1925 with his father C. F., and his brother Will. At a time when mentally ill persons were regularly institutionalized, Dr Menninger espoused the belief that even custodial patients in asylums were treatable. His pioneering efforts had remarkable results and his clinic swiftly came to the nation's attention as a premier treatment center.

Writing *The Human Mind* in 1930, the best-selling, plainly written book successfully explained Freud and psychiatry to a curious and grateful American lay public. Thereafter, over a lifetime of teaching, lectures, speeches, published books, chapters and papers, Dr Karl, as he was known, demystified psychotherapy and psychoanalysis, while advocating the belief that there was hope for every individual who struggled with mental illness.

Along with cofounders, he set up the world's largest center for psychiatric training, the Karl Menninger School of Psychiatry & Mental Health Sciences, which trained as many as 100 residents per year shortly after World War II. During his lifetime he championed the rights of children and Native Americans, proposed prison reform, and vehemently opposed war.

Over the course of his long career in medicine, he came to be known in some circles as the "dean of American psychiatry." A prolific writer and a dynamic speaker, Dr Karl's ability to capture a thought with a pithy comment or render an insight in a few brief words, reflected a sharp, and often witty, mind. Some of his oft-repeated and revealing quotes include:

> Love cures people – both the ones who give it and the ones who receive it.
> The central purpose of each life should be to dilute the misery in the world.
> Hope is an adventure, a going forward, a confident search for a rewarding life.
> One does not fall into love: one grows into love, and love grows in him.

Above all, Dr Karl was not a shrinking violet and said what he thought. Believing that hope was a vital part of the healing process, Dr Karl took his own profession to task in his famous 1959 presidential address to the American Psychiatric

Association in which he deplored the lack of scientific attention to hope as a key in treating mental illness. Later studies affirmed Dr Karl's lifelong belief that instilling hope in patients produced favorable outcomes.

Dr Karl died July 18, 1990, four days short of his 97th birthday, the last cofounder to pass away. The Menninger Clinic continues to operate in Houston, Texas, where it is affiliated with Baylor College of Medicine and The Methodist Hospital. The Clinic's adopted slogan is "Discovering hope, one life at a time," words that echo Karl Menninger's beliefs.

SEE ALSO: ▶ Hope   ▶ Mental illness

Mental Health

Corey L. M. Keyes and Barret Michalec
Emory University

In 1999, the Surgeon General's report focused for the first time on mental rather than physical health. In that report, mental health was defined as "a state of successful performance of mental function, resulting in productive activities, fulfilling relationships with people, and the ability to adapt to change and to cope with adversity" (U.S. Public Health Service, 1999, p. 4). In 2004, the World Health Organization's historic first report on mental health promotion defined mental health as:

> a state of well-being in which the individual realizes his or her own abilities, can cope with the normal stresses of life, can work productively and fruitfully, and is able to make a contribution to his or her community. (World Health Organization, 2004, p. 12)

In contrast, mental disorder (synonymous with *mental illness*) is a persistent deviation from normal functioning that is sufficient to cause emotional suffering and role impairment, diminishing individuals' capacities to execute their responsibilities as a parent, spouse, or employee.

Although it sounds serious, and its name equates it with physical illness, mental illness was not considered a priority by the medical and public health community until the last decade of the twentieth century. In 1996, the World Health Organization published the results of the Global Burden of Disease study. This study calculated the total contribution of acute and chronic medical conditions and illnesses to a measure of the disability life-adjusted year (DALYs). The DALY reflects the total number of years in a population (i.e., in a developed or developing nation) that was either lived with disability (i.e., unable to perform activities of daily living, etc.) or abbreviated prematurely (i.e., as compared against the average life expectancy for that person's race, sex, and age) and could be attributed to a specific physical or mental condition or illness. To the surprise of many, major depression was among the top five illnesses contributing to DALYs in both developed and developing nations. Moreover, the category of mental disorders was second only to the category of cardiovascular diseases in contributing the DALYs.

Health economic studies calculate the cost of health conditions in terms of their contribution to direct costs – i.e., the costs of treating the condition – and in terms of indirect costs – i.e., the costs accrued due to lost productivity from the illness causes sick-days, work cutbacks, and presenteeism (i.e., remaining at work but not being as productive as would be estimated without the illness). Major depression alone has been estimated to cost annually in excess of $40 billion in total costs (i.e., combined direct and indirect). Mental disorder, as a class of conditions, is among the three most costly conditions in the US (along with cardiovascular diseases and physical rehabilitation), resulting in a higher amount of combined cost than diabetes, cancers, stroke, arthritis, digestive disorders, or HIV/AIDS.

Studies of the population estimate that as much as one-half of adults will experience at least one episode of mental illness in a lifetime. Furthermore, research has also revealed that a prior episode of mental illness increases the chances of a future episode of mental disorder. During the twentieth century, the average age of the first onset of any mood disorder (e.g., depression), of any anxiety disorder (e.g., generalized anxiety disorder), and any substance disorder (e.g., alcohol dependence) decreased, while the average life-expectancy at birth increased by 30 years. It should not be surprising, then, that mental health advocates cite population studies showing rising rates of mental illness in the U.S. population and argue these changes reflect actual change in the mental health of the U.S. population rather than merely being artificial changes in the measurement and diagnosis of mental illness and decreased sensitivity of the population to reporting mental illness symptoms.

From Treatment of Mental Illness to the Study of Mental Health

Treatments for mental disorder have come a long way from trephening – i.e., drilling a small hole in the patient's skull to release the pressure or demons that were presumed to cause the disorder – to prescription medicines designed to enhance neurotransmission and psychotherapies that aim to enhance patient's cognition and coping strategies. Starting in the 1990s, *Consumer Reports* magazine – which tests and then reports on the quality of consumer products – periodically devotes a section to the effectiveness of mental illness treatments. Most patients, by some estimates as many as 7 of every 10, who receive either prescription medications, psychotherapies, or a combination of the two, benefit substantially. Unfortunately, studies suggest that barely half of individuals in the population who would need treatment, because they fit the criteria for a mental disorders, also report receiving treatment.

Remission from a mental disorder following a course of treatment tends to be partial or short lived for up to 60%, and sometimes more, of patients. Moreover, current treatments for mental illness are palliative, providing symptomatic relief but not a cure. As such, the director of the NIMH has recently discussed the new research goal of cure therapeutics and the overall need for and likelihood of finding cures for mental disorders. Advocates and scientists of mental illness believe, and convey to the public, that the treatment, cure, or prevention of mental illness is the only and the best way to promote the overall mental health of the population. However, Corey Keyes believes that this is "promising too much" at best, and a "false promise," at worst.

Keyes' research on mental health as a *complete* state suggests that the paradigm of mental health research and services in the US must include two, complementary, ongoing strategies: the promotion and maintenance of mental health as "flourishing," as well as the treatment and prevention of mental illness. Research on the national sample of U.S. adults has shown that measures of mental illness and measures of mental health form two distinct continua. In other words, the absence of mental illness does not translate into the presence of mental health as flourishing. In turn, measures of work productivity, disability, chronic physical illness, cardiovascular disease, psychosocial functioning, and healthcare utilization reveal that anything less than mental health as flourishing is associated with increased impairment and burden to self and society. In other words, the absence of mental health is as problematic as the presence of mental illness, and only mental health as flourishing is associated with the desired quality of execution of social roles and responsibilities as well as health and work productivity outcomes. Whereas more US adolescents (i.e., ages 12 to 18) are flourishing than adults (i.e., ages 25 to 74), barely one-half of adolescents and barely 20% of adults are flourishing. In other words, only a small proportion of those otherwise free of common mental disorders are mentally healthy, i.e., flourishing.

In sum, mental health is a positive state of well-being, as conceptualized by the Surgeon General, the World Health Organization, and as studied in the concept of flourishing. Mental illness is a persistent deviation of normal functioning that results in emotional suffering and significant impairment of functioning at a high cost to society. However, it is now clear that the absence of mental illness is not the presence of mental health. Moreover, mentally healthy, i.e., flourishing, individuals function markedly better than all others, even those who are otherwise free of a mental illness but have moderate or low levels of well-being. While the surplus of mental illness is a serious public health issue, so too is the deficit of flourishing, i.e., mental health, in the US.

SEE ALSO: ▶ Flourishing   ▶ Mental illness   ▶ Well-being

References

U.S. Public Health Service. (1999). *Mental health: A report of the Surgeon General*. Rockville, MD: Author.

World Health Organization (2004). *Promoting mental health: Concepts, emerging evidence, practice* (Summary report). Geneva: Author.

Mental Illness

Stephanie E. Petersen
Private practice, Houston, Texas

The term *mental illness* refers to severe emotional or thought disturbance that negatively affects one's health and safety. It is a collective term for all of the diagnosable mental disorders. Those with any of the severe mental disorders present with disturbances of thought and perception, dysregulation of mood, excessive and inappropriate anxiety, and/or cognitive abnormalities. People with disorders such as schizophrenia may be viewed as experiencing serious mental illness, but other disorders are best considered to have symptoms which occur on a continuum of severity. Mental disorders are a relatively common occurrence; in a given year an estimated one in four American adults experiences a diagnosable mental disorder. Serious mental illness is concentrated on a smaller group, approximately 6% of the US population. Many individuals suffer from more than one mental disorder at a time, with nearly half of those with a mental disorder meeting criteria for two or more disorders. Mental disorders often demonstrate an onset of symptoms by adolescence, with half of lifetime cases of mental illness beginning by 14 years of age, although many do not seek treatment until long after the first onset of symptoms. Untreated mental illness can lead to more severe, more difficult to treat illness, and the development of cooccurring mental illness.

The Diagnostic and Statistical Manual of Mental Disorders, fourth edition, consists of a classification of mental disorders which are conceptualized as clinically significant behavior or psychological syndromes associated with distress, disability, and impairment in functioning. Schizophrenia and other psychotic disorders include prominent psychotic symptoms which include positive symptoms such as delusions, hallucinations, and disorganized speech/behavior. There may also be negative symptoms which involve deficits such as flat affect, anhedonia, or a lack of motivation or initiative. Disturbances of mood involve sustained feelings of sadness and/or a sustained elevation of mood. Such symptoms correspond to diagnoses of either a depressive or bipolar disorder. Anxiety disorders are characterized by excessive fear in response to a threatening event and may include symptoms such as panic attacks (i.e., a sudden, discrete episode of an extreme anxiety reaction) or agoraphobia (i.e., avoidance of different places or situations). Specific diagnoses include specific phobias, generalized anxiety disorder, obsessive-compulsive disorder, post-traumatic stress disorder, and panic disorder. Somatoform disorders include the presence of physical symptoms that suggest a general medical condition and are not fully explained by a general medical condition, by the side effects of a substance, or another mental disorder. It is not intentional or under one's voluntary control. Factitious disorder consists of physical or psychological symptoms intentionally produced or feigned to allow one to assume a sick role. Mental disorders may be diagnosed by a mental health professional through the use of clinical assessment techniques such as clinical interview (which may include some form of mental status examination), behavioral observation and assessment, and psychological testing (such as projective testing, personality inventories, and intelligence testing).

The U.S. Surgeon General released a report on mental illness in 1999 which emphasized the importance of treatment and the need for increased public awareness to decrease the stigma associated with mental illness and encourage individuals to seek treatment when necessary. Those with mental illness must deal with the disability itself, as well as negative public reaction and social stigma which may affect opportunities for work and achievement of goals. The stigma often prevents people from seeking needed treatment. Laws such as the Americans with Disabilities Act have helped, as well as an increased understanding of mental disorders and recognition of the need for treatment. Roughly one-third of individuals with mental illness receive adequate treatment, while many receive no treatment at all. Beyond medication, there is increasing recognition of a need for rehabilitative and recovery-oriented services for those with serious mental illness, including the development of evidence-based treatments which would allow individuals to gain the skills need to live productively in the community. Therapeutic approaches to treatment of mental disorders include psychodynamic, interpersonal, and cognitive-behavioral approaches. Many members of racial and ethnic minority groups are underserved by the mental health services system, thus there is a need for linguistically and culturally competent services to provide treatment for individuals from different cultural groups. The etiology or causes of mental illness are not completely known, but thought to be shaped by biological, psychological, and social/cultural factors (and the interaction among each). This biopsychosocial model of disease provides a framework for understanding health and disease which takes into account the interaction among each of those factors.

SEE ALSO: ▶ Abnormal psychology   ▶ *Diagnostic and Statistical Manual*   ▶ Mental health   ▶ Psychopathology

Mindfulness

Ellen Langer
Harvard University

Mindfulness is the feeling of involvement or engagement. It is an active state of mind that is achieved by simply noticing new things. It doesn't matter how smart or silly the new distinctions are, just that they are novel. By actively drawing novel distinctions we become situated in the present, sensitive to context and perspective.

We can follow rules and routines, however, when we are mindful they guide rather than govern our behavior. Many extol the virtues of being in the present. When in the present we can take advantage of new opportunities and avert the danger not yet arisen. Indeed, everyone thinks they are in the present. When we are mindless, however, we are unaware that we are not in the present.

What is *mindlessness*? It is not the same thing as ignorance, stupidity or vigilance. Mindlessness is an inactive state of mind that is characterized by reliance on distinctions drawn in the past. When we're mindless we are trapped in a rigid perspective, insensitive to the ways meaning changes depending on subtle changes in context. The past dominates and we behave much like automatons without knowing it, where rules and routines govern rather than guide what we do. Mindless behavior is characterized by a reliance on old, often outdated categories, a lack of spontaneity and a reduced awareness of one's social and physical world. Mindlessness freezes our responses and closes us off to needed change. While some have argued that mindless behavior may be positive at times, a closer examination reveals that mindlessness is rarely, if ever, beneficial because it closes us off to possibility. Essentially we freeze our understanding and become oblivious to subtle changes that would have led us to act differently, if only we were aware of them. Mindlessness is pervasive and costly and operates in all aspects of our lives. Although we can see it and feel it in other people we are blind to it in ourselves.

Ignorance is not knowing and stupidity may be understood as knowing wrongly. Mindlessness, on the other hand refers to a way of knowing irrespective of content. It refers to information that is essentially frozen in the form in which it was originally learned. Vigilance may seem like mindfulness to some but is more akin to mindlessness in that when vigilant, we hold our attention still and focus on a single stimulus. If we were on horseback and were vigilant of the trees in the path we very well might not notice the boulder soon to cause the horse to trip.

Mindlessness comes about in two ways. It may occur either through repetition or on a single exposure to information. The first case is the more familiar. Most of us have had the experience, for example, of driving and then realizing, only because of the distance we have come, that we made part of the trip on "automatic pilot," as we sometimes call mindless behavior. Another example of mindlessness through repetition, is when we learn something by practicing it so that it becomes like "second nature" to us. We try to learn the new skill so well that we don't have to think about it. The problem is that if we've been successful, it won't occur to us to think about it even when it would be to our advantage to do so. If, for example, we practiced holding our tennis racket in a particular way so that we don't have to think about it any more and then found that we had to use someone else's racket that was heavier than ours, we may perform poorly because we're unlikely to change our grip to meet the new circumstances. Moreover, many of us learn "the basics" mindlessly without thinking to question whose basics we're learning. What is basic for some may not be the best approach for others.

We also become mindless when we hear or read something and accept it without questioning it. Most of what we know about the world or ourselves we have mindlessly learned in this way. An example I'm particularly fond of is of my own mindlessness that I wrote about in *The Power of Mindful Learning*. I was at a friend's house for dinner and the table was set with the fork on the right side of the plate. I felt like some natural law had been violated because the fork "goes" on the left side! I knew this was ridiculous. Who cares where the fork is placed. Yet it felt wrong to me, in spite of the fact that I could generate many ways it was better for it to be placed on the right. How had I learned this? I didn't memorize how to set a table. One day as a child, my mother simply said to me that the fork goes on the left. Forever after that is where I am destined to put it, no matter what circumstances might suggest doing otherwise. I became trapped without any awareness that the way I learned the information would stay in place in the future. Much of what we know now we mindlessly learned in the past under different circumstances that closed the future to potentially new and helpful alternative understandings. Whether we become mindless over time or on initial exposure to information, we unwittingly lock ourselves into a rigid understanding of information.

Mindlessness is pervasive and the costs are great. For those of us who learned to drive many years ago, we were taught that if we needed to stop the car on a slippery surface, the safest way was to slowly, gently, pump the brake. Today most new cars have anti-lock brakes. To stop on a slippery surface, now the safest thing to do is to step on the brake firmly and hold it down. Most of us caught on ice will still gently pump the brakes. What was once safe is now dangerous. The context has changed but our behavior remains the same, the essence of mindlessness.

Much of the time we are mindless yet thirty years of research reveals that mindfully noticing new things results in nursing home residents living longer; students learning better; and results in more intelligent and creative products, and positive affect, to name a few of the findings. Moreover, in our most recent research we have found that dolphins, children and adults are more attracted to people when they are mindful. Thus it may be the essence of charisma. Research also has shown that the more distinctions we draw, the more we like the target of our mindfulness and the more we remember about it. It can even be recognized in the products we produce. In recent research, for example, orchestras performed mindlessly or mindfully. (To accomplish the latter, all they were instructed to do is to make their performance new in very subtle ways that only they would notice.) The musicians preferred playing this way and when the recorded pieces were played for audiences, they too overwhelmingly preferred the mindfully played piece. In other research we found the same to be true for drawings and essays, i.e. those that were mindfully produced were preferred.

Most of what we learn we learn in an absolute way, without regard to how the information might be different in different contexts. We are taught that $1 + 1 = 2$. Yet if we added one wad of chewing gum to one wad of chewing gum, $1 + 1 = 1$. If we used a binary system, then $1 + 1 = 10$. When we learn mindlessly, we take the information in as true without asking under what conditions it may not be true. This is the way we learn most things. As a result, although we may be confident, we're often in error.

When information is given by an authority, appears irrelevant, or is presented in absolute language, it typically does not occur to us to question it. We accept it and become trapped in the mindset, oblivious to how it could be otherwise. Authorities are sometimes wrong or overstate their case and what is irrelevant today may be relevant tomorrow. Indeed, most of the information we receive is typically couched in absolute language that we accept without regard to context or nuance. Mindful learning is more like learning probable "truths" rather than mindlessly accepting absolutes.

Language too often binds us to a single perspective with mindlessness as a result. In one of our studies, Alison Piper and I introduced people to a novel object in either an absolute or conditional way. They were told that the object "is" or "could be" a dog's chew toy. We then created a need for an eraser. The question we considered was who would think to use the object as an eraser? The answer was only those subjects who were told "it could be a dog's chew toy." The name of something is only one way an object can be understood. If we learn about it as if "the map and the territory" are the same thing, creative uses of the information will not occur to us. Learning conditionally, i.e. mindfully, results in increased creativity, higher attention levels, and improved memory. One hallmark of how information is traditionally imparted is to reduce or eliminate uncertainty. We want to know what things are and mean with no ambiguity. Unfortunately, however, this mindset increases mindlessness. Ironically, people seem to like choice but to dislike doubt. Without uncertainty there can be no meaningful choice. In contrast, when we exploit the power of uncertainty, we learn what things can become and as a result, the world becomes richer in possibility.

Everything is always changing. Even the cells in our bodies are constantly changing. When we experience stability, we are confusing the stability of our mindsets with the stability of the underlying phenomenon. Instead, we should consider exploiting the power of uncertainty so that we can learn what things can become. Mindfulness that is characterized by novel distinction-drawing will lead us in this direction. When we stay uncertain, we stay in the present and we notice and when we notice we become mindful.

The antidote, then, to mindlessness is to learn to be more mindful, which is often an easier task than it first appears to be. When we are mindful, we are actively drawing novel distinctions rather than relying on distinctions drawn in the past. Although similar to the concept of mindfulness found in Eastern religions, mindfulness, as I've researched it for over 30 years, comes about in a different, more immediate, way and springs from a Western, scientific perspective. Becoming more mindful requires learning to switch modes of thinking about ourselves and the world. Meditation, regardless of the particular form, is engaged to lead to post-meditative mindfulness. Meditation grew up in the East. Whether practicing Zen Buddhism or Transcendental Meditation, for example, typically the individual is to sit still and meditate for 20 minutes twice a day. If done successfully over time, the categories we mindlessly committed ourselves to start to break down. The two are by no means mutually exclusive. In our work we provoke mindfulness by active distinction-drawing. Noticing new things about the target reveals that it looks different from different perspectives and thus categories break down and become more malleable.

The idea that mindfulness can result without meditation, has been confirmed by the results of years of research that also makes clear its importance to health and well-being. When we learn our facts in a conditional way, we are more likely to draw novel distinctions. Mindfulness that is characterized by novel distinction-drawing or meditation that results in post-meditative mindfulness both lead in the direction of health and well being.

SEE ALSO: ▶ Charisma   ▶ Meditation

Moral Development

John C. Gibbs
The Ohio State University

The emergence, socialization, and growth of morality are of major importance in the social and behavioral sciences. Psychological theories have conceptualized three main sources of moral development and prosocial behavior. First, theorists have posited *biology* as the source of moral development, emphasizing the natural emergence of an empathic predisposition. Second, theorists have located morality's source in *society*, focusing on the socialization or internalization of a society's prescriptive norms and values. Finally, theorists have identified the *mental coordination of perspectives* as the primary source, focusing on the construction of mature moral judgment. Integrative views have recently appeared.

Biology as the Source of Moral Development

Prosocial or cooperative behavior has been observed in ethological studies of mammalian social groups. Chimpanzee groups may cooperatively hunt, share meat after a kill, groom one another, and adopt a motherless infant. Humans beyond infancy are likely to help others in distress, at least when egoistic motives do not compete and other potential helpers are absent. Sociobiologists emphasize that prosocial behavior can be adaptive not only for the group but also for the helper insofar as the individual helped is genetically related. Even if the helper does not survive, some portion of the helper's genes may pass on through the helped individual. Prosocial behavior is also adaptive for the individual in the case of reciprocal altruism, that is, when the recipient may eventually reciprocate the help.

The tendency of higher animals to help one another may derive at least partially from a capacity for empathic arousal. Empathic responses are widely observed among primates. Human newborns spontaneously cry upon hearing other infants' cries (more so than upon hearing their own cry or a comparably loud nonhuman sound), suggesting an early capacity for conditioning and vicarious arousal. The biological (genetic, neural) basis of empathy has been established by various research findings: greater empathic responding in identical than fraternal twins; brain images depicting prefrontal regions activated by others' distress in normal individuals; poor empathic responding in patients with ventromedial prefrontal damage; and poor aversive conditioning of psychopathic individuals.

Moral development and prosocial behavior entail the emergence, then, of a biologically based capacity for empathic arousal. The mechanisms of empathy emergent in infancy, however, are insufficient to support mature moral behavior in adults. Empathy must gain cognitive subtlety or depth, balance, accuracy, and social breadth for mature moral behavior, a point emphasized in integrative views.

Society as the Source of Moral Development

Other theorists have focused on society, or social institutions such as the family, as the source of moral development and prosocial behavior. Moral socialization or internalization theories address morality's movement from society to the individual. Among sociologists, Emile Durkheim emphasized the inculcation in the child of a sense of respect for society's collective norms and standards. Alvin Gouldner studied the reciprocity norm, comprised of prescriptions that one should reciprocate if one receives help and, indeed, should take into account how anyone would wish to be treated in the way one treats others (the Golden Rule). The reciprocity norm is taught and internalized in many societies. Gouldner attributed the reciprocity norm's universality to its adaptive value in supporting cooperative behavior.

Developmental psychology traditionally features internalization theories. In Freudian theory, one posits that internalization takes place as the young child identifies with the same-sex parent, thereby incorporating the parent's moral standards and values. In social learning theory, children develop morally as they observe and imitate the prosocial behavior of nurturant models (typically the parents). Children are rewarded or praised or are disciplined for transgressions. Attachment theory warns that child maltreatment can undermine identification with the parent or moral internalization. Maltreatment prompts the child to see the world as a hostile place. Accordingly, the child may engage in destructive behavior against others or the self.

Hoffman's Integrative View

Taking into account both biological and societal origins of morality is developmental psychologist Martin Hoffman's integrative view. Hoffman's theory begins with empathic arousal but emphasizes its development and socialization. The biologically based empathy of infancy is not only unsophisticated but egocentric. The empathic predisposition is rendered less egocentric in part through cognitive development and social perspective-taking. The adolescent and adults typically sympathize with the plight of entire groups of unfortunate or victimized individuals. The availability and potential activation of multiple mechanisms or modes (such as social perspective-taking) render the empathic predisposition more complex and reliable. Advanced cognitive and social modes can promote – but do not assure – mature (balanced, subtle, expanded) morality.

To promote mature morality, the motive power of empathy must be cultivated and prosocially channeled in the course of socialization. Hoffman emphasizes the discipline encounter in moral internalization and prosocial behavior. By pointing out how their child's transgression has harmed others, parents induce empathy-based guilt (a technique Hoffman termed "inductive discipline") and thereby empower internalized prosocial norms of reciprocity and restitution. Inductive appeals can become more subtle as the growing child's empathic predisposition becomes more cognitively sophisticated.

Although Hoffman's view encompasses the child's empathy and cognitive development, it still shares with other internalization theories certain limitations. If mature morality moves from a given society to the individual, then morality becomes relative to various given cultural norms and ground is lost for evaluating cultural practices such as female genital mutilation, suttee, and slavery. In other words, internalization theories (as well as the relativistic assumptions prevalent in cultural anthropology) may not adequately capture the universal or cross-culturally general aspects of moral development, moral maturity, and prosocial behavior. Anne Colby and William Damon studied contemporary moral exemplars, or persons dedicated to moral integrity, promoting social justice, and helping unfortunate or victimized others.

Mental Coordination of Perspectives as the Source of Moral Development

Rather than biology or society, the child's mental coordination of perspectives on a situation is emphasized as the source of moral development and maturity in the cognitive developmental theories of Jean Piaget and Lawrence Kohlberg. Piaget conceptualized mature morality as the construction through social interaction of a logic or rationality inherent in social relations. Particularly relevant to moral development is the coordination of self's with other's perspectives in peer conflict situations. John Flavell and colleagues noted that social construction mitigates – but does not eliminate – egocentric bias in human development and behavior.

Mental coordination or construction may supplement internalization in moral development. The cross-cultural universality of moral reciprocity, for example, may reflect not only widespread moral internalization of a norm (as Gouldner asserted) but also the social construction of an *ideal* as children (perhaps with the help of inductive parents or teachers) interact. Piaget (1932/1965) wrote that reciprocity as an "ideal equilibrium" is "born of the actions and reactions of individuals upon each other" (p. 318). Concrete forms of moral reciprocity (prescribing the reciprocation of favors or blows, or crude equality) precede the Golden Rule or ideal form (prescribing reciprocation according to how you or anyone would wish to be treated, or equity according to situational circumstances). Piaget suggested that the child during preadolescence gains hypothetical and reflective abilities that enable him or her to ponder the "deeper" meaning of moral reciprocity. The child may set "forgiveness above revenge, not out of weakness, but because "there is no end to revenge (a boy of 10)" (p. 323).

Cognitive developmental theorists suggest that the transition from concrete to ideal forms of reciprocity is part of a cross-culturally general age trend. Prior to moral judgments of concrete reciprocity, especially in the preschool years, children tend to center upon the superficial or highly salient in situations and accordingly confuse morality with physical size or power or with momentary egocentric desires. Through social construction, children "decenter" or become less egocentric and develop concrete and ideal moral reciprocity. As adolescents and adults mentally coordinate social perspectives in complex work or university settings, their mutualistic ideals expand from interpersonal to broader societal or humanitarian concerns.

Based on Piaget's work are other conceptualizations. Lawrence Kohlberg proposed a six-stage model of lifespan moral judgment development, but the rarity of his highest stages meant that they were poor candidates for defining cross-culturally general moral judgment maturity. John Gibbs proposed a four-stage model of standard moral judgment development. Immature stages are: 1) superficial centerings; and 2) pragmatic exchanges (or concrete moral reciprocity). These gradually give way in childhood to mature stages: 3) mutualities (or ideal moral reciprocity); and 4) systems (or expansion of mutual ideals to represent the bases of complex social systems). The four stages define a rough age trend seen in numerous cultures, such that basic moral judgment maturity is commonly evident by the adolescent or adult years.

Other Integrative Views

Besides Hoffman's, other integrative views of moral development or morality are noteworthy. Gibbs offered a comprehensive view of moral development that encompasses biological, societal, and mental coordinative sources. Gibbs pointed out that Hoffman's integrative view and Piaget's or Kohlberg's cognitive developmental theory refer, respectively, to the "right" and "good" strands of moral development. Similarly, Tom Beauchamp and James Childress conceptualized morality in terms of two primary principles: first, justice and respect for the person; and, second, nonmaleficence or beneficence. Although distinct, the right and the good interrelate and complement one another – as do cognitive development and Hoffman's theories of moral development.

SEE ALSO: ▶ Altruism   ▶ Effective parenting   ▶ Empathy
▶ Moral judgment   ▶ Values

Reference

Piaget, J. (1965). *Moral judgment of the child* (M. Gabain, Trans.). New York: Free Press. (Original work published 1932.)

Moral Judgment

Charles C. Helwig
University of Toronto

Moral judgment encompasses how people think about ethical or moral issues. Moral issues are distinguished from other sorts of issues, such as issues of personal choice or aesthetics, in that they entail a sense of obligation or *should* that is believed to hold for all people in similar circumstances. Depending on the theoretical perspective, morality may be defined either more narrowly or broadly to include such issues as justice, rights, and the welfare of others, laws and social customs, religious obligations, or questions of virtue or the good life.

The study of moral judgment in psychology has been conducted in the main by developmental psychologists, who have been interested in charting how thinking about morality is transformed from its beginnings in early childhood throughout adolescence and into adulthood. The field of moral judgment began in earnest with the efforts of the Swiss psychologist Jean Piaget, published in his seminal work *The Moral Judgment of the Child* in 1932. Piaget applied his clinical interview method to the study of children's moral conceptions. He questioned children of various ages about rules in children's games, and asked them to evaluate the actions of characters in stories in which children committed violations of moral rules of different kinds (e.g., property damage, physical harm, lying). From his investigations, Piaget outlined several levels in children's understanding. After an initial premoral level, in which social rules are understood merely as analogous to physical regularities without any attendant sense of obligation, children at around five years of age enter a period of *heteronomy*, in which they show a strong sense of respect for rules and authority in their moral thinking. Children at this level trace the origins of rules to authorities (e.g., usually parents) and view social rules as fixed and unalterable. When making judgments about moral actions, these young children focus on the letter rather than spirit of the law, and give greater priority to consequences over intentions.

In middle childhood, children's morality shifts to one of moral *autonomy*. Children's ability to take the perspective of the other increases and hence they become capable of reciprocal social interactions with peers. Out of these reciprocal interactions emerges a sense of morality as reciprocity or justice, embodied in maxims such as the Golden Rule (or "do unto others as you would have them do unto you"). Correspondingly, the child's moral judgments shift from a focus on rigid obedience to rules to a more nuanced application of morality that takes into account subjective, psychological features of acts such as the intentions of the transgressor. Older children and adolescents now understand morality in terms of true principles of justice, with rules no longer seen as good in and of themselves but only insofar as they serve these principles.

Building on Piaget's research, the American psychologist Lawrence Kohlberg developed an extremely influential theory of the development of moral judgment from an extensive program of research that began in the late 1950s and continued until his death in the late 1980s. Kohlberg's method involved presenting individuals with a series of moral dilemmas or conflicts and exploring their thinking through in-depth interviews. In one such conflict, known as the Heinz dilemma, a man's wife is dying from cancer. There is a drug that can cure her. However, the druggist who invented the drug is selling it for an exorbitant price and Heinz is unable to pay. In desperation, Heinz breaks into the druggist's store to steal the drug. To explore their moral reasoning, participants are asked a series of questions, such as whether it is acceptable for Heinz to steal the drug, and whether or not Heinz is obligated to steal even for strangers.

Kohlberg identified a six-stage sequence of moral judgment development, grouped into three broad levels, in which moral reasoning becomes increasingly abstract and oriented to general moral principles. At the first stage of the *preconventional* level, people (usually young children) reason in terms of punishment and obedience to authority. For example, individuals reasoning at this stage typically state that Heinz should not steal the drug because he may get caught and be sent to prison. In the second stage of this level, people take the perspective of others (such as the dying wife), but reason about relationships and obligations in tit-for-tat terms, arguing, for example, that Heinz should steal the drug because he needs his wife to help take care of him or do things for him in the future.

The next two stages comprise the *conventional* level, usually reached in adolescence or early adulthood. Here, people are aware of shared social or cultural norms that transcend personal wishes or desires and become the basis for moral obligation. For example, at stage 3, it may be argued that Heinz should steal the drug because it is what any good husband would do. These shared obligations, however, are mainly formulated in terms of the norms and values of the group with whom the individual identifies; they are not conceptualized as general obligations (such as a universalizable moral principle to respect all human life). Thus, there is no corresponding obligation to save the life of a stranger who is not part of one's reference group. At the fourth stage, the individual takes the perspective of society, including societal laws and institutions and the existing social order. The vantage point here is one of maintaining existing societal laws or institutions for the purpose of preventing a breakdown of the social system and the disorder that would ensue (e.g., "If people were allowed to steal, then society would break down").

At stage 5, the first stage of the *principled* level, the individual reasons in terms of universal moral principles that people in any society would be able to assent to. These may include notions such as the social contract, the common good, and universal human rights. Instead of the law maintaining position of stage 4, the person adopts a law creating perspective in which the focus is explicitly on the underlying principles that are necessary to legitimize a just and fair social system. Hence, at this level, individuals may perceive a conflict between existing societal laws and conventions and moral principles, and they will tend to give priority to moral principles over law or convention in such conflicts. Kohlberg initially identified a sixth stage, but later dropped this stage from his scoring system because he could not find enough examples of participants who reasoned at this stage for empirical validation. Even stage 5 was reached by only a fairly small minority of people in North American studies.

Kohlberg's stage sequence was extremely influential throughout the 1960s and 1970s, yielding a large body of evidence from both cross-sectional and longitudinal studies that corroborated the general pattern of development. However, Kohlberg's claims about moral development have sparked considerable controversy and continuing debates. For example, critics have maintained that Kohlberg's definition of morality as justice is too narrow to encompass the broad range of ideas subsumed within the term morality, or they have questioned whether his stage sequence accurately captures the morality of everyone.

One such critic is Carol Gilligan, a former colleague of Kohlberg, who took issue with Kohlberg's theory in her best-selling book *In a Different Voice*, published in the early 1980s. Gilligan noted that Kohlberg's original doctoral dissertation, upon which subsequent longitudinal investigations were based, included only a male sample. Gilligan argued that Kohlberg's definition of morality as justice, in which abstract, rights-based principles define the higher stages, is biased toward a male way of thinking and inadequate in capturing the unique features of women's moral reasoning. According to Gilligan, the reasoning of women is oriented not to rights or justice but to notions of care and interpersonal responsibility. Correspondingly, women's moral reasoning is mainly focused on the avoidance of harm in close, interpersonal relationships. However, within Kohlberg's system, these features of reasoning are relegated to stage 3, leading to an implicit bias against women. In addition, Gilligan believed that the hypothetical dilemmas used in Kohlberg's research appeal more to men, whereas woman are more likely to be engaged by real life moral dilemmas related to their own personal experiences.

Gilligan proffered her own sequence of moral development, derived from research she conducted on the reasoning of pregnant women of various ages and backgrounds who were contemplating having an abortion. In Gilligan's model of women's moral development, there is an initial, egocentric focus on the self, followed by a shift to a way of thinking that entails self-sacrificial caring for others. This level is unstable and eventually leads to a synthesis of the needs of the self and those of others, resolved through the application of a generalized moral principle of nonviolence.

Gilligan's claims about sex bias in Kohlberg's theory, and sex differences regarding moral reasoning in general, received intensive scrutiny throughout the 1980s and early 1990s. Contrary to Gilligan's claims, extensive reviews of the voluminous research on moral judgment tended to show no differences in the level of moral development reached by women and men on studies using Kohlberg's measure. Evidence of sex bias appeared to be confined mainly to a few early studies that confounded sex with other variables, such as occupation and level of education. However, when men and women of the same occupational and education levels are compared, sex differences disappear. Moreover, there is little evidence that men predominately use a rights orientation in their reasoning and women use a care orientation. Instead, most studies show that men and women use both orientations in ways that depend on the particular situation. For example, more impersonal dilemmas, such as reasoning about conflicts with strangers in institutional settings, tend to pull for rights-based reasoning, whereas more personal dilemmas, such as conflicts in close interpersonal relationships, tend to elicit care-based reasoning, regardless of gender. Although most of her empirical claims about gender differences in moral reasoning have not received much support, the theoretical debates spawned by Gilligan's work did draw attention to the inadequacy of Kohlberg's theory in accounting for important aspects of moral life, such as the particular obligations of care that may operate within close personal relationships.

A second area of heated controversy centers around the cross-cultural universality of Kohlberg's stage sequence. Some critics, such as Richard Shweder, have argued that Kohlberg's theory is ideologically biased because it reflects the influence of Western belief systems such as democratic liberalism and secular humanism. At the principled level, the moral worth of the individual is abstracted from the social roles and relationships in which he or she participates, and expressed in terms of abstract, human rights held by everyone. Questions have been raised about whether Kohlberg's theory is applicable to those cultures that may define higher morality in terms of divine duties or obligations of filial piety or obedience to authority (e.g., China), or that view human dignity as residing not in an abstract human nature but rather in the position one holds within a social system, as in societies with strictly defined caste or gender hierarchies, such as India.

A fairly large body of cross-cultural evidence has accumulated exploring the universality of Kohlberg's developmental sequence, including longitudinal studies conducted in the United States, Israel, Turkey, India, Indonesia, and China. The results of these studies indicate that individuals in diverse cultures do appear to move through the first three or four stages in the order prescribed by the theory. As well, principled or post-conventional reasoning has been documented in a variety of non-Western cultures, including India and China.

However, two caveats are in order. First, studies of village populations in a variety of cultures indicate that reasoning among villagers tends to remain at stage 3, even in adulthood, and that principled reasoning is virtually nonexistent in such societies. Second, in supporting their judgments, postconventional reasoners from non-Western cultures sometimes appeal to other principles besides the standard stage 5 focus on individual rights or social contract. For example, people from India were found to draw on concepts from indigenous religious or philosophical traditions, such as the Hindu principal of nonviolence (ahimsa), when taking a postconventional perspective. These sorts of responses were difficult to score within the standard stage definitions in Kohlberg's coding manual.

Contrary to certain claims of the cultural critics, however, these postconventional perspectives found within non-Western cultures did not simply equate the good with existing social arrangements, or deny the universal dignity of all human beings. Instead, postconventional reasoners from non-Western cultures applied concepts from their own religious and cultural traditions in universalizable ways, and took a critical perspective on existing social conventional arrangements when these failed to meet the demands of morality and justice – all hallmarks of the postconventional level. Nevertheless, the findings of these cross-cultural studies highlight the need to expand the definition of the postconventional level in Kohlberg's system in order to accommodate the diverse moral principles and concepts found across the world's cultures.

More recently, new perspectives have arisen based on questions about the methodological adequacy of Kohlberg's dilemma and interview approach. Kohlberg's method relies heavily on the ability of people to formulate arguments and to explicitly articulate complex notions, such as moral principles. As such, it is high on production demands and may be biased against less verbal individuals, such as young children or those without formal education. Researchers such as James Rest have devised an objective (multiple choice) measure of moral comprehension (the Defining Issues Test, or DIT), in which participants must identify from a list of statements associated with the different stages what they believe to be the most important issues that should be considered when deciding about a course of action in a moral dilemma. Studies using the DIT have generally found the same developmental pattern as Kohlberg; however, many more people score as principled on the DIT than on Kohlberg's measure. These findings suggest that comprehension measures such as the DIT may be more sensitive to principled moral intuitions held by many people who would otherwise have trouble articulating these ideas within Kohlberg's interview method.

A more extensive revision and critique comes from social domain theory, a perspective developed by Elliot Turiel in the late 1970s and early 1980s that has gained prominence in the last two decades. Turiel and colleagues have suggested that children's understanding of morality emerges neither from an initial orientation to authority and upholding existing social rules that are seen as defining the right and the good (as in Piaget's heteronomous morality), nor out of a prior stage of social convention (e.g., Kohlberg). Instead, morality is a distinct domain of social understanding that stems from children's reflections on their direct experiences with harm and unfairness.

Rather than employing complex dilemmas such as those used by Kohlberg, social domain theorists have explored children's and adults' reasoning about different kinds of acts and rules by directly probing the basis of their judgments. In these studies, participants were asked whether a particular act (e.g., a child hitting another child or calling a teacher by his or her first name) would be acceptable if it were not punished, if there were no explicit social rule prohibiting the act, or if it were common practice in a variety of social contexts (e.g., at home, in school, in another country). Participants across a wide age span distinguished acts entailing harm and unfairness from arbitrary social customs or conventions. The former, termed *moral* acts, were seen as wrong even in the absence of punishment and explicit social rules or authority sanctions, or when commonly practiced, whereas the rightness or wrongness of violations of *social conventions* were seen as dependent on rules, authority commands, or social consensus. When making these distinctions, children and adults appealed to issues of welfare and fairness regarding the moral acts, and social order, authority, and rules in reasoning about social conventions.

Researchers working within this approach have also uncovered a domain of *personal* issues that are seen as up to individuals to decide and beyond the bounds of legitimate authority. Personal issues include recreational pursuits or personal preferences regarding food and dress, with the scope of actions seen to fall within the personal domain expanding in late-childhood or adolescence to encompass issues such as rights to privacy and more abstract freedoms such as freedom of speech or religion. Distinctions among the moral, social-conventional, and personal domains have been found in a variety of cultures, including non-Western cultures such as India, Korea, Indonesia, China, and Nigeria.

The social domain approach suggests that the social reasoning of children and adults is multifaceted and cannot be encompassed within broad orientations such as Kohlberg's or Piaget's stages of reasoning. Even young children do not view the moral in terms of what is punished or prescribed by authorities or dictated by custom, at least for some issues. It is important to stress that, although young children do distinguish morality from social convention, they do not always reason about all such issues in the same way as adults. Children's ability to apply and distinguish social domains depends on a number of factors, such as development within each of the domains and the ability to coordinate judgments in situations that entail components of different domains. For example, as children's moral thinking develops, they may be better able to perceive the moral implications (e.g., social injustice) inherent in certain social arrangements (e.g., sex-role differentiations, exclusionary practices) and to subject their society's laws and social conventions to greater moral scrutiny.

Moreover, although these distinctions are made by both children and adults, there can be disagreement both within and between cultures over the types of actions falling within each domain. For example, in the United States, adolescents sometimes define certain issues as personal (e.g., unconventional styles of dress or the cleanliness of their own room) that their parents see as social conventions and therefore within the bounds of legitimate parental authority. Within cultures, even adults may vary in whether they view some actions (e.g., homosexuality) as matters of personal choice or as linked to religious or social conventional systems of regulation. And, across cultures, some actions that are seen as matters of personal choice (e.g., dietary preferences) may take on moral significance through their association with belief systems entailing harm to persons or supernatural entities, such as deceased ancestors. The social domain perspective stresses the complexities inherent in how individuals apply different social conceptual systems to comprehend and evaluate their social world.

Nevertheless, some psychologists, such as Larry Walker, recently have noted that research and theorizing on moral judgment remains dominated by a focus on issues such as justice and concern for others. The field has paid little attention to *eudaimonia* or self-regarding virtues, associated with normative ideas about self-development and human flourishing. Eudaimonia are often conceived as aspects of the good believed to be desirable but that are not usually thought of as subject to social regulation (unlike justice). Exploring how people reason about these virtues could broaden the field of moral judgment, open up fruitful new avenues of investigation, and strengthen potential connections between this field and the positive psychology movement.

SEE ALSO: ▶ Altruism ▶ Justice ▶ Moral development ▶ Values ▶ Virtue ethics

Motherhood

Melinda J. Key-Roberts
University of Kansas

Motherhood is most frequently defined as a set of socially constructed activities involved in nurturing and caring for dependent children. While early work on mothering focused on the quality of mothering and its effects on the child, the study of mothering has recently expanded to include the activities, understandings, and experiences of motherhood. Thus, as scholarly work on mothering shifted to focus on the person who does the child rearing, definitions of motherhood also began to broaden.

Ideologies of Motherhood

Studies undertaken in the 1970s and early 1980s routinely reported that both men and women tend to see the mother as being more vital to the needs of young children than the father. By the early 1990s a more egalitarian approach to parenting appears to have emerged; however, it is clear that women continue to carry out more childcare and domestic tasks than their partners.

Beliefs about motherhood often reinforce traditional gender-based divisions of labor. According to Terry Arendell, in her comprehensive article *Conceiving and*

Investigating Motherhood: The Decade's Scholarship, the prevailing ideology in North America is that of *intensive mothering*. Proponents of intensive mothering suggest that mothering should be exclusive, wholly child-centered, emotionally involving, and time consuming. The good mother portrayed in this ideology is devoted to the care of others, often neglecting her own needs and interests. When asked to articulate their notion of what makes a good mother, women often endorse the ideal of the good mother put forward by the intensive mothering ideology.

Inconsistencies between the ideologies of motherhood and the experiences of real women are widespread. According to the good mother model, mothers should be passionate about their parental duties. In reality, however, raising a child can result in frustration, depression, and anxiety. In theory, the ideal mother is one who has a constant presence and guiding role in her child's life, putting the child's needs ahead of her own. In practice, however, achieving the ideal can pose a challenge to a woman's sense of self and desire for autonomy. Given the sometimes difficult work associated with mothering, meeting the criterion for a good mother can feel overwhelming, particularly to new mothers. In truth, mothering is a very distinctive and individual experience. For many mothers, tension between the good mother ideal and the reality of mothering is resolved by the emergence of a personal and evolving definition of a good mother.

Maternal Psychological Well-Being

It is not unusual for mothers to feel constrained by the tasks of motherhood one moment, only to experience significant emotional rewards from parenting their children the next. While the responsibilities associated with parenting sometimes weigh heavily on mothers, they also derive great satisfaction from the powerful role they play in the positive outcomes of their offspring. For the majority of women, parenting is both challenging and rewarding. Mothers understand that they are essential to their children's identity formation and socialization. They clearly see their contribution to the care of children as extremely important and unique. Many mothers see themselves as the primary source of comfort for their children. Mothers also believe that they are more naturally attuned to children's emotional needs than other caregivers.

Assuming primary responsibility for children's day to day upbringing can be stressful. Marital dissatisfaction, economic hardship, and difficulty locating and affording childcare can all contribute to greater stress and dissatisfaction among mothers. Mothers living in crowded conditions with young children feel more overburdened than other mothers. Similarly, young mothers, especially those with multiple children, experience greater distress and have fewer psychological resources than older mothers. While popular discourse on motherhood often emphasizes the pressure and stress mothers experience, a national survey of more than two thousand mothers found that mothers generally report high levels of satisfaction with their lives. Results of *The Motherhood Study* suggest that women nearly always tie their satisfaction with their lives as mothers to how their children are doing. In particular, mothers find satisfaction from watching children grow-up well. They also find specific satisfaction in learning from and with their children. While mothers experience more parental strain over the course of child rearing than fathers, they also report more satisfaction with parenting. As cited in Arendell's article *Conceiving and Investigating Motherhood*, mothers are generally more positive and supportive of their children than fathers, and both mothers and children report that children feel more closely attached to their mothers than their fathers.

Research indicates that maternal satisfaction and well-being increase with income and education; satisfaction and well-being are also higher for married mothers and those with high levels of religious involvement. Employed mothers who are able to locate and afford high-quality childcare, who are supported by their partners, and who have flexible workplace options also experience increased well-being. Research by Stacy Rogers and Lynn White also related parenting approach to maternal satisfaction. Specifically, they found that mothers who utilize an authoritative parenting style – characterized by warmth, autonomy, and consistency and clarity in use of discipline – report more satisfaction with parenting than those who use an authoritarian approach.

Satisfaction with social support also appears to be a key factor underlying some of the variation in maternal psychological well-being. Both quality of intimate relationships and quantity of social ties are related to mothers' satisfaction and well-being. While mothers benefit from both emotional support and practical support, differences exist along racial and ethnic lines in mothers' reliance on family and friends for childrearing assistance. In comparison to white mothers, who rely more on neighbors and friends for assistance, African American mothers rely mostly on extended family for help with childcare. In contrast to both black and white mothers, Hispanic mothers rely mostly on other household residents and less on extended family or nonrelatives.

Working Moms

Over the past 30 years, maternal employment has steadily increased for all racial and ethnic groups. According to traditional definitions, a mother is expected to be her child's primary caregiver, particularly when her children are young; this emphasis on mothers as exclusive caregivers may result in feelings of loss, sadness, or guilt when mothers are separated from their children. The unique bond between mother and child may also make it difficult for mothers to relinquish care to others.

Mothering requires sacrifices in alone time, time with friends, and sleep. Many mothers also make sacrifices in their careers, by stepping off the career path or passing up opportunities for advancement. For women who continue to work following the birth of a child, the potentially conflicting demands of motherhood and employment may result in role strain. Many women struggle to balance work and family responsibilities. Employed women who are deeply committed to their role as mother and worker may be more likely to experience role conflict, especially when the demands of both roles are simultaneous and ongoing.

The research findings of Debra DeMeis and H. Wesley Perkins indicate that full-time employed women reduce the amount of time they spend on household chores, but they do not decrease their overall range of responsibilities. Mothers in part-time and full-time paid employment spend an equivalent amount of time with their children as full-time mothers. Furthermore, employed and full-time mothers generally engage in the same childcare activities, with the exception that full-time mothers watch more educational television with their children. Overall, mothers' mental health and parenting satisfaction benefit from maternal employment. However, commitment to both work and family may result in less sleep, curtailed leisure time, and greater stress for working mothers.

When combining parenting and paid work, employed African American mothers may experience greater psychological satisfaction and less stress than white mothers. While they, like all employed mothers, must contend with role conflicts, employment rates among African American women have been higher for a longer period of time and working mothers are seen as vital to family survival. From such a perspective, the ideology of intensive (exclusive) mothering is neither practical nor desirable. As a result, racial-ethnic mothers have carved out alternative childrearing practices to those favored by white, middle-class mothers. Within the black community, raising children is not an individual undertaking; instead the honor and responsibility of caring for children is shared among sisters, grandmothers, and "other-mothers."

Working mothers use a variety of strategies to cope with the increased demands on their time and attention. Research on strategies that employed mothers use to cope with role conflict indicates that working mothers frequently modify their standards for what constitutes a good mother. Because feelings of adequacy may hinge on the relationship between the actual mothering work women perform and their perception of a mother's role, redefinition of the maternal role is critical for both employed and homemaker mothers. Working mothers who do not alter their definition of a 'good mother' may be more likely to experience dissatisfaction with their performance at work and home.

In addition to cognitively restructuring their attitudes and assessments, working mothers may also seek to emphasize the positive and downplay the negative aspects of being a working mother. For example, mothers in part-time and full-time paid employment are more likely to stress the positive outcomes of placing children in alternative care. When asked how they cope with the demands of motherhood and employment, working mothers also emphasize efficiency and organization, planning ahead, and relaxed attitudes about housework.

Future Directions

Research on mothering and motherhood is rapidly expanding. Historically, research on motherhood has been guided by the dominant ideology of intensive mothering. In order to fully understand the experience of mothering, however, inclusion of minority and working-class definitions and perceptions of mother-hood is imperative. As more mothers join the workforce, additional information is also needed on the strategies working mothers use to meet the demands of work and family. Finally, mothers self-report of satisfaction warrants further exploration. As the primary caretaker for their children, most women encounter stress and anxiety. However, the majority of mothers also experience great joy and fulfillment in motherhood.

SEE ALSO: ▶ Attachment   ▶ Subjective well-being

Myers, David G.

Martin Bolt
Calvin College

David G. Myers' integrative review of research on happiness shifted attention to the study of positive emotions and facilitated the emergence of positive psychology. His important work on subjective well-being has reached both scholarly and general audiences and has brought the field closer to understanding the core principles of human flourishing. He has provided direction to empirical work as well as guidance for fostering healthier and happier individuals, families, and societies.

Born in Seattle on September 20, 1942, Myers received his PhD in psychology from the University of Iowa in 1967. He has spent his career at Hope College in Holland, Michigan, where he is presently the John Derk Werkman Professor of Psychology. An award-winning researcher, Myers received the Gordon Allport Prize for his work on group polarization. With his wife Carol, he has established a charitable foundation endowed by royalties from his introductory psychology texts and his general audience trade books. In 2004 the David and Carol Myers Foundation endowed the American Psychological Society Fund for Teaching and Public Understanding of Psychological Science.

Myers' studies of happiness have appeared in numerous scientific and popular journals including *American Psychologist, Psychological Science, Scientific American*, and *Psychology Today. The Pursuit of Happiness: Who is Happy and Why* meticulously surveys research on subjective well-being and dispels popular but mistaken ideas about the factors that enable happiness. *The American Paradox: Spiritual Hunger in an Age of Plenty* explores the personal and social consequences of materialism and individualism and points the way to a communitarian synthesis of individual rights with communal need.

Myers has devoted special attention to understanding religion's positive links with well-being. Devout faith, he suggests, may offer communal support, a sense of meaning and purpose, and enduring hope. Myers has also fostered dialogue between psychology and religion by relating central ideas about human nature found in psychological science and in religious literatures.

Many students first encounter positive psychology in Myers' best-selling psychology textbooks that are renowned worldwide for coupling scientific rigor with a warm writing style that engages both mind and heart. In addition to his multiedition psychology textbooks, Myers's articles have appeared in three dozen magazines, and he has authored 15 books. By effectively digesting psychological science for the general public, he has been a foremost leader in "giving psychology away."

In *Intuition: Its Powers and Perils*, Myers provides a comprehensive survey of recent research that demonstrates both the remarkable capacity and predictable pitfalls of the human mind. *A Quiet World: Living With Hearing Loss* explains the psychology of hearing loss and describes powerful new hearing technologies. *What God Has Joined Together: The Christian Case for Gay Marriage* explores the scientific literature on the roots of sexual orientation and demonstrates how same-sex marriage strengthens the institution for all people. Each highly accessible, provocative book couples authoritative review of the relevant research with insightful reflection on its practical implications.

SEE ALSO: ▶ Enjoyment ▶ Happiness ▶ Prayer ▶ Religiousness
▶ Spirituality

N

Narrative Identity

Dan P. McAdams

Northwestern University

Narrative identity is the story a person constructs and internalizes to organize and make sense of his or her life as a whole. Complete with characters, plots, and other literary features learned from culture, narrative identity includes the person's reconstruction of the autobiographical past and his or her vision or plan for the future. The person's story is likely to incorporate or suggest an imagined beginning (where I came from, how I came to be), middle (who I am now, what my life is now about), and ending (where my life is going in the future, how things will turn out for me). As such, narrative identity is not so much an objective recording of past events as it is an internalized and evolving personal myth of the self, a product of autobiographical reasoning whereby the past is selected and construed in such a way as to set the stage for an anticipated future. Narrative identity integrates a life in time and provides life with some sense of psychological unity and purpose. Contemporary theorists of narrative identity argue that people living in modern societies begin to construct narrative identities in their adolescent and young-adult years as they explore the various economic, ideological, social, and psychological options that society affords for living life as an adult. Through introspection and social interaction, furthermore, people continue to work on and articulate their life stories across the adult life course, often in response to various expected and unexpected life transitions.

The Challenge of Identity

In his famous stage model of psychosocial development, Erik Erikson described *identity versus role confusion* as a critical life challenge that first arises in adolescence. Before the teenage years, Erikson argued, people are not typically concerned with identity questions like "Who am I?" and "What gives my life unity, meaning, and purpose?" Instead, infancy and childhood are taken up with such basic psychological issues as the security of attachment bonds (Erikson's first stage of trust versus mistrust), developing independence in the toddler years (autonomy versus shame and doubt), the Oedipal struggles of early childhood (initiative versus guilt), and the socialization challenges of the elementary-school years (industry versus inferiority). With the advent of puberty, the emergence of abstract thought, and the cultural expectations that attend the move into the teenage years, adolescents find themselves in a new psychological world – Erikson's fifth stage of psychosocial development – wherein they are challenged to formulate a new understanding of the self that will prepare them for adult life.

For many adolescents, Erikson argued, identity construction involves questioning some of the assumptions that implicitly guided their lives as children, even rejecting mores and conventions that are now seen, from the standpoint of adolescence, as immature, authoritarian, simplistic, inauthentic, or, in some sense, no longer true to the new sense of self adolescents now feel they are experiencing. Therefore, adolescents and young adults may experiment with new ideologies (both political and religious), lifestyles, and points of view as they endeavor to figure out who they "really" are and how their lives as adults will eventually unfold. For many people living in modern industrialized societies, identity exploration is expected to run well past adolescence proper and into their 20s and 30s. The development of identity prepares the individual for the challenges of Erikson's sixth stage – intimacy versus isolation. One is best prepared to give oneself to another in long-term bonds of intimacy if one first has established a coherent identity, Erikson argued. Identity, furthermore, paves the way for the midlife challenges of generativity versus stagnation and Erikson's last stage of ego integrity versus despair.

Erikson described identity as a particular configuration or arrangement of the self that is designed to situate the young person in a meaningful and socially-validated niche within the adult world while integrating the person's understanding of who he or she was (as a child), is now, and will be in the future. This configuration of self provides the person with a sense that he or she is fundamentally the same person across different situations and roles while also providing a convincing explanation, for others and for the self, of how the person came to be who he or she is now and will be later. Erikson was never especially clear, however, about just what such a configuration or arrangement of the self might look like. How is the identity configuration structured? What does it contain?

The Turn to Narrative

In the 1980s, psychological theorists began to suggest that the configuration of identity about which Erikson spoke may look something like *a story*. Dan McAdams recast Erikson's concept of identity in narrative terms. McAdams argued that identity is, in part, an internalized and evolving life story and that identity construction in late adolescence and young adulthood is the process of developing a convincing and vivifying story of the self, a personal myth that lends coherence and meaning to a life. Emphasizing individual differences in narrative identity, McAdams suggested that people's life stories can be analyzed, classified, and categorized in terms of such dimensions as narrative tone (the overall emotional quality of the story), recurrent motivational themes (the extent to which the characters in the story pursue ends of power or love, for example), critical scenes (such as high points, low points, and turning points in the plot), central characters (what McAdams called *imagoes*, or personified and idealized images of the self), an *ideological setting* within which the plot develops, and an envisioned ending for the story (typically one that envisions how the story's protagonist will leave something positive behind – or what McAdams called a *generativity script*). McAdams's life-story model stimulated a flurry of research in personality and lifespan developmental psychology into the relations between dimensions of life stories on the one hand and such variables as personality traits, motives, and values on the other. In a broad reformulation of personality psychology, McAdams and Pals described how integrative life narratives define one of three different levels in human personality itself, layered over and influenced by Level-2 constructs, called *characteristic adaptations* (such as motives, goals, and developmental tasks), and Level-1 *dispositional traits* (such as extroversion and neuroticism). Of the three levels, narrative identity most closely and intricately links a person's life to culture.

The emergence and articulation of the life-story model of identity was part of a larger movement toward narrative theories and research in psychology and the social sciences in the 1980s and 1990s. Jerome Bruner, Theodore Sarbin, Kenneth Gergen, and others proposed that human beings are fundamentally storytellers who make meaning in life through narrative and that human lives should be viewed as psychosocially-constructed narrative texts. Cognitive psychologists began to study autobiographical memory, scripts, and narrative styles of information processing; developmental psychologists explored mother-child patterns of storytelling and the development of narrative understanding in children and adolescents; social psychologists began to conceive of situational encounters, social relationships, and even love and attachment in narrative terms; health psychologists documented the salutary effects of personal storytelling; and industrial-organizational psychologists began to write about the narratives of groups and organizations. In a landmark series of books and monographs, Josselson and Lieblich first described *the narrative study of lives* as the interdisciplinary effort to collect, analyze, and disseminate life stories, with a special emphasis on those life narrative accounts, such as those provided by women and people of color, that have historically been marginalized or even silenced. In a related vein, psychotherapists proposed new conceptions of *narrative therapy* that explicitly detailed how therapists might aim to edit or rewrite their clients' life stories.

Research Trends, Issues, and Controversies

Empirical psychologists have conducted many studies on how people incorporate negative life events into narrative identity. Experiences of pain, loss, failure, and human suffering may challenge people's assumptions about how the world works and what their own lives are fundamentally about. Research has suggested that individuals who are able to translate their own negative experiences into coherent stories that entail both the depth of their pain and a sense of positive closure show the best adaptation to negative experiences, the highest levels of psychological maturity, and the greatest degree of life satisfaction. Researchers have also shown that life stories featuring themes of intrinsic motivation, personal growth, and psychological integration tend to be associated with higher levels of well-being. By contrast, narrative identities that contain a large number of contamination sequences – discrete life-story scenes that begin with strong positive emotion but suddenly turn negative – tend to be associated with low self-esteem and depression.

In *The Redemptive Self: Stories Americans Live By*, McAdams described two decades of research into the narrative identities of highly generative (caring and productive) American adults. McAdams identified a common life story prototype constructed by many highly generative American adults in their midlife years – what he calls the "redemptive self". In brief, the story follows this plot: The protagonist learns as a child that he or she is blessed or special and that the world is a dangerous place in need of help; motivated by strong moral convictions, the protagonist journeys forth into the world in an effort to make a positive difference; he or she encounters many negative experiences on the way, but many of these are transformed into positive outcomes (redemption sequences); the protagonist struggles to reconcile competing desires for power and love; at the end of the story, he or she looks forward to leaving a positive legacy for future generations. McAdams argues that the redemptive self reinforces a caring and productive life in the adult years while translating into a psychological narrative some of the most cherished and contested cultural themes in American life, such as the notion of a personal manifest destiny.

While many researchers have examined the content and structure of people's life stories, others have focused their attention on the storytelling process itself, especially as it plays out in social interaction. Researchers have documented how audiences shape the stories people tell about themselves and how different genres to self-telling develop in different kinds of situations. Research into the social construction of life stories highlights ongoing controversies in the study of narrative identity. For example, while some psychologists conceptualize narrative identity as a broad-based story that serves to integrate a life in full, others insist that people tell many different kinds of stories about themselves and that the different accounts cannot readily be incorporated into a larger and synthetic narrative. Researchers and theorists have developed different viewpoints on a number of other important issues in the study of narrative identity. These include: 1) the extent to which a person has one life story or many; (2) the role of individual agency versus the role of situational constraints and performance norms in the construction of narrative identity; and 3) the extent to which life stories are stable versus the extent to which they change over time.

SEE ALSO: ▶ Possible selves

National Institute of Mental Health

Janice E. Jones
Cardinal Stritch University

The National Institute of Mental Health (NIMH) is a division of the National Institute of Health. Located in Rockville, Maryland, the NIMH conducts research on the brain, mind and behavior in order to reduce the pain of mental illness and other disorders related to behavior. The NIMH is a division of the National Institute of Health which is under the jurisdiction of the United Stated Department of Health and Human services. Mental disorders can occur at any age across a person's life span and it is important to note that the NIMH works with any age group. Research is an integral component of the work of the institute and through grant awards both individual and collaborative research efforts are under way which will improve the lives of people with mental illness and improve the quality of care they receive. The NIMH also performs leadership functions for research on the brain and behavior. Education and activism are also important aspects of work at the Institute. The institute disseminates information on mental illness to schools, governments, and volunteer organizations throughout the world.

In 1946 President Truman signed the National Mental Health Act which allowed the federal government to develop the NIMH. Three years later, in 1949, the NIMH was established under the umbrella of the National Institute of Health. As the institute grew it changed to meet the needs of society and the people it was serving. In the 1960s President Lyndon Johnson vowed to link scientific research to societal problems. The institute responded to this call and established centers for research on a variety of mental health issues such as suicide, family mental health, schizophrenia, children's mental health and problems associated with urban living. Additionally, in the mid-1960s alcohol abuse and alcoholism were recognized as major public health problems and again the institute addressed a societal concern and established the National Center for Prevention and Control of Alcoholism.

As technology improved and our understanding for the need for continued research into how the brain works, the NIMH has been on the cutting edge of computer-aided systems and networks that enable scientists to see into the brain and to understand its functions more fully. As such in the 1990s the institute developed the Human Brain Project which is a database of information on neuroscience that scientists around the world can access to improve the human condition. Another important contribution that the advanced technology of the computer age has provided to the NIMH is improved tracking and trends in mental illness. Increased and improved information has allowed the institute to continue to meet the needs of society and to be prepared to offer assistance in times of crisis through information dissemination, providing a network of trained workers and resources. In 2005, the worst natural disaster ever to hit the United States struck the Southeastern states, in the form of hurricanes. The NIMH sent scientists, doctors, nurses and other trained practitioners to these states to provide mental health services and emergency response care. Along with the victims of the storms, the institute provided service and care to the emergency responders. Understanding emergency responder trauma will improve training of emergency responders and mental health service providers in the future. The institute is working to ensure all people affected by a natural disaster receive the help they need to return to the life they knew before the disaster.

In 2004 the NIMH established five divisions for extramural research to address cross-disciplinary collaboration, to allow translation of new inventions from scientific discoveries and to take advantage of recent scientific breakthroughs in the field of mental health. Currently, the institute is working with other divisions of the National Institute of Health to mesh physical and mental health recognizing the interaction between the two. The causes, diagnosis, treatment and prevention of physical health related illnesses have been found to play a significant role in a person's mental health. Ongoing exploration of the interplay between physical and mental health will improve the quality of life for all people.

The NIMH is also responding to the changing demographics of the United States. As researchers and practitioners become more culturally responsive to design and evaluate treatments that meet the needs of a diverse population, the disparities that currently exist will be eliminated and everyone who needs mental health services will be able to access them. The institute is working to make research opportunities available to researchers who are interested in eliminating disparity. In addition to the disparity that exists among diverse populations and access to mental health services, researchers are also examining women, children, minority groups and the elderly.

Addressing the needs of a changing population continues to be of paramount importance to the NIMH as evidenced by recent findings of adolescents and the elderly. In 2006, researchers found that for adolescents a combination of psychotherapy and medication provided the best outcome. Other researchers focused on patients with Alzheimer's disease. The institute continues to evolve and change to meet the needs of the populations and to address the findings that the researchers working either in the field or at the institute discover about mental health. This work helps to ensure that the public is receiving the best care available and that practitioners have the support they need to improve the lives of their patients.

Neurobiology

Mark D. Holder
University of British Columbia, Okanagan

Neurobiology combines biology and neuroscience to study the relation between behavior and cells and cell circuits of the nervous system. The relation between biology and positive psychology is more than a simple correlation. In particular, experimental research suggests that enhancing one's positive psychological state causes changes in one's biology. For example, volunteers who were exposed to the virus that causes the common cold were less likely to develop a cold if they experienced experimentally-induced happiness prior to the exposure. As another example, immune functioning was enhanced after people viewed a humorous video.

The neurobiology of positive psychology has been investigated by examining the neurochemistry of the brain. One research approach has been to study the relationship between mood and serotonin (5-hydroxytryptophan; 5-HT). Serotonin is a monoamine neurotransmitter that regulates many different behaviors including sleep, appetite, arousal, and aggression. Serotonin has also been associated with different aspects of mood, including mood disorders. According to a widely accepted model of depression, when dysfunction occurs in systems that involve serotonin, symptoms of depression may be evident. This model receives support from antidepressant therapies that attribute their success in relieving symptoms of depression to drugs that increase the functional level of serotonin at synapses. Studies have assessed the relationship between serotonin and both positive and negative emotions. However, the results are not always simple and consistent. One reason for this is that serotonin is difficult to measure and consequently, researchers must often rely on indirect measures. One indirect measure of serotonin found that the strength of both positive and negative emotions is associated with decreases in serotonin. However, clinical research suggests that a decrease in serotonin is related to a decrease in positive mood, and that the administration of drugs that increase serotonin levels in the brain also increase positive mood, even in nondepressed people. This is consistent with research hypotheses and studies that claim that low levels of serotonin are linked to an absence of positive mood. However, studies using more direct measures of serotonin, obtained from blood samples, have suggested that although increases in serotonin levels are associated with increases in positive emotions, serotonin may not be clearly related to negative moods.

In addition to studies of neurochemistry, neurohormonal influences on positive psychology have also been assessed. For example, optimism and morning cortisol levels are inversely related; as optimism increases, cortisol levels tend to decrease. Cortisol is a corticosteroid hormone with several functions in the body, including that it is involved in our reactions to stressful events.

One of the most exciting new areas of neurobiology involves the use of cutting-edge technologies that allow scientists to actually see the workings of the brain in living people. These techniques, referred to as brain-imaging or neuroimaging techniques, have recently been applied to positive psychology. In one study, the brain activity was assessed in a person who had meditated for many years. This person was highly accomplished at meditating and was recognized as possessing a very high level of happiness and well-being. The researchers found that he showed an unusually high level of activity in the cells of his frontal lobes. This area is in the front of the brain just behind the forehead. Similarly, experienced meditators were able to focus their attention to increase their positive emotions and achieve what was referred to as a "blissful experience." This state was accompanied by increased electrical activity in cells, including those in the frontal lobes. A low level of activity in this area of the brain is associated with the apathy and lack of emotional expression in patients with disorders such as schizophrenia. Interestingly, the frontal brain regions show increased activity when people hear a joke, but only if they find the joke amusing.

Future research challenges in the area of the neurobiology of positive psychology include identifying the neurobiological correlates of happiness, subjective well-being, and life satisfaction. To do this, techniques such as enzyme immunoassays (EIAs), which have been used extensively to determine the biological markers of depression, could be used. Positive and negative dispositions are not necessarily opposite anchors of a single dimension. Positive dispositions like happiness are independent of negative dispositions. For example, one study reported that family environments accounted for 22% of the variance in positive emotions, but only 2% of negative emotions. Though general and short-term measures of happiness and depression are negatively correlated, more specific and long-term measures of positive and negative affect are not. Therefore, the biological markers of depression, such as those identified with EIAs, may not be associated with happiness; happiness may have unique markers. Thus, the relation between positive psychology and biological markers of negative dispositions (e.g., erythrocytes and neurotrophins such as brain-derived neurotrophic factor [BDNF]) needs further assessment. In addition, the association between aspects of positive psychology and neurotransmitters linked to pleasure and reward (e.g., dopamine) should also be assessed. An advantage of the biological research in positive psychology is that unlike research on depression, there are fewer ethical concerns in increasing positive emotions in humans. Therefore, the causal links between positive psychology and the biological markers can be more easily determined.

SEE ALSO: ▶ Optimism ▶ Serotonin

Neurofeedback

Donald Moss
Saybrook Graduate School and Research Center

Neurofeedback is an evidence-based behavioral therapy based on monitoring brain processes; the neurofeedback therapist displays information on brain processes to the patient, guiding the patient to modify brain activity. Neurofeedback is an extension of biofeedback, which may use electronic instruments to monitor and feed back information about diverse physiological responses, such as muscle tension, hand temperature, or respiration activity. The basic biofeedback paradigm suggests that when we provide a human being with feedback about a biological process, that feedback enables the individual to increase awareness of the process and gain conscious control.

Most neurofeedback relies on an electroencephalograph (EEG) to monitor areas of excessive or deficient brain activation, as well as more intricate patterns in brain activity, such as the coherence of EEG frequencies at two different scalp locations.

The growing appeal of neurofeedback is that it offers an evidence-based complementary therapy which is noninvasive and oriented to enhanced self-regulation. Neurofeedback therapy modifies brain function, through training and behavioral conditioning, and provides relief from many medical illnesses and behavioral problems, without the adverse effects of medication.

History of Neurofeedback

Neurofeedback began with research by Joseph Kamiya in the 1950s and 1960s. Initially Kamiya discovered that one of his subjects could learn through EEG feedback to discriminate between alpha (slow wave) dominant and beta (fast wave) dominant brain states, and further, to produce either brain state on demand. Kamiya's research inspired the hope that human beings could voluntarily modify brain states through feedback learning, enhancing learning potential and alleviating brain-based disorders. Four decades of research since Kamiya's initial publications have shown this hope to be a realistic one, with research showing that neurofeedback can help musicians, dancers and athletes to achieve optimal performance, and can assist students to overcome attention deficits and learning disabilities. In addition, neurofeedback has been shown to assist medical and psychiatric patients in reducing the effects of a wide variety of disorders.

Current Practice

Neurofeedback has improved in effectiveness as advances in computer hardware and software have produced more complex recording and analysis of brain activity, allowing nearly instantaneous feedback of derived information. Feedback can be displayed in a variety of creative ways, ranging from line graphs of the raw biological signal, to bar graphs, and to digital displays. Animations keyed to specific changes in brain activity also allow treatment for younger children who may be asked to make a skeleton dance or to navigate a maze, by changing a brain pattern in a desired direction.

Today an initial evaluation using a digitized quantitative EEG (QEEG), typically employs multisite recording and allows comparison of an individual's brain function to a normative database that contains information on thousands of individuals with known brain-based disorders. The QEEG identifies abnormalities in the electrical activity in the individual's cortex – areas of overactivation, underactivation, asymmetries between the left and right brain hemispheres, and excesses or deficiencies in coherence among brain areas. This initial brain map serves to guide the neurofeedback treatment, which seeks to normalize the abnormal aspects of the patient's QEEG.

Documented Applications

Current research shows clinical value for biofeedback for a growing number of disorders. The two prominent organizations in the field, the Association for Applied Psychophysiology and Biofeedback and the International Society for Neurofeedback and Research have developed standards for rating the clinical efficacy of biofeedback and neurofeedback for medical and psychiatric disorders. The two associations have also sponsored a series of white papers documenting the efficacy of neurofeedback for specific disorders. To date, a white paper has appeared on neurofeedback treatment of Attention Deficit Hyperactivity Disorder (ADHD), and additional white papers are scheduled on neurofeedback for traumatic brain injury, seizure disorders, substance abuse disorders, and anxiety disorders. Already published research supports the use of neurofeedback for ADHD and learning disabilities, depression, mood disorders, anxiety disorders, seizure disorders, addictive disorders, and traumatic brain injury.

SEE ALSO: ▶ Biofeedback   ▶ Complementary and alternative medicine
▶ Neurobiology

Occupational Health Psychology

Jo-Ida C. Hansen
University of Minnesota

The National Institute for Occupational Safety and Health (NIOSH) defines *occupational health psychology* (OHP) as a field concerned with "the application of psychology to improving the quality of worklife and to protecting and promoting the safety, health and well-being of workers." Although OHP is an emerging specialty in psychology, the fields of counseling and vocational psychology and social, industrial-organizational, health and clinical psychology have been engaged in research and applications relevant to OHP for decades. The term occupational health psychology provides a name for the intersection of these specialties around broad issues related to the applications of psychology to prevent illness, injury and occupational stress in the workplace. Simply put, OHP is concerned with stressors that are the antecedents or predictors of stress as well as with the consequences of that stress, in other words the psychological and physical symptoms that result from stress. Another broad focus of OHP is to identify ways in which individuals can learn to tolerate or cope with stress related to their work lives.

The earliest work on stressors and stress stemmed from medical researchers who, through correlational research, noticed that psychological variables served either as predictors of health problems or as a response to physical illness (e.g., the correlation between hard-driving Type A personalities and migraines or the correlations between anxiety, anger, or depression and heart disease and high blood pressure). Other early work related to OHP came from vocational psychology where the emphasis is on improving the fit between worker characteristics – especially interests, abilities, and values – and demands of the work environment.

Vocational psychology also has a long history of counseling application designed to help people adjust to work. These interventions may be oriented towards resolving work-related or personal problems that have a negative impact on work behaviors and performance or on-the-job satisfaction.

In the 1980s, psychological disorders made the top ten list of work-related illnesses as measured by number of worker compensation claims. Not coincidently, during the same period dramatic changes that increased the potential for a stressful workplace environment were occurring, and still are occurring. For example, the wide-spread use of technology has reduced the possibility of leaving work at the office and employees often are expected to be available 24/7; work loads in general have increased with the expectation that people will multitask; and more teamwork is encouraged which can lead to increased stress on interpersonal relationships. In addition, the number of temporary workers has increased substantially which has populated the workforce with employees that have inadequate benefits. Finally, the intersection of work and family is more complex than at any time in history with more dual career couples, increasing eldercare responsibilities for individuals who also are fully engaged in the work force, as well as continuing childcare responsibilities. As these examples suggest, many workers are exposed to stressful circumstances that can lead to emotional exhaustion. OHP is concerned with issues such as these and others that influence the health and well-being of workers.

In response to increased concerns about worker well-being, NIOSH and the American Psychological Association (APA) have collaborated on initiatives designed to introduce researchers and practitioners to OHP. Since the 1990s they have supported the development of 12 graduate training programs in OHP, sponsored 6 international conferences on occupational stress and health, founded the *Journal of Occupational Health Psychology* in 1996, and supported the organization of the Society of Occupational Health Psychology.

One of the challenges for OHP practitioners has been to convince employers that excessive stress does have an impact on the workers as well as the profitability of the company. Many chief executive officers view stress as a motivating factor that energizes workers. Psychological research shows that meeting challenges in the workplace can be rewarding and satisfying and that challenge is an important ingredient for the productive worker. However, research also shows that a fine line exists between challenges and stressors. Whereas challenge can invigorate, stressors actually act on the body in much the same way that infection does leading to poor health and often increasing the probability of injury on the job.

Two schools of thought about the cause of job stress drive the research and application in OHP. One approach examines individual differences and their relation to stress, coping and coping styles. In other words, workplace factors that are stressful for one person may not be stressful for another. This approach views developing a person's resources and coping mechanisms as a way to decrease job stress. Another approach is to study work conditions, identify those that are stressful to most people, and then modify the environment to reduce or eliminate the stressors.

Three broad categories of workplace stressors are job demands, organizational factors, and physical conditions. A fourth category is traumatic stressors. Job or demands that can be stressors include heavy work loads or those that require more ability than the worker has; shift work that interferes with sleeping patterns, eating habits, or normal biorhythms; occupations with high interpersonal demands; repetitive or monotonous work that leads to boredom; and work that involves responsibility for the fate of others. Organizational factors that can create stress include a lack of control over work decisions; unclear responsibilities, goals and objectives; conflicting values; conflicting work and nonwork roles; faulty performance appraisals; inadequate rewards; organizational change; over- or under-promotion; job insecurity; incongruence between person and environment; dead-end jobs; inadequate supplies, assistance, budget, space, training, information or authority. Physical conditions that can create stress include excessive noise; exposure to toxins and chemicals; heat or cold; inadequate lighting; poor fitting work stations; dangerous equipment, and poor ventilation. Traumatic stressors include many of those experienced by medical personnel, police, firefighters, insurance investigators, and natural disaster workers such as death, violence, injury, and destruction of property.

Nonwork factors also can be stressors that affect workplace performance and satisfaction. These include family variables such as dual careers, childrearing and eldercare responsibilities; inadequate finances; insufficient education; and substance abuse. Individual differences variables that can have an impact on workplace adjustment include personality variables; career stage; level of self-esteem and self-efficacy; commitment to work or to an organization; and work-related interests, values and abilities. Variables that may serve as buffers to reduce the effect of job stress include social support, the use of coping strategies, healthy lifestyles, and adequate training and preparation for change and stress.

In addition to understanding the relation between the predictors and the outcomes of stress, OHP emphasizes the prevention of organizational risk factors as well as interventions to manage the stress. For example, fitness health promotion, stress management and environmental safety programs can help to foster growth and development of individuals in organizations. The integration of individual coping strategies with organizational change can help to convert stress from a negative threat to employees' well-being to a positive opportunity that challenges workers to grow and develop through the experience and to achieve success.

SEE ALSO: ▶ American Psychological Association ▶ Vocational psychology

Reference

National Institute for Occupational Safety and Health. http://www.cdc.gov/niosh/ohp.html

Open Source

Y. Joel Wong
Indiana University Bloomington

In its original sense, open source refers to a computer software production and development practice in which the source code is available to the public, enabling anyone to copy, modify, and redistribute it for free. More recently, the meaning of open source has been expanded to include any practice characterized by open and heterogeneous membership, community ownership, convergence of producer and consumer statuses, egalitarianism, and large-scale peer review. Applications of the open source concept include diverse areas such as books and encyclopedias, educational practices, journalism, and psychotherapy. Open source is important in positive psychology because it can be characterized as a positive community practice that spurs innovation.

History

The open source movement emerged in tandem with the Internet explosion in the 1990s. In contrast to traditional commercial software companies that use copyright laws to safeguard the rights of the innovator, several open source software projects released their source codes and harnessed the Internet to enable hundreds of volunteer software developers to make improvements to their software. The open source movement attained prominence on April 7, 1998, when a group of influential software developers gathered in Palo Alto for a summit to discuss ways to increase the use and acceptance of open source practices, especially among commercial businesses. The summit generated a significant amount of interest from the media, resulting in the introduction of term open source to the general public.

Applications

Historically, open source refers to computer software development practices. The source code of an open source software is available to anyone for free to encourage others to make improvements to the software. Contributors to open source projects are allowed to freely distribute the software on condition that their recipients also receive the source code for free. Examples of open source software include *Linux* (an operating system for personal computers), *Sendmail* (an Internet mail utility) and *Apache* (a widely used web server).

Other applications of the open source concept have emerged in recent years. Open source online books (e.g., *Wikibooks*) and encyclopedias (e.g., *Wikipedia*) have become popular because of wiki technology that enables website visitors to easily add, remove, and edit existing content. Open source educational practices often involve online forums where educators share, download, and modify educational materials (e.g., see Open Source Schools at www.opensourceschools.org). Open source journalism refers to forms of online journalism where a diverse group of citizen journalists contribute to the reporting of news rather than relying on a professional journalist. Some scholars have suggested that the open source concept can be applied to psychological practices such as the collaborative development of innovative therapeutic practices by a diverse group of scholars and therapists.

Characteristics

At its core, an open source community is one that is open to anyone who wishes to contribute to the development of a product that is generally available to anyone. In addition, open source communities tend to have the following features:

Heterogeneous Membership

Because open source communities are typically open to anyone who is interested in contributing to their projects or using their products, they tend to be large and attract members with varying degrees of skill and reputation. For example, in the development of open source computer software, it is not uncommon to have hundreds of volunteer software developers testing, examining, and fixing bugs for a computer program.

Community Ownership

Typically, anyone can join an open source community or use, modify, or distribute its products for free. No single person owns the rights to the products. Instead, a sense of community ownership is fostered in an open source community.

Convergence of Producer and Consumer Statuses

In traditional commercial industries, producers and consumers perform distinct roles: producers develop a product for sale while consumers pay for its use. In open source communities, consumers who have an interest in using a product may also contribute to the development and distribution of that product, thus blurring the traditional boundaries between consumers and producers.

Egalitarianism

An open source community tends to lack formal authority or control. Although an open source project may be initiated by a specific individual or organization, anyone, regardless of status or skill, has the right to make changes to a given product.

Large-Scale Peer Review

In an open source community, modifications to a product are subject to peer review not unlike the process in an academic community, although on a much larger scale. Modifications to products are constantly and quickly evaluated by members of the open source community.

Potential Benefits

The development of a product in an open source community has the following potential benefits: cost; innovation and flexibility; speed; and meritocracy.

Cost

A critical advantage of open source is the availability of low-cost technology transfer. Costs related to intellectual property rights, e.g., copyright, are eliminated in favor of community ownership and free exchange of information.

Innovation and Flexibility

The pooling of large, diverse contributions from members of an open source community coupled with the constant flow of ideas and feedback facilitated by the Internet often leads to innovation. In addition, members of the open source community can modify a given product to fit their own needs, resulting in tremendous flexibility and multiple versions of the product.

Speed

A product developed in an open source community has the potential to develop much faster than in traditional projects because of a much larger group of contributors. Moreover, improvements to a product are freely made available to all members of a community, thus allowing members to rapidly build on each other's work.

Meritocracy

In traditional organizations, the contributions of certain members may be recognized or favored on the basis of their rank (e.g., the Chief Executive Officer of a company) or affiliation (being the spouse of the boss) rather than on the basis of their skills. Because of the lack of a formal hierarchy, open source communities are more likely to operate on meritocratic principles; members' contributions are recognized by other members on the basis of their skills.

SEE ALSO: ▶ Organizational psychology

Open-Mindedness

Blaine J. Fowers
University of Miami

Open-mindedness makes it possible to make something of new experiences, learn from errors and blind spots, and engage productively with those who are different from oneself. The capacity for open-mindedness is essential for living a fully human life, as, in the course of living, individuals inevitably encounter new experiences, discover shortfalls in their knowledge and abilities, and confront others who present different views and practices.

The understanding that open-mindedness is necessary for living the best kind of life (flourishing) has led some authors to see it as a virtue because virtues are the character strengths that make it possible to flourish. Peterson and Seligman (2004) call "open-mindedness a strength of character" that involves "the willingness to search actively for evidence against one's favored beliefs, plans, or goals, and to weigh such evidence fairly" (pp. 144–145). If open-mindedness is seen as a virtue, it must have cognitive affective, motivational, and behavioral elements, and be practiced with wisdom, each of which is outlined below.

Open-mindedness is the character strength that comes into play in situations in which one confronts the limits of one's knowledge and experience. Therefore, the key cognitive element of open-mindedness is the understanding that these limits are an inescapable feature of the human condition. Open-mindedness requires an appreciation of the multiple sources of these limits, which include the finite quality of human knowledge and experience, the natural biases to which humans are subject (e.g., ingroup bias), the power of custom and well-worn practice to narrow one's perceptions, self-deception, and the possibility of ideological distortions. In the absence of this knowledge, it is difficult to practice open-mindedness because all of these limiting factors can lead one to see one's viewpoint as complete and beyond the need for correction and expansion. On reflection, it is clear that no human can have an error-free perspective, so open-mindedness is a way to grow and expand one's world. With respect to diversity, "knowledge about cultural matters helps to elevate naïve goodwill to a solid capacity to reach out to others across cultural differences" (Fowers & Davidov, 2006, p. 587).

Individuals are motivated to exercise open-mindedness by the recognition of the limits of their knowledge and their curiosity about what they do not understand. In other words, one wants to be receptive to influence because it provides a way to grow, learn, and overcome error and limitation. This motivation fosters an affective attunement to open-mindedness such that open-minded individuals embrace opportunities to expand their knowledge gladly. Receptivity to what is outside one's experience is spontaneous. One of the key differences between a virtue and a sense of obligation is that "individuals of character are spontaneously drawn to the good" which "encourages the best kind of desires" and actions in the service of that good (Fowers, 2005, p. 45). Of course, obligatory open-mindedness is better than none at all, but the best expression of this capacity occurs as a kind of second nature.

Open-mindedness is not just an internal experience; it manifests behaviorally as well. This involves communicating directly and consistently that one is interested in alternative points of view, that one is comfortable with differences, and that one actually takes steps to expand one's knowledge. Individuals can exercise open-mindedness occasionally or as a settled habit. Having the character strength of open-mindedness would manifest in consistent behavioral expressions of receptivity to influence.

Aristotle famously describes virtue as a mean between deficiency and excess. In the case of open-mindedness, the deficiency-excess dimension could be termed the degree of *receptivity to influence*. (One cannot have too little or too much of a virtue or it ceases to be a virtue. Therefore, the question is not how open-minded to be, but rather how much receptivity to influence constitutes beneficial open-mindedness.) A deficiency of receptivity to influence would be close-mindedness, which can be motivated by a self-protective fear or a self-certain arrogance. An excess of receptivity to influence would occur when one accepts influence from other perspectives willy-nilly, without due deliberation and respect for one's own viewpoint.

Open-mindedness involves a midrange of receptivity to influence such that one remains attached to one's own standpoint even as one allows it to come into question. The most productive form of open-mindedness occurs when genuine dialogue takes place. Dialogue goes beyond an exchange of ideas to engage individuals and groups in a process through which they actively question their own standpoint in light of what the dialogue partner brings to the conversation. Dialogue partners include each other in their ongoing self-exploration and learning, which can result both in greater appreciation for the other and in greater self-understanding. Sometimes, open-minded dialogue results in the accepting influences from the other through coming to recognize key areas of human fallibility such as limited knowledge, self-deception, or ideological blindness.

Open-mindedness allows individuals to expand their knowledge because they recognize that their understanding is limited. Fallibilities of knowledge and ability are endemic to humans and tend to be self-perpetuating. Open-mindedness provides a pathway for exposing self-deception and ideology because alternate perspectives are not subject to the same biases. It is crucial to human flourishing because limitations and blind spots are inescapable and can seriously constrain individuals who are not open to having them questioned. Open-mindedness is therefore necessary for learning and growth, which are key elements in human flourishing.

Although open-mindedness is often extremely valuable, there are times when dialogue leads one to better appreciate one's own deepest commitments with less acceptance of influence. This makes it clear that decisions about how and when to exercise open-mindedness must be made wisely. One must be able to recognize what actions constitute beneficial open-mindedness in a given circumstance. Practical wisdom guides the individual in understanding how much authority to grant to a dialogue partner, and the degree to which one's own standpoint might be erroneous or misguided. To give a few examples, wisdom illuminates areas in which one's perspective seems problematic through leading to undesirable consequences, repetitive errors, undue limitations, and so forth. Seeking input from alternative viewpoints is desirable in such cases. In contrast, wise individuals would also recognize situations in which others are seeking to impose undue influence through manipulation, coercion, or obfuscation and eschew such bids for influence. The judicious exercise of open-mindedness provides an essential corrective to human fallibility.

SEE ALSO: ▶ Flourishing   ▶ Virtue   ▶ Wisdom

References

Fowers, B. J. (2005). *Virtue and psychology: Pursuing excellence in ordinary practices.* Washington, DC: APA Press.

Fowers, B. J., & Davidov, B. J. (2006). The virtue of multiculturalism: Personal transformation, character, and openness to the other. *American Psychologist, 61*, 581–594.

Peterson, C., & Seligman, M. E. P. (2004). *Character strengths and virtues: A handbook and classification.* Washington, DC: American Psychological Association.

Optimism

Michael F. Scheier[a] and Charles S. Carver[b]

[a]*Carnegie Mellon University;* [b]*University of Miami*

Optimists are people who expect good things to happen to them; pessimists are people who expect bad things to happen to them. Folk wisdom has long held that this difference among people is important in many aspects of living. In this case, folk wisdom appears to be right. Optimists and pessimists differ in ways that have a big impact on their lives. They differ in how they approach problems, and they differ in the manner – and the success – with which they cope with adversity. These differences have important implications for their psychological and physical well-being.

The Centrality of Expectancies

The concept of expectancy is pivotal in understanding optimism. Defining optimism and pessimism in terms of expectancies creates a link to expectancy-value theories of motivation (some of which date back to the first few decades of the twentieth century). Expectancy-value models assume that behavior occurs in order to attain desired values or goals. If engagement of effort is to occur, there must be a goal that matters enough (has enough value) to try to reach it. The other element in the equation is expectancy: confidence or doubt that the goal can be obtained. If the person lacks confidence, again there will be no action. If the person loses confidence along the way, action will stop. Only when confidence is sufficiently high do people act and remain engaged in goal-directed efforts. Of the two elements in expectancy-value models, it is the expectancy component that matters in discussing optimism.

Expectancies exist at many levels of generality. A person growing old can have a variety of different expectancies. The person can have an expectancy about being able to move her fingers enough to tie her shoes when getting dressed, an expectancy about still being able to drive to the hair stylist to get her hair cut, as well as an expectancy about living a fulfilling life for several more years. Presumably, the principles in expectancy-value theories pertain equally well to expectancies that are specific in nature and expectancies that are more general. They should even apply to the most general kinds of expectancies, those that characterize optimists and pessimists. The "confidence" that is at issue is simply broader in scope, relevant to a larger class of situations and behaviors. From this perspective, optimism and pessimism are simply broader versions of confidence or doubt, pertaining to most situations in life rather than just one or two.

Effects of Optimism on Well-Being

Measuring Optimism

Research on the effects of optimism has flourished over the past 20 years. This research has taken several different routes to assessing optimism, leading to somewhat distinct literatures. One approach measures expectancies directly. Some researchers who take this approach ask respondents about their expectancies in *specific situations*, trying to sample from as many domains of life as possible. An optimism score is then derived by adding responses to the particular items. Others do not ask about particular situations, but rather ask people whether they think their outcomes will be good or bad *in general*, by asking people to respond to statements such as "I'm optimistic about my future." The advantage of this approach is that a shorter scale can be used to assess optimism, thereby making it easier for respondents. In addition, scales that sample particular domains run the risk of not including all domains that are important. On the other hand, if a researcher is only interested in one specific domain, it might be better to assess expectancies in that domain directly, and not use a measure of generalized optimism at all.

Another, quite different, approach to assessing generalized optimism derives from work on attributional style. The idea behind this approach is that people's expectancies for the future stem from their interpretations of the past. Explaining bad outcomes in terms of causes that persist into the future and influence a broad range of events implies pessimism. This explanation carries the implication that negative outcomes will continue to occur in the future. The opposite attributional style, explaining negative events in terms of causes that are more time limited and narrower in their effects, implies a more optimistic orientation.

Researchers who work on optimism often refer to optimists and pessimists as though they were distinct groups. However, this usage is a verbal convenience. All approaches to the measurement of optimism provide scores that vary continuously across large numbers of people. Thus, people actually range from very optimistic to very pessimistic, with most falling somewhere between.

Historically, researchers have viewed optimism and pessimism as comprising of a single, bipolar dimension. From this perspective, pessimism is simply the opposite of optimism. Most people working in the field still continue to construe optimism and pessimism in this fashion, and analyze their studies accordingly. However, a growing number of researchers are exploring the possibility that optimism and pessimism are somewhat distinct constructs. This view is consistent with the fact that scales of generalized optimism are often shown to be comprised by two separate components – one measuring the person's expectancies for positive outcomes and one measuring the person's expectancies for negative outcomes. It remains unclear how questions involving the structure of optimism and pessimism will be resolved.

Psychological Well-Being

Dozens of studies have been conducted examining relationships between optimism, pessimism, and distress among people undergoing adversity of one type or another. The stressors studied have varied widely. Studies have examined the experiences of students entering college, employees of businesses, and survivors of missile attacks. Studies have measured the reactions of people caring for cancer patients and people caring for patients suffering from Alzheimer's disease. Research has examined experiences of people dealing with medical procedures such as childbirth, abortion, coronary artery bypass surgery, and attempts at in vitro fertilization, as well as heart and bone marrow transplantation. Other studies have looked at how people deal with a diagnosis of cancer, the pain of arthritis, and the progression of AIDS.

The results of these various studies all point in the same direction: Optimistic persons experience less distress during times of adversity than do pessimists. This conclusion holds for studies that are cross-sectional – that is, that assessed optimism and distress at the same point in time. This conclusion also holds true for studies that are prospective – that is, that assessed optimism and distress at some base-line and then reassessed distress later in time. The results of the prospective studies are particularly important, in that they suggest that optimism is associated with beneficial changes in distress over time. Thus, these prospective studies also help to get around the potential problem inherent in cross-sectional research of confounding optimism with subjective well-being.

Optimism, Pessimism, and Coping

If optimists experience less distress than pessimists when dealing with difficulties, is it just because optimists are cheerful? Apparently not. If so, optimism would not predict *changes* in distress over time, which findings from prospective studies show it does. There must be other explanations. One possibility, now thoroughly explored, is that optimists and pessimists differ in the way in which they react to and cope with adversity. In many ways, the work relating optimism to coping simply provides a more detailed depiction of the broad behavioral tendencies that were used to characterize optimists and pessimists earlier in this entry. That is, people who are confident about the future continue trying, even when it's hard. People who are doubtful try to escape the adversity by wishful thinking, they employ temporary distractions that don't help solve the problem, and they sometimes even stop trying.

Such differences in coping have emerged in a number of studies. The majority of these studies have examined different types of patient populations or people undergoing different types of medical procedures. The findings from these projects suggest that optimistic people differ from pessimistic people in a number of ways, in terms of both their situational coping responses and their general, more stable coping styles. Some of the major differences are summarized in Table 4.

The studies on coping help to establish that optimists cope differently to pessimists. However, they do not show that these differences in coping tendencies are responsible for the differences seen in psychological well-being. Perhaps both the psychological outcomes and the coping findings are being driven by some third unmeasured variable. Fortunately, a number of prospective studies have contained measures of coping tendencies in addition to measures of well-being. This

Table 4 Differences in the Coping Tendencies of Optimists and Pessimists.

Optimists	*Pessimists*
Seek information about the problem	Suppress thoughts about the problem
Plan and use problem-focused coping	Engage in self-distraction tactics
Use positive reframing	Focus on their distress
Try to find benefits in their adversity	Use cognitive and behavioral avoidance
Use humor	Overtly deny that the problem exists
Try to accept the reality of their situation	Give up trying to cope with the problem

allowed researchers to examine whether the differences they observed in well-being were mediated by differences in coping. This body of research has consistently shown that psychological well-being and coping responses are linked. Thus, optimists receive better psychological outcomes than pessimists in part because of the differences between them in coping.

Physical Well-Being

Much more is known about the effects of optimism on psychological well-being than is known about the effects of optimism on physical well-being. Still, a number of studies have explored links between optimism and physical health, and between optimism and aspects of physiological functioning. The findings from this research mirror those just presented with respect to psychological functioning: Optimistic persons typically show better outcomes. In this case, they show signs of better physical health or signs of more adaptive physiological responses when under adversity than do persons more pessimistic in orientation.

For example, compared to pessimists, optimists report fewer physiological symptoms during times of duress and maintain a higher health status across their lives. Other studies show that optimists are less likely to suffer negative medical side effects from major surgery or to be rehospitalized within the first few months after major surgery. They are also more likely to benefit longer from the effects of their surgery. In a similar vein, less pessimistic persons have been found to outlive more pessimistic persons when diagnosed with a life-threatening illness such as recurrent cancer. They also exhibit less extreme cardiovascular reactivity during the course of their daily lives. On a somewhat different note, optimists tend to show signs of more adaptive immune functioning than do pessimists, but the evidence on this point is a bit more mixed than the other physical health outcomes that have been examined.

Health-Promoting and Health-Damaging Behavior

As noted, extensive research has documented that optimists and pessimists cope differently with stress and that these differences in coping are partly responsible for producing beneficial psychological outcomes for optimists. In part, coping differences may also be responsible for the more beneficial physical health outcomes as well. The studies making this case involve reactions to particular health threats or illness episodes. As a group, these studies demonstrate that optimists are more likely than pessimists to face health threats head-on, and do whatever they can to improve the situation they are confronting. In this respect, the behavior seems to reflect problem-focused coping, an attempt to engage in proactive processes that promote good health and well-being.

For example, following coronary artery bypass graft surgery, optimistic patients are more likely than pessimistic patients to enroll in cardiac rehabilitation programs and to take vitamins and eat low-fat foods. Optimistic patients are also more likely to benefit from cardiac rehabilitation programs than are pessimistic patients. In a similar vein, HIV-negative gay men who are optimistic report having fewer anonymous sexual partners than those who are more pessimistic in outlook, suggesting that optimists are making efforts to reduce their risk, safeguarding their health. Finally, optimists are more likely than pessimists to seek out information about risk factors for major diseases.

Optimists appear to take action to minimize health risks. They do not simply stick their heads in the sand and ignore threats to well-being. They attend to risks, but do so selectively. They focus on risks that are applicable to them and relate to potentially serious health problems. If the potential health problem is minor, or if it is unlikely to bear on them, their vigilance is not elevated. Optimists appear to scan their surroundings for threats to well-being but save their behavioral responses for threats that are truly meaningful.

If optimists face health threats head-on and try to do as much as they can to make themselves less vulnerable to poor health outcomes, pessimists do just the opposite. It was noted earlier that pessimists tend to give up when confronting serious problems in life. Giving-up can become manifest in ways that have negative health consequences. For example, giving up may underlie various forms of substance abuse, such as excessive alcohol use, which is often seen as an escape from problems. This suggests that pessimists should be more vulnerable than optimists to maladaptive behavior of this type. Evidence supports this reasoning.

Clearly, giving up can be reflected in many ways. Alcohol dulls awareness of failures and problems. People can ignore problems by distracting themselves with other activities. In other cases, though, giving up is more complete. Sometimes people give up not just on trying to deal with the problems they are confronting, but on their lives, by suicide. Some are more vulnerable to suicide than others. It is commonly assumed that depression is the best indicator of suicide risk. But pessimism is actually a stronger predictor of this act, the ultimate disengagement from life.

Is Optimism Always Better Than Pessimism?

The evidence suggests optimists are better off than pessimists. They are less distressed when times are tough, they cope in ways that foster better outcomes, and they're better at taking the steps necessary to ensure that their futures continue to be bright. Although there are situations in which optimists are only slightly better off than pessimists and probably some where they have no advantage, there is remarkably little evidence that optimists are ever worse off than pessimists.

Several theorists have suggested that such situations do exist, that optimism may be potentially damaging. The logic is this: Too much optimism might lead people to ignore a threat until it's too late, or might lead people to overestimate their ability to deal with it, resulting in poorer outcomes. As previously noted, this appears to be generally not the case. However, occasional studies do suggest adverse effects of optimism. For example, there is some evidence that optimism predicts poorer immune response under relatively high challenge and that the buffering effect of optimism reverses when life stress accumulates over time. In addition, cross-cultural work suggests that optimism and pessimism may function quite differently in different cultural groups. Findings such as these suggest that some caution is warranted in concluding that optimism is invariably beneficial.

Development of Optimism

At present, not much is known about the origins of optimism, but the determinants must necessarily fall into two broad categories – nature and nurture.

On the nature side, the available evidence suggests that individual differences in optimism-pessimism are partly inherited. The evidence comes from twin studies, in which the similarity between identical and fraternal twins is compared. The available evidence suggests that between 25% and 30% of the variability in optimism is due to genetic factors, depending on how the estimate of heritability is made. Thus, at least some of the differences in optimism and pessimism among people are due to genetic influence.

On the environmental side, it makes sense to suggest that prior experience with success and failure might play a role. Prior success breeds anticipation of future success, and prior failure should create the expectation of future failure. Consistent with these ideas, research has shown that childhood socioeconomic status (SES) predicts adult levels of optimism and pessimism, even when adult levels of SES are taken into account. Children from low SES families, who presumably experience more failure experiences and who have fewer opportunities to be successful, grow up to be more pessimistic in outlook.

Children might also acquire a sense of optimism (or pessimism) from their parents, a possibility supported by at least some twin studies that show that shared environment is also an important determinant of optimism. Parental transmission of optimism could occur indirectly through the expression of optimistic or pessimistic thoughts, or by modeling appropriate or inappropriate behavioral responses to adversity. Parents might also influence their children more directly by instructing them in problem solving. Parents who teach adaptive coping skills are likely to produce children who are more successful. Thus, the basis for an optimistic orientation to life is provided. The idea that optimism is somewhat malleable has spawned a treatment approach, called *learned optimism*. In essence, this approach tries to reduce a person's level of pessimism by altering the person's tendency to process information in a pessimistic way.

Future Directions

Extensive work on optimism and pessimism has been done over the past two decades. Still, more work is needed. In this regard, more research is needed to help answer questions about the structure of optimism and pessimism – whether optimism and pessimism are bipolar in nature or constitute separate constructs. More research also needs to be done on the developmental antecedents of optimism and pessimism, especially on the environmental side. In addition, the field needs to investigate more thoroughly the influence of optimism and pessimism on physical well-being. Assuming that this link is made, studies will also then be needed to identify the biophysiological mechanisms that produce differences in physical well-being. Finally, although the field has started to make progress in the intervention area, there is still a way to go. Greater effort needs to be made to develop interventions that allow pessimistic persons to deal more effectively with the adversity of life.

SEE ALSO: ► Learned optimism ► Attribution theory ► Coping ► Well-being

Organizational Psychology

Roni Reiter-Palmon, Marcy Young Illies, and Joseph M. James
University of Nebraska-Omaha

Positive organizational psychology is characterized as the application of positive psychology principles to the study of organizational phenomena. While positive psychology focuses on the study of positive emotions and traits at the individual level, positive organizational psychology focuses on using knowledge from positive psychology to enhance the experience of work.

A useful framework to understand positive organizational psychology phenomena is to look at person-, process-, and outcome-oriented domains. Specifically, a *person domain* refers to a positive state of mind experienced by organizational members (e.g., intrinsic motivation or job satisfaction). A *process domain* is a construct or intervention intended to positively affect organizational members (e.g., transformational leadership or job enrichment). An *outcome domain* refers to the positive results organizations seek to elicit from organizational members (e.g., creativity or team collaboration). While all three domains are important in the context of positive organizational psychology, this review will focus primarily on the process and outcome domains, as those are unique to positive organizational psychology. Specifically, from the process domain, leadership will be reviewed, while creativity and team collaboration will be the outcome domains reviewed.

Implicit to the person-, process-, and outcome-domain framework is the existence of interrelationships across the domains. Specifically, process domain constructs or interventions may have a direct influence on outcomes, for example, leadership may directly influence team collaboration and creativity. These constructs or interventions may also have an indirect influence on outcomes by way of person domain constructs, for example, leadership may affect follower job satisfaction. Equally so, person domain constructs may influence outcomes exclusive of any explicit process interventions such as the relationship between intrinsic motivation and creativity. Additionally, positive outcomes may be influenced by the outcomes from other domains as exemplified in the relationship between team collaboration and creativity. In other words, constructs across the three domains may influence or be influenced by the other two domains, either independently or in combination.

Leadership

Leadership is of relevance to positive organizational psychology due to the broad range of influence leaders have on organizations and organizational members. Leadership can be a vital part of an organization's success. Leaders can create a positive work environment in numerous ways, such paying attention to employees' needs, empowering employees to fulfill these needs, and providing a positive role model. Many of these leadership practices are captured in the transformational and charismatic leadership models.

House defined the charismatic leader as a leader who typically has a combination of dominance, self-confidence, need for influence, need for conviction, and that they use these characteristics to articulate goals, provide a role model, motivate others, demonstrate confidence, and build his or her image. The effect of these characteristics is seen by the effect on followers. Followers of charismatic leaders exhibit trust in and affection to the leader, identify with the leader, are emotionally involved with the task, adopt the goals of the leader and show confidence in completing the task.

Similar to charismatic leadership, transformational leadership also addresses the leader's relationship with the follower. Transformational leadership is defined through its four components: a) idealized influence – the leader is charismatic, admired, and followers identify with him or her; b) inspirational motivation – the leader motivates and inspires followers by providing significance to work; c) intellectual stimulation – the leader supports creativity and innovation and promotes intelligent thinking; d) individualized consideration – the leader treats follower as individuals and tries to pay attention to each individual and their needs.

While some argue that there are differences between charismatic and transformational leadership, others suggest that there is a large degree of overlap. Research on charismatic and transformational leadership tends to focus on the positive influence these leadership styles have on organizations and followers. For example, Zaccaro and Banks suggested that transformational and charismatic leadership could create a positive work environment by creating a positive vision for which the organization strives to achieve. House stated that charismatic leadership influences subordinates to accept this vision by establishing a bond with leader and followers.

Using the framework presented previously, transformational and charismatic leadership, exemplifying the process domain can influence the person and outcome domains of positive organizational psychology in a variety of ways. Transformational leadership was found to be related to person-domain constructs such as follower job satisfaction and motivation as well as positive job perceptions. Additionally, transformational and charismatic leadership are linked to several positive organizational outcomes. Transformational leadership was found to positively influence project team performance, organizational commitment, and creativity.

Creativity

Today's ever-changing markets coupled with job changes due to outsourcing, have caused an increase in the demand for employee creativity. In addition, creativity is no longer limited to a subset of positions. This surge in the need for creativity has made it an important component for organizational success. Creativity is relevant to the present discussion of positive organizational psychology because it represents an outcome domain of positive organizational psychology. As such, creativity is somewhat dependent upon the process- and person-domains.

Researchers define creativity as something that is novel and of value. Woodman, Sawyer, and Griffin suggested that from an organizational perspective, creativity is typically a subset of innovation. Innovation is viewed as the act of implementation and actually using the creative idea, whereas creativity focuses mainly on the idea development stage.

Models of organizational creativity suggest that creativity can be developed at an organizational level, a group level, and an individual level. As an outcome, creativity is affected by factors from the person and process domains of positive psychology, as well as other outcomes. At the individual level, creative people have been known to apply the appropriate cognitive process, have domain relevant knowledge, have intrinsic motivation to engage in the task, and are independent, persistent and open to experiences. Factors that affect these variables are known to effect creativity, such as job enrichment programs that increase job challenge and intrinsic motivation, or training programs that are designed to increase the application of cognitive processes. This indicates the importance of the process domain of positive organizational psychology for fostering creativity in organizations.

The workplace environment also plays a critical role in facilitating or hindering creative performance by individuals and groups. Research on organizational climate has found that organizations that are able to provide environments compatible with creative individual needs improve creativity. Creative climates that promoted freedom, risk-taking, openness, and trust had more creative employees. Leadership, a process variable, has been found to affect creative performance directly through the support of the leader, as well as through the development of an organizational and group climate that supports creativity. Process domains of positive organizational psychology related to group-level creativity may be team-building activities designed to enhance trust among team members in order to foster the open exchange of ideas.

Team Collaboration

Research on team functioning has focused on many aspects of team behavior that are negative in nature such as conflict, social loafing, team member dominance, misunderstanding or lack of communication, groupthink, and lack of resource or information sharing, to name a few. Further, when team collaboration or cooperation is studied, it is typically in the context of the factors that hinder collaboration. It is also important to study what does work when teams work together. Positive team collaboration is an important aspect of positive organizational psychology. Team collaboration is viewed as part of the outcome domain, and similar to creativity, it is affected by factors from person, process and outcome domains.

Person-domain factors include motivation and willingness to work in a team and commitment to the team. Team cohesion is the direct result of individual team member commitment to the team. Team cohesion further enhances member satisfaction from team interaction and these factors increase the likelihood that team members collaborate and work together.

The process domain includes several possible interventions that may facilitate team collaboration. For example, research suggests that shared mental models lead to better collaboration, as team members have a shared understanding of the task and expected behaviors. Training can be used to facilitate the development of these shared mental models. Team composition variables, such as homogeneity or diversity of team members, can also influence collaboration. Diversity can be defined as surface-level, focusing on social categories such as gender or race, or deep-level, reflecting diversity in education, experience, personality, and values. Research on team diversity suggests that deep-level diversity can facilitate some aspects of team collaboration such as information sharing and creative problem-solving, however, research has also suggested that diverse teams are not always beneficial. To facilitate the attainment of the benefits associated with diverse teams, interventions that improve group process and collaboration skills as well as develop a group identity have been suggested.

One can view the process domain (leadership) and outcome domains (creativity and team collaboration) as a means to influence employees in order to elicit positive organizational outcomes. Implicit in this is the goal of enhancing organizational members' well-being, which fits within positive psychology in general. One final point should be mentioned, the intent here is not to argue for enhancing organizational member well-being solely in the pursuit of positive organizational outcomes. Rather, the intent is to illustrate the benefits of putting people first within an organization.

SEE ALSO: ▶ Charisma ▶ Creativity ▶ Job satisfaction ▶ Leadership ▶ Positive organizational behavior

Oxytocin

C. Sue Carter
University of Illinois at Chicago

Oxytocin is a small peptide molecule, made primarily in the brain, and with a major functional role in mammalian sociality. Oxytocin was probably pivotal in permitting the evolution of the human nervous system by facilitating the birth process and protecting the fetal nervous system during the birth. Oxytocin also facilitates milk ejection and thus lactation, which is the defining feature of Mammalia. Lactation in turn allows the birth of immature infants, permitting post-natal cortical and intellectual development in young that are dependent on their mother as a source of both food and caregiving.

Oxytocin also sits at the center of a neuroendocrine network that coordinates social behaviors and concurrent response to various stressors, generally acting to reduce reactivity to stressors. Oxytocin tends to decrease fear and anxiety, and increase tolerance for stressful stimuli. At the same time oxytocin appears to encourage various forms of sociality including maternal behavior, social contact and social bonds, and even "trust."

Oxytocin is released and works in conjunction with a related neuropeptide known as vasopressin. Vasopressin is structurally similar to oxytocin, differing by only two of nine amino acids. The genes regulating the synthesis of these pep-tides are on the same chromosome and are modifications of a common ancestral gene. The similarity of the oxytocin and vasopressin molecules also allows them to influence each other's receptors. The actions of oxytocin and vasopressin are often – but not always – in opposite directions. Oxytocin reduces behavioral and autonomic reactivity to stressful experiences. Vasopressin, in contrast, is associ-ated with arousal and vigilance.

Various brainstem neural systems, including those that rely on peptides such as oxytocin and vasopressin, help to regulate emotional states including approach-avoidance reactions and the tendency of mammals to immobilize, permitting sexual or maternal behavior. Oxytocin and vasopressin are synthesized in and are particularly abundant in the brain structure known as the hypothalamus, but may reach distant receptors including those in the cortex and lower brain stem areas responsible for autonomic functions, thus helping to integrate behavioral and emotional responses.

Oxytocin and vasopressin have the capacity to move through the brain by diffusion, rather than acting only across a synapse or requiring transport by the circulatory system; for this reason these neuropeptides have pervasive effects on the central nervous system. Oxytocin is unique in having only one known receptor and in using the same receptor for many functions, thus allowing coordinated effects on behavior and physiology, although oxytocin also can bind to vasopressin receptors (and vice versa). Dynamic interactions between oxytocin and vasopressin may be of particular importance to the approach and avoidance components of sociality and the subsequent formation of selective social bonds. For these reasons, it is possible that oxytocin, and perhaps also vasopressin, may have a role in the behavioral responses necessary for positive social behaviors.

The importance of social interactions can be understood in part by examining the consequences of placing animals in social isolation. In this context, oxytocin can be elevated, especially in females, possibly as a protective mechanism against possibly negative consequences of isolation. Oxytocin, often in conjunction with vasopressin and dopamine, influences various social behaviors, including the formation of social bonds, suggesting one mechanism through which social interactions have powerful effects on reward systems.

Oxytocin and vasopressin receptors are found in many brainstem structures including the extended amygdala, and also in the neocortex and hippocampus. The amygdala and its connections serve a role in integration of reactions to various kinds of sensory stimuli, including approach and avoidance. In human males, intranasal administration of oxytocin inhibited the activity of the amygdala and altered down-stream connections to brainstem structures involved in the regulation of the autonomic nervous system. Vasopressin, acting centrally (in areas including the bed nucleus of the stria terminalis, BNST, amygdala and lateral septum), may elevate vigilance and defensiveness, possibly serving in some cases as an antagonist to the effects of oxytocin. Thus, oxytocin has the capacity to reduce fear and calm the sympathetic responses to stressful stimuli.

It is reported that females are more social than males. Explanations for sex differences typically focus on steroid hormones. However, neuropeptides also may be involved. Oxytocin is estrogen-dependent, but has functions in both males and females. However, the hypothalamic synthesis of vasopressin is androgen-dependent and this molecular may be of particular importance to behavior in males. Working together these molecules may allow sexually-dimorphic responses to emotionally contradictory tasks such as forming social bonds or showing empathy, while also permitting rapid behavioral and autonomic reactions, including defensive behaviors or aggression, in the face of other social cues.

The release of oxytocin may encourage social interactions including those associated with detecting and responding to the emotions or experiences of others. Emotional and visceral states influence how we feel about and react to others, and thus our capacity for positive social interactions. Awareness of factors that regulate emotional responses and feeling lead us to a deeper understanding of the evolved neurobiology of positive social behaviors. Selective social behaviors can facilitate survival and reproduction, promoting safety and a sense of emotional security. Sociality is essential to human existence and it is likely that the neural substrates and hormonal conditions for positive social behaviors are shared with those for other forms of sociality including the willingness to approach or trust others or show sensitivity to the emotional cues from others. This strategy for understanding sociality also has been extended to the level of genetic analysis.

As just one example, the genetic substrates responsible for the production of oxytocin and vasopressin receptors have been linked to disorders such as autism. Individual or sex differences in the genetics of this system might be associated with individual differences in social behavior.

SEE ALSO: ▶ Appetitive motivational systems ▶ Aversive motivational systems ▶ Cortisol ▶ Dopamine ▶ Social support

P

Paragons

Silvia Osswald, Dieter Frey and Tobias Greitemeyer
Ludwig-Maximilians-University Munich

A *paragon* is a person of outstanding merit who serves as a model of some quality. Throughout their lives, human beings allow themselves to be guided by the influence of paragons. Especially during childhood and adolescence, paragons play an important role in personality development. Paragons are widely used to change attitudes and behaviors as people not only learn by classical or operant conditioning processes, but also by models. For instance, in antidrug campaigns, famous athletes express that they are against drugs. People like Martin Luther King, Mahatma Gandhi, or Mother Theresa set extremely high standards and it is questionable if such paragons do really play a role in daily life. Thus, when children and adults are directly asked what paragons they have, it is not well-known personalities that are primarily named, but rather friends and most often, one's own parents. For instance, White and O'Brien asked children and adolescents what heroes they have. The 8- to 16-year-olds most often named their parents – ahead of athletes, entertainers, or political leaders. This underscores the importance parents have as models. With increasing age, however, people seem to have fewer paragons – or they are less likely to admit to having some. The reason might be found in a misunderstood individualization (misunderstood because there is no contradiction between being unique and having a paragon) and a desire for matchlessness. On the contrary, Simonton has shown that paragons played an important role in the lives of famous artists. When asking people about their exemplars, it is clear that the answers will differ depending on the area in question: Moral exemplars are different from paragons of intelligence; Einstein is more likely to be a paragon for science-engineering students, whereas Shakespeare would be among arts-education students. Paragons are also gender-dependent: Female students have more female paragons, whereas male students have mostly male. The paragon *par excellence* does not exist – the choice of a model is always a subjective process. According to Paulhus and Landolt, those who are chosen are familiar, likeable, occupationally and attitudinally similar and often members of the same sex as the individual making the choice.

Aside from the question of who is selected, it is also important to know in what ways exemplars can exert an influence on people. To find answers to such questions, the social cognitive theory of Albert Bandura could be employed as a theoretical framework with special emphasis on the parts of this theory that deal with observational learning. Observational learning means that "observers can acquire cognitive skills and new patterns of behavior by observing the performance of others (i.e. models)" (Bandura, 1986, p. 49). To display their influence, models should be attractive (possess prestige, power or competence) but also similar to the observer. The literature distinguishes between mastery (who already perform perfectly) and coping models (who perform better step by step). In some cases coping models may be preferred to mastery models as the former are more similar to the observer: Models (and paragons) can only affect persons when they are seen as reachable. If a paragon is out of reach (too demanding, too good), those attempting to model him or her will become depressed and frustrated. A special type of observational learning that is significant in this respect is abstract modeling, whereby judgmental skills and general rules are acquired through the observation of a real or symbolic model (e.g., a person described in a text). On a descriptive and prescriptive level, abstract moral rules and ethical norms can be learned from paragons. They can therefore be characterized as direct, informative and motivational models. Paragons, however, also display a more subtle impact: Activated exemplars unconsciously influence cognitive processes or behavior. Baldwin and colleagues demonstrated that priming practicing Catholics subliminally (they were not aware of what they had seen) with pictures of the Pope affected their self-ratings. For nonpracticing Catholics, however, the Pope was not a paragon and therefore had no influence.

More research should be dedicated to this topic, like studies that examine how paragons change through the course of life or whether people act *better* (i.e., more morally) when reminded of their paragons. Furthermore, future research should address how every one of us could become a paragon, a person that acts authentically to make the most (positive) out of one's own life.

SEE ALSO: ▶ Self-efficacy   ▶ Social cognitive theory

Reference

Bandura, A. (1986). *Social foundations of thought and actions. A social cognitive theory.* Englewood Cliffs, NJ: Prentice-Hall.

Peace

Ilana Shapiro, Rezarta Bilali, and Johanna Vollhardt
University of Massachusetts

Whether it is defined negatively as the absence of hostilities, violence, or war, or more positively as a state of social harmony, tranquility, and equilibrium, the concept of *peace* is undoubtedly complex. Most seem to agree that peace is a human virtue and a noble goal, yet there is no consensus on a definition to help guide in operationalizing the concept or developing measurement procedures and indicators. As a result, both within the field of psychology and across disciplines, researchers apply very diverse theoretical frameworks to its study and often examine different levels of analysis.

At an individual or intrapersonal level, psychologists focus on peace as an internal state of untroubled calm, serenity, and contentment. Both psychological and medical research demonstrates an important relationship between inner peace and physical health. Research in affective neuroscience has examined the effects of meditative practice designed to transcend internal agitation, chatter, and craving and findings suggest a striking difference between trained and untrained individuals' brain activity and capacity to maintain states of inner peace, even in the face of difficult situations and disputatious people. In addition, cognitive-behavioral therapies often include methods for cultivating inner peace as a stress reduction and cognitive restructuring tool useful in the treatment of anger and anxiety disorders, addiction, obsessive compulsive disorders and a variety of other problems.

Perhaps the largest areas of psychological research on peace, however, focus on relations between individuals, groups, and nations. The subdisciplines of social, political, and peace psychology cover vast territory in understanding processes for preventing violence, reducing prejudice and discrimination, resolving conflict, and promoting cooperation. Research focuses on issues such as nonviolence, intergroup contact, interdependence, social justice and morality, prosocial attitudes and behaviors, collaborative problem-solving, integrative negotiation, forgiveness, reconciliation, and posttraumatic growth.

A fairly recent area of research in the field of psychology focuses on more macrolevel issues of peaceful cultures, structures, and systems. Examining how social, economic, political, and military institutions promote or inhibit the development of peaceful attitudes, behaviors, and relationships highlights the psychological impact of situations or contexts on people. This work is concerned with promoting nonviolent social change as well as societal conditions and practices that foster peace.

There is disagreement about how connected these levels of analysis are to each other. Some argue that they are integral: Inner peace is required to be at peace with others and build peaceful societies. Yet others suggest that people can experience inner peace even amidst the chaos and violence of war. Disagreement also exists about whether peace is an end state – a goal toward which one works – or a dynamic process – a way in which one works.

While issues such as aggression, violence, and conflict have received widespread attention in the field of psychology, the positive construct of peace has been relatively neglected. The development in recent years of the subdiscipline *peace psychology* has only begun to redress this concern and pull together disparate threads of research and theory. Positive psychology, with its focus on optimal functioning, human virtues, and what is right with people, has an important role to play in contributing to this growing area of study.

An Evolving Psychology of Peace

A number of prominent scholars in the history of psychology have contributed to the study of peace. William James, for example, wrote extensively on militarism and psychological alternatives to war. William McDougall devoted himself to the analyses of peace strategies during World War I, and both Gordon Allport and Otto Klineberg were involved with United Nations' efforts to study international tensions that lead to war. The Society for Psychological Study of Social Issues (Division 9 of the American Psychological Association [APA]) was formed after an appeal to psychologists in 1966 to address issues related to peace and conflict. In 1990, the Society for the Psychological Study of Peace, Conflict, and Violence (Division 48 of the APA) was organized specifically to encourage psychological research and education on this topic. Only a few years later, *Peace and Conflict: The Journal of Peace Psychology* was established as a forum for publishing empirical, theoretical, clinical, and historical work at the intersection of psychology and peace.

Much research in social psychology following World War II focused on psychological processes believed to underlie war such as prejudice, authoritarianism, aggression, obedience, conformity, and attributional biases. Beyond the study of violence, intolerance, and enmity, psychologists also began to explore positive factors that promote and maintain peaceful relations. For example, Mary Parker Follett's innovative work on conflict resolution in organizational settings emphasized the importance of reciprocal relationships and power sharing in fostering peaceful and productive environments. Work on the contact hypothesis by Gordon Allport, and experiments by Muzafar Sherif on intergroup conflict and its resolution, examined conditions that promote cooperative intergroup relations.

During the Cold War, psychological research focused on important related issues such as enemy images (e.g., Ralph White), tension reduction strategies (e.g., Charles Osgood), as well as cooperative interdependence and trust (e.g., Morton Deutsch). In more recent years, the psychological study of peace has shifted to include a greater focus on cultural contexts, differentiated meanings of peace as a construct, and a more systemic perspective on the nature of peace.

The Psychology of Positive Peace

Current work in the field of psychology related to peace spans a broad array of research areas, theoretical orientations, and practical applications. A useful framework for summarizing work that specifically supports the positive dimensions of peace involves examining issues relevant before (prevention), during (intervention), and after (reconciliation) conflict.

Before, or in the absence of conflict, perspective-taking increases the ability to understand others and make appropriate attributions in potentially contentious situations. This reduces the likelihood of anger, blame, and the escalation of conflict, and conversely, increases positive responses such as forgiveness and helping behavior. Empathy with others enhances altruism, an unselfish concern for others that motivates prosocial behavior, and can help inoculate against participation in a destructive conflict spiral. Prosocial behavior is essential for peace because it is the basis of cooperation, interdependence, and sharing of resources with other individuals and groups. In practice, training and educational programs for youth and educators, community leaders, political leaders, journalists, policy makers, etc. have been one of psychologists' main tools for primary prevention.

During social conflicts, morality – particularly the inclusion of outgroup members in the realm of those to which moral values and positive norms are applied – plays a crucial role in cultivating peace. Likewise, the acknowledgement of shared humanity with members of other groups is important in maintaining peaceful relations in society and the global community. Positive attitudes and relations between members of different social groups are enhanced through cooperative, intergroup contact under optimal conditions. Generally, situations with friendship potential reinforce the development of positive relations between individual members of different social groups, and positive attitudes resulting from outgroup friendships can generalize to the entire group. Many nonviolent interventions focus on creating positive contact situations for parties in the conflict to dialogue with each other, develop joint analyses of the conflict, improve communication and cooperative problem-solving skills, and develop strategies for building peace.

Positive individual characteristics and behaviors can also reduce harm and contribute to the reestablishment of peace once violence has started. Resilience supports normal and prosocial functioning even under adverse conditions such as war. Active bystandership, or responding to the suffering of others with the moral courage to oppose violence or act nonviolently, plays an important role in limiting and counteracting harmful societal movements. Such characteristics have been prevalent among individuals who rescued outgroup members in times of ethnic persecution, such as Christians hiding Jews during the Holocaust.

In the wake of violent conflict, posttraumatic growth among individuals who have experienced mass violence can include enhanced empathy, compassion, and altruism, and result in a strong commitment to positive social change. It can also manifest as a positive survivor mission to prevent future suffering among individuals and nations.

Forgiveness and reconciliation are positive constructs that foster and sustain peace after conflict. On an interpersonal level, this often involves dialogue processes where both sides have the opportunity to tell their stories about the violent event and receive some form of recognition of grievances, acknowledgement of pain and injustices, and acceptance of responsibility and contrition from the other. On the societal level, establishing truth and a shared history are crucial for both justice and reconciliation. This involves discussing the collective memories of different groups, as well as organizing public rituals that promote collective healing and social transformation. The complex and difficult processes of postconflict peacebuilding are often sought through truth and reconciliation committees.

Methodological Challenges in Studying Peace Psychology

The complexity of peace as a construct has had consequences for its scientific study. For example, different conceptualizations and definitions of peace have created disconnected and disputed lines of study. In addition, while considerable research exists on elements directly relevant to peace such as empathy, altruism, aggression, and prejudice, difficulties in defining positive peace have made research on the construct itself rare.

Characterized by a focus on individuals and microlevel analysis, recent research funding and publishing trends in psychology have constrained the study of peace at intergroup and societal levels. Research on a multifaceted concept like peace, increasingly needs to draw from triangulated methodologies and address a variety of levels of analysis. Advances in statistical tools such as structural equation modeling and hierarchical linear modeling can support such studies by considering the interplay of multiple variables and levels of group membership.

Within social psychology, the trend of laboratory experiments and survey studies involving college students has been useful in understanding basic psychological processes underlying peace and violence. However, as an applied area of study, research on peace should be supplemented with rigorous studies conducted in real-world settings with representative populations. This is particularly important because both conflict and peace are embedded in specific contexts and involve variations across cultures and situations.

Field research on this topic, however, is wrought with a variety of practical and ethical challenges. Working in conflict zones raises concerns about the physical safety of the researchers and the participants. In addition, conducting research with representative populations can be difficult because of limited access to such groups and their small numbers. Research instruments are often not appropriate or validated across cultures. Finally, addressing sensitive topics such as participants' experiences perpetrating and/or surviving violence carry significant ethical constraints.

Future Directions in Developing a Psychology of Peace

Advancing a psychology of peace requires strengthening links between theory, research, and practice. Currently, many practitioners do not articulate the theories that inform their work, nor are they necessarily familiar with research that could impact their methods. At the same time, scholars rarely have grounding in practical experience and a disjunction often exists between theoretical issues being studied at universities and the practical needs of psychologists working in the field. In order for this area of study to mature and contribute more effective models and methods for fostering peace, future work must better integrate the work of scholars and practitioners.

In addition, the vast majority of research and practice in the realm of peace has been problem-focused and reactive – exploring ways to reduce aggression, violence, and war after it has already begun. Both psychologists and policy makers seem to agree that a stronger emphasis on prevention is needed. This involves identifying, understanding, and reinforcing positive characteristics and conditions that promote peace and creating environments in which violence is less likely to emerge in the first place. In this way, a positive psychology approach to studying these issues is essential for developing sustainable peace.

SEE ALSO: ▶ Empathy   ▶ Justice   ▶ Posttraumatic Growth   ▶ Prosocial Behavior   ▶ Resilience

Penn Resiliency Program

Jane E. Gillham[ab] and Karen J. Reivich[b]
[a]*Swarthmore College;* [b]*University of Pennsylvania*

The Penn Resiliency Program (PRP) is a group intervention designed to promote resilience in children and adolescents. PRP teaches a variety of cognitive and behavioral skills that are relevant to the wide range of challenges and stressors that are common during the late elementary and middle school years. PRP uses a group format and a structured curriculum, and it can be implemented in schools, after-school programs, clinics and other community settings.

PRP originated as a depression-prevention program. Many of the PRP skills come from cognitive-behavioral therapy, which is one of the most effective therapies for depression. PRP aims to prevent depression by teaching these cognitive and behavioral skills before students encounter the common interpersonal and academic challenges associated with the transition from childhood to adolescence. Rates of depression begin to climb in early adolescence, making this an important period for prevention efforts. In fact, by high school, depression is one of the most common public health problems affecting approximately 5–10% of adolescents each year. Even more adolescents suffer from high but subclinical levels of symptoms, and these symptoms cause great distress and interfere with functioning.

In PRP, students learn about Albert Ellis's ABC model which states that beliefs and interpretations of events have powerful effects on our emotions and behaviors. Students learn to identify thinking styles that can interfere with problem-solving and exacerbate sadness and anxiety. They learn to identify and challenge inaccurate beliefs by examining the evidence for the belief and by considering alternative ways of understanding the situation. Research suggests the PRP increases optimism; however, it's important to note that the focus in PRP is on increasing optimistic thinking within the bounds of what is accurate. In addition to these cognitive skills, PRP teaches skills for solving problems, coping with uncontrollable stressors and being comfortable with a full range of emotions. Students also learn assertiveness, negotiation, and relaxation techniques as well as skills for overcoming procrastination. PRP includes approximately 18–24 hours of content (usually delivered in 12 sessions lasting from 90 to 120 minutes). PRP is typically delivered to small groups (approximately 8–14 students) by teachers, counselors, and clinicians who have received training in the intervention.

PRP has been evaluated in 13 controlled studies, making it one of the most extensively evaluated depression-prevention programs. These studies have included a total of approximately 2,000 children from a variety of socioeconomic and cultural backgrounds. In most studies, PRP has reduced or prevented symptoms of depression. In some studies PRP's effects have been large. For example, the first study of PRP found the intervention halved the rates of moderate to severe symptoms two years after the program ended. A few studies have not found positive effects on depressive symptoms. PRP appears to be less effective when group leaders receive minimal training or do not cover the intervention content adequately.

Current work on PRP focuses on expanding and strengthening the intervention, and achieving effective dissemination. Studies are evaluating booster sessions for students and a parallel intervention for parents that teaches them to use the PRP skills in their own lives, so that they can model resilience for their children. Research on the effectiveness of the parent program is underway. Results from a pilot study indicated that combining PRP with parent training may more powerfully prevent symptoms of depression and anxiety.

Although initially developed to prevent depression, PRP is currently conceptualized as a program that teaches valuable life skills. These skills are relevant to a variety of academic, social, and family situations, and are helpful to most children. This view of PRP is supported by studies that evaluate effects on outcomes. For example, several studies have documented beneficial effects on anxiety, behavioral problems, cognitive styles, and hopelessness. Evaluations of PRP's effects on positive emotions and achievement are underway.

SEE ALSO: ▶ Empirically-supported interventions ▶ Resilience

Disclosure

The Penn Resiliency Program for Children and Adolescents is owned by the University of Pennsylvania. The University of Pennsylvania has licensed this program to Adaptiv Learning Systems. Dr Reivich and the University of Pennsylvania own stock in Adaptiv and could profit from the sale of this program. Dr Gillham does not have a financial interest in Adaptiv.

Perseverance

Cynthia L. S. Pury
Clemson University

Definition

Perseverance is the intentional continuation or reapplication of effort toward a goal despite a temptation to quit.

Intellectual and Social Context

Perseverance (also called *persistence* or *industriousness*) allows us to continue to work towards a goal when, at some level, we would prefer to be doing something else. Nearly all of the advances that make modern civilization possible require extended or repeated effort in the face of failure, fatigue, or boredom. Remove modern civilization and its precursors and perseverance is needed to keep searching for edible plant matter in winter or to stalk yet another antelope after the first two have fled.

Living in modern society likewise requires perseverance, as anyone who has earned a degree, taught a child to tie her shoes, or even tracked down the right person in customer service can attest. Modern sayings attest to the fact that "Quitters never win, and winners never quit," and "If at first you don't succeed, try, try again."

Major Dimensions of the Topic

Intentional and Goal-Directed

Intentionality in pursuit of a goal may differentiate perseverance from *perseveration*, unintentional repetition of movement or vocalization, and from automatic habits.

The goal may or may not be socially desirable, and may or may not be attainable. Stalkers, terrorists, and embezzlers may show perseverance, as may a blind person who wants to obtain a commercial pilot's license.

Continuation or Reapplication of Effort

Perseverance has been measured by researchers as both time-on-task, representing continuation of effort; and as number of attempts, representing reapplication of effort. Some tasks, such as studying for a test, may be best represented by time-on-task; other tasks, such as perfecting a dive, may be best represented by number of attempts.

Temptation to Quit

There is no perseverance needed to continue actions that are enjoyable, relaxing, or producing flow. Temptation to quit is required. This temptation may be due to internal factors, such as boredom or low self-esteem; due to situational factors, such as task difficulty or other people; or a combination of both. Moreover, it must be possible to quit: Coping well with an unpleasant but inescapable experience such as grief or pain may elicit endurance but not perseverance.

Changes Over Time in Perseverance Research

The history of perseverance research mirrors the history of psychology. The early 1900s saw an interest in measurement of individual differences in a laboratory setting. Persistence was measured by various physical tests, such as standing on the balls of one's feet or holding a small dumbbell at arms length for as long as possible. By the 1930s, many of these tasks were collected into batteries designed to measure perseverance. Sample battery items include solving anagrams, code deciphering, inhibition of free association, inhibition of patellar reflex, continuous addition, arm extension, resistance to shock, and maintained grip. Persistence on such batteries has been associated with grades in school, emotional stability, and resistance to suggestion. Scores increase with age to adolescence, and college students score higher than high school students.

Trait approaches to persistence continued to flourish, and followed the same trajectory as trait psychology in general. Introduction of factor analytic techniques indicated both general and task-specific components of persistence. Trait approaches were expanded to include life-data performance measures (e.g., completion of a course of study) and ratings made by self and others. These measures correlate with emotional stability and extraversion.

A parallel trend in psychology was the rise of behaviorism. Learning models of perseverance came to dominate, and the most dominant of these was based on the partial reinforcement extinction effect (PREE). PREE has most commonly been observed in operant conditioning paradigms. During the learning phase of the experiment, a given response is rewarded on either a continuous reinforcement schedule (after every correct response) or on a partial reinforcement schedule (after only some correct responses). During the extinction phase, the reinforcement is withdrawn. The extent to which the organism continues to respond without reinforcement is the measure of perseverance. PREE occurs when organisms trained on a partial reinforcement schedule continue responding to a greater extent than organisms trained on a continuous reinforcement schedule. PREE is very robust: observed in both humans and nonhumans for a wide variety of behaviors, ranging from lever pressing and maze running to schoolwork and housekeeping tasks. It is worth noting that in this paradigm, continued goal-directed behavior during extinction is objectively maladaptive, as the rewards have ceased.

Cognitive motivational approaches, exemplified by Feather's extension of Lewin's achievement motivation, examined perseverance as a measure of how quickly goals change when individuals encounter obstacles. Perseverance on laboratory tasks is predicted by the interaction of expectation of success and achievement motivation. Individuals high in achievement motivation persist longer on a task presented as easy; individuals high in failure avoidance motivation persist longer on a task presented as difficult.

Attributional or explanatory style likewise presents a cognitively-mediated model of low perseverance and other motivational deficits present in depression. Attributional style refers to an individual's habitual explanations for negative events. Those with depressogenic attributional styles explain failures as due to internal, stable, and global causes. Thus, following a failure, they conclude that it is due to something about them that will not change and will affect multiple areas of their life. Learned helplessness begins and motivational deficits, including a lack of perseverance, begin.

Current Emphases in Perseverance Research and Theory

Individual Differences

Individual differences in perseverance, like other traits, have been increasingly explained in terms of differences in cognitive processes. Most directly relevant to perseverance theory is Dweck's social–cognitive approach. Dweck and her colleagues propose that, when faced with a task, an individual can hold performance goals or learning goals. Performance goals motivate behavior as a means to reward. Learning goals motivate behavior as a means to increase skill. Both are related to the individual's theory of intelligence or performance in the domain of interest: An individual can see his or her performance as due to immutable abilities or as learnable. If the person believes the task taps fixed abilities, the individual will hold performance goals. If the person believes the task taps into skills that improve with learning, the individual will hold learning goals. In general, research indicates that learning goals lead to greater perseverance in the face of failure than performance goals. However, if the individual is confident in his or her abilities, performance goals will lead to greater perseverance than learning goals.

Self-efficacy involves a person's belief in his or her own ability to bring about a desired outcome. Individuals higher in self-efficacy have shown increased perseverance on a wide variety of tasks.

Self-esteem, or self-appraisal, also influences perseverance. In situations in which persistence is likely to lead to success eventually, individuals with high self-esteem show greater perseverance than those with low self-esteem. However, in situations in which perseverance is unlikely to lead to success, individuals low in self-esteem persevere longer than individuals high in self-esteem.

The values in action system (VIA) considers persistence as one of four character strengths that, along with bravery, integrity, and vitality, comprise the larger virtue of courage. Recent research suggests that persistence is the most common strength in courageous actions.

Learning Models

Eisenberger's learned industrious theory explains and expands on PREE. The experience of exerting effort is both aversive and an experience in itself, subject to the same conditioning effects as any other experience. Partial reinforcement involves the pairing of reward with higher levels of effort during learning. The experience of expending greater effort under partial reinforcement becomes a secondary reinforcer itself, leading to enhanced perseverance during extinction. Beyond partial reinforcement, other ways of rewarding high effort, including rewarding higher levels of performance or explicit verbal acknowledgment of high effort, also yield increased persistence.

Rewarding high effort creates generalized perseverance in a variety of ways. Individuals with a history of learned industriousness training will later persist in the face of other obnoxious stimuli, not just absence of reward. Generalized cognitions during training (e.g., "I'm good at school") lead to greater generalized persistence than more specific cognitions (e.g., "I'm good at remembering pictures"). Learned industriousness can lead to greater self-control and greater integrity in other situations, and can immunize participants against the effects of learned helplessness. Finally, highly persistent individuals report a greater history of strong reinforcement for high effort.

Methodological Issues and Future Directions

Future time perspective is an individual difference in how one's present effort fits with future goals. Greater perseverance is seen when the future goals are internally motivated and the relationship between action and future goal is made explicit. Future time perspective may provide a framework for understanding perseverance in larger goals and their component subgoals. For example, "graduation from college," "completion of foreign language sequence," "pass French 102," and "study for tomorrow's French test" represent different levels of nested goals, each of which may require perseverance.

Self-efficacy theory has been expanded to include other forms of human agency, including moral agency and agency at a societal level. The extent to which moral and societal agency also increase perseverance is unknown.

While a general attitude of perseverance may be associated with greater life satisfaction and greater success, continued persistence in the face of clear evidence that reward is not forthcoming may be maladaptive. This is objectively the case in PREE paradigms: Rewards have ceased during extinction. Self-esteem has been shown to increase the chance of appropriate perseverance; other strengths and values, such as wisdom or practical intelligence, may come into play as well.

The desirability of the goal may also be an issue. While history of drug and alcohol abuse shows a negative relationship with persistence, it is not difficult to imagine that persistence may be required to obtain substances illegally. Likewise, perseverance may be required to seek revenge, carry out a terrorist plot, or engage in other negative behaviors. Perseverance has been shown to be related to success in societally-valued activities such as educational attainment and work; the extent to which it is related to undesirable goal attainment remains for future research.

SEE ALSO: ▶ Character strengths (VIA) ▶ Courage ▶ Hope ▶ Self-efficacy ▶ Self-regulation

Personal Growth Initiative

Christine Robitschek and Cynthia Spering
Texas Tech University

Personal growth initiative, a construct operationalized by Christine Robitschek, is intentional engagement in the process of trying to change oneself. It grew out of her work with students in a wilderness program, Outward Bound, which focuses on personal growth. Personal growth initiative includes cognitive and behavioral elements. The cognitive elements, such as believing that change within the self is possible, valuing this type of change, and knowing how to change the self function as precursors for the behavioral elements. The behavioral elements involve actually engaging in the behaviors that lead to changes in the self, when confronted with a need to change or when the person simply desires to change.

Personal growth initiative exists on a continuum from low to high levels, with the individual's level of personal growth initiative determining, in part, how the person will respond in a situation that either requires the person to change or presents an opportunity for change and growth. For example, if a person with a high level of personal growth initiative wants to become more assertive, this person most likely will believe that it is possible to become more assertive (that the change is possible), will value this change, and will either know what steps to take to become more assertive or will take the initiative to find out how to become more assertive. Then this person most likely will follow through with these steps and actually succeed in becoming more assertive (i.e., will enact the behaviors). In contrast, a person with a low level of personal growth initiative may share the desire to become more assertive but may not believe that this change is possible, may not value the change, may not know what steps to take to make this change or how to get assistance to learn these steps, or may not follow-through with these steps even if the knowledge is obtained.

Personal Growth Initiative in Contrast with Other Constructs

Given the plethora of positive psychology constructs that center on human agency, it is important to clarify how personal growth initiative is differentiated from other dimensions of human agency.

Personal Growth

Perhaps the greatest potential source of confusion is the difference between the constructs of personal growth and personal growth *initiative*. Carol Ryff defined personal growth as awareness that one is changing and developing as a person across the lifespan. The important distinction is that personal growth initiative involves *intentional* cognitions and behaviors; Ryff's personal growth only requires *awareness* that the growth is occurring.

Self-Actualization

Both personal growth initiative and self-actualization address intentional actions directed at self-improvement. However, self-actualization is theorized to be a human *need*, an imperative within each person that will inherently motivate humans if all other needs are met. In contrast, personal growth initiative can be present in a person regardless of the extent to which other needs have been met. In some situations, a person may need to grow in a personal way to get basic needs met; for example, a person who is in an abusive relationship may need to increase his or her self-esteem to get basic safety needs met. To seek out counseling explicitly to gain this self-esteem is to enact one's personal growth initiative.

Self-Efficacy

Albert Bandura defined *self-efficacy* as the belief that one can perform a specific behavior necessary to obtain a specific outcome. A person can have self-efficacy for intentional personal growth in a specific domain. But the cognitive components of personal growth initiative are both more basic than self-efficacy (e.g., believing that change within the self is possible) and go beyond self-efficacy for intentional change (e.g., valuing intentional change and possessing the requisite knowledge to change the self).

Achievement

Personal growth initiative can be confused with the outcomes of growth, in other words, *achievement*. Sometimes personal growth is needed for achievement to occur. For example, a person with a fear of heights may need to actively work on reducing this fear (thereby growing as a person) to become an accomplished rock climber. But intentional personal growth is not inherent in the resulting achievement. This same person may be very disciplined about weight lifting and have no need to change anything *within the self* (i.e., no personal growth is required) to build stronger muscles to become an accomplished rock climber.

Personal Growth Initiative in Relation to Human Functioning

Personal growth initiative has been related to a broad range of dimensions of human functioning, including both adaptive and maladaptive functioning. Research has shown that people with high levels of personal growth initiative tend to have higher levels of psychological, social, and emotional well-being than people with low levels of personal growth initiative. Similarly, people with high levels of personal growth initiative may be better prepared to cope with common developmental tasks, such as career decision making, which requires developing one's vocational identity. People with high levels of personal growth initiative also tend to have high levels of adaptive coping skills, specifically a reflective coping style. They are better able to cope with transitions in life because they know how to make changes in themselves and their lives; they know how to grow. Conversely, people with low personal growth initiative tend to have somewhat high levels of depressive and anxious symptoms, although these symptoms are not always at clinically significant levels.

Measuring Personal Growth Initiative

Personal growth initiative is measured by the Personal Growth Initiative Scale (PGIS). The PGIS is a 9-item scale, with each item rated on a 6-point Likert scale ranging from 0 (*definitely disagree*) to 5 (*definitely agree*). A single scale score is calculated by summing the responses to all items; total scores can range from 0 to 45. Higher scores indicate higher levels of personal growth initiative. Research has provided evidence of strong internal consistency, test-retest reliability, and convergent, discriminant, and cultural validity (for Mexican Americans and European Americans) for the PGIS. In the research to date, women and men generally have had similar scores on the PGIS and scores have been similar across ethnic groups in the United States.

One limitation of this research is that it has been conducted almost exclusively with non-Hispanic white and Latino college student samples. Further assessing the cultural validity of personal growth initiative and its relevance across life-span and life situations will be important contributions. A second limitation is the unidimensional construction of the PGIS. By definition, personal growth initiative is multidimensional, including both cognitions and behaviors, with multiple dimensions within the cognitions. Yet the current version of the PGIS blends cognitions and behaviors into a unidimensional measure. Refining the measurement of personal growth initiative so that these multiple dimensions can be independently assessed would be a welcome addition to the field of positive psychology. This new measure would allow psychologists and other mental health practitioners to determine where clients are limited in their personal growth initiative so that interventions can be targeted to these specific areas.

Personal Growth Initiative in Psychotherapy

Many theories of psychotherapy state that one of the purposes of counseling is to teach the process of personal growth so that clients will be able to transfer this process to situations they encounter outside the therapy hour and after the therapy experience. Although this process may be called something quite different from personal growth, for example, disputing irrational thoughts, as in cognitive therapy, the shared notion is to teach the self-change process to clients within therapy. Mental health practitioners can assess a client's level of personal growth initiative at the beginning of therapy to determine if clients are entering therapy ready to make changes in themselves or needing to learn to value intentional personal growth. Research has shown that clients with higher levels of personal growth initiative are likely to be more ready to take action in making changes in themselves and their lives, as opposed to being in a contemplative stage. In addition, personal growth initiative theory indicates that engaging in the process of growth or change will increase clients' overall levels of personal growth initiative. This, in turn, may make these clients more likely to create additional positive changes in themselves in the future. It is noteworthy, however, that although personal growth initiative theory has made this claim, there is limited research, to date, to either support or challenge it. Future research can begin to investigate these propositions.

SEE ALSO: ▶ Change (stages of)   ▶ Growth goals

Personal Responsibility

P. Alex Linley[a] and John Maltby[b]
[a]*Centre for Applied Positive Psychology, UK;* [b]*University of Leicester, UK*

Personal responsibility is concerned with people taking individual accountability for their decisions and actions, together with the outcomes they create and their impacts on others. It is about feeling that one is the author of one's own life, accountable for the life that is created and the impacts caused through one's decisions and actions, both on oneself and on others. Within philosophy, the concept has been referred to as *moral responsibility*, although with a narrower focus on causal accountability for actions either undertaken or not undertaken.

Personal responsibility is differentiated from *civic* or *social responsibility*, which is concerned with our collective responsibilities to each other as human beings. The constructs are, however, related. Personal responsibility is understood at the level of the individual; civic or social responsibility is understood at the level of the collective. Responsibility is often also defined from the perspective of legal culpability, but the concept of personal responsibility differs from this constrained definition, being focused more widely on a prospective, future-focused sense of the need to take actions that will deliver appropriate outcomes over time, rather than a retrospective, past-focused accountability and culpability for previous actions.

On this basis, personal responsibility can be understood as actively *taking* responsibility, rather than passively *being* responsible. Personal responsibility is about one's willingness to be held accountable for one's life and one's impacts on others. When one chooses the behavior in knowledge of the outcome, one is also holding oneself accountable for that outcome, whether the outcome is achieved or not. The opposite of personal responsibility may be considered *entitlement*, the sense that someone or something else is accountable for one's life, rather than oneself, or more directly, *irresponsibility*, that is, acting without responsibility.

Personal Responsibility and Empirical Research

Personal responsibility is a core virtue within positive psychology, but it has received remarkably little empirical or theoretical attention, despite being cited as one of the core virtues in the opening article of the positive psychology special issue of the *American Psychologist* in January 2000.

This relative lack of empirical attention to the topic of personal responsibility also extends more widely; there are, however, themes across certain domains. In education, personal responsibility has been regarded as a topic that should be taught and developed in students to render them better members of civilized society. In health, personal responsibility has been advocated as a means of increasing healthy choice behaviors with attendant positive consequences for disease prevention and health promotion. In organizations, personal responsibility has been studied in relation to people acting together to create better working environments, and holding themselves accountable for the effective and appropriate discharge of their professional duties. In forensic settings, personal-responsibility therapy has focused on changing the cognitive errors that are believed to lead to criminal behavior, and developing a sense of remorse and regret as a mainstay for future responsible living.

There are two self-report measures of personal responsibility, the Student Personal Responsibility Scale-10, which assesses students' acceptance of personal responsibility in their day to day living, and the scale developed by Bierhoff and colleagues to assess personal responsibility in the context of work. Neither scale has been used widely. There are not yet either descriptive or explanatory models of personal responsibility, although the triangle model of responsibility, developed by Barry Schlenker and colleagues, has been influential. This model, however, is concerned with responsibility retrospectively as culpability, rather than with personal responsibility prospectively as life authorship.

Personal Responsibility and Social Well-Being

Personal responsibility is regarded as a central virtue of a civic society. In *Man's Search for Meaning*, the eminent psychiatrist Viktor Frankl wrote "I recommend that the Statue of Liberty on the East Coast be supplemented by a Statue of Responsibility on the West Coast" (1984, p. 134), and this Statue of Responsibility, showing two interlocking hands, is now under construction through the auspices of the Statue of Responsibility Foundation. Frankl's argument was that too much focus had been given to individual liberty, and not enough to personal responsibility. It is axiomatic, but rights need to be balanced by responsibilities. This is also the essence of the philosopher Immanuel Kant's categorical imperative: the idea that we must act toward others as we would wish them to act toward us, and further, that we must reject any course of action that cannot be universalized in this way. In this way, acting from a sense of personal responsibility is regarded as a requirement of living in a civilized world: When people do so, the quality of life for all citizens is enhanced as a result. This theme of personal responsibility enhancing the lives of all citizens has been identified in public policy in both the United States and the United Kingdom.

In seeking to balance the freedoms of individualism with recognition of the responsibilities that those freedoms bring, Western governments are paying increasing attention to the role of personal responsibility in a well-functioning society. In Britain, for example, the Prime Minister's Strategy Unit in 2004 published a report entitled *Personal Responsibility and Changing Behaviour: The State of Knowledge and Its Implications for Public Policy*. This paper cited three key reasons for the growing interest in personal responsibility. First, improvements in public service require greater public engagement, and personal responsibility is a core factor of that engagement, whether in health through better diet and exercise, or in education through children's willingness to learn and parents' willingness to help them. Second, protecting and enhancing personal responsibility is regarded as a moral and political good in its own right, and UK social policy is largely premised on this fundamental assumption. Enhancing personal responsibility strengthens individual character and moral capacity, as well as enhancing the quality of life of the whole community. Third, across a range of policy areas, including health, education and crime, behavioral interventions underpinned by personal responsibility are more cost effective and deliver better outcomes. For example, a change in diet which prevents heart problems is better and cheaper than dealing with the consequences of poor diet and subsequent heart surgery. Overall, this strategy paper concluded that through enhancing personal responsibility, more effective public services and a stronger society would result.

In the United States, similar principles were enacted into law with the *Personal Responsibility and Work Opportunity Reconciliation Act* of 1996. This act essentially sought to end the culture of welfare as an entitlement, by requiring that claimants met certain conditions, including being in work or actively looking for work – a shift in personal responsibility that transferred at least a degree of the accountability for their individual welfare to the individual, rather than allowing that welfare to rest entirely with the state. The underlying principle of the act, as suggested by its title, was to enhance personal responsibility as an explicit public policy aim.

Personal Responsibility and Irresponsibility in Business

The question of personal responsibility, and indeed irresponsibility, is a topical one in the business world. For example, with the scandals of irresponsibility at Enron and at Arthur Andersen, there have been calls for a greater focus on responsibility. One response to those calls has been the volume *Responsibility at Work*, edited by Howard Gardner, which draws from the findings of the initial efforts of the GoodWork Project, concerned with understanding work that is excellent, engaging and ethical. In *Responsibility at Work*, William Damon and Kendall Cotton Bronk define three types of ultimate personal responsibility that people may take at work: responsibility for the ethical conduct of the organization and its employees; responsibility for the fulfillment of the organization's professional or business purposes; and responsibility for the wider social good to which the organization can contribute. Gardner concludes the volume with a clarion call for personal responsibility at work:

> As aspiring trustees, we see our responsibility clearly: to portray what it means to be responsible, to model responsibility to the best of our ability, and to pass on a sense of responsibility to the future stewards of the workplace and the wider world. (Gardner, 2007, p. 335)

Future Directions

It is clear that personal responsibility can be regarded as a personal, social and civic good in its own right. It is also clear that most people subscribe to this view, rather than advocating irresponsibility or entitlement, which is presumably premised on the implicit understanding that a society where people act with personal responsibility is a society that delivers a better quality of life for all its citizens. Equally clear is that people do not always act in accordance with this sense of personal responsibility. Future research should therefore be focused on exploring, explicating and advocating the most effective means through which personal responsibility can be practiced as well as understood, developed as well as recognized. To do so, future work should seek to understand the implicit theories that people hold about personal responsibility, recognizing that these implicit theories evolve over time and across cultures, and using them as the basis for further work, empirical and applied, that underpins the development of individual practices, social institutions and public policies that are enhancing of personal responsibility and the broader benefits this virtue enables.

SEE ALSO: ▶ Character education ▶ Civic responsibility and virtues ▶ Frankl, Viktor ▶ Moral judgment ▶ Virtues ▶ Well-being

References

Frankl, V. (1984). *Man's search for meaning: An introduction to logotherapy* (3rd ed.). New York: Touchstone Books.

Gardner, H. (2007). Conclusion. In H. Gardner (Ed.), *Responsibility at work: How leading professionals act (or don't act) responsibly* (pp. 332–335). San Francisco, CA: Jossey-Bass.

Personality

Mark D. Holder and Andrea Klassen
University of British Columbia, Okanagan

In the study of psychology, *personality* refers to the internal traits that contribute to people behaving in consistent ways over time and across situations. Our personalities are our unique set of individual differences that govern how we behave and how we react to the environment. Our personalities are relatively enduring components that describe who we are; they are not momentary and fluctuating states. Research has demonstrated that different dimensions of personality are strongly associated with aspects of positive psychology, including happiness and life-satisfaction.

Two personality variables that have been consistently and strongly connected with positive psychology are extroversion (a trait typified by being social, assertive, lively, and sensation seeking) and neuroticism (a trait typified by being anxious, depressed, and emotional, as well as having low self-esteem). For example, people who are highly extroverted tend to be happier, and people who are highly neurotic tend to be less happy. One study reported that extroversion and neuroticism together accounted for 42% of the variance in the happiness of adults and that extroversion and neuroticism also predicted well-being more than a decade later.

In addition to extroversion and neuroticism, additional variables related to personality are associated with happiness in adults. For example, optimistic people (i.e., those people with a bright, positive outlook and relatively low levels of hope-lessness and pessimism) tend to rate highly in aspects of positive psychology, includ-ing happiness. Additional variables related to personality that have been associated with positive psychology include assertiveness (those who are more assertive report higher levels of happiness), attributional style (those who attribute life events to their own actions and, therefore, believe they have the capacity to effect change report higher levels of happiness), emotional stability (those who are emotionally unstable report lower levels of happiness), loneliness (those who are lonely report lower levels of happiness), and self-esteem (those with high self-esteem report higher levels of happiness).

Although the majority of research on the relationship between personality and positive psychology has used adults, many of the findings from this research have been extended to the elderly, adolescents, and children. For example, in a group of people aged 51 to 95, happiness was associated with extroversion, neuroticism, and self-esteem. Similarly, self-esteem, optimism, neuroticism, and introversion were found to predict happiness in adolescents. In addition, life satisfaction in chil-dren was positively correlated with extroversion and negatively correlated with introversion. Furthermore, one study showed that for four different measures of children's happiness, a variable akin to neuroticism accounted for a significant proportion of the variance. Thus, though personality may continue to develop until past the mid-twenties the early underpinnings of factors that may be related to aspects of neuroticism and extroversion are associated with happiness. It is import-ant to study different age groups to determine whether the relationship between personality and positive psychology changes throughout the lifespan.

Though personality and positive psychology are associated, research has not established a clear causal relationship between personality and positive life out-comes. Individuals' personalities may predispose them to experience higher levels of happiness and life satisfaction. This position is supported by research showing that extraverts report higher levels of happiness, whereas introverts report lower levels of happiness. It is unlikely that aspects of positive psychology cause the development of particular personality traits due to the fact that personality traits appear early in life and appear to be regulated by genetics. However, it is possible that one or more external variables may influence both personality and positive psychology, thus accounting for their association.

The relationship between personality and optimal well-being may be mediated by external factors. For example, social affiliations have been strongly linked to happiness and life satisfaction (i.e., happy people have more friends and participate in more social activities than less happy people). Thus, rather than extroversion caus-ing happiness, the fact that an individual is extroverted increases the likelihood that this individual will seek out social relationships, social situations, and social leisure activities, and these social affiliations in turn may promote happiness. Conversely, a neurotic person would be less likely to seek out social affiliations and this may contribute to why individuals who score highly on neuroticism are also less happy. Similarly, assertiveness has been shown to act as a mediator between happiness and personality. Assertiveness was found to predict happiness, and its mediating effects largely explained the contributions of extroversion and neuroticism. Furthermore, though personality factors were found to predict happiness, attributional style, which was correlated with extroversion and neuroticism, was important in explaining happiness. In essence, our personalities may predispose us to use certain behavioural strategies, some of which may influence our positive and negative emotions.

Personality may influence the effectiveness of behavioral strategies that people choose to achieve happiness. Rather than a single set of strategies being effective for all people, research suggests that in order to achieve happiness, a person must pursue goals that are consistent with their personalities. For example, people with high levels of extroversion and agreeableness (i.e., people who are cooperative, forgiving, and kind), will be more successful in achieving happiness if they pursue social goals. People with high levels of introversion may not be as successful if they pursue these same goals.

Though aspects of positive psychology are clearly and strongly related to personality variables, they are distinguishable. For example, though high self-esteem has been used as an indication of global happiness, the factors that predict happiness and self-esteem differ. Self-esteem may be required to achieve well-being, happiness, and satisfaction, but self-esteem alone does not guarantee these aspects of positive psychology.

Assessing the relationship between personality and positive psychology is a fertile ground for future research. Researchers still need to explore potential mediators and explain how they influence the relationship between personality and positive psychology. In addition, the relationship between the different dimensions of children's temperament and positive psychology requires additional study. Temperament is thought to be the foundation for adult personality and there is little research exploring its links with positive psychology. Furthermore, children have been a largely ignored population in positive psychology research. Therefore, it is important to explore whether research with children shows similar or different results than the adult literature. For example, it is possible that the relation between personality and positive psychology may be stronger in younger people. Finally, research should continue to explore individual differences in all age groups to discover how they contribute to, influence, and possibly mediate the relationship between personality and positive psychology.

SEE ALSO: ▶ Allport, Gordon   ▶ Five factor model   ▶ Optimism

Person-Environment Fit

W. Bruce Walsh
Ohio State University

The match between characteristics of the person and characteristics of the environment reflects the concept of *person-environment fit*. Theoretically, person-environment

fit is a fulcrum concept that is assumed to influence a wide variety of psychological phenomena, ranging from satisfaction to performance to personality consistency to subjective well-being. As noted by Walter Mischel, we can't take the person
out of personality; but at the same time, we can't ignore the fact that environments and social cultures, like people, have personalities and influence behavior
and well-being.

A number of person-environment fit theories have clear implications for
positive psychology and well-being. These theories include Holland's theory
of personality types and model environments; the theory of work adjustment
by Dawis, England, and Lofquist; social cognitive theory by Lent, Brown, and
Hackett; the situation selection theory by Diener, Larson, and Emmons; the self-
concordance theory by Sheldon and Elliott; the demands control model by
Karasek and Theorell; the attraction, selection, attrition model by Schneider, Smith,
and Goldstein; the social-ecological model of well-being by Little; the transitional
approach by Pervin; and the life domains approach by Moos. Taken together, these
theories and their related research, in one way or another, suggest that persons
in environments that are congruent with their personalities tend to be psychologically healthier, more satisfied, and more productive than persons in incongruent
environments.

Related reviews of the literature have further focused on individual motivation and the pursuit of relevant goals. Overall, the evidence suggests that individuals who pursue personal goals that are self-selected and self-congruent tend
to experience enhanced levels of subjective well-being. Research in this area also
suggests that subjective well-being is enhanced when we pursue goals that have
a long-term orientation rather than goals that satisfy short-term needs. In addition, intrinsic goals which are group enhancing and focus on the contributions
we can make to others tend to be more positively related to well-being than more
self-serving goals. Overall, goals are important to us; they give our lives meaning
and an identity.

With respect to person-environment fit and the research, there are a number
of conceptual and methodological issues. For example, studies of personal-
environment congruence frequently implement a point-in-time view of congruence or fit. The primary approach has been to describe the person and the
environment and explore their independent and interaction effects. In essence,
the research generally is conducted at one point in time. However, a number of
theoretical frameworks note that people tend to seek out complementary or congruent environments and that environments attract, retain, and influence these
individuals. Bandura, for example, suggests that humans act on the environment;
they create, uphold, and transform their environment in an interplay between the
personal agency, and environmental influences. According to Bandura, people are
producers of their life circumstances and not just the products of them. Thus, these
assumptions further suggest the need for research designs that run across time.
Very few studies have empirically investigated the person-environment hypothesis from a longitudinal perspective.

In addition, major methodological issues continue to revolve around ways of measuring people's personality, interests, and environment, and congruence itself. From all indications people are the strength. The person concept has been operationalized using a variety of traditional inventories of personality, interests, competencies, and values that have proven reliability and validity. The measurement quality of the instruments used is such that we can be reasonably certain that we have obtained a good estimate of the person side of the equation. However, actually measuring the environment or the situation has been far more difficult. There is no question that we need more reliable and valid assessments of the environment. We are still in the early stages of our understanding of the characteristics of the situation or the environment that affect behavior. Different from personality, we have no well-accepted taxonomies that we can use to describe the significant dimensions of environmental variability.

Finally, there are a number of important issues in the person-environment domain that need to be mentioned. One such issue that cross-cuts all social sciences is that concerning cultural relativism vs. universals in human behavior. What is culture general and what is culture specific? There is no question that definitions of the person and the environment are culturally rooted and any assessment of the person and the environment cannot be value free. An additional issue is that of wealth. How might wealth influence the person-environment process and worker satisfaction, well-being, and performance? For example, a poor infrastructure within a nation would tend to restrict opportunities for stable relationships, personal expressiveness, and productivity. Thus, as noted by Ryan and Deci, not only can national poverty interfere with the satisfaction of physical needs (such as food and shelter), but it can also arrest and block access to expressing competencies, pursuing interests, and maintaining relationships which would provide psychological need satisfaction. Also, freedom appears to be an important issue. A book by Sen titled *Development as Freedom* argued that freedom is a more rationale goal for national development than is gross national product. He shows that in cultures where relative freedoms have been augmented, both quality of life and economic growth are improved.

In summary, the assertion that satisfaction, performance, and well-being are related to congruence remains intuitively appealing and paramount in work and person-environment psychology. Researchers have tried to address this assertion, but the work remains incomplete. Given this context, it is the interaction of the environment (cultural, situational, physical, technological and informational) and the person (cognitive, affective, and behavioral) that we need to understand more effectively in order to improve our knowledge of the process by which person-environment congruence becomes reflected in certain outcomes. This includes how personality is related to goal-setting behavior and well-being; how personality affects the choice of situations at work; how job satisfaction and performance are affected by personality and choice of situations; and in general, how personality affects behavior and well-being in certain kinds of situations.

SEE ALSO: ▶ Subjective well-being ▶ Vocation

Peterson, Christopher

Nansook Park
University of Rhode Island

Christopher Peterson, PhD, (1950–) is best known for his work on good and bad adaptation, with a focus on the role played by such individual differences as optimism, personal control, and strengths of character, in a variety of populations with respect to outcomes like health, work performance, achievement, and life satisfaction. He is currently Professor of Psychology at the University of Michigan.

Dr Peterson's main contribution to positive psychology is his role as research director of the Values in Action (VIA) Project, which is arguably the most ambitious empirical undertaking to date within positive psychology. The goals of the project are to provide: a) a coherent classification of human strengths and virtues; and b) reliable and valid strategies for assessing these aspects of excellence.

Dr Peterson has authored or coauthored 10 books, 70 book chapters, and 140 journal articles. His most recent books are *Character Strengths and Virtues* and an introductory text: *A Primer in Positive Psychology*. In 2003, he was named by the Institute for Scientific Information (ISI) as among the world's 100 most widely-cited psychologists over the past 20 years. His work has been featured on numerous newspapers and popular magazines worldwide including *The New York Times*, *Time*, *Newsweek*, *U.S. News and World Report*, *USA Today*, and *Reader's Digest*.

In 1999, Dr Peterson was named an Arthur F. Thurnau Professor at the University of Michigan, in honor of his excellence in undergraduate teaching. On two different occasions, a psychology course that he taught at Michigan was named "best university course" by the Ann Arbor Weekend Magazine. At the University of Michigan, Peterson served as the Director of the APA-approved clinical psychology program from 1996 to 2000 and again in 2002. He has been the Ferne Forman Fischer Lecturer at the University of Kansas, the Clifford Fawl Lecturer at Nebraska Wesleyan University, and the Thomas Hawkins Johnson Visiting Scholar at the United States Military Academy.

Dr Peterson earned his PhD from the University of Colorado in Boulder with emphases in social psychology, personality psychology, and learning and completed post-doctoral respecialization in clinical psychology at the University of Pennsylvania.

Dr Peterson's work spans subdisciplines within psychology and has often entailed the creation of new methods and measures for assessing individual differences, including content analysis strategies for measuring explanatory style and various measures of character strengths. He developed the CAVE technique – an acronym for Content Analysis of Verbatim Explanations – that allows optimism to be assessed from how individuals explain the causes of events. One of the best-known of Dr Peterson's findings, from his pioneering studies in the 1980s, is that optimism longitudinally predicts good health operationalized in a variety of ways, from self-reported symptoms to physician-rated health to longevity. He found that optimists are healthy because they behave in health-promoting ways.

Dr Peterson is a member of the Positive Psychology Steering Committee, a consulting editor of the *Journal of Positive Psychology*, a Templeton Senior Fellow at the Positive Psychology Center of the University of Pennsylvania, and the editor of the Oxford University Press Series in Positive Psychology.

SEE ALSO: ▶ Character strengths (VIA)

Physical Health

Heather N. Rasmussen[a] and Sarah D. Pressman[b]
[a]University of Kansas; [b]University of Pittsburgh Medical Center

Physical health can be described as a state of optimal well-being, free of disease or illness. When considering personal physical health, however, some might think about exercising outside on a summer day, whereas others might think about going throughout the day without experiencing physical pain. Accordingly, many researchers in psychology interested in studying health actually measure it in a variety of ways such as assessing illness, disease survival, or quality of life during an illness. In the following section, the definitions and measurement of physical health and illness will be discussed. This is followed by examples of research on positive psychological constructs and physical health/illness and finally, suggestions for future research in the field are identified.

What is Physical Health?

The term *physical health* is quite broad. Physical health can be framed in terms of *absence* of symptoms or objective indicators of disease or injury, whereas physical illness is the *presence* of subjective and objective indicators of disease or injury. Health also can be thought of as the presence of positive states, such as well-being or pregnancy, rather than simply the absence of illness or injury. Studying health and illness also is a broad endeavor as it could include research with healthy participants as well as patient populations. Studies of healthy participants are wide ranging, from smoking prevention efforts to investigating the health effects of everyday stress. Within the patient populations, patients with diverse types of diseases are represented across studies, from those with a common cold to those with HIV. It should be clear that studying physical health from a psychological perspective is as vast as the science of psychology.

Measuring Physical Health and Illness

Just as there are many ways to define physical health and illness there exists a variety of measures used to assess physical health and illness. Some examples include examining mortality and survival, physical symptoms, disease morbidity, pain, and perceived health in both healthy and diseased populations. One approach to categorizing the variety of measures, is to consider whether the health outcome is self-reported by the research subject or achieved objectively via a medical professional or some other unbiased source.

Objective Health Outcomes

Objective health outcomes represent measures that can be objectively determined via physician assessment, medical records, or biological testing. For example, measures might include biopsies for cancer, clinical assessments, or other technologically achieved medical tests (e.g., brain imaging, x-ray, EKG) and physiological measures (e.g., heart rate, blood pressure, respiration, immune function) intended to help with the diagnosis of disease. The key to objective measures is that these are not self-reported by the patient or research subject but are instead indicated by an unbiased medical professional.

Subjective Health Outcomes

Subjective health outcomes are primarily measured using self-report measures, such as questionnaires, surveys, or interviews. These are medical indices that are reported by the participant or a close other (e.g., family member). There are a wide variety of subjective health outcomes, including reports of pain and physical symptoms, perceived health, quality of life, and self-reported adherence to treatment to name a few.

Concerns with Measurement

Although a thorough discussion of the concerns with measurement of physical health and disease is beyond the scope of this entry, a few of these issues will be highlighted. First, subjective measures of health can be problematic in that it is difficult to tease out the psychological and social processes that influence symptom reports. For example, it is known that negative affect (NA) can influence the way people respond to self-report measures, primarily by increasing their report of negative symptoms and body sensations. Conversely, optimism and positive affect (PA) influence the report in the opposite fashion making it difficult to discern whether subjective measures are a true indicator of objective health, or if they are instead gauging participant mood and disposition. Self-reports of health and illness could also be subject to socially desirable responding. For instance, studies of smoking behaviors or sexually risky practices may lead participants to *underreport* behaviors considered socially undesirable or unhealthy and *overreport* desirable behaviors such as exercise and nutritional adherence.

Many illnesses have symptoms that are confounded with emotional disorders. A person with cancer may be experiencing a loss of appetite and increased sleep, both of which also are diagnostic symptoms of depression. As a result, it is desirable not only to consider the effect of the disease on affect, but to also ensure that your study research design accounts for this problem. For example, if you are interested in whether affect plays a causal role in a health outcome (e.g., does happiness decrease the probability of getting a disease?), it is best to find a healthy population and assess affect *before* the disease is present to ensure that your independent variable is not confounded with health at baseline.

Finally, although it is tempting to interpret some objective measures of physiology as health outcomes, this conclusion is not warranted. For example, changes in immune parameters, heart rate, or blood pressure are interesting because of their theorized pathways to various disease outcomes (i.e., cancer, heart disease); however, in studies examining the psychosocial impact on these outcomes, the magnitude of change found is rarely outside of normal levels. Furthermore, it is even rarer for these changes to be tied to true illness outcomes making their interpretation suggestive of health at best.

From this brief discussion, it should be clear that relying solely on subjective reports of health and illness is problematic and the most rigorous designs should include objective as well as subjective measures of health and/or disease (depending on the nature of the investigation). With these issues in mind, we now provide an overview of the literature on positive psychological constructs and physical health. This review is not meant to be exhaustive; rather it is to provide a snapshot of the physical health outcomes that have been tied to positive feelings and cognitions, specifically positive affect and optimism.

Summary of Health Evidence

Longevity

The best evidence for the beneficial effects of positive traits on health is in studies of life duration in healthy populations. Most studies have been conducted with elderly persons living either on their own or with their families. This work provides virtually unanimous evidence that positive dispositions are linked to increased longevity. Similarly, studies of young and middle-aged adults have similarly found benefits of positive feelings on longevity, including a well-publicized study by Danner, Snowden, and Frieson in 2001 showing that a more positive writing style in early adulthood predicted longevity 65 years later in a sample of nuns. One earlier study of children by Friedman and colleagues, on the other hand, found that cheerfulness at an early age predicting *greater* risk for earlier death; however, in this case PA was reported by parents and teachers and not by the participants themselves making the interpretation of the PA measure unclear.

Morbidity

Cross-sectional studies not surprisingly show that having one of many types of diseases is associated with lower PA than healthy controls. It is, however, likely that reports of lower PA in those suffering from disease, pain and disability are primarily attributable to the influence of the disease on PA rather than the influence of PA on disease. Interestingly, although PA may decrease in response to the onset of serious physical illness, there is some evidence of adaptation over time where PA returns to levels reported by healthy people. Prospective studies of morbidity also are consistent in the positive effects of PA on a variety of outcomes. For example, PA has been associated with lower rates of stroke, rehospitalization for coronary problems, fewer injuries, decreased incidence of the common cold and improved pregnancy outcomes. Researchers have also found that higher levels of optimism are associated with morbidity such as fewer post surgical complications, and fewer new coronary events in a sample of cardiac patients. Similar, to the previously mentioned pregnancy finding, several studies have also found that optimism benefits gestational age, birth weight, and is associated with decreased pregnancy loss.

Disease Severity

Naturally occurring positive emotions and optimism have been associated with a variety of benefits for disease severity. For example, naturally occurring PA has been associated with better lung function in asthmatics and decreased hospitalization. Optimism has been tied to better outcomes in cardiovascular disease patients, but to date there is no evidence that PA benefits cardiovascular disease patients most likely due to the focus in the heart disease literature on negative emotions such as hostility and depression.

Laboratory studies of patient populations (e.g., irritable bowel, asthma) studying the impact of induced emotion on symptoms tend to *not show* benefits of positive emotions, and in fact often show symptom exacerbation. This is likely due to the physiological arousal experienced along with the laboratory mood manipulations that attempt to induce intense emotions.

Survival

Survival studies are prospective studies of groups of those suffering from serious (often fatal) diseases. Although it is a popular idea that staying happy can lengthen one's life when facing a life-threatening illness, *few* studies have examined whether this is the case. To date, the evidence suggests that individuals with diseases with the potential for long-term survival (i.e., years) such as early stage HIV and breast cancer benefit from higher levels of PA, while those with end-stage illness such as metastatic breast cancer, lung cancer and end-stage renal disease are not helped by PA and optimism and are sometimes harmed possibly due to the underreporting of symptoms resulting in poorer care and decreased treatment adherence. It may be that at disease end stages, once the body has progressed to an advanced weakened state, positive feelings and expectations are most beneficial for quality of life outcomes rather than extending life duration. Along these lines, studies of institutionalized elderly, who often have an array of health difficulties and are often in a weakened state, similarly find no objective benefit of PA on survival.

Subjective Health

Recently, Pressman and Cohen noted in their review of the health benefits of PA that there is a great deal of evidence indicating that PA is associated with reporting less physical pain (both naturally and when experimentally induced), fewer symptoms and reports of better health. Although these outcomes have practical importance, as we stated previously, findings have suggested that this association may be driven primarily by PA influences on *how* we perceive our bodies rather than by affect-elicited changes in physiological processes. Although these data are provocative, many of these studies also found that NA was associated with greater symptom reporting and poorer self-reported health, begging the question of whether NA or PA is responsible for the found effects. Although problematic for interpretation purposes, there are several studies that provide evidence that PA effects on self-reported health are independent of and often stronger than those of NA.

There are also a number of studies tying optimism to subjective health measures. For example, several researchers have found more optimistic samples of older individuals and patient populations report less pain. Similarly, there are ample studies tying optimism to better perceived health and physical function in both patient and healthy populations. Finally, there is consistent evidence that optimism is tied to the report of fewer physical symptoms (e.g., upper respiratory infection symptoms, disease specific symptoms) in both diseased and nondiseased populations.

How do Positive Psychological Constructs Improve Health?

Higher trait PA is associated with better health practices such as improved sleep quality, more exercise, and with lower levels of the stress-hormones epinephrine, norepinephrine and cortisol. PA has also been tied with other health relevant hormones including increases in oxytocin, growth hormone and secretion of endogenous opioids as well as to alter various aspects of immune function. Finally, PA may also influence health by improving social relationships that have been repeatedly associated with both lower risk for morbidity and mortality.

Positive cognitions such as optimism, on the other hand, may influence health in a different fashion. The expectation that good things will happen or that one has control over a situation is more likely to operate via a person's ability to cope with stressful life events and potentially by increasing feelings of PA. Interestingly, researchers have also have hypothesized that PA plays a role in the stress buffering process via its association with the building of resources (social, intellectual, and physical) that might help when negative life events occur suggesting both direct and stress-buffering pathways for PA's influence on health.

There is a great need for further studies assessing health outcomes to measure these psychosocial and biological pathways to understand better the mediators of these associations as well as whether PA and optimism influence health in a direct or indirect fashion.

Discussion

Overall, the literature to date is provocative and shows many benefits of positive psychological constructs on physical health; however, many studies reviewed here also suffer from methodological and conceptual limitations. For example, in many cases, it is difficult to distinguish between the effects of positive and negative emotions. Many studies include bimodal measures of PA/NA or do not statistically control for levels of negativity. This raises the question of whether any found benefits of PA are due to its presence or merely the absence of NA. There are, however, promising results from the few studies that have controlled for NA which suggest that when it is statistically controlled, the PA effects remain associated with better health and are often more powerful than those of NA.

Another important issue to consider is the adequacy of measures of baseline health in prospective studies. Inadequate measurement allows the possibility that being healthier at baseline contributes to both greater baseline PA and to subsequent longevity. As mentioned in the introduction and in the reviewed literature, perceived health is highly correlated with positive constructs. This suggests then that any study using a self-reported health measure at baseline may be inadvertently assessing PA and/or optimism. On a related topic, some PA adjectives such as *alert* and *full of pep* might directly tap perceived health; a predictor of mortality above and beyond objective health assessments. To the extent that PA measures are actually markers of perceived health, it is possible that the association between PA and mortality may be attributable to existing medical conditions or subclinical illness. It is noteworthy that the PA-health association remains in the majority of studies that control for perceived health.

Another important issue to consider is *what it is* about these constructs that benefits health. Pressman and Cohen recently raised the issue that many measures used in assessing PA and physical health are confounded by nonemotional items such as those assessing optimism, esteem, extroversion, and perceptions of control. Since it is rare for studies to assess one type of positive construct while statistically controlling for other positive measures, it remains unclear whether various types of positive measures uniquely predict different health outcomes or if some scales are more powerful than others. Furthermore, even within measures of one type of positive construct, it remains unclear which components of that construct are necessary for health benefits (e.g., within PA is it calm, happiness or vigor?). Future research should assess whether it is overall positive nature driving these effects or whether we should be considering specific types of positive items.

Suggestions for Those Interested in Assessing Physical Health and Positive Constructs

We suggest that if you are interested in moving forward in this field, there are several strategies to consider. First, given the limitations of subjective reports of health and their strong associations with positive psychological constructs, objective measures of health should be included in studies whenever possible to prevent limited interpretative ability of the study. Second, given the large literature on NA measures and health (e.g., depression, hostility) it is important to measure both positive and negative measures to determine if found effects are independent from the negative measures, confounded, or more powerful. Research must begin to determine whether these constructs are merely bipolar opposites predicting the same health outcomes in reverse directions, or whether in some health outcomes one is a better predictor than the other. Finally, if you are interested in whether positive constructs *cause* differences in physical health, cross-sectional designs are not sufficient. One must design longitudinal, prospective studies with baseline measures of PA and baseline controls for both perceived and objective health to get around any potential confounds of the influence of positive measures on self-reported health measures as well as the influences of health on report of PA and optimism.

SEE ALSO: ▶ Cortisol ▶ Immune system ▶ Optimism ▶ Oxytocin ▶ Positive affectivity

Play

Sandra W. Russ, Beth L. Pearson, and Sarah Cain Spannagel
Case Western Reserve University

Pretend play is a resource for children that relates to adaptive functioning in the developing child. Because processes in play have been associated with optimal functioning, play can be considered within the positive psychology framework. Pretend play has long been recognized as important in child development. Pretend play involves the use of fantasy, make-believe and symbolism. In 1987, Fein defined *pretend play* as symbolic behavior in which "one thing is playfully treated as if it were something else" (p. 282). Both cognitive and affective processes are utilized in play. Jerome and Dorothy Singer in 1990 identified many cognitive processes in play. For example, play involves practice with divergent thinking – the ability to generate ideas. Play also involves the ability to store and recombine images; transformation abilities; and organization of narratives. They also emphasized the importance of affective processes in play. Sandra Russ in 2004 identified possible affective processes such as the expression of emotions and affect themes and enjoyment of the play process. Play is also an arena where children learn to process and regulate emotions. Anna Freud was one of the first to recognize the importance of play in helping children to express and resolve emotional problems and conflicts. Her work led to the utilization of play in play therapy approaches.

In the research literature, play has been found to relate to or facilitate areas of adaptive functioning including creativity, perspective-taking and emotional understanding, and general well-being and adjustment. Pretend play has been found to relate to measures of creativity in children, especially to divergent thinking, ability in a number of different studies, in different research labs with different ages of children. The relationship between pretend play and creativity is one of the most robust in the play research literature. There have been a number of well-executed experimental studies that have found that play facilitated divergent thinking in preschool children. Methodological issues have been raised about possible experimenter bias in the play and divergent thinking literature. However, both Dansky in 1999 and Russ in 2004 pointed out, that studies controlling for experimenter bias also found positive results. Theoretical explanations of the relationship between pretend play and creativity have focused on the cognitive variables of divergent thinking, recombination of objects and ideas, symbolic transformation, breadth-of-attention deployment, and the loosening of old cognitive sets. Russ has focused on the affective processes in play as another possible explanation for the link between play and creativity. Theoretical explanations for the links between play, affect and creativity have been in existence for some time, although research that tests the theory is relatively recent. Both psychoanalytic theory and more recent cognitive-affective theories of mood and memory hypothesize that the search process for associations is broadened by the involvement of emotion. This broadened search process increases the generation of ideas and original associations in divergent thinking and other creativity tasks. In order to test these theories, measures of play must assess affective components of play. Using the Affect in Play Scale, a standardized play task developed by Russ, studies have found that the amount of affect expressed in a 5-minute play session relates to divergent thinking in children, usually independent of IQ. Future research in the play and creativity area should investigate specific components of both play and creativity.

Play also has been found to relate to perspective-taking and understanding the point of view of the other person. In 2000, Harris proposed that imaginative understanding may enable children to understand others' mental states and affective experiences. The research is beginning to support this hypothesis. The ability to understand others' emotions provides the basis for empathy. There is also a literature on "rough and tumble" play, discussed by Pelligrini in 1992, that relates this kind of interpersonal playful interaction with prosocial problem-solving ability.

Play also relates to aspects of general adjustment in children. Pretend play ability is related to coping ability in children. Children who show imagination in play can think of more ways to cope with stressful situations. It is possible that divergent thinking ability is the common ability that links play to the ability to generate problem-solving strategies. Play helps well-being and adjustment in other ways. A number of studies have found that play reduces anxiety. When play intervention studies are focused and well-controlled, play has been found to reduce fears and anxiety around medical procedures and around issues of separation. Several studies suggest that imagination and fantasy components of the play are key factors in reducing anxiety.

Play should also enable children to be hopeful. One aspect of hope, according to Snyder, is agency, or a child's sense that he can reach his goals. Part of what makes play so pleasurable for children is that within play, unlike the rest of their day, children can be powerful. In play, children can arrange toys anyway they like; they can choose which character to be and how to respond. In this way, the child feels a sense of agency.

Intervention and Prevention Programs

Given the important role that pretend play has in child development and in children's adaptive functioning, it is essential that we determine whether we can teach children to be better players. There is some evidence that play skills can be improved. Dansky (1999) reviewed the play tutoring literature and found that "more than a dozen studies have shown that play tutoring can increase not just the quantity of play displayed but also the richness and imagination of children's pretense" (p. 404). These play tutoring sessions usually involved 8 to 12 sessions with an adult who modeled and encouraged participation in social interactive pretense over a 3- to 6-week period. In his review, he concluded that there were consistent positive results in studies with adequate control groups. He concluded that play tutoring, over a period of time, resulted in increased imaginativeness in play and increased creativity on other measures.

J. Singer and D. Singer in 1999 have developed a video-based program for parents and other caregivers of preschool children. The video and manual provide clear examples and instructions for parents and caregivers that model how to use play to help children use their imagination and to learn through play. For example, in a going-to-a-restaurant pretend play situation, just a few of the skills the children learn include taking on different roles, doing tasks in sequential order, and counting. In a recent study using this intervention, Bellin and Singer found that play helped children develop literacy skills.

Russ, Moore, and Pearson have been developing play interventions that target creativity, well-being, hope, anxiety, and school adjustment. Results of these pilot intervention studies have been promising.

Future Research

Because play is so important in child development and there is a growing body of research that relates play to many areas of adaptive functioning, future research programs in the play area are crucial. Important future research programs need to:

- Identify which play process relate to different areas of adaptive functioning.
- Develop play intervention manuals that target specific processes in play.
- Integrate play intervention and prevention programs into a child's day at school and at home.

The importance of pretend play in child development is being rediscovered. In this age of heavy scheduling and increased demands on children and parents, it is important that children have the time to play – so they can develop optimally. Research studies are building an empirical foundation for the importance of pretend play.

SEE ALSO: ▶ Creativity ▶ Hope ▶ Positive emotions

References

Dansky, J. (1999). Play. In M. Runco & S. Pritzker (Eds.), *Encyclopedia of creativity* (pp. 393–408). San Diego: Academic Press.

Fein, G. (1987). Pretend play: Creativity and consciousness. In P. Gorlitz & J. Wohlwill (Eds.), *Curiosity, imagination, and play* (pp. 281–304). Hillsdale, NJ: Lawrence Erlbaum Associates.

Pleasure

Danielle Johnson
University of Kansas

Pleasure is a term used to describe a range of positive affective, emotional, and physical sensations. Pleasure is a major component of the developing field of positive psychology, as it encompasses the essence of what is associated with positive functioning. The aspect of pleasure as it relates to positive functioning, describes a niche of how we interpret and understand positive functioning. For example, a state of gratification implies a more sensate or physical pleasure, whereas "a source of delight or joy" implies an emotional state. Most people can reach a consensus that getting a back rub (sensation) is pleasurable, or immediate response when surprised with a dozen roses (affect), or the feeling evoked when being praised for a great performance by a demanding boss (emotion) as pleasing, but there is no blanket or objective rule to describe what pleasure is for every person, although some of the physiologic responses related to pleasure can be identified. The broadness and subjectivity of pleasure has long been examined and debated and has been examined from a number of perspectives.

The historical context from which pleasure is most notably recognized is from the writing of the psychoanalyst Sigmund Freud. In his writings and discussions of human behavior he wrote about the "pleasure principle." Freud explained the pleasure principle as the motivating force in human behavior, the need for immediate gratification of pleasure and avoidance of pain. In this context pleasure has been characterized as something that is negative or problematic. The negative association attached to the use of pleasure in this manner stems from pleasure being described as something that needed to be satisfied regardless of the outcome or consequence. A shift from using pleasure to describe that level of extremity in the pursuit of pleasure has been relegated to a term that dates back to the 1800s, *hedonism*, which is pleasure being the purpose in life. Today, hedonism would be analogous to Freud's pleasure principle. The definition of pleasure has broadened since its usage by Freud to include things other than a behavioral reaction and has taken on a general descriptor of something that positive or good.

As the research and understanding into human strengths and positive emotions expands so does the subjective understanding of pleasure. Pleasure at its widest definition can be described as an umbrella term to describe positive emotions and sensations. Although pleasure encapsulates a number of descriptors, it can be viewed as being on a continuum of positive emotions in which pleasure is close to an extreme form of happiness. To understand the range of possibilities that fit under the pleasure umbrella an examination of the key terms, concepts, and theories will be discussed.

The exploration of positive emotions has allowed for the development of a number of theories that account for or explain the presence of pleasure. The *broaden-and-build* theoretical model is one such model that suggests that positive emotions can expand the number of possible reactions one has to choose from. The implications of this model suggest that the higher the number of positive emotions, the more options we are able to perceive to accomplish tasks and goals. The model is represented by an upward spiral of emotions. *Need/goal satisfaction theories* postulate that pleasure is achieved when tensions are reduced. Freud's pleasure principle fits under this group of theories. *Process/activity theories* espouse that certain activities can generate happiness. There is a debate within this camp in regards to if engaging in certain activities produces happiness or if the process of engaging causes happiness. A related concept under these theories is flow. *Flow* is the engagement in completing an activity in which one's skills are matched to complete the challenge. The emotional response of being in flow with the task is one that would be described as pleasure.

Another group of theories that account for pleasure is the *genetic and personality predisposition theories*. This group of theories suggests happiness is a stable variable that does not change significantly due to environmental or situational events. A term that is related to this group of theories that lends to an overall stable view is *subjective well-being*. Subjective well-being is a term to describe how the world is viewed subjectively, taking into account level of life satisfaction and presence of positive affect, with no negative affect being present. Subjective well-being is associated with *happiness* and as already mentioned, a subjective term, which is assessed with the use of self-report measures.

As pleasure is described as an emotional reaction to an event, current research is focused on pleasure being segmented into two categories, one being the biological basis and reactions of pleasure and the other category being pleasure as it relates to other variables. The research into the biological basis of pleasure, looks at the concept at a neurochemical level, attempting to understand how we respond neurologically to pleasure. This type of research seems to be working towards making the mind-body connection a more concrete idea, allowing a greater understanding of the physical response of pleasure on a microlevel. The other category of current research on pleasure aims to understand the circumstance in which pleasure is evoked and how that can impact other areas of functioning.

Pleasure in and of itself is not an isolated concept and is more of a response to stimuli. The other arm of research looks at pleasure from its relationship to other variables. Pleasure and such items as food intake, health behaviors (i.e. exercise, smoking, and sex for example) motivation, risk taking, and learning are some of the current focuses of research. Personality functioning and the impact of pleasure seeking is an area in which psychological research is being executed, to identify how pleasure seeking affects overall personality functioning. Much of the research on personality and pleasure is being examined from a psychoanalytic perspective, and serves to explain how the pursuit of pleasure fits into certain personality types. The defining and researching of pleasure, has allowed the development of scales to assess pleasure.

There are scales used to assess anhedonia, or the inability to experience pleasure. These scales are used in research to assess depression, in which anhedonia is one criterion that must be met to be diagnosed with clinical depression. Some of the most recognized measures of pleasure are the Snaith-Hamilton Pleasure Scale (SHAPS), the Fawcett-Clark Pleasure Capacity Scale (FCPS), and the Revised Chapman Physical Anhedonia Scale (CPAS). The SHAPS measures ability to experience pleasure in the last few days, with a higher score indicating greater pleasure capacity. "I would enjoy my favorite television or radio program," is an example of the type of question found in this measure. It assesses anhedonia by measuring: interest/pastimes, social interaction, sensory experience, and food/drink. The FCPS measures ability to experience pleasure by responding to questions based on their current state (i.e., "You sit watching a beautiful sunset in an isolated, untouched part of the world"). Higher scores indicate greater pleasure capacity, by assessing social activities, sensory experiences, and mastery of challenging tasks. The CPAS taps the feelings and interests about normally pleasurable events and activities (i.e., "The taste of food has always been important to me"). The CPAS is different from the other two measures discussed previously, in that this scale measures pleasure characteristics over the lifetime, instead of recent experiences.

All three measures were able to differentiate between depressed and non-depressed, with some measures being able to differentiate between melancholic and nonmelancholic depression (FCPS, CPAS). The close correlation between anhedonia and depression, is one that often prevents the ability to find or feel pleasure in events of daily life. The implications of this research will be valuable in the development of tools to assist in increasing the ability to find or feel pleasure in those that are depressed. The availability of psychometrically validated instruments will further inform the field of psychology's understanding of the measurement and quantification of positive emotions.

As mentioned when discussing the concepts and theories associated with pleasure and the scales used to measure it, there is no way to objectively measure pleasure. The inability to objectively measure pleasure limits the context in which the term is applied. The word is also limited by another context in which it may be used, the cultural context. In some cultures pleasure is not in the vocabulary or something that has a positive connotation. While this term is something to further understand in the pursuit of positive psychology it is one that must utilized in the correct cultural context. The understanding of pleasure as an emotion and a sensation is one that continues to be developed through continued research, to guide the development of strength's based approach in psychology and in the promotion of positive human functioning.

SEE ALSO: ▶ Amusement   ▶ Broaden and build theory of positive emotions   ▶ Euphoria   ▶ Hedonics   ▶ Positive emotions

Positive Affectivity

Kristin Naragon and David Watson
University of Iowa

Positive affectivity is a trait that refers to stable individual differences in the experience of positive emotions and active engagement with one's surroundings. Along with negative affectivity (the parallel tendency to experience negative emotions), positive affectivity is one of the two basic dimensions that define long-term affective experiences. Individuals who are high in positive affectivity tend to be cheerful, enthusiastic, energetic, confident, and alert. In contrast, those who are low in positive affectivity tend to experience lower levels of happiness, excitement, vigor, and confidence. Positive affectivity is a moderately stable trait over time and individuals tend to report consistent levels across different situations, such as being alone, interacting with others, or working.

Defining Positive Affectivity

Biobehavioral Links

Positive and negative affectivity are relatively independent of one another, which means that they can occur in a widely varying range of combinations (e.g., an individual can be high in both traits or low in both traits). They may be seen as the subjective components of larger biobehavioral systems that have evolved to promote the survival of animals. Positive affectivity is related to the behavioral facilitation system, an approach system that directs organisms towards rewarding and pleasurable situations, such as food, shelter, and sex. This system is linked primarily to dopamine activity and the level of resting activity in the left prefrontal cortex. In contrast, negative affectivity is related to the behavioral inhibition system, which protects organisms by encouraging the cessation of actions that may result in injury or death. The behavioral inhibition system is associated with activity in the right frontal cortex. Given the different evolutionary pressures that gave rise to these biobehavioral systems, it is not surprising that positive and negative affectivity are relatively independent and have different correlates.

Specific Content

There is not a strong consensus regarding the specific content that defines positive affectivity, with different prominent self-report measures containing different sets of scales. In these measures, respondents rate the extent to which each mood adjective or phrase is characteristic of them. The Differential Emotions Scale (DES) has positive affectivity scales assessing enjoyment (e.g., *happy, joyful*) and interest (e.g., *excited, alert, curious*), while the relevant scales in the Multiple Affect Adjective Checklist – Revised (MAACL-R) consist of a broad measure of positive affect that includes terms from both DES positive affectivity scales, and a second scale assessing sensation seeking (e.g., *daring, adventurous*). In contrast, the Profile of Mood States (POMS) has a single scale (vigor) that assesses the domain of positive affectivity.

The Expanded Form of the Positive and Negative Affect Schedule (PANAS-X) has the most differentiated conceptualization of positive affectivity, consisting of three core scales: Joviality (e.g., *cheerful, happy, lively*); Self-assurance (e.g., *confident, strong*); and Attentiveness (e.g., *alert, concentrating*). The structure of the PANAS-X has been supported by numerous factor analyses; moreover, the data have established that these positive affectivity scales measure related but ultimately distinctive mood states. Unfortunately, little information is currently available regarding the convergent validity of the above commonly-used measures of positive affectivity.

Related Constructs

Positive affectivity can be distinguished from several related constructs. Happiness, subjective well-being, and self-esteem are all correlated with positive affectivity; however, in addition to high positive affectivity, they also include an element of low negative affectivity. The personality trait of extroversion is also related to positive affectivity, although extroversion is a broader construct that includes social and interpersonal components, in addition to positive affectivity.

Causes and Correlates of Positive Affectivity

Genetic Influences

The small relevant literature indicates that positive affectivity is a moderately heritable trait. Twin studies utilizing the Well-being scale from the Multidimensional Personality Questionnaire (MPQ) have reported heritability estimates ranging from .40 to .50, while other heritability estimates range from .36 to .45. These studies found that the common rearing environment essentially has no effect on the development of the trait. The larger literature on the heritability of the related trait of extroversion supports these findings: Heritability estimates hover around .50 and the data again show little effect from the shared rearing environment.

Demographic and Cultural Variables

The above genetic studies indicate that the rearing environment plays a very minor role in the development of positive affectivity; similarly, a substantial body of evidence suggests that demographic variables also generally have little impact on positive affectivity. For instance, age, gender, marital status, ethnicity, income, and socioeconomic status are all relatively weak predictors of positive affectivity and happiness. However, there are two demographic variables that seem to be important for positive affectivity: social activity and religious/spiritual involvement. Positive affectivity is correlated with various indices of social behavior, such as the number of friends and the number of hours spent socializing. The influence of positive affectivity and social activity seems to be bidirectional: those high in positive affectivity are motivated to seek out social and affiliative activities; conversely, socializing tends to increase state positive affect. In addition, those who consider themselves religious or spiritual also report increased positive affectivity. This association may be due to a stronger sense of meaning or purpose in life, as well as the fact that religious groups provide a community and, hence, the opportunity for social activities.

There is no clear evidence for mean level differences in positive affectivity across cultures, but some studies suggest that individualist, rich, and democratic cultures may have higher levels of subjective well-being than collectivistic, poor, and totalitarian cultures. Cultural individualism versus collectivism may be especially important in determining how consistent an individual's level of positive affectivity is across various situations, such as working or being alone. For instance, Oishi and colleagues found that the situation had a greater impact on the positive affectivity levels of members of more collectivist cultures, whereas members of individualist cultures tended to remain consistent in their positive affectivity levels, regardless of the situation.

Current Research Applications

Psychopathology

Numerous clinical disorders are characterized by low positive affectivity, including social phobia, agoraphobia, posttraumatic stress disorder, schizophrenia, eating disorders, and the substance use disorders. However, low positive affectivity plays an especially salient role in the mood disorders. In particular, prospective data have shown that low positive affectivity levels predict the future development of depression. These findings raise the intriguing possibility that a lack of positive affectivity may be an important vulnerability factor for the mood disorders. The association between the mood disorders and positive affectivity also may help to explain the cyclic course of the mood disorders. Given that positive mood normally follows a daily cyclical course of waxing and waning, the mood disorders may be seen as a dysregulation or exaggeration of this pattern. The cycling of mood disorders is most apparent in the bipolar disorders, in which the individual fluctuates between well-defined episodes of mania (or hypomania) and depression. Melancholic depression and seasonal affective disorder also are characterized by marked cyclical patterns.

Job and Marital Satisfaction

Positive affectivity plays an important role in both job and marital satisfaction: Because people high in positive affectivity tend to feel good about themselves and their life, it is not surprising that they also report greater satisfaction in these import-ant life domains. For instance, positive affectivity was a significant predictor of job satisfaction, even when it was measured two years prior to the measurement of job satisfaction. Other studies have shown that positive affectivity is strongly related to personal accomplishment (i.e., an individual's sense of adequacy and effectiveness on the job) and organizational commitment. Positive affectivity is also moderately associated with marital satisfaction, with correlations ranging from .24 to .48. It should be noted that marital satisfaction and job satisfaction are them-selves linked, and there is some evidence that mood (particularly positive affect) may mediate this relationship.

Physical Health

Positive affectivity is associated with physical health, with high positive affectivity predicting increased longevity in the elderly population and resistance to devel-oping infectious illnesses. Positive affectivity is also correlated with better physical health in studies using subjective report: Among both diseased and healthy populations, those who are higher in positive affectivity report fewer symptoms and less pain. In addition, there is some evidence that positive affectivity may have more impact on how people *perceive* their health and bodies, rather than their actual physical condition. Positive affectivity may also affect health through its association with healthy behaviors such as sufficient sleep and increased exercise. Finally, positive affectivity levels may directly impact physiological processes (such as neurological and hormonal activity) that are relevant to physical health.

SEE ALSO: ▶ Appetitive motivational systems ▶ Happiness
▶ Job satisfaction ▶ Physical health ▶ Self-esteem ▶ Well-being

Positive Emotions

Jeffrey J. Froh
Hofstra University

Positive emotions are brief experiences that feel good in the present and increase the chances that one will feel good in the future. They seem to be essential ingredients in the recipe of living the good life. Understanding positive emotions is a core objective of positive psychology.

The study of emotions in psychology is relatively recent, with emotions only being the subject of sustained empirical scrutiny since the 1960s. Even then, the empirical focus was almost always – and almost always exclusively – on negative emotions. Groundbreaking researchers, including first Alice Isen and subsequently Barbara Fredrickson, started to give systematic attention to positive emotions from the 1980s onwards, and there is now a growing body of evidence to support their occurrence and implications. There is, however, consistent evidence that people generally have a bias toward attending to the negative, which may in large part account for the absence of research into positive emotions until the last 20 years or so.

Neglecting Positive Emotions

There is a general bias to give more weight to negative entities (e.g., emotions and personal traits) compared to positive entities. Generally, negative events and information seem to command more attention over positive ones. This makes sense from an evolutionary perspective. Someone who misses a positive outcome may later experience regret for not experiencing pleasure or growth, but they'll survive. In comparison, someone who fails to notice danger may suffer the ultimate negative outcome – death.

Baumeister and colleagues argue that bad is stronger than good across many psychological phenomena. For example, bad impressions and stereotypes form more quickly and are more difficult to alter compared with good ones. People get more upset over losing $50 than they are happy winning $50. Bad events influence both good and bad moods, whereas good events only influence good moods. Having a good day will unlikely influence someone's next day, but having a bad day will likely influence someone's next day – for the worse. Numerous types of trauma, even if it's a sole occurrence, can have severe and lasting negative effects on behavior, but research doesn't support the idea that a sole positive event can have similarly strong and lasting effects. For example, being sexually abused once can have long-term deleterious effects. One experience of sexual bliss has not been shown to predict comparable long-term positive effects.

Thanks largely to Isen and Fredrickson, empirical evidence supporting the role of positive emotions in promoting personal growth and development is accumulating. By increasing our thought-action repertoires (i.e., by broadening our cognitive and behavioral flexibility and options) and subsequently engendering physical, intellectual, and social resources, positive emotions improve coping and thus build resilience. Resiliency, in turn, predicts future occurrences of positive emotions. With positive emotions demonstrating such robust relationships to goal-achievement, physical and mental health, and other positive outcomes, it makes sense for psychology to further the understanding of positive emotions.

In her seminal article *What Good Are Positive Emotions?* Fredrickson suggested that positive emotions receive less attention than negative emotions for several possible reasons. First, compared with negative emotions, positive emotions are limited in quantity. The English language reflects this disparity. More words exist describing negative emotions relative to positive ones. Positive emotions, compared with negative ones, also don't have distinct facial expression or autonomic responses. Someone experiencing gratitude may express appreciation with relatively little behavioral or physiological change. An angry person, in contrast, may have snarled lips, a fist pumping, and a raised sympathetic nervous system response (e.g., increased blood flow to the muscles). While uncertain if the beneficiary experienced gratitude, it's evident that the fist-pumping individual is angry.

Second, some argue that psychology wears problem-focused lenses. It focuses on the negative. Although aiming to reduce negative emotions is an integral part of treatment, it may be insufficient for facilitating positive emotions, especially since some suggest that negative and positive emotions operate largely independently. Mental illness, usually involving negative emotions, is associated with more missed workdays, unhealthy psychosocial functioning, poorer physical health (e.g., cardiovascular disease), and limited daily activities. It therefore makes sense, some argue, to put the investigation of negative emotions ahead of positive ones. Positive emotions, however, have been shown to both undo and decrease physiological responses triggered by negative emotions (e.g., increased heart rate). Promoting positive emotions may be a fruitful psychological investment in the long-term.

Finally, emotion theorists have aimed to appreciate emotions in general. Emotion specific models largely reflecting prototypic emotions (e.g., anger, fear) have thus developed. But understanding anger doesn't necessarily lead to a greater understanding of joy, hope, or gratitude. A different theory is needed for positive emotions, and it was this theory that Fredrickson developed.

The Broaden-and-Build Theory of Positive Emotions

A single general-purpose model of emotions inadequately describes positive emotions. This realization sparked Fredrickson to develop her broaden-and-build theory of positive emotions. Negative emotions narrow our focus and restrict our behavioral range. Fredrickson argued that positive emotions yield nonspecific action tendencies beyond physical action. She proposed that positive emotions generate broad thought-action repertoires that ultimately build enduring physical, intellectual, and social resources.

Regarding physical resources, certain species use similar maneuvers during play and survival situations. For instance, while playing young patas monkeys run into foliage and catapult themselves away from their playmate. Adults in this species do the same when running from predators. The physical skills used and acquired during play apparently aid in survival.

Intellectual resources can be built via experiencing positive emotions such as joy. Here, joy will trigger explorative behaviors, subsequently engendering greater knowledge about one's environment. This information may prove useful in the acquisition of basic and applied knowledge. To illustrate, a young child who is securely attached to his caregiver will likely feel comfortable exploring his surroundings. Doing so he may learn both who is in the environment (i.e., basic knowledge) and who is approachable enough to help in the future if needed (i.e., applied knowledge). Hence, he has built enduring intellectual resources.

Social resources can be built via the experience and expression of gratitude – one of the more popular empirically studied positive emotions. Gratitude doesn't prompt one to reciprocate benefits in a tit-for-tat fashion. Instead, it can stretch one to repay kindness creatively. Fredrickson suggests that these new methods for repaying kindness can become enduring skills in someone's repertoire for strengthening relationships and building social capital. Indeed, grateful individuals may act prosocially as a way of merely expressing their gratitude. Over time, however, these actions can have lasting impacts on people's social relationships. Gratitude helps build trust in social relationships. Thus, gratitude may serve to maintain and build social resources.

A recent meta-analysis by Lyubomirsky, King, and Diener, in which the results of over 300 studies were aggregated, suggests that success engenders positive emotions – but also that positive emotions engender success. Indeed, happy people tend to live longer, make more money, and enjoy enduring loving relationships. One reason that positive emotions (e.g., happiness) might cause human flourishing could be because of the durable resources – physical, intellectual, and social – that were built over time. These resources can then be tapped into during times of adversity, as well as in times of growth.

Positive Emotions: Past and Present

Research on positive emotions has changed over the past few decades. Beginning in the 1980s and continuing today, much of the research conducted by Isen is focused on the role of positive emotions in cognitive processes. Specifically, several studies investigated the effect of positive emotions on cognitive organization, problem-solving, and decision-making. The findings suggest that when people are experiencing positive emotions, they demonstrate broadened thinking by associating more unusual words with neutral words, and group more stimuli together (suggesting positive emotions are linked with processing material in a more integrated fashion); flexible thinking and creative problem-solving; and more conservative and self-protecting behaviors when meaningful loss is likely.

Although the role of positive emotions in cognitive processes (e.g., own-race bias) is still being studied, much of the focus is now on promoting well-being. Again, Fredrickson is at the forefront. In 1998, Fredrickson and Levenson tested the hypothesis that contentment and amusement speed recovery from the cardiovascular symptoms of negative emotions (i.e., elevated heart period, pulse transmission times to the ear and to the finger, and finger pulse amplitude). In the first study, 60 female undergraduate students were first shown a film-clip eliciting fear and then randomly assigned to view a second film-clip eliciting contentment, amusement, neutrality, or sadness. Compared to the students who viewed the neutrality or sadness film-clips, those who viewed the films eliciting positive emotions demonstrated significantly faster returns to pre-film levels of cardiovascular reactivity. In the second study, 72 individuals between the ages 20 and 35 viewed a film-clip known to elicit sadness. Participants' behavior was analyzed and coded for the occurrence of smiles. The 50 participants who spontaneously smiled at least once during the sad film returned to their pre-film levels of cardiovascular reactivity faster than those who didn't smile. Spontaneous smiling speeded recovery to pre-film levels of reactivity. Negative emotions, with their link to specific action-tendencies (e.g., fight or flight), consistently trigger cardiovascular activation (e.g., increased heart rate and blood flow to the muscles). Certain positive emotions, in contrast, may reduce this cardiovascular activation. This undoing effect of positive emotions will likely bring the organism back to prior levels of physiological activation and increase psychological openness to numerous action tendencies.

In 2000, Fredrickson, Mancuso, Branigan, and Tugade replicated – and extended – the undoing effects of positive emotions. In the first study, 170 undergraduate students were told they had 60 seconds to prepare a 3-minute speech on a to-be-determined topic. While no one delivered a speech, the goal of the experimental manipulation was to induce anxiety. Students were then randomly assigned to watch one of four emotion eliciting film-clips: contentment, amusement, neutrality, or sadness. Again, compared with the neutral or sad films, the positive emotions films produced faster cardiovascular recovery. One could argue, however, that the positive emotions don't undo the cardiovascular reactivity of negative emotions, but instead simply replace the cardiovascular reactivity of negative emotions. The undoing hypothesis states that positive emotions produce specific cardiovascular activation only *after* negative emotions have already caused cardiovascular activation. The replacement hypothesis states that positive emotions – produced after either negative *or* neutral emotion induction – cause their own unique cardiovascular activation. To test the undoing versus replacement explanation, in the second study, 185 undergraduate students viewed the same films as in the first study after a neutral state. Results confirmed the undoing effect of positive emotions. The positive and neutral films produced statistically indistinguishable cardiovascular activation. Together, these studies suggest that positive emotions may help promote well-being by reducing the psychological and physical strain associated with cardiovascular activation, as well as the broadened mindset promoted by positive emotions, which is essential for building physical, intellectual, and social resources.

Fredrickson and Joiner tested if positive emotions triggered upward spirals of well-being. Using the broaden-and-build theory of positive emotions as a framework, they predicted that positive emotions and broad-minded coping (i.e., measured by items such as, "Think of different ways to deal with the problem" and "Try to step back from the situation and be more objective") would reciprocally and prospectively predict each other. A study using 138 undergraduate students completed measures of positive emotions, negative emotions, and broad-minded coping at two time points 5 weeks apart. Initial positive emotions, and not negative emotions, predicted enhanced broad-minded coping 5 weeks later. Initial broad-minded coping predicted enhanced positive emotions 5 weeks later, but not reductions in negative emotions. Furthermore, initial positive emotions predicted positive emotions 5 weeks later partly because of increases in broad-minded coping during the 5 weeks. Initial broad-minded coping predicted broad-minded coping 5 weeks later partly because of increases in positive emotions. Overall, these findings suggest that positive emotions and broad-minded coping mutually build on each other. Positive emotions thus feel good in the present, but also increase the chances of feeling good in the future.

In 2003, Fredrickson, Tugade, Waugh, and Larkin found that gratitude, a particular positive emotion, was the second most commonly experienced emotion in the wake of the terrorist attacks on September 11, 2001 (out of 20 emotions, only compassion was more common). They found evidence that the experience of positive emotions helped resilient people actively cope with the tragedy. Mirroring this work in children, Gordon, Musher-Eizenman, Holub, and Dalrymple conducted a subsequent archival study of newspaper accounts about what children were thankful for before and after 9/11. It produced further evidence that gratitude plays an important role in coping – and for children as well. Themes of gratitude for basic human needs (i.e., family, friends, and teachers/school) increased after 9/11. Evidence suggests, therefore, that gratitude may be a powerful positive emotion for coping with adversity.

The research produced by Isen, Fredrickson, and colleagues strongly suggests that positive emotions are a good thing. They lead to more flexible and creative thinking and, over time, build enduring physical, intellectual, and social resources. Thus, the broaden-and-build theory of positive emotions provides a framework from which we can explain the link between positive emotions and subsequent goodness, resilience, growth, generativity, and longevity.

Future Directions

Moving beyond the investigation of cognitive processes and into human flourishing is likely to continue being the research focus for positive emotions. This makes sense, since some argue that well-being interventions and positive psychotherapy are the most practical tools provided by positive psychology. Within the last decade global well-being has become a mainstream concern. Therefore, investigating the role of positive emotions in the functioning of nations around the world becomes increasingly important. It is likely then, that most positive emotions research in the future will be aimed at addressing the questions: How can we help people achieve sustainable well-being? What are the mediators for this augmentation? As has been shown with adults, counting blessings leads to positive emotions because of an increase in gratitude. What are the moderators for this augmentation? For instance, visualizing best possible selves seems to be an engaging strategy for young adults to become happier, while counting blessings may be more effective in older adults. Age, in this example, seems to matter. Furthermore, what are the specific positive emotions produced by these happiness-boosting interventions, and what are their links to specific life outcomes? Complicating matters even more, Rozin and Royzman state that the determinants of positive emotions are more idiosyncratic compared with negative emotions. Therefore, augmenting positive emotions is not likely to be a "one size fits all" solution. Rather, much time may be needed to tailor specific interventions for specific people. (This may explain why augmenting positive emotions in a laboratory setting seems to be comparatively more difficult than reducing negative emotions; it's also the inherent difficulty of making public policy that's aimed at augmenting citizens' well-being).

With the growing field of positive developmental psychology, the following questions should be addressed: What environmental factors facilitate and inhibit specific positive emotions? Who experiences which positive emotions the most, and why? Why do some people seem to have all of the ingredients to experience positive emotions and don't experience them? Why do some people seem to have a few of the ingredients to experience positive emotions and do experience them? Answering these and similar questions may help us to elucidate the well-springs of positive emotions, as well as develop a better understanding of the mechanisms, processes, and outcomes.

Finally, assessment, statistical analyses, and theories for positive emotions have improved. But more work is needed. First, we need to move beyond the traditional self-report measures of positive emotions. For instance, in addition to using self-report measures, researchers now include behavioral measures of gratitude (e.g., distributing resources between partners as indicating prosocial behavior). Furthermore, according to Isen and Erez, we can also use conceptual validation, converging operations, discriminant validation, implicit measures, and investigate if the obtained results with the chosen operation are compatible with theoretical expectations. Second, advanced statistics such as growth curve analysis, latent class models, and those designed specifically for testing intraindividual differences (e.g., P-technique factor analysis) should be used. These will allow us to understand better the intricacies of positive emotions. Finally, Fredrickson significantly advanced the study of positive emotions with her broaden-and-build theory of positive emotions. Theories now need to be created for discrete positive emotions. Some of this work has already begun. For instance, in relation to gratitude, McCullough, Kilpatrick, Emmons, and Larson extensively reviewed the literature in developmental, evolutionary, social, and personality psychology. They proposed that gratitude serves three moral functions. As a *moral barometer*, gratitude signals to the beneficiary that a benefactor bestowed a gift upon him. As a *moral motive*, gratitude encourages prosocial behavior in the beneficiary either directly towards the benefactor or others. Finally, as a *moral reinforcer*, gratitude increases the probability that the benefactor will act prosocially toward the beneficiary in the future. Fredrickson's theory provides a solid framework for positive emotions in general. But since theory and research serially influence each other – and some positive emotions seem to serve specific functions beyond simply broadening one's thinking and building one's thought-action repertoires – specific theories for some of the specific positive emotions might further the field of well-being.

SEE ALSO: ▶ Broaden and build theory of positive emotions ▶ Eudaimonia ▶ Happiness ▶ Hedonics ▶ Positive affectivity ▶ Well-being

Positive Ethics

Samuel Knapp,[a] Michael C. Gottileb,[b] and Mitchell M. Handelsman[c]
[a]*The Pennsylvania Psychological Association;* [b]*Independent Practice, Dallas, TX;* [c]*University of Colorado at Denver and Health Sciences Center*

Positive psychology attempts to move the discipline of psychology away from an emphasis on pathology or illness to a discussion of the uplifting and emotionally fulfilling aspects of life. Similarly, positive ethics attempts to move the discussion of professional and scientific ethics away from "an almost exclusive focus on wrongdoing and disciplinary responses to a more balanced and integrative approach that includes encouraging psychologists to aspire to their highest ethical potential" (Handelsman, Knapp, & Gottlieb, 2002, p. 731). The ethics of psychologists need not be restricted to a set of specific rules as promulgated by the current code of conduct and/or the laws of a particular jurisdiction. Ethics can also include affirmations of what is good, ideal, and valuable, and embrace the best of the world's rich professional, philosophical and religious traditions. Rather than being a static set of directives or a fixed entity of prohibitions, ethics can be a dynamic enterprise that allows psychologists to respond better to changing conditions and situations. "Most psychologists want to do more than just avoid being punished; they want to have a positive impact on others and excel in their profession" (Knapp & VandeCreek, 2006, p. 4). Traditional approaches to ethics often focus only on the minimum standards of the profession (the "ethical floor") or the sanctions that would be applied to the few who violate them. Positive ethics informs psychologists who strive for the ethical ceiling.

Although Handelsman, Knapp, and Gottlieb first used the term *positive ethics* in a peer reviewed publication, other scholars have expressed similar goals in which they indicate the limitations of looking at ethics only from the standpoint of obedence to rules. For example, Brown warned against concrete ethics that separate us from others, and Tjeltveit noted that ethical codes do not contain the highest levels of ethical excellence. Bricklin notes that ethics and law are not the same and should not be confused, and Kitchener urged psychologists to rely on foundational ethical theories to guide their behavior.

Positive and the Aspirational Principles of the APA Ethics Code

Positive ethics is similar to the aspirational ethics or General Principles of the APA Ethical Principles of Psychologists and Code of Conduct in that it urges psychologists to live up to high ideals. It differs from the APA aspirational principles in that it: a) urges psychologists to integrate personal values and professional ethics; and b) recognizes that ethics may be approached from viewpoints other than the principle-based perspective found in the APA Ethics Code.

The APA Ethics Code clearly applies only to the "psychologists' activities that are part of their scientific, educational, or professional roles as psychologists" (APA, 2002, Introduction and Applicability) and not their private conduct. However psychologists, as most others, seek consistency between their personal and professional ideals, and prefer a career that allows them to live out their personal ideals. They hope for the opportunity to reflect upon their daily work with feelings of accomplishment and pride, and a sense that their work has value. Similarly, a positive ethics perspective encourages psychologists to clarify the ways in which they can fulfill their highest personal ideals through their careers, whether it is: teaching a new generation of students; assisting individuals with health and mental health concerns; or expanding the knowledge base of our discipline.

The positive ethics perspective also differs from the aspirational principles of the APA Ethics Code in that it does not endorse any one particular ethical theory.

Psychologists working from a positive ethics perspective may endorse principle-based ethics, virtue ethics, feminist ethics, Utilitarianism, or an ethical perspective based on a religious tradition.

Implications of a Positive Ethics Approach

Of course a positive ethics perspective does not eschew the necessity for the societal regulation of scientific and professional psychologists' behavior. At times miscreants need to be sanctioned. But, education regarding psychology's standards may be more helpful if it includes an understanding of the ways in which disciplinary codes are consistent with generally accepted moral values. For example, Knapp and VandeCreek analyzed the 2002 APA Ethics Code and found almost all of the enforceable standards could be justified on the basis of principle-based ethics. However, discussions of ethics should go beyond just codes and laws. By themselves, external disciplinary controls are only concerned with minimum obligations; but from the perspective of positive ethics, psychologists should also be concerned with higher ideals.

A focus on positive ethics expands the options available to psychologists because it allows them to draw upon a wide range of philosophical and scientific perspectives when faced with an ethical issue. The criteria for judging an action ceases to be, "What must I do to avoid being disciplined?" and becomes, "What is the best way to promote my highest ethical ideals?" For example, many research psychologists want to protect research participants because it is an intrinsic good and actualizes their professional identities, even if doing so exceeds IRB requirements. Psychologists work to ensure their patients' fullest understanding and participation in the treatment process beyond just obtaining their signatures on an informed consent form. That is, positive ethics encourages psychologists to examine their behavior in light of the higher standard of promoting human welfare.

In addition, positive ethics encourages psychologists to articulate a framework that gives meaning and unity to their work. When one's ethics are alive, vital, pertinent, and creative, a psychologist can respond to ethical dilemmas from a more coherent and multifaceted perspective instead of responding impulsively based upon a potentially ill-considered intuition or a knee-jerk adherence to the rules.

An excessive emphasis on disciplinary ethics may also have adverse consequences. For example, many psychologists view ethics negatively and thus feel alienated from the ethics code or even from general discussions of ethics. Too often psychologists respond to considerations of ethics with dread and avoidance, instead of with curiosity and enthusiasm for professional development. Furthermore, an excessive focus on the disciplinary sanctions may fail to highlight the relationship between the enforceable standards of the Ethics Code and one's personal values. Consequently, some psychologists may view the Ethics Code as something imposed on them that must be obeyed rather than a document that reflects their deepest beliefs and aspirations.

Current and Future Directions in Research and Applications

The major thrust of positive ethics is to review all aspects of professional and scientific psychology from an overarching ethical perspective. Thus, positive ethics is employed any time a commentator looks at the behavior of psychologists from a deeply held overarching ethical perspective. For example, a positive perspective was used when Fisher urged psychologists to consider foundational ethical principles when conducting research. Brown applied a positive approach when she looked at forensic consultation from the standpoint of an overarching feminist theory. Bennett, Bricklin, Harris, Knapp, VandeCreek, and Younggren went beyond the narrow perspective of ethics seen only as a list of laws and punishment when they urged patient-oriented and ethically-based risk management principles. Positive ethics influenced Knapp and VandeCreek's recommendation that psychologists consider civic virtue and community responsibility as one aspect of their moral obligations.

Positive ethics has implications for the training of psychologists. Handelsman, Gottlieb and Knapp argued that psychology trainees undergo an experience akin to acculturation as they learn the ethical standards that are embedded in the culture of psychology. The acculturation model serves as a foundation for developing positive ethics because it helps students to integrate personal values and ideals into their professional behavior and identity.

The documents developed by the Association of Psychology Postdoctoral and Internship Centers Competency Conference also have relevance to positive ethics. The work group on the ethics competency area defined the ethical competencies of psychologists as going beyond just learning disciplinary codes to include, for example, teaching students about themselves as moral individuals. The work group on professional development overlapped considerably with positive ethics in that it urged programs to teach students about self-care, self-understanding, responsibility, accountability, and other personal qualities with ethical valence that help psychologists reach their highest potential.

A final thrust of positive ethics is on learning more about what motivates and reinforces ethical conduct. Cognitive and psychological sciences are uncovering the mechanisms by which humans determine concepts of right and wrong, and how they influence subsequent behavior. Although science cannot tell us what our ideals should be, scholars such as Hauser inform positive ethics when they ask: What propels people to moral judgments? How do ethical intuitions vary across cultures? and What social factors influence ethical behavior. Indeed, a positive ethics perspective appears among the writings of many psychologists, including those involved with positive psychology, when they consider some of the same aspects of human existence (such as empathy, compassion, forgiveness, universal virtues, and wisdom) as have been considered by philosophical and religious ethicists. Positive ethics is a development with great potential to help psychologists improve themselves, their work, and their communities.

SEE ALSO: ► Compassion ► Leadership

References

American Psychological Association. (2002). Ethical principles of psychologists and code of conduct. *American Psychologist, 57*, 1060–1073.

Handelsman, M. M., Knapp, S., & Gottlieb, M. (2002). Positive ethics. In C. R. Snyder & S. J. Lopez (Eds.), *Handbook of positive psychology* (pp. 731–744). New York: Oxford University Press.

Knapp, S., & VandeCreek, L. (2006). *Practical ethics for psychologists: A positive approach.* Washington, DC: American Psychological Association.

Positive Experiences

Elin B. Strand,[a] John W. Reich,[b] and Alex J. Zautra[b]
[a]Faculty of Nursing, Oslo University College; [b]Department of Psychology, Arizona State University

The fundamental building blocks of all emotions, positive as well as negative are the person's experiences: his or her interactions with the physical and most of all the social world. Evidence shows that positive experiences are directly related to positive emotions, they occur frequently in our daily lives, they help buffer the effects of negative events and emotions, and they are intimately connected to the sense of personal control and mastery in our daily living. Positive experiences are a mainspring of the good life, and research shows that when people increase the number of such events, they will report better well-being.

Studying positive experiences is centrally related to the positive psychology movement. This movement has created new vistas for scientists and practitioners who are focused on understanding and improving human well-being. It provides a platform for integrating newly developing knowledge of the positive aspects of well-being with what is already known about stressful and maladaptive aspects of adaptation.

Positive experiences are most clearly identified as positive events which occur to people in the course of their daily lives. The study of events began with the classic study of Holmes and Rahe who developed a survey instrument to assess the frequency of occurrence of major life changes: large, such as marriage and divorce, and a few small events like vacations. Their work focused on classifying the major stresses, working from the premise that important experiences were the ones most likely to be disruptive. They weighed the experiences based on estimates of the degree of readjustment to everyday life that the events would require for the person to regain equilibrium.

There were two problems with this approach to life experiences. First, the focus was on major events, ignoring the vast set of experiences that define the quality of a person's everyday life. This shortcoming was corrected with inventories designed to study hassles and other small events. These events are much more frequent, they are constantly present, requiring coping and resolution, and our lives take on different levels of adjustment or maladjustment depending on how well we deal with them. The second problem with the original focus on major calamities in the study of life experience was the focus on the stressful and otherwise disruptive aspects, ignoring the enriching aspects of positive or favorable life experiences altogether. Early on, Zautra and colleagues recognized this shortcoming and in a series of studies introduced methods of registering positive experiences as a central feature in understanding the quality of life. One of the most significant contributions of this line of research has been the discovery of the distinctive nature of positive events compared with negative events. Dealing with a negative event is obviously very different from dealing with a positive one. Personal successes have a major impact on our well-being; they are frequent, pervasive, and motivating. People strive to have more positive events in their lives, and they strive to avoid the negative ones. Research is now showing that both classes of events have to be considered in an integrative, comprehensive positive psychology.

Several distinctive areas of theory and research have become joined in the positive psychology framework. One important tradition within positive psychology is the research by Csikszentmihalyi and colleagues. Based on their work on positive and optimal experiences they have developed what is called the Flow theory. *Flow* is a concept that refers to a state of optimal experience with total absorption in the task at hand. Flow enhances positive feelings when the person's experience becomes so concentrated that other concerns are eliminated, and attention is focused on the event and the positive feelings that result from such complete focus. It is a powerful characteristic of a good life. An experience may be understood as any of the contents of consciousness such as thoughts, feelings and sensations. Flow theory also makes a distinction between external coordinates, such as one's location and activities, and internal coordinates, for example, concentration, happiness and attention of experiences.

A second development by Diener and colleagues has focused on the measurement of well-being. They have investigated what is called *subjective well-being* (SWB) measurement, defined broadly as peoples' cognitive and affective evaluation of their lives. Their assessments of SWB have even extended to cross-national comparisons of levels of SWB in various countries. Their research has shown that events involved in, for instance, positive social relationships and economic status are central to SWB. In overview, it is a hallmark of these research areas to emphasize the dynamics between the person and their environment. Environmental events and the person's cognitive and emotional reactions to them are central components of an integrative model of health and well-being.

Over the years different design and assessment methods have been developed and employed in studies of peoples' experiences and well-being. Often longitudinal approaches of the same population with one year or more between the measurement points were applied. This is appropriate for studying groups in society but not in the study of individuals. Recent research has used more rigorous study designs and methods such as repeated measures with either weekly or daily and even within-day assessments. Such methods give the opportunity to study both stability and change in a person's everyday experiences. Further, more frequent reports give the opportunity to study life as it goes on and thus, a more detailed and complete picture may be achieved.

The Effects of Positive Experiences

In one experimental study carried through by Csikszentmihayi and colleagues, the study participants were instructed to live their lives as usual except for having fun, playing or doing anything that was nonfunctional. Even small pleasures such as watching a sunset or smiling to a neighbor should be avoided. Headache, fatigue, distress or being less creative were some of the unpleasant responses that were more frequently reported by many of the participants during the registration period. Thus, a continuous diet of even small daily positive experiences seems to be necessary for sustaining well-being.

An early comprehensive review of the research literature on positive events by Reich and Zautra revealed that desirable events were experienced two to three times more commonly than negative events. Further, people appear to feel good most of the time, and on a daily basis, positive emotions (deriving from positive experiences) greatly outweigh negative emotions. As might be expected, high frequencies of positive experiences are related to higher positive emotions such as happiness and contentment, but they are not generally related to *lower* negative emotions. Negative events have been shown to be related to negative emotions such as anxiety or depression and also tend to suppress our positive feelings. There is an asymmetry in our emotional lives, and this asymmetry is to some extent related to the kinds of experiences people have in daily living. In general, our emotional lives are compounded out of two relatively distinct and, in fact, uncorrelated emotion systems, positive and negative. Thus, people should not generally expect to remove feelings of distress, unhappiness, or depression by taking action to increase their positive experiences. On the other hand, "buffering effects" have been found, in which positive experiences do in fact reduce the impact that negative experiences have on our emotional lives. In this context, it is particularly significant that, in a study by Reich and Zautra, research participants were given experimental instructions to engage in either none, a few, or up to a dozen positive experiences in a two-week period, along with return to the laboratory to report how they had been feeling. Those participants who reported having experienced a large number of stressful (negative) events reported *less* psychological distress if they also had engaged in a high number of positive experiences. Buffering effects of positive experiences are possible under high stress, and a valuable finding for developing event-based therapeutic interventions.

The Benefits of Positive Emotional Experiences

Positive emotions reflect pleasurable engagement with the environment, for example, excitement, joy, interest, love, enthusiasm and contentment. Positive events are what create positive emotional states and feelings. They are connected to greater odds of survival and of living long enough to reproduce and strongly connected to innate and underlying systems of motivational, physiological, and cognitive processes. They facilitate approach behaviors that enhance initiative and activity and promote an individual's engagement and connection with the environment. Our repertoire of positive emotions deriving from positive experiences is wide ranging and highly differentiated. For example, interest creates an urge to explore, and joy creates an urge to play, push limits and be creative in social, intellectual as well as artistic contexts. More specific research suggests that positive experiences are related to cognitive strategies for reframing a situation to see it in a more positive light, such as optimism, hope, and finding meaning. Further, positive emotions broaden a person's mindset, such as expanding the capacity to organize ideas in multiple ways and they enhance cognitive elaboration and creative problem solving.

Based on this research and her own investigations Barbara Fredrickson has developed the broaden-and-build theory of positive emotions. The theory posits that positive emotions increase well-being not only in the moment by triggering upward spirals of cognitions and actions but also by, over time, building physiological, intellectual, psychological and social resources. This broadening and building improves our capacity to cope with the many different adversities we experience in the course of our daily living.

Positive Emotional Experiences as Sources of Resilience

The ability to bounce back from negative emotional experiences and show a flexible adaptation to changing demands of stressful experiences is conceptualized as *resilience*. Resilience is important for sustaining health and well-being. Research is showing that high-resilience individuals tend to report more positive experiences when under stress, and those having more positive emotions on average also have greater capacity to recover from aversive states.

In research on patients with different chronic pain conditions, positive emotions as source of resilience with chronic pain have been the subject of investigation. Whether pain is associated with an identifiable cause or not, it may be a highly stressful experience and a burden to the patient's well-being. Pain can be an extremely aversive bodily experience and a potential stressor because of its uncontrollable fluctuations. Research has shown that subjective experiences of pain vary between individuals and across situations in intensity, duration, and unpleasantness, and that negative emotions are significantly associated with and influence the pain experience in more destructive ways. Thus, identifying factors that may diminish and prevent negative feelings of pain may be of considerable value to patients' emotional well-being. In that research, participants were asked to give either daily or weekly reports of their pain as well as to what degree they had experienced positive and negative emotions during different periods of assessment. Results from the analyses confirmed that higher levels of pain increased negative emotions and stress. Moreover, in the days and weeks when the participants were able to mobilize positive experiences, even when pain was at its most intense, their levels of stress and negative emotions were significantly lower. Overall, then, research has shown that increased positive affect seems to protect against negative emotions. Thus, positive emotional experiences may be understood as sources of resilience.

Events and Personal Causation

One may wonder why positive experiences have such favorable effects on our well-being. It is not only their greater frequency or their connection to the above-mentioned benefits of positive emotions, but also other properties have been shown to be directly linked to adjustment and well-being.

Cognitive factors are useful in understanding the impact of positive experiences on health and well-being. A broad range of explanatory style theories have focused on cognitive factors such as the way people explain and judge the cause of an event. Peterson and Seligman have in their attribution theory specified distinct differences between event causation as internal or external and controllable or uncontrollable. Also the reformulated learned helplessness theory posits that the explanations for the cause of an event may vary, that it is of importance and makes a difference to well-being. For example optimistic explanations for negative events are those that are more external, unstable, and specifically related to one single event. In turn, optimistic explanations of positive events are internal, stable, and global while pessimistic explanations for such events are external, unstable, and specific. According to this theory stability relates to duration of helplessness symptoms, globality to generalization of helplessness across events, while the internal causation of the event is associated to deficits in self-esteem in depression. Optimistic and pessimistic explanations in turn will lead to different expectations about future events. Those attributing positive events to internal and stable causes may expect to be in control of such events in the future and thus more resilient.

Numerous studies have shown that a sense of personal (internal) control and mastery in dealing with life's challenges is related to higher levels of mental health. For example, positive events have been shown to be perceived by the person as more under their own personal control, and for desirable events (but not negative events), the perception of being in personal control is related to improved psychological well-being. Furthermore, events are often judged as being positive when people feel that they themselves caused them to occur. When people judge events as self-caused rather than externally-caused, they tend to rate those events as more positive. This apparent bidirectionality may be a major reason why engagement in positive experiences has been shown to broaden and build a person's thought repertoires.

Control and Causation in Positive Experiences

These principles were put to a rigorous assessment in a recent study by Strand, Reich and Zautra. A large sample of adult medical patients as well as healthy participants reported on the frequencies of positive and negative small daily events – including interpersonal events – which they had experienced in the previous week, along with measures of emotional well-being assessed by positive and negative emotions. The events list on which the patients responded contained subsets of daily events which had been independently scored on the underlying dimension of internal personal causation vs. external causation (for example, "played a sport, game, or cards with friends vs. received a compliment from friend/acquaintance"). Analysis of these reports indicated, as predicted, that experiencing a greater number of personally caused positive events was related to higher levels of positive emotions during the same time period. Interestingly, though, and of great significance for the understanding of mental health and positive experiences, the reporting of having experienced a higher number of externally-caused positive experiences, although correlated with positive emotions, was *also* correlated with higher negative emotions. The fact that the positive events which were externally caused were correlated with negative aspects of adjustment shows the power that personal causation, or in this case a lack of it, plays in the overall structure of our mental health. The results also were congruent with an earlier finding of Brickman, Coates, and Janoff-Bulman that a sample of lottery winners reported no greater happiness than lottery nonwinners. The negative outcomes of positive events may also be because even if the events are positive, they are external and uncontrollable and thus hard to interpret as self-caused. According to both the attribution theory approach and the reformulated learned helplessness theory, this may be related to a pessimistic explanation style associated to negative emotional states and reduced well-being such as depression.

In addition to providing a greater sense of personal control, positive experiences are a magnet that draws people together and the glue that holds them in close connection with one another. This connection provides the nourishment of the positive and is central to the sustainability of the good life. Most positive experiences arise out of interpersonal relations, and there is evidence that sharing the positive amplifies and extends positive emotion benefits. Indeed, most meaningful relationships are defined by a rich history of shared positive and negative life experiences, and happy versus troubled relations may be defined in part by a favorable ratio of positive to negative experiences.

In overview, evidence is accumulating that positive experiences play a major role in positive feelings about life. At this point, the data appear to suggest that positive experiences have their effects through their intimate connection with personal mastery, control of the life events, the creation of the kind of life that will allow full growth, emotional well-being, and close, caring relationships. Positive experiences are amenable to manipulation by researchers, therapists and trainers who can encourage their research participants to engage in their own self-chosen positive events. The favorable results of that study should be seen in light of contemporary positive psychology. Improved living is one of the promises of the positive psychology movement, and personal causation and helping people increase the quality of their lives is at least one key to this promise.

SEE ALSO: ► Attributional theory ► Broaden and build theory of positive emotions ► Csikszentmihalyi, Mihaly ► Diener, Ed. ► Flow

Positive Illusions

Shelley E. Taylor
University of California, Los Angeles

Many people hold beliefs about themselves, the world, and the future that are more positive than reality can sustain. These beliefs have been called *positive illusions*. At least three types of positive illusions have been documented. The first is self-aggrandizing self-perceptions. People consistently regard themselves more positively and less negatively than they regard others and than others regard them. The second illusion concerns perceptions of mastery or control. Most people believe that they can exert more personal control over environmental circumstances than is actually the case. Indeed, considerable research shows that people believe they can even affect outcomes that are heavily due to chance. A third positive illusion concerns unrealistic optimism. Most people are optimistic and believe that the present is better than the past and that the future will be better as well, especially for themselves. For example, when asked what they think is possible for themselves in the future, college students report more than four times as many positive as negative possibilities. Typically, people overestimate the likelihood that they will experience a wide variety of pleasant events, such as liking their first job or having a gifted child, and somewhat underestimate their risk of succumbing to negative events, include being fired, getting divorced, or succumbing to a chronic disease.

These positive beliefs are highly prevalent in normal thought and might seem amusing or perhaps troubling, were it not for the fact that they are reliably associated with psychological well-being. Mental health experts generally define the well-adjusted person as possessing particular qualities: the ability to be happy or contented; the ability to care for and about others; the capacity for creative and productive work; and the ability to meet stressful events with relative equanimity, learning or growing from them when possible. Extensive research now suggests that positive illusions are associated with these outcomes.

The positive illusions of self-aggrandizing self-perceptions, an illusion of control, and unrealistic optimism may be particularly helpful for enabling people to combat major stressful events or traumas. These disruptive negative events at least temporarily produce aberrations in psychological functioning, marked by anxiety, depression and other negative emotional states, and may also enhance risks for health-related disorders. Research suggests that people who are able to develop or maintain their positive beliefs in the face of these traumas or potential setbacks, even when illusory, cope more successfully with them and show less evidence of psychological distress.

Research with a broad array of patient groups including heart patients, cancer patients, and people living with AIDS reveal that the majority of people in these circumstances react to their conditions by developing perceptions of themselves as physically better off than others with their condition, as coping more successfully than other patients like themselves, and as having experienced beneficial outcomes in their lives. The themes around which such adaptations occur include a search for meaning in the experience, an effort to regain a sense of mastery, and an attempt to restore a positive sense of self. Many people report that the stressful event revealed or evoked personal qualities that were either previously latent or nonexistent, such as an increased understanding of others and an enhanced sense of meaning in life. These findings suggest that when people experience personal tragedies or setbacks, they respond with cognitively adaptive efforts that may enable them to return to or exceed their previous level of psychological functioning. Not all of the beliefs that people develop in the wake of life threatening experiences are illusory, of course, but the illusory component of these adaptive beliefs is highly prevalent.

Potential Risks of Positive Illusions

There are several potential risks that may arise if people hold positive illusions about their personal qualities and likely outcomes. The first is that they set themselves up for unpleasant surprises for which they are ill prepared when their overly optimistic beliefs are disconfirmed. Research suggests that for the most part, these adverse outcomes do not occur. People's beliefs are more realistic at times when realism serves them particularly well, for example, when initially making plans, when accountability is likely, or following negative feedback from the environment. Following a setback or failure, people's overly positive beliefs may be attached to a new undertaking.

A second risk is that people who hold positive illusions will set goals or undertake courses of actions that are likely to produce failure. This concern appears to be largely without basis. Research shows that when people are deliberating future courses of actions for themselves, such as whether to take a particular job or go to graduate school, their perceptions are fairly realistic, but they become overly optimistic when they turn to implementing their plans. The shift from realism to optimism may provide the fuel needed to bring potentially difficult tasks to fruition.

A third risk is that positive self-perceptions may have social costs. Considerable research suggests that people who are self-promoting in public situations do indeed turn other people off. Initially their upbeat optimistic nature endears them to others, but over time, other people become aware of their self-absorption and turn away from them. People who hold overly positive self-assessments privately, however, do not turn others off and indeed the opposite is the case. They make positive impressions on others, they are well liked by their friends, and they impress clinicians and peers as mentally healthy.

A potential limitation of positive illusions concerns their cultural prevalence. Although it is easy to document positive illusions in Western cultures, people in East Asian cultures are much less likely to self-enhance and indeed, are often self-effacing instead. Positive illusions may be manifest in group-enhancing biases and may also be privately held, but not publicly voiced. Nonetheless cultural differences in manifestations of and prevalence of positive illusions remains an important issue.

Positive Illusions and Physical Health

The ability to develop and sustain positive perceptions in the face of setbacks has health benefits. In a series of studies with men who were HIV seropositive or already diagnosed with AIDS, Reed, Kemeny, Bower, Taylor and their colleagues found that those who held unrealistically positive assessments of their abilities to control their health conditions experience a longer time to developing symptoms and a slower course of illness. In addition, men who were able to find meaning in their experiences were less likely to experience HIV progression that might result from stressful events such as bereavement.

Some of the health benefits of positive illusions may result from several known predictors of health: the ability to attract social support, protection against psychological distress including depression (which has been tied to risk of illness and/or a more rapid course), or better health behaviors. However, evidence supports a more direct biological pathway. Specifically, people who hold overly positive beliefs about themselves, the world, and the future, show somewhat less reactivity to stress. These findings suggest that positive illusions may be health-protective by means of keeping wear and tear on stress systems at low levels. As such, the cumulative damage that might otherwise occur to biological systems as a result of stress exposure may be lessened.

Origins of Positive Illusions

Where do positive illusions come from? Research suggests that there may be genetic origins of positive illusions, although the amount of variance accounted for by genetic factors is relatively modest, perhaps 25–30%. Early environment also plays an important role, such that people are more able to develop positive beliefs and psychosocial resources more generally in nurturant environments than in more harsh ones. Gene-environment interactions may also play a role.

Summary

Positive illusions are overly positive beliefs about the self, the world, and the future that are protective of mental and physical health. Increasingly, scientists are deepening their understanding of the emotional, neural, genetic, and neuroendocrine bases of these beneficial effects. Whether positive illusions can be learned or not remains an open question. There is no reason to think that they cannot be taught and indeed, many well-established therapies that involve teaching people to think better of themselves, their circumstances, and their outcomes may rely, at least in part, on instilling a somewhat illusory positive glow about oneself in the world.

SEE ALSO: ▶ Cognitive appraisal   ▶ Taylor, Shelley

Acknowledgments

Preparation of this manuscript was supported by grants from the National Institute of Mental Health (MH056880) and the National Institute of Aging (AG030309).

Positive Law and Policy

Peter H. Huang[a] and Jeremy A. Blumenthal[b]
[a]*Temple University;* [b]*Syracuse University*

> Gross national product does not allow for the health of our children, the quality of their education, or the joy of their play. It does not include the beauty of our poetry or the strength of our marriages, or the intelligence of our public debate or the integrity of our public officials. It measures neither our wit nor our courage, neither our wisdom nor our teaching; it measures everything, in short, except that which makes life worthwhile. (Robert F. Kennedy, Speech at the University of Kansas, March 18, 1968 [Kennedy, 1968/1993])

Positive law and policy applies insights from positive psychology to design legal rules and public programs that foster a good life. Data measuring people's happiness can inform policy evaluation in diverse arenas. Jury participation and direct participatory democracy improve life satisfaction. Positive psychology has novel implications for paternalism.

Positive law and policy applies insights from positive psychology to design legal rules and institutional policy. Happiness-based measures offer nonmonetary metrics for evaluating policy in financial and securities regulation (Huang, 2005). It would be helpful to policy-makers to quantitatively assess how financial policies impact not only people's happiness, but also investors' confidence and moods. Both investor confidence or trust in financial markets and investors' moods, such as financial anxiety or investment stress, affect and are affected by financial variables, such as consumer debt, consumer spending, consumer wealth, corporate investment, initial public offerings, and securities market demand, liquidity, prices, supply, and volume. Financial and securities regulators can and should consider the emotional impacts that alternative regulations have upon both people's emotions themselves and real consequences of changes in people's emotions on aggregate economic and financial variables. There is evidence that people in many countries have experienced increased wealth over time but not increased self-reported happiness over time. Such evidence suggests that designing financial policies to merely increase people's wealth over time may not lead to people increasing their well-being. Such evidence also supports proposals that policy makers should analyze how financial policies affect measures of people's happiness.

Affective reactions are likely to be just as important, if not more important, for nonfinancial risks, such as environmental, health, and safety risks, than financial risks. But while money provides a common metric for quantifying and measuring financial risks, nonfinancial risks typically lack a universally accepted standardized and unifying metric. Money arises naturally in discussions evaluating regulating financial and securities markets, but not necessarily in discourse analyzing regulating nonfinancial risks. Measures of subjective well-being and happiness can lend insight into nonfinancial contexts as diverse as development economics, environmental protection, macroeconomics, and taxation. In particular, Nobel-prize winning psychologist Daniel Kahneman and coauthors have developed several empirical means of measuring happiness, both at the individual and national levels. For example, Kahneman and economist Alan B. Krueger propose the U-index to measure the fraction of time people spend in an unpleasant emotional state. Instead of designing public policy to achieve higher subjective well-being, there could be greater emotional appeal to and political support for designing public policy to minimize subjective ill-being. For instance, U-index data can identify laws and policies that can improve people's happiness by changes in their allocation of time over such activities as childcare, commuting, and work versus leisure.

Civic participation at various levels can also lead to a flourishing life. Citizens who serve on juries are typically well-satisfied with their experience, satisfaction that may stem from their ability to participate in the mini-democracy of jury deliberation. That is, jurors might be "motivated by a feeling of satisfaction with participation in the democratic process" (Prescott & Starr, 2006, p. 339). Similarly, participating in a democratic political culture, or simply having the chance to do so, can lead to increased happiness. Regardless of political outcome, such participation evidently provides citizens "a feeling of being involved and having political influence, as well as a notion of inclusion, identity and self-determination" (Frey, Benz, & Stutzer, 2004, p. 380).

Government intervention may help enable individuals and communities to thrive. Such a positive approach to law and policy would assist individuals and societies to elevate their well-being from existing baseline levels – rather than the traditional paternalism which limits choices and opportunities. Public policy to promote *beneficial* outcomes might be more politically feasible than remedial policies. An example is government response to problems of poor physical health, including obesity or coronary heart disease. The conventional sort of paternalistic intervention – a "remedial" approach – might remove people's options to buy and eat fatty and other unhealthy foods by prohibiting their sale in restaurants, cafeterias, or even supermarkets. A positive paternalistic approach, in contrast, such as government mandating an exercise program – perhaps even just for those at risk for heart disease – might be seen as less intrusive than the remedial approach, and may achieve the same objectives. Public health experts suggest that reducing youth obesity and other health problems can occur by requiring minimum physical activity levels in schools, with potential accountability for schools failing to provide appropriate physical education programs. Far more speculative and controversial might be for governments to encourage or even mandate such physical exercise programs not for the potential *health* benefits, but for the positive *mood* effects that exercise brings about, in order to reap the benefits of being in a positive mood (Blumenthal, in press). Employer-sponsored, or mandated, meditation programs might also serve such a goal. Clearly, both the acceptability of such interventions by either government or private parties is a matter for further empirical research, as is, of course, such programs' effectiveness.

Environments in which it is challenging for people to learn to want what they like, such as those involving viscerally addictive experiences or substances, decisions having irreversible or very costly to reverse consequences, and infrequently repeated situations, might justify some type of policy intervention. Examples include possible choices about career, children, death, family, health, living wills, marriage, and retirement. Positive paternalism can also encourage people to engage in practicing interventions and strategies that lead to sustainable increases of well-being. Government sponsoring, subsidizing, or even mandating that curricula in elementary schools and high schools include education about positive psychology are other possible policy alternatives to foster increases of well-being among youth. Whether such positive educational policy interventions can and will be successful at increasing and sustaining happiness are currently open empirical questions about which there will be more forthcoming data.

SEE ALSO: ▶ Flourishing   ▶ Civic responsibilities and virtues

References

Blumenthal, J. A. (in press). Emotional paternalism. *Florida State University Law Review, 35.*

Frey, B. S., Benz, M., & Stutzer, A. (2004). Introducing procedural utility: Not only what, but also how matters. *Journal of Institutional and Theoretical Economics, 160,* 377–401.

Huang, P. H. (2005, November). Emotional impact analysis in financial regulation: Going beyond cost–benefit analysis. Institute for Advanced Study School of Social Science Working Paper 62. http://www.sss.ias.edu/publications/papers/econpaper62.pdf.

Kennedy, R. F. (1968/1993). Speech at the University of Kansas (March 18, 1968). In E. O. Guthman & C. R. Allen (eds. 1993), RFK: Collected Speeches (pp. 329–330). New York: Viking.

Prescott, J. J., & Starr, S. (2006). Improving criminal jury decision making after the *Blakely* revolution. *University of Illinois Law Review, 2006,* 301–356.

Positive Organizational Behavior

Carolyn M. Youssef[a] and Fred Luthans[b]

[a]*Bellevue University;* [b]*University of Nebraska, Lincoln*

Drawing from the theory-building, research and applications associated with the Gallup Leadership Institute at the University of Nebraska, Lincoln (see www.gli.unl.edu for further information and updates), *positive organizational behavior* (POB) has been defined as: "the study and application of positively oriented human resource strengths and psychological capacities that can be measured, developed, and effectively managed for performance improvement in today's workplace" (Luthans, 2002b, p. 59). Although positivity in the workplace has a long history, similar to the emergence of positive psychology, applied to the workplace, POB represents a recent focus on positive psychological resource capacities meeting the inclusion criteria of being theory- and research-based, having valid and reliable measures, exhibiting state-like and thus developmental characteristics that can be enhanced through relatively brief interventions, and yielding an impact on work-related performance.

Positive Psychological Resource Capacities

Examples of resource capacities meeting the POB inclusion criteria include self-efficacy, hope, optimism, and resiliency. *Self-efficacy* can be defined as: "one's conviction (or confidence) about his or her abilities to mobilize the motivation, cognitive resources, and courses of action needed to successfully execute a specific task within a given context" (Stajkovic & Luthans, 1998, p. 66). *Hope* is defined as: "a positive motivational state that is based on an interactively derived sense of successful 1) agency (goal-directed energy) and 2) pathways (planning to meet goals)"

(Snyder, Irving, & Anderson, 1991, p. 287). Based on Martin Seligman's research, *optimism* refers to an explanatory style that attributes positive events to personal, permanent and pervasive causes, and negative events to external, temporary and situation-specific ones. In contrast, pessimism explains positive events through external, temporary and situation-specific attributions, and negative events through internal, permanent and pervasive ones. Resiliency is "the capacity to rebound or bounce back from adversity, conflict, failure, or even positive events, progress, and increased responsibility" (Luthans, 2002a, p. 702).

From Positive Organizational Behavior to Psychological Capital

A further development of POB is *psychological capital* (PsyCap), which has been defined as:

> An individual's positive psychological state of development that is characterized by:
> 1) having confidence (self-efficacy) to take on and put in the necessary effort to succeed at challenging tasks; 2) making a positive attribution (optimism) about succeeding now and in the future; 3) persevering toward goals and, when necessary, redirecting paths to goals (hope) in order to succeed; and 4) when beset by problems and adversity, sustaining and bouncing back and even beyond (resiliency) to attain success. (Luthans, Youssef, & Avolio, 2007, p. 3)

Luthans and Youssef explain that PsyCap goes beyond the traditionally recognized financial capital (what you have), human capital (what you know), and even social capital (who you know). According to Avolio and Luthans, PsyCap synergistically adds to the equation one's actual self (who you are today), and developing that self into what one can become in the future (the possible self). Luthans, Avolio, Avey and Norman have recently conceptualized and shown beginning empirical support for PsyCap as a multidimensional, latent core construct, to which self-efficacy, hope, optimism and resiliency synergistically contribute. In addition, Luthans, Avey, Avolio, Norman, Combs, and Patera have recently conceptually and empirically demonstrated successful PsyCap development interventions capitalizing on such synergies.

Current Status and Emphases of POB and PsyCap Research

In line with the POB inclusion criteria, to date, there are valid and reliable measures for self-efficacy, hope, optimism, and resiliency, some of which are specific to the workplace. Moreover, a comprehensive PsyCap measure has also been recently developed and tested by Luthans, Avolio, Avey and Norman, published in *Personnel Psychology*. The external validity of PsyCap is being conceptually and empirically supported through several cross-sectional and cross-cultural applications. Just recently, a comprehensive review of the positive organizational behavior literature to date by Luthans and Youssef has been published in the *Journal of Management*.

Another development in this positivity in the workplace domain of study is *authentic leadership development* (ALD). ALD has been defined as:

> The process that draws upon a leader's life course, psychological capital, moral perspective, and a highly developed supporting organizational climate to produce greater self-awareness and self-regulated positive behaviors, which in turn foster continuous, positive self-development resulting in veritable, sustained performance. (Avolio & Luthans, 2006, p. 2)

In other words, the leader's values, past experiences and PsyCap, along with a positive organizational climate, can accelerate and sustain the ALD process. An accelerated ALD process can then trickle down to the leader's followers, enhancing their performance, positive attitudes and development.

Challenges and Future Directions

Several challenges and opportunities clearly face POB researchers and attempts at effective application. Some on these issues pertain to positivity in general. For example, critics of positivity research doubt the assumption of human benevolence often underlying many of the current positive approaches, making it necessary to examine critical interactions between personal, organizational and other situational factors that may be conducive or restrictive to the applicability of positivity.

Moreover, positivity (and negativity) may vary across cultures and other contexts; this necessitates careful examination of the boundaries of various virtues and positive capacities. In addition, many skeptics have rightfully questioned if and when overemphasis on positivity can result in "too much of a good thing." Such contingencies and limitations may lead to interesting relationships and interactions that should be examined using newly developing theoretical frameworks and research methodologies in order to better capture the contribution of positivity to today's and tomorrow's workplace.

Another critical challenge and relevant area for future research is the need for a clear demarcation and objective criteria for distinguishing what constitutes developmental states, versus dispositional traits. Recent conceptual theory-building, as well as beginning empirical research, have been addressing this critical issue, and it is likely that more will take place in the near future. In the context of POB, Luthans and colleagues have conceptualized states and traits to exist along a continuum. On one end of that continuum are highly stable traits that are believed to be hardwired at a very early age, or even genetically determined, such as one's intelligence and various areas of talent. On the opposite end of the continuum are highly transient states that exhibit very little stability over time and that are subject to change in reaction to momentary situational variables, such as one's mood.

On the other hand, uncertainty often occurs in relation to variables that are not at the extreme ends of the continuum, but rather those referred to as *trait-like* or *state-like*. Although not entirely fixed or hard-wired, trait-like variables are characterized by relative stability over time and applicability across situations. They result in general cognitive, affective, and behavioral tendencies, and are empirically supported by high test-retest correlations. Examples include the Big Five personality traits such as conscientiousness and emotional stability, as well as core self-evaluation traits such as self-esteem and locus of control.

Although state-like variables are not as transitory or short-lived as "pure" states, they are still relatively malleable and open for development and change using relatively brief and practical interventions, thus meeting the POB inclusion criteria, and offering particular relevance to today's fast-paced workplace. One rule of thumb recently suggested by Wright for researchers to consider is to use stability over six months as an operationalization of the temporal demarcation between traits and states. As discussed earlier, examples of state-like capacities include self-efficacy, hope, optimism, and resiliency. However, many other positive psychological resource capacities represent high-potential variables for inclusion in POB and PsyCap research. Luthans, Youssef and Avolio suggest that future research may address potential PsyCap resource capacities such as courage, forgiveness, gratitude, spirituality, creativity, wisdom, well-being, flow, humor, and emotional intelligence for their possible development and performance impact in the workplace.

Finally, POB and PsyCap research will likely benefit from examining various levels of analysis: the individual (micro) level currently emphasized by POB as defined here, as well as the dyad (e.g., leader-follower relations), group (e.g., team, department or business unit), organizational, and even societal levels. Such macro perspectives have been recently addressed by the parallel *positive organizational scholarship* (POS) movement at the University of Michigan (see http://www.bus.umich.edu/positive for further information and updates). POS is defined as:

> the study of that which is positive, flourishing, and life-giving in organizations. Positive refers to the elevating processes and outcomes in organizations. Organizational refers to the interpersonal and structural dynamics activated in and through organizations, specifically taking into account the context in which positive phenomena occur. Scholarship refers to the scientific, theoretically derived, and rigorous investigation of that which is positive in organizational settings. (Cameron & Caza, 2004, p. 731)

Similar to this POS emphasis is the understanding of the social embeddedness of POB and PsyCap in the upward spirals and contagion effects within and across organizational units and participants. In conclusion, positive organizational behavior as summarized here may contribute to competitive advantage through people in present and future organizations.

SEE ALSO: ▶ Organizational psychology ▶ Positive organizational scholarship ▶ Resiliency ▶ Self-efficacy

References

Avolio, B. J., & Luthans, F. (2006). *The high impact leader: Moments matter in accelerating authentic leadership development*. New York: McGraw-Hill.

Cameron, K. S., & Caza, A. (2004). Contributions to the discipline of positive organizational scholarship. *American Behavioral Scientist, 47*, 731–739.

Luthans, F. (2002a). The need for and meaning of positive organizational behavior. *Journal of Organizational Behavior, 23*, 695–706.

Luthans, F. (2002b). Positive organizational behavior: Developing and managing psychological strengths. *Academy of Management Executive, 16*(1), 57–72.

Luthans, F., Youssef, C. M., & Avolio, B. J. (2007). *Psychological capital: Developing the human competitive edge*. Oxford, UK: Oxford University Press.

Snyder, C. R., Irving, L., & Anderson, J. (1991). Hope and health: Measuring the will and the ways. In C. R. Snyder & D. R. Forsyth (Eds.), *Handbook of social and clinical psychology* (pp. 285–305). Elmsford, NY: Pergamon.

Stajkovic, A. D., & Luthans, F. (1998). Social cognitive theory and self-efficacy: Going beyond traditional motivational and behavioral approaches. *Organizational Dynamics, 26*, 62–74.

Positive Organizational Scholarship

Jane E. Dutton and Scott Sonenshein
University of Michigan

Introduction

Positive organizational scholarship (POS) and positive psychology are focused on understanding the conditions and processes that explain flourishing. What differentiates POS is an explicit interest in understanding and explaining flourishing in organizational contexts (including individuals, groups, units and whole organizations). *Flourishing* refers to being in an optimal range of human functioning and as Fredrickson and Losada have suggested, flourishing is indicated at the individual level by goodness, generativity, growth and resilience. At the collective level of groups and organizations, flourishing may be indicated by creativity, innovation, growth, resilience, thriving, virtuousness or other markers that a collective is healthy and is performing in an "above normal" or positively deviant range. POS also focuses on the development of individual, group and collective strengths that represent forms of individual and collective excellence.

POS unites existing domains of organizational inquiry focused on flourishing. This includes work on flourishing indicators such as creativity, engagement, flow, growth, health and well-being, as well as contributors to flourishing that consider features of the organization, group and job contexts. POS opens up new topics of study, such as compassion, courage, energy and energy networks, forgiveness, resilience, thriving, and work callings – just to name a few. POS scholarship includes a growing body of theoretical work and an emerging set of empirical studies (for examples, see publications in mainstream organizational journals).

In this brief review of POS, we will trade depth for breadth to provide the reader with a basic understanding of POS as both a domain and lens.

The Topic's Intellectual and Social Context

Many intellectual disciplines have influenced the development of POS including appreciative inquiry and community psychology. POS also reinvigorates ideas from humanistic psychology that were foundations for the field of organizational studies. The first POS conference was in 2001 and it generated the first edited book devoted to POS by Cameron, Dutton and Quinn in 2003. However, the most widespread influence comes from positive psychology. Both POS and positive psychology urge scholars to focus not only on improvements from "negative" states (such as illness or corrosive relationships) to normal states (such as mental health and helpful relationships), but also from normal states to extraordinary ones (such as thriving and life-giving relationships). This shift in explanatory focus from negative→normal towards normal→positive reflects a common concern that current theories are limited by a focus on explaining how individuals, groups and organizations move from below normal to normal states, which may be very different from explaining how individuals, groups and organizations move from normal to above normal, or positively deviant states. From a POS perspective, negative states may be important for explaining flourishing or the cultivation of strengths. For example, work on resilience shows that negative setbacks are critical. But POS scholars emphasize the building of strengths in the recovery from setbacks. POS is not synonymous with only positive phenomena but rather treats them as figure, and not ground.

Several research streams with a more positive focus have developed within organizational studies. Positive organizational behavior (POB) focuses on understanding how to develop a particular set of psychological states (confidence, hope, optimism and resiliency) in individuals. Models of healthy work and healthy work practices also inform the positive organizational scholarship agenda. A focus on positive organizational relationships at work emphasizes the forms, functions, consequences and enablers of relationships between people at work that are mutually beneficial. Researchers have called for a more positive approach to leadership and group research, and other organizational researchers have integrated business ethics and POS research, either through a strengths-building approach to understanding business ethics and corporate responsibility or focusing on how ethics as a field provides important philosophical foundations for POS. Finally, some have called to revise the work-family literature with a focus on explaining conditions where individuals are flourishing in both life domains as opposed to emphasizing trade-offs between the two.

While positive psychology originally sought to understand "positive institutions," POS provides the thought leadership in this domain. To date, POS scholars tend to focus on the situations and states of individuals and groups in work organizations. POS shares many assumptions and goals with positive psychology, but brings a unique focus on processes, states and behaviors in and between organizational contexts. This necessitates the use of multiple levels of analysis and a greater social processes focus.

Major Dimensions of the Topic

The domain of POS is appreciated from three vantage points: the dependent variables studied, the core mechanisms considered and the core enablers identified. Given the newness of POS, these descriptors mark the beginnings of this field of inquiry.

Dependent Variables

Because of its interest in explaining flourishing at all levels within and of organizations, the range of dependent variables of interest to POS is broad. At the individual level, foci have included: well-being and health, growth, optimism, self-efficacy, happiness and satisfaction, thriving, resilience, integrity, and other markers of optimal human functioning and the building and exercising of individual strengths and virtues in organizations. At the dyadic level, POS focuses on high quality connections that may be manifest in a variety of relationships in organizations e.g., between subordinates and supervisors and among peers. At the group, team or unit level, POS invites inquiry into flourishing as indicated by collective levels of creativity, learning, flow, synergy and resilience. Finally at the organizational level, POS focuses on the development and display of virtues and strengths such as organizational courage, compassion, forgiveness, wisdom, integrity, and virtuousness as well as explaining other forms of organizational flourishing such as collective resilience, collective optimism and collective hope.

Explanatory Mechanisms

Another way of viewing POS is to examine explanatory mechanisms, which emphasize positive dynamics within individuals, groups and organizations. Positive dynamics refer to processes that strengthen or improve the functioning of individuals, groups or organizations. A POS focus directs attention to generative (e.g., life-building, capability-enhancing, capacity-creating) dynamics in organizations. Consider three possible mechanisms.

First, the dynamics of positive emotions are keys to understanding human flourishing in and of organizations. Positive emotions refer to shorter-term states of felt activation of individuals or collectives that are associated with "a pleasantly subjective feel" (Fredrickson, 1998, p. 300). Positive emotions of individuals and of collectives broaden "momentary thought-action repertoires" and the experience "builds enduring personal resources" (Fredrickson, 2003, p. 166). Studies directly and indirectly support this idea when accounting for the effects of positive emotions on creativity, patterns of group interaction in problem-solving tasks and levels of cooperation in negotiation.

Second, the dynamics of positive meanings help to explain how individuals, groups and whole organizations construct and institutionalize meanings that facilitate individual and collective functioning. For example, studies of how individuals craft positive work identities through seeing their work as a calling, through changing the relationships that people have with others on their jobs, or through emphasizing positive distinctiveness of one's social group memberships illustrate how cultivating positive meaning about the self in organizations can direct people toward more optimal states of functioning. However, positive meaning can also be a collectively shared construction among unit members that fosters flourishing. For example, in a study of compassion organizing by Dutton and colleagues, shared positive meaning around the collective valuing of the whole person and the valuing of expressing one's humanity were shown to help explain the activation and mobilization of compassion. More generally, shared positive collective meaning can alter the connection between people, provoke positive emotions, and foster interactions that elevate functioning and capability.

A third mechanism that is studied in POS involves positive relationships between people that are marked by mutuality, positive regard, trust and vitality. While called by different names (e.g., positive ties, positive social capital, or high quality connections), a focus on these types of relationships and their functions (e.g., task accomplishment, career development, sensemaking, provision of meaning and personal support), Kahn has unearthed possibilities for explaining different forms of flourishing in and of organizations. For example, Vogus has found in his studies in nursing units find that units marked by higher levels of respectful interaction between members (a form of high-quality connecting) are more attentive to errors, which, is associated with fewer accidents and a better safety record.

Core Enablers

A final mapping of the POS domains extends the interest from a focus on process to a focus on contextual enablers of different forms of flourishing in and of organizations. Included in this approach is research on how organizational cultures, structures, practices, systems and leadership create conditions in which individuals, teams or units flourish, and consideration of how features of organizations, unit or team contexts create dynamics that contribute to individual and collective flourishing.

Methodological and Conceptual Challenges

While POS research has progressed, pressing methodological and conceptual concerns remain. Methodologically, POS researchers have often "sampled on the dependent variable," studying instances where people, units or organizations are flourishing, which may obscure the more intricate dynamics of the full spectrum of variation needed to explain these outcomes. On the other hand, the types of enablers and mechanisms that underlie states and behavior associated with flourishing may differ from those that focus on negative and normal behavior.

A second methodological challenge involves developing valid measures of the new variables being considered – e.g., energy, vitality, high-quality relationships, thriving – and to establish their convergent and discriminant validity. Finally, future work will need to include experimental and field study designs that allow for inferences about underlying causal dynamics and processes, while at the same time, remaining open to the insight and descriptive richness afforded through more qualitative and narrative approaches.

Several conceptual challenges invite consideration. First, POS scholars must account for the role of the "negative" in explaining positive outcomes and positive dynamics within and of organizations. As recent reviews of POS suggest, negative phenomena – such as negative emotions – are often adaptive in human functioning. Yet, as suggested above, POS scholars are attentive to "the negative"; they examine what may be positive about seemingly neutral or negative states.

Second, POS researchers need to clarify the referent groups for determining positive, to address the question, "positive to whom?" For example, research in organizational-citizenship behaviors identifies a set of prosocial behaviors individuals engage in, but some of these prosocial behaviors may compromise organizational functioning. Is something that helps individuals but harms organizations considered positive? Or consider traditional positive phenomenon such as empowerment. Would POS scholars consider such concepts positive if they are used to exploit individuals? Have point critical theorists considered this?

A third challenge is to more comprehensively determine the range of positive and negative enablers that explain human flourishing in and of organizations, and to carefully identify at what level of analysis these enablers and processes are operating. This means carefully attending to what is uniquely organizational about the underlying causes and processes.

Fourth, while some indicators of flourishing and some individual and organizational strengths have been studied, much remains unexplored. For example, Peterson and Seligman have developed a classification of 6 core virtues thought to capture positive human strengths highlighted across a broad range of philosophical and religious traditions. While organizational scholars have considered some of these virtues and strengths (e.g., justice and wisdom) they have paid less attention to emotional strengths such as courage, interpersonal strengths such as humanity and temperance or transcendence-related strengths. Organizational researchers have opportunities to contribute to understanding how organizational contexts develop and sustain these kinds of positive strengths as well as how these strengths are manifest at collective levels.

SEE ALSO: ▶ Positive organizational behavior

Reference

Fredrickson, B. L. (2003). Positive emotions and upward spirals in organizations. In K. Cameron, J. Dutton, & R. Quinn (Eds.), *Positive organizational scholarship* (pp. 163– 175). San Francisco: Berrett-Koehler Publishers, Inc.

Positive Psychology (History)

P. Alex Linley
Centre for Applied Positive Psychology

Positive psychology as we know it today was inaugurated with Martin E. P. Seligman's Presidential Address delivered to the 107th Annual Convention of the American Psychological Association in Boston, Massachusetts, on August 21, 1999. Shifting focus from an established career as an international authority on depression, pessimism, and learned helplessness, Seligman proposed to his audience that psychology had largely neglected the latter two of its three pre-World War II missions: curing mental illness, helping all people to lead more productive and fulfilling lives, and identifying and nurturing high talent. The advent of the Veterans Administration (in 1946) and the National Institute of Mental Health (in 1947) had largely rendered psychology a healing discipline based upon a disease model and illness ideology, and Seligman resolved to use his APA Presidency to initiate a shift in psychology's focus toward a more positive psychology.

Positive Psychology Meetings, Conferences, and Awards

Seligman's presidential initiative began with a series of meetings in Akumal, Mexico, of mid-career scholars who could inform the conceptualization and early development of positive psychology. The Akumal meetings ran annually from January 1999 (Akumal I) through January 2002 (Akumal IV). The first Positive Psychology Summit was held in September 1999 in Lincoln, Nebraska, followed by two further national Positive Psychology Summits in Washington, DC (October 2000, October 2001), which were then superseded by the First International Positive Psychology Summit in October 2002. Subsequent International Positive Psychology Summits have since run annually each October.

In addition to the International Positive Psychology Summits in the United States, there have been a number of European positive psychology conferences. The first was the British Psychological Society Student Members Group Conference, themed "Positive Psychology: A new approach for the new millennium," held in Winchester, England, in April 2000. Subsequently, biennial European conferences have been organized by the European Network for Positive Psychology, including the First European Conference on Positive Psychology in Winchester, England (June 2002); the Second European Conference in Verbania Pallanza, Italy (July 2004); and the Third European Conference in Braga, Portugal (July 2006). The First Applied Positive Psychology Conference was held at the University of Warwick, England (April 2007). Outside the United States and Europe, the first South African Conference on Positive Psychology was held in Potchefstroom (April 2006), the first Asian Conference on Positive Psychology was held in Hong Kong (May 2006), and the First Iberoamerican Conference on Positive Psychology was held in Buenos Aires, Argentina (August 2006).

As well as the research summits, there have been a number of dedicated initiatives to support, build and recognize the research capabilities of early and mid-career positive psychology researchers. The Positive Psychology Summer Institutes were designed to bring together early career researchers and more senior scholars for intense intellectual exchange and interaction. Five Summer Institutes were held: Sea Ranch, California, August 2001; Montchanin, Delaware, August 2002 and August 2003; Lago D'Orta, Italy, July 2004; and Philadelphia, Pennsylvania, June 2005. The prestigious Templeton Positive Psychology Prize, administered by the American Psychological Association, ran for 3 years and offered the largest monetary prize in psychology. The winners of this Prize were Barbara Fredrickson (2000) for her work on positive emotions; Jon Haidt (2001) for his work on the positive moral emotion of elevation; and Suzanne Segerstrom (2002) for her work on the beneficial effects of optimism on physical health. In October 2006, Shelley Taylor was awarded the inaugural Clifton Strengths Prize, which recognized the life work of Donald O. Clifton (1924–2003), and is awarded biennially in acknowledgement of an individual's enduring influence on the field of strengths psychology.

Publication and Education Landmarks

Significant publication landmarks in the history of positive psychology include the millennial special issue of the *American Psychologist* on happiness, excellence, and optimal human functioning, edited by Martin E. P. Seligman and Mihaly Csikszentmihalyi; the *Handbook of Positive Psychology*, edited by C. R. Snyder and Shane J. Lopez; Martin E. P. Seligman's bestselling *Authentic Happiness: Using the New Science of Positive Psychology to Realize your Potential for Lasting Fulfillment*; the first volume to focus on positive psychology applications, *Positive Psychology in Practice*, edited by Alex Linley and Stephen Joseph; and the supporting manual of the VIA Inventory of Strengths, *Character Strengths and Virtues: A Handbook and Classification*, by Christopher Peterson and Martin E. P. Seligman. The first issue of the *Journal of Positive Psychology* was published by Taylor and Francis in January 2006, with Robert Emmons serving as Editor-in-Chief, the opening article of which included an appendix detailing all journal special issues on positive psychology to October 2005.

The world's first Master of Applied Positive Psychology was launched at the University of Pennsylvania in September 2005, while the first European Masters in Applied Positive Psychology commenced at the University of East London, UK, in February 2007.

Historical Lineage

Clearly, positive psychology has had a major impact in a relatively short period of time, but it is also eminently clear from a cursory examination of the research literature that positive psychology did not "begin" in 1997, or 1998, or 1999, or 2000. Positive psychology has always been with us, but as a holistic and integrated body of knowledge, it has passed unrecognized and uncelebrated, and one of the major achievements of the positive psychology movement to date has been to consolidate, lift up and celebrate what we *do* know about what makes life worth living, as well as carefully delineating the areas where we need to do more.

Taking a longer historical view of positive psychology, it is important to note that more than fifty years ago, Abraham Maslow lamented psychology's preoccupation with disorder and dysfunction:

> The science of psychology has been far more successful on the negative than on the positive side. It has revealed to us much about man's shortcomings, his illness, his sins, but little about his potentialities, his virtues, his achievable aspirations, or his full psychological height. It is as if psychology has voluntarily restricted itself to only half its rightful jurisdiction, and that, the darker, meaner half. (Maslow, 1954, p. 354)

Maslow even talked specifically about a positive psychology, by which he meant a more exclusive focus on people at the extremely positive ends of the distribution, rather than the meaning which is today understood of positive psychology. More broadly, there are strong themes of convergence between the interests of humanistic psychology and modern positive psychology, and one might even trace the study of positive psychological topics back as far as William James and his writings on healthy mindedness. The oldest historical antecedents of positive psychology that have been identified are the writings of Aristotle on virtue and what it means to live a good life.

Historical Critiques

Initially at least, positive psychology came in for some criticisms about the fact that it did not do enough to acknowledge the rich philosophical and psychological heritage on which ideas about a good life and optimal human functioning might be based. This is perhaps understandable in the early days of a "new" research endeavour, but increasing maturity should be recognized by an increasing acknowledgement of what has gone before and how new work can build on its historical foundations. Similarly, early critiques of the positive psychology movement often centred on positive psychology's perceived attention only on the positive sides of human experience, leading to a number of rebuttals that sought to demonstrate how positive psychology could actually serve as an integrative force for psychology, rather than a divisive one. Other early critiques of the positive psychology movement were directed at the perceived inability of psychologists and others to assess states such as happiness and traits such as character strengths in any meaningful way, compounded by the view that these were in any event irrelevant epiphenomena. Substantial subsequent research, much of it conducted under the positive psychology umbrella, has now faced down many of these criticisms by demonstrating the reliable and valid measurement of happiness and character strengths, as well as articulating their roles within and importance for optimal human functioning.

Looking Forward

The study of the history of positive psychology can also inform us about the directions that it may take in the future. The specialization argument, which divorces positive psychology from other areas of psychology, whether described as negative psychology or business-as-usual psychology, versus the integration argument, which sees positive psychology as an integrative force for the study of holistic human experience, are two of the trends that will determine how positive psychology's future evolves. A second fault line will be whether positive psychology succeeds in reaching out to other branches of psychology and other disciplines more broadly, or whether it becomes a narrowly focused home for people only interested in happiness. If positive psychology is to realize its own potential for optimal scientific functioning and powerful preventative and curative applications, it requires both integrative energy and inclusive policies. Its reach and influence in such a short time indicates the appetite that exists for the ideas and applications of positive psychology, but only time will tell whether it will take the steps toward genuine transformational actions.

SEE ALSO: ▶ Applied positive psychology   ▶ Aristotle   ▶ Positive psychology   ▶ Seligman, Martin   ▶ Strengths perspective (positive psychology)

Reference

Maslow, A. H. (1954). *Motivation and personality*. New York: Harper.

Positive Psychology Network

Peter Schulman
University of Pennsylvania

The intellectual birth of positive psychology came in 1998 when Dr Martin Seligman was President of the American Psychological Association and made positive psychology one of his presidential initiatives. The organizational and financial birth of positive psychology arrived in 1999, when Seligman raised millions of dollars of funding to carry out numerous initiatives, some of which are described below. The term *Positive Psychology Network* was the name of the network of leading scholars he assembled to chart the course of this new field and carry out these initiatives.

The birth and fast growth of positive psychology was due largely to Seligman's vision, organizational skills, public lectures, and fund-raising. Donations and grants from several organizations enabled Seligman to attract many leading scholars of all ages through research grants, awards, conferences and summer institutes. In addition, and importantly, many supportive colleagues of Seligman's played key roles in the many initiatives, as did a receptive public with whom the ideas resonated, enabling positive psychology to spread around the globe in a few short years.

It is important to note that Seligman does not claim that positive psychology is a new field, but has many distinguished ancestors. Since at least the time of Socrates, Plato, and Aristotle, the good life has been the subject of philosophical inquiry and many psychologists have been working in positive psychology topics for decades. The contribution of contemporary positive psychology has been to make the explicit argument that what makes life most worth living deserves its own empirically based field of study, to bring together isolated lines of theory and research under one scientific umbrella and call this field positive psychology, to promote the cross-fertilization of ideas through different social sciences, to develop a broader conceptual view of happiness, to bring this field to the attention of various foundations and funding agencies, to raise money for research, and to firmly ground all assertions in the scientific method.

The Positive Psychology Network (PPN) was first created with a generous gift from the Atlantic Philanthropies to Dr Seligman at the University of Pennsylvania. Matching funds quickly flowed from several other organizations, including the Annenberg Foundation, the Hovey Foundation, the Mayerson Foundation, the Mellon Foundation, the Pew Charitable Trusts, and the John Marks Templeton Foundation.

The following are some of the initiatives spearheaded by Dr Seligman, as a result of the generous support of these organizations.

Key Personnel

First, Seligman assembled the intellectual and organizational infrastructure to carry out the positive psychology initiatives. He created the Positive Psychology Steering Committee, a group of leading scholars, to help him plan the goals and initiatives. This committee was initially comprised of Mihaly Csikszentmihalyi, Ed Diener, Ray Fowler, Kathleen Hall Jamieson, Robert Nozick, Christopher Peterson, and George Vaillant. He pegged his longtime colleague, Peter Schulman, to lead the organizational and financial running of the initiatives.

Classification of Strengths and Virtues

The first great intellectual task, and the foundation of much that followed, was the creation of the classification and measurement of strengths and virtues, which led to a book and a self-report measure by Peterson and Seligman. These were made possible by generous support from the Mayerson Foundation and its Values In Action Institute.

Akumal Conferences

In the first four years of the PPN, annual conferences were held in Akumal, Mexico. About 30 leading researchers, including the steering committee, attended each year to build research collaborations, cross-fertilize, and brainstorm future directions in positive psychology. One particular focus was to encourage and help fund young scientists.

Research Funding

The PPN supported the research of about 30 groups of researchers (the pods) from over 50 universities. The pods included the Teaching Task Force, which created resources for teachers of positive psychology in high schools and colleges. The PPN also awarded over 25 microgrants, providing research seed funds to encourage promising early-career scholars who were developing innovative lines of empirical research in positive psychology.

Young Scholar Research Grants

The PPN awarded more than 20 Young Scholar Grants to promising young researchers in positive psychology.

Templeton Positive Psychology Prize

The first place prize ($100,000) was the largest prize ever awarded in the field of psychology and was given each year for three years in recognition of excellence in positive psychology research.

Gallup International Positive Psychology Summit

Starting in 1999, Gallup has sponsored the annual Positive Psychology Summit at their Washington, DC headquarters. This is a large conference open to the public, where cutting edge research is presented by leading researchers. The Summit is attended by hundreds of scholars and practitioners from around the world.

Positive Psychology Summer Institute

The PPN convened five summer institutes from 2001 to 2005. As one of the most popular initiatives, the purpose of the institute was to provide support and mentoring for beginning researchers, as well as to develop a network of young, mid-career, and senior scholars interested in positive psychology.

Websites

The PPN created two websites. They created www.positivepsychology.org to provide practical resources for people interested in positive psychology, including researchers, students, teachers, and the general public. These resources include information on opportunities, upcoming conferences, resources for researchers (e.g., questionnaires and research summaries), resources for teachers (e.g., syllabi), educational programs, and general information and readings to help people learn about positive psychology. They created www.authentichappiness.org to disseminate information about positive psychology to the general public in three languages – English, Chinese, and Spanish. This website has numerous online questionnaires that provide people with instant feedback.

SEE ALSO: ▶ Seligman, Martin

Positive Psychotherapy

Tayyab Rashid
University of Pennsylvania

Positive psychotherapy (PPT) is a therapeutic movement within positive psychology to broaden the scope of traditional psychotherapy. It rests on the central hypothesis that building positive emotions, strengths and meaning, in addition to undoing symptoms, is efficacious in the treatment of psychopathology. Positive emotions, strengths and meaning serve us best not when life is easy but when life is difficult. For a depressed client, having and using strengths such as optimism, hope, zest, and social intelligence can be more important to counter depression than they are in good times.

PPT is based on three assumptions. First, psychopathology results when a person's inherent capacity for growth, fulfillment and happiness is thwarted. Most traditional psychotherapies, with the exception of client-centered therapy, assume that psychopathology engenders when: symptoms leak from the unconscious; maladaptive behaviors are strengthened by conditioning or environmental reinforcement; irrational and faulty thinking effects behavior and feeling; or troubled relationship patterns lead to resentment. On the contrary, PPT assumes that a client has good and bad states and traits, which influence each other and are also influenced by the larger culture and environment in which clients live. All clients have an inherent capacity for growth, fulfillment, flourishing and happiness, when this tendency is blocked, psychopathology results. Second, positive emotions and strengths are as authentic and real as symptoms and disorders. These are not defenses, Pollyannaish illusions, rose-tinted eye-glasses or clinical by-products of symptom relief which lie at the clinical peripheries and do not need exclusive attention. PPT regards positive emotions and the strengths of clients as authentic and values them in their own right. Within the framework of PPT, Mother Theresa's compassion for poor, Gandhi's and Martin Luther King Jr's struggle for civil rights, Eleanor Roosevelt's altruism, Aung San Suu Kyi and Shareen Abadi's political and social courage are considered as authentic and valuable in their own right, rather than as mere attempts to deal with anxiety, anger and an inferiority complex. According to the PPT perspective, human strengths are as authentic and real as weaknesses and therefore should command equal merit and as much therapeutic attention as do weaknesses.

Third, most traditional therapy is conducted by discussing troubles in-depth. The portrayal of psychotherapy in popular films and on television has socialized clients to the belief that therapy exclusively entails talking about troubles, ventilation of the inner child's bottled up emotions and recovering injured self-esteem. Exacerbated by negative bias, most clients come to therapy viewing themselves as deeply flawed, fragile, and see themselves as victims of cruel environmental or genetic causalities. Their anger stands out as compared to their gratitude. So talking about troubles with an empathic, warm and genuine therapist is indeed a powerful cathartic experience. Any perceived failure to take clients' problems seriously may violate their expectations and could undermine the therapeutic relationship. Nevertheless, PPT believes that even clients who bring the weightiest psychopathological burden to therapy, care much more about their lives than just relief from their suffering. Clients want more satisfaction, contentment and joy; not just less sadness and worry. Therefore, PPT assumes that therapy is not a place where only resentment, frustration, jealousy, anxiety and competition is discussed and treated, but also a venue where active doses of hope, optimism, gratitude, compassion, contentment, modesty and emotional and social intelligence can be delivered. PPT also assumes that it is not an absolute *sine quo non* that only discussion of troubles builds strong therapeutic relationship and is essential for cure. Rather using the same therapeutic basics such as warmth, unconditional positive regard and empathic listening, the therapist can draw clients' attention to positive emotions and strengths in their lives in a gentle and careful manner. Doing so takes added importance because human beings in general, and clients coming to therapy in particular, are biased towards remembering the negative, attending to the negative, and expecting the worst. Riding on this negative bias, if the therapist is an authority in eliciting and interpreting negatives only, then clients' strengths will likely receive less attention and assume less importance. A therapist in traditional therapy may ask: *What personal weaknesses have lead to your troubles?* Whereas in PPT therapist may ask: *What strengths do you bring to deal with your troubles?*

Acknowledging that due to negativity bias and symptomatic stress, positives may not be readily accessible to the consciousness and memory of troubled clients, PPT actively elicits positive emotions and memories, in addition to discussing troubles. It is, as Duckworth, Steen and Seligman (2005) put it, a "build-what's-strong" approach to supplement the traditional "fix-what's-wrong" approach (p. 631). Thus, PPT discusses with clients the transgressions as well as acts of kindness; insults as well as compliments, selfishness as well as compassion and kindness of others; hubris as well as humility; hurry as well as harmony; hate as well as love; pain of trauma as well as potential growth from it. PPT purports that to create peaceful, fulfilling and flourishing selves, families and communities; we have to understand both the causes of anger and aggression and the determinants of empathy, kindness and love. PPT acknowledges that human beings are naturally biased toward remembering the negative, attending to the negative, and expecting the worst. Troubled clients coming for therapy are most proximally driven by negative memories, attention and expectations and often exaggerate this natural tendency. PPT through structured exercises aims to reeducate clients' attention, memory and expectations away from the negative toward the positive and hopeful" (Seligman, Rashid & Parks, 2006, p. 783). PPT believes that the equal and explicit discussion of weaknesses and strengths establishes a strong therapeutic relationship in which the therapist no longer remains an authority with expertise in diagnosing what is wrong with someone, but becomes a witness of the client's deepest and authentic psychological assets.

Any number of happiness and well-being interventions may constitute the content of PPT. However, so far PPT conducted in randomized clinical trials has followed happiness exercises which are devised from Seligman's three-tiered theory of happiness. According to this theory, *authentic happiness* is decomposed into three empirically distinguishable lives; the pleasant life, the engaged life and the meaning-ful life. These exercises are described in the PPT manual. An idealized individual PPT follows a 12 to 14 session protocol and includes exercises such as positive introduction, identification and building of signature strengths, good versus bad memories, forgiveness letter, gratitude visit, three nightly blessings, satisficing plan, three doors that closed and three doors that opened, active-constructive respond-ing, family trees of strengths, savoring activity and gift of time. However, PPT can easily be incorporated in other treatments as an adjunct. An outcome measure, the Positive Psychotherapy Inventory (PPTI) to evaluate the effectiveness of PPT has been devised and validated.

Drawing systematic attention towards positives and engaging clients in inten-tional activities which utilize their strengths, are argued to be possible mechanisms of change in PPT. Intentional behavioral activities which are designed to create engagement and flow are vital to PPT. These are everyday, ordinary, normative, human experiences. Examples of such activities include painting, pottery, baking, reading, writing, socializing, helping others, savoring natural or artistic beauty, and rock climbing, for example. PPT emphasizes that these are not mere doings, rather they serve to bring clients' focus to the process rather than to the product.

Compared to experiences of sensory satisfaction to which clients adapt quickly, these engaging activities utilize clients' signature strengths, last longer and clients do not habituate easily. In addition, these activities offer numerous creative avenues for growth and flourishing, and even the pursuit of meaning.

Like any good therapy, PPT is sensitive and appreciative of the complexities of human beings. How positive states and traits interact with a client's person-ality disposition may differ markedly from one another. Clients may also differ in their motivational orientation to change long-standing behavioral patterns. For example, an introvert client may readily engage in activities which do not require lots of socialization yet provide her/him deep satisfaction. The therapist in PPT, therefore is encouraged to refrain from adopting a "one-size-fits-all" approach as it may not work with all clients. Additionally, the structure and sequ-ence of exercises is kept flexible to accommodate and adapt to the uniqueness of each client.

Another daunting task for PPT therapist is to ensure that what is purported as "positive" is not perceived by clients as prescriptive. Just as medical research shows that eating vegetables and exercising is "good" for us, the contents of PPT are presented as descriptive with clear explanations of the documented benefits of positive emotions, strengths and meaning. Furthermore, negatives are never dismissed nor artificially replaced. Instead, when clients bring negatives, they are empathetically attended and offered time-proven traditional interventions to undo negatives. However, slowly and gradually attention is drawn to positive emotions, strengths and meaning to widen the perspective about negatives. Thus, PPT does not compete with, but rather complements traditional therapeutic approaches.

SEE ALSO: ▶ Applied positive psychology   ▶ Positive therapy   ▶ Quality of life   ▶ Well-being therapy

References

Duckworth, A. L., Steen, T. A., & Seligman, M. E. P. (2005). Positive psychology in clinical practice. *Annual Review of Clinical Psychology, 1,* 629–651.

Seligman, M. E. P., Rashid, T., & Parks, A. C. (2006). Positive psychotherapy. *American Psychologist, 61,* 774–788.

Positive Social Media

Naif Al-Mutawa
Kuwait University

From the perspective of Albert Bandura's social cognitive or social learning theory, the advent of social media will have a prospectively significant and, on balance, a highly positive impact upon its participants, most notably through their potential for contributing to positive self-efficacy beliefs on the part of children and adolescents. According to Wikipedia (2007), "social media describe the online tools and platforms that people use to share opinions, insights, experiences and perspectives with each other." Not only is participation in *social media* growing at an astounding pace, new categories of social media are emerging as users innovate and experiment with existing Internet-based communication modalities. Individuals and organizations having a vested interest in the growth of social media typically envision an optimistic scenario for its influence upon users and, indeed, upon society at large. Thus, for example, Anthony Mayfield, the Head of Content and Media at the online company Spannerworks, has proclaimed that as a consequence of Internet-based social media, "people can find information, inspiration, like-minded people, communities, and collaborators faster than ever" (2006, p. 7). In the course of taking part in social media, the users themselves are likely to undergo changes in their attitudes and beliefs, notably in core identity constructs such as self-efficacy.

As Albert Bandura wrote in the opening chapter of *Social Foundations of Thought and Action*, no other form of cognition has a "more central or pervasive" influence on human behavior "than people's judgments of their capabilities to deal effectively with different realities" (p. 21). In an article appearing in the *Encyclopedia of Human Behavior* (1994), Bandura alluded to "a growing body of evidence that human accomplishments and positive well-being require an optimistic sense of personal efficacy" (p. 76). Consistent with its antideterministic and inherently optimistic thrust, social cognitive theory posits that "perceived self-efficacy results from diverse sources of information conveyed vicariously and through social evaluation, as well as through direct experience" (Bandura, 1986, p. 411). The common and, indeed, the defining attributes of social media may well facilitate the acquisition of positive self-efficacy beliefs through three channels: mastery experiences, modeling, and social persuasion. Moreover, these processes are likely to have their greatest impact upon individuals in the formative stages of their development, that is, children and adolescents, the age groups in which users of social media are most heavily concentrated.

According to Mayfield (2006), there are, at present, five generic types of social media: 1) blogs; 2) social networks; 3) content communities; 4) *wikis*; and 5) podcasts (p. 6). Alternative classifications abound, attesting to the rapid evolution of social media and the associated difficulty of delineating boundaries between categories or classes of social media. Of the diverse forms of social media, however, *social networks* represent the most prevalent type and they are, in fact, the salient form from the standpoint of prospective impact upon self-efficacy. In their introduction to a study conducted as part of the Pew Internet and American Life Project, Amanda Lenhart and Mary Madden (2007) explained that "a social network is an online place where a user can create a profile and build a personal network that connects him or her to other users" (p. 1). It has been estimated that 55% of all American adolescents between the ages of 12 and 17 have created an online personal profile within a social network, using such Internet sites as MySpace.com or Facebook.com (Lenhart & Madden, 2007, p. 2).

Somewhat ironically, while the vast majority of children and teenagers in the United States are keenly aware of the rise of MySpace.com and of other types of social media, their adult counterparts (many of whom still report the status of "novice" in their understanding of consumer digital technology) are generally ignorant of these new forms of cyber-communication. Social media are in their infancy, so to speak: Indeed, the term social media is generally ascribed to Chris Shipley, who first used it in early months of 2004 to denote a "new form of participatory media" (Wikipedia, 2007). Since that time, individual participation in social media has expanded at an exponential and accelerating pace. In November of 2006, there were an estimated 60 million personal *blogs* in existence with their ranks literally doubling every six months, and there were over 107 million registered members of the social network website MySpace.com alone (Mayfield, 2006, p. 4).

Writing for an online edition of *Newsweek*, Steven Levy and Brad Stone (2006) reported that the founders of MySpace.com were motivated to go beyond "social computing" into full-fledged "social media" by their shared notion that "younger people get more out of the Internet if they could express themselves by putting information where their friends could see it." Participation is, in fact, a primary characteristic of all types of social media. In Mayfield's (2006, p. 5) estimation, five attributes are common among social media: 1) participation, the encouragement of contributions and feedback from everyone who is interested; 2) openness, with few technical or resource barriers (including money) to individual access; 3) conversation, two-way, informal exchanges as opposed to one-way broadcasting of conventional media; 4) community, as all social media allow communities to form around common interests; and, 5) connectedness, with links to and combinations of different kinds of media accessibly in one place.

With this background in mind, we now turn to Bandura's work on self-efficacy. In his 1994 encyclopedia entry, Bandura defined the term *perceived self-efficacy* as "people's beliefs about their capabilities to produce designated levels of performance over events that affect their lives" (p. 97). Self-efficacy beliefs, in his view, "determine how people feel, think, motivate themselves and behave" (p. 71); positive self-efficacy beliefs generate desirable psychological and social outcomes through cognitive, motivational, affective, and selection processes (p. 71). Elaborating upon the potential effects of positive self-efficacy, Bandura asserted:

> A strong sense of efficacy enhances human accomplishment and personal well-being in many ways. People with high assurance in their capabilities approach difficult tasks as challenges to be mastered rather than as threats to be avoided. Such an efficacious outlook fosters intrinsic interest and deep engrossment in activities. They set themselves challenging goals and maintain strong commitment to them. They quickly recover their sense of efficacy after failures and setbacks. They attribute failure to insufficient effort or to deficient knowledge and skills which are acquirable. They approach threatening situations with assurance that they can exercise control over them. Such an efficacious outlook produces personal accomplishments, reduces stress, and lowers vulnerability to depression. (1994, p. 71)

The possession of positive self-efficacy beliefs does not guarantee success in task performance or within any of life's domains: negative self-efficacy, however, clearly contributes to under-performance, isolation, and an array of psychosocial pathologies.

Bandura identified three basic ways in which an individual can acquire a strong sense of self-efficacy. The first of these, *mastery experiences*, unfold when individuals achieve challenging goals that require them to overcome obstacles through perseverant effort. Indeed, in social learning theory, mastery experiences are identified as the principal means through which personality changes take place. Social media furnish individuals, particularly children and adolescents, with an inherent opportunity to undergo mastery experiences. In Sonia Livingstone and Magdalena Bober's summary of the findings from a study sponsored by British government under the title of *UK Children Go Online*, we find that interviews with 1,511 children aged between 9 and 19 disclosed that most of these youthful participants recalled that they had not been taught Internet skills within their respective school systems. Instead, most had learned how to use the Internet through "trial and error" procedures supplemented by periodic communication with more technically-advanced peers or older children. Based on these results, Livingston and Bober commented that "children often prefer to learn how to use the Internet by playing around with the medium and working things out for themselves"

(2004, p. 9). As a consequence of recent progress in making Internet tools more "user-friendly," even children can now utilize a wide range of social media. In this context, Mayfield has remarked, "even five years ago, it was still beyond most people's technical skills to create and maintain their own websites" (2006, p. 8). Today, however, many people, especially young people, can readily perform this task on their own or with a modicum of assistance. Indeed, studies of *Internet self-efficacy* or *Internet confidence* have uniformly found that children and teenagers are far more likely to state that they command "advanced" Internet skills than are adults (Livingstone & Bober, 2004, p. 11). Simply being able to set up a MySpace.com website and fill it with personally-relevant content frequently constitutes a potent mastery experience.

As Bonnie Strickland has noted, social learning theory presumes that a "child can learn without actually being rewarded or punished himself," through a process which Bandura referred to as *vicarious learning* (2001, p. 65). Vicarious learning takes place through the observing others demonstrate or model behaviors and inferable attitudes. "Seeing people similar to oneself succeed by sustained effort," Bandura argued, "raises observers' beliefs that they too possess the capabilities to master comparable activities to succeed" (1994, p. 72). For children and adolescents, modeling by age-peers amounts to "the most important points of reference for comparative efficacy appraisal and verification" (Bandura, 1986, p. 416). In the course of utilizing a social network like MySpace.com or Facebook.com, children will encounter and communicate with at least some age-peers who have been able to attain very high levels of digital sophistication but who are, at bottom, otherwise similar to themselves. Indeed, by dint of visiting MySpace.com or some other youth-oriented social network website, they are likely to gain access to informal social media use tutoring by children in their particular developmental stage. As Bandura also observed, in conventional "real world" relationships, "children tend to choose peers who share similar interests and values. Selective peer association will promote self-efficacy in directions of mutual interest, leaving other potentialities underdeveloped" (1994, p. 77). While participation in an online social network is often organized around interest or topical areas, the range of interests available in cyberspace is substantially greater than in the "real world." Consequently, the diversity of interests found in the "blogosphere" helps to overcome the limitations of relying upon "physical" contact with a much smaller universe of peers. Bandura also noted that "because peers serve as a major influence in the development and validation of self-efficacy, disrupted or impoverished peer relationships can adversely affect the growth of personal efficacy" (1994, p. 77). The likelihood that peer relations will be disrupted through, for example, a friend's relocation, is minimal in cyberspace; the presence of over 100 million MySpace.com users clearly militates against the "impoverishment" of peer relationships.

The third (and weakest) modality through which self-efficacy can be enhanced in Bandura's model is *social persuasion*. Such persuasion can contribute to the development of positive self-efficacy beliefs through credible messages from others that individuals can succeed even at difficult tasks, if they mobilize greater efforts to accomplish ends in view (Bandura, 1994, p. 72). Participation in social networks exposes individuals, particularly young people, to a range of explanatory styles. Consistent with Bandura's social learning theory, Martin Seligman argued that cognitive styles are learned and that a child can acquire a pessimistic style for interpreting personally-relevant events that leads to a pervasive sense of helplessness that is associated with clinical depression. However, in *Learned Optimism*, Seligman noted that people, particularly younger individuals, can also learn positive explanatory styles, through direct or vicarious experiences. By taking part in a social network, users come into contact with individuals harboring a range of explanatory styles and they are exposed to optimistic templates for interpreting life events.

A fourth prospective self-efficacy "benefit" of social media that does not have an explicit correlate in Bandura's theory but that is nonetheless entirely congruent with it involves identity management. As Lenhart and Madden (2007) reported, in their use of online social networks, many adolescents reported making frequent visits to their own profile, checking in on a daily basis: among the teenagers in the Pew Internet Study, "those who are most interested in maintaining an appealing profile must make frequent visits to social network sites, both to edit one's own profile and to view the profiles of others" (p. 4). By the same token, a large proportion of the subjects in the *UK Children Go Online* research project told investigators that, in some instances, they prefer online communication to face-to-face contact with peers because it enables them to "manage to intimacy, embarrassment, or privacy" more effectively (Livingstone & Bober, 2004, p. 2). Given that negative evaluations from others can exert a destructive and enduring negative influence on self-efficacy, being able to: 1) manage the identity that they present to "visitors"; and 2) to "escape" negative assessments with a simple "double-click" on "exit" or "delete," furnishes young people with a means for avoiding the negative judgments of others that has no counterpart in real-world settings.

According to Livingstone and Bober (2004), while "online opportunities should surely engage children creatively, support their social, intellectual and personal development, and facilitate their active and critical participation in social and civic forums" (p. 22), there are, in fact, several prospective hazards entailed in children's entrance into virtual social networks. The most widely publicized of these dangers pivots on adult sexual predators cruising chat rooms in search of under-age victims. In the Pew study, however, most of the children and teenagers interviewed were assiduously aware of this danger and took steps to counteract it. Thus, for example, most (66%) of the respondents in the study who had created online profiles reported that they were not visible to all Internet users and that they had limited access to their personal information to known friends and contacts (Lenhart & Madden, 2007, p. 2). Similarly, while adults may be concerned that minors browsing the web in search of information lack the critical capacity to assess the trustworthiness or reliability of the content that they encounter, the majority of the children in the UK study expressed a "healthy" skepticism about the trustworthiness of content on some, or even all, websites (Livingstone & Bober, 2004, p. 13).

From a social learning standpoint, the most serious problem posed by social media entails the possibility that virtual or cyber relationships will replace "conventional," face-to-face interactions. The bulk of the evidence indicates that this is not likely to be the case for most youthful users of social media. In fact, the UK researchers found that children and teenagers generally used the Internet to strengthen already existing relationships, particularly hard to maintain contacts with friends living abroad, distant relatives, or companions who have moved (Livingstone & Bober, 2004, p. 16). Concurrently, as Mayfield has stated, "the growth in use of social networks by young people in recent years has come at the expense of their consumption of traditional media such as TV and magazines" (2006, p. 24). From the standpoint of conventional media business interests, this is clearly a negative trend. But given the negative effects associated with excessive television watching by youngsters in Western societies, a reduction in television usage can be construed as a secondary benefit of social media. Finally, the use of the Internet in general appears to steer children and teenagers towards pursing voluntary interests in important social domains. A full 55% of the UK youths indicated to researchers that they had actively sought out information on the Internet about political, environmental, human rights, or other "participatory issues" (Livingstone & Bober, 2004, p. 20).

As it now stands, it is "unclear whether the opportunities facilitated by the Internet represent a significant change in young people's lives or, less dramatically, simply a new means of achieving familiar ends" (Livingstone & Bober, 2004, p. 4). The same, of course, can be said of social media that entail Internet usage. Nonetheless, when assessed against its likely influence on the development of positive self-efficacy perceptions, it does appear that social media have the capacity to enhance self-efficacy beliefs by providing and enlarging the channels identified by Bandura as sources of positive self-efficacy beliefs.

SEE ALSO:　▶ Self-efficacy　▶ Social cognitive theory　▶ Social support　▶ Positive youth development

References

Bandura, A. (1986). *Social foundations of thought and action: A social cognitive theory*. Englewood Cliffs, NJ: Prentice-Hall.

Bandura, A. (1994). Self-efficacy. In V. S. Ramachaudran (Ed.), *Encyclopedia of human behavior* (Vol. 4, pp. 71–81). New York: Academic Press.

Lenhart, A., & Madden, M. (2007). *Social networks sites and teens: An overview*. Retrieved January 7, 2007, from http://www.pewinternet.org/pdfs/PIP_SNS_Data_Memo_Jan_2007.pdf

Levy, S., & Stone, B. (2006, April 3). The new wisdom of the web [Electronic version]. *Newsweek*. Retrieved January 7, 2007, from http://vtech.canalblog.com/docs/The_New_Wisdom_of_the_Web___Next_Frontiers___MSNBC.pdf

Livingstone, S., & Bober, M. (2004). Taking up online opportunities? Children's uses of the Internet for education, communication and participation [Electronic version]. *E-Learning, 1*(3): 395–419. Retrieved January 7, 2007, from http://eprints.lse.ac.uk/archive/00000418/01/e-learning_article_vol_1(3).pdf

Mayfield, A. (2006). *What is social media?* Retrieved January 7, 2007, from http://www.spannerworks.com/seotoolkit/search-and-social-media-ebooks-white-papers-and-articles/

Strickland, B. (Ed.) (2001). Albert Bandura. In *The Gale encyclopedia of psychology* (pp. 65–66). Detroit: Gale Press.

Wikipedia contributors (2007). Social media. In *Wikipedia, the free encyclopedia*. Retrieved January 7, 2007, from http://en.wikipedia.org/w/index.php?title=Social_media&oldid=101065143 Page Version ID: 101065143

Positive Therapy

Stephen Joseph[a] and P. Alex Linley[b]
[a]*University of Nottingham;* [b]*Centre for Applied Positive Psychology, UK*

Positive therapy has been used to describe counseling and psychotherapeutic approaches that are consistent with the ambition of positive psychology to facilitate well-being and not simply to alleviate distress and dysfunction. The exemplar is client-centered therapy (CCT) originally developed by Carl Rogers. CCT is based on the meta-theoretical principle that people are intrinsically motivated toward fully functioning, but that intrinsic motivation can be distorted by unfavorable social environmental conditions resulting in distress and dysfunction. Thus, the therapist aims to provide a social environment that is facilitative of the client's intrinsic motivation. The term positive therapy has been used specifically by Joseph and Linley (2006) to describe positive psychological approaches that are based on this meta-theoretical principle:

> positive therapy is based on the fundamental assumption that the client is their own best expert and that the role of the therapist is to facilitate the client in listening more attentively to their own inner voice, and to learn how to evaluate their experiences from an internal locus rather than an external locus . . . The essence of client-centred therapy is the belief in the self-determination of the client. (p. 140)

Positive therapy takes as a fundamental assumption about human nature the view that the actualizing tendency is the universal motivation of people to move toward growth, development, and autonomy. Given this constructive directional tendency in people, the role of the therapist within positive therapy is to enable the client to hear his or her own inner voice, or organismic valuing process, and to establish and then follow the directions that are right for him or her. This view found favor with advocates of the humanistic psychology movement, but lost currency as humanistic psychology became marginalized from mainstream psychology. The advent of positive psychology has caused a reemergence and reexamination of some of these classical ideas from earlier humanistic psychology.

Research evidence in support of this fundamental assumption is not systematic, because it does not easily lend itself to empirical scrutiny. However, the available evidence is consistent. Self-determination theory has repeatedly demonstrated the role of intrinsic motivation in health and well-being, and Ken Sheldon and colleagues have demonstrated that when people shift their goal choices over time they do so in more intrinsic directions, taken to be indicative of the organismic valuing process that is operating within people. More broadly, Linley and Joseph have argued that the meta-theoretical stance of the actualizing tendency is the only view of human nature that can account for the broad research findings of positive psychology: All are interpretable within the framework of an actualizing tendency, but not within other fundamental assumptions.

Other psychological therapies that are considered as positive therapies because they share this meta-theoretical stance include many approaches derived from humanistic, existential, and experiential psychotherapy. In recent years there has been much interest in developing positive therapies and newly developed approaches include positive psychotherapy, well-being therapy, quality of life therapy, mindfulness-based cognitive therapy, and clinical approaches to posttraumatic growth. Future research should seek to extrapolate and empirically assess the evidence for the meta-theoretical stance of an actualizing tendency, and to examine the efficacy and effectiveness of positive therapies for both the alleviation of distress and the enhancement of well-being.

SEE ALSO: ▶ Actualizing tendency   ▶ Humanistic psychology
▶ Positive psychotherapy   ▶ Quality of life therapy   ▶ Rogers, Carl
▶ Well-being therapy

Reference

Joseph, S., & Linley, P. A. (2006). *Positive therapy: A meta-theory for positive psychological practice*. London: Routledge.

Positive Youth Development

Richard F. Catalano[a] and John W. Toumbourou[b]
[a]*University of Washington;* [b]*Deakin University and Murdoch Children's Research Institute VicHealth Fellow, Australia*

In the twentieth century, childhood and adolescence have increasingly become regarded as special periods of development in which children were provided extra support to learn and develop. Programs that focus on enhancing positive youth development are part of the response to providing extra support. Early in the century a number of important changes emerged including universal education delaying the entry into the workforce, and later changes in conceptualization of school and community practices to support the family to raise healthy children. At mid-century, federal funding initiatives began to address reducing juvenile crime, substance use, and academic failure through treatment and remedial programming. Prevention programs became part of the supports for childhood and adolescent development late in the twentieth century, with the first programs being trialed in the late 1960s and early 1970s, with the science of prevention being described in the 1990s.

Many early prevention efforts were not based on child development theory or research and most failed to show positive impacts on youth problems including drug use, pregnancy, sexually transmitted disease, school failure, or delinquent behavior. Faced with early failures, prevention program developers became increasingly aligned with the science of behavior development and change and began designing program elements to address predictors of specific problem behaviors identified in longitudinal and intervention studies of youth. A second generation of prevention efforts sought to use this information on predictors to interrupt the processes leading to specific problem behaviors.

In the 1980s, these prevention efforts which focused on predictors of a single problem behavior came under increasing criticism. Critics urged prevention program developers to consider the cooccurrence of problem behaviors and the extensive overlap in predictors across multiple problem behaviors. Further, many critics advocated a focus on factors that promote positive youth development in addition to focusing on reducing factors that predict problems. Such concerns, expressed by prevention practitioners, policy makers, and prevention scientists, helped expand the design of prevention programs to include components aimed at promoting positive youth development. These critics suggested that successful childhood and adolescent development required more than avoiding drugs, violence, school failure, or risky sexual activity. The promotion of children's social, emotional, cognitive, and moral development began to be seen as key to preventing problem behaviors themselves.

In the 1990s, practitioners, policy makers, and prevention scientists adopted a broader focus for addressing youth issues. Supported by a growing body of research on the developmental etiology of problem and positive behaviors and results from randomized and nonrandomized controlled trials of positive youth development programs, policy makers, practitioners, and prevention scientists were now converging in their focus on the developmental precursors of both positive and negative youth development.

In the late 1990s, youth development practitioners, the policy community, and prevention scientists reached similar conclusions about promoting better outcomes for youth. They all called for expanding programs beyond a single problem behavior focus and considering program effects on a range of positive and problem behaviors. Prevention and developmental research provide substantial evidence that many youth outcomes, both positive and negative, are affected by the same predictors, including risk factors that increase the likelihood of problems and protective factors that appear to promote positive behavior or buffer the effects of risk exposure. The evidence that risk and protective factors are found across family, peer, school, and community environments led to recommendations that positive youth development interventions address multiple socialization forces – across family, school, community, peer, and individual development. This convergence in thinking has been recognized in forums on youth development including practitioners, policy makers, and prevention scientists who have advocated that models of healthy development hold the key to both health promotion and prevention of problem behaviors.

In reviewing the literature and conducting a consensus meeting of leading scientists, an operational definition of positive youth development constructs was created in 1997. This definition was further developed by a meeting of scientists organized by the Annenberg Sunnylands Trust. Space limitations preclude a full description of these constructs that are described in Catalano, Berglund, Ryan, Lonczak, & Hawkins (2002). The constructs included under the umbrella of positive youth development have emerged through consensus meetings involving scientists, practitioners, and policymakers synthesizing findings across the developmental, evaluation, and behavioral sciences. These efforts have married diverse science and practice across a range of disciplines and achieved an encompassing scope in the characterization of positive youth development. Constructs addressed by youth development programs include: promoting bonding; fostering resilience; promoting social, emotional, cognitive behavioral, and moral competence; fostering self-determination; fostering spirituality; fostering self-efficacy; fostering clear and positive identity; fostering belief in the future; providing recognition for positive behavior; providing opportunities for prosocial involvement; fostering prosocial norms; promoting life satisfaction; and promoting strength of character.

In the early twenty-first century, efforts have begun to emerge that attempt to tie this long list of youth developmental constructs together in theories of positive youth development. These theories attempt to improve our understanding of the mechanisms through which different risk and protective factors influence positive youth development and problem behavior.

A review of the efficacy of positive youth development programs used both evaluation design and program content as selection criteria (Catalano et al., 2002). Research designs had to be experimental or quasi-experimental without critical flaws that would affect conclusion validity. Programs had to address at least one positive youth development construct across multiple socialization domains, and the population served could not be selected because of their need for treatment. In addition, the review included only programs addressing youth between the ages of 6 and 20. These selection criteria produced a range of diverse youth development programs for review, some of which may be described as positive youth development, some as health and well-being promotion programs, and others as universal prevention. This diverse selection was due in part to the convergence from multiple sectors of the call for positive youth development programs. For example, a number of programs traditionally considered primary prevention interventions incorporated many of the same positive youth development constructs as did programs viewed primarily as positive youth development programs.

Of the programs considered, 161 were identified as potentially within the scope of that review. Of these 77 of these positive youth development programs had evaluations that met the initial criteria for the review. Of the 77 programs, 8 with evaluations had to be removed from the review due to missing information. On closer inspection, 44 programs had evaluations with design flaws that affected conclusion validity (39) or did not have positive effects on behavioral outcomes (5). There were 25 programs that incorporated positive youth development constructs, had strong evaluation designs (experimental or quasi-experimental with viable comparison groups), provided adequate methodological detail to allow an independent assessment of the study's soundness, and produced evidence of significant effects on behavioral outcomes.

Program results are briefly summarized below. Illustrative references to articles describing outcomes of these programs are provided when the program is first mentioned. More complete descriptions of the programs, research designs, behavioral outcomes, and complete references are available elsewhere.

The following presents a selection of the positive youth outcomes. These included a variety of improvements in emotional competence, including greater self-control (PATHS, Bicultural Competence Skills), frustration tolerance (Children of Divorce), increased empathy (PATHS), and expression of feelings (Fast Track, PATHS). Improvements in social competence, including interpersonal skills (Adolescent Transitions Program, Child Development Project; Life Skills Training, Social Competence Promotion Program, Children of Divorce, Fast Track), greater assertiveness (Bicultural Competence Skills, Children of Divorce), greater self-efficacy with respect to substance use refusal (Project Northland), healthy and adaptive coping in peer-pressure situations (Bicultural Competence Skills), improvements in acceptance of authority (Fast Track), and improvements in race relations and perceptions of others from different cultural or ethnic groups (Woodrock Youth Development Project). Increases in cognitive competence included decision making (Life Skills Training) and better problem-solving (Children of Divorce, PATHS, Social Competence Promotion Program). Increases in behavioral competence included better health practices (Growing Healthy, Know Your Body) and greater self-efficacy around contraceptive practices (Reducing the Risk). Positive youth development programs were associated with improvements in parental bonding and communication (Seattle Social Development Project, Big Brothers/Big Sisters, Reducing the Risk). Positive outcomes also included increased acceptance of prosocial norms regarding substance use (Project ALERT, Life Skills Training). A variety of positive school outcomes were also achieved by some youth development programs, including higher achievement (Teen Outreach, Valued Youth Partnerships, Success for All, Big Brothers/Big Sisters, Seattle Social

Development Project), higher school attachment (Seattle Social Development Project), increased high school attendance (Quantum Opportunities, Big Brothers/Big Sisters), increased high school graduation (Across Ages, Quantum Opportunities Program, Seattle Social Development Project, Valued Youth Partnerships), and increased post-secondary school and college attendance (Quantum Opportunities Program, Seattle Social Development Project). Other positive youth outcomes included higher levels of voluntary community service (Across Ages) and use of community services when needed (Creating Lasting Connections).

Problem behaviors were also reduced or prevented. Substance use was lower for several programs, including alcohol or other drug use (Midwestern Prevention Project, Bicultural Competence Skills, Big Brothers/Big Sisters, Child Development Project, Life Skills Training, Project Alert, Project Northland, Seattle Social Development Project, Woodrock) and tobacco use (Child Development Project, Growing Healthy, Know Your Body, Life Skills Training, Midwestern Prevention Project, Project ALERT, Project Northland, Woodrock). Several programs reduced delinquency and aggression (Responding in Peaceful and Positive Ways, Metropolitan Area Child Study, Adolescent Transitions, Big Brothers/Big Sisters, Fast Track, PATHS, Seattle Social Development Project, Social Competence Promotion Program). Youth contraception practices increased and initiation and prevalence of sexual activity were reduced in two programs (Reducing the Risk, Seattle Social Development Project) and Teen Outreach and the Seattle Social Development Project reduced teen pregnancy. Negative school outcomes were reduced, including truancy (Big Brothers/Big Sisters) and school suspension (Responding in Peaceful and Positive Ways).

A summary of the characteristics of these 25 effective positive youth development programs is instructive but may not be typical of programs in general. These programs were fortunate to have attracted funding to support strong evaluations, thus, they may be at a later stage of development, having convinced funding sources of their evaluability. Evaluability usually entails a strong adherence to scientific behavior theory or empirical evidence in the rationale for the program components and resources that enable replicability, e.g., manualization of procedures and curricula specifying the logical links between procedures and outcomes.

In overview, these programs tended to be highly integrative, bringing together activities and components across multiple youth development domains and environments to achieve improvements in a range of positive and prevention constructs. All of the effective programs in this review addressed a minimum of five positive youth constructs and most interventions addressed at least eight constructs. Three constructs were common in all 25 well-evaluated programs: competence, self-efficacy, and prosocial norms. Several other constructs were addressed in over half of the 25 programs, including: opportunities for prosocial involvement (88%), recognition for positive behavior (88%), and bonding (76%), and 50% of the well-evaluated programs addressed positive identity, self-determination, belief in the future, resiliency and spirituality.

Having a structured curriculum or structured activities is critical for program replication. Of the well-evaluated effective programs, 24 (96%) incorporated a structured curriculum or program of activities. One program, Big Brothers/ Big Sisters, did not focus on a structured strategy to build social competence. Big Brothers/Big Sisters assumed that positive outcomes are mediated by the bonding and other aspects of positive interaction (such as the presumed modeling of effective behavior by the adult) within the mentoring relationship. Of the effective, well-evaluated programs, 20 (80%) were delivered over a period of 9 months or more. In the interventions shorter than 9 months, programs ranged from 10 to 25 sessions, averaging about 12 sessions per intervention.

Fidelity of program implementation is one of the most important topics in the positive youth development field. Implementation fidelity has repeatedly been shown to be related to effectiveness. The effective positive youth development programs reviewed here consistently attended to the quality and consistency of program implementation. The majority of evaluations (24 [96%]) addressed and/or measured how well and how reliably the program implementers delivered the intervention.

Evaluation of a wide range of positive youth development approaches demonstrated that they can promote positive youth behavior and prevent youth problem behaviors. Positive changes in youth behavior were demonstrated in 19 effective programs and included significant improvements in interpersonal skills, quality of peer and adult relationships, self-control, problem-solving, cognitive competencies, self-efficacy, commitment to schooling, and academic achievement. Of the effective programs, 24 showed significant improvements in problem behaviors, including drug and alcohol use, school misbehavior, aggressive behavior, violence, truancy, high-risk sexual behavior, and smoking. The conclusion is clear that promotion and prevention programs that address positive youth development constructs are making a difference to important outcomes in studies with strong designs.

Although a broad range of strategies produced these results, the themes common to success involved methods to: strengthen social, emotional, behavioral, cognitive, and moral competencies; build self-efficacy; shape messages from family and community about clear standards for youth behavior; increase healthy bonding with adults, peers and younger children; expand opportunities and recognition for youth; provide structure and consistency in program delivery; and intervene with youth for at least 9 months. Although one-third of the effective programs operated in a single setting only, it is important to note that for the other two-thirds, combining the resources of the family, the community, and the school was important to success.

In sum, although the full promise of youth development rests on demonstration of long-term effectiveness in reducing problems and promoting positive development, there is clear evidence from well-conducted trials that positive youth development programs can be effective. Looking toward the future, there is potential to encourage the application and dissemination of these programs to achieve positive youth development in new areas aligned with international priorities, including the United Nations Millennium Development goals aimed at eliminating poverty and ensuring peace, justice, and environmental survival.

SEE ALSO: ▶ Character education ▶ Developmental psychology ▶ Moral development

Reference

Catalano, R. F., Berglund, M. L., Ryan, J. A. M., Lonczak, H. S., & Hawkins, J. D. (2002). Positive youth development in the United States: Research findings on evaluations of positive youth development programs. *Prevention and Treatment*, 5(15). Retrieved from: http://journals.apa.org/prevention/volume5/pre0050015a.html

Possible Selves

Michael F. Hock, Irma F. Brasseur and Donald D. Deshler
University of Kansas

The term *possible selves* has been reintroduced to the field of psychology by Hazel Markus, professor of psychology at Stanford University. Markus defined possible selves as, "the ideal selves that we would very much like to become. They are also the selves we could become and the selves we are afraid of becoming" (Markus & Nurius, 1986, p. 954). Markus stated that these ideas are motivating and can inspire us to attain goals related to future possible selves. When individuals have clear goals and specific plans for attaining those goals, they become motivated and willing to put forth the effort necessary to fulfill the desired goals. For example, a student who likes video games might have a hoped-for possible self as a highly successful video game programmer. She might be more likely to work hard in her algebra class if she saw the connection between attaining the desired possible self and the skills she would learn in algebra.

Markus also reports that individuals work just as hard to avoid possible selves they fear. For example, if a student has a feared possible self of having a job they dislike, he may be motivated to work hard and put forth effort to avoid such a future. Whether the person is working hard to attain or to avoid a possible self, thinking about possible selves can increase a person's motivation to put forth effort to attain specified goals. In short, possible selves are a connection between one's desired self-concept and motivation.

The nature of possible selves has been explored in descriptive research studies. These descriptive studies have shed light on whether certain groups do indeed, have future visions of possible selves and whether these possible selves are motivating. The results of these studies are somewhat mixed in terms of the effect of possible selves on achievement, but the studies show that most individuals seem to have visions of themselves in the future and they try to attain these positive future selves and to avoid negative possible selves. For example, Markus and Nurius assessed the possible selves of college students. Most of the college students they assessed had some conceptual knowledge of what they hoped, expected, and feared in the future. In addition, most of the students identified more positive possibilities for the future than negative possibilities. Importantly, these future possible selves were different from their current selves, and the students believed they could attain their hoped-for selves.

Similar findings were reported for youth aged between 13 and 16. Youths attending a public school had no problems explaining what their possible selves were, and their explanations were diverse in nature. This finding also held true for youths who had been adjudicated and placed in delinquency programs. However, the nature of the possible selves of the groups differed. The adjudicated youth were focused on feared possible selves more so than hoped-for or expected possible selves, suggesting less balance between positive and negative selves and a sense of hopelessness.

In another study, college students were classified as being schematic (good problem-solvers) or aschematic (poor problem-solvers). Then the relationship of possible selves and self-schema to performance was assessed. While performance on problem-solving measures did not distinguish between the groups, those who were schematic and endorsed more positive possible selves enjoyed attacking problem-solving tasks and required less failure feedback than did the aschematic group. Open-ended questionnaires were administered in another study. Researchers reported that the use of open-ended questionnaires seemed to be an effective way to identify current and future possible selves, and that associations can be made between positive visions of one's self in the future and academic performance and deep processing or self-regulating strategy usage.

The Possible Selves Program: Nurturing Motivation

Nurturing the motivation of students who are not motivated to engage in learning can be a challenge. In an effort to address this challenge, possible selves interventions have been developed to enhance academic and personal motivation in elementary through to postsecondary students. Preliminary studies indicate that when students become aware of their possible selves, they can increase the number of life roles they identify as possible for themselves in the future and the number of career, learning, and personal goals they wish to achieve.

In an early attempt at a possible selves program, Estrada developed an intervention based upon the construct of possible selves and designed to build awareness and clarity to the possible selves of Hispanic students in 2nd through to 7th grade. The intervention consisted of career, family, leisure, and friends awareness activities, discussion of the relationship between possible selves and high school graduation, how to deal with negative feedback, and coping with failure. The effects of the intervention were positive, with most gains in the number and specificity of roles and goals identified as possible for the learner. Effects for increased grade performance in classes were moderate.

Building on the foundational principles described above (positive vision of oneself in the future, identification of goals, development of plans to attain goals), Hock, Schumaker, and Deshler developed and validated the Possible Selves Program to increase student motivation by having students examine their future and think about goals that are important to them. Students describe their hoped-for, expected, as well as feared possible selves. Once they have described their possible selves, they go on to create a "possible selves tree." Serving as a metaphor for their possible selves, the tree helps students examine the roles they will assume in life, their hopes, expectations, and fears for the future, as well as the overall condition of their tree. Based on an examination and evaluation of their possible selves tree, students take action by formally writing goals to nurture their trees, make plans for reaching their goals, and then work toward those goals. As a result of this process and evidence from research studies, students begin to view learning as a pathway to their hopes and expectations and as a way to prevent feared possible selves from happening. Thus, learning becomes more relevant because it is directly tied to students' personal interests and goals. Typically, an increase in student effort and commitment to learning follows.

The Possible Selves Program consists of six components designed to guide students in identifying and sharing their possible selves through goal setting and monitoring of progress toward goal attainment. The first component, *discovering*, helps the student answer the question, "What are my strengths and interests?" Here, the teacher engages students in activities designed to help them identify areas in which they have interests and skills and that make them feel good about themselves. The goal is to find an area in which each student has had positive experiences and that they are willing to share. By finding an area about which the student feels positive, the "pump is primed," and the student becomes more willing to share information related to areas about which he or she may not feel so positive (e.g., learning).

Thinking, the second component of the program, is designed to help the student answer the question, "Who am I?" During this phase, students complete a structured but open-ended interview, either individually or as part of a group. During the interview, students are asked to identify words and phrases that describe them individually as a learner, person, worker, and in the strength area that they identified during the discovering phase. They also define their hopes, expectations, and fears for the future in each area. In this way, an outline of the current self and possibilities for the future are developed within each area. Suggested interview questions include: "What statements or words best describe you as a learner?" "What do you hope to achieve as a learner?" "What do you expect to achieve as a learner?" "What do you fear as a learner?" As the students respond to questions and describe themselves, they write down their answers. Additional questions about the student's hopes, expectations, and fears for the future in at least two other domains are also recorded.

Once the interview has been completed, the third component of the Possible Selves Program, *sketching*, is introduced. Sketching helps students answer the question, "What am I like and what are my possible selves?" During this activity, students draw a possible selves tree. The teacher models how to draw each part of the tree and the students follow suit. The tree limbs represent students as a learners, persons, and workers. The branches represent hoped-for and expected possible selves in those three areas. Feared possible selves are represented by threats to the tree, such as lightning, termites, poison in the soil, and so on. Finally, the roots of the tree represent the words used by the student to describe him or herself. After the tree is drawn, preliminary goals are discussed concerning how to keep the tree strong, make it fuller, protect it from fears, and provide it with nourishment. In short, the student is asked to briefly think about the tree and ways to nurture and protect it.

The fourth component of the program, *reflecting*, helps students answer the question, "What can I be?" This phase provides an opportunity for students to evaluate the condition of their tree and set goals for the future. This reflection activity also includes a discussion of how learning can support the health of the student's tree.

The fifth component, *growing*, helps the student answer the question, "How do I accomplish my goals?" The purpose here is to get students to start thinking about specific ways to nurture and "grow" their trees and attain identified goals. If, for example, a student identified a hope-for a career as the owner of a music business, a singer, a diesel technician, or a player in the National Football League (NFL), the student can develop the short- and long-term goals that are necessary to attain this "possible self" and generate a plan to reach these goals. In addition, students may discover that the same goals help them avoid the "feared selves" that have been identified (e.g., no job, no money, no friends). In short, during the growing activities, the student constructs a well-developed action plan that serves as a pathway to support the attainment of long-term goals and hopes for the future.

The sixth and final component is *performing*. This component helps students answer the question, "How am I doing?" During this phase, the possible selves tree, the goals established to nurture the tree, and the action plans are revisited and revised regularly. Task completion is reviewed, goals and action plans are modified, goal attainment is celebrated, new goals are added, and hopes, expectations, and fears are continually examined. For example, if the stated goal of playing football in the NFL is no longer considered viable by the student, new and perhaps related goals are identified. The student may see coaching middle school football as a more realistic career, and that goal then becomes the focus of the revised action plan.

The Future of Possible Selves

While there is a growing literature on the construct of possible selves, the majority of the research has focused on describing the various dimensions of possible selves in populations with different characteristics under different conditions. Thus, there is a paucity of studies investigating how to effectively teach individuals to become aware of their possible selves and how to set and work toward meaningful goals in light of their possible selves knowledge. Research is needed to determine the sustainability of effects of possible selves intervention programs, the ecological conditions that are most conducive to teaching and learning components of possible selves programs, the role that behaviors such as self-advocacy play in enabling people to use their possible selves to set and work toward goals, and strategies for operationalizing a possible selves program across ages and grade levels – how to optimally structure programs for students of different ages and reinforced by different teachers and adults (e.g., counselors) who interact with them. In short, much work needs to be done to determine the ultimate impact of possible selves as a tool for improving student engagement in the learning process and how it can be best leveraged to improve academic and social outcomes.

SEE ALSO: ▶ Actualizing tendency ▶ Narrative identity

Reference

Markus, H., & Nurius, P. (1986). Possible selves. *American Psychologist, 41*, 954–969.

Posttraumatic Growth

P. Alex Linley[a] and Stephen Joseph[b]
[a]*Centre for Applied Positive Psychology, UK;* [b]*University of Nottingham*

Posttraumatic growth refers to the constellation of positive changes that people may experience following a trauma or other stressful event. The term was introduced by Richard Tedeschi and Lawrence Calhoun in 1995, in the context of the Posttraumatic Growth Inventory, a self-report assessment of the construct that was first presented in their book *Trauma and Transformation: Growing in the Aftermath of Suffering*. Conceptually, posttraumatic growth is described as consisting of three broad dimensions. First, people often report that their relationships are enhanced in some way, for example that they now value their friends and family more, and feel an increased compassion and altruism toward others. Second, survivors change their views of themselves in some way, for example, that they have a greater sense of personal resiliency and strength, perhaps coupled with a greater acceptance of their vulnerabilities and limitations. Third, there are often reports of changes in life philosophy, for example, survivors report finding a fresh appreciation for each new day, and renegotiating what really matters to them in the full realization that their life is finite. Unlike resilience, which connotes a stability of functioning in the face of adversity, posttraumatic growth refers to a nonnormative positive shift in functioning, and has been likened to using the traumatic experience as a springboard or trampoline to achieve a higher level of posttrauma functioning than existed at the pretrauma baseline.

Although it has only been the focus of research attention since the 1990s, the concept of posttraumatic growth, or positive change following trauma, has been recognized throughout human history. The value of suffering is a theme of many of the world's religions (e.g., the crucifixion of Jesus within Christianity), as well as being recurrent throughout existential philosophy (e.g., Nietzsche's dictum: "What does not kill me, makes me stronger," 1889/2003, p. 33), literature (the Russian novelist Fyodor Dostoevsky drew on his own experiences of a mock execution to inform his writing; the Italian poet Dante Alighieri wrote of the loss of his own great love in his masterpiece *The Divine Comedy*), and psychology itself (Viktor Frankl tested his own theories of logotherapy when being held in the Nazi concentration camps; Aaron Antonovsky developed his theory of salutogenesis as a way to explain the recovery and growth of his Jewish compatriots following the Second World War).

While the term posttraumatic growth is the most widely used label for the construct of positive change following trauma and adversity, a number of other terms have been developed and are often used interchangeably. These include *stress-related growth*, *adversarial growth*, *positive adaptation*, *positive changes*, *positive by-products*, *benefit finding*, *perceived benefits*, *thriving*, *flourishing*, and *growth following adversity*. Importantly, posttraumatic growth does not require the presence of a DSM-IV Criterion A traumatic stressor for the use of the term posttraumatic growth to be considered appropriate. Posttraumatic growth is considered a much more normative and dimensional phenomenon than posttraumatic stress disorder, which, coming from a medical model perspective, requires the presence of a specifically defined traumatic stressor before a diagnosis can be made. In contrast, posttraumatic growth is considered a more normative developmental experience, and as such may be reported following apparently more minor difficulties and stresses, and not just major traumatic events.

The events for which posttraumatic growth outcomes have been reported include transportation accidents (shipping disasters, plane crashes, car accidents), natural disasters (hurricanes, earthquakes), interpersonal experiences (combat, rape, sexual assault, child abuse), medical problems (cancer, heart attack, brain injury, spinal cord injury, HIV/AIDS, leukemia, rheumatoid arthritis, multiple sclerosis, illness) and more normative life experiences (relationship breakdown, parental divorce, bereavement, immigration). Further, vicarious experiences of posttraumatic growth have been shown in a variety of populations not directly suffering themselves, but exposed to the suffering of others, including counselors, therapists, clinical psychologists, funeral directors, disaster workers, spouses of people with cancer, and even British people who saw the September 11, 2001, terrorist attacks on television.

Several variables have been found to be consistently related to posttraumatic growth, including appraisals of greater threat, harm, and controllability (although it is likely that there is a curvilinear relationship with threat and harm); problem-focused, acceptance, and positive reinterpretation coping; optimism; religion; cognitive processing; and positive affect. Studies have shown inconsistent associations between a number of sociodemographic variables (gender, age, education and income) and psychological distress variables (depression, anxiety, posttraumatic stress disorder), although the evidence suggests that people who report posttraumatic growth and maintain that growth over time are likely to report less subsequent psychological distress.

Models of Posttraumatic Growth

The two most elaborated models of posttraumatic growth are the functional-descriptive model proposed by Richard Tedeschi and Lawrence Calhoun, and the organismic valuing model proposed by Stephen Joseph and Alex Linley. The functional-descriptive model is premised on the importance of appraisal processes, and discusses how traumatic events serve as seismic challenges to the pretrauma schema, by shattering prior goals, beliefs, and ways of managing emotional distress. The shattering of these schemas leads to ruminative activity, as people try to make sense of what has happened and to deal with their emotional reactions to the trauma. In the initial stages, this ruminative activity is more automatic than deliberate (consistent with the reexperiencing and avoidance symptom clusters within posttraumatic stress disorder, PTSD). Although this automatic ruminative activity is often distressing, it is indicative of cognitive activity that is directed at rebuilding the pretrauma schema. This ruminative process is influenced by social support networks that provide sources of comfort and relief, as well as being influenced by new coping behaviors and the options that are available for the construction of new, posttrauma schemas.

Successful coping at this stage facilitates disengagement from goals that are now unreachable, and beliefs that are no longer tenable in the posttrauma environment, together with decreased emotional distress. As successful coping aids adaptation, the initial ruminative activity that was characterized by its automatic nature shifts towards a more effortful ruminative activity. This effortful ruminative activity is characterized by narrative development, part of which may be the search for meaning. Interacting with this process is the experience and self-identification of adversarial growth. Importantly, although this shift toward more effortful ruminative activity represents growthful adaptation, it does not exclude the possibility of some enduring distress from the trauma, but at a lower level than was experienced in the immediate aftermath.

Building on positive psychological perspectives and the person-centered approach, Stephen Joseph and Alex Linley developed the organismic valuing theory of growth following adversity. The *organismic valuing process* (OVP) refers to people's innate ability to know what is important to them and what is essential for a fulfilling life, based on the view that human beings can be relied on through their physiological processes to know what they need from their environment and what is right for them to grow and develop. As with the functional-descriptive model, the confrontation with an adverse event has a shattering effect on the person's assumptive world, and following the completion tendency there is a need to integrate the new trauma-related information. The completion principle is the foundation of a number of cognitive-emotional processing models in the posttraumatic stress literature, and within the organismic valuing theory, the completion principle is viewed as an aspect of the organismic valuing process. Organismic valuing theory posits that when the social environment is able to provide for the basic human needs of autonomy, competence, and relatedness, then growth will be promoted. The theory holds that it is human nature to modify existing models of the world to positively accommodate new trauma-related information when the social environment provides the basic nutrients for growth; however, the social environment does not always provide the nutrients for growth, and as such people may assimilate or negatively accommodate the trauma-related information.

The new trauma-related information is stored in active memory, awaiting processing, and this in turn leads to the intrusive states. However, this leads to high states of distress and arousal that need to be defended against, hence the avoidance states. The person goes through a series of oscillating phases of intrusion and avoidance as the new trauma-related information is processed. When a baseline is reached and intrusive and avoidant states are no longer present this is explained as resulting from cognitive assimilation of the traumatic memory or a revision of existing schemas to accommodate new information. Following adverse events, new trauma-related information can only be processed in one of two ways. Either, the new trauma-related information must be *assimilated* within existing models of the world, or existing models of the world must *accommodate* the new trauma-related information which requires people to change their worldviews.

Theoretically, the alleviation of posttraumatic stress disorder symptoms can come about either through assimilation or through accommodation of the new trauma-related information, as the person must somehow integrate the material, thus allowing them to return to a pretrauma baseline. However, to move beyond the pretrauma baseline requires accommodation as opposed to assimilation, given that as growth is, by definition, about new worldviews.

Thus, within the organismic valuing theory, three cognitive outcomes to the psychological resolution of trauma-related difficulties are posited. First, that experiences are assimilated, leading to a return to pretrauma baseline, but also leaving the person vulnerable to future retraumatization. Second, that experiences are accommodated in a negative direction, leading to psychopathology and distress because the person feels helpless and hopeless. Third, that experiences are accommodated in a positive direction, leading to growth because the person has evolved and developed their world view in light of the new traumatic information. The distinctions between these three cognitive outcomes are a major novel contribution of the organismic valuing theory of posttraumatic growth. One of the most important aspects of OVP theory is that it provides an integrative social-cognitive model that integrates what we know about posttraumatic stress with what is known about posttraumatic growth. Building on this, recent theoretical work by Joseph and Linley has been concerned with the integration of posttraumatic stress and posttraumatic growth within a unitary psychosocial framework from a positive psychological perspective, an approach which is premised on the value of examining and integrating both the positive and negative aspects of human experience.

Assessment of Posttraumatic Growth

The assessment of posttraumatic growth has typically depended on retrospective self-report measures, the most widely used of which are the Posttraumatic Growth Inventory and the Changes in Outlook Questionnaire. The Posttraumatic Growth Inventory measures five dimensions of posttraumatic growth, namely relating to others, personal strength, new possibilities, appreciation of life, and spiritual change. The Changes in Outlook Questionnaire measures two dimensions of positive changes and negative changes. Other generic self-report measures of positive changes following trauma and adversity include the Stress-Related Growth Scale, the Perceived Benefits Scales, and the Thriving Scale, as well as a number of other measures developed for use with specific trauma populations (e.g., cancer, multiple sclerosis).

The accuracy and reliability of these retrospective self-report measures of growth have been called into question by Julian Ford, Howard Tennen, and David Albert, who identified the five mental processes through which a respondent must work in order to answer a posttraumatic growth rating statement: evaluate his/her current standing on a dimension; recall his/her previous standing on the same dimension; compare current and previous standings; assess the degree of change; and finally determine how much of that change is attributable to the traumatic or stressful event in question. Taking into account the complexity of these mental operations, and the likelihood that respondents to posttraumatic growth questions do not systematically compute all of them, a number of methodological issues have been raised for research into and assessment of posttraumatic growth. One of the biggest challenges for the posttraumatic growth field as it moves forward will be to establish empirical findings on a more rigorous methodological and statistical footing.

SEE ALSO: ▶ Benefit finding ▶ Frankl, Viktor ▶ Resilience ▶ Suffering

Reference

Nietzsche, F. (2003). *Twilight of the idols and the anti-Christ*. (Trans. R. J. Hollingdale). London: Penguin Books. (Original work published 1889.)

Prayer

Maggie Syme[a] and Rebecca Syme[b]
[a]*University of Kansas;* [b]*Bethel Seminary*

Prayer is an act of communication between an individual and a specific reality, such as a supernatural being or natural force. It is a central practice of many religions, typically the means of connecting the individual or group to the divine. However, prayer has been shown to be prevalent among both religious and nonreligious persons. The multidimensional nature of prayer makes it easily adaptable to a variety of human experiences.

Though prayer is used by both religious and nonreligious alike, the dominant function of prayer is as a means of religious expression. Each religion, however, utilizes prayer in a slightly different way. In some religions, for instance, prayer is a daily requirement, whereas other religions encourage regular prayer with no stipulated practice. Some faiths encourage public prayer and some emphasize private prayer. The monotheistic religions emphasize both ritual (or sacramental) and spontaneous prayer. Most religions believe that the divine being or force (god, universe, nature) reciprocates communication with the individual or group and may measure the effectiveness of prayer by external signs or circumstances.

Different religions emphasize different elements of prayer. The Second Pillar of Islam is ritual prayer – five prayers each day at set times with accompanying bodily positions of veneration. Buddhists practice *metta*, which is a combination of concentrated visioning and directed words or thoughts of loving kindness. Jews use a prayer book called the *siddur* to guide them through daily prayers and place a high value on corporate prayer. Catholic Christians memorize prayers that can be used as either acts of worship or signs of repentance or penance, such as the Divine Praises and the Act of Contrition. Some Christians practice listening prayer where the person silently awaits words from the divine. Yet as different as they are, many of these traditions overlap or practice prayer in ways virtually indistinguishable from one another. Among religions that worship a deity, prayer is the way humans commune with the object of worship and receive communication in return.

A multitude of research has been conducted on prayer, which has illustrated its complex nature. These studies have been primarily based on theoretical hypotheses about the nature of prayer and its possible typology. Subsequently, few empirically based studies have been conducted to ascertain distinct prayer types. Of those, there is considerable semantic overlap and little consistency in the number of prayer types. This may be due to the diverse ways in which prayer is viewed and used by individuals. It has been proposed that the type of prayer utilized will often depend on the context, the individual, the goal of prayer, and several other factors. Types of prayers include expressions of suffering, contemplations, intercessions for others, personal petitions, confessions, adorations, sacraments, and giving thanks.

Assessments of prayer have been developed to encompass the dimensions of prayer, such as the Multidimensional Prayer Inventory and the Inward, Outward, Upward Prayer scale. These measures seek to improve upon the early measures of prayer determining only the frequency of prayer, which were comprised of one item relying solely on the frequency of occurrence; these have been criticized as an incomplete representation of the multidimensional nature of prayer and its many uses. These new measures also provide assessments focused specifically on prayer, as opposed to being a part of an overall spiritual coping or religious practices scale.

Research has repeatedly demonstrated the benefits associated with prayer, including improved mental health, greater marital satisfaction, recovery from substance abuse and many other mental and physical health benefits. These benefits may be due to the fact that prayer often functions as a resource and coping strategy for individuals across sociodemographic variables.

For example, prayer can be a way to exercise control over an otherwise uncontrollable situation by appealing to a sovereign power. Research conducted with various medical populations suggests that prayer may be used as a reminder of the sovereignty and omnipotence of the deity being addressed and may result in a feeling of peace, knowing that an all-powerful deity is watching over the individual. Prayer may also provide a sense of belonging through the connection to both a deity and a larger group of worshipers. This connection is reportedly present in private as well as corporate worship.

Prayer has also been described by professional black women as a way to meditate, quiet the self, increase personal strength, assist in decision-making and gain some perspective in a stressful situation. People experiencing suffering have also been known to utilize prayer to help understand and accept their situation. Individuals with an illness or severe injury may use different types of prayer to explain and accept their circumstances as being part of God's plan. The coping function of prayer in those with physical impairments has received considerable attention in the research literature. It has been shown to be a primary resource for those suffering from chronic pain, terminal illness, and various physical ailments, as well as a resource for their caregivers.

Whether prayer directly or indirectly causes positive effects in people's lives is unknown. One role of prayer may be to bolster other positive psychological factors, such as optimism and hope, which in turn lead to other benefits. For example, personal fulfillment through prayer and meditation has been linked to greater optimism and social support, both being positively related to life satisfaction. Prayer has also been positively correlated with the agency factor of hope as well as finding increased meaning in life. The conclusion that prayer is a direct cause of improved physical and mental health has been a contention among scholars. Researchers continue to call for further investigation into the specific role of prayer as a coping resource and protective factor.

SEE ALSO: ▶ Buddhism ▶ Coping ▶ Mental health ▶ Religiousness ▶ Spirituality

Prevention Focus

E. Tory Higgins
Columbia University

Prevention focus is one of two distinct regulatory systems that has developed to deal with a distinct survival concern – security. To survive, people (and other animals) need both nurturance and security; they need support or nourishment from the environment (often provided by others), as well as protection from dangers in the environment (social and physical dangers). When people succeed in satisfying a concern they experience pleasure, and when they fail they experience pain. Thus, both nurturance and security systems involve approaching pleasure and avoiding pain. However, the nurturance and security systems differ in *how* pleasure is approached and pain is avoided.

The security system is associated with the development of *prevention focus* and concerns safety, with meeting duties and obligations (oughts). People can succeed or fail to fulfill their prevention focus concerns, and thus experience pleasure from success and pain from failure. But hedonic experiences are not the end of the story. There are distinct emotional and motivational consequences of self-regulation in a prevention focus.

Individuals with a prevention focus use ought self-guides in their self-regulation. Self-guides are self-directive standards, which function as a major source of people's emotions and motivation. They both directly prompt action as desired end-states (i.e., goals to be attained), and, through their use in self-evaluation (i.e., standards to be met), arouse emotions that are themselves motivating. Ought self-guides represent a person's beliefs about his or her duties, responsibilities and obligations. Ought self-guides vary in strength across persons (between individuals) and across situations (within individuals). There are different modes of strong socialization that produce strong ought self-guides. Strong ought self-guides are produced by interactions with significant others that involve protection and safeguarding, as well as punishment and criticism for failure to meet an ought self-guide. When self-guides are strong from socialization, they have high chronic accessibility. They predominate in self-regulation for years. When strong ought self-guides predominate, people have a prevention focus on duties and obligations.

When people are in the prevention focus system, they experience quiescence-related emotions following success (e.g., calm, relaxed) and agitation-related emotions following failure (e.g., nervous, tense). This is true whether people are in a prevention focus from a chronic predisposition to be in that system or from a current situation activating that system. Individuals in a prevention focus more readily appraise objects and events in the world (e.g., exams, money, garbage, music) along a quiescence-agitation dimension than a cheerfulness-dejection dimension.

Individuals with a prevention focus not only have a distinct emotional life, they also have a distinct motivational life. Importantly, they have distinct *strategic preferences* when they pursue goals and make decisions. Individuals in a prevention focus prefer to use *vigilant* strategies to pursue goals or make decisions (a nonloss). Vigilant strategies are strategies of carefulness, strategies to prevent movement from a current neutral or satisfactory status quo to a less desirable or negative state. Individuals in a prevention focus experience positive and negative events in the world as nonlosses and losses, respectively, because their concerns are about safety and meeting obligations. Strategic vigilance is also about trying to be careful to ensure nonlosses and not wanting to commit mistakes that produce a loss, so vigilance fits a prevention focus.

Strategic vigilance is also about ensuring nonlosses and not wanting losses, so vigilance sustains or fits a prevention focus. Indeed, many studies have found that individuals in a prevention focus prefer to use vigilant strategies to pursue goals or make decisions. There is also evidence that when the strategic approach to an achievement task is experimentally manipulated, individuals in a prevention focus perform better when instructed to use vigilant means than when instructed to use eager means. Persuasive messages with a vigilant tone (vs. an eager tone) are more effective in changing the attitudes of individuals with a prevention focus. The prevention focus on vigilant nonlosses also influences how ingroup bias is displayed. For individuals in a prevention focus, outgroup members are treated with a negative bias ("preventing them") rather than ingroup members being treated with a positive bias ("promoting us").

The fact that vigilance sustains or fits a prevention focus has other implications as well. It means that individuals with a prevention focus will be motivated to imagine or anticipate the possibility of future failure in order to create a vigilance in the present that will sustain their motivation ("defensive pessimism"). Because of this, individuals who are effective at maintaining their prevention focus are less optimistic than other people, without being pessimistic. They also have lower self-esteem, without having low self-esteem. In addition, when they succeed at a task they are less likely than other people to raise their expectations and expect success the next time. After success they will even lower their self-esteem if they need to remain vigilant for the next task. The relatively lower self-esteem associated with individuals who have effective prevention has been found not only in the United States but also in other nations, such as Italy, India, Israel, and Japan. There is also evidence from several nations that individuals with effective prevention are also generally less extroverted than others.

Regulatory fit increases strength of engagement, which intensifies evaluative reactions, and regulatory nonfit decreases strength of engagement, which deintensifies evaluative reactions. This contributes to the emotional responses of individuals with a prevention focus. When individuals succeed in a prevention focus it decreases their vigilance, creating a regulatory nonfit that reduces engagement strength, which is then experienced as low-intensity calmness. When individuals fail in a prevention focus it increases their vigilance, creating a regulatory fit that strengthens engagement, which is then experienced as high-intensity nervousness. When failures become severe and prolonged, individuals with a strong prevention focus are vulnerable to suffering from generalized anxiety.

Regulatory focus differences in strategic approaches are especially likely to be revealed when there is a conflict between different choices or different ways to proceed on a task. One prevalent conflict is between being "risky" or being "conservative" when making a judgment or decision. When people are uncertain, they can take a chance and treat something as being correct that could actually be incorrect (a possible error of commission). Alternatively, they can be cautious and reject something as being incorrect that could actually be correct (a possible error of omission). Studies on memory, judgment, and decision making have found that, when the status quo is satisfactory, individuals with a strong prevention focus tend to more conservative than other people. When the current state is not satisfactory, however, and the conservative option would improve things but not get all the way back to the satisfactory status quo, then individuals with a prevention focus tend to be even riskier than other people – doing whatever is necessary to get back to the satisfactory status quo.

There is also evidence that individuals in a prevention focus are less creative than those in a promotion focus, and are also less willing to change and try something new when given the opportunity. Under conditions of uncertainty (and a satisfactory status quo), individuals in a prevention focus, compared to other people, are less willing to consider new alternatives and more likely to stick with the established state of affairs. Although individuals in a prevention focus tend to be less creative than others, they are more likely to carry out a creative decision in the face of obstacles. More generally, they are more likely to maintain commitments. Individuals in a prevention focus are also more analytic than others.

There are other conflicts on which individuals in a prevention focus act differently than other people. One classic conflict on many tasks is between speed (or quantity) and accuracy (or quality). Compared to others, individuals with a prevention focus emphasize accuracy more than speed. A third conflict concerns whether to represent objects or events in a more global and abstract manner or in a more local and concrete manner. Compared to others, individuals with a prevention focus are more likely to represent objects and events in a local and concrete manner (as well as less temporally distant) than in a global and abstract manner.

SEE ALSO: ▶ Goals and goal-setting theory ▶ Hedonics ▶ Promotion focus ▶ Self-esteem ▶ Self-regulation

Pride

Sara Cho Kim
University of Wisconsin – Madison

Pride is commonly defined as a positive emotion that contributes to the development of healthy self-esteem. The behavioral and emotional components of pride are often associated with success, achievement, and group membership. At an extreme level, pride is associated with narcissism, a personality trait, which can negatively affect an individual's ability to interact in social situations. In addition, the lack or loss of pride can contribute to an increase in aggressive, hostile, and destructive attitudes and/or behavior.

Major Dimensions of Pride

In experiencing pride, areas of achievement are where pride is most widely cited. Pride encourages prosocial behaviors like achievement and success. The achievement domain can span areas such as performance in an athletic competition, school grades and earning top honors in the military. In addition, pride is intricately involved with the functioning and maintenance of self-esteem. Pride is considered one of the primary emotional components to self-esteem. Based on socialization, pride is involved in a number of interpersonal processes from boosting one's self-esteem to signaling to others that his or her behavior is valuable and an important member of the group. In other words, pride can be interpreted as an evaluation of self-worth and can be highly subjective.

Understanding pride involves examining the affiliative and intersubjective components where social comparisons are expected. For example, an athlete running in a sporting event is competing against his or her peers to win first place. The affiliative or social component of pride involves social status and distinction from others. Individuals desire esteem for their accomplishments, recognition for their achievements, and increased social status in the social hierarchy. Public recognition of achievement contributes to pride. For example, when individuals in Western cultures outperform others and receive recognition for their success, they feel proud. The feeling of pride, however, occurs when there is a sense of personal responsibility (e.g., I trained diligently for the race) and a favorable outcome (e.g., I won because I trained hard).

The expression of pride is another integral component to consider. The outward expression of pride serves the purpose of conveying the message that this individual warrants attention from the social group that he, she, or the group merits acceptance, respect, and recognition. For example, some nonverbal expressions of pride may include a picture of an individual with their head tilted upwards, arms up in the air as a sign of victory, or hands on their hips denoting confidence and pride. Associated with feelings of satisfaction and self-worth, outward expressions of pride are publicity for a job well done.

Pride Based on Group Membership

In one's life, pride is expressed based on group membership. One example is the concept of ethnic pride, which involves positive attitudes toward and association with one's group of origin. Ethnic pride provides a sense of belonging as a member of a group. Strong identification with a group is a form of self-empowerment. By identifying as a member of a cultural group – racial or ethnic group, sexual orientation, occupation, or special interest group (e.g., motorcycle club membership) – one's pride is based on affiliation and involvement with the group.

A sense of belonging and contributing to a group elicits feelings of pride, a sense of security, and acceptance. Individuals may choose to retain distinct qualities based on their group membership as a result of pride in their shared ethnic heritage. For example ethnic pride serves several protective factors that can contribute to increased positive regard for self and others, resilience, and positive well-being. Ethnic pride and affiliation has been shown to buffer the effects of racism, discrimination, and microaggressions that assault members of disenfranchised groups.

Not all cultural groups may agree on the positive attributes of pride. For example, in collectivistic cultures, feelings of pride are based on the "collective good" where one's accomplishment reflects positively on the group and not only on the individual. For members in Judeo-Christian religious groups, pride is often referred to as a sin. References in the Bible extol the virtues of humility, while pride is to be avoided.

Methodological Issues and Problems Associated with Pride

Researchers have noted the difficulty in determining the complexity of the emotion of pride. Adding to this difficulty is a shortage of well-constructed scales that can be used to measures the construct of pride.

Relegated to a secondary emotional status, it has not received much attention over the years. Yet, research has demonstrated that children as young as five years old are able to recognize expressions of pride and distinguish it from other positive emotions like happiness.

Future Directions

Developing an interdisciplinary understanding and expansion of the topic of pride would increase our understanding of this complex, multifaceted positive emotion. A well-constructed and empirically sound scale would also serve to increase interest in studying pride. Including cultural variations on experiencing and understanding pride would also expand the study of pride.

SEE ALSO: ▶ Humility ▶ Self-esteem

Proactive Coping

Ralf Schwarzer[a] and Nina Knoll[b]

[a]*Freie Universität Berlin, Germany;* [b]*Charité – Universitätsmedizin Berlin, Germany*

Proactive coping entails striving for more resources, desiring to maximize gains, and building up resistance factors either to ward off future crises or to grow and cultivate their capabilities for their own sake. Proactive coping's forward time perspective opens new research questions and helps to overcome traditional coping models that overemphasize the reactive nature of coping. There is a general trend to broaden stress and coping research by including *positive strivings* that were formerly domains of motivation and action theories. The notions of mastery, such as Baltes and Baltes' optimization, Lazarus' challenge and benefit, and Hobfoll's resource gain, are in line with proactive coping theories as proposed by authors such as Aspinwall, Greenglass, or Schwarzer.

The recent broadening of coping theory might be a reaction to earlier conceptualizations of coping that neglected goals, purpose, and meaning. As these become more salient and explicit in the current thinking, it is appropriate to redesign coping theory in order to extend it into volition and action theory. In line with ideas presented by Beehr and McGrath in the late 1990s, the present approach makes a systematic distinction between proactive coping and three other kinds of coping that might shed more light on some previously neglected aspects.

Four Coping Perspectives as a Function of Timing and Certainty

Situational demands can be continuous or changing. They can reflect an ongoing harmful encounter, or they can exist in the near or distant future, creating a threat to someone who feels incapable of matching the upcoming demands with the coping resources at hand. For instance, critical events at the workplace may have occurred in the past, leading to layoff, demotion, or adverse restrictions. In light of the complexity of stressful episodes, coping cannot be reduced to either relaxation or fight-and-flight responses. Coping depends, among others, on the temporal perspective of demands and the subjective certainty of the events. Distinctions are made between reactive, anticipatory, preventive, and proactive coping. Reactive coping refers to harm or loss experienced in the past, whereas anticipatory coping pertains to inevitable threats in the near future. Preventive coping refers to uncertain threats in the distant future, whereas proactive coping involves future challenges that are seen as self-promoting (see Figure 6).

Reactive coping can be defined as an effort to deal with a stressful encounter that is ongoing or has already happened. Moreover, it might aim at compensation for

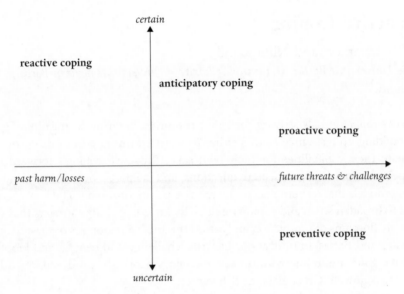

Figure 6   Four Coping Perspectives as a Function of Timing and Certainty.

or acceptance of harm or loss. Examples are losing a loved-one, being diagnosed with a severe or chronic disease, failing an exam, or having been demoted. All of these events happened in the past with absolute certainty; thus, the individual who needs to cope has to either compensate for loss or alleviate harm. Other options might entail readjusting goals or searching for meaning. Reactive coping may be problem-focused, emotion-focused, or social-relation-focused.

Anticipatory coping can be defined as an effort to deal with imminent threat. In anticipatory coping, individuals face a critical event that will occur in the near future. Examples are speaking in public, taking a difficult exam, having to undergo painful medical procedures, anticipating increased workload, children moving out, a loved-one's severe illness, etc. There is a risk that the upcoming event may cause harm or loss later on, and the person has to manage this perceived risk. The function of coping may lie in solving the actual problem at hand, such as increasing effort, getting help, or investing other resources. Another function may lie in feeling good in spite of the risk, for example by redefining the situation as less threatening, by distraction, or by gaining reassurance from others.

Preventive coping can be defined as an effort to build up general resistance resources that result in less strain in the future (minimizing severity of impact), less severe consequences of potential distress, and an overall reduced risk of stressful events. In preventive coping, individuals face a critical event that may or may not occur in the distant future. Examples are anticipated job loss, physical impairment, disaster, separation, or poverty. The individual plans for the occurrence of such nonnormative life events that are appraised as threatening. Since all kinds of harm or loss could materialize one day, the individual builds up general resistance resources, accumulating wealth, social bonds, and skills, "just in case."

Proactive coping can be defined as an effort to build up general resources that facilitate promotion toward challenging goals and personal growth. In proactive coping, people have a vision. They see risks, demands, and opportunities in the far future, but they do not appraise these as threats, harm, or loss. Rather, they perceive difficult situations as challenges. Coping becomes goal management instead of risk management. Individuals are not reactive, but proactive in the sense that they initiate a constructive path of action and create opportunities for growth. The proactive individual strives for improvement of life or work and builds up resources that ensure progress and quality of functioning. For instance, proactively creating better work conditions and higher performance levels may be experienced as an opportunity to render life meaningful or to find purpose in life. Stress is interpreted as "eustress," that is, productive arousal and vital energy.

Preventive and proactive coping are partly manifested in the same kinds of overt behaviors such as, skill development, resource accumulation, and long-term planning. However, the motivation can emanate either from threat appraisal or from challenge appraisal, which makes a difference. Worry levels are high in the former and low in the latter. Proactive individuals are motivated to meet challenges and commit themselves to personal quality standards. Self-regulatory goal management includes an ambitious manner of goal setting and tenacious goal pursuit.

The distinction between these four perspectives of coping is useful because it moves the focus away from mere responses to negative events toward a broader range of risk and goal management that includes the active creation of opportunities and the positive experience of stress.

Proactive Coping: Assessment and Findings

Psychometric analyses have resulted in the Proactive Coping Inventory (PCI) which was constructed by Greenglass, Schwarzer, and Taubert in the 1990s. A preventive coping subscale is included in the PCI. Typical items are, "I plan for future eventualities," and "I prepare for adverse events." It also includes the Proactive Coping subscale that has been tested in various samples and that is available in several languages. Its 14 items form a unidimensional scale. Examples: "I visualize my dreams and try to achieve them"; "After attaining a goal, I look for another, more challenging one." It has satisfactory psychometric properties, and there is growing evidence of its validity. Several studies have found that proactive coping is positively correlated with perceived self-efficacy and negatively with job burnout in different professions. In 316 German teachers, the internal consistency of the Proactive Coping scale was alpha = .86, and correlations were $r = .61$ with perceived self-efficacy, $r = .50$ with self-regulation, and $r = -.40$ with procrastination.

Proactive teachers reported less job burnout as reflected by less emotional exhaustion, less cynicism, and more personal accomplishments than their reactive coping counterparts. Other recent work by Greenglass, Fiskenbaum, and Eaton, involving rehabilitation settings and addressing functional disability in the elderly, has also found positive effects of proactive coping, particularly on walking behavior and independence functioning and on feelings of vigor and vitality, emotions seen as important for psychological well-being.

The field of coping is becoming broader and now includes positive striving and emotions, goals, benefit finding, and search for meaning. Proactive coping theory is one example of a construct that embodies all of these dimensions. This theory builds upon Lazarus's cognitive appraisal approach and adds other dimensions to earlier work, including a temporal one. Moreover, proactive coping theory may be seen as bridging the gap between the construct of coping and those of action and volition. Extending the concept of coping to tenacious goal pursuit and personal growth offers a more comprehensive and precise depiction of human beings in their struggles and strivings. In light of daily obstacles and disappointments, one may assume that life is inherently stressful. Thus, *coping* becomes an appropriate label for behaviors that are over and above simple routines and habits. There may not necessarily be a concrete "stressor" that elicits coping behavior, as is depicted in the concept of reactive coping. Rather, self-imposed goals and visions may elicit opportunities and risks, and thus, the struggle for rewards and growth. Building a career or a house, writing a book, leading others to success, all represent situations with a continuous potential for the experience of stress. Use of proactive coping can be a valuable tool to improve one's quality of life.

SEE ALSO: ▶ Appetitive motivational systems   ▶ Coping   ▶ Self-efficacy

Problem-Solving Appraisal

P. Paul Heppner,[a] Dong-gwi Lee,[b] and Yuhong He[a]
[a]*University of Missouri – Columbia;* [b]*Yonsei University, Korea*

Problem-solving appraisal refers to one's self-perception or assessment of his or her problem-solving skills, attitudes, and styles to resolve everyday problems as well as stressful life events. In line with positive psychology, which focuses on identifying and promoting human strengths that can help people live more fulfilling lives as well as buffer stress, an important way to facilitate or optimize the process of promoting human strengths involves helping people develop effective problem-solving skills. One of the important components of problem-solving that has been studied extensively in psychology is a person's problem-solving appraisal. To date, there are more than 120 empirical studies conducted on problem-solving appraisal, which provided strong support for a significant overlap between problem-solving appraisal and actual problem-solving skills.

Brief History of Applied Problem-Solving

Psychologists have been interested in how people solve various problems for many years. Conceptualizations of the problem-solving in early literature include various learning, Gestalt, and computer-simulation approaches. In the 1970s psychologists began to divide problem-solving into two general categories, laboratory-type problems (e.g., water jar problems) and personal problems which often include emotional elements (e.g., difficult career choices). Intuitively, it made sense that people who had learned effective problem-solving skills would be more successful in a wide array of life tasks, and also would be psychologically adjusted. Researchers started identifying critical skills for helping individuals become more effective applied problem-solvers. Subsequently, more scholars joined in the study of how people solve real life problems and its implications for mental health issues and in helping professions. Conceptualizations of applied problem-solving in early literature include a constellation of relatively discrete, cognitive abilities or thought processes, and sequential models. For instance, researchers include Spivack and Shure who, in the 1960s and 1970s, studied interpersonal cognitive problem-solving skills such as problem sensitivity, means-ends thinking, alternative solution thinking, causal thinking, and consequential thinking. There was also the introduction by D'Zurilla and Goldfried of a sequential stage model (general orientation, problem definition and formulation, generation of alternatives, decision making, and verification). This model not only led to the development of problem-solving training interventions but also was used for conceptualizing psychotherapy activities. During the 1980s and 1990s, more sophisticated information processing theories were developed by researchers such as Anderson, which allowed further refinement of applied problem-solving models and training. For instance, at the beginning of the cognitive revolution in psychology, psychologists began to broaden the conceptualization of applied problem-solving not just in terms of the specific knowledge that individuals may apply directly to resolve problems, but with higher-order or metacognitive variables that affect how they will solve problems. In essence, an individual's self-appraisal of his or her problem-solving ability was hypothesized to be a central component of applied problem-solving as well as linked to coping effectively with stressful life events. A great deal of research has subsequently supported this hypothesis.

Measuring Problem-Solving Appraisal

A number of measures of applied problem-solving have been developed over the years, such as the Means-End Problem Solving Procedure, Problem-Solving Inventory (PSI), and Social Problem Solving Inventory. However, only the PSI is conceptualized as a measure of problem-solving appraisal. In addition, the PSI has been widely researched in over 120 studies across many countries, and is the most widely used measure of problem-solving appraisal. The rest of this entry will focus on problem-solving appraisal as measured by the PSI.

The PSI aims to access individuals' perceptions of their problem-solving ability, style, behavior and attitudes. It consists of 35 items, each having six possible responses from *strongly agree* (1) to *strongly disagree* (6), with lower scores indicating positive problem-solving appraisal. A person taking this instrument would receive scores on the following three subscales: 1) *Problem-Solving Confidence* is defined as an individual's general tendency to believe and trust in one's problem-solving abilities, a self-assurance in a wide range of problem-solving activities. 2) *Approach-Avoidance Style* is defined as a general tendency to approach or avoid different problem-solving activities. 3) *Personal Control* is defined as a general tendency to believe in one's emotional and behavioral control while engaging in problem-solving. An extensive body of empirical research supports the reliability and validity of the inventory across a range of populations and cultures. The PSI is an easy inventory to administer. It typically requires 15 minutes for completion and can be easily scored by hand or computer. The readability level is at the 9th grade (an adolescent version with 4th grade reading level also is available).

Associations with Problem-Solving Appraisal

Over 120 empirical investigations have been conducted on the relationships between problem-solving appraisal as measured by the PSI and psychological adjustment, physical health, coping, and educational and vocational issues. The literature suggests that peoples' application of their problem-solving capabilities is useful for understanding a broad range of human behaviors and that in general problem-solving appraisal is related to effective problem-solving skills as well as enhanced psychological and physical well-being.

Psychological Adjustment

Since problem-solving was first claimed to be linked to psychological adjustment in the early 1970s, numerous studies have been conducted to examine the relationship between problem-solving appraisal and psychological adjustment, particularly in five areas: a) general psychological and social adjustment; b) depression; c) hopelessness and suicidal behavior; d) alcohol use/abuse; and e) personality variables.

General Psychological and Social Adjustment

A positive problem-solving appraisal is related to positive self-concepts, greater locus of control, fewer personal problems, higher racial identity statuses in African American students, and better coping with grief experiences. In addition, it has been found that a positive problem-solving appraisal is associated with more advanced social skills, social easiness/trust, and more social support. Moreover, there seems to be an important chain of events in that the more people attempt to solve their problems, the more confident they are as problem-solvers, and subsequently they report higher levels of psychological adjustment. Thus, a positive problem-solving appraisal is related to higher levels of general psychological and social adjustment.

Depression

A more positive problem-solving appraisal is associated with lower levels of depression across a wide range of populations. For instance, a positive problem-solving appraisal in people such as college students, prisoners, patients with chronic low-back pain, adults with spinal-cord injuries, and a variety of cultures such as South Africa, Turkey, and China all reported lower levels of depression. In addition, a positive problem-solving appraisal seems to play a protective role with stress. That is, when people are under a great deal of stress, those who have a positive problem-solving appraisal experience less depression than those with a negative problem-solving appraisal. Thus, a positive problem-solving appraisal is associated with lower levels of depression, even when people are under a great deal of stress.

Hopelessness and Suicidal Behavior

A positive problem-solving appraisal, particularly problem-solving confidence, is associated with fewer feelings of hopelessness and suicidal ideation across a variety of populations (e.g., college students, correctional inmates, psychiatric patients, outpatient suicide ideators and attempters). Problem-solving appraisal also seems to play a protective role in warding off hopelessness when people are under a great deal of stress. There also seems to be a chain reaction among problem-solving appraisal, hopelessness and suicidal ideation, such that those with a more positive problem-solving appraisal, even if they experience hopelessness, tend to have lower levels of suicidal ideation. Thus, a positive problem-solving appraisal is associated with people feeling more hopeful in their lives and experience less suicidal ideation.

Alcohol Use and Abuse

A positive problem-solving appraisal is associated with less alcohol use and abuse. In addition, other research has found that there may be different drinking patterns associated with different components of problem-solving appraisal (i.e., those who lacked confidence but approached problems drank to enhance their mood, but those who lacked confidence and avoided problems drank to escape problems). Moreover, there is an interaction between alcohol abuse and parental drinking (i.e., students with more negative problem-solving appraisal and whose parents had more drinking problems reported more alcohol abuse).

Personality Variables

A positive problem-solving appraisal is associated with less trait anxiety (even when under a great deal of stress), less trait anger, and more trait curiosity. Moreover a positive problem-solving appraisal (particularly problem-solving confidence), is associated with less worrying, a sign of anxiety. In addition, a positive problem-solving appraisal has been linked with a stronger sense of instrumentality or agency to handle normal daily events as well as stressful life events. Thus, problem-solving appraisal is related to a number of personality variables that are related to important psychological constructs.

Physical Health

There is now a great deal of evidence that psychosocial factors have an important influence on physical health; problem-solving appraisal is one of those psychosocial factors that is related to physical health. Positive problem-solving appraisal is linked to positive health expectancies, more health promotion behaviors, as well as fewer health complaints about premenstrual and menstrual pain, chronic pain, cardiovascular problems, and health problems in general, particularly with clinical patients.

Additionally, a positive problem-solving appraisal is associated with fewer physical health outcome complications such as urinary track infections. Moreover, problem-solving appraisal is identified not only as one of the most successful measures to differentiate brain injured adults from controls (even over standard neuropsychological measures of problem-solving), but also the best predictor of community integration. Thus, there is an association between problem-solving appraisal and a range of physical health indices, which provides useful information about the role of psychosocial factors in positive physical health.

Coping

Problem-solving appraisal is related to the manner in which people respond to stressful life events, whether they respond to resolving the problem itself (problem-focused coping) or whether they tend to primarily respond to their emotions (emotion-focused coping). A positive problem-solving appraisal was associated with the consistent report of actively focusing on the problem and attempting to resolve the cause of the problem. One probable explanation for this relationship has been that those people with a positive problem-solving appraisal who tend to engage in problem-focused coping also tend to assume responsibility for personal problems and attempt to cope actively. In addition, problem-solving confidence and approach-avoidance style appear to be the strongest contributors to problem-focused coping activities, and a sense of personal control was particularly related to disengaging, denial, and emotion-focused coping. People's strategies for seeking and using helping resources are also related to their appraisal of the problem-solving skills. A positive appraisal is associated with more aware-ness of the availability of helping resources, higher rates of utilization, and more satisfaction with those resources. Similarly, when people seek counseling, those with a more positive problem-solving appraisal tend to report more positive out-comes in personal and career counseling.

Educational and Vocational Issues

People's problem-solving appraisal is also related to a wide range of educational and vocational issues. For example, a more positive problem-solving appraisal is related to less test anxiety, test irrelevant thinking, and better study skills even in at-risk students, across different educational levels and ages. However, problem-solving appraisal is related to measures of intelligence and academic aptitude. In addition, problem-solving appraisal is positively related to vocational adjustment, such as vocational identity, more certainty in career decision making, and more knowledge of career choices and career planning. Thus, how people appraise their problem solving in general is related to how they approach a specific task, such as career decision making and vocational adjustment in general.

Problem-Solving Training Interventions

In general, problem-solving training has involved teaching: a) specific components of problem-solving (e.g., problem definition skills, decision-making skills); b) a gen-eral problem-solving model; and c) specific problem-solving skills in conjunction with other interventions.

D'Zurilla, Nezu, and others have tried to enhance participants' problem-solving skills by teaching specific problem-solving skills associated within a specific prob-lem-solving stage (e.g., decision making). Usually the training lasts 45 minutes. People in the specific problem-solving skills training group typically have out-performed those in the control group on brief tasks or inventories designed to assess the particular problem-solving stage (e.g., decision making). However, questions remain about the generalizibility of such brief training to resolving complex and stressful real-life problems. Thus, other problem-solving training strategies have focused on teaching a general problem-solving model (such as the sequential-stage model), which usually includes didactics and practice in each of the stages over several training sessions, along with an applied integration step. This approach is effective with many populations (e.g., psychiatric patients) and target goals (e.g., substance abuse and addictions, depression, stress and anxiety). Teaching specific skills in conjunction with other interventions such as anxiety management, communication skills, or study skills often consists of one or more problem-solving component skills. Such training has been effective in a wide range of populations (e.g., academic underachievers, psychiatric patients) and target goals (e.g., depression, phobias, marital and family problems, cigarette smoking, weight problems). In short, problem-solving training offers a great deal of promise to enhance people's strengths to lead more effective and meaningful lives.

Future Directions

Future research and theory development could enhance our understanding of problem-solving appraisal and its role in psychological adjustment and coping. One promising direction may be to examine the construct in diverse populations (e.g., various U.S. racial/ethnic minority groups, people from countries other than the US, noncollege populations) and to distinguish between universal (*etic*) and culture-specific (*emic*) problem-solving appraisal. Another direction may be to examine the effect of individual components of problem-solving appraisal and the combination of the PSI factors (e.g., reporting being confident but avoiding problems) on people's development and life satisfaction. Finally, because we now know the connection between problem-solving appraisal and important life outcomes such as psychological adjustment and physical health, it is imperative that we train future generations to appraise their problem-solving capabilities positively.

SEE ALSO: ▶ Coping   ▶ Hope   ▶ Self-efficacy

Promotion Focus

E. Tory Higgins
Columbia University

Promotion focus is one of two distinct regulatory systems that has developed to deal with a distinct survival concern – nurturance. To survive, people (and other animals) need both nurturance and security; they need support or nourishment from the environment (often provided by others), as well as protection from dangers in the environment (social and physical dangers). When people succeed in satisfying a concern they experience pleasure, and when they fail they experience pain. Thus, both nurturance and security systems involve approaching pleasure and avoiding pain. However, the nurturance and security systems differ in *how* pleasure is approached and pain is avoided.

The nurturance motive is associated with the development of *promotion focus* which is concerned with accomplishment, with fulfilling hopes and aspirations (ideals). People can succeed or fail to fulfill their promotion concerns, and thus experience pleasure from success and pain from failure. But hedonic experiences are not the end of the story. There are distinct emotional and motivational consequences of self-regulation in a promotion focus.

Individuals with a promotion focus use ideal self-guides in their self-regulation. Self-guides are self-directive standards, which function as a major source of people's emotions and motivation. They both directly prompt action as desired end-states (i.e., goals to be attained), and, through their use in self-evaluation (i.e., standards to be met), arouse emotions that are themselves motivating. Ideal self-guides represent a person's hopes, wishes and aspirations. Ideal self-guides vary in strength across persons (between individuals) and across situations (within individuals). There are different modes of socialization that produce strong ideal self-guides. Strong ideal self-guides are produced by interactions with significant others that involve bolstering and supportiveness, as well as love withdrawal for failure to meet an ideal self-guide. When self-guides are strong from socialization, they have high chronic accessibility. They predominate in self-regulation for years. When strong ideal self-guides predominate, people have a promotion focus on accomplishment and advancement.

When people are in the promotion focus system, they experience cheerfulness-related emotions following success (e.g., happy, joyful) and dejection-related emotions following failure (e.g., sad, discouraged). This is true whether people are in a promotion focus from a chronic predisposition to be in that system or from a current situation activating that system. Individuals in a promotion focus more readily appraise objects and events (e.g., exams, money, garbage, music) along a cheerfulness-dejection dimension than along a quiescence-agitation dimension.

Individuals with a promotion focus not only have a distinct emotional life, they also have a distinct motivational life. Importantly, they have distinct *strategic preferences* when they pursue goals and make decisions. Individuals in a promotion focus prefer to use *eager* strategies to pursue goals – strategies of advancement (a gain), which move the actor from a current neutral or satisfactory state (the status quo) to a more desirable state. Individuals in a promotion focus experience positive and negative events in the world as gains and nongains, respectively, because their concerns are about accomplishments and aspirations.

Strategic eagerness is also about ensuring gains and not wanting to miss gains, so eagerness sustains or fits a promotion focus. Indeed, many studies have found that individuals in a promotion focus prefer to use eager strategies to pursue goals or make decisions. There is also evidence that when the strategic approach to an achievement task is experimentally manipulated, individuals in a promotion focus perform better when instructed to use eager means than when instructed to use vigilant means. Persuasive messages with an eager tone (vs. a vigilant tone) are more effective in changing the attitudes of individuals with a promotion focus. The promotion focus on eager gains also influences how ingroup bias is displayed. For individuals in a promotion focus, ingroup members are treated with a positive bias ("promoting us") rather than treating outgroup members with a negative bias ("preventing them").

The fact that eagerness sustains or fits a promotion focus has other implications as well. It means that individuals with a promotion focus will be motivated to imagine or anticipate future success in order to create an eagerness in the present that will sustain their current motivation. Because of this, individuals who are effective at sustaining their promotion focus are more optimistic than other people and have higher self-esteem. In addition, when they fail at a task they are less likely than other people to lower their expectations and, instead, continue to expect success the next time. After failure they will even raise their self-esteem if they need to remain eager for the next task. The higher self-esteem associated with individuals who have effective promotion has been found not only in the United States but also in other nations, such as in Italy, India, Israel, and Japan. Because extroversion also involves eagerness to meet new people and being enthusiastic, there is also evidence in each of these nations that individuals who have effective promotion behave in a more extroverted manner than other people.

Regulatory fit increases strength of engagement which intensifies evaluative reactions, and regulatory nonfit decreases strength of engagement which deintensifies evaluative reactions. This contributes to the emotional responses of individuals with a promotion focus. When individuals succeed in a promotion focus, it increases their eagerness, creating a regulatory fit that strengthens engagement, which is then experienced as high intensity joy. When individuals fail in a promotion focus, it decreases their eagerness, creating a regulatory nonfit that reduces engagement strength, which is then experienced as low intensity sadness. When failures become severe and prolonged, individuals with a strong promotion focus are vulnerable to suffering from dejection-depression, which is an extreme state of underengagement ("having no interest in doing things").

Regulatory focus differences in strategic approaches are especially likely to be revealed when there is a conflict between different choices or different ways to proceed on a task. One prevalent conflict is between being "risky" or being "conservative" when making a judgment or decision. When people are uncertain, they can take a chance and treat something as being correct that could actually be incorrect (a possible error of commission). Alternatively, they can be cautious and reject something as being incorrect that could actually be correct (a possible error of omission). Studies on memory, judgment, and decision making have found that, when the status quo is satisfactory, individuals with a strong promotion focus tend to more risky than other people. There is also evidence that individuals in a promotion focus are more creative than those in a prevention focus, and are also more willing to change and try something new when given the opportunity. Under conditions of uncertainty (and a satisfactory status quo), individuals in a promotion focus, compared to other people, are more willing to consider new alternatives and not simply stick with the established state of affairs.

There are other conflicts on which individuals in a promotion focus act differently than other people. One classic conflict on many tasks is between speed (or quantity) and accuracy (or quality). Compared to others, individuals with a promotion focus emphasize speed more than accuracy. A third conflict concerns whether to represent objects or events in a more global and abstract manner or in a more local and concrete manner. Compared to others, individuals with a promotion focus are more likely to represent objects and events in a global and abstract manner (as well as more temporally distant) than in a local and concrete manner, whereas the opposite is true for those in a prevention focus.

SEE ALSO: ▶ Goals and goal theory ▶ Hedonics ▶ Prevention focus ▶ Self-esteem ▶ Self-regulation

Protective Factor

Ann S. Masten and Janette E. Herbers
University of Minnesota, Twin Cities

Protective factors are predictors of positive outcomes among people at risk for developing problems as a result of adverse life events or experiences. Interest in protective factors emerged in the context of research on resilience in the 1970s, as scientists began to search for explanations of unexpectedly good adjustment among individuals exposed to negative experiences. Initially, research was focused on identifying the qualities of individuals, their relationships, or other qualities in their environments that were associated with positive adaptation to risk or adversity. Eventually, research turned to deeper questions about how protective factors work and how to facilitate resilience by mobilizing protective processes.

Pioneering scientists recognized that protective factors represented important clues to resilience processes, with the potential to inform intervention. Early researchers, such as Norman Garmezy, Michael Rutter, and Emmy Werner, observed striking consistencies in the protective factors found across diverse studies of individuals who overcame significant challenges in their lives. Subsequently, this "short list" of protective factors would be corroborated many times across diverse studies of resilience.

Widely Reported Protective Factors

The short list of protective factors for resilience in young people includes attributes of the individual, family, and neighborhood that are associated with positive adaptation in the context of risk or adversity. At the top of the list is an involved and competent parent figure or mentor. Effective parenting in the context of a close relationship with a caring and capable adult appears to be the key protective factor in the lives of young children undergoing adversity. As children grow older, close relationships with additional supportive people such as friends, romantic partners, and mentors also become more important. By adulthood, the protective factors based in relationships are often described in terms of social capital or social support.

Individual attributes strongly associated with resilience in childhood and adulthood include an array of cognitive skills related to problem solving and intelligent behavior; motivation and self-efficacy related to achievement; and hope for the future, faith, and beliefs that life has meaning. Self-regulation skills appear to be crucial protective factors for children and adults as they overcome difficult times, including capabilities for controlling and directing one's own attention, arousal, emotion, and behavior in order to achieve goals.

Community-based protective factors include effective schools, resources such as health care, recreational centers, religious institutions and emergency services. As research on protective factors for midlife and aging adults expands, the list of protective factors in the community is also growing.

As research advances, there is more attention to the changing role of protective factors across development and also to the possibility that the same factor may be protective for one person at one point in time but not for the same person at another point in time or in a different situation. Similarly, the same factor may be protective for one person and not another, such as for a boy but not a girl in the same community. The importance of friendship as a protective factor increases across childhood; infants are not protected by close friendships (or their own cognitive abilities) in the same ways as older children or adults. It is also conceivable that the same personality characteristic, such as shyness, could create difficulties for a child entering school for the first time, yet serve to protect a young person from risky behavior in deviant peer groups during adolescence.

Distinguishing Protective Factors from Assets and Other Positive Factors

As research on resilience expanded, it became evident that many of the protective factors associated with positive adaptation under risky or hazardous circumstances were the same factors that predict positive outcomes in general. Good intellectual skills and good parenting, for example, predict favorable development at all levels of risk or adversity. This observation led to a differentiation between factors that play a special role under negative or risky conditions and those that play the same role no matter what level of adversity is experienced. The terms *promotive factors* or *assets* are widely used to denote factors that are generally associated with positive outcomes, regardless of risk level, whereas the term *protective factors* denotes a special role when there is high risk or adversity exposure. Some factors function both ways. There is considerable evidence that good problem-solving skills and good parenting generally promote healthy development, but also that in very challenging life situations these factors play a particularly important role in protecting children from the worst ravages of adversity.

There also can be protective factors that *only* play a role when there is exposure to hazardous conditions, much like the airbag in an automobile or a vaccine that creates antibodies against specific infectious diseases. In communities, emergency social services, such as a crisis nursery or a domestic violence shelter, operate in this way.

Vulnerability versus Protection

It has also been tricky to distinguish promotive and protective factors from risks and vulnerabilities, because many positive factors reflect underlying bipolar dimensions that have a positive and negative pole. It is often difficult to tell where the action is occurring, for example, when analysis indicates a moderating effect of a variable such as parenting quality on adaptive behavior. Ineffective parenting can function as a vulnerability or a risk factor for a child growing up in hazardous circumstances, just as effective parenting can function as a promotive or pro-tective factor. In many cases, the role of the factor is probably occurring along a continuum, with effects extending from the negative to the positive.

Research on How Protective Factors Work

Once the evidence on sets of protective factors associated with positive outcomes in the resilience literature began to accumulate, investigators were interested in understanding how protective factors work and also what could be done to facil-itate the processes behind these factors. Answers to "How?" questions are crucial for designing effective programs and interventions to help people adapt well or recover in the face of adversity. Yet it is not easy to study how protection works during a crisis or following a disaster. One cannot randomly assign people to conditions that vary in hazards or protections. Instead, investigators have begun to design preventive interventions and programs on the basis of resilience models, attempting to reduce risk, boost resources, or mobilize powerful protective systems strongly implicated by research on protective factors.

Protective factors frequently implicated in developmental resilience research probably reflect powerful human adaptive systems that are the legacy of biolog-ical and cultural evolution. These basic adaptive systems include the attachment system and the family; the central nervous system as manifested in problem-solving, learning, and other aspects of adaptive behavior; religion and other cul-tural systems; the mastery motivation system; stress response systems; and other systems that humans engage in in the course of adapting to threatening, destab-ilizing, or traumatic circumstances. When these fundamental adaptive systems are operating normally, human individuals have considerable capacity for weather-ing the storms of life and recovering from temporarily overwhelming trauma. The greatest damage to human functioning and development occurs when catas-trophic or cumulative experiences destroy, harm, or overwhelm these systems or their development in a lasting way.

The most powerful experiments to test resilience theory are intervention experiments to engage the power of these adaptive systems for resilience and ascertain whether positive change results from the intervention. Thus, experiments have been designed, for example, to improve the effectiveness of parenting for children faced with bereavement or divorce, to provide a mentor or build self-regulation skills for highly disadvantaged children, to boost self-efficacy or school bonding for adolescents living in dangerous neighborhoods, or to recover a sense that life has meaning and hope in the future for survivors of war or natural disasters, all in an effort to mobilize protective processes for people undergoing adversity. Evidence is accumulating that it is possible to promote and prepare for resilience by boosting assets and protections in individuals, their relationships, and their environments.

Emerging Research Directions

A fourth wave of research on resilience is now rising, characterized by integrative studies of resilience across levels of analysis, species, and disciplines. There is intense interest in the biology and neuroscience of protective processes and also in the possibility that protective systems affected by early adversity in development can be corrected or reprogrammed. At the same time, there is growing interest in protective systems beyond the individual, embedded in religion and other cultural traditions, organizations, ecosystems, information or communication systems, and the many other systems that humans interact with every day. There is increasing recognition, for example, that preparation for disasters requires a better understanding of how protective systems for human life work across many interdependent systems, from the level of individuals and families to the level of communities, nations, and global systems.

SEE ALSO: ▶ Attachment theory   ▶ Developmental psychopathology
▶ Resilience   ▶ Self-regulation   ▶ Werner, Emmy

Psychological Adjustment

Cherisse L. Seaton
University of Northern British Columbia

In psychological research, *adjustment* refers both to an achievement or outcome as well as a process. As an achievement, *psychological adjustment* is a phrase used to denote positive mental health. The concept of positive mental health is detailed extensively in Jahoda's classic conceptualization and refers to an individual's state of mind and overall well-being. The process conceptualization of psychological adjustment reflects whether an individual is able to cope effectively with the demands of the environmental context as well as with the stress created by these demands. Thus, as a process, psychological adjustment reflects the relative adaptation of an individual to changing environmental conditions.

The Dimensions of Adjustment in Research and Theory

Psychological adjustment is a popular outcome measure in psychological research, and often measures such as self-esteem, or the absence of distress, anxiety, or depression are used as indicators of adjustment. Researchers may also measure an individuals' level of adjustment or well-being in response to some stressful event, such as divorce, or as the absence of deviant behavior, such as drinking or drug use. Although adjustment is a broad concept as well as an abstract construct by definition, it can generally be broken down into four major dimensions. The major dimensions include: 1) psychological adjustment as the absence of psychological symptoms (e.g., depression, anxiety); 2) psychological adjustment as normality, or the condition of the majority; 3) measures of well-being as indicators of positive adjustment (e.g., self-esteem, life satisfaction); and 4) psychological adjustment as an individual's characteristic level of positive adaptation (e.g., resilience, emotional intelligence). The first three dimensions of psychological adjustment refer to adjustment as an achievement (mental health), and the fourth dimension is a measure of adjustment as a process.

A great deal of psychological research has been dedicated to the assessment of adjustment as the absence of psychological symptoms over the century. In this area, researchers have studied a range of symptoms from clinical diagnoses of mental illness to recovering from stress. The presence or absence of depression is a popular indicator of psychological adjustment as well as the presence or absence of anxiety. Adjustment to stress-inducing life events, such as divorce, as well as the level of adjustment in groups considered to be disadvantaged (e.g., at-risk youth) are also commonly studied in mainstream psychology. However, defining adjustment or mental health as the opposite or absence of mental illness has disadvantages. For example, the definition of what constitutes mental illness is vague, and is subject to social and cultural standards. Jahoda suggested that the absence of mental illness may be necessary, but not sufficient to the construct of mental health and psychological adjustment.

The dimension of psychological adjustment as normality is apparent in research that defines adjustment as the absence of "deviant" behavior (e.g., drinking, drug use, gang membership). In this line of research, adjustment refers to how closely an individual conforms to statistical norms, and those who deviate from the norm are considered abnormal or maladjusted. The operationalization of adjustment as normality is often observed in research conducted in the health psychology field; for example, obesity reflects a marked deviation in weight from that considered to be normal for the individual's height and age. A low IQ relative to the majority is also considered a marker of abnormality, or poor mental health; however, in the dimension of psychological adjustment as normality, individuals who are doing extremely well relative to the population are also considered abnormal (e.g., those with abnormally high IQ scores). Another problem with this operationalization is that norms are defined by culture; belief in witchcraft in present day North America would be considered abnormal, while in previous centuries such beliefs were normal and acceptable.

The dimension of psychological adjustment as well-being has been widely studied and more recently drawn under the wing of the positive psychology movement. Life satisfaction, for example, is a measure of subjective well-being and has been of interest to psychologists for years. Self-esteem has also been considered to be closely linked with adjustment and coping, and consequentially has been promoted in youth for years. An individual's current level of happiness, or positive affect, is also a measure of well-being.

Assessing adjustment as well-being alone also has drawbacks. For one, self-reported well-being is subject to social desirability. An individual may also be consciously unaware of and therefore unable to report his or her disturbance or mental illness. Likewise, individuals with severe mental illnesses may nonetheless report being happy and satisfied with their lives. Finally, subjective well-being is necessarily dependent on situation. A parent who has recently lost a child should not be expected to report happiness in response. Thus, the dimension of well-being may also be necessary but not sufficient to the construct of adjustment.

Emotional intelligence is one example of a concept that is used to assess characteristic levels of adaptation. Emotional intelligence consists of the ability to identify, express, understand, and regulate emotions in one's self and others and reflects individual differences in skills for handling emotion-laden problems. Overall, emotional intelligence is an underlying skill that promotes adaptive coping, greater adaptation to changing environments, as well as positive psychological adjustment.

Resilience is another construct that reflects positive psychological adjustment. Ego resiliency, in particular, reflects the strength or maturity of the ego in dealing with adversity.

> Ego-resiliency refers to the dynamic capacity of an individual to modify a characteristic level of ego-control, in either direction, as a function of the demand characteristics of the environmental context, so as to preserve or enhance system equilibration. (Block & Kremen, 1996, p. 351)

Resilience is effective coping when faced with adversity and provides a protective buffer against the effects of stress, resulting in health benefits for the resilient individual. It is not that resilient individuals do not recognize conflicts (which would not be adaptive); they are just better able to adjust to or integrate negative events. For example, Tugade and Fredrickson reported that resilience did not predict the magnitude of participants' cardiovascular reactions to stress, but that resilient participants' cardiovascular activation returned to baseline faster following a stressful task. The concept of resilience overlaps that of psychological adjustment, as resilience reflects the ability to adapt or adjust to changing circumstances.

A Theory of Positive Adaptation

The most comprehensive work to date, in the area of positive psychological adjustment, is Shelly Taylor's theory of cognitive adaptation. This theory holds that positive psychological adjustment following adversity involves finding meaning, regaining perceived control (mastery) and enhancing self-esteem. Meaning and mastery are often inseparable, as knowing the cause of the experience (e.g., believing that a high-fat diet causes cancer), allows an individual to feel he or she can control the experience (i.e., cancer can be prevented from reoccurring by changing diet). Individuals enhance their self-esteem by making downward comparisons, for example, by believing they are coping better than others whose condition is not as severe. It is evident that the concept of effective coping also corresponds closely to psychological adjustment or adaptation, as well as overlaps the concept of resilience.

The Subtle Difference between Resilience and Flourishing

Researchers have been interested in the process of resiliency for a long time; however, the process by which individual's are able to flourish following adversity is not well understood. When an individual undergoes a traumatic experience or life-threatening event, it challenges their personal adjustment or adaptation. A traumatic experience brings into question an individual's worldviews, or their assumptions about the world (for example, the view that the world is just), and forces the individual to realize that he or she is fragile. Recovering from or adjusting to such an experience must involve one of two processes: the individual will either *assimilate* the trauma into his or her existing worldview or he or she will *accommodate* his or her worldview to accept the new information. For example, using assimilation, a person might reason that he or she personally caused his or her own traumatic experience (e.g., "I was attacked because I was walking too late at night in a dangerous neighborhood"). Perceiving the experience in this way allows the individual to maintain a sense of perceived control over his or her experience (i.e., he or she believe he or she can prevent it from happening again), as well as to maintain his or her worldview that the world is just. This is the process described by the theory of cognitive adaptation.

Conversely, an individual can change his or her worldview via accommodation. The process of accommodation can be either negative (e.g., "The world is unjust and random"), leading to feelings of helplessness and depression, or it can be positive (e.g., "Life is short, so I should enjoy each day as if it were my last"). Joseph and Linley argue that an individual can attain positive growth following adversity only through the process of positive accommodation, and that the process of assimilation will only lead to increased defense use and vulnerability to posttraumatic stress disorder. The process of positive assimilation may allow an individual to be resilient in the face of adversity, but not necessarily experience positive growth, as positive growth requires the adoption of a new worldview. It is only via positive accommodation, and changing existing worldviews that an individual can truly transcend the event and flourish.

Criteria of Psychological Adjustment

Several researchers have outlined criteria for psychological adjustment, including Jahoda's review of positive mental health, Ryff's dimensions of well-being, and Keyes and Lopez's more recent concept of "complete mental health." The criteria described by these authors are meant to better define the broad construct of mental health as well as to distinguish characteristics that may be necessary for psychological adjustment.

Jahoda outlined six criteria or approaches to the concept of mental health or adjustment: 1) an individual's attitude towards themselves; 2) an individual's level of growth, development or self-actualization; 3) an integration of personality or a balanced and flexible consciousness; 4) autonomy; 5) an accurate perception of reality; and 6) environmental mastery. Thus, according to Jahoda's criteria, in order to have positive mental health, an individual must have a positive and accurate view of him- or herself, be striving toward goals, be balanced, independent, not distort reality, and be able to successfully adapt to environmental demands.

Carol Ryff integrated several theoretical perspectives to generate six dimensions of psychological well-being and positive functioning. These theory-guided dimensions include: 1) self-acceptance; 2) positive relations with others; 3) autonomy; 4) environmental mastery; 5) purpose in life; and 6) personal growth. Thus, to be considered to have high psychological well-being, or adjustment, an individual must be accepting of both the positive and negative aspects of him- or herself and his or her past, be intimate and effective in human relationships, independent, competent in managing his or her environment, have goals and a sense of direction, be open to new experiences and see him- or herself as continually growing.

Keyes and Lopez's concept of complete mental health is currently the most integrated approach to psychological adjustment. In this model, complete mental health includes psychological well-being, emotional well-being, social well-being combined with low levels of mental illness. The concept of psychological well-being in this model is taken from Ryff's definition, described above. Emotional well-being is subjective well-being, such as happiness, life satisfaction and positive affect. Finally, social well-being in this model consists of five dimensions that indicate how well an individual is functioning in their social world. The dimensions are from Keyes' social well-being model and include: 1) social integration, or the sense of belonging; 2) social contribution, or one's value in society; 3) social coherence, or a perception of society that is organized and meaningful; 4) social acceptance, or positive attitudes towards others; and 5) social actualization, or the belief in the potential of society. Keyes and Lopez's model comprises a four-fold typology, in which positive functioning (psychological, emotional and social well-being) and mental illness are two distinct dimensions. In this model, an individual who has both high well-being and low mental illness is considered to be flourishing, while an individual who has low well-being and high mental illness is floundering. Individuals with high well-being but high mental illness are deemed to be struggling, and those with low well-being and low mental illness are considered to be languishing.

Measures of Psychological Adjustment

Although many outcome variables are employed as indirect assessments of an individual's adjustment (as discussed earlier), more direct measures have been developed as well. These measures typically employ a mix of mental health, well-being and positive adaptation or growth dimensions. For example, Ryff's Psychological Well-being Scales, which includes six subscales (positive growth, autonomy, environmental mastery, positive relations with others, purpose in life and self-acceptance), mirror her six theoretical dimensions of psychological well-being. Ryff's measure is a self-report instrument to which participants respond on a Likert scale. Keyes created a social well-being measure to assess the five dimensions of social well-being, and this measure, along with Ryff's well-being scales, and other measures of emotional well-being and mental illness are employed by Keyes and Lopez to capture their model of complete mental health. Other scales include the Crawford Psychological Adjustment Scale and more specific measures of adjustment, such as the Personality Adjustment Questionnaire, to measure psychological adjustment in children.

SEE ALSO: ▶ Adaptability   ▶ Emotional intelligence   ▶ Flourishing
▶ Mental health   ▶ Resilience

Reference

Block, J., & Kremen, A. M. (1996). IQ and ego-resiliency: Conceptual and empirical connections and separateness. *Journal of Personality and Social Psychology, 70*(2), 349–361.

Psychological Capital

Mihaly Csikszentmihalyi and Jeanne Nakamura
Claremont Graduate University

The concept of psychological capital emerged from three decades of research on flow, a state of complete experiential involvement in the activity at hand. In particular, the idea of psychological capital builds upon the prior concept of the "autotelic personality." It was observed that some individuals were able to enjoy, or find flow in, even the routine and the difficult aspects of their lives, whereas others would report being bored or stressed. For instance, surveys conducted in the US and in Germany reported that about 15% of representative samples of the adult population in both countries reported never having experienced flow, whereas a similar proportion claimed to experience it every day, with the remainder reporting various frequencies between these two extremes. These and later studies suggested that there might be a trait-like disposition to achieve flow, or a subjective state that is "autotelic" (i.e., being its own goal), even when the external conditions were not conducive to it. This is what came to be called the *autotelic personality*.

It became apparent, however, that important as the concept of the autotelic personality was, it had its limitations. Because flow can be experienced in a variety of settings, some of which are undesirable – for example, extreme risk, or activities such as gambling that become addictive without providing positive developmental outcomes – the concept of the autotelic personality could not distinguish between people who were on a trajectory of positive personal growth, and those whose flow experiences in the moment were likely to lead to a developmental dead end.

Because of these considerations, the authors began to extend the idea of autotelic personality into a lifespan concept, and called the resulting construct *psychological capital*, or PK. We argued that the quality of our lives depends on the habits of attentional investment we develop. These attentional structures are the basic resources needed to access and interpret information. How we invest attention, and in what objects, will determine the experiences we have, and thus the quality of life. We call PK the ability to allocate attention so as to generate positive experiences in the present, and in ways that are likely to provide positive experiences in the future as well. Table 5 summarizes how various ways of investing attention result in different experiential outcomes. When a person is able to derive positive experiences from the moment, while at the same time doing something that is likely to improve the quality of experience in the future, that person is *forming psychological capital*. The ability to choose a desirable focus for one's attention, and the ability to keep attention concentrated on desired objects, is what makes the building of capital possible. For a child, this means developing interests and focused curiosity as well as habits of attention that are likely to provide positive experiences in adulthood.

Table 5   Four Ways of Investing Attention.

		Is the experience positive now?	
		Yes	No
Is it likely to be	Yes	Capital Formation	Postponed Gratification
positive in the future?	No	Resources Consumed	Resources Wasted

Positive experience in the moment that is unlikely to provide positive experiences in the future corresponds to the process of *consuming* one's attentional resources. One might derive pleasure or even flow, but fail to add to one's meta-skills for enjoying experience. Many forms of entertainment provide immediate positive experiences without increasing the likelihood that the person will be able to enjoy future events.

The opposite situation obtains when the present activity is not positively experienced, but it promises to improve the quality of experience in the future – as is common in classroom learning or when practicing a difficult skill. As with any form of investment, future outcomes are not entirely predictable. In attentional as in financial investment the odds of having more positive returns in the future might be enhanced, but never assured. Thus *postponing gratification* could be a wise choice, but not necessarily the best: What if the years of boring preparation do not result in the expected positive outcomes? Much of the developmental research on self-discipline and self-regulation assumes that these processes require voluntary, effortful investments of attention that are experienced as difficult and tedious. But if one learns to enjoy an activity that promises to help us reach a distant goal, the effortful concentration required when we postpone gratification begins to turn effortless. This is the kind of process that leads to capital formation.

When neither present nor future provides enjoyment, one's limited opportunities to experience are truly *wasted*. Unfortunately, studies with the experience sampling method (ESM) suggest that many adolescents and young adults often feel that what they do is neither enjoyable now, nor is it likely to be so later. If such a condition persists through life, it threatens to deprive existence of its experiential rewards. In other words, the person who fails to derive enjoyment from the past as well as from the future will reach the end of life with nothing positive to show for it.

Intellectual Context

The concept of psychological capital thus stands in instructive contrast to such well-established concepts as delay of gratification, and the associated developmental theories that chart the acquisition of impulse control. These lines of work are concerned with the future yield of acquired self-regulatory habits, but they do not focus on the yield in terms of present – or future – experiential rewards. In addition, much as the flow model has held implications for the nature and conditions of suboptimal experience, particularly the states of boredom and anxiety, we anticipate that the concept of PK will cross-fertilize productively with theory and research on pleasure and addiction.

The term psychological capital was chosen to highlight the parallel to a number of other characteristics that the social sciences have recognized as resources individuals possess in varying degrees, which yield returns in the future: economic capital, or means of production; human capital, or credentials and expertise; cultural capital, or assets that derive from the symbolic culture (e.g., "taste"); and social capital, or relational resources. Organizational psychologist Fred Luthans and his colleagues have recently introduced a concept that they call *positive psychological capital* or PsyCap, to label a set of positive personality traits that have been shown to be assets in the workplace: hope; optimism; confidence or efficacy; and resiliency. Like PK, the concept of PsyCap attempts to identify personal resources that affect an individual's capacity to take advantage of the other resources that he or she possesses.

What differentiates the present notion of PK from all of these other constructs, including PsyCap, is the fact that it is psychological in both its *nature* and *effect*. Whereas the other forms of capital derive their significance from the returns they provide in terms of productivity and material accomplishment, PK has its yield in enhanced subjective well-being.

Directions for Future Research and Application

The shift from the concept of autotelic personality to the idea of PK opens up a number of directions for the future. The measurement of PK will entail assessing the psychological resources for: 1) regulating one's own attention; 2) deriving rewards from present experience; and (3) investing attention in directions likely to yield experiential rewards in the future, as well. Research on autotelic personality has used the ESM to assess naturalistically individuals' capacity to structure their own experience so that it provides subjective rewards. We anticipate that the quality of experience *in vivo*, and the way that individuals allocate attention in everyday life, will also be an ideal window on psychological capital. Among the many intriguing questions for future research and theory are: 1) the origins of PK; 2) the contributors to its development and deployment over the life course; and 3) the dynamics of its expression in interactions with the environment, both at the microlevel of attention regulation and at the more macrolevel of navigating the life course.

PK is most immediately relevant to scholarship addressing such developmental issues as self-regulation, resilience, and postponement of gratification. It promises to have substantial application to research in parenting, education, and preparation for adulthood. How psychological capital is best used in later life, and how it is passed down to future generations, open up new directions for research. Finally, the relevance of PK to psychology in general consists in pointing out that the main measure of a good life is not how much success a person has achieved, or how much knowledge, power, or material resources he or she has accumulated, but rather the quality of the experiences one has had over the course of life.

SEE ALSO: ▶ Csikszentmihalyi, Mihaly   ▶ Flow   ▶ Future mindedness

Psychoneuroimmunology

Kathi L. Heffner
Ohio University

Definition and Historical Grounding

Psychoneuroimmunology (PNI) is the scientific study of bidirectional communication between the brain and immune system, and it is grounded in a fundamental health perspective linking mind and body. The domain of PNI research includes the examination of the nervous and endocrine system pathways mediating brain-immune communication, the psychosocial and behavioral factors that play a role in these nervous (neuro), endocrine, and immune system interactions, and aspects of physical, psychological, and social well-being that can be provoked, modulated, or attenuated by these processes.

In 1964, George Solomon first used the term *psychoimmunology* in what has become a landmark publication describing his theoretical approach to understanding relationships among emotions, immune functioning, and disease. In his 1980 presidential address to the American Psychosomatic Society, Robert Ader coined the term psychoneuroimmunology when summarizing research on the interactions among bodily systems that maintain health and their associations with social, psychological and behavioral factors. Although these moments were pivotal in formally defining the field, psychoneuroimmunology has historical roots in mind-body research dating back to the early half of the twentieth century. It was at this time that investigators began to observe associations among psychological, emotional, and behavioral characteristics and immune-related diseases such as allergy, asthma, rheumatoid arthritis, and infectious disease. These early studies paved the way for the brain-immune communication research subsequently advanced by Ader and Solomon, and by the mid-1970s two foci in psychoneuroimmunology emerged. As highlighted by Solomon's work, close attention to the role of emotion and stress in immune pathways contributing to health and disease grew. Concurrently, investigators in the tradition of Pavlov and led by Ader and Nicholas Cohen were investigating how the immune system could be conditioned to respond to non-pathogenic stimuli like sugar water and pain. These empirical traditions continue in PNI research and have grown to include the study of psychosocial factors related to resiliency of the immune system, as well as behavioral and psychological interventions that protect and strengthen immune function.

The Immune System: Form, Function and Measurement

The immune system functions to defend our bodies against invading pathogens, like bacteria or viruses, and to assist with control of malignant disease, such as cancerous cell growth. Thus, the first task of the immune system is to recognize *self* from *nonself.* This task is accomplished initially and primarily by cells termed *phagocytes*, which include cell-ingesting macrophages and neutrophils, by complement proteins that can destroy bacteria and help up-regulate phagocytes, and by natural killer (NK) cells which can destroy virus-infected cells, bacteria, and cancerous cells. Together, this first line of nonself recognition is referred to as *innate* or *natural immunity*, and is responsible for the generalized inflammation response to pathogens. A continued inflammatory response that is unable to resolve an infection will initiate the next phase of defense known as *adaptive* or *specific immunity.*

The adaptive immune response is characterized by the activation and proliferation (replication) of cells called *lymphocytes* that have receptors for specific pathogens. The lymphocytes primarily responsible for the adaptive response include cytotoxic T-cells, B-cells, and T-helper cells. Cytotoxic T-cells destroy infected or transformed cells. B-cells produce proteins called *antibody* that serve many functions, including tagging pathogens for recognition and destruction by phagocytes and preventing viruses from entering cells. There are two arms of adaptive immunity. The *cellular* arm is characterized by activation of the cytotoxic T-cells in response to intracellular viruses or bacteria, whereas the *humoral* arm is characterized by activation of B-cells to produce antibody in response to extracellular viruses, bacteria or parasites. T-helper cells produce chemical mediators called *cytokines* that coordinate the cellular and humoral responses to pathogens: the Th-1 subclass of T-helper cells produce cytokines associated with proinflammatory, cellular responses. Th-2 cytokines function to inhibit inflammation and activate the humoral arm of immunity. In general, natural immunity occurs quickly, is a generalized response to infection that does not require specific recognition of a pathogen, and requires less energy on the part of the organism; adaptive immunity follows natural immunity, results in the proliferation of cells and production of antibody that are specific to the pathogen, and requires more energy mobilization.

Measurement of the immune system entails the quantification of cell numbers, immune-relevant protein levels, and function of immune cells by immune assaying techniques. *Enumerative* immune assays provide basic measures of cell counts, that is, the numbers of immune cells in a sample of peripheral blood. Other assaying techniques provide quantification of levels of immune-relevant proteins in the blood, including cytokines and antibodies. *Functional* immune assays assess the performance capacity of cells. More commonly used functional assaying techniques provide measurement of proliferative responses of lymphocytes to foreign substances, the ability of NK cells to kill other cells, and cells' ability to produce cytokines in response to stimulation.

Communication Pathways Between the Brain and Immune System

Although once thought of as an autonomously functioning system, the immune system is now known to communicate bidirectionally with the central nervous system (which includes the brain and spinal cord) via the peripheral nervous and endocrine systems. These two systems operate in parallel in response to both infection and psychological stress. For example, as the activating branch of the peripheral nervous system, the sympathetic nervous system regulated by the hypothalamus in the brain has direct input – via neural pathways – into lymphoid organs (tissues that house lymphocytes and other immune cells). Activation of the sympathetic nervous system by pathogens, environmental threats or emotional states can stimulate lymphoid tissue to release immune cells into circulation. Immune cells also have receptors for norepinephrine that is released by the sympathetic nervous system when activated: Norepinephrine can affect both NK cell activity and lymphocyte proliferation.

In addition to activating sympathetic pathways, the hypothalamus controls aspects of the hormone-producing endocrine system. Much of the emphasis in psychoneuroimmunology has been on two regulatory endocrine pathways that support bodily responses to pathogenic and psychological challenges.

The first is the *sympathetic-adrenal medullary* (SAM) axis, which is responsible for the release of epinephrine (adrenaline) by the adrenal glands in response to sympathetic nervous system activation. Epinephrine, once in circulation, can quickly increase cardiac activity to help support immediate responses to threats. Epinephrine also has affects on lymphocyte function and trafficking, and in general, appears to have immediate stimulating effects on aspects of immune function.

Activated in parallel to the SAM axis during infection or environmental threat is the *hypothalamic-pituitary-adrenocorticotropin axis*. It is during activation of this axis that the hypothalamus releases corticotropin-releasing factor (CRF) which then stimulates the pituitary gland to release adrenocorticotropin hormone (ACTH). ACTH travels through circulation to the adrenal glands where it stimulates the adrenals to release glucocorticoids. Cortisol is the key glucocorticoid in humans. Cortisol can have powerful regulatory effects on the immune system by, for example, reducing the activity of lymphocytes and modulating inflammatory processes.

This brain-neuroendocrine-immune pathway includes feedback loops that create a system of bidirectional communication such that increases in hormones and other substances released via the endocrine and nervous systems are detected by the brain. The brain can in turn increase or decrease activity of the SAM and HPA pathways as necessary. Other aspects of immune function can also communicate with the brain to modify subsequent immune activity and, most intriguingly, can also interact with the central nervous system to affect behavior. Cytokines released by T-helper cells in response to infection interact with the central nervous system and signal to the brain the presence of immune activation. In this role, the immune system can serve as a sensory system communicating the status of the body to the brain. In response to increasing cytokine levels, the brain also activates behavioral systems that contribute to recovery from infection. These *sickness behaviors* that result can include social withdrawal, fatigue, and anhedonia (reduced pleasure). Understanding the role of the immune system in behavior has led to greater attention to neuroimmune mechanisms involved in links between disease, such as cardiovascular disease or chronic pain, and mood disturbances characterized by sickness-related behaviors, such as clinical depression.

Psychosocial Factors and Immune Function: Focus on Stress

Contemporary PNI inquiry has predominantly focused on relationships between stress and the immune system, with attention to the nervous (SAM) and endocrine (HPA) system mediators that coordinate stress responses which, in turn, interact with the immune system. A 2004 review by Segerstrom and Miller provides strong evidence for effects of distinct stressors on immune function. Generally, short-term, time-limited (acute) stressors appear to be associated with an upregulation of natural immunity, including redistribution of immune cells and mobilization of natural immunity in preparation for potential injury or infection, with a return to resting function at the conclusion of the stressor. These changes are seen as adaptive in the context of short-term fight or flight responses to acute challenges. Brief, naturalistic stressors, involving coping with a shorter-term real-life challenge, such as an academic examination period, are characterized by a shift in the Th-1/Th-2 cytokine balance from cellular responses to humoral responses. Studies of this shift help explain the increase in allergy and autoimmune disease in the context of stress. Finally, long-term, uncontrollable chronic stressors are related to overall suppression of immune system function, including reductions in lymphocyte proliferation and natural killer cell function. Research has linked global immunosuppression to chronic stressors such as caregiving for a loved one with dementia, unemployment, and clinical depression.

PNI's traditional emphasis on stressful negative events and states has begun to evolve toward understanding the individual factors that promote immune resilience in the face of threat. For instance, optimism, social support, and general positive affect are related to better immune function, although again, the emphasis has been on the role of these factors in promoting coping with stress. As such, evidence supports the likelihood that positive psychological and environmental factors protect the immune system through their attenuation of prolonged SAM and HPA stress responses. Similarly, intervention studies are helping to delineate the components of stress management, relaxation techniques, cognitive-behavioral and psychotherapeutic processes, and alternative and complimentary medical approaches that contribute to a strengthened immune system in healthy individuals, as well as those with immune-related diseases, including rheumatoid arthritis, asthma, and HIV.

Challenges for PNI

Since the 1970s, burgeoning evidence has implicated psychosocial factors in immunocompetence, but much remains to be understood with regard to the connection between psychosocial factors, the immune system and actual mental and physical health outcomes. Most support for this tricomponential relationship comes from distinct lines of evidence linking psychosocial factors to the immune system, and for relations among psychosocial factors and immune-related disease. The challenge for PNI researchers is to incorporate simultaneous, longitudinal measurement of psychosocial factors, neuroendocrineimmune parameters, and health outcomes, both positive and negative. Doing so will allow the field to more fully delineate the impact of social and psychological characteristics on physical and mental well-being, and the role of the neuroendocrine and immune systems in this important link.

SEE ALSO: ▶ Cortisol ▶ Immune system ▶ Neurobiology

Psychopathology

Stephen Joseph
University of Nottingham, UK

Psychopathology is the study of the thoughts, feelings, or behaviors that are either distressing (feeling emotionally upset), dangerous (doing something that is harmful to ourselves or to another person), deviant (doing something that seems really odd or strange to other people), or dysfunctional (having difficulty functioning in our everyday lives), or a combination of these.

Although this sounds straightforward, defining psychopathology is problematic, and we must be wary always of how judgments of distress, dangerousness, deviance, and dysfunctionality are subjective and likely to vary cross-culturally and throughout history.

Models of Psychopathology

Historically, psychopathology has been understood in many ways, the result of supernatural forces, the wrath of gods, demonic possession, for example, and at different times, psychopathology has attracted ridicule, fear, pity, anger, and been variously treated, from attempts to exorcise demons to taking cold baths. Within modern psychology and psychiatry there are seven major theoretical models, or paradigms, from which we can understand psychopathology. These are: biomedical model; psychodynamic model; behavioral model; cognitive model; humanistic model; transpersonal model; and sociocultural model. Each model provides us with its own boundaries of inquiry, a way of looking at the world, and a shared set of assumptions about reality. Each of these seven models presents a view of how psychopathology develops and how it can be prevented and treated. In brief, the biomedical model suggests that psychological problems are the result of physical dysfunction; the psychodynamic model suggests that psychological problems are caused by conflict between unconscious forces; the behavioral model suggests that psychological problems are a result of maladaptive learning; the cognitive model suggests that psychological problems are caused by irrational or distorted thinking; the humanistic model suggests that psychological problems are caused by a failure to know and accept oneself; the transpersonal model is concerned with spirituality and experiences beyond the person; and the sociocultural model suggests that psychological problems result from social factors.

Most mental health professionals today would agree that human experience is so diverse that no one model of psychopathology is able to offer the full explanation for all psychological problems for all people all of the time, and current approaches attempt to adopt a biopsychosocial approach which understands the models as providing explanations at different explanatory levels and at different temporal etiological stages. For example, research suggests that people who are depressed have lower levels of social resources (evidence for the sociocultural model), particular negative patterns of thinking (evidence for the cognitive model) and lower levels of the neurotransmitter serotonin (evidence for the biological model) than people not suffering from depression.

Classification of Psychopathology

Psychopathology refers to the study of a range of seemingly very different psychological conditions; thus one task of psychiatry has been to produce a classification system of various so-called psychiatric disorders, such as major depressive disorder, panic disorder, posttraumatic stress disorder, obsessive-compulsive disorder, anorexia nervosa, to name but a few of the more commonly known disorders described in the *Diagnostic and Statistical Manual of Mental Disorders*, fourth edition (DSM-IV). The DSM-IV provides psychiatrists, as well as others who use the manual, with a shared frame of reference, a common language, and a fundamental tool for scientific investigation into the causes and treatment of each of the various so-called disorders. This classification system has been influential and most modern textbooks on abnormal psychology are arranged around discussions of empirical evidence about what is known about the causes and treatment of each of the various psychiatric disorders.

Current Issues

Although widely adopted, the classification of psychiatric disorders is however controversial. The current DSM-IV classification system is based on the underlying medical model assumption that psychological problems can be grouped in a way analogous to physical illness symptoms (i.e., by observing the symptoms people experience, what symptoms always seem to occur together, what symptoms do not seem to occur together, a taxonomy is created) and that such a taxonomy is a necessary first step because each of the conditions will have its own specific etiology and treatment.

Taking a social constructionist approach, the classification of psychiatric disorders in DSM-IV is not an objective value-free task but one which is based on the medical model and an illness ideology that implicitly prescribes certain ways of thinking about psychological problems. First, it promotes the idea of dichotomies between normal and abnormal behaviors, between clinical and nonclinical problems, and between clinical populations and nonclinical populations. Second, it locates human maladjustment inside the person, rather than in the person's interactions with the environment and their encounters with sociocultural values and social institutions. Third, it portrays people who seek help as victims of intrapsychic and biological forces beyond their control, and thus leaves them as passive recipients of an expert's care.

Over the years, various theoretical alternatives to the DSM classification system have however been proposed from various quarters. For example, personality theorists such as Eysenck argued that psychopathology can be understood as combinations of extreme scores on factor analytically derived continuous personality traits, such as extroversion, neuroticism, and psychoticism; evolutionary psychologists have argued for the need to provide a taxonomy based on functional explanations; and humanistic psychologists such as Rogers have argued to reject the medical model, instead proposing an understanding based on an organismic growth model.

Debate around the scientific validity and ethical base of DSM and the search for alternative ways of thinking about psychopathology continues within the mental health system, and within the field of critical psychology. Critics such as Bentall and Boyle argue that traditional diagnostic-based approaches have failed to be of benefit to the vulnerable people in society.

Positive Psychological Perspective

More recently, positive psychologists such as Maddux have also urged that we reconsider our underlying conceptions of psychopathology, pointing to how our understanding of psychopathology rests ultimately on social construction rather than empirical fact, thus raising questions as to whether psychopathology would be more constructively viewed as differing *only in degree*, rather than in kind, from normal problems in living; and whether psychological disorders are indeed analogous to biological or medical diseases, or rather if they are reflective of problems in the person's interactions with his or her environment. Positive psychology has been seen as the study of optimal functioning, in contrast with the traditional focus on psychopathology, but what becomes evident is that these need not be two separate domains of enquiry if the illness ideology of traditional psychology and psychiatry is rejected in favor of a positive psychological conception, such as the organismic growth model originally developed by Rogers, and more recently applied to the study of posttraumatic stress by Joseph and Linley. In contrast to the medical model, a positive psychological conception of psychopathology seeks to explore the idea of continuity between normal and abnormal behaviors, between clinical and nonclinical problems, and between clinical populations and nonclinical populations.

SEE ALSO: ▶ Abnormal psychology ▶ *Diagnostic and Statistical Manual* ▶ Mental illness

Purpose in Life

Nicholas E. Pisca and David B. Feldman
Santa Clara University

Scholarship on purpose and meaning in life spans centuries, religions, and world-views. The modern approach to these constructs, however, began with existential philosophers like Nietzsche, Sartre, and Camus. In general, existentialists concluded that it was impossible to determine life's meaning objectively. Thus, they reframed the age-old question "What is the purpose of life?" to reflect a more contemporary perspective – "How do people arrive at their own senses of purpose?" To echo this distinction, researchers still tend to use the term "purpose *in* life" rather than "purpose *of* life."

Of note, *meaning* and *purpose* have somewhat different connotations. According to Irvin Yalom (1980), " 'Meaning' refers to sense or coherence. . . . 'Purpose' refers to intention, aim, function" (p. 423). Although some authors have suggested that purpose is only one aspect of meaning, these terms generally are used interchangeably.

Definitions and Theoretical Foundations

Many theories of purpose in life have been developed. Due to space limitations, only four are included here. Viktor Frankl was one of the first to develop a psychological theory of meaning. At the core of his theory, called *Logotherapy*, is the "will to meaning" – the universal drive toward life meaning – which, when frustrated, can lead to mental illness. Based partially on his experience as a prisoner in a Nazi concentration camp, however, Frankl observed that life can have meaning in any situation. People find meaning through acting on three types of values: 1) creative values (by creating or producing something); 2) experiential values (by experiencing something, especially love); and 3) attitudinal values (through the attitude that one takes to situations).

A second approach to purpose, the *sense of coherence*, was developed by Anton Antonovsky. Believed to serve as a stress buffer preserving psychological and physical well-being, the sense of coherence consists of three components. First, people must *comprehend* how their environments function. Second, people must believe that they can *manage* those environments so as to achieve their desires. Last, as people cope with the demands of their environments, they must believe that they do so for *meaningful* or worthy ends.

A third approach to purpose is *terror management theory*. Developed by Jeff Greenberg, Tom Pyszczynski, and Sheldon Solomon based on the work of Ernest Becker, this theory conceptualizes meaning as linked with culture and self-esteem. The theory begins with the premise that, as human beings, we must ultimately die – a prospect that could engender great anxiety. To avoid this, people cling to their cultural worldviews, most of which promise potential immortality. Through Christian culture, for instance, people who live up to cultural standards are promised immortality in heaven. Likewise, secular culture promises symbolic immortality in such forms as monuments, works of art, and children. When people meet cultural standards, they feel increased self-esteem and thereby are buffered against death anxiety. Terror management theory represents an important development, as it acknowledges the centrality of culture in meaning.

Roy Baumeister has developed a fourth theory that integrates concepts cutting across various other theories of meaning. He posits four needs for meaning. Notably, the first need is for *purpose*. That is, people have a need to see their current activities "in relation to future or positive states" or goals (Baumeister, 1991, p. 32). The second need, for *value*, consists of people's desire to see their actions as right, good, or justifiable. Third, people have a need for *efficacy*, for a sense that they have control over events. Last, people have a need for *self-worth*; that is, they desire to see themselves as having positive value. Baumeister believes that when these needs are satisfied, a sense of meaning ensues. When unsatisfied, people show "signs of being thwarted – some frustration, malaise, discontent, or instability" (p. 47). This approach to meaning represents an important development because of its integration of research and theory on such diverse topics as goal striving, self-efficacy, and self-esteem.

Measurement

Researchers have developed many measures of purpose in life with reasonable reliability and validity. The instrument most extensively used in research, the Purpose in Life Test (PIL), was developed by James Crumbaugh and Leonard Maholick to tap Frankl's meaning construct. The PIL consists of 20 items rated on 7-point scales. An example item is "In thinking of my life, I . . ." with a scale ranging from 1 (*often wonder why I exist*) to 7 (*always see a reason for my being here*). However, the PIL has been criticized on psychometric grounds; some of its items appear to tap depression or life satisfaction rather than exclusively purpose in life.

The Sense of Coherence scale (SOC) consists of 29 items rated on 7-point scales, although short-forms also are available. Developed by Antonovsky, the SOC is comprised of three subscales: comprehensibility, manageability, and meaningfulness. A sample meaningfulness item is "You anticipate that your personal life in the future will be:" with a scale ranging from 1 (*totally without meaning or purpose*) to 7 (*full of meaning and purpose*); a sample manageability item is "When you think of difficulties you are likely to face in important aspects of your life, do you have the feeling that:" with a scale ranging from 1 (*you will always succeed in overcoming the difficulties*) to 7 (*you won't succeed in overcoming the difficulties*); and a sample comprehensibility item is "Do you have the feeling that you are in an unfamiliar situation and don't know what to do?" with a scale ranging from 1 (*very often*) to 7 (*very seldom or never*).

John Battista and Richard Almond's Life Regard Index (LRI) taps a meaning construct similar to that described in terror management theory. The LRI is a 28-item measure with two subscales. The framework subscale measures the perception that one has a structure or philosophy from which to derive life goals. The fulfillment subscale measures the perception that one is fulfilling that framework. Items are rated on scales ranging from 1 (*totally disagree*) to 5 (*totally agree*) and include "I have really come to terms with what's important for me in my life" (framework) and "I feel that I'm really going to attain what I want in life" (fulfillment).

Although the aforementioned instruments are the most frequently used, Michael Scheier and his colleagues have recently developed the Life Engagement Test (LET) which is designed to assess life purpose. The LET measures the extent to which individuals are engaged with goals of personal value. The LET consists of 6 items rated on scales ranging from 1 (*strongly agree*) to 5 (*strongly disagree*). An example item is, "To me things I do are all worthwhile." This instrument represents an important development, as it systematically incorporates goal striving into a measure of life purpose.

Although most measures of purpose in life consist of closed-ended items, open-ended instruments have also been developed. Developed by Peter Ebersole and his colleagues, the Meaning in Life Depth instrument provides a standardized strategy for coding the depth of meaning present in respondents' written descriptions of their life purposes. Roy Baumeister and Dan McAdams, among others, have also developed strategies for coding elements of meaning in research participants' life stories.

Relationships to Other Constructs

In contrast to the well-developed status of theory, empirical research on purpose in life is relatively sparse. Traditionally, purpose has been investigated within a pathology-focused framework. For instance, the PIL was developed in part to identify "pathological groups in contrast to 'normal' populations" (Crumbaugh & Maholick, 1964, p. 201). Research demonstrates that purpose and meaning inversely relate to depressive symptoms, anxiety, substance abuse, and suicidal ideation.

Purpose also has been shown to relate to positive psychology constructs including greater happiness, self-esteem, resilience, and hope.

Research findings on purpose in life and physical health are less consistent. Some studies show relationships between life purpose and perceived health, whereas others do not. Similar mixed results have been found for purpose's ability to predict mortality from medical illness. Perhaps because it was developed in part to predict health, studies utilizing the SOC in contrast to other measures tend to find positive results more often. Studies show that the SOC relates to blood pressure and cholesterol levels, glycemic control in diabetes, incidence of cancer, and functional status in Parkinson's Disease, among other variables.

Promising Directions for Research

Although there undoubtedly are many profitable directions in which to take research, three are highlighted here. First, researchers are beginning to explicitly view purpose in life through the lens of goals. This certainly is not a new idea, but one that historically has been incorporated only obliquely into research. Snyder (1997) has suggested that purpose in life can largely be explained by the notion of *control*, which he defines as "a cognitive model whereby people strive to comprehend the contingencies in their lives so as to attain desired outcomes" (p. 48). Researchers such as Brian Little, Eric Klinger, and Robert Emmons have attempted to explain in greater detail how different goal constructs relate to life meaning. Although we doubt that purpose can be fully reduced to goals, this approach may provide a useful framework within which to understand meaning more deeply.

Another direction in which some scholars have begun to take work on purpose in life involves exploring the phenomenon from a societal or collective perspective. That human goal pursuits are affected by others and by culture is undeniable. Michael Lerner (1997) writes, "There are societal and psychological obstacles to our pursuit of meaning. . . . Meaning cannot be fully supplied by an existential choice . . . nor can it be fully supplied by service to society" (p. 29). Most research on life purpose within the field of psychology addresses the personal existential dimension of meaning but neglects the social or cultural aspects.

Finally, moving forward with research on purpose in life, there is a need for more studies with longitudinal and true experimental designs. Much of the extant research is either descriptive or correlational in nature, rendering it difficult to draw distinctions between the consequences versus causes of having a sense of life purpose. The issue of life's meaning has been of great concern to scholars for centuries. With such an overwhelming topic, it can seem daunting to perform empirical research. For this reason, purpose in life has often been avoided by those who consider it too "vague" or "philosophical" a topic. In the future, it will be important for positive psychology researchers to have courage and perseverance in investigating this difficult, often murky, but extremely rewarding issue.

References

Baumeister, R. F. (1991). *Meaning of life*. New York: Guilford.

Crumbaugh, J. C., & Maholick, L. T. (1964). An experimental study in existentialism: The psychometric approach to Frankl's concept of noogenic neurosis. *Journal of Clinical Psychology, 20,* 200–207.

Lerner, M. (1997). *The politics of meaning*. New York: Addison-Wesley.

Snyder, C. R. (1997). Control and the application of Occam's razor to terror management theory. *Psychological Inquiry, 8,* 48–49.

Yalom, I. (1980). *Existential psychotherapy*. New York: Basic Books.

Quality of Life

Tiffany M. Greene-Shortridge and Heather N. Odle-Dusseau
Clemson University

Quality of life (QOL) has most often been defined as the assessment of one's own well-being and is affected by both physical and psychological health, as well as personal beliefs, social relationships, and relationships with salient features of the environment. Most researchers agree that the concept of QOL came about during the social indicators movement of the 1960s. This movement approached QOL as a population concern, such that QOL was looked at as the importance of objective and subjective indicators of social well-being. Objective indicators were represented by societal facts, such as health, poverty, and crime, whereas subjective indicators took into account the individual perceptions of societal conditions (e.g., job satisfaction, sense of safety, happiness, etc.). Currently, much more work is concentrated on the subjective indicators of QOL, or as some have coined this research, focusing on the eye of the beholder.

Here, we first concentrate on defining QOL, both as a population-level construct and an individual-level construct. We then examine the measurement issues that have resulted from QOL research, and explore what we consider to be valued measurements of QOL. Next, we summarize the literature on the indicators, or antecedents of QOL, and then introduce the major outcomes of QOL. We conclude with a section on future research for the field of QOL and provide insight for the QOL concept and practice. Throughout this entry we hope to provide the reader with a better understanding of the concept of QOL and its implications for individuals and society.

Defining Quality of Life

Unfortunately, a uniform definition of QOL used by researchers across the board is lacking. Furthermore, while most researchers would agree that QOL is a multi-dimensional construct, the number of dimensions or a compilation of them has yet to be agreed. QOL is often used interchangeably with other constructs, such as subjective well-being or overall happiness. Nonetheless, most researchers have come to a consensus that QOL can be defined as a population-level construct *and* as an individual-level construct. Both of these dimensions of QOL are discussed next.

Concerning the definition of this construct at the population level, most researchers equate QOL to normative, objective components of peoples' experiences, such as income. On the other hand, QOL at the individual level is often addressed as the satisfaction that individuals have with their lives. Some researchers conceptualize these subjective and objective indicators of QOL as comprising a 2×2 matrix, such that good objective living conditions and good subjective well-being comprise the highest level of well-being (i.e., the happy rich). However, if one has good objective living conditions, but poor subjective well-being, one can experience dissonance, which is characterized as having good living conditions, but being unsatisfied with life in general (i.e., the unhappy rich). If one encompasses bad objective living conditions, but has good subjective well-being, he/she may experience adaptation (i.e., the happy poor). In contrast though, if people experience both bad objective living conditions and bad subjective well-being, they are likely to experience deprivation (i.e., the unhappy poor). While this framework proposes a means to better define QOL overall, there still exist disagreements as to what conceptualizes the objective and subjective dimensions of QOL.

Measurement Issues in Quality of Life

In accordance with attempting to define QOL, the measurement of the construct revolves around the approaches formerly mentioned. Hence, the first approach concentrates on objective indicators of QOL, such as economic and social indicators; examples of such include crime rates, literacy rates, life expectancy, and health care. Furthermore, research on social indicators has been conceptualized as being composed of four dimensions. These include security (e.g., crime rate, life expectancy), mastery (e.g., health, poverty rate), harmony (e.g., unemployment rate, income per capita), and intellectual autonomy (e.g., percentage completing college). One criticism of the objective measurement approach suggests that wealth is likely to explain a large part of differences in these social indicators. Nonetheless, in utilizing objective assessments, researchers are often able to make regional comparisons of QOL. The second approach to measuring QOL concentrates on the subjective assessments of well-being (SWB). In operationalizing QOL as a subjective construct, numerous assessment tools have been created. The major focus of these instruments is on global assessments of well-being, as well as physical health.

Measures of QOL have been criticized for excluding important content domains, such as social and emotional realms. Furthermore, measures of QOL often fail to encompass a uniform theory of the construct, thus inevitably failing to show how QOL antecedents are often related to the outcomes of QOL. Additionally, QOL instruments have commonly included items that call for judgmental comparisons and causal considerations, as opposed to simply descriptive items that do not require assessment of causes or results. Finally, because QOL measures often focus on physical symptoms, researchers often find it difficult to compare across samples. For example, items are often specific to the symptoms experienced to particular samples (e.g., cancer patients), and are therefore inapplicable to healthy individuals.

In an attempt to alleviate these criticisms of QOL assessments, Kreitler and Kreitler developed a new, multidimensional measure. Great care was taken for the sample to be as heterogeneous as possible, which included individuals from multiple socioeconomic levels, and both males and females between the ages of 25 and 65. This sample varied in both health and types of sicknesses, stressful experiences, as well as educational and cultural backgrounds. In developing this new QOL measure, five dimensions were identified: physical functioning, emotional functioning, cognitive functioning, social functioning, and perceived coping. While this measure is relatively new, support has been found for both the reliability and validity of the measure within various samples.

Additionally, a comprehensive quality of life (ComQOL) scale was developed by Cummins and colleagues. The scale is made up of seven domains: material well-being, health, productivity, intimacy, safety, community, and emotional well-being. Each domain contains both objective and subjective items in order to measure one's overall QOL. Psychometric support for this measure has been found.

Frisch and colleagues have also developed the Quality of Life Inventory (QOLI), which seeks to measure life satisfaction and is suggested to be used in conjunction with Quality of Life Therapy. In combination, the QOLI and Quality of Life therapy are aimed at treating mental disorders and physical illnesses, as well as community social problems. Internal consistency and test-retest reliability has shown to be adequate for the QOLI.

Furthermore, the World Health Organization also has a Quality of Life group that has developed a measure which includes four QOL domains: physical health, psychological/bodily image and appearance, social relationships, and the environment. However, critics of this measure argue that it fails to include all content domains, items refer too often to physical symptoms, findings are often unable to be compared across sick and healthy samples, and the suitability of the measure restricts it to only assessing QOL as impaired by one's health.

While researchers and practitioners have attempted to define and measure QOL more effectively, there still exists a discrepancy among subjective and objective measurements, such that objective measurements of QOL and subjective estimates of well-being are often found to be unrelated, and sometimes even contradictory to one another. Thus, it has been suggested that proponents of QOL ask themselves which side seems to be the most compelling, not necessarily which side seems to be correct.

Antecedents of Quality of Life

Quality of life is typically measured in research as an outcome of multiple antecedences that are subjective and objective in nature. Bulbolz, Eicher, Evers, and Sontag's ecological perspective of QOL entwines subjective and objective indicators at the individual, family, community, and global level. At the individual or more personal level, objective indicators of health and subjective assessments of well-being predict QOL. At the interpersonal or family level, interactions and relationships with family members and close friends, as well as norms and obligations, are indicative of QOL. These two levels encompassing the personal and interpersonal indicators of QOL are referred to as the *microsystem*. Finally, the external and global "outer" levels are comprised of community and national indicators of QOL, such as income, housing, societal wealth, health, natural resources, and sustainability. Research concerning this model has found support for individual components of the ecological model. For example, the experience of role responsibilities in work, family, and social domains has been found to predict QOL. Additionally, the *amount* of responsibilities within multiple roles predicts QOL in both positive (benefits of being involved in multiple roles) and negative ways (stress of balancing multiple roles).

In addition to Bulbolz's and colleagues' ecological perspective on QOL, there are four other approaches that are often used in assessing predictors of QOL. The first of these includes utility, or one's overall mental state of pleasure or happiness, which is most often measured in terms of income. Needs is the second predictor of QOL and is usually measured by the degree or amount of resources one is able to provide in order to lead an acceptable life (in terms of nutrition, shelter, health and education). While less clear cut than needs, prudential values are the third predictor of QOL. These values do not encompass actual desires, but instead include one's informed desires, or desires that would make any human life better. Last, capabilities, or the freedom to pursue what one wishes to be or do in order to flourish as a human, comprise the last major predictor of QOL. Together, these predictors of QOL have implications for social action, subjective well-being, and human nature in general.

Outcomes of Quality of Life

At the societal level, the major outcomes of high QOL are social capital and social cohesion. However, it is important to note that QOL should not predict maximal social capital and social cohesion, but instead should predict optimal levels of these outcomes. Thus, too much or too little social capital and cohesion can lead to negative effects; instead, QOL should predict just the "right amount" of these societal outcomes. These two major outcomes of QOL are discussed next.

Unlike social cohesion, social capital is multi-dimensional in nature. Social capital encompasses society's trust, reciprocity, values, and norms. Additionally, social capital is often broken down into two dimensions: bonding and bridging. Bonding encompasses the tight relationships between members within a group, while bridging refers to the networks between groups. Furthermore, social capital encompasses all other forms of capital as well (e.g., financial capital, economic capital, and human capital). While these forms of capital are usually individually based, taken together, they encompass a social capital. However, it is important to note that social capital only belongs to a collective group; it should never be used on an individual basis.

Unlike social capital, there lacks a clear operationalization of what social cohesion is. Indeed, some researchers refuse to offer a definition for social cohesion, but rather suggest that we explore different constructs and understandings to come to a better conclusion of what social capital could encompass. The construct of social cohesion can be traced back to Tonnies' research in which QOL is thought to lead to family and peer group cohesion, as well as an increased societal structure. Today, it seems that most researchers would agree that social cohesion includes societal expectations and norms.

Future Research and Concluding Thoughts

In the study of QOL, researchers are recommended to take into account the use and development of both objective and subjective assessments. While research has found that there are benefits and drawbacks to the measurement of each dimension, both allow for a better overall picture of the construct, and are assumed to be complimentary to each other. Additionally, if QOL researchers only use one type of measurement, it is advised that they clearly specify which QOL definition they are attempting to measure, as the field has yet to come to a consensus on a concrete operational definition. Moreover, we recommend that researchers continue to further validate the multidimensional nature of QOL, as well as concentrate on additional antecedents and outcomes of such. It is our hope that future research addressing these issues will allow for a more comprehensive approach to QOL that all researchers can use consistently.

SEE ALSO: ▶ Family quality of life; Quality of Life Inventory ▶ Quality of life therapy ▶ Well-being

Quality of Life Inventory (QOLI)

Michael B. Frisch

Baylor University

The QOLI® or Quality of Life Inventory is an evidence-based positive psychology test of "psychometric soundness" (Biswas-Diener & Dean, 2007, p. 96) that is useful both in intervention planning and in outcome evaluation, that is, documenting positive outcomes that result from positive psychology interventions. In a study involving 3,927 clients, "the QOLI was found to be sensitive to treatment-related change in two samples and the predictive validity of the QOLI was supported in terms of its ability to predict academic retention in college students 1 to 3 years in advance" (Frisch et al., 2005, pp. 72–73). In a second independent review of the measure, Michael J. Lambert, Benjamin Ogles, and Kevin Masters (2006, p. 92) assert: "The most promising quality of life instrument available is the Quality of Life Inventory."

The QOLI is published by Pearson Assessments – see pearsonassessments.com – the publisher of the Minnesota Multiphasic Personality Inventory (MMPI)-2 and the Millon Inventories; it may be ordered with the least expense by obtaining the "Hand-Scoring Starter Kit." Because the QOLI is nonpathology-oriented and is relatively simple to use and interpret, a college degree is all that is required of those who wish to use the test in their coaching or therapy practice, etc.

The QOLI is a measure of life satisfaction or quality of life. It was intended to be a measure of *positive mental health* or life satisfaction based on a well-articulated theory which could augment or replace existing measures of negative affect and symptoms of disease or psychological disturbance such as those symptoms listed in the *Diagnostic and Statistical Manual.*

Based upon an exhaustive review of the literature in general, "cognitive mapping" studies of human concerns, quality of life and social indicators research, and studies identifying particular areas of life associated with overall life satisfaction and happiness a comprehensive list of human concerns, "domains," or areas of life was developed and reduced to the 16 areas of life that make up the QOLI. These 16 items have been selected to include all domains of life that have been empirically associated with overall life satisfaction. Respondents rate how important each of the 16 domains is to their overall happiness and satisfaction (0 = "not at all important," 1 = "important," 2 = "very important") followed by rating of how satisfied they are in the area (−3 = "very dissatisfied" to 3 = "very satisfied"). The importance and satisfaction ratings for each item are multiplied to form weighted satisfaction ratings ranging from −6 to 6. A "weighted satisfaction profile" akin to an MMPI profile (or an Un-MMPI profile of health; see Figure 7) is generated which gives a comprehensive overview of clients satisfaction in 16 areas of life (weighted for each area's importance to the respondent). The overall life satisfaction is then computed by averaging all weighted satisfaction ratings with nonzero importance ratings; the total score thus reflects one's satisfaction in only those areas of life one considers important. Respondents can also indicate what problems interfere with their satisfaction in each area on a narrative section of the QOLI test booklet. Figure 7 shows a portion of a QOLI profile – without the accompanying interpretation and without the client's listing of problems that interfere with their satisfaction in each area of life.

QOLI° Profile Report   ID: 12345
07/13/2005, Page 2

INTRODUCTION

The Quality of Life Inventory (QOLI) provides a score that indicates a person's overall satisfaction with life. People's life satisfaction is based on how well their needs, goals, and wishes are being met in important areas of life. The information in this report should be used in conjunction with professional judgment, taking into account any other pertinent information concerning the individual.

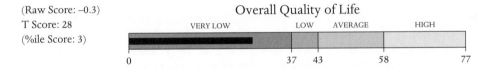

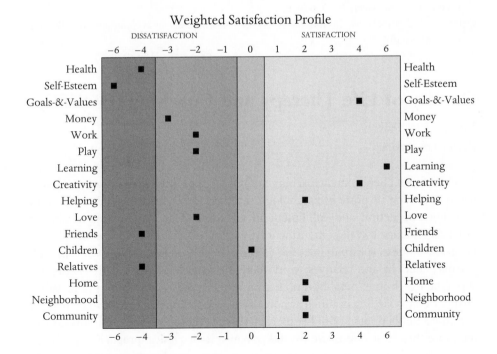

Figure 7   QOLI Profile Report.
Source: Pearson Assessments – see pearsonassessments.com

Use of the QOLI in Documenting Outcomes, Planning Interventions, and Fine-Tuning Interventions

A QOLI profile such as this yields an overall score useful in demonstrating that a client has moved into the average range or above in quality of life or life satisfaction after a positive psychology intervention. A QOLI weighted satisfaction profile, as in Figure 7, may also help in intervention planning by suggesting strengths or areas of satisfaction in the white area of the profile on the right, while showing valued areas of dissatisfaction on the left side of the profile in gray. These gray areas may be listed as targets of intervention, with the larger negative numbered items considered the most serious and in need of intervention.

SEE ALSO: ▶ Quality of life   ▶ Quality of Life Therapy

References

Biswas-Diener, R., & Dean, B. (2007). *Positive psychology coaching*. Hoboken, NJ: John Wiley and Sons.

Frisch, M. B., Clark, M. P., Rouse, S. V., Rudd, M. D., Paweleck, J., & Greenstone, A. (2005). Predictive and treatment validity of life satisfaction and the Quality of Life Inventory. *Assessment, 12*(1), 66–78.

Ogles, B. M., Lambert, M., & Masters, K. (1996). *Assessing outcome in clinical practice*. Boston: Allyn & Bacon.

Quality of Life Therapy and Coaching (QOLTC)

Michael B. Frisch
Baylor University

Quality of Life Therapy and Coaching or QOLTC is a comprehensive and evidence-based approach to positive psychology intervention. Clients are given tools for boosting satisfaction and fulfillment in any one of 16 *specific* areas of life in order to enhance *overall* contentment or quality of life. These areas include: life goals-and-values; spiritual life; self-esteem; health; relationships with friends; partner; children and relatives; work; play; helping; learning; creativity; money; surroundings–home; neighborhood; community; and relapse prevention. While quality of life coaching is aimed at nonclinical populations who wish to be happier and more fulfilled, quality of life therapy teaches therapists and clinicians how to integrate the latest in positive psychology into their clinical practice.

Quality of life coaching and therapy is evidence-based in so far as this package of interventions has been evaluated as successful in two separate trials conducted at different laboratories with different clients, that is, a coaching sample from Beth Israel Medical Center in Boston and a clinically depressed sample at Baylor University. For example, in a randomized controlled trial, Rodrigue and his colleagues (2005, p. 2430) conclude: "Quality of Life Therapy leads to significant improvement in quality of life, mood disturbance, and social intimacy. Second, improvements in quality of life and mood appear to be maintained for as long as 3 months. Third, while supportive therapy/treatment as usual appears to yield some short-term benefits in mood, Quality of Life Therapy is a more effective treatment overall." Other grant-supported randomized controlled trials of QOLTC are currently underway. The evidence-based Quality of Life Inventory (QOLI) is also a part of quality of life therapy and coaching where it is used to plan interventions, identify areas of strength, and scientifically measure the effect of intervention by showing if clients' overall scores move into the average or normal range of life satisfaction for a nationwide sample of adults that approximate the US Census in ethnic composition. Psychometrically speaking, in a study involving 3,927 clients, "the QOLI was found to be sensitive to treatment-related change in two samples and the predictive validity of the QOLI was supported in terms of its ability to predict academic retention 1 to 3 years in advance" (Frisch et al., 2005, pp. 72–73). Finally, as part of an independent assessment of the approach, Ed Diener (2006) evaluates quality of life therapy and coaching as "research-based," "science based," "comprehensive," and representative of the "state of the art" in positive psychology today (pp. vii–viii), while Christopher Peterson (2006) states that "Quality of Life Therapy and Coaching is psychology at its best – theoretical and practical" (back cover).

The quality of life theory which undergirds the approach attempts to integrate the findings from the fields of positive psychology, coaching, well-being, life satisfaction, happiness, quality of life and social indicators research, psychotherapy, and Beck's cognitive therapy. The theory itself is practical, serving as it does as the basis for the five paths to happiness or CASIO intervention applicable to any area of life. The theory attempts to integrate the latest in positive psychology and 30 years of quality of life research with Aaron T. Beck's and David A. Clark's latest cognitive theory of psychopathology and depression. In fact, David A. Clark authored a second foreword to the book *Quality of Life Therapy*, which constitutes an intervention manual for conducting quality of life therapy and coaching.

Quality of life coaching and therapy begins with an assessment of life goals and quality of life using the QOLI or similar instrument and the Three Pillars of Quality of Life Therapy and Coaching. Clients do well to begin any positive psychology intervention program with a modicum of self-care or "inner abundance" such that some basic physical and emotional needs are being met. Without this physical or emotional reserve, clients will often feel too tired or overwhelmed by the demands of the moment to try to build a better quality of life. Fostering inner abundance in clients is the first pillar of QOLTC.

Inner abundance means feeling deeply calm, rested, centered, loving, alert, and ready to meet the challenges of your day and your life after caring for yourself in a thoughtful, loving, compassionate, and comprehensive way. When you do the very best for you, there is a lot more of you available for other people and activities. We must feel centered, calm, and good on the inside – hence the "inner" of inner abundance – to serve others or to find fulfillment in any of the 16 areas of life in quality of life therapy and coaching. We need a modicum of self-care – both physical and emotional – or self-maintenance so that we have the energy, clarity, wisdom, and calmness to identify and pursue our most important life goals, including service to others.

Finding meaning in life, the second of the Three Pillars in QOLT/C, helps clients to articulate goals for each valued area of life. Finally, clients benefit from "quality time" or periodic times for rest, reflection, and problem-solving in their quest for greater fulfillment. Quality time is the third pillar of quality of life therapy and coaching. Clients are introduced to the Three Pillars at the same time that they begin to try interventions associated with the 16 areas of life that make up quality of life coaching and therapy.

SEE ALSO: ▶ Quality of Life Inventory

References

Diener, E. (2006). Foreword. In M. B. Frisch, *Quality of life therapy: Applying a life satisfaction approach to positive psychology and cognitive therapy* (pp. vii–viii). Hoboken, New Jersey: John Wiley & Sons.

Frisch, M. B., Clark, M. P., Rouse, S. V., Rudd, M. D., Paweleck, J., & Greenstone, A. (2005). Predictive and treatment validity of life satisfaction and the Quality of Life Inventory. *Assessment, 12*(1), 66–78.

Peterson, C. (2006). Critical review. In M. B. Frisch, *Quality of life therapy: Applying a life satisfaction approach to positive psychology and cognitive therapy* (back cover of book). Hoboken, New Jersey: John Wiley & Sons.

Rodrigue, J. R., Baz, M. A., Widows, M. R. & Ehlers, S. L. (2005). A randomized evaluation of quality of life therapy with patients awaiting lung transplantation. *American Journal of Transplantation, 5*(10), 2425–2432.

Rehabilitation Psychology

Timothy R. Elliott[a] and Gitendra Uswatte[b]

[a]Texas A&M University; [b]University of Alabama at Birmingham

Rehabilitation psychology is committed to the development and application of psychological knowledge and services to promote the health and well-being of individuals who live with disabling conditions. The specialty has been historically linked with institutions that serve individuals who have disabling conditions (including hospitals, schools, universities, nonprofit organizations, and federal and state agencies). Rehabilitation psychologists, therefore, have actively participated in multidisciplinary service and research endeavors, program development and evaluation, administration, policy formation, advocacy, and training. Rehabilitation psychology was originally construed to serve those who encounter "deprivation and disability" that devalued their role in society in any fashion (including institutionalization, racism, poverty, older age, and chronic disease; Dembo, Diller, Gordon, Leviton, & Sherr, 1973, p. 719). However, the specialty is typically associated with the provision of psychological expertise on behalf of persons with congenital or acquired physical, neuromuscular, and developmental disabilities.

Historical Context and Development

Many psychologists, educators, and counselors responded to federal legislation to assist workers injured in the early twentieth century during the industrialization of the American working environment. The general thrust of this legislation and accompanying programs was directed toward compensating injured workers who could not return to their jobs, and to study work-related accidents to determine preventative measures. These efforts were complimented and expanded by legislation to assist soldiers injured in World War I and World War II. Legislation following World War II, in particular, was highly influential in addressing the psychological issues of personnel who incurred permanent disabilities.

These policies and programs addressed the psychological, vocational, educational and medical issues germane to the individual who had acquired a disability. Rehabilitation psychology gained prominence at this time, and psychologists inspired by Lewinian field theory were influential. Beatrice Wright and Tamara Dembo recognized the environmental and social factors that defined and characterized disability. Collaborating with other invested colleagues (including many notable social, clinical and counseling psychologists of the day), they received support from federal agencies and the American Psychological Association to convene and define the initial parameters of rehabilitation psychology.

Theoretical Foundations

Wright and Dembo advanced the premise that behavior associated with disability was best understood within the classic Lewinian equation, $b = f(p \times e)$. From this perspective, psychologists were to appreciate how characteristics of everyday situations impose disability vis à vis architectural barriers, negative and stereotypic attitudes, limited access, and lack of information. These factors limit opportunities and options and prompt behavioral reactions that are invariably interpreted by observers in a negative fashion and attributed to the presence of the disability. Wright furthered this perspective in the classic *Physical Disability: A Psychological Approach* in 1960, in which core "strengths" of rehabilitation psychology were proposed. These strengths – including somatopsychological relation, individuation, the insider-outsider distinction, and the recognition of assets – perpetuated the value of recognizing the individual (rather than the "diagnosis" of a disability), and an appreciation for abilities and assets of the individual and the need to identify personal goals of the individual. Wright also augmented these strengths with an explicit delineation of values inherent in rehabilitation psychology research and practice. Thus, the roots of rehabilitation psychology orient the field toward examining the strengths of individuals with disability and growth toward personal goals.

Growth and Evolution

The growth of rehabilitation psychology was stimulated by counselors who advanced vocational rehabilitation, by social psychologists who studied the mechanisms associated with stigma, and by psychologists who provided clinical services in medical settings to individuals who had incurred physical and neuromuscular disabilities. Rehabilitation psychologists seized the initiative to develop appropriate norms and psychometric properties of many psychological instruments that were otherwise unsuitable for use with individuals with sensory or physical limitations. Wilbert Fordyce relied on an operant perspective to understand further how environmental factors can shape and reinforce "disabled behavior" and behavioral strategies were successfully integrated in rehabilitation programs for persons with chronic pain conditions. Other psychologists used behavioral paradigms to understand psychophysiological processes that could be targeted in self-regulation strategies for persons with disabilities (e.g., biofeedback). More contemporary research has demonstrated the utility of cognitive-behavioral processes in the prediction of adjustment, health and well-being of individuals with disabilities. Cognitive-behavioral strategies are often utilized by rehabilitation psychologists. Rehabilitation psychologists have worked in federally-funded collaborative studies that mandate data-sharing across medical institutions to further understanding of the health and social needs of people with severe yet low-incidence disabilities. These systems have played a pivotal role in measuring and predicting the quality of life for individuals with these conditions.

Issues and Problems

The early pioneers of rehabilitation psychology envisioned a broad scope for the field that could accommodate psychologists from various psychological specialties. The emphasis on shared core values and beliefs, as espoused in the influential works of Wright and Dembo, were deemed central to the field. As opportunities grew in the clinical rehabilitation setting substantially in the recent decades, the job demands were met by psychologists with backgrounds in clinical health psychology and neuropsychology who had little exposure to the field theory perspectives of Wright and Dembo. Clinicians achieved a great milestone when the American Board of Professional Psychology recognized rehabilitation psychology as a board specialty. With this specialization, however, the possible gaps between problem-oriented practice – a long-standing target of rehabilitation psychology pioneers – and the values of disability rights community may have widened. In an influential body of work, Olkin and colleagues decried the relegation of disability issues to the realm of rehabilitation psychology (as a specialty discipline perceived to be wedded to a traditional medical model), and urged professional psychology to recognize disability issues as a matter of diversity that should be addressed in every APA-accredited training program. This view, which is largely informed by scholarship (and activism) associated with the interdisciplinary field of disability studies, has also advocated an affirmation approach to counseling with individuals with disabilities. The basic principles of affirmation therapy recall many of the original values of Wright and Dembo.

Current health care service delivery systems and shrinking federal and state budgets have placed considerable financial restrictions on rehabilitation therapies, generally. Consequently, interventions that have demonstrated effectiveness but are labor-intensive – such as supported employment techniques (which uses on-site job coaches to return persons with severe disabilities to work) and constraint-induced movement therapy (which features physical therapies to enhance motor function to limbs affected by stroke) – encounter difficulty in receiving reimbursement for services.

Future Directions in Practice and Research

Contemporary trends in health and health service delivery provide many unique opportunities for the advancement of rehabilitation psychology values and principles. For the first time in the history of the United States, over 45% of the population now lives with a chronic health condition (and other estimates place this figure over 50%). The health and well-being of individuals with these conditions are ultimately determined by behavioral and social mechanisms that are addressed in rehabilitation psychology. Moreover, the primary model for understanding chronic conditions advanced by the World Health Organization – the International Classification of Functioning, Disability, and Health (ICF; WHO) – defines disability by the environmental and social factors that limit ability and impose limitations in a fashion consonant with the original ideals promoted by the founders of rehabilitation psychology. The ICF de-emphasizes the explanatory utility of a medical diagnosis, and compliments alternative service models that promote independent living, improved access to institutions, and improved role functioning and mobility to reduce disability across the dimensions in the WHO model.

To promote the health and well-being of community-residing persons with disability, it is essential to form collaborative partnerships between these individuals and health service providers so that appropriate community-based services and ongoing access to information and support are available (and this will likely include an increased use of long-distance technologies to circumvent mobility problems). A greater emphasis is now placed on health promotion programs for individuals with disability. Similarly, the effective and strategic provision and usage of assistive devices and enhanced computer technologies to improve function will involve rehabilitation principles; virtual reality technologies may very well expand rehabilitation therapies to individuals who might otherwise have restricted access to traditional therapies (in-home mobility, driver training).

Theory-driven psychological research continues to inform interdisciplinary practice; behavioral neuroscience now demonstrates that physical therapies may work in informed, concentrated ways to improve function and mobility, and possible neural growth. Contemporary models now acknowledge the essential and subjective role of the individual in a manner that can accommodate the study of other assets and character strengths. To demonstrate the effectiveness of novel interventions and services, researchers will have to find ways to integrate qualitative measures in mixed-model designs, and the current emphasis on randomized clinical trials may be frustrated by the real-life difficulties of recruiting sufficient numbers of individuals with low-incidence disabilities while minimizing volunteer biases (and to approximate meaningful control groups). These methodological problems may necessitate intervention studies to incorporate sophisticated analyses available for single-case designs, and greater familiarity with program evaluation and participatory action methods.

Some of these developments, the affirmation of the Lewinian model of disability by the ICF and the increased emphasis on health promotion, may guide the field back to the roots laid down by Wright and Dembo and increase interest in applying positive psychology approaches to challenges that individuals with disability face. Examples are interventions that enhance the health and well-being of families that live with chronic health conditions and individuals with disability and studies of character strengths that enhance the relationship between the individual with disability and other family members.

SEE ALSO: ▶ Environmental resources ▶ Family quality of life ▶ Four-front assessment approach ▶ Self-determination

Reference

Dembo, T., Diller, L., Gordon, W., Leviton, G., & Sherr, R. L. (1973). A view of rehabilitation psychology. *American Psychologist, 28,* 719–722.

Relaxation

Tamara Coder Mikinski
University of Kansas

Relaxation, a state of rest, recreation, and restoration, is vital to emotional, physical, and intellectual health. Individuals who are accomplished at relaxation are masters of the mind-body connection. They are able to promote health, mental acuity, and positive affect through highly personal and satisfying activities or states of being. Being relaxed is not an optional human condition. It is crucial to life and without the most universal form of relaxation, *sleep*, a person becomes at first tired and cranky, then unable to concentrate or make good decisions, and finally will evolve into a psychotic state. Relaxation is not only a personal value but also a cultural one. Psychologists are actively involved with the creation and maintenance of relaxed states through their clinical work.

Physiological Relaxation

The human heart knows relaxation. If our heads followed the heart muscle's pattern of total contraction followed by total relaxation, there might be fewer stress-related health problems. However, our bodies are wired at the most basic level for fight or flight. During an aroused state, our muscles tense, endorphins course through our systems, and we are in a heightened state of alert. When our safety is threatened, such activation is life-saving. However, when we adopt a prolonged state of arousal, there are unhealthy ramifications. Extended periods of stress without bouts of rejuvenating relaxation have been linked with high blood pressure, increased cortisol levels, muscle tension, gastrointestinal difficulties, and psychological distress.

Individuals who aspire to a balanced and healthy life build daily physical relaxation into their schedules. It is not an option; it is a necessity, habit, and pleasure that is greatly missed when it does not happen. Many individuals seek relaxation through physical exercise such as sport, working out at a gym, or through an activity like yoga which combines physical movement, mental engagement, and meditative states. Physical relaxation is highly individualized. What is pleasurable for one person can be boring or unpleasant to another. Therefore, it is extremely important to select a physical activity which is enjoyable, easy to fit into a regular pattern and works with personal lifestyle issues.

The benefits of physical relaxation also mediate psychological distress such as depression and anxiety. Research has shown that aerobic exercise has had a positive impact on reducing levels of depression and increasing levels of neurotransmitters linked to mood. Therefore, a common intervention for individuals experiencing psychological distress and/or stress is to immediately get moving with exercise.

As research on childhood obesity and early onset of Type-2 diabetes highlights, physical activity must be a lifelong commitment. Children are encouraged to develop good exercise, sleep, and dietary habits early in order to combat serious health problems that can begin early in life and have irreversible consequences. Again, balance appears to be the key. A childhood which includes appropriate academic expectations and family support and responsibilities as well as time for many forms of play and relaxation will most likely result in a happy, healthy individual.

Psychological Relaxation

Many psychologists believe that you can think yourself into a relaxed state. Through cognitive-behavioral therapy, clients learn to transform distress into a more relaxed physical and psychological place. By manipulating our thinking, we can effectively dispute and restructure thoughts which might otherwise lead to depression, anxiety, and physical discomfort.

Clients learn to identify "automatic or irrational thoughts" and are trained to send out a mental lasso to capture these beliefs before they spiral, seemingly, out of control and result in such feelings as worry and anxiety or manifest in stomach upset or muscle tension. The client who is skilled in the slow motion thinking of cognitive-behavioral therapy is able to make in the moment shifts in thinking which can quickly result in reinstating an overall sense of well-being.

In addition to strategies such as cognitive restructuring, many psychologists work with a client's capacity to visualize alternative, positive, and optimal states. Clients may be taught a progressive muscle relaxation accompanied by a guided imagery and eventually will be able to invoke these strategies in times of stress to learn to regulate their own stress responses.

Working with clients' strengths through positive approaches such as solution-focused therapy has revolutionized the practice of psychotherapy. When the psychotherapeutic work centers around building on strengths and maximizing the client's personal ability to attain their goals, the client become more relaxed and confident about their ability to manage life's challenges and bumps.

Culture and Relaxation

Relaxation is a universal value. Throughout world cultures, people value and intentionally create opportunities to obtain relaxed states. From formal governmental initiatives like the 40-hour work week to traditional European extended summer holidays, our world community realizes the necessity of time away from the ordinary routine. Our 24/7 society's struggle with balance is reflected in advances in modern technology that feed the workaholic mentality versus the existence of more leisure time per lifetime than ever before. The rapid transmission of information and quick dissemination of health research, make us keenly aware of the health effects of overwork and a lack of down time.

Ancient cultural traditions all emphasized some type of spiritual dimension that included a connection with life beyond the ordinary. Each year, more and more people are drawn to the teachings and practice of yoga which has its roots in ancient India. Yoga is the ultimate mind-body activity combining ancient teachings directed toward enlightenment with movement that promotes health and relaxation. Quieting the "monkey mind" is one of the wonderful side effects of yoga practice.

Spiritual practices such as prayer and meditation yield peace of mind and larger connection which can be highly comforting and relaxing.

Not all attempts to reach a relaxed state are necessarily positive or healthy. The use of alcohol or drugs to cope with stress, anxiety, and depression can be counterproductive and may create more problems beyond the original discomfort or pain. Images in popular American culture promote alcohol use as a means of obtaining a relaxed and fun social environment. Messages from America's pharmaceutical companies promote the use of prescription medication to promote sleep and other relaxed states; however, these can be just as dangerous as alcohol when wrongly or over used as coping mechanisms.

Quick Relaxation Tips

Both research and clinical evidence point to the powerful impact of simple breath training in promoting a relaxed state that can lower blood pressure and reduce anxiety. Here are two simple techniques to try to invoke a relaxed state.

Find a quiet space and close your eyes. With your mind's eye, do a body scan, noting any points you might be holding tension within your body. When you come across a tense or tight spot, take a moment to do the following four-count breathing. Inhaling to a count of four and holding for two counts and then exhaling to a count of four. Try to imagine directing the exhaling breath directly into the tight muscle. For a particularly troublesome spot, you may need to do a couple of cycles of breathing prior to moving on through your body. Within ten minutes, you probably will be able to scan through your entire body and will notice a decrease in muscle tension and a feeling of calm and increased well-being. Another option is to add a visualization to the breathing, such as imagining that the breath is being warmed by the sun or imagining that you are lying on a beach or in a warm pool of water or some other personally appealing visual picture.

If you only have a moment, perhaps at a stop light or in the heat of a stressful interpersonal moment either at work or home, try just doing two cycles of the breathing with your eyes open. You can do the four-count breathing completely unobtrusively and it will still yield the benefit of a moment relaxation.

SEE ALSO: ▶ Heart–brain connection

Religiousness

Brian J. Zinnbauer
Cincinnati, OH

Religiousness can be understood as a personal or group search for the sacred that unfolds within a traditional sacred context. Vitally concerned with human life, death, morality, virtue, social justice, self-improvement, and "the good life," religious beliefs and behavior have had profound effects on individuals, groups, and cultures throughout the course of history. Within the past century, psychologists and other social scientists have examined religious phenomena through both theoretical description and empirical inquiry.

Brief History in Psychology

Religiousness was considered a positive and central element of human development by many of the early twentieth century American psychologists such as William James, G. Stanley Hall, George Coe, and Edwin Starbuck. During this period Europeans such as Sigmund Freud and Carl Jung also produced influential works that described the relationship between religious experience and mental illness or health. However, this early focus and interest waned within American psychology during the middle of the twentieth century with the rise of behaviorism and efforts to differentiate psychology from religion and philosophy.

Interest in religiousness and spirituality among psychologists rose again in the 1960s and has continued to expand up to the present. In addition to generating theories of religious and spiritual functioning, much work within psychology has focused on scale development and validation. Two research areas of intense inquiry include research designed to determine the relationship between religiousness and various heath indices, and methods of incorporating religiousness into mental health intervention. Of note, spirituality as a distinct concept has recently received increased attention, and in contrast to historical conceptions, it has been explicitly differentiated from religiousness. Currently, most American scholars and believers assume that the two terms represent distinct but related concepts.

Dimensions of Religiousness

How to define religiousness remains the topic of ongoing debate among scholars and researchers within psychology. In general, however, there is consensus that religiousness involves the sacred, is both multidimensional and multilevel, can be associated with both mental health and distress, and is best understood within context. To separate it from the broad concept of spirituality, many characterize religiousness as specifically associated with a traditional context or organized faith tradition.

The Sacred

In Peterson and Seligman's positive psychology work entitled *Character Strengths and Virtues*, religiousness is considered to be one aspect of spirituality and both are distinguished from other related concepts such as hope, gratitude, meaning, and secular transcendence by their focus on the sacred. The sacred in this sense refers to that which is considered holy, worthy of reverence, or associated with the divine. Aspects of human life such as healthy lifestyles, relationships, changes, goals in life, cultural traditions, and formal rituals can acquire sacred qualities through the process of sanctification, or lose them through desanctification. It appears that individuals pursue, maintain, or react differently to sacred phenomena than to secular objects and processes. These processes have recently been investigated empirically by psychologists such as Ken Pargament and Robert Emmons.

Multidimensions and Levels

In the past, popular usage and scientific inquiry have often focused on specific aspects of religiousness such as religious attitudes, frequency of prayer, or religious experiences. However, religiousness is not one-dimensional. Rather, it touches on a wide range of psychological phenomena such as beliefs, behavior, emotions, identity, meaning, personality, and morality. Further, religious correlates and phenomena extend beyond individual intrapsychic functioning to many levels of analysis. In other words, as described by theorist Ken Wilber, concepts such as religiousness can be examined from the micro to the macro in terms of neuroanatomy, intrapsychic phenomenon, states of consciousness, family dynamics, group processes and norms, cultural patterns, social systems, and global concerns. For example, the process of religious conversion may be understood through an examination of neurotransmitter levels, changes in brain activation, emotional experiences, cognitive shifts, alterations in personal and social behavior, role and identity transformations, family impacts, group membership changes, cultural influences, and global events.

Similarly, a full understanding of the relationship between religiousness and positive psychology requires attention to these multiple dimensions and levels. Examples relevant to both domains include faith-inspired resilience, happiness, civic virtues, altruism, social support, family influences, and culture. Likewise, several processes or outcomes may be similarly relevant: the development of character, methods of increasing adherence to healthy proscriptions such as abstinence from alcohol or risky behavior, the process of forgiveness, conversion experiences that solidify identity and resolve suffering, religious aspects of effective coping, and clerical methods of interpersonal influence for health and virtue promotion.

Health Outcomes

A common error when characterizing religiousness and spirituality has been to assume an evaluative component when defining the concepts. For example, at times spirituality has been portrayed as representing only the positive side of life, and religiousness has been described as a hindrance to spiritual expression. In contrast, a scientific approach to the concepts considers the relationships between religiousness and health as empirical questions to be investigated. Accordingly, several current research programs are examining the relationship between religiousness and specific health outcomes. Two of many examples are the SPIRIT research group at Bowling Green State University lead by Ken Pargament and Annette Mahoney, and the Center for Spirituality, Theology, and Health at Duke University lead by Harold Keonig. A consensus conclusion across studies is that there are positive links between religiousness and mental and physical health. However, the nature of those links is not completely understood, and several critics have argued for greater rigor in the methods used to conduct research on this topic.

Research is also beginning to understand those forms of religiousness that are related to poor outcomes or impairments in functioning. For example, religious struggles with God, with others, or within oneself have been related to psychological distress, slower recovery from physical health problems, and mortality. Other consistent results have found that negative religious coping, such as prolonged anger at God or conflict among members of a religious congregation, is also linked to declines in physical and mental health.

Context

Context is one criterion by which religiousness and spirituality are often distinguished: religiousness is that portion of spirituality that unfolds within a sacred traditional context. Cultural context has also been identified as an important aspect of religiousness. Proponents of multiculturalism frequently include religiousness as an aspect of cultural diversity, and professional organizations such as the American Psychological Association and the American Counseling Association explicitly address religion in their codes of conduct as an element of ethnic and cultural diversity that must be considered in professional work.

Future Directions

The general goals of personal development and civic improvement are common to both religion and positive psychology. Many scholars are currently investigating the various ways in which religiousness contributes to positive and negative mental health outcomes, and this is likely to prove a fertile and rewarding avenue for research in the twenty-first century. Further inquiry that includes the range of phenomena from the biological to the global are needed to provide a clear understanding of religiousness, as well as translating this knowledge into applications that can be used to directly improve the lives of individuals, groups, and societies.

SEE ALSO: ▶ Spirituality

Resilience

J. J. Cutuli and Ann S. Masten
Institute of Child Development, University of Minnesota

Resilience generally refers to positive adaptation in the context of risk or adversity. It is a broad concept that encompasses a wide range of phenomena, including the capacity of a system to withstand or recover from significant challenges. In human development, resilience research has focused on three distinct situations: a) functioning well during a time of significant adversity ("stress resistance"); b) returning to a previous level of good functioning following a traumatic or severely disturbing experience ("bouncing back"); or c) achieving new levels of positive or normal adaptation when severely adverse conditions improve ("normalization").

In all these cases, resilience refers to patterns of doing well after exposure to a serious adversity or threat.

People have probably been intrigued with resilience as long as stories have been told of heroes, heroines, and underdogs who overcome great obstacles on the road to success. The science of resilience, however, began only a few decades ago. Resilience research grew out of research on people at risk of developing problems, including children at risk because of their family background (such as having a parent with a severe mental disorder), life experiences (such as premature birth or divorce), or hazardous rearing conditions (such as poverty or neighborhood violence). Investigators seeking to understand the etiology of mental illness began to notice that some individuals "at risk" were doing quite well, even flourishing. Pioneering investigators in the 1970s and 1980s, including Norman Garmezy, Lois Murphy, Michael Rutter, and Emmy Werner, recognized the importance of unexpectedly positive development, and began to search for explanations of resilience. From the outset, these pioneers had the goal of gaining knowledge for promoting better outcomes among individuals at risk for problems.

Resilience and Developmental Psychopathology

Early resilience scientists sought strategies for conducting informative research on resilience at a time when there was little interest in positive psychology and measures of positive adaptation in adults and children were underdeveloped. This mission was facilitated by the emergence of developmental psychopathology, which provided an overarching perspective for conceptualizing different pathways across the lifespan. Developmental psychopathologists emphasized the crucial importance of studying processes that lead to both positive and negative outcomes. This perspective embraced the study of resilience as a key domain of research for preventing problems and also for understanding and promoting positive development. Developmental psychopathology and resilience theory were both deeply influenced by systems theory.

Resilience as Process

In developmental systems theory, all complex patterns of behavior arise from the interaction of many influences acting across multiple levels of analysis. This principle certainly applies to resilience, which emerges from dynamic processes over time. Resilience involves many systems from cells to individuals to families to societies. An individual may be said to have more or less capacity for resilience, but the actual pattern of an individual's behavior will result from many interactions, both within the person and between the person and environment. Because of the many interactions involved, resilience cannot be viewed as a single trait. In any person's life, resilience arises from many resources and processes that shape a positive life trajectory. Many attributes of a person, their relationships, and other resources are involved in these processes. Therefore, efforts to identify a universal trait of "resiliency" that protects people against any adversity are misguided.

Two Judgments

Researchers soon realized that resilience is an inference based on two fundamental judgments about a person's life: a) something has occurred with the potential to seriously harm development or disrupt good functioning; and b) the person is doing OK by some criteria. To study resilience, it is necessary for investigators to define and measure two components of resilience: the threat to positive adaptation, usually termed risk, adversity, or stressful life experiences, and positive development or adaptation, often defined in terms of the person's quality of life or success in major domains of achievement expected for people of a given age in a given culture. In order to explain resilience, it is also important to study predictors of different outcomes among people facing similar threats. Both researchers and practitioners want to know which factors are important in producing resilience among children threatened by adversity and how these factors work.

Defining Positive Adaptation in Resilience Research

Before one can begin to think about factors and processes that bring about positive adaptation, it is necessary to first define what counts as "positive adaptation." Investigators have focused on different aspects of positive functioning and development to define and measure the criteria for positive adaptation. These varying criteria are often the product of the specific research goals of the investigators. Some criteria are broader (such as general competence) and some are narrower (such as academic achievement). Some focus on behavioral development and health, whereas others emphasize physical health.

Many studies have focused on two broad domains of adaptive behavior, often called *psychopathology* and *competence*. Studies with a focus on mental health typically define adaptation in relation to subjective well-being and the absence of clinical levels of symptoms or disorder. Thus, good adaptation is judged from assessments that a person is showing positive mental health rather than emotional or behavior problems. In contrast, developmental scientists often define positive adaptation in terms of competence in age-salient developmental tasks.

Developmental tasks are the standards for behavior by which people of a particular age are judged in a given culture and time in history. Many developmental tasks are common across cultures, whereas some are unique to specific cultures. For small children, common developmental tasks include forming an attachment bond to a caregiver, learning to walk and talk, and following simple commands. In school-age children, key tasks include school success, getting along with peers, and following the rules of home, school, and community. During adolescence, individuals are expected to learn more advanced subjects, behave and follow rules across contexts (including societal laws), form close relationships with peers, and begin to explore the worlds of work and romantic relationships. In adulthood, work and romantic relationships become salient tasks, often followed by family formation and parenting. Successes in these changing developmental tasks indicate that a person is adapting to society in expected ways. Outstanding achievement is not required; instead, the person is expected to meet minimum standards for functioning. Such achievements also carry the implicit expectation for future success.

One of the basic tenets of developmental psychology is the idea that achieving competence in one developmental period facilitates the development of later competence. There are cumulative effects of competence: success in one period of development is carried forward because it provides a strong foundation of skills and achievements on which future competence is built. Along with competence, children develop adaptive tools for life that are honed by experience.

Threats to Positive Adaptation or Development: Risk and Adversity

Attributes of a person or a person's situation that forecast later problems are called *risk factors*. Research on groups of people who have certain factors in their lives has indicated that there is an elevated chance for a specific negative outcome among the group as a whole. Those with these certain risk factors are often said to be "at-risk" for the problematic outcome. Risk factors commonly co-occur, and there may be a much greater likelihood of problems when risk factors accumulate in the lives of individuals. Risk is a general term that includes a wide variety of predictors, including traumatic life events, chronic disadvantages, and status variables. In psychology and resilience science, the risk factors of poverty, low socioeconomic status, violence and maltreatment, prematurity and low birth weight, minority status, war, and natural disasters have all received a great deal of study.

Given the goal of understanding how individuals overcome adversity, it is important for resilience researchers to understand how negative life experiences interfere with competence. Risk factors may exert their deleterious effects in many different ways during various times in development. Some risk factors, such as malnutrition or exposure to toxic substances, interfere directly with the function or development of adaptive biological systems. Other risks can operate through limiting the experiences or opportunities available to the individual, for example when children with a chronic illness are not able to interact with peers in normal social activities, or adolescents living in severely impoverished areas have little access to quality schools. Still others work by increasing the likelihood of experiencing additional adversities: People who are impulsive tend to have more accidents or injuries.

The impact of risk factors also can vary for different periods of development. For example, caregivers are important across many ages, but very young children are highly dependent on others for care. Consequently, young children may be more affected than older youth by risk factors that interfere with the caregiver-child relationship, including the loss of the caregiver or risks that involve substandard levels of care, such as a severe depression in an infant's primary caregiver.

Predictors of Resilience: Promotive and Protective Factors

Given the twin goals of understanding and facilitating resilience, it is important to study the factors that predict resilience and how these work. Resilience researchers have studied many potential factors that might account for better outcomes in the context of risk or adversity. These have come to be called promotive and protective factors. *Promotive factors* are associated with good outcomes in general, regardless of risk exposure. Healthy brain development and good parenting predict many good outcomes in life, regardless of risk exposure. In contrast, *protective factors* moderate risk, showing a special effect when adversity is high. Some protective factors are analogous to airbags in automobiles or the antibodies of the human immune system. They have no function until they are activated by threat and then they serve a protective role. Emergency social services, like child protection, are intended to work in this way.

Other protective factors have a generally promotive role even when risk is low, but also take on special protective functions when adversity is high. Many of the most basic (and flexible) human adaptive systems serve multiple roles in this way, probably as a result of biological and cultural evolution. For example, parents serve many roles in human development, both at low and high levels of adversity. A good parent may routinely feed and care for a child and promote developmental task achievements, such as school success, but also may take special action in the face of a major threat. Thus a parent may intervene to protect the child from impending harm or help the child recover, as when a parent prepares a child for the loss of a loved one or helps a child recover from an assault or a house fire.

Studies of developmental resilience around the world have repeatedly noted a striking consistency in the most frequently reported promotive and protective factors, including attributes of individuals, their relationships, and the contexts that appear to offset or ameliorate risks. The most widely reported of these factors are good relationships, and in the case of young children, a secure attachment bond with a competent caregiver. Close relationships have been found to moderate risk across all ages. Caregivers who provide warmth, security, and reassurance in the face of adversity are robustly associated with favorable outcomes in children, whereas impaired caregiving is particularly damaging. The protection afforded by caregivers is multifaceted. Caregivers are a direct resource of help and security for children, and they also play a major role in the development of other protective factors, including self-regulation skills, cognitive skills, and relationships with other people. Research has documented the role of positive relationships with caregivers on many aspects of development and particularly in the building of adaptive tools for competence.

Social connectedness to people beyond the family is also a key type of protective factor. Connections with adults, including teachers, coaches, or mentors, have positive benefits for children and youth. These adults can be a positive influence and provide stability that is lacking in the child's home life when the family is disrupted by adversity. Peer relationships and acceptance also may serve an important protective role as children grow older. In addition to providing another source of support, peers help a child internalize sociocultural values while affording opportunities to develop and refine good social skills. In these ways, peer relationships may provide a supportive training ground for at-risk children to cultivate the interpersonal abilities that foster later close relationships and building of social support networks over the lifespan.

Another important group of protective factors is related to individual differences in cognitive functioning, self-efficacy, motivation, and self-regulation skills. Children with good problem-solving skills and age-appropriate regulation of emotions, attention, and actions, who believe in themselves and are motivated to adapt, often fare better when confronted with adversity. Such children have a broad range of personal attributes and skills at their disposal; they find more opportunities, they persist in the face of challenge, and they also seem to attract more support from other people, attributes that serve them well in adverse situations.

The Promise of Resilience Science for Prevention and Clinical Intervention

Understanding how risk and resilience processes operate has revolutionized thinking and strategies for prevention and treatment, shifting models, methods, and measures toward a strengths-based approach. In resilience-based frameworks, prevention and practice are oriented to set positive goals, to measure assets and protective factors as well as risks, and to include strategies intended to increase the odds of resilience by reducing risk exposure, increasing promotive factors, and mobilizing protective systems. Preventive interventions and programs are being designed to foster positive outcomes among individuals believed to be at-risk due to existing or anticipated adversities. In addition, prevention research with experimental designs holds the potential to test theories about promotive and protective processes and how they work, thus contributing to resilience theory as well as evidenced-based practice.

As resilience science expands, models of risk and protection are beginning to incorporate multiple levels of analysis and their function across the lifespan. Consequently, comprehensive and integrated accounts of resilience are emerging that include the interactions among genes, neurobiology, behavior, family and peer relationships, and the larger systems represented by neighborhoods, schools, communities, and cultures. As ongoing research on resilience in development continues, diverse stakeholders in the health and well-being of young people have a growing body of knowledge to inform their policies and programs. As a result, there is promising progress toward the goal of evidenced-based interventions to promote resilience in people at risk across the lifespan.

SEE ALSO: ▶ Attachment theory   ▶ Developmental psychopathology   ▶ Protective factor   ▶ Werner, Emmy

Respect

Susan S. Hendrick and Clyde Hendrick
Texas Tech University

Respect is an important component of both personal self-identity and interpersonal relationships. Feeling respected can almost be considered a basic human right.

Studying Respect

According regard or perceived worth to someone conveys a sense of respect, and valuing another person's feelings and thoughts is also part of the respect process. Respect has been studied less than has disrespect, with the latter behavior related to stereotyping, prejudice, issues of power and status, injustices, and the like. *Disrespecting* someone is serious business and can lead to ruptures in relationships, gang violence, and wars between nations.

Respect has been studied in the workplace, since it may play a part in hiring decisions. Jackson, Esses, and Burris found that liking, respect, and gender stereotyping were all related to hiring decisions, but respect was of particular importance. Issues of respect may also differ for women and men. Tannen noted numerous gender differences in communication strategies and observed that women in work settings want to be liked. In order to achieve this, they may forego being respected. Men, on the other hand, may more likely opt for respect, sometimes being liked less as a result.

Important as respect might be in the workplace, it is even more significant in personal relationships, particularly intimate, partnered ones.

Respect in Close Relationships

Although romantic relationships are the primary focus here, some interesting research has explored respect-giving and respect-denying behaviors among cross-sex friends.

Denial of respect to friends impairs the friendship, and indeed, awarding respect may be almost a "rule" in both close friendships and romantic relationships. It is important in relationships such as marriage in many cultures and countries, and its meaning changes over time. For example, Hirsch found that in Mexican marriages, formal respect between partners has been a part of traditional marriage and traditional gender roles. Yet more recently, intimacy has joined respect as an important value for marital partners. Some contemporary scholars believe that mutual and egalitarian respect is an essential characteristic of marital love and an enduring marital relationship. The clinical literature addressing couple therapy and enrichment has openly mentioned respect as an important ingredient for a relationship that "works." Indeed, John Gottman has worked with couples for decades, noting that most couples desire "just two things from their marriage – love and respect" (1994, p. 18). Scholars such as Feeney, Noller, and Ward found that respect was one of five dimensions of marital quality. Yet although respect has been rather widely acknowledged as important, research on respect in romantic relationships has been relatively recent.

Current Research on Respect in Relationships

Frei and Shaver set out to systematically explore respect in the context of close relationships. They first determined the features that people would identify as central to the construct of respect as it might be enacted in both romantic relationships and in parent/caregiver relationships. Across several studies, they found that respect seemed to be an attitude rather than an emotion, that there was relative consistency across people from different ethnic groups in identifying several central aspects of respect, that a partner's "respect-worthiness" was important when measuring respect, and that respect was a better predictor of relationship satisfaction than were measures of love, liking, or attachment. They also developed a measure to assess respect in romantic relationships.

A keen observer of respect, sociologist Sara Lawrence-Lightfoot addressed the topic in *Respect: An Exploration*. She wrote in biographical form about six different people whom she viewed as embodying six different dimensions of respect. Her words bring these people to life. These exemplars of respect include a midwife, who in the drama of birth, gives inner-city women a sense of their own *empowerment*; a pediatrician whose respectful *healing* supports both children and their parents; a high school English teacher whose creative *dialogue* allows her students to be heard; a photographer whose *curiosity* about his subjects makes the photo process a collaboration, a law professor whose goal is to challenge in order to engender *self-respect* in his students, and a chaplain who works with dying persons through *attention*, as a witness to the transition. These embodiments of respect, transcending race and gender, speak the dimensions of respect in their actions.

Consonant with these six dimensions is the concept that relational respect carries, among other things, aspects of both equality/mutuality and caring/supportiveness.

The notion of mutuality is highlighted by other scholars, and the caring aspect is an inevitable part of valuing another person because of their sheer existence in the world and in our lives.

Research by Hendrick and Hendrick built on Lawrence-Lightfoot's conception of respect and was consistent with other work showing respect's fundamental importance to relational satisfaction. For example, in the Hendricks' research, respect was related positively to passionate, friendship-oriented, and altruistic love as well as to commitment, satisfaction, and other positive relationship qualities. These findings were consistent for both college students and older persons in the work force; thus respect is powerful for relational partners who are of different ages and different relational stages. Not surprisingly, respect was related negatively to game-playing love. Respect that is both caring and egalitarian has no place for game-playing. In the actual prediction of relationship satisfaction for people in romantic relationships, the two most powerful relational conditions were passionate love and respect. Passionate love has been shown to positively affect satisfaction in many previous studies, but the results for respect are new and compelling. It appears that respect has always been in the background as a sustaining relational force, but only recently have we begun to understand just how important it is.

Future Directions for Studying Respect

Respect can be viewed through a number of lenses in the years ahead. One interesting conceptual direction is the possible evolutionary basis for respect. It is evolutionarily adaptive for humans to live in groups for purposes of safety and sustenance, and pair-bonding between males and females is necessary for reproduction and species continuation. Positive emotions such as love foster these bonds, and it is logical to assume that respect would also. Respect within the group might allow for both protection of those who do not hold power and a judicious balance between those who do hold power. Within the couple, respect appears to contribute to satisfaction, which in turn is related to the continuation of the relationship.

Another area of investigation might be the relationship between respect and conflict in romantic relationships. When partners have greater respect for each other, their conflict may be reduced. Or perhaps partners who respect each other feel comfortable disagreeing. Perhaps the level of respect in the relationship relates to the ways in which conflict is enacted, such that respectful disagreement characterizes couples in which each partner has both high self-respect and high respect for the other. These issues and questions can help in better understanding the "successful" relationship.

Finally, how does respect influence personal growth and the "self-identity" mentioned earlier? Carl Rogers referred to "unconditional positive regard" as a core facilitative condition for psychological growth. Perhaps respect, given freely and without condition, can contribute to psychological and even relational growth. The future study of respect is rich with promise.

SEE ALSO: ► Romantic love

Reference

Gottman, J. M. (1994). *Why marriages succeed or fail*. New York: Simon & Schuster.

Rogers, Carl

John C. Wade
University of Kansas

Carl Rogers (1902–1987) is known as the founder of client-centered therapy, emphasizing a nondirective, collaborative relationship in which the client determines the focus and pace of treatment. He was a leading spokesperson for humanistic psychology, and fostered advances in psychotherapy research. Rogers studied religion as an undergraduate, before changing his focus to psychology and earning an MA and then a PhD from Columbia University in 1931.

Rogers began to question the prevailing Freudian psychoanalytic climate of the period, and differed from Freud in that he regarded people as basically good and healthy, with the potential to understand themselves and resolve their own problems without direct intervention from the therapist. Rogers' theory is founded upon this principle, termed the *actualizing tendency*, which assumes that we all have an innate motivation not just to survive, but to develop our potential to the fullest extent possible and to find and create meaning in our lives.

Rogers contended that if the therapist created an environment where the client experienced genuineness, acceptance and empathy from the therapist, growth and positive change would naturally occur. Three attributes of the therapist are necessary for a transformative therapeutic environment to occur: 1) congruence – the therapist is genuine and authentic with his/her clients; 2) unconditional positive regard – the therapist is accepting, caring and nonjudgmental; and 3) accurate, empathic understanding – being able to deeply grasp the subjective, lived world of the other person.

Although we have a natural inclination toward self-actualization, Rogers believed that as we develop, our parents, teachers, peers, etc. place "conditions of worth" on us. We are praised and reinforced only for certain behaviors, such as eating our vegetables, and are criticized or shunned for other behaviors such as talking too loudly. This leads us to believe that acceptance and positive regard is conditional, and causes us to shape our behavior to meet the expectations of others instead of allowing our behavior to be guided by our actualizing tendencies. The unconditional positive regard and trust in the client shown by the therapist enables the client to reconnect with his or her authentic self. Because of the belief in the client's capacity for awareness and positive change, the client-centered approach rejects the role of the therapist as the authority and gives responsibility primarily to the client.

Rogers served as president of the American Psychological Association in 1947, and received a distinguished contribution award in 1956 for research in psychotherapy. In his later years, Rogers expanded his focus to education, business and industry, conflict resolution and the search for world peace. Shortly before he died, he was nominated for a Nobel Peace Prize for his efforts at the reduction of interracial tension and achieving world peace. Rogers wrote several influential books, including *Counseling and Psychotherapy* (1942), *Client Centered Therapy* (1951), *On Becoming a Person* (1961), and *A Way of Being* (1980). Rogers' legacy has profoundly impacted the practice of psychotherapy, and is the foundation for many of the key principles of positive psychology today.

SEE ALSO: ▶ Actualizing tendency ▶ Humanistic psychology
▶ Positive therapy

Romantic Love

Clyde Hendrick and Susan S. Hendrick
Texas Tech University

Love consists of great emotional affection, and loving another person and being loved by that person in turn are among the most meaningful aspects of being human. Romantic love and many other types of love are all of great importance in our lives.

Love in the Human Condition

Love is one manifestation of the basic human need for connection, referred to by Baumeister and Leary (1995) as the "need to belong." This need for connection requires that people have some number of "lasting, positive, and significant personal relationships" (p. 497). The actual number of these relationships depends on a person's preferences and life situation, since some people want only a few intimate relationships, whereas other people want numerous meaningful connections with others. To meet human needs for belonging, these relationships must be positive, ongoing, and stable.

People typically begin forming relational bonds in infancy, establishing a template for relatedness that may follow throughout a person's lifetime. Attachment theory describes how infants and their parents develop these bonds during early months and years. Attachment theory has been expanded to include the bonds that adult romantic partners have with each other.

Love is one aspect of intimate attachment. Shaver, Morgan and Wu proposed that love is a basic human emotion, much like joy or sadness. Because virtually all people feel love at one time or another, evolutionary scholars have said that we are "hard-wired" for love, meaning that the ability to love and be loved is part of our biological nature. Some scholars have pointed to the adaptive nature of love, noting that it aids in reproduction and continuation of the species. For example, romantic love guides the mating process that results in reproduction, whereas mother love ensures that mothers feed and nurture their infants.

Many types of love exist, including love of parents for children and children for parents, love of family, love of friends, and so on. Our focus is romantic love – the kind of love that leads to marriage and other long-term partnerships.

History of the Study of Love

For centuries, love has been a major theme of drama, poetry, literature, art, and music. Irving Singer detailed the history of the study of love and identified four broad conceptual ways of looking at love: Agape (divine love); Eros (love for what is beautiful or good); Nomos (love resulting in obedience to a deity or a loved one); and Philia (friendship love). Singer also proposed two fundamental ways of loving another person, *appraisal* and *bestowal*. Appraisal is love that is given because of the perceived value of particular qualities that the loved one is seen to have, whereas bestowal is given simply because the other person exists in the world. It is love given without conditions.

Social scientific study of love is relatively recent. For example, Berscheid and Walster contrasted passionate and companionate love. Passionate love is emotionally intense and characterizes early stages in love relationships. As this "hot" love cools during the course of a relationship, companionate love, cooler and more friendship-oriented, presumably emerges from the ashes of passion. More recently, however, research has shown that both passionate love and friendship-oriented love are important to partners early in their love relationships and much later as well. Contemporary research on love has broadened greatly both our ways of thinking about love and our ways of measuring how people love each other.

Conceptualizing and Measuring Love

Friendship and Love

Davis and Todd conceptualized loving and liking as sharing many of the same characteristics, though in different amounts, and they developed the Relationship

Rating Form to measure those characteristics. The scale was later refined to include six subscales: Care; Conflict; Intimacy; Passion; Satisfaction; and Viability.

Passionate Love

Hatfield argued for the importance of passionate love as an extremely important form of love that is found across historical periods and world cultures and is essentially "universal" to the human condition. Hatfield and Sprecher developed the Passionate Love Scale to measure this form of love.

Prototypes of Love

Fehr took a prototype approach to the study of love, attempting to discover the "best examples" of love. She found that people rated companionate love as the most *typical* example, but friendship, parental and maternal love were also viewed as good examples of love. Fehr was not particularly seeking to find romantic love, and indeed found that passionate and sexual love were rated as less "typical" of love. Other researchers sought the best example of romantic love and found that passion emerged as one of the central features. It seems that characteristics seen as important to love may vary depending on the type of love that is being considered.

Love and Self-Expansion

Aron and Aron took the perspective of Eastern traditions in conceptualizing the growth of the self, referring to it as *self-expansion*. One method of self-expansion is falling in love, wherein the partner is incorporated into one's own self in an expansion process. This expansion is measured by having respondents draw circles (representing self and partner) which overlap each other, thus showing how much of the partner is actually viewed as part of the self.

Love as a Triangle

An important theory of love, the triangular theory of love, was proposed by Sternberg, who viewed love as composed of mixes of three primary components: intimacy; passion; and commitment. These components, when combined in varied proportions, result in eight different kinds of love: consummate love (all three components present); nonlove (all components absent); liking (primarily intimacy); infatuated love (primarily passion); empty love (primarily commitment); companionate love (intimacy + commitment); fatuous love (passion + commitment); and romantic love (passion + intimacy).

More recently, Sternberg has presented the view that people in essence create their own love stories. In *Love Is A Story*, he offered 25 love stories or "guiding metaphors" that people enact in their romantic relationships. If love is indeed a story and people can be helped to understand their own story, they can sometimes "rewrite" aspects of the story to achieve happier relational outcomes.

Love Styles

People have different personality styles, so perhaps they also have different love styles. Still another theory of love was developed by Lee, whose research revealed that people have different love styles. Six major love styles have been studied extensively: Eros is the passionate love style, characterized by intensity, communication, and a tendency toward "love at first sight"; ludus is the game-playing love style, avoiding commitment and just wanting to have a good time; storge is the friendship-based love style, epitomizing stable, companionate love; pragma is the practical love style, characterized by practical searching for an appropriate love partner; mania is the possessive, dependent love style that is insecure and experiences intense emotional highs and lows; finally, agape is the altruistic love style, characterized by concern for the partner's welfare, sometimes above one's own welfare. Questionnaires to measure the love styles were developed and refined over a number of studies. Most recently, a 24-item measure called the Love Attitudes Scale: Short Form is typically used to measure the love styles.

Developing theories about and measures of romantic love is the work of scholars, yet how does this work answer questions and solve problems that happen to real people in real romantic relationships?

Love: Gender, Sex, Age, and Culture

Popular media often gives us the impression that women and men have very different approaches to love, but when it comes to love styles, the genders are more similar than they are different. Yet they are not exactly the same. For example, men tend to report being both more game-playing and altruistic than women, whereas women are more friendship-oriented than men. Yet these differences are small.

Love and sex have often been decoupled by researchers, such that the two topics are studied as though they have nothing to do with one another. Another point of view is that sex and love are linked but that one is more important than or "subsumes" the other. Aron and Aron placed such ideas on a continuum, anchoring "sex is really love" at one end and "love is really sex" at the other end. Research specifically exploring people's everyday perceptions of the links between love and sex indicate that love and sex are linked, not separated, and that both are viewed as important in romantic relationships. When people wrote about how love and sex were linked in their relationships, several themes emerged, including the idea that "love is most important" and "sex demonstrates love." Both relational aspects were deemed significant.

As noted earlier, couples at all ages and stages of relationships appear to value both the passionate and friendship components of love. Research exploring how love might contribute to relationship satisfaction in young, dating couples found that a combination of passionate, friendship, and altruistic love was a positive predictor of relationship satisfaction, but game-playing love was a negative predictor. Montgomery and Sorell (1997) assessed love styles and other constructs in young unmarried adults, married adults under age 30 and without children, married people aged 24 to 50 with children still at home, and married people aged 50 to 70 without children at home. The greatest differences were not between the younger and older couples but rather between the people who were unmarried and those who were married. Other research studies show similar results: younger and older couples simply do not differ as much as we might think. "Individuals throughout the life-stages of marriage consistently endorse the love attitudes involving passion, romance, friendship, and self-giving love" (Montgomery & Sorell, p. 61).

Love does not look drastically different across genders or across ages, but several studies have sought to understand how love might differ across countries and cultures. Although Hatfield argued that passionate love is fundamental across both historical periods and world cultures and is essentially universal to humanity, others noted that love exists within a cultural context and must be understood that way. Cho and Cross considered ancient Chinese literature and proposed that several different types of love (e.g., passionate love, casual love, obsessive love, devoted love) were apparent during historical eras from 3,000 to 500 years ago. So these are not recent innovations in the Eastern (or Western) world. These authors also explored current love styles among Taiwanese students living in the United States, finding that although several love styles existed, they were not exactly the same love styles proposed by Lee. In fact, Agape (altruistic love) and Pragma (practical love) combined to form an "Obligatory Love" type, which was more appropriate to Taiwanese culture than Agape or Pragma considered separately. Pacific Islanders, Japanese Americans, and European Americans (all living in Hawaii) were compared on love and relationship characteristics, with no differences between the groups for either companionate or passionate love. Such findings, which are echoed by other research studies, are not surprising if in fact love is a basic emotion, is part of a fundamental need to be "in relationship," and is part of our biological make-up. We are likely much more the same in our humanity than we are different.

In spite of all the theory-building, measurement development, and accumulating research findings, questions about love remain. It is almost as if our answers to existing questions simply produce more questions.

Future Directions for the Study of Love

Loving others and being loved by them is a basic part of what it is to be a person, so love is clearly an important topic. It appears that many aspects of love have transcended time and culture, and many of the ways in which we experience and express romantic love are similar to the ways in which such love was expressed in ages past. Yet societies are changing rapidly in a world in which technology is exploding, distant cultures are becoming neighbors, and the future in some ways may differ from the present more than the present differs from the past. How might love evolve in a world of constant communication (e.g., via cell phones and email) where real connection may become more and more elusive? Will our increasingly global village result in racial and cultural barriers being lowered, so that more romantic relationships may be formed between persons of different cultures, races, religions? Exploring love's evolution – and its constancy – remains a fascinating task for the future.

SEE ALSO: ▶ Adult attachment security   ▶ Intimacy   ▶ Respect

References

Baumeister, R. F., & Leary, M. R. (1995). The need to belong: Desire for interpersonal attachments as a fundamental human motivation. *Psychological Bulletin, 117,* 497–529.
Montgomery, M. J., & Sorell, G. T. (1997). Differences in love attitudes across family life stages. *Family Relations, 46,* 55–61.

Ryff, Carol

Corey L. M. Keyes
Emory University

Carol Ryff is the Director of the Institute on Aging and a Professor of Psychology at the University of Wisconsin, Madison. Her research centers on the study of psychological well-being, an area in which she has developed multidimensional assessment scales (translated into more than 25 different languages). Her article on psychological well-being, published in 1989 in the *Journal of Personality and Social Psychology,* is a classic in the field of well-being. It is considered by many to be among the seminal articles that launched the study of the eudaimonia tradition of well-being within the discipline of psychology.

Subsequent research by Carol Ryff and colleagues has addressed how psychological well-being varies with age, gender, socioeconomic status, ethnic/minority status, cultural context, as well as by the experiences, challenges, and transitions individuals confront as they move through the life course. Two primary themes characterize her most recent work. First, she has investigated whether psychological well-being is protective of good physical health during life transitions and stress. Second, she is among the leading researchers investigating psychosocial health and its linkages to biological markers in ongoing longitudinal investigations linking positive psychosocial factors to neuroendocrine, immune, cardiovascular, and neural circuitry biomarkers. The guiding theme within Ryff's research is human resilience, i.e., how some individuals are able to maintain, or regain, their well-being in the face of significant life challenge and what neurobiology underlies this capacity.

Carol Ryff was born in Wheatland, Wyoming on October 27, 1950. She earned her PhD in 1978 in lifespan psychology in the College of Human Development at Pennsylvania State University. Her mentors at Penn State were Orville "Bert" Brim in sociology and Paul Baltes in psychology, both of whom were the pioneers in creating the field of lifespan psychology. Starting in 1988, she was among a handful of select scholars chosen to form the nucleus of the John D. and Catherine T. MacArthur Foundation's interdisciplinary Research Network on Successful Midlife Development. She has been honored as being elected a fellow of the Gerontological Association of America, and Division 20, Adult Development and Aging, of the American Psychological Association. She also has been awarded the Henry Murray in 2003 by the Society for Personality and Social Psychology. Carol Ryff has published over 120 publications in the research areas described above. She is currently the director of the MIDUS (Midlife in the US) longitudinal study, which is based on a large national sample of Americans and twins. Funded by a $28 million grant from the National Institute on Aging, the MIDUS longitudinal study has become a major forum for studying health as an integrated biopsychosocial process, reflecting Carol Ryff's passion for fostering interdisciplinary and integrative research on health and human development.

SEE ALSO: ▶ Well-being

S

Saleebey, Dennis

Uta M. Walter

Catholic University of Applied Sciences, Berlin, Germany

Dennis Saleebey, DSW, born August 29, 1936, is Professor Emeritus at the School of Social Welfare, University of Kansas, and perhaps best known for his work on the *strengths perspective* in social work. Saleebey coined this term through various publications, most notably *The Strengths Perspective in Social Work Practice*, currently available in its fourth edition. Saleebey started his professional career as a mental health social worker for the U.S. Air Force in the 1960s in San Antonio, and advanced to Chief Social Worker in the Child Diagnostic Clinic of Wilford Hall Hospital. He received his doctorate from the University of California – Berkeley in 1972, and began his academic career at the University of Maine. Saleebey's interests soon shifted away from the individual and pathology-focused approach he had encountered in clinical social work toward those factors that made people, families, and communities stronger, more resilient, and more hopeful. Particularly inspired by Ernest Becker's scholarship on how humans construct and revise meaning for their lives, Saleebey began to ask how people are capable of overcoming the most difficult of circumstances, and how some are not merely coping but at times even thriving in the face of adversity.

After 17 years at the University of Texas at Arlington, Saleebey, by then a widowed father of four children, joined the faculty of the University of Kansas in 1987. Together with Ann Weick, he challenged the profession's tendencies to focus on problems and dysfunctions. Fervently seeking beyond the bounds of social work, he connected with kindred ideas including those of the late Insoo Kim Berg and Steve de Shazer and their solution-focused approach, Michael White's narrative therapy, Steven and Sybil Wolin's resiliency work, and Roger Mills' approach to community development. Adding to the chorus of social work scholars who championed postmodern ideas, Saleebey argued for the reconnection of social work with its roots of empowerment and for shifting the focus toward strengths and capacities. In his own words:

> I believe, in the long run and in the most generous sense, that the business of social work is to ease or quell oppression and to engage those we help in the search for the liberation of spirit, soul, body, – and community. I also am convinced of the magnificence of the capacity for rebound and resilience in people(s). Surely it can be compromised, even crushed, but it stands as a testimony to our survival as a species, and to the inner beacon of the soul. I believe that, in the end, individual transformation depends to an uncertain degree upon the transformative power of social justice. (Saleebey, 2001, p. xi)

Saleebey's scholarship has consistently dealt with the intersection of culture, meaning, and narrative and most recently with the biopsychosocial perspective promoted in the field of social work. Finding social work's attention to the biological aspects lacking, Saleebey explicates how the neurological and the narrative intersect to make up the human experience in his unusually narrative textbook *Human Behavior and Social Environments: A Biopsychosocial Approach*.

SEE ALSO: ▶ Social work ▶ Strengths perspective (social welfare)

References

Saleebey, D. (2001). *Human behavior and social environments: A biopsychosocial approach*. New York: Columbia University Press.

Saleebey, D. (Ed.) (2006). *The strengths perspective in social work practice*, (4th ed.). Boston, MA: Allyn & Bacon.

Saving

Kimberley R. Monden
University of Kansas

Saving and financial health are related to a number of positive psychological constructs, such as psychological and social well-being, locus of control, and coping. In the current literature, there is not one universally agreed upon definition of *saving*, for example Lunt and Livingstone (1991) tell us that "saving refers to money put in banks or building societies as protection against future insecurities or to save up for particular goods and services" (p. 624). Further, Romal and Kaplan

(1995) define saving as "a matter of putting aside present needs and wants in the expectation of future needs and wants" (p. 10). Katona goes into more detail and distinguishes between 3 different types of saving: contractual, discretionary, and residual. First, *contractual* saving involves paying installments to oneself regardless of circumstances. Second, *discretionary* saving is the deliberate saving of spare income. Finally, *residual* saving is money not yet spent and therefore saved by default. Given the array of definitions currently being used, it becomes clear that a coherent and detailed definition of saving is needed so that one common language can be used across different research domains.

Historically, the topic of spending has been more comprehensively researched than the topic of saving, as economists, market researchers, and consumer psychologists have examined the motives, both economic and psychological, behind people's spending habits. Traditionally, economic theory has held that the amount people save is not reliably predictable by psychological variables, but is better explained by a number of other factors such as income, socioeconomic status, and number of children in the family. Recently however, economic theory has begun to acknowledge the psychological factors involved in saving such as self-control, fear of economic uncertainty, and pessimism about the economy. Furthermore, the amounts of money people commit to regular saving have been predicted by a variety of psychological factors including locus of control, coping, income, valuing enjoyment, shopping behavior, and social networks.

As economic and financial statistics continue to reveal that people are carrying heavier debt loads, and thus are less financially secure, psychologists are now concerned with the burden of carrying an increased amount of debt and the implications of financial insecurity on the quality of our relationships and overall psychological well-being. Recent research has begun to investigate the psychological impact of debt. For instance, in a sample of college students, increased debt and perceived financial instability were found to be related to decreased psychological well-being and dysfunctional impulsivity. Other studies have linked high levels of debt and a disproportionate debt/income ratio with a variety of negative consequences, such as stress-induced health problems, and decreased academic performance. Furthermore, in his book, *The High Price of Materialism*, Kasser describes his and others' research showing that when people organize their lives around extrinsic goals such as product acquisition, they report greater unhappiness in relationships, poorer mood, and more psychological problems.

Since preliminary research seems to support the notion that increased debt is associated with negative consequences on a variety of psychological factors, it appears that financial health is a salient and relevant topic to the field of psychology. If we can begin to build a better understanding of the psychological factors that motivate people to save, or at least avoid debt, then perhaps we can help to bolster these attributes in our clients.

SEE ALSO: ▶ Coping   ▶ Locus of control

References

Lunt, P. K., & Livingstone, S. M. (1991). Psychological, social and economic determinants of saving: Comparing recurrent and total savings. *Journal of Economic Psychology*, *12*(4), 621–641.

Romal, J. B., & Kaplan, B. J. (1995). Difference in self-control among spenders and savers. *Psychology: A Journal of Human Behavior*, *32*(2), 8–17.

Savoring

Fred B. Bryant, Carrie L. Ericksen and Adam H. DeHoek
Loyola University Chicago

Savoring is the capacity to attend to, appreciate, and enhance the positive experiences in one's life. Savoring involves cognitive and behavioral processes that regulate positive feelings; that is, thoughts, and behaviors that influence the frequency, intensity, and duration of positive experience, including joy, pride, gratitude, awe, and pleasure. The term "savoring" was first used in this context by Bryant in 1989.

Savoring processes are largely independent of coping processes. Whereas *coping* moderates the quality of negative experience, savoring moderates the quality of positive experience. In addition, just as coping is distinct from the experience of pain or distress, so is savoring distinct from the experience of joy or pleasure. In contrast to flow, which is short-circuited by self-awareness, savoring requires a conscious meta-awareness of one's positive feelings while one is experiencing them. The process of savoring also requires that one be relatively free from threat or self-esteem concerns, in order to have the cognitive resources necessary to attend to ongoing positive feelings.

Although savoring requires a focus of attention on positive feelings in the present, savoring may also involve a temporal focus on either the past (termed *reminiscence*) or the future (termed *anticipation*). When people savor through reminiscence, they attend to positive feelings that they rekindle from the past, or attend to other positive feelings they experience when looking back on the past. When people savor through anticipation, they attend to positive feelings they imagine they will have in the future, or attend to other positive feelings they experience when looking forward. People may also enhance the quality of an unfolding positive experience by remembering how much they looked forward to it earlier (i.e., *recalled anticipation*) or by looking forward to reminiscing about it later (i.e., *anticipated recall*). Regardless of the source, the positive feelings that one experiences when savoring are in the here-and-now.

In explicating the nature of savoring, it is important to distinguish four inter-related conceptual components: savoring experiences, savoring processes, savoring responses (or strategies), and savoring beliefs. At the broadest level, a *savoring experience* consists of one's sensations, perceptions, thoughts, behaviors, and feelings when mindfully attending to and appreciating a positive stimulus (e.g., listening to a virtuoso musical performance).

At the intermediate level, a *savoring process* is a sequence of mental or physical operations that unfolds over time and transforms a positive stimulus into positive feelings to which a person attends and savors. Different savoring processes regulate different positive emotional states. For example, marveling regulates awe, thanksgiving regulates gratitude, basking regulates pride, and luxuriating regulates physical pleasure.

At the smallest level, a *savoring response* or *strategy* is the operational component of the savoring process – that is, a specific, concrete thought or behavior that amplifies or dampens the intensity, or prolongs or shortens the duration, of positive feelings (e.g., mentally congratulating oneself while basking in response to a personal achievement). The distinction between savoring processes and savoring strategies parallels the distinction between coping processes (such as mourning, that change over time as people interact with their environment) and coping strategies (such as denial, which are specific cognitions or behaviors that influence the coping process).

Bryant and Veroff have identified ten savoring strategies that people use in relation to positive experience: sharing with others, memory building, self-congratulation, sensory-perceptual sharpening, comparing, absorption, behavioral expression, temporal awareness, counting blessings, and kill-joy thinking. Bryant and Veroff developed the 60-item Ways of Savoring Checklist as a self-report instrument for assessing people's use of savoring strategies in response to positive outcomes. Different cognitive appraisals are associated with the use of different savoring strategies. For example, stronger internal causal attributions for a positive outcome predict higher levels of self-congratulation, greater perceived outcome rarity predicts greater memory building, and greater perceived event desirability predicts greater use of counting blessings. Women, compared to men, tend to engage more in sharing with others, behavioral expression, and counting blessings (all of which are associated with greater enjoyment) in response to positive outcomes, whereas men report a greater use of kill-joy thinking (which is associated with less enjoyment).

Savoring experiences can be differentiated in terms of whether one's dominant focus of attention is on the external world or the internal self. In *world-focused* savoring, the source of positive feelings is primarily identified with something or someone outside oneself (e.g., a spectacular sunset). In such experiences, savoring is largely experienced as an involuntary, uncontrollable positive emotional response to an external stimulus. In *self-focused* savoring, on the other hand, positive feelings are primarily perceived as originating within the self. Savoring experiences can be further distinguished in terms of whether they primarily involve *cognitive reflection* (in which one introspects about one's subjective experience) or *experiential absorption* (in which one minimizes introspection in favor of perceptual engrossment).

Combining the distinctions between world- versus self-focused attention and between reflection versus absorption produces a 2 × 2 classification model of four primary savoring processes (and their associated positive feelings): a) thanksgiving (gratitude) is a form of world-focused cognitive reflection; b) marveling (awe) is a form of world-focused experiential absorption; c) basking (pride) is a form of self-focused cognitive reflection; and d) luxuriating (physical pleasure) is a form of self-focused experiential absorption.

Savoring beliefs reflect people's perceptions of their ability to enjoy positive experiences, as distinct from their ability to obtain positive outcomes in the first place. In 2003, Bryant developed the Savoring Beliefs Inventory as a self-report instrument for assessing savoring beliefs, and in 2007, Bryant and Veroff presented a Children's Savoring Beliefs Inventory. Compared to males, females tend to perceive themselves as more capable of savoring positive experiences – a sex difference that emerges as early as 5th grade, persists throughout adulthood, and has been found in the United States, Canada, Australia, and Japan. Comparing levels of savoring beliefs across temporal domains within individuals, people typically report that they are most capable of savoring through reminiscence, moderately capable of savoring the moment, and least capable of savoring through anticipation.

SEE ALSO: ▶ Capitalization ▶ Enjoyment ▶ Positive emotions ▶ Positive experience ▶ Self-regulation

School Psychology

Patricia A. Lowe and Jennifer M. Raad
University of Kansas

School psychology is a profession where individuals apply psychological principles to educational issues. School psychology is a young profession in comparison to the physical sciences. The practice of school psychology did not begin until the turn of the twentieth century. School psychologists work with children, adolescents, families, and school personnel to help students succeed in academic and nonacademic settings. School psychologists collaborate with parents and educational professionals to create positive school environments for all children and youth. These individuals are trained in psychology and education, and their role is to address the educational, behavioral, and socioemotional needs of children and adolescents.

School Psychologists and Related Professions

The distinction between school, clinical, and counseling psychologists has blurred over the years. Historically, clinical and counseling psychologists worked with adults, but they had a different focus. Clinical psychologists focused on abnormal behavior and counseling psychologists focused on normal development, adjustment issues, and careers. In contrast, school psychologists worked with children, adolescents and families. Now, many school, clinical, and counseling psychologists with doctorate degrees perform similar duties and may work with the same-age clientele. However, school psychologists are somewhat unique from clinical and counseling psychologists with a specific focus on children and adolescents' educational and learning needs in school settings.

Employment Settings for School Psychologists

School psychologists work in a variety of settings, with the public schools being the most common place of employment. In the public school setting, school psychologists provide direct (e.g., counseling) and indirect (e.g., consultation) services to students, school personnel, parents, and families. Direct services involve directly working with a client, such as a student, whereas indirect services involve working with an individual, such as a parent or teacher, and helping an individual develop skills to work directly with a client. Other school psychologists who work in the public schools have administrative positions. They may serve as a director of school psychological services or a director of pupil personnel services for a school district. School psychologists also work in other settings, including academia, community-based mental health facilities, medical centers, private practice, private schools, residential treatment centers, and state departments of education. In these different settings, they may perform different roles and functions.

Roles and Functions of School Psychologists

The duties performed by school psychologists may vary depending on their work setting. School psychologists may engage in a variety of activities in these different settings. Activities may include assessment, consultation, intervention, prevention, and research and program evaluation. Assessment is one of the major roles performed by school psychologists. School psychologists may conduct comprehensive evaluations in the school setting to determine whether a child or adolescent may benefit from special education and related services, or they may conduct comprehensive evaluations in a nonschool setting for diagnostic purposes. In these comprehensive evaluations, school psychologists may use a variety of formal and informal assessment techniques such as intelligence tests, academic achievement tests, curriculum-based measures, behavior rating scales, classroom observations, and clinical interviews. Consultation is another service that school psychologists may provide. Consultation is an indirect service and involves a consultant (e.g., a school psychologist) working with one or more consultees (e.g., a teacher and/or parent) to bring about a change in a client (e.g., a student). The consultant and consultee(s) work together using a problem-solving approach to determine the problematic area of concern (e.g., homework completion problems or disruptive behavior in the classroom) and then develop an intervention such as an academic or behavioral intervention that is implemented by the consultee(s) to change the client's behavior. School psychologists may also conduct systems-level consultation. In systems-level consultation, school psychologists may work with an entire organization such as a school or school district to bring about a change in the organization. As systems-level consultants, school psychologists may assist organizations in the development of prevention programs such as alcohol and drug abuse prevention programs. Once developed, these prevention programs are implemented by personnel in the organization. Another role performed by school psychologists is in the area of intervention. School psychologists may work directly with children, adolescents, and/or parents either on an individual basis or in a group setting. For example, school psychologists may provide individual counseling to alleviate a child's anxiety, parent training to assist parents in decreasing their child's noncompliant behavior, and problem-solving skills training to improve a group of adolescents' interpersonal skills. School psychologists may also be engaged in research activities, especially if they work in a university setting. Most school psychologists who work in a university setting conduct research relevant to the educational, behavioral, and socioemotional needs of children, adolescents, and adults. They may also engage in program evaluation research where they evaluate the effectiveness of school programs, for example different reading programs used in the schools. As noted, school psychologists perform a wide range of duties in their work setting and in order to perform these different roles and functions, they need to obtain an advanced degree (i.e., a masters, specialist, or doctoral degree) and participate in continuing professional development.

Educational and Training Requirements of School Psychologists

Training programs in school psychology are found throughout the US. These programs differ in theoretical orientation and models of training. However, general curriculum domains and credit hour requirements of these various training programs are similar. Students who enter into these training programs have at least a bachelor's degree from a university or college. Most students who are admitted to these training programs majored in psychology or education. However, some students received undergraduate degrees in other disciplines.

Although some states allow an individual to be certified or licensed to practice in the schools with a master's degree, other states require a specialist degree. The specialist degree is recognized as the entry level for the practice of school psychology in most cases. According to the standards set forth by the National

Association of School Psychologists (NASP), a professional school psychology organization and an accreditation body, specialist-level training includes 60 semester credits and a 1,200 hour internship. Students who are trained in specialist-level programs typically are required to take two years of course work, including courses in assessment, consultation, intervention, prevention, mental health, learning, child and adolescent development, behavior, and effective teaching, and school-based and sometimes clinic-based experiences, followed by a full-time internship for one academic year or a half-time internship for two academic years in a school setting. Those students who are enrolled in NASP-approved doctoral training programs are required to complete a minimum of 90 semester credits beyond the bachelor's degree and a 1,500 hour internship. The doctoral curriculum would include courses taken by specialist students in addition to advanced courses in such areas as statistics, measurement, and research design, as well as school-based and clinic-based experiences. The doctoral internship may be completed in a school or nonschool setting. However, if a student did not complete a specialist-level internship as defined by NASP standards before the doctoral internship, then the student's doctoral internship must include a minimum of 600 hours of school-based experience. Like NASP's doctoral training standards, the American Psychological Association (APA), a professional organization of psychologists, including school psychologists and another accreditation body, has guidelines for doctoral training programs. Students who are enrolled in APA-accredited doctoral training programs are required to complete three years of full-time study beyond the bachelor's degree and a one-year full-time internship. Some doctoral training programs are both NASP- and APA-accredited and students in these programs follow both NASP standards and APA guidelines in completing their doctoral studies.

Credentialing of School Psychologists

Once students complete their specialist or doctoral degree, they need to apply for the appropriate credentials in order to practice. For specialist and doctoral students who wish to work in a school setting, they will need to apply for a certificate, sometimes referred to as a license, from their State Department of Education in the state where they plan to practice. Endorsement from the training program is usually required for students who graduate from in-state programs. Some states may have additional requirements and students need to be aware of those requirements in the state where they wish to practice. In contrast, students who attended out-of-state programs may be required to submit their transcripts for review by state officials to determine whether the program meets state standards to practice in their state. In addition to the transcript review, students may need endorsement from their training program.

Students with a specialist or doctoral degree may also apply and be awarded the Nationally Certified School Psychologist (NCSP) credential. The NCSP credential was established by NASP and is a measure of professionalism for those individuals who hold the credential. To be eligible for the NCSP credential, individuals must have graduated from a 60 semester credit hour training program in school psychology, completed a 1,200 hour internship of which 600 hours were in a school setting under a credentialed school psychologist, and pass a national exam. Some states require the NCSP for certification/licensure, whereas other states may grant a certificate or license to an individual who holds the NCSP credential.

For doctoral students interested in working in a nonschool setting, they must apply for a license from a state board of examiners in psychology. To obtain a license, the individual, in most cases, must have a doctoral degree in psychology, two years of supervised experience in the practice of psychology under a licensed psychologist, and pass the Examination for Professional Practice in Psychology (EPPP). A state or provincial jurisprudence exam may also be required. Individuals who obtain a license for the independent practice of psychology from a state board of examiners may provide psychological services to individuals or groups of individuals in a variety of settings such as a medical center, community-based mental health facility, or private practice and are not required to work under the supervision of another licensed mental health professional.

Employment Trends and Salaries of School Psychologists

The current outlook for employment for individuals who earn a degree in school psychology is excellent. A shortage of school psychologists exists throughout the US. The shortage is the result of several factors, including the retirement of many school psychologists who entered the profession shortly after the enactment of the Education for All Handicapped Children Act of 1975. This piece of federal education legislation guaranteed a free appropriate public education for children with disabilities and created positions in the schools for school psychologists to assess children who might be eligible for special education and related services. The current shortage is expected to continue for some time and is most prevalent in the northeastern and midwestern sections of the US. However, many university trainers have noted an increase in the number of applicants applying to school psychology programs. Thus, a steady supply of new school psychologists is expected in the future.

Salaries of school psychologists are influenced by geographical region, state, and school district where they work, type of employment setting, number of years of experience, and educational degree held. Curtis, Lopez, Batsche, and Smith conducted a survey of NASP members during the 2004–2005 school year and found the average salary was $60,581 for practitioners, university trainers, and administrators working in the US.

Future Directions for the Profession of School Psychology

The future of the profession of school psychology looks bright, with its strong commitment to children, adolescents, families, and schools. Individuals who pursue a career in school psychology will find it to be a rewarding profession. However, the profession is not without its challenges. The diversity of students who attend US schools has increased, and school psychologists will need to respond effectively in working with students and families from culturally and linguistically diverse backgrounds. Role expansion is another challenge facing the school psychology profession. Although many university trainers, practitioners, and school psychology professional organizations advocate the delivery of comprehensive psychological services in school and nonschool settings, most school psychologists continue to focus on the assessment aspect of service delivery. To meet the future service needs of children, adolescents, families, and schools, school psychologists will need to focus on prevention and promoting wellness of the individuals they serve, become more familiar with the different contexts (home, school, cultural, and societal contexts) that influence children and adolescents' lives, and establish home-school-community partnerships to address the needs of their constituency.

SEE ALSO: ▶ American Psychological Association ▶ Counseling psychology ▶ Developmental psychopathology

Self-Compassion

Kristin D. Neff and Lindsay M. Lamb
The University of Texas at Austin

Self-compassion is an open-hearted way of relating to negative aspects of oneself and one's experience that enables greater emotional resilience and psychological well-being. According to the definition proposed by Neff, self-compassion is composed of three key factors: (a) self-kindness – extending kindness and understanding to oneself in instances of perceived inadequacy or suffering rather than harsh judgment and self-criticism; b) common humanity – seeing one's experiences as part of the larger human experience rather than seeing them as separating and isolating; and c) mindfulness – holding one's painful thoughts and feelings in balanced awareness rather than overidentifying with them in an exaggerated manner.

Western psychologists have only recently begun to examine self-compassion, but the construct is central to the 2,500-year-old tradition of Buddhist psychology. Interest in self-compassion has been fueled by a larger trend towards integrating

Buddhist constructs such as mindfulness with Western psychological approaches, exemplified in clinical interventions such as mindfulness-based stress reduction (MBSR) and mindfulness-based cognitive therapy. While mindfulness has received more research attention than self-compassion (with dozens of studies supporting the effectiveness of mindfulness-based interventions), the two constructs are intimately linked. *Mindfulness* refers to the ability to pay attention to one's present-moment experience in a non-judgmental manner. Self-compassion entails holding negative self-relevant emotions in mindful awareness, generating feelings of kindness towards oneself and insight into the interconnected nature of the human experience. There is some evidence to suggest that increased self-compassion may actually help explain the success of some mindfulness-based interventions: for instance, one study found that increased self-compassion levels after participation in a six-week MBSR program mediated reductions in stress associated with the program.

While self-compassion has similarities to the concept of unconditional self-acceptance proposed by humanistic psychologists such as Maslow, Ellis or Rogers, self-compassion is a broader construct. In addition to accepting oneself with kindness and non-judgment, self-compassion entails emotional equanimity and recognition of interconnectedness. Moreover, while self-acceptance may theoretically entail passivity toward personal shortcomings, self-compassion involves the desire to alleviate one's suffering, and is therefore a powerful motivating force for growth and change.

Most research on self-compassion has been conducted using the Self-Compassion Scale (SCS), a self-report measure created by Neff. The scale has strong psychometric properties and demonstrates concurrent, discriminate, and convergent validity (e.g., significant correlations with therapist and partner reports of self-compassion, positive correlations with emotional intelligence and negative correlations with self-criticism). Research suggests that self-compassion is strongly related to emotional well-being. For instance, higher levels of self-compassion have been associated with greater life satisfaction, social connectedness, self-determination, self-concept accuracy and emotional equanimity when confronting daily life events. Self-compassion has also been associated with less anxiety, depression, rumination, thought suppression, and perfectionism. One study, for example, examined how self-compassion levels predicted behavior in a mock job interview task in which participants were asked to write about their greatest weakness. Those scoring higher in self-compassion experienced less anxiety during the writing exercise, and also used more interconnected and less isolating language when discussing their weaknesses.

A study designed to examine the link between self-compassion and other positive psychological strengths found that self-compassion was associated with greater happiness, optimism, positive affect, wisdom, curiosity and exploration, and personal initiative. The study also examined relations with the Big Five personality traits, and found that self-compassion was associated with less neuroticism and more agreeableness, extroversion, and conscientiousness, though self-compassion was still a significant predictor of psychological strengths when controlling for personality.

Self-compassion appears to be adaptive in academic contexts. Self-compassion is positively associated with mastery goals, which focus on the joy of learning for its own sake, and negatively associated with performance goals, which involve defending or enhancing one's sense of self-worth through academic performances. Research suggests that the link between self-compassion and mastery goals is mediated through the greater perceived competence and lesser fear of failure associated with self-compassion. By not harshly judging the self or blowing one's failures out of proportion, self-compassion engenders self-confidence in one's ability to learn and lessens the self-condemning aspects of failure, which in turn helps to foster mastery goal adoption. Research also indicates that self-compassionate students exhibit more adaptive ways of coping with academic failures.

Self-compassion appears not only to benefit oneself, but also others within interpersonal relationships. In a study of heterosexual romantic partners, self-compassionate individuals were described by partners as being more emotionally connected, accepting and autonomy-supporting while being less detached, controlling, and verbally or physically aggressive. Self-compassion was also associated with more relationship satisfaction (as reported by oneself and one's partner) and greater attachment security. Because self-compassion includes recognition of human connectedness, it allows for caring behavior with partners while reducing the need for ego-defensiveness associated with the desire to control or strike out against others.

In many ways, self-compassion is a useful alternative to the construct of self-esteem, providing similar psychological health benefits while avoiding its more problematic aspects. As Seligman has argued, self-esteem programs tend to emphasize feeling good about oneself rather than building competence, and may hamper the giving of critical feedback to children out of fear of protecting their self-esteem. High self-esteem is often associated with inflated and inaccurate self-concepts, making self-improvement difficult. Individuals may put others down in order to feel better about themselves, with high rather than low self-esteem being associated with narcissism and prejudice. High self-esteem is also associated with anger and aggression towards those perceived to threaten the ego. Because self-esteem is contingent on success in particular domains, it tends to falter in failure situations, leading to unstable feelings of self-worth.

Self-compassion, in contrast, is not based on self-evaluations, social comparisons, or personal success. Rather, it stems from feelings of human kindness and understanding in the face of life's disappointments. For this reason, self-compassion does not require feeling "above average" or superior to others, and provides emotional stability when confronting personal inadequacies. In a large community-based study, it was found that self-compassion displayed a moderate correlation with self-esteem, as should be expected given that both constructs tap into positive self-affect. However, self-compassion was a stronger predictor of healthy self-to-self relating than was global self-esteem, including more stable and less contingent feelings of self-worth, less narcissism, anger, social comparison, and public self-consciousness. In a series of lab-based studies conducted by Leary and colleagues, self-compassion was also associated with more emotional balance than self-esteem when participants encountered potentially humiliating situations or received unflattering inter-personal feedback. When feelings of self-compassion versus self-esteem were fostered through a mood induction exercise, participants in the self-compassion condition were more likely to take responsibility for their role in painful life events without feeling overwhelmed with negative emotions (as compared to those in the self-esteem or control conditions).

Many theorists assume that high self-esteem is essential to psychological health. For instance, proponents of terror management theory argue that self-esteem is necessary because it provides individuals with a sense of meaning, symbolic immort-ality, and security that buffers existential anxiety. At the same time, they acknow-ledge that the need for self-esteem can create a type of ego-defensiveness that may harm relations with others and inhibit growth and change. Self-compassion offers a sense of meaning, belonging and security that is not dependent on bolstering one's ego or on evaluating the self in contrast to others. Rather, it stems from recognizing and feeling tenderness for the shared human experience. Self-compassion provides a caring motivation for personal growth, while reducing the need for distorting, positive illusions about the self.

Given the strong association between self-compassion and mental health, self-compassion is likely to have important applications in clinical settings. The com-passionate mind training (CMT) program developed by Gilbert is an intervention program designed for individuals who experience chronic shame and self-criticism. In the program, clients are taught how to be self-soothing and to generate feel-ings of compassion and warmth towards themselves when they feel threatened, defensive, or self-critical. A pilot study on the effectiveness of CMT found that clients experienced significant reductions in depression, anxiety, self-criticism, shame, inferiority and submissive behaviors.

Researchers are beginning to examine group differences in self-compassion, includ-ing variables such as age, gender, and culture. For instance, a recent cross-cultural study compared average levels of self-compassion in Thailand, Taiwan and the United States. It was found that self-compassion levels were highest in Thailand, where original Buddhist teachings on self-compassion are integrated with daily life, and lowest in Taiwan, where there is a strong Confucian emphasis on self-improvement through self-criticism. Americans fell in between these two poles. Self-compassion was associated with interdependent self-construal in Thailand but with indepen-dent self-construal in Taiwan and the US. In all three cultures, increased levels of self-compassion were associated with less depression and greater life-satisfaction. Such findings suggest that the prevalence of self-compassion is linked to specific societal features such as parenting practices and philosophical worldviews rather than general East-West differences in culture or self-construals, and that self-compassion may have universal psychological benefits.

SEE ALSO: ▶ Buddhism ▶ Mindfulness ▶ Self-esteem

Self-Determination

Michael L. Wehmeyer and Todd D. Little
University of Kansas

Positive psychology is the pursuit of understanding optimal human functioning and well-being. As Seligman and Csikszentmihalyi (2000, p. 5) observed,

> The field of positive psychology at the subjective level is about valued subjective experiences: well-being, contentment, and satisfaction (in the past); hope and optimism (for the future); and flow and happiness (in the present). At the individual level, it is about positive individual traits: the capacity for love and vocation, courage, interpersonal skill, aesthetic sensibility, perseverance, forgiveness, originality, future mindedness, spirituality, high talent, and wisdom.

Ryan and Deci (2000) asserted that in this pursuit for understanding optimal human functioning and well-being, researchers must take into account the agentic nature of human action, noting:

> The fullest representations of humanity show people to be curious, vital, and self-motivated. At their best, they are agentic and inspired, striving to learn; extend themselves; master new skills; and apply their talents responsibly. That most people show considerable effort, agency, and commitment in their lives appears, in fact, to be more normative than exceptional, suggesting some very positive and persistent features of human nature. (p. 68)

Self-determination is a general psychological construct within the organizing structure of theories of human agentic behavior. An agentic person is the "origin of his or her actions, has high aspirations, perseveres in the face of obstacles, sees more and varied options for action, learns from failures, and overall, [and] has a greater sense of well being" (Little, Hawley, Henrich, & Marsland, 2002, p. 390). Human agentic theories "share the meta-theoretical view that organismic aspirations drive human behaviors" (Little, Snyder, & Wehmeyer, 2006, p. 61). An organismic perspective views people as active contributors to, or *authors* of, their behavior, which is self-regulated and goal-directed *action*. Such actions are motivated by biological and psychological needs, directed toward self-regulated goals linked to these needs, precipitate self-governance of behavior, and require an explicit focus on the interface between the self and the context.

The construct's origins lie in the philosophical doctrines of *determinism* and *free will*. Determinism is the philosophical doctrine positing that events, such as human behavior, are effects of preceding causes. Free will is conceptualized as the human capacity to act (or not) as we choose or prefer, without external compulsion or restraint. According to philosophers like John Locke, though, human behavior can be both caused and free, as long as the distinction is made between the agent, as actor, and the action, as caused. That is, a person (the agent) is free to act or not, as one chooses, even if the action itself is caused by some deterministic factor.

This early focus in personality psychology carried forward into theory in human agentic behavior. Bandura (1997) observed that in discussions of human agency, referents to the term determinism imply the "production of effects by events, rather than the doctrinal sense meaning that actions are completely determined by a prior sequence of causes independent of the individual" (p. 7).

It is this notion of human action as caused or determined by either by the person (the agent) or another factor that became the focus of early psychologists. In *Foundations for a Science of Personality* (1941), Angyal proposed that an essential feature of a living organism is its autonomy, where *autonomous* means self-governing or governed from inside. According to Angyal, an organism "lives in a world in which things happen according to laws which are heteronomous (e.g., governed from outside) from the point of view of the organism" (p. 33). Angyal noted, though, that "organisms . . . can oppose self-determination to external determination" (p. 33), and suggested that the *science of personality* is, fundamentally, the study of two determinants to human behavior, autonomous-determinism (self-determination) and heteronomous-determinism (other-determined).

Self-determination, then, as a psychological construct, refers to self- (vs. other-) caused action – to people acting volitionally, based on their own will. *Volition* is the capability of conscious choice, decision, and *intention*. Self-determined behavior is volitional, intentional, and self-caused or self-initiated action.

Theories of Self-Determination

A number of psychological theories of self-determination have been forwarded. *Self-determination theory* (SDT) merged research on innate human tendencies, social contexts, and motivators for human action to posit congruence between one's basic needs and core values that spurs individual agency and, ultimately, results in overall well-being. SDT proposed three basic psychological needs – competence, autonomy, and relatedness – that are either supported or challenged by social contexts. The context also contributes to intrinsic and extrinsic motivators that are self-regulated at either conscious or unconscious levels. This perspective views the process of self-regulation as an organizational function that coordinates systemic behaviors and serves as a foundation for autonomy and the sense of self.

In SDT, the inherent psychological need for competence refers to the motivation to be competent and effective within environments, which in turn stems from the theory of effectence motivation, which describes an innate drive for environmental mastery. This drive leads to behavioral responses that sustain and augment individual capabilities. The psychological need for relatedness is the sense of connectedness and belonging with others. This sense is distinct from the status of role-identification or group membership, as the focus is on personal perceptions of relatedness instead of goal outcomes. Variously, competence, relatedness, and autonomy needs may compliment each other, or may conflict.

Satisfying these needs enhances well-being. Within SDT, autonomous actions are based on one's core or "higher order values." Sometimes outside influences (e.g., social context) force values to conflict and a choice must be made that reflects the true self. Intrinsic and extrinsic motivation plays a role here and these motivators are not simply polar opposites. Instead, the rationale and outcome of negotiating and integrating the demands of intrinsic and extrinsic sources of motivation determines the autonomy of an action. Thus, an autonomous action is one in which the rationale behind an action-response (behavior) to an extrinsic pressure reflects one's core values.

Early SDT research focused on the role of social contexts in supporting or thwarting intrinsic motivation and found that conditions fostering autonomy and competence were positively associated with intrinsic motivation. When extrinsically motivated behaviors were acted on, individuals were more likely to integrate the behavior with core values when the social context supported autonomy, competence, and relatedness. Recent SDT research has examined the relationship between implicit/explicit motives (conscious or unconscious) and intrinsic/extrinsic motivation.

Wehmeyer proposed a functional theory of self-determination (fSDT), in which self-determination is conceptualized as a dispositional characteristic (enduring tendencies used to characterize and describe differences between people) based on the *function* a behavior serves for an individual. Self-determined behavior refers to "volitional actions that enable one to act as the primary causal agent in one's life and to maintain or improve one's quality of life" (Wehmeyer, 2005, p. 117). Broadly, *causal agency* implies that it is the individual who makes or causes things to happen in his or her life. Causal agency implies more than just causing action; it implies that the individual acts with an eye toward *causing* an effect to *accomplish* a *specific end* or to *cause* or *create change*. Bandura noted that:

> In evaluating the role of intentionality in human agency, one must distinguish between the personal production of action for an intended outcome, and the effects that carrying out that course of action actually produce. Agency refers to acts done intentionally. (Bandura, 1997, p. 3)

According to fSDT, self-determined *actions* are identified by four essential characteristics: 1) the person acts *autonomously*; 2) the behavior is *self-regulated*; 3) the person initiates and responds to the event(s) in a *psychologically empowered* manner; and 4) the person acts in a *self-realizing* manner. These essential characteristics refer not to the behavior performed, but to the *function* the behavior serves for the individual; that is, whether the action enabled the person to act as a causal agent.

fSDT's use of behavioral autonomy draws from two sources: autonomy as synonymous with individuation and autonomy as roughly synonymous with independence. Developmental psychologists view the process of individuation, or the formation of the person's individual identity, as a critical component of social and personality development. Individuation is, generally, the progression from being dependent on others for care and guidance to self-care and self-direction, the outcome of which is autonomous functioning or behavioral autonomy.

Self-regulation is:

> a complex response system that enables individuals to examine their environments and their repertoires of responses for coping with those environments to make decisions about how to act, to act, to evaluate the desirability of the outcomes of the action, and to revise their plans as necessary. (Whitman, 1990, p. 373)

Zimmerman and Rappaport forwarded the construct of psychological empowerment to account for the multidimensional nature of perceived control, which, according to these authors, had been previously treated as if it were a univariate construct. Through the process of learning, using problem-solving skills and achieving perceived or actual control in one's life (e.g., learned hopefulness), individuals develop a perception of psychological empowerment that enables them to achieve desired outcomes.

The term *self-realization* was used originally by Gestalt psychologists to refer to the intrinsic purpose in a person's life. It also has more global meaning related to the "tendency to shape one's life course into a meaningful whole" (Angyal, 1941, p. 355). People who are self-determined are self-realizing in that they use a comprehensive, and reasonably accurate, knowledge of themselves – their strengths and limitations – to act in such a manner as to capitalize on this knowledge. This self-knowledge and self-understanding forms through experience with and interpretation of one's environment and is influenced by evaluations of significant others, reinforcement, and attributions of one's own behavior.

The primary research focus of fSDT has been on people with intellectual disability, although the theory itself is not specific to people with disabilities. In another theoretical model derived from research in special education, Mithaug suggested that self-determination is an unusually effective form of self-regulation markedly free of external influence in which people who are self-determined regulate their choices and actions more successfully than others. Mithaug suggested that individuals are often in flux between existing states and *goal* or desired states. When a discrepancy between what one has and wants exists, an incentive for self-regulation and action becomes operative. With the realization that a discrepancy exists, the individual may set out to achieve the goal or desired state. Because of a previous history of failure, however, individuals may set expectations that are too low or too high. The ability to set appropriate expectations is based on the individual's success in matching his or her *capacity* with present *opportunity*. Capacity is the individual's assessment of existing resources (e.g., skills, interests, motivation), and opportunity refers to aspects of the situation that allow the individual to achieve the desired gain. Mithaug referred to optimal prospects as "just-right" matches in which individuals are able to correctly match their capacity (i.e., skills, interests) with existing opportunities (e.g., potential jobs). The experience generated during self-regulation is a function of repeated interaction between capacity and opportunity.

Mithaug (1998) noted that "self-determination always occurs in a social context" (p. 42) and suggests that the "social nature of the concept is worth reviewing because the distinction between self-determination and other-determination is nearly always in play when assessing an individual's prospects for controlling their life in a particular situation" (p. 42).

Wehmeyer and Mithaug proposed *causal agency theory* (CAT) to explain how and why people become *self-* verses *other-*determined. Wehmeyer and Mithaug refer to the "class of behavioral events" that CAT explains as *causal events, causal behavior,* or *causal actions*. These function as a means for the person (the causal agent) to achieve valued goals and, ultimately, become more self-determined. CAT proposes a number of "operators" that lead to self-determined behavior. These operators involve the capability to perform causal actions or behaviors, subdivided into *causal* and *agentic capabilities*. People are "caused" to implement causal and agentic capabilities in response to challenges that serve as catalysts for causal behavior. Causal actions are provoked by two classes of challenges to self-determination: opportunities or threats. *Opportunity* refers to situations or circumstances that provide a chance for the person to create change or make something happen based upon his or her individual *causal capability*. If a person has the causal capability to act on the situation or circumstance, that situation or circumstance can be construed as an opportunity. Opportunities can be *found* (unanticipated, happened upon through no effort of one's own) or *created* (the person acts to create a favorable circumstance). The second challenge condition involves situations or circumstances that threaten the organism's self-determination and provoke the organism to exercise causal action to maintain a preferred outcome or to create change that is consistent with one's own values, preferences, or interests, and not the values, preferences or interests of others. A third operant in CAT is *causal affect*: those emotions, feelings, and other affective components that regulate human behavior, including causal behaviors.

People who are causal agents respond to challenges (opportunities or threats) to their self-determination by employing causal and agentic capabilities that result in causal action and allow them to direct their behavior to achieve a desired change or maintain a preferred circumstance or situation. In response to challenges, causal agents use a *goal generation process* leading to the identification and prioritization of needed actions. The person frames the most urgent action need in terms of a goal state, and engages in a *goal discrepancy analysis* to compare current status with goal status. The outcome of this analysis is a *goal-discrepancy problem* to be solved. The person then engages in a *capacity-challenge discrepancy analysis* in which capacity to solve the goal discrepancy problem is evaluated. The person maximizes adjustment in capacity (e.g., acquires new or refines existing skills and knowledge) or adjusts the challenge presented to create a "just-right match" between capacity and challenge to optimize the probability of solving the goal discrepancy problem.

Next, the person creates a discrepancy reduction plan by setting causal expectations, making choices and decisions about strategies to reduce the discrepancy between the current status and goal status. When sufficient time has elapsed, the person engages in a second goal discrepancy analysis, using information gathered through self-monitoring to self-evaluate progress toward reducing the discrepancy between current and goal status. If progress is satisfactory, they will continue implementing the discrepancy reduction plan. If not, the person either reconsiders the discrepancy reduction plan and modifies that or returns to the goal generation process to reexamine the goal and its priority and, possibly, cycle through the process with a revised or new goal.

Finally, numerous scholars and theorists provide complimentary views of human agency as a process of self-determination. Recent discussions of self-efficacy, for example, draw upon key concepts that underlie self-determination. Similarly, other theoretical perspectives examine self-determined behavior at either higher or lower levels of analysis. At the lower level, for example, action-control theory examines the perceptions of control from the perspective of behavior as self-determined action. At the higher level of analysis, Snyder's body of work on hope theory emanates from a perspective of self-determined behavior whereby hope is conceptualized as the confluence of agency and pathways thinking – both of which are hallmarks of self-determined behavior.

Conclusion

That self-determination is a critical construct to the study of a positive psychology seems self-evident. An organismic perspective of self-determination that views people as active contributors to, or "authors" of their behavior, where behavior is self-regulated and goal-directed, provides a compelling foundation for examining and facilitating the degree to which people become "causal agents" in their lives.

SEE ALSO: ▶ Agency   ▶ Intentional self-development

References

Angyal, A. (1941). *Foundations for a science of personality*. Cambridge, MA: Harvard University Press.

Bandura, A. B. (1997). *Self-efficacy: The exercise of control*. New York: W. H. Freeman and Co.

Little, T. D., Hawley, P. H., Henrich, C. C., & Marsland, K. (2002). Three views of the agentic self: A developmental synthesis. In E. L. Deci and R. M. Ryan (Eds.), *Handbook of self-determination research* (pp. 389–404). Rochester, NY: University of Rochester Press.

Little, T. D., Snyder, C. R., & Wehmeyer, M. (2006). The agentic self: On the nature and origins of personal agency across the lifespan. In. D. K. Mroczek & T. D. Little (Eds.), *Handbook of personality development* (pp. 61–80). Mahwah, NJ: LEA.

Mithaug, D. (1998). Your right, my obligation? *Journal of the Association for Persons with Severe Disabilities, 23,* 41–43.

Ryan, R. M., & Deci, E. L. (2000). Self-determination theory and the facilitation of intrinsic motivation, social development, and well-being. *American Psychologist, 55,* 68–78.

Seligman, M. E. P., & Csikszentmihalyi, M. (2000). Positive psychology: An introduction. *American Psychologist, 55,* 5–14.

Wehmeyer, M. L. (2005). Self-determination and individuals with severe disabilities: Reexamining meanings and misinterpretations. *Research and Practice in Severe Disabilities, 30,* 113–120.

Whitman, T. L. (1990). Self-regulation and mental retardation. *American Journal on Mental Retardation, 94,* 347–362.

Self-Efficacy

James E. Maddux
George Mason University

Self-efficacy beliefs are people's beliefs about their ability to produce desired outcomes through their own actions. These beliefs are among the most important determinants of the behaviors people choose to engage in and how much they persevere in their efforts in the face of obstacles and challenges. Therefore, they also are among the most important determinants of psychological well-being and adjustment. Although the term *self-efficacy* is of recent origin, interest in beliefs about personal control has a long history in psychology. Albert Bandura's 1977 *Psychological Review* article "Self-Efficacy: Toward a Unifying Theory of Behavior Change" formalized the notion of perceived competence as self-efficacy, defined it clearly, and embedded it in a theory of how it develops and influences human behavior.

Self-efficacy beliefs can be distinguished from a number of related concepts. Self-efficacy beliefs are not beliefs about skill; they are beliefs about one's ability to exercise one's skills under certain conditions – especially under changing and challenging conditions. Self-efficacy beliefs are not predictions or intentions about behavior; they are concerned not with what one believes one *will* do but with what one believes one *can* do. Self-efficacy is not self-esteem, although self-efficacy beliefs in a given domain will contribute to self-esteem in direct proportion to the importance one places on that domain. Self-efficacy is not a motive, drive, or need for control. One can have a strong need for control in a particular domain, and still hold weak beliefs about one's ability to perform effectively in that domain. Self-efficacy is not a personality trait. Although measures of general self-efficacy have been developed and are used frequently in research, they have not been as useful as specific self-efficacy measures in predicting how people will behave under specific conditions.

The Development of Self-Efficacy Beliefs

The early development of self-efficacy beliefs is influenced primarily by two interacting factors. The first is the development of the capacity for symbolic thought, particularly the capacity for understanding cause-and-effect relationships and the capacity for self-observation and self-reflection. These abilities begin developing in infancy and move from the infant's perception of the causal relationship between events, to his or her understanding that actions produce results, to the recognition that he or she can be the origin of actions that affect their environments. As children's understanding of language increases, so does their capacity for symbolic thought and, therefore, their capacity for self-awareness and a sense of personal agency.

Second, the development of self-efficacy beliefs is influenced by the responsiveness of environments to the infant's or child's attempts at manipulation and control. Environments that are responsive to the child's actions facilitate the development of self-efficacy beliefs, whereas nonresponsive environments retard this development. The development of self-efficacy beliefs encourages exploration, which in turn enhances the infant's beliefs about self-efficacy. The child's social environment (especially parents) is usually the most important part of his or her context. Thus, children usually develop a sense of efficacy from engaging in actions that influence the behavior of other people, which then generalizes to the nonsocial environment. Parents can facilitate or hinder the development of strong self-efficacy beliefs by their responses to the infant's or child's actions and by encouraging and enabling the child to explore and master his or her environment.

Self-efficacy beliefs develop throughout the lifespan as people continually integrate information from five primary sources. The most powerful influences on self-efficacy beliefs are *performance experiences*, one's own attempts to control one's environment. Successful attempts at control that one attributes to one's own efforts will strengthen self-efficacy beliefs for that behavior or domain. Self-efficacy beliefs also are influenced by *vicarious experiences*, or observations of the behavior of others and the consequences of those behaviors. People use these observations to form expectancies about their own behavior and its consequences. People can also influence their self-efficacy beliefs by *imagining* themselves or others behaving effectively or ineffectively in hypothetical situations. Such images may be derived from actual or vicarious experiences with situations similar to the one anticipated, or they may be induced by verbal persuasion, as when a psychotherapist guides a client through interventions such as *systematic desensitization*, a traditional behavioral therapy technique that relies on the person's ability to imaging coping effectively with feared situations and objects. Self-efficacy beliefs also are influenced by *verbal persuasion* – what others say to a person about what they believe that person can or cannot do. The power of verbal persuasion to affect self-efficacy beliefs will be influenced by such factors as the expertness, trustworthiness, and attractiveness of the source. *Physiological and emotional states* influence self-efficacy when a person learns to associate poor performance or perceived failure with aversive physiological arousal and success with pleasant feeling states. When a person becomes aware of unpleasant physiological arousal, he or she is more likely to doubt his or her competence than if his or her physiological state is pleasant or neutral. Likewise, comfortable physiological sensations are likely to lead people to feel confident in their ability with the situation at hand.

The Measurement of Self-Efficacy Beliefs

As noted previously, self-efficacy is not a trait and should not be measured as such. Instead, self-efficacy measures should be specific to the domain of interest (e.g., social skills, exercise, dieting, safe sex, arithmetic skills). Within a given domain, self-efficacy beliefs can be measured at varying degrees of behavioral and situational specificity, depending on what one is trying to predict. Thus, the measurement of self-efficacy should be designed to capture the multifaceted nature of behavior and the context in which it occurs. Specifying behaviors and contexts improves the predictive power of self-efficacy measures, but such specificity can reach a point of diminishing returns if carried to far. Therefore, the researcher must "know the territory" and have a thorough understanding of the behavioral domain in question, including the types of abilities called upon and the range of situations in which they might be used.

The Influence of Self-Efficacy Beliefs

Self-efficacy beliefs are important in all aspects of human psychological functioning. Four domains are especially important: psychological adjustment; physical health; self-regulation; and psychotherapy.

Psychological Adjustment

Most philosophers and psychological theorists agree that a sense of control over our behavior, our environment, and our own thoughts and feelings is essential for happiness and a sense of psychological well-being. Feelings of loss of control are common among people who seek the help of psychotherapists and counselors. Self-efficacy beliefs play a major role in a number of common psychological problems. Low self-efficacy expectancies are an important feature of depression. Depressed people usually believe they are less capable than other people of behaving effectively in many important areas of life. Dysfunctional anxiety and avoidant behavior can be the direct result of low self-efficacy beliefs for managing threatening situations. Self-efficacy beliefs also play a powerful role in substance abuse problems and eating disorders. For each of these problems, enhancing self-efficacy beliefs for overcoming the problem and for implementing self-control strategies in specific challenging situations can contribute to the success of therapeutic interventions.

Physical Health

Self-efficacy beliefs influence health in two ways. First, they influence the adoption of healthy behaviors, the cessation of unhealthy behaviors, and the maintenance of behavioral changes in the face of challenge and difficulty. All of the major theories of health behavior, such as protection motivation theory, the health belief model, and the theory of reasoned action/planned behavior include self-efficacy as a key component. In addition, enhancing self-efficacy beliefs is a part of successful change and maintenance of virtually every behavior crucial to health, including exercise, diet, stress management, safe sex, smoking cessation, overcoming alcohol abuse, compliance with treatment and prevention regimens, and disease detection behaviors such as breast self-examinations.

Second, self-efficacy beliefs influence a number of biological processes which, in turn, influence health and disease. Self-efficacy beliefs affect the body's physiological responses to stress, including the immune system. Lack of perceived control over environmental demands can increase susceptibility to infections and hasten the progression of disease. Self-efficacy beliefs also influence the activation of catecholamines, a family of neurotransmitters important to the management of stress and perceived threat, along with the endogenous painkillers referred to as endorphins.

Self-Regulation

Research on self-efficacy has added greatly to our understanding of how we guide our own behavior in the pursuit of desired goals. Self-efficacy beliefs influence self-regulation in several ways. First, they influence the goals we set. The stronger a person's self-efficacy in a specific achievement domain, the loftier will be the goals that person sets in that domain. Second, they influence people's choices of goal-directed activities, expenditure of effort, persistence in the face of challenge and obstacles, and reactions to perceived discrepancies between goals and current performance. Strong self-efficacy beliefs are associated with perseverance in the face of difficulties and setbacks. Perseverance usually produces desired results, and this success then strengthens self-efficacy beliefs.

Third, self-efficacy beliefs influence the efficiency and effectiveness of problem-solving and decision-making. When faced with complex decisions, people who have confidence in their ability to solve problems use their cognitive resources more effectively than people who doubt their cognitive skills. Such efficacy beliefs usually lead to better solutions and greater achievement. In the face of difficulty, people with strong self-efficacy beliefs are likely to remain *task-diagnostic* and continue to search for solutions to problems. People with weak self-efficacy beliefs, however, are likely to become *self-diagnostic* and reflect on their inadequacies. This diminishes their ability to evaluate and solve problems.

Psychotherapy

The term *psychotherapy* refers broadly to professionally guided interventions designed to enhance psychological well-being. Different psychological interventions, or different components of an intervention, may be equally effective because they equally enhance self-efficacy for crucial behavioral and cognitive skills. The success of psychological interventions can be enhanced by arranging experiences designed to strengthen self-efficacy beliefs for specific behaviors in specific problematic and challenging situations. Some basic strategies for enhancing self-efficacy beliefs are based on the five sources of self-efficacy previously noted.

Performance Experience

When people see themselves coping effectively with difficult situations, their sense of mastery is likely to be heightened. For example, the most effective interventions for phobias and fears involve gaining gradual experience with the feared object or situation during therapy sessions or between sessions as homework assignments. Recent advances in computer technology now allow for the use of virtual reality experiences in the treatment of phobias and fears. In cognitive treatments of depression, clients are provided structured guidance in arranging success experiences that will counteract low self-efficacy expectancies.

Vicarious Experience

Vicarious learning and imagination can be used to teach new skills and enhance self-efficacy for those skills. For example, modeling films and videotapes have been used successfully with people who have phobias. Research has shown that changes in self-efficacy beliefs for approaching feared objects and situations lead to adaptive behavioral changes. Common everyday (nonprofessional) examples of the use of vicarious experiences to enhance self-efficacy include advertisements for weight-loss and smoking cessation programs that feature testimonials from successful people. The clear message from these testimonials is that the listener or reader also can accomplish this difficult task. Formal and informal support groups – people sharing their personal experiences in overcoming a common adversity such as addiction, obesity, or illness – also provide forums for the enhancement of self-efficacy.

Imagined Experience

Imagining ourselves engaging in feared behaviors or overcoming difficulties can be used to enhance self-efficacy. For example, cognitive therapy of anxiety and fear problems often involves modifying visual images of danger and anxiety, including images of coping effectively with the feared situation. Systematic desensitization, noted previously, relies on the person's ability to imaging coping effectively with a feared situation. Because fearful and depressive images are important components of anxiety and depression, various techniques have been developed to help clients modify and reduce these images and to replace them with more positive images.

Verbal Persuasion

Most formal psychological interventions rely strongly on verbal persuasion to enhance a client's self-efficacy and encourage small risks that may lead to small successes. In cognitive and cognitive-behavioral therapies the therapist engages the client in a discussion of the client's dysfunctional beliefs, attitudes, and expectancies and helps the client see the irrationality and self-defeating nature of such beliefs. The therapist encourages the client to adopt new, more adaptive beliefs and to act on these new beliefs and expectancies. As a result, the client experiences the successes that can lead to more enduring changes in self-efficacy beliefs and adaptive behavior. People also rely daily on verbal persuasion as a self-efficacy strengthener by seeking the support of other people when attempting to lose weight, quit smoking, maintain an exercise program, or summon up the courage to confront a difficult boss or loved one.

Physiological and Emotional States

People usually feel more self-efficacious when they are calm than when they are aroused and distressed. Thus, strategies for controlling and reducing emotional arousal (specifically anxiety) while attempting new behaviors should enhance self-efficacy beliefs and increase the likelihood of successful implementation. Hypnosis, biofeedback, relaxation training, meditation, and medication are the most common strategies for reducing the physiological arousal typically associated with weak self-efficacy beliefs and poor performance.

Collective Efficacy

Accomplishing important goals in groups, organizations, and societies has always depended on the ability of individuals to identify the abilities of other individuals and to harness these abilities to accomplish common goals. This idea is captured in the notion of *collective efficacy*, the beliefs that people in a group hold about their ability to work together effectively to accomplish shared goals. Collective efficacy has been found to be important to a number of settings and groups. The more efficacious couples feel about their ability to accomplish important shared goals, the more satisfied they are with their relationships. The collective efficacy beliefs of an athletic team can be raised or lowered by giving them false information about ability and can influence its success in competitions. The collective efficacy beliefs of teachers can affect the academic achievement of school children. The effectiveness of self-managing work teams also seems to be related to collective efficacy beliefs. Collective efficacy beliefs also can be important in people's attempts to create social and political change. Individual success and happiness depends to a large degree on the ability to cooperate, collaborate, negotiate, and otherwise live in harmony with other people. In addition, the ability of businesses, organizations, communities, and governments (local, state, and national) to achieve their goals will increasingly depend on their ability to coordinate their efforts, particularly because these goals often conflict. In a world in which communication across the globe is often faster than communication across the street, and in which cooperation and collaboration in commerce and government is becoming increasingly common and increasingly crucial, understanding collective efficacy beliefs will become increasingly important.

SEE ALSO: ▶ Bandura, Albert   ▶ Self-regulation

Self-Esteem

John P. Hewitt
University of Massachusetts

Self-esteem is the evaluative dimension of self-regard, combining a cognitive and an affective aspect. People acquire knowledge of themselves, organized into schemas derived from direct experience as well as the real or imagined judgments of others. And they respond emotionally to this knowledge. They feel about themselves essentially the same range of affect that they are capable of directing toward any object. Fear, anger, hatred, love, pride, satisfaction, anxiety, loathing, shame, guilt, embarrassment, and other named emotions which may figure in the experience of self. Self-esteem may exist as a global sense of worth or value; it may be felt in relation to particular accomplishments or spheres of competence; and it may be experienced in relation to the person's real or desired membership in racial, ethic, or other collectivities, with a sense of worth derived from identification with them.

Social scientists most commonly emphasize global self-esteem, measuring it by asking individuals to agree or disagree with self-referential statements. Typical of self-esteem measures, and still the most widely used, is the ten-item global scale developed by Morris Rosenberg (Rosenberg, 1965, pp. 305–307):

1. On the whole I am satisfied with myself.
2. At times I think I am no good at all.
3. I feel that I have a number of good qualities.
4. I am able to do things as well as most other people.
5. I feel I do not have much to be proud of.
6. I certainly feel useless at times.
7. I feel that I am a person of worth, at least on an equal plane with others.
8. I wish I could have more respect for myself.
9. All in all, I am inclined to feel that I am a failure.
10. I take a positive attitude toward myself.

Such statements elicit cognitive and affective responses to the self. By scaling responses to such items, researchers create self-esteem scores for individuals and examine their relationship with other variables in an effort to discern the antecedents and consequences of various levels of self-esteem.

Self-esteem is an intensively studied topic, not only in academic psychology and sociology but also in such applied fields as education, social work, clinical psychology, and psychiatry. Although the psychologist William James wrote about self-esteem in the nineteenth century, researchers began intensive study of its origins and consequences only during the last third of the twentieth century. During the same period self-esteem became the focus of a "self-esteem movement," which advanced the notion that an epidemic of low self-esteem was responsible for many social and personal problems – such as delinquency, poor school performance, and drug use. Proponents argued that these problems could be alleviated by programs, especially in schools, specifically designed to raise self-esteem. The psychological concept of self-esteem thus became imbued with broader cultural meanings, and it is often difficult to separate one from the other.

The Nature of Self-Esteem

We can best examine the interlinked psychological and cultural meanings of self-esteem by considering it as a *socially constructed emotion*. Placing self-esteem within the realm of socially created emotions fosters consideration of its cultural meanings while also recognizing its underlying visceral, physiological, and neurological correlates. Not simply universal psychological states, socially constructed emotions are created when social expectations and cultural meanings are laid over universal affective responses to experience. Self-esteem is a reflexive emotion that arises in response to the person's own thoughts and actions. It has developed over time in social processes of invention, which over the past century have been strongly influenced by scientific psychology and its advocates and popularizers. Individuals must *learn* to experience and to talk about self-esteem, which, like other emotions, arises in predictable social circumstances and is subject to social control.

The key term for grasping the socially constructed emotion of self-esteem is *mood*, which is a generalized aroused or subdued disposition. At one end of a mood continuum, *euphoria* is a pervasive good feeling that the individual might describe in such terms as energized, happy, "psyched," self-confident, or elated. At the other extreme, *dysphoria* is a feeling described in such opposite terms as listless, sad, fearful, anxious, or depressed. In a positive mood, the individual is aroused, organized, and ready to act; in a negative mood, the individual is reserved, fearful, and reluctant to act. Mood is a normal animal response to experience, promoting activity when success seems likely and restraining or cautioning it in the face of potential failure or harm. For human beings, culture provides the words and ideas that label and interpret mood, transforming it into a more or less self-conscious experience.

Batson's distinction between *affect*, *mood*, and *emotion* helps explicate the relationship between self-esteem and mood. *Affect*, which is the most general and primitive of the terms, tells the organism about the more and less valued "states of affairs" it experiences. Events leading to valued states of affairs produce positive affect, whereas events leading to less valued states produce negative affect. *Mood*, in contrast, entails more or less well-formed *expectations* about the future experience of positive or negative affect. Mood thus refers to "the fine-tuning of one's perception of the general affective tone of what lies ahead" (Batson, 1990, p. 103). *Emotions* are oriented to the present and are focused on the person's relationship to a specific goal. The person in a positive mood expects more positive affect in the future. The person experiences the emotion of joy in the present as his or her goals are attained or attained more fully than imagined. Likewise, the socially constructed emotion of self-esteem arises as the person interprets mood in relation to feelings about the self. High self-esteem entails positive mood and the perception of an efficacious and socially valued self. Low self-esteem entails the opposite – negative mood and a self that is incapable and socially at risk.

Variations in mood are describable by a variety of culturally provided terms, which vary both across historical periods and from one situation to another. The contemporary individual has access to the social machinery of psychiatry and its array of diagnostic categories, therapies, and medicines; to religious interpretations that emphasize sin and repentance over medicine; to political ideologies that emphasize personal responsibility and eschew scientific causal explanations of conduct; and, of course, to scientific and popular ideas that view self-esteem as central to personal satisfaction and social responsibility. People tending toward euphoria may report that they are "happy," "excited," or "self-confident," or that they "feel good" or are "in a good mood." They may respond to self-esteem measures in ways that lead a social scientist to attribute high self-esteem to them. They may see themselves in terms of religious ecstasy. They may strike a psychologist or psychiatrist as healthy or, if too euphoric, as manic. And if they have access to the discourse of self-esteem, as nearly everyone nowadays does, they may say that they have high self-esteem and thus experience the socially created emotion of self-esteem.

Origins of Self-Esteem

Self-esteem is thought by contemporary behavioral scientists and laypersons alike to be rooted in four conditions – acceptance, evaluation, comparison, and efficacy. Self-esteem is believed to depend on unqualified acceptance of the child early in life, the provision of positive evaluations by significant others, favorable comparisons with others and with an ideal self, and the capacity for effective conduct. It is thought to require the child's acceptance within the social fold and to be built early in life on a foundation of security, trust, and unconditional love. Later, positive evaluations enhance self-esteem and negative evaluations damage it. Likewise, self-esteem is enhanced when the person is able to make favorable comparisons with other people or with an ideal self, and also when the person acts effectively in his or her world.

Both the idea of self-esteem and the science that has created it are deeply embedded in and in some ways mirror American culture. This culture makes the individual responsible for creating a social world or finding a place in an existing one. It is the individual who must develop friendships, establish an occupational or professional network, or find a mate or life partner. Likewise, American culture exposes the individual to numerous situations of evaluation by self and others. Children earn grades for academic work, get cheers or jeers for their athletic or musical accomplishments, and are assigned to "popular" or "unpopular" peer groups. Adults are evaluated for their appearance and work performance, and think about their success or lack of it in comparison with their peers. Parents compare their own children with those of their friends and strive to "keep up with the Joneses". And it is the individual who must act independently and effectively.

American culture does not, however, present a consistent set of expectations. The social world often is portrayed as an interpersonal oyster for the individual to crack and enjoy, but Americans also look wistfully for places where acceptance is guaranteed and "everybody knows your name." Schools apply evaluative criteria unevenly, sometimes enforcing academic standards weakly while requiring talent and hard work for membership on the varsity football squad or the school chorus. Children are told to work hard, but also that they are entitled to feel good about themselves no matter how well they do and that failure does not make them less worthy human beings. Finally, a communitarian impulse in American culture often works against its intense individualism. Sometimes people are urged to base their estimate of self-worth simply on their membership in a group and to take personal pride from group accomplishments.

This ambivalence about acceptance, evaluation, comparison, and efficacy arises from several fault lines in American culture. Americans feel entitled to the "pursuit of happiness" and believe that each person deserves a chance at success. But happiness and success are ambiguous, ill-defined qualities. Happiness is defined both as future enjoyment earned by individual effort and as contentment with one's place in life. Everyone deserves a chance at success, but for some it is social and financial advancement, and for others the contented application of effort to a vocation even without hope of fame or fortune. Americans are also ambivalent about equality. Sometimes they emphasize equality of opportunity, believing that each person should have a fair start in life and obey the same rules on a level playing field. But Americans also sometimes emphasize equality of condition or outcome, with happiness and success defined as entitlements of membership in the society rather than as prizes to be sought and won.

Differing meanings of self-esteem reflect these contrasting meanings of success, happiness, and equality. One set of meanings views self-esteem as a privilege to be achieved by displaying socially appropriate attitudes and engaging in hard work. The other set views self-esteem as an entitlement requiring no changes in behavior or attitudes. Indeed, the individual is held able to bootstrap himself or herself to self-affirming feelings.

The language of self-esteem transforms deeply rooted cultural issues into personally relevant questions: Do others like or respect me? Am I as happy or as successful as I could be? Do I deserve to think better of myself than I do? How can I feel better about me? What must I do to feel better? How can I justify the way I feel about myself? For those in *pursuit* of happiness and success and who feel themselves well along on the path, self-esteem is a way of characterizing – and experiencing – their positive feelings about their lives. For those who feel themselves falling behind in the quest, talk of earning self-esteem motivates further effort. In contrast, those who favor communitarian definitions of self, as well as those whose future-oriented quest for success and happiness has faltered, also can find reassurance in the discourse of self-esteem. "I have the right to feel good about myself," one might say, "because friends and family value me for virtues that are more important than financial success. I am content with my life and with myself."

Whichever version of self-esteem is emphasized, it is a culturally important emotion, perhaps even a necessary one, since it expresses and resonates with important cultural dilemmas. By creating the concept of self-esteem and providing the knowledge and ideas for a popular discourse about it, social scientists thus inadvertently create what Michel Foucault called "technologies of the self," manufacturing the very terms and instruments whereby the self is experienced. They have been joined in this effort by legions of "conceptual entrepreneurs" who market the idea of self-esteem as well as techniques for its improvement.

The Consequences of Self-Esteem

In spite of considerable scientific and entrepreneurial effort devoted to its study and promotion, there is little evidence that efforts to enhance self-esteem provide significant leverage in improving individual well-being or solving social problems. Studies of the distribution of self-esteem suggest that there is neither an epidemic of low self-esteem nor an outbreak of unearned high self-esteem. Low self-esteem is not the cause of such social problems as poor academic achievement, drug abuse, or teenage pregnancy, nor is the improvement of self-esteem a remedy for these conditions. And although no one would maintain that low self-esteem is desirable, it can be argued that high self-esteem is not an unqualified good.

An exhaustive review of self-esteem research has made clear that the effects of self-esteem are generally far less impressive than proponents of the self-esteem movement have claimed. Although high self-esteem is positively and strongly related to happiness, they found it is "not a major predictor or cause of almost anything" (Baumeister, Campbell, Krueger, & Vohs, 2003, p. 37). (The sole major exception is that high self-esteem appears to insulate girls from bulimia.) Self-esteem correlates most strongly with *subjective* perceptions of success, intelligence, likeability, and attractiveness. Thus, they report, "people with high self-esteem seem sincerely to believe they are smarter, more accomplished, more popular and likeable, and more attractive than other people" (p. 37). But such self-perceptions are not borne out in the judgments of other people; people with high self-esteem are not thought by others to be smarter, more successful, or more likeable. When objective measures of outcomes, such as school performance, are employed, correlations with self-esteem become much smaller. And the evidence suggests that high self-esteem is a result of good school performance, not a cause of it.

Moreover, self-esteem may not be the unqualified good that its proponents claim. High self-esteem does seem to enable people more readily to speak up in groups, and to take the initiative. But it also seems to dispose people to regard members of their own group as preferable to outsiders, and thus may promote prejudice and discrimination as readily as group pride. Moreover, high self-esteem is not a homogeneous attribute. The relatively high measured self-esteem of some individuals reflects a reasonably accurate picture of how they view their strengths and accomplishments. But others respond defensively to self-esteem measures, and thus only appear to have high self-esteem because they are so strongly motivated to deny they have any negative qualities. Others are merely conceited, with highly inflated self-perceptions, and some are narcissistic. Finally, while high self-esteem fosters initiative and independence from the group, it also renders the person less susceptible to influence by group norms and expectations.

The value of self-esteem is thus less than previously thought. High self-esteem is associated with the pleasant feelings we call happiness and with the fostering of initiative. But there is no convincing reason to believe that raising self-esteem by itself is a useful means of improving the quality of the individual's life or solving social problems. With the important qualification that some manifestations of high self-esteem are the result of defensive tactics, conceit, and narcissism, high self-esteem is best conceived as an *indicator* of the individual's mental health, well-being, and social capabilities rather than as a desirable goal or end state in itself. Conditions that promote optimal human functioning also promote self-esteem, and these fundamental conditions are the ones worth pursuing: acceptance within a social fold, a sense of security, cultural competence, and the capacity to reconcile personal goals and social expectations.

SEE ALSO: ▶ Affective forecasting   ▶ Collective self-esteem   ▶ Emotions   ▶ Happiness   ▶ Individualism

References

Batson, C. D. (1990). Affect and altruism. In B. S. Moore & A. M. Isen (Eds.), *Affect and social behavior* (pp. 89–125). Cambridge, UK: Cambridge University Press.

Baumeister, R. F., Campbell, J., Krueger, J., & Vohs, K. (2003). Does high self-esteem cause better performance, interpersonal success, happiness, or healthier lifestyles? *Psychological Science in the Public Interest, 4,* 1–44.

Rosenberg, M. (1965). *Society and the adolescent self-image.* Princeton: Princeton University Press.

Self-Monitoring

David V. Day[a] and Deidra J. Schleicher[b]

[a]*Singapore Management University;* [b]*Purdue University*

Self-monitoring personality was introduced into the psychological literature more than three decades ago by Mark Snyder as a dispositional construct reflecting differences in the extent to which individuals monitor their self-presentations, expressive behavior, and nonverbal affective displays. High self-monitors are generally more flexible and pragmatic in their interpersonal orientations, adopting social interaction patterns that promote fitting in and meeting others' expectations. As such, they have sometimes been labeled as "chameleons." Low self-monitors are regarded as generally more principled in their interactions in that they are more likely to display a high correspondence between their emotions or attitudes and their behavior. These individuals are very consistent and predictable in terms of acting in accord with their beliefs, and thus operate according to the philosophy of "to thine own self be true." Self-monitoring is considered to be relatively enduring over time and captures aspects of both the motivation and ability to monitor verbal and nonverbal behavior in social situations.

From this early conceptualization, self-monitoring has evolved in meaning. Specifically, the concept has been elaborated to reflect differences in: a) how high and low self-monitors think about and organize the social world around them; b) the types of interpersonal strategies that are adopted by high and low self-monitors; and c) how high and low self-monitors construct aspects of their identity to make sense of themselves and their social relationships. The most recent conceptualization is that self-monitoring reflects individual differences in the tendency to engage in or avoid certain forms of image and impression management. That is, high self-monitors embrace impression management as a way of enhancing their own personal status (status enhancement motive), whereas low self-monitors are more concerned with making sure that their true self is portrayed as accurately as possible in social situations (self-congruency enhancement motive).

The popularity of self-monitoring as a focus of both basic and applied research is evident in the number of different areas in psychology in which it has been examined. The construct of self-monitoring emerged from the literature in social psychology and has been especially associated with the disciplinary subareas of social interactions and close relationships such as friendships, romantic relationships, and marriage. Research in these areas has generally found that high self-monitors are likely to have more interpersonal relationships that are less committed and intimate in nature, whereas low self-monitors are likely to have fewer relationships, although these relationships are characterized by deeper levels of commitment.

Other disciplines in which self-monitoring has received substantial attention include consumer psychology (such as the differential reactions of high and low self-monitors to specific advertising approaches) and industrial/organizational psychology (in terms of the role of self-monitoring in work and organizational contexts). The latter includes empirical studies linking self-monitoring with job attitudes, job performance and organizational advancement, and leadership.

It is also the case that there is conceptual and empirical overlap between self-monitoring personality and a number of variables studied in the positive psychology literature such as subjective well-being, job and life satisfaction, self-esteem, positive affectivity, authenticity, resilience, and empathy. Thus, self-monitoring personality has important implications for the study of positive psychology. Although the empirical findings in these areas are somewhat inconsistent and complex, there appears to be substantial evidence to support the general conclusion that there are positive characteristics associated with both high and low self-monitors. For example, in the authenticity literature, it has been noted that although low self-monitors are more likely to be true to themselves and more sincere, high self-monitors have more flexibility to cope with the increasing diversity of social roles. Similarly, in terms of job-related well-being (composed of job satisfaction, job involvement, and organizational commitment), meta-analyses have indicated that although low self-monitors are likely to have higher levels of organizational commitment, it is high self-monitors who tend to have greater job involvement (no consistent differences have been found with regard to job satisfaction). The list of positive characteristics that low self-monitors may be more likely to possess include greater sincerity and authenticity, more principled behavior, an internal locus of control, higher self-esteem, and greater commitment to friends, relationship partners, and employing organizations. High self-monitors, on the other hand, are likely to have higher levels of extroversion, agreeableness, and positive affectivity (they not only express but also evoke higher levels of positive affect in their interpersonal relationships), greater interpersonal, social, and communication skills, more flexible orientations that allow them to face change with greater resilience and optimism, greater confidence in their judgments, better job performance (particularly in sales positions), and increased likelihood of emerging as leaders.

Self-monitoring has been examined in a number of contexts and has been found to relate to a number of important variables, including those in the positive psychology domain. It is likely that research in these areas will continue in the future, taking into account the challenges and controversies surrounding self-monitoring that are reviewed in the following section. One of the more pressing needs for future research in this area is to become more focused on low self-monitors, as much less is known about the characteristics and behavioral outcomes of low self-monitors than high self-monitors. Similarly, there is a need for continued research and debate on the question of whether low self-monitors lack the ability, or merely the motivation, to monitor their social behavior.

Challenges and Controversies in Measuring Self-Monitoring

The major controversies associated with self-monitoring concern its measurement, including its scoring and dimensionality. The most popular measurement instrument is the Self-Monitoring Scale (SMS), which has been revised from 25 items to an 18-item format. The recommended scoring format according to Snyder is true-false responses for each item, and the scale is keyed such that higher scores indicate a higher self-monitoring tendency. It has also been argued that self-monitoring personality is a *discrete class variable*, as opposed to a continuous variable, meaning that respondents can be classified discretely as a low self-monitor (scores of 10 and below on the 18-item SMS) or as a high self-monitor (scores above 11), rather than falling along a self-monitoring continuum. This idea in particular has been controversial among researchers. However, meta-analytic findings suggest that relationships between self-monitoring and work-related constructs at least do not differ significantly if self-monitoring is measured or scored in a continuous (as opposed to discrete) manner.

The SMS was originally composed of the subcomponents of *extroversion* (e.g., "In a group of people I am rarely the center of attention," reversed scored), *acting* (e.g., "I would probably make a good actor"), and *other-directedness* (e.g., "I would not change my opinions . . . in order to please someone or win their favor," reverse scored). Based on extensive factor analyses, some researchers have questioned whether the self-monitoring construct as measured by the SMS would be better represented by two, not three, subcomponents, or whether one general factor underlies individual differences in self-monitoring. The most recent analysis of the evidence suggests that there is a conceptually meaningful general self-monitoring construct that relates to other constructs differently as compared with its subcomponents of extroversion, acting, and other directedness. Because of the questions raised about the self-monitoring construct and its measurement, other researchers, most notably Lennox and Wolfe, have suggested an alternative theoretical model for self-monitoring, along with a revised measurement scale.

SEE ALSO: ▶ Agreeableness ▶ Authenticity ▶ Life satisfaction ▶ Meaning

Self-Regulation

James E. Maddux
George Mason University

The study of self-regulation is concerned with understanding how people go about trying to accomplish valued goals and how and why they succeed or fail. The term *self-regulation* is often viewed as synonymous with *self-control*, implying that people can exercise some degree of voluntary control over their behavior, feelings, and thoughts. The term self-regulation, however, is usually used to refer to self-control that is directed toward a valued goal, especially a goal that extends beyond the immediate situation. Of course, to assume that humans *can* exercise control over their own behavior is not to assume that human behavior is always or even usually under intentional control but only that people are capable of controlling their own behavior in the pursuit of valued goals. Even currently automatic, habitual, or seemingly mindless behavior may have been at one time deliberate, mindful, and intentional.

People are usually more satisfied with their lives when they believe that they are making good progress in moving toward valued goals. For this reason, effective self-regulation is crucial to psychological adjustment and well-being. In addition, ineffective self-regulation can lead to serious psychological problems, including depression and anxiety disorders. This is not to say, however, that the happy and psychologically healthy person is one who is capable of exerting perfect control over his or her behavior, feelings, and thoughts at all times. Self-regulation in the pursuit of perfectionistic, unrealistic, or unhealthy goals can lead to unhappiness and dissatisfaction with life, as when the pursuit of the "perfect" body leads to eating disorders or to excessive worry about normal physical imperfections.

When most people think of a person's ability control his or her own behavior, they think of the concept of *willpower*. People commonly say such things as "I just can't control my eating. I have no willpower." or "You were able to lose 20 pounds in three months? I sure wish I had your willpower." In such statements, willpower is viewed as a fixed and unchanging property of the person – similar to the way that many people view intelligence or a personality trait – that each person has a certain amount of and that determines each person's ability to control his or her behavior. The problem with the notion of willpower is that it sounds like an explanation but really it is not. Someone observes another person's success at losing weight and attributes that success to the person's willpower. The only evidence for the person's willpower, however, is the person's success at losing weight. For this reason, explaining the person's success by referring to the person's willpower explains nothing. What were not observed were the person's decision-making processes concerning how much weight to lose and by when to lose it and the person's plan for doing so. What were not observed were the hundreds or thousands of decisions the person made about his and her food consumption (not to mention exercise) in hundreds or thousands of situations over a period of weeks, months, or even years. What were not observed were the trials and errors of various strategies for reducing food intake and resisting temptation and how the person learned to deal with challenges and setbacks along the way, including the distressing emotions that often accompany attempts to accomplish a difficult goal. What were not observed were the ways in which the person's confidence gradually strengthened along the way and how this confidence influenced the person's ability to deal with challenges and setbacks. Essentially, what were not observed were the specific self-regulation *skills* and *strategies* that the person employed in the attempt to lose weight.

It is these specific skills and strategies that are the topic of theories and models of self-regulation. Unlike willpower, self-regulation is viewed not as a fixed and unchanging property of the person but as a set of skills that can be learned, can be improved through practice, and can be adapted from one situation to another. Numerous models of self-regulation have been proposed over the past several decades. Taken together, these models identify ten components of self-regulation: a) goals – what a person is either trying to accomplish or trying to avoid; b) plans – the person's strategy for accomplishing the goals; c) self-efficacy beliefs – the person's confidence in his or her ability to implement specific aspects of the plan; d) standards of evaluation – the person's "yardstick" for measuring progress along the way; e) goal-directed action – actual attempts to implement specific aspects of the plan; f) self-monitoring – observing one's behavior and the impact of one's behavior on progress toward a goal; g) feedback – information about progress toward a goal (as compared to standards of performance) that people either gather themselves or that is provided by other people or automatically by the situations (e.g., a computer video game); h) self-evaluation – judgments about one's progress toward a goal; i) emotional reactions to these evaluations; and (j) corrective action – attempts to changes one's behavior to move oneself toward one's goal more efficiently based on feedback, self-evaluation, and emotional reactions. Self-regulation does not, of course, consist of an invariable sequence of ten steps, beginning with a goal and ending with correction action. Instead, self-regulation consists of a number of *components* that interact continually in complex ways.

As the above list of self-regulation components indicates, human self-regulation is a complex process. One way to get a better idea of how it works is to understand the operation of a *cybernetic device* – a self-regulating system or machine such as a guided missile or a robot. A simple thermostat provides a good example of a cybernetic device. A thermostat may be programmed to maintain the temperature of a room at 72°F. The thermostat's *goal* is 72°F. The thermostat can also be set to be alert for deviations from 72°F of a certain magnitude – its *standard of evaluation*. The thermostat continually collects information or *feedback* about the temperature of the environment. The thermostat then compares this information with the standard – a process of *self-monitoring*. If the thermostat detects a sufficiently large discrepancy between the room's temperature and the standard, it then sends a signal that turns the heating or cooling unit on, depending on the direction of the discrepancy (i.e., warmer vs. cooler than the reference criterion) – the goal-directed *action*. The result of this action is a reduction of the discrepancy between the perceived room temperature and the goal of 72°F. When the thermostat senses that the goal has been attained, it sends a signal that turns the heating or cooling unit off. As long as the thermostat does not detect a sufficiently large discrepancy between the room temperature and the reference criterion (72°F), it will do nothing. However, when the thermostat once again detects a discrepancy, it sends a signal that turns the heating or cooling unit on. If the thermostat is reset for 74°F, it will have a new goal that it will work to attain and maintain.

Perhaps the human behavior that most resembles the operations of a cybernetic device and that is familiar to most people is driving an automobile. Driving usually begins with a goal – getting from point A to point B quickly but also safely. Of course, this situation already presents a complication not presented by the thermostat – a conflict between goals, because driving quickly may be incompatible with driving safely. Under relatively good conditions (clear weather, good roads, moderate traffic) and in familiar territory (e.g., driving to work for the 1,000th time), the driver behaves much as the thermostat does and behaves almost as automatically as does the thermostat. The driver has a goal (getting from A to B) and has standards of evaluation in that the driver, like the thermostat, is alert for deviations from the goal of a certain magnitude, such as drifting too close to the curb or the middle of the road or approaching the car in front too quickly or too closely. The driver constantly gathers information or feedback about how well he or she is doing in maintaining these standards and constantly self-monitors his or her deviations from these standards. If the driver detects a sufficiently large discrepancy between the current situation and the standard (e.g., drifting too close to the middle line), then the driver performs an action to reduce this discrepancy (e.g., a slight turn of the wheel to the right). Even in a short drive of a few miles, an experienced driver will make thousands of these automatic adjustments in pursuit of the goal of arriving from point A to point B relatively quickly but also safely.

The "driver-as-cybernetic-device" analogy holds up fairly well as a model of human self-regulation as long as the driving conditions are fairly good, the terrain and route fairly familiar, and the driver fairly confident and calm. But because people are thinking and feeling beings, driving can easily become more complicated than the operation of a thermostat. Consider the driver who is late for an important appointment. This driver may be preoccupied with thoughts about the consequences of being late for the appointment and therefore may self-monitor his or her behavior and collect feedback about his or her driving less efficiently than otherwise. The driver's reaction time and thus his or her ability to quickly engage in discrepancy-reducing action may be impaired. If this hurried and anxious driver also is driving in unfamiliar territory, he or she will have the added distraction of having to pay closer attention to the surroundings (e.g., looking for exit ramps and street signs) and the anxiety that results from not being quite sure how to get to where one wants to go. Bad weather could produce additional distractions and additional anxiety. If the driver tries to use the cell phone to call the person with whom the appointment is, there is another major distraction with which to deal. If the driver is unaccustomed to driving in bad weather in unfamiliar territory, he or she may have little confidence in the ability to drive under these conditions. This lack of confidence can result in anxiety, which can further hinder performance. The driver may be hungry and may suddenly decide that the goal of satisfying hunger is more important than the goal of arriving on time for the appointment (the temptation of competing situational goals). There may even be a decision not to go to the appointment because of extreme anxiety about the appointment.

It is easy to understand, therefore, how human self-regulation can become more complicated than the operation of even the most complex cybernetic device. These complications are the result of several major differences between machines and people. First, although a cybernetic device has goals, it does not choose its goals, nor can it choose to reject them. Humans often are assigned goals (e.g., in the workplace) but can decide to reject them or work on them only half-heartedly while giving the appearance of working diligently. Cybernetic devices begin with an established goal and then operate automatically to attain and maintain the goal. Machines, unlike people cannot "fake it." Regardless of their complexity and their ability to self-regulate once set into action, not even the most sophisticated self-regulating devices (e.g., robots) design themselves or set themselves into action – at least not yet. They initially depend on human goal-directed behavior and human self-regulation. When they malfunction, they depend on humans to fix them.

Second, cybernetic devices do not make their own plans. Human beings make plans and install them in machines. Third, cybernetic devices do not develop self-efficacy beliefs – beliefs about their ability to accomplish their goals – that can change with time and experience and can influence their ability to function effectively. Fourth, machines do not have self-esteem. Although cybernetic devices can measure their progress toward a goal, they cannot evaluate themselves as good or bad or strong or weak based on how well or how quickly they believe they are accomplishing their goals. Finally, machines do not feel. Cybernetic devices (even the most sophisticated computerized robots) lack the human capacity for emotion. Research has demonstrated that a person's evaluation of his or her progress toward a valued goal produces emotional reactions (e.g., anxiety, sadness, satisfaction, joy) and that these emotional reactions can either facilitate or disrupt self-regulation. Likewise, because self-regulation requires effort and can be emotionally taxing, self-regulatory efforts in one situation (e.g., not eating those additional cookies) can leave the person temporarily depleted or less able to exert his or her self-regulatory skills in a new situation (e.g., studying for an exam.) Machines do not become tired or depleted in this same way.

Therefore, a model of *human* self-regulation must allow for self-set goals, self-made plans, self-evaluation, the experience of emotion during self-regulation, and the influence of emotion on self-regulation, including the experience of self-regulatory depletion.

SEE ALSO: ▶ Agency ▶ Self-efficacy

Self-Report Inventory

Neal M. Kingston
University of Kansas

A *self-report inventory* is a type of assessment intended to measure a person's interests, attitudes, or personality. As the name implies, a self-report inventory is one where individuals are asked to respond to questions about themselves, rather than a measure which obtains information from direct observation (in either a natural or artificial setting) by one or more third parties.

Self-report inventories use a variety of item formats. Many use a Likert format, where respondents, in response to a statement, select from choices like: 1) very much like me; 2) somewhat like me; 3) neither like nor unlike me; 4) somewhat unlike me; or 5) very much unlike me. Others require examinees to respond *Yes* or *No* to statements such as "I would rather go to watch a play than go to a party." Others require respondents to endorse one of two statements as being more like themselves.

The advantages of self-report inventories are that they are fast, inexpensive, and collect information from the person with the most intimate knowledge of the subject. The primary disadvantage is that they are subject to bias, both because a person is responding to fairly subjective questions from a single point of view, and because those responses may be tinged by a desire to look good or to look bad.

Early History

The assessment of personal characteristics has been of interest since at least the beginnings of astrology, approximately 5,000 years ago in Babylonia. In China 4,000 years ago a more rigorous, assessment center type approach was implemented to select government leaders based on both ability and personality traits. The Chinese system evolved over the millennia but continued in well-documented form until about 1900 CE. In the first half of the twentieth century free-association and projective approaches of personality assessment were developed, as well as other interview approaches used by trained psychologists.

In the late 1930s Starke Hathaway and J. C. McKinley gathered numerous questions that he and his colleagues used while interviewing patients or that had appeared in other questionnaires. They administered about 1,000 true-false questions to 221 patients who had previously been diagnosed with psychopathology and to 724 people who were friends or relatives of the patients but who had no psychopathological diagnoses. About 500 items for which self-reports differentiated the different diagnostic categories from each other and from the "normal" group were retained and used in research for several years and then published in 1943 as the Minnesota Multiphasic Personality Inventory, the first widely used self-report inventory.

In 1946, Raymond Cattell applied a statistical technique, factor analysis, to data derived from adjectives used commonly to describe personality. This led to the development of the 16 PF (16 personality factors), a self-report inventory intended to be used broadly, not just for diagnosing psychopathology. Replications of Cattell's work led to a reduction of Cattell's 16 primary personality factors to five. Other early widely used self-report inventories include the California Psychological Inventory and the Thurstone Temperament Schedules.

While self-report inventories have been critiqued for their aforementioned methodological flaws, their use has grown and self-report inventories have been created to be congruent with a variety of different personality models as well as for career interests and attitudes.

Minimizing the Impact of Social Desirability and Other Response Sets on Self-Report Inventories

Various approaches have been taken to minimize intentional and unintentional distortions on self-report instruments. An example of an intentional distortion is lying (or exaggerating) to appear less prone to violence than one really is. An example of an unintentional distortion might be a tendency to agree with statements (acquiescence), regardless of how they are worded. One approach requires that respondents choose between alternatives that have been matched on social desirability. So, for example, an examinee would be forced to choose between endorsing one of the following statements: 1) I am more prepared at work than most of my colleagues; or 2) I have more friends than most people. Examinees who choose the first statement might have points added to a conscientiousness score scale while examinees endorsing the second statement would have points added to their extroversion scale score. But despite the social desirability of both scales, they can only add points to one of the scales. Such an approach is called *ipsative*.

An ipsative approach does not allow people to score very high on all scales. Two people might be viewed from external evidence (or any nonipsative approach) as equally extroverted, but if one was also highly conscientious this would tend to lower that person's extroversion scale score on an ipsative measure, as sometimes he or she would choose a response that loaded on conscientiousness when it was paired with a response for extroversion. In other words, ipsative measures are a zero sum game – you can't be high or low on everything. Because of this, ipsative scores allow comparison of the strength of different characteristics within an individual, but not the strength of any one characteristic across individuals.

An alternative approach to minimizing social distortions on self-report inventories is to ask questions for which it is not clear the scale and direction to which a response contributes. The scale loadings for such questions are determined by statistical analysis, and not by any theoretical linkage. An example of such a question might be, "Who was the better president, John Adams or Thomas Jefferson?" It might well be that people who choose one rather than the other are more likely to be neurotic, but it is unlikely that the examinee would determine that this question contributed to the neuroticism scale or was more indicative of neuroticism.

A third approach to minimizing the impact of any respondent tendency to skew results is to determine the extent that the test taker answers in socially desirable ways by asking questions where the socially desirable response is uncommon. A set of such questions appropriate for the particular population taking the test, such as, "I never lie," or "I have never gossiped" are asked. While any respondent might honestly answer one or two such question in the affirmative, too many affirmative responses to a set of such questions suggests that consideration be given to the impact of social desirability on this person's scores.

Another response set that should be addressed is acquiescence. Some examinees tend to respond in the affirmative when they are truly ambivalent or even close to ambivalent. Others tend to respond in the negative. Either tendency can skew results. Thus it is desirable to balance questions phrased in the positive and the negative. For example, if asked if this statement describes an individual accurately, a *yes* response to "I like to be the center of attention at parties" will load positively on an extroversion scale, as will a *no* answer to the statement, "I seldom talk in large groups."

Self-Report Inventories and Positive Psychology

Most measures used in a positive psychology context (e.g., constructs such as hope, optimism, life satisfaction, or curiosity) have been self-report in nature. In fact this is true for most personality measures and precedes the development of Positive Psychology as a field by about 70 years.

More recently, one emphasis of positive psychology has been the development of a classification of human strengths in some ways parallel to the *Diagnostic and Statistical Manual of Mental Disorders* (DSM) published by the American Psychiatric Association. This schema, the positive psychology Values in Action Classification of Strengths and Virtues, proposes 24 strengths grouped into six virtues (wisdom and knowledge, courage, humanity and love, justice, temperance, and transcendence). While there has not yet been developed a comprehensive instrument to assess of all these strengths and virtues, and thus there is not yet empirical support for the details of this model, much progress has been made in assessing components of this model.

Research in positive psychology often requires measures of happiness. Scientifically developed general measures of happiness have been used in research since at least Fordyce's work in 1977. As positive psychology's model of happiness evolved into three parts – pleasure, engagement, and meaning, the need for new measures has become clear. Several such assessments have been developed by researchers, but at this time none are widely used outside research studies.

SEE ALSO: ▶ Character strengths (VIA)

Seligman, Martin

Peter Schulman
University of Pennsylvania

Martin Seligman has made significant contributions to research on learned helplessness; depression; interventions that prevent depression; the relationship between optimism/pessimism and depression, achievement and physical health; positive psychology; and interventions that build strengths and well-being. Born in 1942 in Albany, New York, Seligman and his older sister, Elissa Beth, were raised by loving parents, Irene and Adrian. Seligman graduated from Princeton University in 1964 with a BA in Philosophy and attended the psychology program at the University of Pennsylvania for his PhD, graduating in 1967. His faculty advisor at Penn was Richard Solomon, a leading researcher in learning and motivation.

While a graduate student at the University of Pennsylvania, Seligman's animal research led him, along with Steve Maier and Bruce Overmier, to a discovery they called *learned helplessness*. This is considered an important discovery, as it identified a new kind of learning in which an organism recognizes there is no relationship between its behavior and desired outcomes, which can lead an organism to give up trying to achieve desired outcomes. Seligman noticed that this animal model of helplessness bore similarities to human depression, which led him to study helplessness and depression in humans.

In his research, Seligman also discovered that when exposed to uncontrollability, not all animals or humans give up in their efforts to control outcomes, and that experiences with controllability can buffer against the learning of helplessness. He next investigated the distinguishing features of those who give up from those who do not, which led him to develop the attributional style theory of depression. This theory asserts that individuals with pessimistic explanations of good and bad events are at greater risk for depression, and research has shown that optimistic explanations buffer against depression and enhance motivation, physical health, and achievement in different domains. Seligman's research further showed that optimism can be measured and it can be learned. He subsequently developed cognitive-behavioral interventions with his colleagues to teach optimism and prevent depression among children and young adults. These interventions have proven effective in preventing depression.

In the 1990s, Seligman became increasingly interested in the flip side of human deficits and psychopathology – human strengths and happiness. Elected President of the American Psychological Association in 1996, he made one of his presidential initiatives the promotion of positive psychology. Seligman made the case that psychology had largely focused its efforts on the understanding and treatment of psychological problems, with many successes. One consequence of this focus on psychological problems, however, was that psychology has had little to say about what makes life most worth living.

Seligman therefore proposed to correct this imbalance by focusing on strengths as well as weaknesses, on building the best things in life as well as repairing the worst, asserting that human goodness and excellence are just as authentic as distress and disorder, and that the mission of psychology entails more than the undoing of problems. He believes psychology's concern with remedying human problems is understandable and should not be abandoned. Human suffering demands scientifically informed solutions. Suffering and well-being, however, are both part of the human condition, and psychologists have a responsibility to be concerned with both.

Since 2000, Seligman's main mission has been the promotion of the field of positive psychology. One of his primary goals is to produce large-scale public health benefits by building strengths and happiness through positive psychology interventions. His research covers both classroom-based and web-based versions of these programs, with the hope of achieving widespread, cost-effective dissemination of programs to schools and other organizations.

Seligman is a humanist and a pragmatist with a vision for improving the human condition. He believes the ultimate value of his scientific research lies in its ability to improve the quality of human life. His commitment to broad intellectual questions of practical importance coupled with a rigorous respect for the empirical method has given him a leading role in psychology.

Seligman does not claim that positive psychology is a new field; rather, it has many distinguished ancestors. Since at least the time of Socrates, Plato, and Aristotle, the good life has been the subject of philosophical and religious inquiry and many psychologists have been working on positive psychology topics for decades. It just hadn't been brought under one scientific umbrella – positive psychology – until recently. The contribution of contemporary positive psychology has been to make the explicit argument that what makes life most worth living deserves its own empirically based field of study, to provide a legitimate discipline that brings together isolated lines of theory and research, to promote the cross-fertilization of ideas in related fields through conferences, summer institutes and research grants, to develop a comprehensive conceptual view of broad notions of happiness, to bring this field to the attention of various foundations and funding agencies, to help raise money for research, and to firmly ground assertions using the scientific method.

Since 1976, Seligman has been Professor of Psychology in the Department of Psychology at the University of Pennsylvania. He has written more than 20 books and 200 scholarly publications. His publications include several popular books, such as *Learned Optimism, Authentic Happiness*, and *The Optimistic Child* (with Karen Reivich, Lisa Jaycox, and Jane Gillham), and several scholarly books, including *Helplessness*, and *Character Strengths and Virtues* (with Christopher Peterson). His popular books have appealed broadly to the public, yet are built on firm scientific foundations. He is the recipient of four Distinguished Scientific Contribution awards from the American Psychological Association, the Laurel Award of the American Association for Applied Psychology and Prevention, and the Lifetime Achievement Award of the Society for Research in Psychopathology, among many other awards and honors. For more information on Seligman's activities and initiatives, see the following website: www.positivepsychology.org

Seligman is married to Mandy McCarthy Seligman and they have seven children – Amanda, David, Lara, Nicole, Darryl, Carly, and Jenny. His wife and children are a great joy to him.

SEE ALSO: ▶ Positive Psychology Network

Serotonin

Robyn McKay
University of Kansas

The chemical serotonin, or 5-hydroxytryptamine (5-HT), acts as a neurotransmitter in the brain. However, only a small amount of the body's serotonin concentration is actually localized in the brain. Most serotonin concentrations are produced in the gastrointestinal tract and assist in the regulation of gastric secretions and peristalsis. Serotonin has also been found to be located in blood platelets where it acts as a vasoconstrictor. An imbalance of serotonin often is considered the primary culprit in psychiatric disorders such as depression and mania. In fact, serotonin and other neurotransmitters that act on the limbic system are part of a much larger neurochemical network that has a role in the maintenance of well-being.

The Serotonin Cycle

In part, brain functions are carried out by a network of nerves. Neurotransmitters, which are packets of biochemicals, are involved in the transmission of electrical impulses from one nerve to another. Electrical impulses generated by nerves are used to carry out communications within the neural network. Although there are many different neurotransmitters that are involved in a variety of brain functions, serotonin is one of three neurotransmitters, along with norepinepherine and dopamine, which are used by some of the nerves that regulate the limbic system. The limbic system is the part of the brain that controls emotions such as joy, fear, sadness, and anger. Although there is still much that researchers do not understand about how the limbic system functions, serotonin is often implicated in the identification and treatment of mood disorders. Though all neurotransmitters are thought to function similarly, the serotonin release and reuptake cycle has been studied in detail because of its theorized role in mood disorders, as well as anxiety, obsessive-compulsive disorder, and eating disorders such as anorexia nervosa. Key features of the serotonin cycle are briefly discussed here.

When a nerve is stimulated, an electrical impulse travels down the axon, which is the long, thin part of the presynaptic nerve. The presynaptic nerve is simply the nerve that precedes the synapse (the space that exists between two nerves). Even though the distance between two nerves is small, the electrical impulses that nerves generate are too weak to leap across the synapse. For the electrical impulse to continue across the synapse, serotonin molecules are released from the presynaptic nerve into the synaptic fluid. The molecules are transmitted across the synapse where they attach to serotonergic receptors on the surface of the postsynaptic nerve membrane. (A postsynaptic nerve is one that follows the synapse.) Once attached to the receptors, additional biochemical reactions are triggered, which cause the postsynaptic nerve to fire. As a result, the electrical impulse continues its journey along the neural network. After the postsynaptic nerve fires, serotonin molecules are released from the postsynaptic receptors back into the synaptic fluid. Rather than remaining in the synapse, serotonin molecules are pumped back across the presynaptic membrane, a process that is referred to as *reuptake*. Once the presynaptic reuptake process is complete, serotonin molecules are recycled; or if serotonin concentrations are in excess, the molecules are metabolized by monoamine oxidase, another biochemical that resides in the presynaptic nerve. The metabolized form of serotonin (5-hydroxyindoleacetic acid or 5-HIAA) is absorbed into the blood stream, processed in the kidneys, and excreted in the urine, which completes the serotonin cycle.

Presynaptic nerves also function to produce enough serotonin so that neural transmissions remain in balance. When serotonin and the other neurotransmitters involved with mood regulation are functioning properly, i.e., produced in proper concentrations, the limbic system seems to work well. In other words, positive mood states such as joy, self-confidence, energy, and enthusiasm are associated with appropriate concentrations of serotonin and other neurotransmitters that act on the limbic system.

Pharmacologic Solutions for Improved Well-Being

Since there is much left to be understood about how the brain functions, psychiatric researchers have offered theories to explain the etiology of depression and well-being. Early research suggested that serotonin concentrations are depleted in the case of depression, and are in excess in the case of mania. More recently, the postsynaptic serotonergic receptors, instead of serotonin itself, have been implicated in mood dysregulation. Furthermore, other neurotransmitters, including dopamine and norepinepherine have also been implicated in the regulation of mood and emotions. In any case, three main classes of antidepressants are typically prescribed to treat of depression: selective serotonin reuptake inhibitors (SSRIs), tricyclic antidepressants, and monoamine oxidase inhibitors (MAOIs). Each class of antidepressants is theorized to act slightly differently. For example, SSRIs are thought to block the reuptake of serotonin to the presynaptic nerve. If this mechanism is the case, then serotonin concentrations are theorized to increase, which in turn leads to reductions in symptoms of depression. In contrast, MAOIs are thought to inhibit the action of monoamine oxidase, which is involved in the metabolism of serotonin after it has been reabsorbed into the presynaptic nerve. Importantly, the mechanism of action of antidepressants, or the way that antidepressants act on the body system, is continuing to be understood.

Antidepressants typically take approximately 6 weeks to become fully effective. Researchers theorize that the number of postsynaptic receptors may change in response to antidepressant medications, a biological process that may take time. Neurogenesis (the generation of new neurons), a theory that has gained attention in recent years, is another possible explanation for the delay in the efficacy of antidepressants. Specifically, the neuorgenesis theory proposes that increased serotonin concentrations in the brain are associated with the growth of new neurons, which in turn, has been linked to reduced symptoms of depression and increased feelings of well-being.

Mind-Body Solutions for Improved Well-Being

Along with norepinepherine and dopamine, serotonin is regarded as a key neurotransmitter that is affected by the body's response to stress. Increased serotonin concentrations also are associated with subjective feelings of well-being. However, during prolonged periods of stress, the brain's biochemistry may become unbalanced when an excess of the neurochemical cortisol is produced. The continuous production of cortisol may reduce the availability of tryptophan, the precursor to serotonin. In turn, reductions in serotonin concentrations result in changes in sleep and appetite, depression, and other mood disorders. Other stress-related disorders that can result include anxiety, gastrointestinal disorders, substance abuse, eating disorders, cardiovascular disease, obesity, and diabetes.

Antidepressants are one means of managing the effects of chronic stress. Psychiatric researchers often consider the mind-body connection when examining the biological basis mood regulation. The body's response to stress (the fight or flight response) has been implicated in the regulation mood and emotions. The stress response is governed by the central nervous system. However, genetics, social and cultural influences, critical life events such as traumas, and behaviors such as sleep, nutrition, substance use, as well as individual differences in emotional regulation each play a role in the stress response.

Behavioral medicine interventions targeted at stress management are gaining empirical support as well. One of the goals of the behavioral medicine approach is to repair the stress response in an effort to treat chronic disorders. Theoretically, serotonin production may be changed in some way in response to behavioral interventions. Emerging evidence suggests that mind-body interventions are associated with increases in serotonin concentrations, which in turn may relieve the stress response, and improve subjective feelings of well-being.

Relaxation response training, social support, modifications to nutrition, increased exercise, cognitive-behavioral therapy, and meditation are behavioral interventions that have been demonstrated to improve coping and health outcomes. In particular, relaxation training has been shown to have psychological and physical benefits, such as reductions in chronic pain, depression, and anxiety. Regular meditation practices provide benefits that are associated with elements of positive psychology. In addition to reductions in anxiety and depression, people who meditate regularly report improvements in awareness, calmness, and control. They also seem to have more positive outlooks than those who do not regularly practice meditation. Finally, journaling about traumatic events (which are associated with chronic stress) is associated with symptom reduction and fewer doctors' visits.

Conclusion

The neurotransmitter serotonin is part of the larger mind-body system that functions to maintain well-being. Balanced serotonin concentrations are associated with positive mood and emotions, including happiness, joy, self-assurance, and optimism. When serotonin concentrations are altered in response to chronic stress, negative emotions, as well as anxiety and depression can result. Antidepressant medications have been demonstrated to recalibrate the biochemistry of the limbic system, which is in turn associated with improvements in mood and emotions. In addition, relaxation response training, meditation, cognitive-behavioral therapy, and journaling are among the behavioral medicine interventions that are associated with improved mood and well-being. The combination of pharmacotherapy and behavioral interventions may be appropriate for the treatment of symptoms related to chronic stress, depression, and other mood disorders.

SEE ALSO: ▶ Neurobiology ▶ Positive emotions

Smiles

Anthony Papa
Department of Veterans Affairs, Boston Healthcare System

Smiles are facial expressions characterized by upward curving of the corners of the mouth and lips. In addition to upturned lip corners, some smiles include crinkling or crow's feet at the outer eye corners.

Brief History of Smile Research

The history of smile research is linked to research into facial expressions of emotion in general. Charles Darwin (d. 1882) was one of the first to scientifically explore facial expressions of emotion in his 1872 book, *The Expression of Emotions in Man and Animals*. In this book, Darwin attempts to prove that humans were subject to evolution and natural selection by demonstrating commonalities of expressions across mammalian species (e.g., bared teeth mean anger for both you and your dog). For Darwin, facial expressions of emotion were vestigial traces of our evolutionary past that linked us to other "lower" mammals that also seem to aid communication within and between species.

While research and theorizing on emotions continued in the subsequent years, research into facial expressions, smiles, and smiling was mainly anthropological in nature. In the 1960s, Sylvan Tompkins defined and described the basic human emotions and associated behaviors (such as smiling). His students provided the necessary tools to continue the scientific inquiry into basic emotions by creating objective, observational coding systems to measure facial expressions. One of those students, Paul Ekman, whose work into the types, functions, and behaviors associated with basic human emotions has been very influential, has given particular attention to the types and function of smiles. Research by Ekman and others influenced by him continue to focus on the types and functions of smiles and the behaviors and situations associated with smiling.

Because coding facial expressions is very labor intensive, new technologies are being used and developed to measure smiles and facial expressions in general. Currently, research on smiles often uses electromyography (EMG) to measure related muscle movements, and recently there is work to utilize infrared cameras, and computer algorithms that automatically recognize emotion related facial expressions.

Types of Smiles

Voice, posture, and gesture all communicate emotion, but facial expressions are hypothesized to be the primary means of communication. Facial expressions of emotion have been shown to communicate individuals' internal states, social intent, and information about the environment. Only in the last few decades has research begun to explore what smiles communicate. A crucial insight into the functional nature of smiling emerged with the demonstration of two physically discrete types of smiles, associated with unique neuroanatomical correlates.

Genuine Smiles

Genuine or *Duchenne* smiles involve not only an upward turn of lip corners caused by contraction of the zygomaticus major muscles associated with a prototypical smile, but also the tightening of the orbicularis oculi muscle around the eye, typically causing crow's feet. They are named Duchenne smiles after the French neurologist, Guillaume Benjamin Amand Duchenne de Boulogne, who first noted in 1862 in *Mecanisme de la Physionomie Humaine* that orbicularis oculi muscle contraction occurs during spontaneous, not posed, smiles of enjoyment. This observation remained unexplored and unreplicated until Paul Ekman and colleagues provided further evidence that Duchenne smiles consistently cooccur with positive emotion such as happiness and amusement.

Nongenuine Smiles

People often smile in nonpositive affective states. These polite, *non-Duchenne* smiles typically consist of the upward turn of lip corners caused by contraction of the zygomaticus major muscles, without crow's feet caused by the contraction of orbicularis oculi around the eye. Non-Duchenne smiles are not typically associated with positive emotion.

Smiles in Infants

While Duchenne and non-Duchenne smiles appear to have different functional roles in adults, infants' smiles appear to be less differentiated. Infants' smiles appear to be consistently associated with positive stimuli, and the difference between non-Duchenne and Duchenne smiles may be a matter of degree. Recent work suggests, though, that infants' non-Duchenne, Duchenne, and Duchenne smiles with an open mouth (called *duplay* smiles – a distinction not explored in adult research) are associated with specific situational contexts, implying different functions. It remains unclear at what age humans begin to display nongenuine smiles.

Trends and Limitations in Current Research

A large percentage of studies on smiles and smiling, both past and present, have not made the distinction between Duchenne and non-Duchenne smiles, and consequently have often produced inconclusive or contradictory results. While differentiating smiles based on the action of the orbicularis oculi muscle has been fruitful scientifically, it is unclear at this time if these two types of smiles represent the entire repertoire of distinguishable smiles communicated by adults. Due to the methodological constraints of facial coding, little work has been done examining human interactions in naturalistic settings to identify other possible smile exemplars.

Functions of Smiles

Smiles are Social Signals

Fridlund found that people smiled more often in social contexts than alone, despite being exposed to the same stimuli and reporting the same amount of positive emotion. He hypothesized that smiles were not related to emotional experience but are social signaling behaviors. Subsequent research has replicated but qualified Fridlund's basic findings. Smiling alone, while less frequent than in social situations, is associated with the intensity of the stimuli and reflects positive emotional arousal.

Duchenne expressions have been shown to elicit positive emotional reactions in others, positive personal attributions, affiliative responses and even increased forgiveness. In terms of well-being and adjustment, Duchenne expressions have also been associated with greater marital satisfaction in middle-aged and older couples, and less likelihood for divorce. Strong Duchenne smiles in college yearbook pictures have been associated with less daily distress and greater overall emotional and physical well-being up to 30 years later. Beyond merely signaling current emotional states that reflect current adjustment, Duchenne smiles may promote positive adjustment by eliciting positive responses in other people, encouraging social affiliation, and increasing availability of social resources for coping with adversity.

The scientific literature is mixed about the social effects of non-Duchenne expressions. Some studies have shown that non-Duchenne smiles evoke less positive responses in others than Duchenne smiles, whereas others do not. Non-Duchenne smiles have been shown to function as polite social markers, to mask feelings, and to communicate appeasement.

How Smiles Shape the Social Behavior of Others

Evolutionary based, social functional theories of emotion hypothesize that expressions of emotion in mammals are evolutionary adaptations to social environments, related to the creation and maintenance of social relationships and the organization of interindividual (and interspecies) interactions. Emotional facial expressions shape the responses of others in social environments by evoking specific emotional responses and reinforcing or discouraging social behaviors. Positive and negative emotional reactions appear to be elicited automatically in people exposed to positive and negative facial displays, even when exposure is at speeds below the level of conscious perception.

Keltner and Bonanno found that bereaved individuals who displayed Duchenne expressions and laughter while talking about their bereavement evoked more positive emotion and less frustration in observers, reported better relationships with others, and were found to have better long-term grief outcomes. They hypothesized that Duchenne expressions, by evoking positive emotions in others, increased positive social interactions and social integration, thus promoting well-being. Social integration and regular positive interactions with others are thought to promote better mental and physical health by fostering the development of meaningful social roles, self-worth and self-efficacy, and a stable sense of self.

Differences in Displays of Smiles Based on Social Status, Gender, and Power

Research indicates that females smile more than males, and subtle reminders of culture-based, gender roles heighten this effect, suggesting that rather than a biological sex difference, the frequency of smiles is socially and culturally constrained. Indeed, social role, status, and power (i.e., employer vs. employee) have also found to be related to frequency and types of smiles in social interactions.

Smiles Are an Important Part of Emotional Self-regulation

A major component in regulating emotion is the ability to modulate emotional responding with dispositional differences in individuals' emotional expressive behaviors having a broad effect on adjustment across life span.

Facial feedback

With emotion regulation partially related to modulating emotional responses and expressions, an important component of this process is facial feedback. Mimicking the key muscle movements of emotional facial expressions are associated with autonomic nervous system arousal and increases in the subjective experience of the associated emotions, even when the facial display is unfelt and even when participants are not aware that they are contracting muscles that are part of a specific emotional facial display. Mimicking Duchenne, but not non-Duchenne smiles, is associated with increases in positive emotion, and may have a strong impact on individuals' ability to regulate emotion.

Undoing the effects of negative emotion

Fredrickson hypothesizes that one primary function of positive emotions is to reduce or undo the effects of negative emotion on individuals, by acting as a self-regulatory "emotional reset." A number of studies have found that experience of positive emotion after a negative emotional induction or event is associated with faster cardiovascular recovery to baseline compared to exposure to a neutral or sad film. In the only study looking at expressive behaviors, Keltner and Bonanno found that bereaved participants who exhibited Duchenne laughter (Duchenne smiles with audible laughter-related vocalizations) while being interviewed about an unexpected death had reduced negative affect at the end of an interview.

Broaden and build

Given that positive affect has been linked to increases in problem-solving and decision making ability, cognitive flexibility, variety-seeking, and motivation, Fredrickson has also proposed that positive emotion serves to broaden and builds one's ability to cope with life events by offsetting cognitive narrowing associated with the experience of stress. Self-reported emotional responding has been associated with changes in cognitive appraisal and increased coping, but the relationships of smiles to this phenomenon remains to be explored.

Trends and Limitations in Current Research

Much work remains in elaborating on the situational constraints of how smiles function and how they relate to adaptation and maladaptation in individuals' social interactions and ability to self-regulate. Again, research into the effects and functions of smiles have been mostly lab-based or inferential, due to the time costs of fine-grained facial coding, and as a result, naturalistic responding in normal social interactions or during environmental challenges remains largely unexplored.

SEE ALSO: ▶ Broaden and build theory of positive emotions ▶ Laughter ▶ Positive emotions

Snyder, C. R.

Shane J. Lopez and Candice A. Ackerman
University of Kansas

Charles Richard "Rick" Snyder (1944–2006) was the Wright Distinguished Professor of Clinical Psychology at the University of Kansas, and is probably best known for his work on hope. Snyder is internationally known for research in clinical, social, personality, health, and positive psychology. His career in psychology began in his studies at Southern Methodist University, his subsequent doctoral training in clinical psychology at Vanderbilt University, and his post-doctoral training at the Langley Porter Institute. He spent the remainder of his career as a psychology professor at the University of Kansas, during which he produced many important contributions to the field of positive psychology. Some of his most relevant publications include *Positive Psychology* (the first textbook in this area), *The Handbook of Positive Psychology*, *Positive Psychological Assessment*, *Uniqueness: The Human Pursuit of Difference*, and *The Psychology of Hope*. In addition to his theories on hope and forgiveness, Snyder also developed theories on how people react to personal feedback, the human need for uniqueness, and the ubiquitous drive to excuse and forgive transgressions.

Snyder, through his publications and his 12-year editorship with the *Journal of Social and Clinical Psychology*, demonstrated how studying psychology at the social-clinical interface promotes understanding of human functioning. Additionally, his analysis of the motivational forces that disconnect individuals from the negatives of the past – excuse-making and forgiveness – and connect them to the possibilities of the future – hope – help people around the world to live more positive lives. Furthermore, Snyder demystified hope for researchers, clinicians, and laypersons, and the robust hope literature remains a touchstone for future research on human strengths. As one of the leading positive psychologists, Snyder charted a sustainable future course for studying and applying positive psychology principles.

Though Snyder's contributions were numerous and influential, he probably is most closely associated with his work on hope. His theory of hope emphasizes goal-directed thinking in which the person utilizes both pathways thinking (the perceived capacity to find routes to desired goals) and agency thinking (the requisite motivations to use those routes). In 2000, he had the opportunity to demonstrate his hope theory in action on *Good Morning America* by conducting a live experiment with the show's correspondents. The experiment was a success, and Snyder was able to demonstrate his theory of hope to millions of viewers.

In his career, Snyder won 27 teaching and mentoring awards, including twice being selected for the University of Kansas' prestigious Honor for an Outstanding Progressive Educator (known as the HOPE award) by the undergraduate seniors. In 1995, APA's Division of Teaching awarded him Fellow status. Snyder also mentored 41 doctoral students as their dissertation chair, and a group of them nominated him for the American Psychological Association's Raymond Fowler Outstanding Graduate Mentor Award, which he received in 2000. In 2005, Snyder accepted an honorary doctorate from Indiana Wesleyan University. His research on uniqueness received rare recognition as the subject of a Sunday Doonesbury cartoon sequence, a signed copy of which hangs in his study at home. And yet, in Snyder's own words, "these accomplishments are packaged in a graying and self-effacing absent-minded professor who says of himself, 'If you don't laugh at yourself, you have missed the biggest joke of all!' "

SEE ALSO: ▶ Hope

Social Cognitive Theory

Robert W. Lent[a] and Gail Hackett[b]

[a]*University of Maryland;* [b]*Arizona State University*

Social cognitive theory is an influential approach to understanding human thought processes, motivation, affect, and behavior. The theory focuses on the inter-action among the person, his or her behavior, and the environment. A key feature of the theory is its emphasis on the ways in which people assert agency, or self-direction. Developed by Albert Bandura, it has been used to study many aspects of psychosocial functioning, both positive and problematic in nature. Originally termed *social learning theory*, Bandura's framework emerged in the 1960s, emphasizing the social context of human learning. It has been subjected to a great deal of subsequent research and conceptual development, culminating in his 1986 landmark work, *Social Foundations of Thought and Action: A Social Cognitive Theory*. In its current form, the theory encompasses a wide array of determinants of human behavior and behavior change, bringing them together within a coher-ent integrative system that highlights people's capacity for self-regulation. The theory has been applied to many topics of relevance to positive psychology, such as health-promoting behavior, academic motivation and performance, career development and work adjustment, and adaptive coping with diverse physical and psychological problems.

Basic Concepts and Elements

Social cognitive theory incorporates and extends Bandura's previous work on social learning and self-efficacy theories. The shift from social learning to social cogni-tive theory did not represent a radical departure from his earlier position but rather an evolving, maturing view that emphasizes the important role of cognitive processes in guiding human behavior. This view acknowledges that behavior is responsive to environmental conditions, yet that people also possess agentic (i.e., self-directing) capabilities. In particular, Bandura offered a *triadic reciprocal* model of person-situation transaction in which three major classes of factors affect one another bidirectionally: a) person variables, such as internal cognitive and affective states, and physical attributes; b) external environmental conditions; and c) people's overt behavior. The ongoing interaction among this set of causal factors is viewed as essential in understanding the dynamic nature of human behavior and the means by which people both affect and are affected by their environments.

In its analysis of the personal determinants within the triadic-reciprocal causal system, social cognitive theory highlights a variety of cognitive capabilities that enable humans to guide their own behavior. In particular, *symbolizing capability* refers to the ability to form cognitive representations of the world, allowing one to build internal models that guide future action. *Forethought* is the ability to anticipate the future, including imagining the possible consequences of one's actions, which can provide motivation for pursuing courses of action that do not have immediate payoffs. *Vicarious capability* allows people to learn via observation. People learn not only in an imitative sense, reproducing observed behavior, but they also learn rules and expectations, and can absorb lessons from the consequences experienced by models. This can significantly reduce the time and risks associated with learning particular skills (e.g., driving). *Self-regulatory capability* refers to people's ability to govern their own behavior by developing internal standards, exercising self-evaluation, influencing the environment, and creating their own performance incentives. *Self-reflective capability* involves humans' meta-cognitive capacity to review their own experiences and analyze and alter their own thinking.

Much research on social cognitive theory has examined person variables that derive from the above basic cognitive capabilities, in particular, self-efficacy beliefs, outcome expectations, and personal goals. *Self-efficacy beliefs* refer to "people's judgments of their capabilities to organize and execute courses of action required to attain designated types of performances" (Bandura, 1986, p. 391). These beliefs are seen as constituting the most central and pervasive mechanism of personal agency, helping to determine such outcomes as behavioral choices, effort expenditure, persistence in the face of obstacles, thought patterns, and emotional reactions. Self-efficacy is not viewed as a global trait but rather as a dynamic set of beliefs about one's capabilities to perform particular tasks or courses of action. Such beliefs do not substitute for objective ability; they complement ability by affecting the manner in which people organize and deploy their skills.

Self-efficacy beliefs are assumed to be acquired and modified through four primary sources of information: personal performance accomplishments; vicarious learning or modeling (observing similar others); social persuasion (e.g., verbal encouragement or support from others); and physiological and affective states (e.g., experiencing anxiety when performing a particular behavior). The impact that these informational sources have on self-efficacy depends on a variety of factors, such as how the individual attends to, interprets, and recalls them. However, in general, personal accomplishments (e.g., successes or failure) have the potential to exert the greatest influence on self-efficacy.

Outcome expectations refer to beliefs about the consequences or outcomes of performing particular behaviors. Whereas self-efficacy beliefs are concerned with one's capabilities (e.g., "can I do this?"), outcome expectations involve imagined consequences of particular courses of action (e.g., "if I try doing this, what will happen?"). Bandura maintains that self-efficacy and outcome expectations both help to determine a number of important aspects of human behavior, such as the activities that people choose to pursue and the ones they avoid. People are more likely to choose to engage in an activity not only to the extent that they view themselves as competent at performing it but also to the extent to that they expect their efforts to lead to valued, positive outcomes (e.g., social and self-approval, tangible rewards). However, self-efficacy may be the more influential determinant in many situations, for instance, where complex skills or potentially costly or difficult courses of action are involved. In such situations, people may hold positive outcome expectations but still avoid a course of action if they doubt they have the capabilities required to succeed at it (i.e., where self-efficacy is low).

Personal *goals* may be defined as one's intention to engage in a particular activity or to produce a particular outcome. Goals afford an important means by which people exercise agency. By setting personal goals, people help to organize, direct, and sustain their own behavior, even over long intervals without external pay-offs and despite inevitable setbacks. Social cognitive theory maintains that people's goals are importantly affected by their self-efficacy and outcome expectations. In particular, people tend to select goals that are consistent with their self-efficacy and the outcomes they expect to attain from pursuing a particular course of action. Success or failure in pursuing one's goals, in turn, has a reciprocal influence on self-efficacy and outcome expectations. Successful goal pursuit, for example, may further strengthen self-efficacy and outcome expectations within a positive cycle.

Illustrative Application: Subjective Well-Being

Social cognitive theory has been used as a basis for research and practice on a wide array of topics that are relevant to positive psychology. One recent example involves the study of subjective well-being (SWB) – a key aspect of positive emotional functioning. SWB is often defined as a three-component construct that includes life satisfaction, positive affect, and negative affect. Reviewers have concluded that SWB is likely to be determined by a variety of factors, such as personality, cognitions (e.g., goals), and environmental resources. They have also recommended that the three aspects of SWB be disaggregated so that research can better establish how they function together and what variables uniquely affect each of them.

Observing that social cognitive variables, such as self-efficacy and goals, have been individually linked to SWB, Lent proposed a unifying perspective in which cognitive, behavioral, social, and personality / affect variables are seen as joint determinants of domain-specific and global life satisfaction. This framework employs social cognitive theory as the foundation for its integrative view of SWB, yet also incorporates personality elements in order to accommodate findings showing that affective traits are reliably linked to SWB. The resulting model attempts to reconcile "top down" (dispositional) and "bottom up" (situational) approaches to the study of SWB. At a practical level, and in keeping with the spirit of social cognitive theory, the model emphasizes determinants of SWB over which people can exercise agency and that are readily susceptible to therapeutic efforts (e.g., the setting and pursuit of personal goals, involvement in valued life tasks, building social supports), while also acknowledging factors (e.g., personality dispositions) that may be more resistant to traditional approaches to therapy.

Lent's framework consists of two interconnected models, one aimed at the experience of well-being under normative life conditions and the other focusing

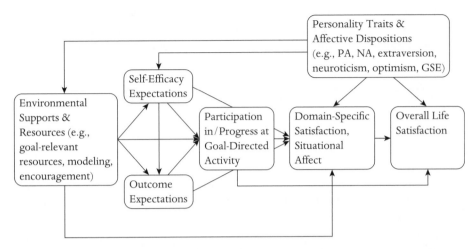

Figure 8 Contributions of Personality, Affective, and Social-Cognitive Variables to Well-Being under Normative Life Conditions.
Notes: NA = negative affectivity; PA = positive affectivity; GSE = generalized self-efficacy.
Source: From Lent, R. (2004). Toward a unifying theoretical and practical perspective on well-being and psychosocial adjustment. *Journal of Counseling Psychology*, *51*, 500. Copyright 2004 by the American Psychological Association. Reprinted with permission.

on the recovery of well-being subsequent to stressful or traumatic life events. The normative well-being model is displayed in Figure 8. According to this model, overall life satisfaction is influenced by certain personality variables (e.g., trait positive and negative affect), satisfaction in one's central life domains (e.g., work, family), participation in valued life tasks, and progress at fulfilling salient personal goals.

Domain satisfaction, one of the precursors of overall life satisfaction, is seen as partly determined by personality factors, but is also posited to be affected by agentic, social cognitive mechanisms, in particular, goal-directed activity, self-efficacy, outcome expectations, and environmental supports and resources. In other words, in addition to benefiting from particular traits, people are more likely to be satisfied within a given life domain when they actively pursue and make progress at their personally valued goals; feel competent at the tasks required for successful performance and goal pursuit; anticipate the receipt of favorable outcomes; and perceive their environment as supportive and as offering resources to enable their goal pursuit in that life domain. Both for theoretical reasons and because of their assumed relevance to preventive and therapeutic interventions, the model is also concerned with the nature of the relations among the social-cognitive precursors of domain satisfaction.

Given the newness of this extension of social cognitive theory, it has thus far received limited empirical study. However, a few studies have found good support for the model of normative well-being in samples of college students. The model has also been adapted as a theoretical approach to the study of work satisfaction and as a source of clinical ideas for assisting the emotional recovery of cancer survivors. Further research, particularly involving longitudinal and experimental designs, is needed to more fully test the causal hypotheses of this model and to explore its clinical utility.

SEE ALSO: ▶ Agency   ▶ Bandura, Albert   ▶ Future mindedness
▶ Goals and goal theory   ▶ Self-efficacy

Reference

Bandura, A. (1986). *Social foundations of thought and action: A social cognitive theory.* Englewood Cliffs, NJ: Prentice-Hall.

Social Skills

Ya-Ting Tina Yang
University of Kansas

Social skills are the complex set of skills that include the development of effective social behaviors, an awareness of the social norms that affect social behavior in different situations, and the abilities to select effective responses, to perceive accurate feedback from others, and to modify one's social behavior based on the feedback received. In other words, social skills involve communication, assertion, peer and group interaction, problem-solving and decision making, and self-management. Social skill or interpersonal skill is not a single entity, but a collection of many basic socially desirable skills. Researchers have been able to develop standardized instruments to measure constructs and dimensions related to interpersonal and social skills, which include: empathy, shyness, assertiveness, sociability, self-monitoring, and verbal and nonverbal communication skills. Although a vast amount of research has been conducted, one of the limitations is that many of the studies assess a single dimension of social skill even though the construct may be multidimensional.

Based on the interactions among the individuals, the response elicited from others, and the social context, social skills allow individuals to perform competently within social situations. With good social skills, individuals are able to establish more confidence, resilience, and peer acceptance, whereas people with poor social skills may experience peer rejection, low self-esteem, and mental health problems such as depression, conduct disorders, and social phobia.

Social skills training (SST) was developed and popularized to teach more effective social behaviors. Although a variation of approaches and names might have been given to SST programs, training components usually consist of acquiring desirable social response, practicing response obtained, shaping response by corrective feedback and reinforcement, and applying learned response in natural environment settings via cognitive restructuring.

In recent years, SST also served as an intervention for specific problems, populations, and settings. For example, it has been used with children and college students with or without disabilities, mental patients in psychiatric units, adults in the workplace, etc. Evidence from several studies has shown positive outcomes of SST, resulting in less anxiety and greater improvement of social adjustment. However, training of social skills has its limitations; the results were often not long-lasting and changes did not transfer from clinical settings to real-life environments. Furthermore, SST did not generate as powerful results when used alone. Nonetheless, SST has been widely accepted and integrated into the broader treatment and intervention programs as an important component. Future studies must attend to basic social skills as well as SST outcome maintenance and generalization from one setting to another.

SEE ALSO: ▶ Social support

Social Support

Benjamin H. Gottlieb
University of Guelph

Social support refers to the social-psychological and interpersonal processes that maintain and promote health and well-being. The sources of social support usually inhabit the inner circle of the individual's social network, typically composed of close friends and family members. The types of social support they can provide include practical aid, socializing and companionship, cognitive guidance, reassurance of worth, and emotional nurturance. The beneficial effects of such support arise either through interaction with these close associates or through the social-psychological representation of them as resources for resisting stress and meeting basic human needs.

Formal study of social support commenced in the final quarter of the twentieth century when converging research in the fields of epidemiology and community mental health identified the important role of the social network in health protection and in the help-seeking process, respectively. Several international studies showed that people who experienced higher levels of social integration, indexed by their private and public social ties, had significantly lower morbidity and mortality rates than those who were relatively isolated. Community mental health studies showed that members of the close social network were the first to hear and be consulted about the stressors and strains of everyday life, such as marital difficulties and depressive episodes. These studies in turn set the stage for psychologists, communication researchers, epidemiologists, and behavioral and medical investigators to examine the power and means through which social support affects health, morale, and life quality. In the process, much has been learned about the fallibility of social support and its promise as a strategy for social intervention.

The preponderance of empirical inquiry on social support has centered on its role in the stress process that arises from people's exposure to stressful life events, chronic hardships, and role transitions. With few exceptions, the evidence reveals that *perceived support* accomplishes a stress-buffering or cushioning impact. This means that people who believe that their close associates are able and willing to provide needed support do not experience as much stress as those who do not harbor such beliefs. Paradoxically, it appears that confidence in the supportive provisions and good will of the network can empower the individual to "go it alone." However, the process whereby perceived support accomplishes its stress-moderating functions is not yet well understood, with competing theories ranging from the biochemical to the purely psychological receiving empirical study. For example, perceived support may effect salutary immune system responses, instill greater self-efficacy, or shape more benign appraisals of the stressful situation. Knowledge of how perceived support arises, how stable it is, and how it affects health behaviors and status can inform the planning of interventions aimed to foster greater resiliency among populations at risk.

Actual or enacted support transactions that transpire in naturalistic settings have received less attention than perceived support, partly because of the challenges involved in their documentation. A handful of laboratory studies and even fewer field studies have observed interactions between marital partners, mothers and their children, and students in contrived situations, the majority of studies relying on self-reported descriptions of support-relevant interactions. No study has compared the information gained from observation of the support mobilization process and subjective reports on the same process. This means that we know little about how people experience and interpret interactions that observers define as supportive in nature. Again, such information is vital for planning programs that marshal support.

The direct or main effects of social support are often contrasted with its stress-moderating effects. That is, in everyday life social ties are among the most valued and meaningful of treasures. Spirits are buoyed by interactions with family members and friends, thereby elevating levels of positive affect and self-worth. The close network provides a sense of belonging and purpose, and perhaps the motivation to keep oneself well to ensure the wellness of others. The network can also contribute directly to health by sheltering individuals from exposure to certain controllable stressors, such as unwanted pregnancy or job loss. It can also provide information about and reinforce self-care practices while also exerting pressure to relinquish self-injurious health behaviors such as smoking, poor dietary practices, and substance abuse. Whether viewed as a contributor to morale and general well-being or as an antidote to loneliness and anomie, this perspective spotlights the basic feedback functions of the network in the process of regulating emotions, cognitions, and behaviors.

The distinctions among the sources, types, and behavioral versus perceptual manifestations of social support are reflected in the abundant measures of the construct that have appeared in the literature. Measures of perceived support are far more numerous than measures of actual support. Some measures gain information about support in a global manner, while others call for information about the sources, types, and sufficiency of support, and may even solicit the recipient's evaluation of its quality. The choice of measures should be predicated on careful consideration of study aims. Investigators may be more interested in capturing information about certain actors in the network than gaining a global measure of perceived or enacted support. Moreover, some types of support may be of greater interest than others, and in some studies the support provider's perspective may be more important than the recipient's perspective. For example, studies of the family caregivers of persons affected by Alzheimer's disease or of the spouses of persons who are trying to quit smoking may focus on the impediments to the provision of support that they experience. Finally, epidemiological investigations that explore social support from a social integration perspective tend to delve into the structural properties of the personal community or network in which people are embedded. They examine the network's size, composition, dispersion, density, and clustering in order to gain insight into the features that best predict the delivery and durability of support as a mediator of health behaviors and health outcomes.

A final set of basic studies on social support bring into sharp relief the misgivings that people can have about soliciting and accepting aid from peers, as well as the injudicious behaviors of well-intentioned donors of aid. Social-psychological studies of the helping process have revealed that people are often reluctant to seek support because of the threat it poses to their sense of competence and self-worth, and because of concerns about social indebtedness and social control. We tend to resist seeking support from associates who may blame us for bringing our calamities upon ourselves, or who may castigate us for our failures to manage our troubles independently. Studies have also demonstrated that our associates can be overzealous in their supportive behaviors, becoming emotionally overinvolved, limiting our sense of decisional control, and even robbing us of a sense of agency and mastery. We have also learned that support tends to be miscarried when the would-be supporters are faced with a highly emotional associate or with an associate who for some reason is incapable of effectively using the provider's support. Collectively, these studies of the fallibility of social support not only dispel some of the romanticism attached to the concept of informal support systems, but also invite further study of the conditions and actors that contribute to both the miscarriage and felicitous expression of support.

Social programs and community interventions involving social support have long preceded the initiation of these varied lines of investigation. Community services such as Big Brothers/Sisters and self-help mutual aid (MASH) organizations such as Alcoholics Anonymous have recognized and harnessed the power of social ties as sources of influence on matters of health and well-being. However, even though the idea that social ties can be "good medicine" is not novel, the knowledge gained from research has brought new measurement tools, better evaluation practices, and more exacting program design to these historic initiatives. It has also provided blueprints for a new generation of intervention studies that promise to refine this stream of positive psychology practice.

Support groups are among the most widely implemented community interventions. Led by one or more professional practitioners, the support group combines expert information and the experiential knowledge of the participants. It is usually time-limited, composed of 10 to 12 participants who share a common stressor, life event, transition, affliction, or noxious habit, and involves a balance of expert guidance and experience-swapping among participants. Processes of social comparison, (re)attribution, emotional validation, and problem-solving lie at the heart of the beneficial effects that are produced by these groups. However, as research accumulates, it is also becoming evident that they are not universally attractive, benefit some participants more than others, and tend to be too short in duration to be effective, especially in chronically stressful circumstances. Evidence also suggests that support groups for people affected by cancer demonstrate improved psychosocial and life quality outcomes but do not slow down disease progress or increase survival time.

Whereas support groups introduce a new set of similar peers, interventions involving the introduction of a single new supporter have also received greater currency. In some instances, the supportive ally is a close associate such as the spouse, and in others the ally is a stranger who must first form a trusting relationship with the focal individual as a basis for rendering support. Examples include home visitors who reach out to young, low-income mothers, and therapeutic "buddies" who are helping one another lose weight, quit smoking, or achieve dietary or exercise goals. Research on the factors that contribute to effective matches, and on the optimal intensity and duration of these dyadic strategies of marshaling, specializing, or augmenting support is sorely needed.

Growing evidence of the importance of supportive social ties for the health and well-being of the population will undoubtedly spur continued research and practice. By refining our knowledge of the people who most need and can benefit from social support, of the contexts in which social support can make a positive contribution, and of the most attractive and effective ways of mobilizing support, research will help to illuminate yet another domain of a positive psychology built on human relationships.

SEE ALSO: ▶ Health psychology   ▶ Social skills   ▶ Well-being

Social Work

Uta M. Walter
Catholic University of Applied Sciences, Berlin

Social work is the applied science and art of professional assistance for individuals, groups, or communities with the goal of improving or maintaining the functioning, well-being, and human potential of all people. Highly diverse in its fields and forms of practice as well as in its use of various psychological and sociological theories and philosophies, the profession is bound together by shared aims and values. With roots in humanitarian and democratic ideals, social work holds central such values as the respect for the equality, worth, and dignity of all human beings, enhancing the welfare of all people, and promoting social justice and human rights. Social work values are embodied in the profession's national and international codes of ethics.

Shifting Identities: Historical Developments and Tensions

Since its beginnings as a profession during the nineteenth century, social work history and identity have been characterized by a diversity of roots and influences sometimes perceived as complementary, and sometimes as contradictory. Prominent among the early roots for social work in the United States is the settlement movement with its focus on community work, most famously represented by Jane Addams' Hull House in Chicago, and the tradition of individual case work which was strongly promoted by Mary Richmond's publication of *Social Diagnosis* in 1917.

In the following decades, social work struggled to extricate itself from the devaluing perception as a female activity and instead establish social work as a legitimate profession with its own scientific base and theory. In the course of this struggle, social work continually shifted preferences and emphases and allied itself with various schools of thought borrowed from psychology and sociology, ranging from psychoanalytic and psychodynamic theories, to Habermas' critical theory, or Bateson's ecosystems theory. Another ongoing tension concerns social work's identity as a change agent seeking to liberate oppressed populations and its simultaneous tradition of ensuring societal stability as an agent of the state or other societal powers. These philosophical and theoretical tensions in the discourse about social work only somewhat abated as the profession was able to establish itself more firmly but never ceased entirely, thus continuing the tradition of social work as a profession with multiple and shifting identities.

Person-in-Environment

Social workers today perform in a wide array of fields and functions that include direct practice with clients, as well as administrative, research, or advocacy functions in academic, governmental, and nongovernmental organizations. They work with individuals and families (micro-level), groups and organizations (mezzo-level), as well as with communities, or as political change activists (macro-level). Social work typically intervenes at the nexus of system boundaries where different social systems interact with people. Trying to remove barriers, inequities or injustices, responding to crises as well as to everyday personal and social problems, the profession underscores the importance of holding the dual focus of a person-in-environment perspective. In other words, social work is focused on understanding and helping individuals within their unique familial, social, and cultural circumstances and also attempts to influence larger societal systems to enhance people's opportunities. Because it recognizes the complexity of interactions between human beings and their environment, social work draws on various theories of human behavior and social systems, and utilizes a variety of skills and methods consistent with a holistic biopsychosocial focus. Current discourse frequently focuses on the question of how to establish and define evidence-based practices (EBP). Various authors suggest that EBP ought to consist of a sound knowledge base for social work that includes necessary empirical data, but also recognizes local and indigenous knowledge that is specific and relevant to a given context, as well as the wisdom born of practitioners' experience and insights, the experiences and voices of clients, and should heed the values espoused by the profession.

The Strengths Perspective

One central value in social work is dedicated to empowering disadvantaged and oppressed populations by recognizing and supporting the strengths and capacities inherent in individuals, families, and communities. The *strengths perspective*, a term coined by Dennis Saleebey, acknowledges personal and societal difficulties and dysfunctions but emphasizes the need to elicit and build upon the resources, hopes, and resiliencies in people and communities. This approach traces back to social work pioneers such as Jane Addams, Virginia Robinson, and Bertha Capen Reynolds, and finds more recent contributions in the empowerment work of Paulo Freire, Barbara Solomon, Lorraine Gutierrez and others. The strengths perspective rests on humanistic and postmodern constructionist assumptions that all people and communities have resources and capacities, and that foregrounding and investing in these capacities helps coconstruct opportunities for hope, agency, resiliency and positive development. The strengths perspective has been operationalized and researched for case management with people with persistent and severe mental illnesses. It seeks and awaits additional forms of operationalization for fields other than case management by, for instance, looking to philosophically related approaches such as solution-focused and narrative work in therapy, or the community development approach by psychologist Roger Mills. Further work toward a more expansive and rigorous evaluation of the theoretical and practical merits of the strengths perspective is still needed.

SEE ALSO: ▶ Saleebey, Dennis

Solution-Focused Brief Therapy

Insoo Kim Berg
Brief Family Therapy Center

As the name suggests, the *solution-focused brief therapy* (SFBT), also called *solution-focused therapy* or *solution-building practice*, is future-focused, goal-directed, and focuses on solutions, rather than on problems that brought clients to seek therapy. This approach to therapy was developed by de Shazer, and Insoo, Kim, Berg, and their colleagues beginning in late the 1970s in Milwaukee, Wisconsin. The developers observed hundreds and hundreds of hours of therapy over the course of many years, noting the questions, behaviors, emotions, and human aspects of the interactions. In addition to paying attention to what impact these activities had on the clients, they also observed therapist activities. Questions and activities related to clients' reports of progress were saved and those that were not were discarded. The entire model was developed inductively in an outpatient mental health service setting without screening of clients. Since then, SFBT has not only become one of the leading schools of brief therapy, but it has become a major influence in such diverse fields as business, social policy, education, criminal justice services, child welfare, and domestic violence offenders treatment.

Described as a goal-driven model, SFBT emphasizes clear, concise, behavioral and realistic goal negotiations as its hallmark. Based on its core assumptions that clients hold keys to their solutions, the professionals' task is to guide the client to construct solutions that fit his or her vision of improved life. Known for its highly respectful approach with clients, it assumes that all clients have some knowledge of what would make their life better, even though they may need some (at times, considerable) help describing the details of their better life. In addition, SFBT also presupposes that everyone who seeks help already possesses all the minimal skills needed to create solutions. Unlike most psychology and therapy approaches, SFBT is very aware of client's social contexts as a resource because the practitioners are aware of how important client's social environments are to maintaining solutions, as well as influencing the intensity of problems. Many practitioners have taken the model and expanded its scope to contexts in which people want to get along or must work together for greater goods. For example, businesses are finding that the principles of SFBT apply in management and supervision practices.

Key Concepts and Tools of SFBT

All therapy is a form of specialized conversation and SFBT pays close attention to how this conversation is directed toward achieving clients' visions of solutions. Several tools, including finding exceptions, the miracle question, scaling questions, and coping questions, characterize the use of SFBT.

Finding Exceptions

In the early 1980s the team discovered that problems do not occur all the time; that is, even the most serious and difficult problems are a little bit less severe at times. For example, couples who fight can get along at times, depression can be more and less severe, and clients who hear voices have times when they do not hear voices, or even if they do, they can still function reasonably well in such tasks such as housekeeping and taking care of themselves. Recognizing this led to a discovery that rather than paying attention to how a problem starts and is maintained, it may be more profitable to learn about how and when a person notices a slight improvement in their situation. For example, when a person is a bit less depressed, what else is going on in his or her social context at that time, and what they do differently as a result of this small change. Once details of this exception are described in concrete, behavioral and measurable form, the next step is to get clients to repeat those successful steps they already knew how to do, until their life is better enough that they are satisfied with therapy. Depending on a client's confidence about how well they can keep making these small changes that increase the likelihood of maintaining solutions, the case can be terminated. This aspect of treatment is what leads to the brief part of the name. Since the solutions are generated by the client, based on what they already know how to do, there is no need to impose new and unfamiliar behaviors that take time and consistent repetition to master and maintain.

Miracle Question (MQ)

This unique tool is a powerful technique in generating the first small steps of solution states by helping clients to describe small, realistic, and doable steps they can take as soon as "tomorrow morning." Developed out of desperation from a client case of a suicidal woman with an alcoholic husband and four "wild" children who gave her nothing but grief, the woman was desperate for solutions. Since this initial encounter with this woman who thought that she might need a miracle to get her life in order, the MQ has been tested hundreds and thousands of times around the world, in many languages. The most recent version is as follows:

T: I am going to ask you a rather strange question . . . that requires some imagination on your part . . . do you have good imagination?
C: I think so, I will try my best.
T: Good. The strange question is this: After we talk, you go home (go back to work), and you still have lots of work to do yet for the rest of today (list usual tasks here). And it is time to go to bed . . . and everybody in your household is sound asleep and the house is very quiet . . . and in the middle of the night, there is a miracle and the problem that brought you to talk to me about is all solved. But because this happens when you are sleeping, you have no idea that there was a miracle and the problems are solved . . . so when you are slowly coming out of your sound sleep . . . what would be the first small sign that would

make you wonder . . . there must've been a miracle . . . the problem is all gone! How would you discover this?

C: I suppose I would feel like getting up and facing the day, instead of wanting to cover my head under the blanket and just hide there.

T: Suppose you do, get up and face the day, what would be the small thing you would do that you didn't do this morning?

C: I suppose I would say good morning to my kids in a cheerful voice, instead of screaming at them like I do now.

T: What would your children do in response to your cheerful "good morning?"

C: They would be surprised at first to hear me talk to them in a cheerful voice, and then they would calm down, be relaxed. God, it's been a long time since that happened.

T: So, what would you do then that you did not do this morning?

C: I would crack a joke and put them in a better mood.

These small steps become the building blocks of an entirely different day. Notice how the solutions are generated by the client and the mothers' knowledge of her children's needs. This question, the longest of SFBT, has a hypnotic quality to it. Most clients visibly change in their demeanor and some even break out in smiles as they describe their solutions states. The next step is to find out when was the most recent times when client has had small pieces of miracles (called exception) and get them to repeat these forgotten experience. It is usual to see clients' outlooks change, in recognition that they have had those good mornings in a not-too-distant past.

Scaling Questions

Scaling Questions (SQ) can be used when there is not enough time to use the MQ or it would be useful to help clients assess their own situations, track their own progress, and how others would evaluate their progress on a scale of 1 to 10. It is versatile to use in different situations, including with children and others who have impaired verbal skills. A therapist can ask about a client's motivation and hopefulness, how depressed and how confident they feel, progress they have made, and a host of other topics to track their performance and determine what the next small steps might be. For example, consider the following situation in which a couple sought help to decide whether their marriage could survive or they should get divorced. They reported that they have fought for 10 of the 20 years of their marriage and they do not want to fight anymore.

T: Since you two know your marriage better than anybody, suppose I ask you this way: On a scale of 1 to 10, where 10 stands for you have every confidence that this marriage will make it, and 1 stands for the opposite, that we might just as well walk away right now and it's not going to work, what number would you give your marriage? (After a pause, the wife speaks first.)

W: I would give it a 9. (Husband flinches as he hears this.)

T: (To the husband.) What about you? What number would you give it?
H: (He thinks about it a long time.) I would say I am at 1.1.
T: (Surprised.) So what makes it a 1.1 rather than a 1?
H: I guess it's because we are both here tonight.

SFBT looks for the smallest possible solutions to build on, as well as viewing clients as the experts on their own situations. SQ makes problems and solutions much more tangible and concrete, while recognizing that clients' scales are entirely subjective and one client's 5 might be very different than another client's 5. Even so, SQ gives us a general idea of a client's perception that their life is getting better or worse in ways that words might not be able to convey. Most disagreements or arguments are conducted with words, and people in many intimate relationships often assume they know what the other means. The scale gives much clearer picture of the differences or similarities. The wife in the above case was shocked to discover that her husband saw things in much bleaker ways than she did, and their marriage at such high risk of divorce, after 10 years of fighting, using words. She realized that she really did not want the divorce and sprang into action of changing herself from being a critical person to a more "reasonable" person. When both agreed, they were about 6 or 7 in their confidence about the marriage making it, and the couple eventually ended the therapy.

Coping Questions

These types of questions are powerful reminders that all clients are doing much more than they first think and recognize, and that they have been doing a great deal of useful things in spite of overwhelming difficulties. Even in the midst of despair, many clients do manage to get out of bed, get dressed, feed their children, and engage in other activities that take enormous effort to do. The therapist's ability to notice these small, but significant hidden resources and strength and determination helps cast an entirely different light on their abilities and motivations. "How do you do it?" is an empowering question that opens up a different way of looking at client's resiliency and determination.

Benefits of the SFBT Model

As mentioned previously, the SFBT model was developed in real-life settings without screening clients, including those who were mandated by the courts, employers, schools, and other institutions. SFBT principles can and are being adapted to work with many populations outside of therapy or counseling offices. SFBT believes that problems and solutions are defined in social contexts; therefore, we cannot separate these issues outside of their environmental concerns, mandates, and resources.

The simple and easy to understand principles and tools for useful conversations with SFBT are written about extensively, not just by developers of the model but also their affiliates and students. SFBT is widely accepted as a useful, efficient practice model across languages and cultures.

More than anything else, the efficiency and brevity of SFBT is attractive at a time of ever-diminishing resources within mental health care. Because all people, even children, have ideas of what kind of solutions might work for them best, the principle of listening and soliciting client's ideas for solutions is an attractive alternative to expert-driven therapy models. Many clinicians report reduction of professional burnout and stress of feeling like they are dealing with "resistive" clients.

As simple and easy to learn the SFBT model may seem, however, it is difficult to practice, simply because the nonexpert orientation may seem counterintuitive to some. The radical acceptance of clients as people who have sufficient wisdom to know what they need, and that they do not need to be told what to do by the "expert" seem difficult to practice for some. Minimum intrusiveness in the life of the client is the rule, and this is sometimes a difficult concept to accept for those young and inexperienced therapists who are eager to offer help to those in great deal of pain and suffering.

Research about SFBT

Even though SFBT is an inductively developed model, there has been consistent interest in learning whether or not the approach really works. Because of its clinical philosophy, initial research efforts tended to rely on client self-reports. Since then, increasing number of studies have been generated, many with randomized comparison groups. For example, researchers have studied the effects of SFBT on the prison recidivism in Hageby Prison in Stockholm, Sweden. This randomized study compared those clients who received an average of 5 SFBT sessions and those who received their usual services, and participants were followed at 12 and 16 months after discharge from prison. The SFBT group consistently did better than the control group.

Other reviews of strongly controlled and randomly controlled studies of SFBT with adults and youth in the United States and Europe have provided initial support for the effectiveness of its use. In 2001 Gingerich and Eisengart reviewed 18 controlled-outcome studies of SFBT and identified client improvement in 17 of the studies, with statistically significant changes in 10 of these. In the 11 studies that compared SFBT to other treatment options, 7 studies reported more positive outcomes with SFBT. Outcome studies of SFBT offer preliminary support for the effectiveness of SFBT to clients. More microanalysis research into the coconstruction process in solution-focused conversation is needed to develop an additional understanding of how clients change through participating in these conversations.

SEE ALSO: ▶ Strengths perspective (social welfare)

Spiritual Well-Being

Edward R. Canda
University of Kansas

Spiritual Well-Being in Historical Context

Spiritual well-being, a perennial and universal concern in human cultures, can be considered a quality of developing and being that is oriented to ultimate or sacred concerns, alleviates personal and collective suffering, provides a sense of meaning and purpose to life and death, and fosters optimal human development and fulfilling relationships. On the most general level, all religions posit beliefs about the nature and fundamental causes of human suffering (such as associated with illness, death, disasters, and life crises); ways to prevent, cope with, and transcend suffering (such as personal behaviors, collective rituals, moral codes, and mutual support systems for happiness, healing, salvation, or enlightenment); and positive spiritual qualities of persons and communities that facilitate a morally good and personally satisfying life.

To this point, writings in positive psychology on spirituality and spiritual well-being have been influenced most by European and American traditions of psychology and allied disciplines and professions, with some allusion to cultural and religious diversity. Some significant precursors to positive psychological study of spiritual well-being include G. Stanley Hall (1844–1924), who advocated for the objective study of religion, including use of questionnaires and statistical analysis, while also advocating for appreciation of Jesus as an exemplar of transformation toward higher positive ideals; William James (1842–1910), who utilized introspective and religious autobiographical studies to explore the varieties of religious experience and their fruits in virtue, saintliness, and social benefit; Carl Jung (1875–1961) who analyzed clinical observations and cross-cultural study of mythology and religions to discuss spiritual aspects of human nature and development; and Abraham Maslow (1908–1970) who focused on the highest human potentials for creativity, love, spiritual insight, and self-transcendence. Positive psychological study of spiritual well-being reflects some of their interests, such as empirically based knowledge, optimal human development, character strengths, and resilient response to challenges. The concept of spiritual well-being is usually defined and operationalized for use in empirical research (especially as subject to statistical analysis) or clinical assessment.

Defining, Measuring, and Assessing Spiritual Well-Being

Definitions of *spiritual well-being* rest on definitions of spirituality and religion. "Both spirituality and religion are complex phenomena, multidimensional in nature, and any single definition is likely to reflect a limited perspective or interest" (Hill et al., 2000, p. 52). These authors point out that the terms *religion* and *spirituality* are not used or defined consistently in psychology or related fields. Further difficulties may arise because definitions often reflect theoretical and worldview assumptions that are not made explicit, may create religious or cultural biases, and may be conceptually and operationally problematic. Variations in use of these terms – and related terms such as *spiritual well-being, spiritual wellness, spiritual health, religiousness,* and *religiosity* – make it difficult to compare and evaluate both empirical and theoretical studies.

Yet it has become common in psychology, social work, psychiatry, nursing, and related fields to differentiate between spirituality and religion as related but distinct concepts. Spirituality often refers to feelings, beliefs, values, experiences, and behaviors that concern the search for a sense of meaning, purpose, and fulfilling relationships in the context of a person's understanding of that which is ultimate, sacred, or of fundamental life significance. Religion involves the expression of spirituality through participation in organized communities and traditions that share these ultimate concerns. For example, the positive psychologists Snyder and Lopez (2007, p. 262) define spirituality as, "the thoughts, feelings, and behaviors that fuel and arise from the search for the sacred." In such formulations, spirituality may be expressed in religious and/or nonreligious ways.

Similar distinctions impact operationalization of spiritual well-being in tools for measurement research and clinical diagnosis and assessment. For example, the Spiritual Well-Being Scale, developed by Craig Ellison and Raymond Paloutzian, includes 10 items each for existential well-being (i.e., related to a person's level of life perspective, meaning, and purpose) and religious well-being (i.e., view of God and sense of positive relationship with God). The concept "religious" is distinguished here by belief in God or a higher power. The more extensive Spiritual Well-being Questionnaire, developed by David Moberg, addresses beliefs and attitudes, social activities, feelings about life, religious activities and identity. Various items relate to the theme of meaning and purpose while others relate to specifically religious issues. Some items use Christian terms. The more recent Spirituality Index of Well-Being (developed by Timothy Daaleman and Bruce Frey) focuses on self-assessments of insight, ability to solve problems, and sense of purpose and meaning in life. There are numerous other instruments dealing with religious and spiritual beliefs, behaviors, values, and coping practices that are relevant to spiritual well-being. Two helpful compendia with critical reviews are: *Measures of Religiosity* edited by Peter C. Hill and Ralph W. Hood and *Handbook of Religion and Health* by Harold Koenig, Michael McCullough, and David B. Larson.

A new clinical diagnostic category has been added in the field of nursing, "readiness for enhanced spiritual well-being" (Anonymous, 2002, p. 68). This is defined as, "ability to experience and integrate meaning and purpose in life through a person's connectedness with self, others, art, music, literature, nature, or a power greater than oneself." In positive psychology, Peterson and Seligman include in the VIA classification of virtues and strengths a category with qualities commonly associated with the concept of spiritual well-being, such as transcendence, a strength that facilitates connections to the larger universe and provides purpose and meaning. This category includes appreciation of beauty and excellence, gratitude, hope, humor, and spirituality. Spirituality is defined as "Having coherent beliefs about the higher purpose and meaning of the universe."

Within tools currently available through the Authentic Happiness website, www.authentichappiness.sas.upenn.edu, hosted by Martin Seligman, various items address spiritual well-being related qualities. For example, the Authentic Happiness Inventory includes an item about sense of purpose or meaning in life. The Approaches to Happiness Questionnaire includes items about a sense of one's life having a higher purpose and meaning and being of benefit to other people. The Meaning in Life Questionnaire focuses entirely on sense of life meaning and purpose. VIA Signature Strengths includes a self-rating of how spiritual a person one is.

Tools for clinical assessment of spiritual strengths and resources related to spirituality and positive forms of spirituality have emerged within counseling psychology and social work, though they do not always use the term spiritual well-being. These tend to address both religious and nonreligious forms of spirituality, encompass more detail than the structured quantitative research tools, and allow flexibility and adaptability for in-depth ongoing conversations that match the terms and beliefs of the client. For example, the Spiritual Strengths Assessment, developed by Eichler, Deegan, Canda, and Wells:

> offers a method for identifying the spiritual strengths and resources of clients who wish to mobilize spiritual aspects of their lives to promote their mental health and overall well-being, to respond to life challenges resiliently, and to help recover from crises and mental illness. (2006, p. 69)

An inventory developed for the counseling field explores dimensions of spiritual wellness, including conception of the absolute/divine, meaning, connectedness, mystery, spiritual freedom, experience/ritual, forgiveness, hope, knowledge/learning, and present-centeredness (Faiver, Ingersoll, O'Brien, & McNally, 2001). Some of the items use theistic language.

Challenges and Opportunities

Within positive psychology and related fields, the burgeoning attention to spirituality and religion highlights a significant aspect of life. The concept of spiritual well-being, in particular, aids in research and clinical assessment revealing intrapersonal, interpersonal, and institutional strengths and resources that may promote resilience, coping, and optimal human development. This early stage of the field offers challenges and opportunities.

The variability of terms, definitions, and measures can create confusion. But care can be taken to make these clear in each study, in comparative or meta-analytical studies, and in clinical tools. Perhaps the most commonly used features of the concept of spiritual well-being are: positive sense of meaning and purpose in life. Some instruments focus exclusively on this, while some include relatedness with the sacred, transcendence, and a general sense of positive connectedness. Some scholars prefer a broad conceptualization, without reference to religion or sacredness, in order to be widely applicable. Other scholars believe that a conceptualization is vacuous without reference to particular religious contexts or at least the dimension of sacredness.

Structured surveys, conducive to nomothetic research, can be complemented by qualitative studies of spiritual well-being that elucidate rich detail and depth of meanings and daily life for individuals and communities. Positive psychological study of spiritual well-being might be enhanced by greater use of multiple methods of inquiry and wider connection across disciplines.

Measurement and clinical assessment of spiritual well-being could be advanced by the development of population-specific definitions, tools, and methods that are sensitive to diverse cultures and spiritual perspectives. Research and assessment tools that are intended for large populations or comparative study can be revised to eliminate religious or worldview biased language, unless these are options from among many that respondents may choose.

Philosophical questions arise from the assumptions implicit in common measures of spiritual well-being. There is an assumption that a clear sense of life meaning and purpose is positive and that it can contribute to other aspects of well-being, such as coping with illness. Although this may be supported by empirical evidence in general, many religious traditions and spiritual perspectives point out that spiritual well-being is a process that may involve crises of meaning, purpose and faith that are crucial for spiritual development. For example, according to the Biblical story of Job, he did not find a satisfactory answer about why he was tormented with personal loss, pestilence, and sickness. In a vision, God spoke from an awesome whirlwind about that which is beyond human understanding. In existential psychology, despair, doubt, confusion, alienation, shame, and guilt can be signs of spiritual well-being (i.e., authenticity) in response to confrontations with oppression, conformist faith, and narcissism. In transpersonal psychology, optimal adult spiritual well-being is associated with transcendence of a view of self and reality rooted in egocentric identifications, pleasures, meanings, and purposes. Some approaches to spiritually based activism, such as the nonviolent resistance of Gandhi and King, view spiritual well-being as a collective ideal and quality for loving and just communities in which well-being of self and others are inextricable. Positive psychology could further explore these insights in refining the concept of spiritual well-being.

SEE ALSO: ▶ James, William ▶ Religiousness ▶ Spirituality ▶ Well-being

References

Anonymous. (2002). Diagnosis review committee: New and revised diagnoses. *Nursing Diagnosis*, 13, 68–69.

Eichler, M., Deegan, G., Canda, E. R., & Wells, S. (2006). Using the strengths assessment to mobilize spiritual resources. In K. B. Helmeke and C. F. Sori (Eds.), *The therapist's notebook for integrating spirituality in counseling* (pp. 69–76). NY: Haworth.

Faiver, C., Ingersoll, R. E., O'Brien, E., & McNally, C. (2001). *Explorations in Counseling and Spirituality*. Belmont, CA: Wadsworth/ Thomson Learning.

Hill, P. C., Pargament, K. I., Hood, R. W., Mccullough, M. E., Swyers, J. P., Larson, D. B., & Zinnbauer, B. J. (2000). Conceptualizing religion and spirituality: Points of commonality, points of departure. *Journal for the Theory of Social Behavior, 30*, 51–77.

Peterson, C. & Seligman, M. E. P. (2004). *Character strengths and virtues: A handbook and classification*. Washington, DC: American Psychological Association.

Snyder, C. R. & Lopez, S. J. (2007). *Positive psychology: The scientific and practical explorations of human strengths*. Thousand Oaks, CA: Sage.

Spirituality

Kenneth I. Pargament
Bowling Green State University

The term *spirituality* comes from the word *spirit* (to breathe) and there is general agreement that spirituality is a living, dynamic process that is oriented around whatever the individual may hold sacred. The *sacred* refers to concepts of God and transcendent reality as well as other aspects of life that take on divine character and significance by virtue of their association with the holy. Thus, the sacred can encompass material objects (e.g., crucifix, American flag), special times (e.g., the Sabbath, birth and death), special places (e.g., cathedral, the outdoors), relationships (e.g., marriage, parenting), and psychological attributes (e.g., soul, virtues). Spirituality can be defined as a search for the sacred, that is, an attempt to discover and hold onto the sacred and, when necessary, transform the sacred.

In their search for the sacred, people take a variety of spiritual pathways. These paths include traditional or nontraditional organized religious beliefs (e.g., God, afterlife, karma), practices (e.g., prayer, meditation, rituals), experiences (e.g., mysticism, conversion), and institutions (e.g., church attendance, Bible study). Pathways to the sacred may also take nonreligious forms, such as walking in the outdoors, journaling, listening to music, scientific study, intimate relations with others, or participating in sociopolitical action.

Over the course of the lifespan, the search for the sacred can unfold in many directions. For some, spirituality is a relatively smooth, stable process. For others, spirituality involves sharp shifts in spiritual pathways and understandings of the sacred itself. Some embed their spirituality in a traditional religious milieu. Others leave traditional religious settings and pursue more individualized spiritual pathways and destinations. Still others join and leave a variety of religious contexts, traditional and nontraditional, over their lives. Spirituality is, in short, a rich, complex, and multiform process.

History

The topic of religion was a vital concern for the founding figures of psychology. Psychologists such as William James, Edwin Starbuck, and G. Stanley Hall viewed religious and spiritual phenomena (e.g., mystical experience, conversion) as central to the study of human behavior. For much of the twentieth century, however, psychology distanced itself from religion, perhaps because the young field was concerned about demonstrating its credentials as a scientific discipline. Those who did devote attention to religious issues, such as Sigmund Freud, tended to be highly critical about religious matters. Religion was often described as irrational, delusional, or a source of pathology.

This picture began to change in the latter part of the twentieth century for several reasons. First, the *zeitgeist* of the field shifted to a focus on positive psychological constructs, including constructs often laden with spiritual meaning (e.g., forgiveness, gratitude, meaning, growth, acceptance, love). Second, theorists and researchers distinguished spirituality more sharply from institutional religious affiliation, beliefs, and practices. Third, empirical studies revealed that spiritual beliefs and practices are commonplace in the United States, with a large majority of people reportedly believing in God, believing in an afterlife, defining themselves as spiritual and religious, and seeing "God's presence in all of life." Finally, empirical research also demonstrated significant, often positive, linkages between spirituality and health and well-being. Thus, there was an eightfold increase in the number of published articles on spirituality in psychological and behavioral science journals from 1965 to 2000.

How Spirituality Works

Having shown that many people in the United States are spiritually involved and that spirituality is linked to health and well-being, researchers are currently taking a closer look at how spirituality works in peoples' lives. Although this research is still in process, several preliminary conclusions appear to be warranted.

The Sacred Elicits Spiritual Emotions

The experience of sacredness is accompanied by a sense of transcendence (i.e., being connected to something that goes beyond oneself), boundlessness (i.e., infinite time and space), and ultimacy (i.e., being in touch with what is "really real"). Theologian Rudolf Otto noted that the idea of the divine is often accompanied by a *mysterium*, a complex of feelings of attraction (e.g., love, adoration, gratitude) and repulsion (e.g., repulsion, fear, dread). More recently, researchers have linked perceptions of the sacred to a variety of emotion-based responses, including peak experiences, mystical experiences, and feelings of responsibility, duty, humility, awe, elevation, and uplift.

The Sacred becomes an Organizing Force

As the source of powerful emotions, the sacred becomes a passion and a priority. People feel drawn to, or even grasped by, the sacred and, as a result, they begin to invest more and more of themselves in sacred pursuits. For example, studies have shown that people who sanctify the environment (i.e., view the environment as sacred) are more likely to invest financially in environmental causes. Similarly, people direct more of their time and energy to sacred strivings than nonsacred strivings. In the process of building their lives around the sacred, people look to the sacred to lend greater coherence to disparate thoughts, feelings, actions, and goals by integrating their competing aspirations into a unified life plan.

The Sacred becomes a Resource

Sacred beliefs, practices, experiences, values, and relationships often serve as resources that people can draw on for strength, support, and satisfaction in their lives. A large body of research points to the positive implications of several spiritual pathways for individual health and well-being. Prayer and meditation, beliefs in a loving God, attendance at religious services, positive spiritual coping, and perceptions of various aspects of life as sacred have all been associated with indices of greater psychological, social, physical, and spiritual well-being. For example, in one study of patients undergoing kidney transplant surgery and their loved ones, those who engaged in positive religious coping reported greater life satisfaction 3 months and 12 months after transplantation. In a meta-analysis of 42 studies on the effects of transcendental meditation, this practice was tied to a greater number of transcendental experiences and these experiences were, in turn, associated with significant psychological and physical change. Yet another longitudinal study focused on 100 people with HIV. People who reportedly became more spiritual and religious after their diagnosis showed significantly greater preservation of T-helper (CD4) cells and better control of their viral load over the 4-year period of the study.

The Sacred becomes a Source of Struggle

Despite the clear benefits of spirituality for health and well-being, spirituality can become a source of stress and strain when people perceive that the sacred has been threatened, damaged, or violated. In times of stress, people may experience divine struggles (e.g., feeling angry at, abandoned or punished by God), intra-psychic struggles (e.g., questions and doubts about dogma, beliefs, and behaviors), or interpersonal struggles (e.g., spiritual conflicts with clergy, family, friends, or others). Spiritual struggles such as these are by no means trivial. They appear to represent a fork in the road to decline or growth. On the one hand, spiritual struggles have been consistently and robustly tied to a variety of poorer outcomes, including poorer mental health, poorer physical health, and even greater risk of mortality. On the other hand, spiritual struggles have been linked to reports of greater stress-related growth and transformation. Researchers are currently attempting to identify those factors that determine whether spiritual struggles lead to growth or decline.

Future Directions

The psychology of spirituality has advanced rapidly in recent years. In the future, advances are likely to continue both in research and in practice.

Why Spirituality Works

Although it has become clear that spirituality has important implications for individuals' health and well-being, a key question remains: how do we account for the spirituality-health connection? Theorists and researchers have offered and begun to examine a number of potential explanations for the relationships between spirituality and health and well-being. These include:

- Behavioral explanations (e.g., spirituality encourages good health practices that are, in turn, tied to better health and well-being).
- Psychological explanations (e.g., spirituality offers a sense of meaning, coherence, esteem, identity, hope, empowerment, and comfort that facilitates health and well-being).
- Social explanations (e.g., spirituality facilitates social connectedness, social support, and a sense of intimacy that promotes health and well-being).
- Physiological explanations (e.g., spirituality produces changes in brain, immune system, and autonomic system functioning that are associated with better health and well-being).

As yet, researchers have not been able to fully account for the links between spirituality and health through the explanations noted above. It is possible that further empirical studies will provide a clearer picture. However, it is also possible that there is something distinctive, even unique, about spirituality that accounts for the spirituality-health connection. The power of spiritual pathways such as prayer, meditation, rituals, attendance at religious services, and spiritual coping methods may lie in the fact that they are tied to perceptions of the sacred. Similarly, at least part of the power of the great virtues – forgiveness, humility, gratitude, compassion – may lie in the fact that they are often grounded in spiritual values and worldviews.

Spiritually-Sensitive Change

For a number of years, practicing psychologists tended to minimize or overlook the spiritual dimension of clients' lives. Yet, this stance has become increasingly untenable with the growing recognition that: many clients are spiritually-oriented; many clients prefer spiritually-sensitive practitioners; that spirituality is a potent resource for many people who experience problems; and that spirituality can also be a part of the problem that leads people to seek help.

Recently, psychologists have begun to develop and assess the efficacy of spiritually integrated forms of psychotherapy. Treatments drawing on spiritual resources (e.g., prayer, meditation, spiritual reframing, ritual) have been implemented for a variety of groups facing a variety of problems: women with eating disorders, drug abusers, people with HIV/AIDS, ex-spouses dealing with anger and resentment, survivors of sexual abuse, and people with social anxiety, depression, and serious mental illness. Spiritually-integrated treatments are still in an early stage of development and further evaluation is needed. Nevertheless, initial studies have yielded promising results.

Psychologists have also started to attend more closely to spirituality in other contexts, including premarital education, medical care, and preventive programming in congregations. In short, psychologists are beginning to weave sacred matters more fully into their efforts to understand human behavior, prevent problems, ameliorate distress, and promote well-being.

SEE ALSO: ▶ Coping ▶ James, William ▶ Religiousness

Sport Psychology

Megan E. Brent[a] and Adrienne Leslie-Toogood[b]
[a]*University of Kansas;* [b]*Kansas State University*

Sport psychology is the scientific study of psychological factors associated with sport participation and performance and the practical application of this knowledge to assist athletes in enhancing performance and achieving optimal mental health. Sport psychology as a discipline is similar to positive psychology in that the primary focus is on building human strengths and striving for optimal experiences. Topics researched and applied by sport psychologists include peak performance, mental skills such as imagery and self-talk, relaxation techniques, leadership, goal setting, motivation, attention and concentration, team dynamics, personality factors, gender and multicultural issues, coaching effectiveness, athletic identity, injuries, burnout, unhealthy behaviors such as substance abuse, psychological concerns such as depression and anxiety, ethical issues of research and practice, and the impact of sport participation on development and well-being.

Sport psychology is a relatively new field, and the origins can be traced to the former Soviet Union and Eastern Europe. The exceptional performances of athletes from these respective countries at various Olympic Games led to increased interest in the application of this sport science. Weinberg and Gould suggest that the historical development of the field can be divided into six eras:

the early years (1895–1920), the Griffith era (1921–1938, named after Coleman Griffith, who established the first sport psychology research lab at the University of Illinois), preparation for the future (1939–1965), establishment of academic sport psychology (1966–1977), multidisciplinary science and practice in sport and exercise psychology (1978–2000), and contemporary sport and exercise psychology (2000–present).

Currently, sport psychology professionals engage in several activities including teaching, research, consulting, and counseling. Team consulting, coaching clinics, individual and group counseling, and life-skills programs may be utilized to address topics such as team dynamics, performance enhancement, and developmental issues. Sport psychologists with clinical training may work with athletes in counseling to manage psychological concerns such as depression, anxiety, and eating disorders. This has training implications for students interested in pursuing a career in sport psychology, and the preferred educational background of future professionals is a topic of frequent debate within the field. In general, students are trained within either a sport science/kinesiology program or a clinical/counseling program. Those trained within a psychology program may be eligible for licensure as a psychologist, and they are the only professionals legally allowed to use this title as a component of their practice. Notably, the Association for the Advancement of Applied Sport Psychology strongly encourages consultants to have training from both kinesiology and psychology, and this is a requirement for their certification process.

Peak performance is a notion that athletes, coaches, and sport psychologists constantly strive to understand and facilitate in the world of sport. In 1975, Mihaly Csikszentmihalyi introduced the concept of *flow*, which is discussed in both sport psychology and positive psychology literature. Flow is associated with enjoyment of an activity for its own sake and the occurrence of peak performances. According to Jackson and Csikszentmihalyi, when athletes were asked to describe the experience of flow, nine fundamental components emerged: balance between challenge and skills, action-awareness merging, clear goals, unambiguous feedback, concentration on the task at hand, sense of control, loss of self-consciousness, transformation of time, and autotelic experience. In 1980, Yuri Hanin introduced the individualized zones of optimal functioning (IZOF) model. Research by Jokela and Hanin has validated this concept that an athlete will perform best with an arousal level within the individual's optimal zone. Sport psychologists assist individual athletes in identifying their own optimal mental, emotional, and physical states for peak performance. Strategies such as positive self-talk, imagery, relaxation, and biofeedback training may help athletes in regulating arousal level, reaching the zone of optimal functioning, and facilitating the flow state.

Sport psychologists teach many skills when working with athletes, including imagery, relaxation, concentration, goal-setting, and positive self-talk. Self-talk refers to a person's cognitions (i.e., thoughts). In the field of positive psychology, the importance of positive thinking is discussed relative to concepts such as optimism, attribution theory, and self-efficacy. In the field of sport psychology, self-talk typically refers to the messages athletes give themselves regarding their abilities and sport performance. The sport psychology literature demonstrates that positive self-talk is linked to athletic success, while negative self-talk such as "I'm not good enough" contributes to performance-hindering anxiety. Sport psychologists guide athletes in monitoring and managing their self-talk. One popular strategy developed by Beck is known as *cognitive restructuring*, a technique that involves identifying negative patterns of thinking and learning to replace them with realistic, self-affirming, success-oriented statements. For example, an athlete who thinks, "This is going to be impossible, and I am afraid I will lose," may replace that thought with the thought, "This is going to be a challenge, and I am going to perform to the best of my abilities." Negative thoughts are inevitable in athletics; the key to positive thinking is awareness of one's thoughts and the ability to transform negative self-talk into positive messages.

For many athletes, participation in sport is a primary source of self-worth. An individual who places great importance on sport involvement is described as possessing a strong athletic identity. Research has shown that athletes with strong athletic identities may benefit from high self-esteem, life satisfaction, and purpose in life while they are still involved in athletics. The positive psychology literature refers to the importance of pursuit of meaningfulness in life. The transition out of athletics is often more difficult when an individual has focused solely on sport at the expense of other possible interests, a phenomenon known as *role foreclosure*. At the end of their athletic careers, former athletes may wonder who they are and what purpose they have in life. This is a particularly difficult transition when retirement from athletics is involuntary following an injury. Individuals may believe they were unable to realize their full athletic potential or accomplish their sport-related goals. They may also miss the strong support system they had as an athlete. Sport psychologists assist individuals in preparing for the transition out of sport, coping with the transition process, identifying transferable skills such as teamwork and leadership, exploring interests outside of sport, and engendering hope for a meaningful future beyond athletic participation.

There are several professional associations connected with the field of sport psychology, including the Association for the Advancement of Applied Sport Psychology (AAASP), Division 47 of the American Psychological Association (APA), the North American Society for the Psychology of Sport and Physical Activity (NASPSPA), and the International Society of Sport Psychology (ISSP). Most of these associations host annual conferences, with the latter hosting a World Congress every few years. Key professional journals include *The Sport Psychologist, The Journal of Sport and Exercise Psychology, The Journal of Applied Sport Psychology, The Psychology of Sport and Exercise*, and *The International Journal of Sport Psychology*. Publishers in the area include Fitness Information Technology (housed at West Virginia University) and Human Kinetics. *The Directory of Graduate Programs in Applied Sport Psychology* includes a listing of graduate preparation programs in Canada, the United States, Australia, Great Britain, and South Africa. *The World Sport Psychology Sourcebook* includes a good description of key sport psychology applications from around the world. *The Directory of Psychological Tests in Sport and Exercise Sciences* includes a listing of most tests used by sport psychology practitioners.

SEE ALSO:　▶ Flow　▶ Hope　▶ Meaning

Stanton, Annette

Jennifer Austenfeld
University of Kansas

Annette Stanton (b. 1955) has provided new insights into the adaptive role of emotion in the coping process and has elucidated factors that enhance adjustment to cancer, reproductive problems, and other adverse health conditions. Stanton, a graduate of the University of Kansas and the University of Connecticut, has received numerous awards recognizing excellence in research, teaching, and mentorship, including the Senior Investigator Award for Outstanding Contributions to Health Psychology by Division 38 (Health Psychology) of the American Psychological Association. She became interested in stress and coping research during her early clinical work when she observed the substantial individual variability in coping responses to illness. She began to study the role of emotion in coping and identified an intriguing discrepancy between the coping research literature and studies of emotion in other diverse fields. Many coping studies described an association between "emotion-focused coping" (i.e., attempts to palliate negative emotions in stressful situations) and maladaptive outcomes, such as symptoms of anxiety or depression. These findings conflicted with work in other disciplines establishing the adaptive importance of emotion in response to environmental challenges through, for example, focusing attention and prioritizing behavioral responses. In a series of studies, Stanton provided insight into this discrepancy by demonstrating that many items designed to measure emotion-focused coping in several widely used coping questionnaires also contain expressions of distress or self-deprecation. These negatively biased items overlap with other measures of poor functioning and confound the observed association between emotion-focused coping and maladaptive outcomes.

Stanton and her research team then developed a new construct encompassing efforts to cope through the acknowledgment, understanding, and expression of emotion which they designated *coping through emotional approach*. This designation emphasizes approach toward emotional experience as a coping process, contrasted with avoidant strategies such as denial. Stanton's team validated a new instrument to assess emotional approach coping (EAC) using items free of negative bias. The EAC measure contains two subscales: emotional processing (EP), consisting of active attempts to acknowledge and understand emotion (sample item, "I acknowledge my emotions"); and emotional expression (EE), consisting of active verbal and/or nonverbal attempts to communicate or symbolize emotion (sample item, "I feel free to express my emotions"). Subsequent studies by Stanton and others have indicated that EAC can be adaptive in the context of several stressors such as infertility, breast cancer, and chronic pain. This research has further identified individual and environmental factors that moderate the relationship between EAC and adjustment. In general, EAC appears to be most adaptive when the stressor is perceived as relatively uncontrollable and when the individual's social environment is receptive to emotional expression.

In a literature dominated by research identifying risk factors for maladjustment, Stanton has made significant contributions in delineating protective processes that enhance adjustment to chronic illness, with much of her work focusing on cancer and infertility. She demonstrated that women completing treatment for breast cancer who wrote either about emotions or perceived benefits of the breast cancer experience reported fewer medical appointments for cancer-related problems at 3-month follow-up, relative to a control group. In ongoing research, Stanton continues to illuminate factors that facilitate well-being and health in individuals confronting adversity.

SEE ALSO: ▶ Coping ▶ Health psychology ▶ Psychological adjustment

Stereotype Threat

Leoandra Rogers and Joshua Aronson
New York University

In 1995 Claude Steele and Joshua Aronson coined the term *stereotype threat* to describe the discomfort people experience when confronted with a negative stereotype associated with their social identity. Steele and Aronson proposed that in certain situations, people become apprehensive about validating a negative group image – both in the eyes of others and in their own eyes – and this often unconscious fear can impair performance in situations where stress or distraction are disruptive (e.g., high stakes testing, public speaking, etc.).

The stereotype threat hypothesis was supported in a series of social psychology experiments evaluating the intellectual test performance of African American college students. The long-standing stereotypic image that portrays African Americans as less intelligent than whites is widely known and well established, making the academic sphere a prime context for eliciting stereotype threat. To test their hypothesis, Steele and Aronson gave African American and White students at Stanford University a difficult standardized test of verbal ability, varying the description of the test such that some students believed the purpose of the test was to measure their intelligence, whereas others were told that the test was purely a nonevaluative laboratory exercise.

The results from these landmark experiments showed a marked difference in performance among the African American students; they performed significantly worse when they believed the test was being used to diagnose their intelligence.

Moreover, in subsequent experiments, simply asking African American students to indicate their race prior to taking the test resulted in impaired performance. Importantly, these declines did not occur among the White test-takers. Because the tests were identical across testing conditions and the students were randomly assigned, the results indicated that African Americans' depressed test performance was the direct result of the way the test was presented suggesting that stereotype threat phenomenon may play a central role in African American students' much discussed academic underperformance.

These experiments garnered a good deal of attention – both in academic circles and in the popular press – because they were seen as a viable alternative explanation for the Black-White test score gap, which had been notoriously described as evidence for the genetic inferiority of African Americans in the controversial book *The Bell Curve*, published in 1994. Steele and Aronson's research was cited in two Supreme Court cases on affirmative action and is one of the most frequently cited articles in the social sciences the past decade, earning a designation as a "modern classic" in the psychological literature. Parallel findings showing that gender stereotypes likewise suppress women's test performance in mathematics further suggested the relevance of stereotype threat to sex differences in mathematics and science achievement.

Because of its relevance to politically charged issues such as affirmative action, racial and gender differences in intellectual capacity, and the predictive value of standardized tests, stereotype threat has also been the subject of controversy, its validity questioned by critics of affirmative action, proponents of genetic theories of intelligence, and by psychologists working in the testing industry. Such critics tend to accept the experimental results but question whether stereotype threat operates outside the confines of the research laboratory, and whether it contributes to the test score gap between blacks and whites and the gender gap in mathematics in the "real world." Proponents of the theory regard it as an important advance because it illuminates the role of tractable situational factors in the test score gap, and thus suggests practicable means for addressing achievement disparities that do not require massive social changes. A series of publications report field interventions based on stereotype threat theory have successfully narrowed racial and gender achievement gaps, strongly suggesting the relevance and utility of the theory for addressing achievement disparities.

Stereotype threat can affect a variety of social groups – anyone for whom a negative stereotype exists or for whom comparisons with a "superior" group can be made salient. For instance, an elderly man forgets his keys and becomes distracted and anxious that his forgetfulness indicates, or will be seen to indicate, senility; a Latino student refuses to engage in class discussions as he is wary that his accent will mark him as intellectually inferior in the eyes of his classmates; a White male feels mathematically incompetent in class when Asian classmates are present and avoids taking advanced courses if too many Asians are enrolled – and so on. These instances exemplify the psychological impact of stereotype threat, and the physiological and behavioral responses evoked by the activation of relevant stereotypes that serve to undermine immediate performance and ultimately lead to adaptations that can turn short-term performance deficits into enduring skill deficits. Experiments confirm that all of the above social groups suffer significant deficits in performance when stereotypes disadvantaging their group are activated.

Although stereotype threat clearly exerts a direct impact on the individual's immediate performance, the indirect pathways and the precise mechanisms through which stereotype threat interrupts performance are continuously under research. It is clear however, that stereotype threat is mediated through heightened physiological arousal, which leads to deficits in both short-term memory and what psychologists refer to as *executive function* – the ability to focus and manipulate cognitive resources. As evidence of this mediating process, researchers have shown that prior to the stereotype threat induction, if subjects are informed that they may experience anxiety and are told to attribute their heightened arousal to a factor completely unrelated to the current task, the effects of stereotype threat are attenuated.

Not all individuals experience stereotype threat to the same degree; there are important moderators. Steele and Aronson proposed that identification – the degree to which one cares about the domain or about his or her social identity – is a critical factor in stereotype threat, arguing that the impact of a stereotype will be negligible if a person cares little about task domain or the relevant social identity. For a person for whom being an African American or being a woman is a central self-definition, a negative stereotype about blacks or women is likely to be more salient and more threatening than for a person whose self-esteem is rooted in other social identities. Likewise, an individual who prides herself on her academic ability will find a stereotype threat especially meaningful and thus, more harmful. One implication of stereotype threat then, is disidentification from either the stigmatized task or social identity, in an effort to preserve self-esteem. This psychological disengagement has grave implications, particularly in the sphere of academics, and may explain the hypothesized lack of interest or concern associated with academic failure among underperforming students.

Maintaining a positive image is critical for social well-being; thus individuals subjected to stereotype threat often engage in self-image protective behaviors that can be counterproductive. A common self-protective behavior is self-handicapping, in which individuals adopt strategies (e.g., not studying prior to an exam) that deliberately preclude their success, enabling them to attribute failure to low effort rather than low ability. Likewise, stigmatized individuals often discount important feedback regarding their performance, refusing to admit their lack of knowledge or understanding. In a similar manner, some individuals will simply avoid new or challenging tasks that offer the opportunity to expand their knowledge and skill in order to resist appearing incompetent. Such adaptations protect self-esteem in the short term, but they virtually guarantee that competence in the domain will stagnate rather than grow. Thus, over the long term, psychological barriers such as stereotype threat can stunt intellectual growth just as surely as poverty or other structural barriers.

Researchers have developed a number of promising interventions for helping students cope with stereotype threat in ways that do not compromise academic achievement. By and large, these studies reveal that knowledge is perhaps the strongest defense against stereotype threat. For instance, coaching students to conceive of intelligence as malleable as opposed to a fixed, immutable entity significantly decreases the impact of stereotype threat. Likewise, teaching students about stereotype threat – how it works and its power to undermine performance in stressful situations – has shown to disrupt the phenomenon. Along with understanding the psychological mediators of stereotype threat, applying research from the laboratory and real-world settings (e.g., schools) in order to develop programs that can buffer the effects of stereotype threat continues to be a central focus of this work.

SEE ALSO: ▶ Cognitive appraisal   ▶ Intelligence

Stone, Phil

Connie Rath
Gallup

Philip J. Stone, a Harvard professor of psychology, was a pioneer in the field of positive psychology who also revolutionized the use of computers in the social sciences. He was ahead of his time technologically and academically. He entered the University of Chicago at age 15 and earned a doctorate in psychology and social sciences from Harvard at the age of 23. He started his teaching career at Harvard in 1960 and was on the faculty until he died in 2006.

Stone became intrigued with finding the strengths of people and led one of the first studies of Clifton StrengthsFinder with Harvard undergraduates. He became an avid writer and teacher about individual talents and their role in developing students. Students cited him as unusual in the way he saw them as more than intelligent high achievers. He was one of the first senior scientists for Gallup. He contributed to the theories of talent identification and strengths measurement through his work with Gallup professionals and senior scientists from other institutions. His innovative ideas contributed to statistical methodologies to study talents and successes and technical advances to report results of psychological assessments.

He was known internationally for the General Inquirer program which made it possible for computers to analyze text. The programs were applied to surveys and to interviews of leaders to quantitatively understand qualitative information.

Stone also consulted about workplace psychology from an environmental perspective. He helped design spaces to encourage people to interact more positively and waste less space. His consulting extended to a wide range of clients including the National Cancer Institute and the US State Department.

The positive psychology course he developed at Harvard grew to become the most requested course at the university. Tal Ben-Shahar, a protégé of Stone, has continued the course and received wide media attention for its demand and success.

SEE ALSO: ▶ Clifton StrengthsFinder   ▶ Gallup

Strengths (Gallup)

Jim Asplund
Gallup

Definition

Gallup defines *strengths* as those activities for which one can provide consistent, near-perfect performance. Strengths are composed of:

- Skills: the basic abilities to perform fundamental tasks, such as operating a particular piece of machinery. Skills are not naturally occurring – they must be acquired through formal or informal training and practice.
- Knowledge: an acquaintance with, and understanding of, facts and principles accumulated through education or experience.
- Talents: natural ways of thinking, feeling, and behaving, such as an inner drive to compete, sensitivity to the needs of others, or the tendency to be outgoing at social gatherings. Talents must come into existence naturally and cannot be acquired like skills and knowledge.

Some aspects of personality are situation-dependent; an individual with low conscientiousness can be occasionally conscientious. Similarly, many persons can exhibit a degree of discipline when it is needed, but for most, it is not a reliable trait. To be a talent, the disposition needs to be a reliable component of one's personality.

There is growing evidence that these stable traits begin to develop at relatively young ages, and in some respects, it is those very relatively fixed talents that define an individual, in that they represent the product of all the billions of choices and circumstances that brought him or her to the present moment. These choices and the emotions associated with them lead to measurable neurochemical changes that provide a scientific basis for why talents do not change significantly over time. Individuals can develop a heightened self-awareness, they can add knowledge and skills, and they can stabilize their values and beliefs as means of developing their talents into strengths.

A person's most powerful talents represent the best of his or her natural self. Accordingly, these talents are a person's best opportunities to perform at levels of excellence. Dominant talents naturally appear frequently and powerfully, in a variety of situations. They can take the form of yearnings, or areas of rapid learning. They can be areas of great personal satisfaction, or in which one experiences a sense of timelessness:

- A yearning can be described as an internal force that leads one to a particular activity or environment time and again.
- Rapid learning reveals talent through the speed at which one anticipates the steps of a new activity, acquires a new skill, or gains new knowledge.
- Satisfaction is a positive emotional response to successfully meeting challenges that engage one's greatest talents. These energizing experiences are often evidence of a dominant talent at work.
- Timelessness also can serve as a clue to talent. Being engaged in an activity at a deep, natural level can result in a lack of the sense of time passing, and indicates a level of engrossment in that activity that is consistent with a deep natural talent.

Once dominant talents are identified, a person can thoughtfully appeal to them and determine how often they will be expressed. The more a talent is exercised, and the more it is refined through added knowledge and skills, the more integrated and stronger it becomes.

In the 1990s, under the leadership of Educational Psychologist Donald O. Clifton, Gallup developed the Clifton StrengthsFinder (CSF) as an objective measure of personal talent that could be administered online in less than one hour.

Clifton believed that talents could be operationalized, studied, and capitalized upon in work and academic settings. He also considered success to be closely associated with personal talents and strengths in addition to the traditional constructs linked with analytical intelligence. In accordance with those beliefs, he worked to identify hundreds of themes of personal talents that predicted work and academic success, and he constructed empirically-based, semi-structured interviews for identifying these themes.

When developing the interviews, Clifton and analysts examined the prescribed roles of a person, visited the job site or academic setting, identified outstanding performers in these roles and settings, and determined the long-standing thoughts, feelings, and behaviors associated with situational success. Many of the interviews developed provided useful predictions of positive outcomes. In the mid-1990s, when considering the creation of an objective measure of talent, Clifton and colleagues systematically reviewed these interviews and the data they generated to capitalize on the accumulated knowledge and experience of Gallup's talent-based practice.

The prominence of dimensions and items relating to motivation and to values in much of the interview research informed the design of a CSF instrument to identify those enduring human qualities. The result was an instrument that identified 34 strengths. To date, CSF has been taken by more than 2 million individuals, in 18 languages.

Strengths Application

Clausen, and also Aldwin, Sutton, and Lachman have studied self-perceived psychological growth and change (psychological turning points) and found positive events can trigger many enduring turning points in individual lives. Identifying and understanding talents can become positive turning points, triggering changes in how people view themselves in the context of the world around them.

Numerous studies of personality, behavior genetics, intelligence, interests, and values have documented high variability across individuals. Genetic research suggests a substantial trait component in personality and intelligence constructs, among other constructs. The findings of high genetic composition may hint that how people most efficiently grow and develop is dynamically related to who they are to begin with. Other "attitudinal" constructs, such as job satisfaction, have a less strong genetic component. People can change the "changeables" (satisfaction, subjective well-being, engagement, performance, etc.), most efficiently through who they are to begin with (their inherent talents).

A development program designed to develop strengths would be mapped to the following course:

1. measure constructs most likely to be predisposed;
2. identify talents and weaknesses;
3. focus maximum learning on talents;
4. integrate activities of one's life around talents, and manage around weaknesses; and
5. focus change on constructs that are changeable, rather than the missing traits.

In a business setting, strengths-based management uses the uniqueness of each employee to maximize the team's output. Teams that operate this way are more engaged and, as a consequence, more productive. In a recent study, Gallup researchers have shown that an employee whose supervisor focuses on employee strengths is over two and a half times as likely to be engaged as one whose supervisor focuses on employee weaknesses. Even worse is the supervisor ignores an employee; there is virtually no chance of being engaged at all.

The strengths approach not only improves team engagement and cohesion, it also generates better performance. Gallup researchers recently completed a study that shows significant financial returns to investing in employees' strengths development. The study included an estimated 90,000 employees in 900 business units, from 11 different organizations representing five different industries. In addition to large increases in employee engagement, teams whose managers received a strengths intervention had trailing productivity measures that were 12.5% higher than teams whose managers received no such treatment, and 8.9% higher profitability. Individual employees who learned to apply their strengths were also less likely to terminate their employment; they turned over at a rate 14.9% lower than employees who did not learn their strengths.

SEE ALSO: ▶ Clifton, Donald   ▶ Employee engagement
▶ Organizational psychology   ▶ Personality   ▶ Person–environment fit

Strengths (Personality)

P. Alex Linley
Centre for Applied Positive Psychology, UK

The label *personality strengths* was adopted from a project of the same name, which set out to identify, name, define, and assess the several hundred strengths believed to exist, but which were not represented by existing strengths groupings or classifications. The project involves the natural observation of strengths from an ethological perspective, understanding strengths and their evolution in relation to explicit theoretical underpinnings, and reviewing existing literature and empirical evidence to inform the understanding of strengths that was developed through the work of the Personality Strengths Project.

The Evolution of the Personality Strengths Project

Personality researchers – albeit still with some dissenting voices – are now broadly agreed on the structure of personality, but it has taken many decades of research for them to arrive at this point, whether that was through systematic observation and theory development (type theory), or lexical analysis of natural language (trait theory). Being much earlier in this process, strengths researchers are still in the early days of exploring how many strengths may exist, let alone how best to classify them most appropriately. Notwithstanding this, important advances have been made with the development of the Clifton StrengthsFinder from Gallup, and the development of the VIA Inventory of Strengths, developed by Christopher Peterson and Martin Seligman. The Clifton StrengthsFinder assesses 34 themes of talent developed through occupational interviews, whereas the VIA Inventory of Strengths assesses 24 character strengths, believed to be universally valued across cultures and time.

Taken together, these two most popular strengths tools assess 58 nonoverlapping strengths. Even so, it is unlikely that they could be considered fully representative of the universe of strengths, and other researchers, including Shane Lopez and colleagues in a special positive psychology issue of *The Counseling Psychologist*, have suggested a myriad of other strengths that merit consideration. Similarly, people have reported taking strengths assessments but being left with a sense of dissatisfaction that it had not captured themes that they considered to be integral to their performance and personality. From these perspectives, the Personality Strengths Project set out to attempt to identify, name, define, and assess the potentially several hundred (or more) strengths that are believed to exist. Recognizing this, the project's focus on identifying strengths is open-ended. Ongoing work is dedicated to exploring newly identified strengths, defining them, and developing assessment tools to measure them, with a goal of developing a comprehensive classification of strengths that is drawn from extensive observational, theoretical and empirical work, and refined through that ongoing process.

Understanding and Defining Strengths

Extensive work has been undertaken to understand strengths more comprehensively through reviewing existing literature and empirical evidence, naturalistic observation and field interviews with strengths exemplars, and reference to theoretical perspectives that would provide a deeper understanding of the evolution of, reason for, and prevalence of strengths within human life.

On the basis of this multimethod approach, a strength was defined as "a preexisting capacity for a particular way of behaving, thinking, or feeling that is authentic and energizing to the user, and enables optimal functioning, development and performance" (Linley, in press).

A strength being a preexisting capacity refers to the fact that it already exists within us, to a greater or lesser extent. While it can be developed and grown, we cannot simply choose to "add in" strengths that we do not have. This is because our biological or psychological structure has predisposed us to have particular strengths, through the integrative processes of nature and nurture throughout our lives.

A strength being authentic reflects the fact that when people are using their strengths, they feel like they are being the "real me," behaving in a way that is right for them and freely chosen by them. For example, Govindji and Linley established empirically that strengths use was significantly associated with organismic valuing: people who used their strengths more were more authentic. This authenticity is also reflected in the fact that strengths are identifiable across many different situations in the same people.

Strengths are defined as energizing because when people are using their strengths, they feel like they have more energy available to them. For example, Govindji and Linley demonstrated that strengths use was associated with higher levels of subjective vitality, the feeling of having energy available to the self. This does not mean that they can use the strength forever without ever needing to rest (physical and biological constraints still apply), but it does mean that people are able to work more effectively, and with more engagement, when they are using their strengths. This may reflect the fact that, to a degree, using strengths recharges people, in the same way that an alternator in a car recharges the battery as the car is used.

Strengths enable optimal functioning, development and performance because using strengths allows people to be at their best in terms of their psychological functioning. This is reflective of strengths as preexisting capacities (we learn best in areas where we are already strong, probably because of the strength of existing neural networks and connections), and strengths as authentic and energizing (we perform better as a result of both of these, including having better health). For example, Govindji and Linley demonstrated overall that strengths use was associated with higher levels of subjective and psychological well-being, and that these associations held when controlling for self-esteem and self-efficacy, clearly indicating the unique contribution of strengths use to optimal functioning and fulfillment.

There is one thing that is missing from this definition – and deliberately so. Strengths are often interpreted as being "positive" qualities, and the understanding of "positive" can be taken in different ways. Rendering something "positive" is, however, inherently a value judgment and no such value judgments are assumed in relation to strengths as they are defined within the Personality Strengths Project. That is, it is recognized that strengths are inherently neutral in terms of their outcomes, except that the outcomes for the individual using the strengths (energy, authenticity, optimal functioning) could almost always be considered "positive." But the wider outcomes of the use of the strength, that is, whether the strength is used "positively" or "negatively" in any given context, is a question outside the purview of a definition of strengths. For example, both Hitler and Stalin could be considered to have had exceptional strengths. The ends to which they applied those strengths were destructive and genocidal, but that was not a function of the strengths themselves. In contrast, Mahatma Gandhi and Mother Theresa also had considerable strengths, but these were applied to more benevolent ends, even so, not being a function of the strengths themselves.

The Nature and Origins of Strengths

In seeking to understand the nature and origins of strengths, the work of the Personality Strengths Project involves examining theories of evolution and human nature, in order to understand, on the basis of existing deep theory, how strengths may best be accounted for in terms of their relation to human nature, and their origins in human development, at both the individual and species-typical level.

As described by Buss in relation to evolutionary personality psychology, there are three perspectives on how human beings came into existence: evolutionary theory, creationism, and seeding (the idea that Earth was visited by aliens who started human life as we know it). Of these three perspectives, only evolutionary theory is supported by extensive theoretical and scientific evidence, and as such is able successfully to organize and explain thousands of diverse findings in a logical and coherent way.

Evolutionary personality psychology suggests that personality characteristics, as we know them today, evolved because they offered adaptive solutions to evolutionary problems – typically, problems of survival and reproduction. Building from this basis, personality strengths theory proposes that strengths evolved similarly because they provided adaptive solutions to more specific environmental problems throughout human evolution. The greater specificity of strengths as adaptive solutions accounts for their multiplicity: Being geared to more specific problems, and with many more specific problems than general problems, it follows that there will be a multiplicity of strengths as adaptive solutions. As described by Buss (1991, p. 463): "Different problems typically select for different adaptive solutions; natural selection results in a multiplicity of specific adaptations over time. Evolutionary psychologists expect psychological mechanisms to be many and domain-specific."

Hence, evolutionary theory can account for the development of strengths at the species-typical level. These species-typical adaptations are then pruned and shaped further by the integrative processes of nature and nurture in any given individual, with a role played both by genetic endowment and by early environmental experiences, thus accounting for the wide range of strengths, and the widely differing strengths profiles, of given individuals.

Turning to theories of fundamental human nature, three broad views were put forward by Karen Horney in *Neurosis and Human Growth: The Struggle toward Self-Realization*. First, that people are inherently sinful and destructive and hence need to be controlled. Second, that people are possessed of tendencies for both good and bad, and so the good must be supported in its battle with the bad. Third, that people are possessed of an inherently constructive directional tendency toward growth and development, and that, given the right social environmental conditions, they will grow and develop positively and constructively in the directions that are right for them. Importantly, as people pursue these constructive directions, authenticity, congruence, energy and optimal functioning will follow.

The parallels identified between the outcomes of people using strengths and the outcomes specified by this third theory of human nature suggested that this view could be used most accurately and parsimoniously to locate a theory of strengths in relation to a deep theory of human nature. As described by Aristotle, Karen Horney, and Carl Rogers, among others, people are believed to have an inherent motivation toward growth, development and fulfillment, which Rogers described as the actualizing tendency. Following the actualizing tendency enables optimal functioning, because people are pursuing the directions in life that are right for them and their fulfillment, as they are guided to by their organismic valuing process. Strengths and strengths use is considered within personality strengths theory to be reflective of this actualizing tendency at work, and is empirically supported by the work of Govindji and Linley, who found that strengths use was significantly associated with organismic valuing.

Optimal Strengths Use

A clarion call of the strengths movement has often been taken to be – rightly or wrongly – play to your strengths and ignore your weaknesses. This led to the counterclaims around strengths overplayed, and the idea that strengths overplayed become weaknesses themselves.

The Personality Strengths Project is explicit about the approach taken to this issue. Given that strengths are ultimately about performance (whether in work or life more generally), strengths should always be used in a way that enables optimal functioning and performance. This can mean that strengths need to be turned up or turned down, like a volume control, as described by Bob Kaplan and Rob Kaiser in *The Versatile Leader*. It always means that Aristotle's concept of the golden mean is at the heart of strengths being used optimally: doing the right thing, to the right amount, in the right way, at the right time.

Understood from this perspective of optimal strengths use, many of the criticisms and questions around strengths come into relief. Strengths can be overplayed, but that does not mean that there is no room for a focus on strengths. It does mean that one should always be mindful of and attend to the context in which strengths are being used: a strength used effectively in one context may not translate so well to another, and when the context changes, strengths deployment may need to change too; this issue is at the heart of much of the literature on why great leaders have failed.

While recognizing the desirability of focusing on strengths, the approach set out in personality strengths theory is also explicit that weaknesses too will sometimes need to be attended to – if they are performance critical. If a person excels in a particular area, but his or her performance is undermined by a weakness elsewhere in his or her repertoire, it makes sense to do what can be done to deal with this – whether that is through skill development, remedial coaching, complementary partnering, strengths-based teamworking, or even job shaping to make the weakness irrelevant.

The starting assumption of the personality strengths approach in practice is to establish whether the weakness can be made irrelevant, or whether it is inescapably central to a person's optimal performance. Given that a weakness is relevant, it can be made irrelevant by complementary partnering – working with somebody else who will compensate for the weakness in that area, or by strengths-based teamworking – working in this way across a functional or project team. Both of these approaches can be complemented by job or role shaping, whereby a person's responsibilities are redesigned so that something that once required the deployment of a weakness is moved outside of their remit.

Applications

The personality strengths approach has been applied most broadly so far to applications with organizations, specifically as a philosophy and approach for building strengths-based organization. Strengths-based recruitment has involved mapping personality strengths to specific role outcomes, and recruiting candidates with a propensity to love to do the job, as well as being able to do the job. Strengths-based leadership development has focused on enabling leaders to identify strengths in themselves and others, to build strong teams, to use strengths optimally, and to build an organizational climate of appreciation and celebration that creates the conditions for human flourishing and the attendant organizational benefits: A major advantage of the strengths approach is this double-win for individuals and organizations.

In another application of the personality strengths approach, Linley and Harrington set out the theoretical underpinnings of strengths coaching, describing how the central premises of the positive psychology initiative accorded with those of coaching, and demonstrating how the actualizing tendency as a central thesis of human nature was consistent with the assumptions both of many coaching approaches and the strengths approach specifically. Subsequent empirical work by Govindji and Linley demonstrated that strengths use was associated with organismic valuing (authenticity), self-esteem, self-efficacy, vitality, subjective well-being and psychological well-being, and that strengths use was a unique predictor of well-being and fulfillment, even when controlling for self-esteem and self-efficacy.

Future Directions

As noted at the outset, there is much more ahead in this field than has been established to date. As such, the future directions that the field takes will be imperative in determining where it arrives and what is discovered through the process.

At the heart of the personality strengths approach will be a continued emphasis on strength-spotting, that is, the identification, definition, and assessment of new strengths through natural observation and ongoing literature reviews, together with theoretical, empirical and experimental work.

Specific empirical attention should be paid to establishing the role of strengths in areas including goal attainment, well-being, child development, educational attainment, business performance, and social contribution. Is strengths use predictive of goal attainment, and if so, how? Is strengths use predictive of well-being, and by what pathways? Do children raised with more of a focus on their strengths demonstrate enhanced developmental outcomes? Does schooling and education that is personalized around students' strengths enable improved academic attainment? Do organizations focused on employees being able to use their strengths deliver tangible business benefits? Can attention to strengths and strengths use be a means to building stronger societies on the basis of improved social contributions from all? In each case, hardening the data will be imperative, so that objective, quantifiable outcomes can be demonstrated that then underpin the case for change in, for example, parenting guidance, learning outcomes, organizational policy and culture, educational policy, and social policy.

Some of the applications of personality strengths are in the early stages of being used in relation to personal development, education and learning, health promotion, social care, and parenting and child development. Given that these applications are just beginning, future research and evaluation should be targeted at understanding what works, and how it works, in relation to the desired outcomes of these various applications.

Overall, the explicit position of the Personality Strengths Project is that using strengths is the smallest thing we can do to make the biggest difference. Strengths and strengths use are not claimed as a panacea for all modern ills, but they do appear to have tangible benefits, for individuals, families, communities, and organizations, with a benevolence that extends well beyond the initial actions required. Future work should be relentlessly focused on the smallest thing that can be done to make the biggest difference, whether that is through strengths or through another medium yet to be established.

SEE ALSO: ▶ Authenticity ▶ Character strengths (VIA) ▶ Strengths (Gallup) ▶ Strengths perspective (positive psychology) ▶ Strengths perspective (social welfare)

References

Buss, D. M. (1991). Evolutionary personality psychology. *Annual Review of Psychology, 42,* 459–491.

Linley, A. (in press). *Average to A+: Realising strengths in yourself and others.* Coventry, UK: CAPP Press.

Strengths Coaching

Dominic Carter and Nicky Page
Centre for Applied Positive Psychology

Strengths coaching is concerned with facilitating the identification, use and development of strengths to enable optimal functioning, performance and development. It may be understood as an *approach* to coaching, where the focus is on achieving other goals through harnessing strengths, or it may be understood as an *outcome* of coaching, where the intention is for the coaching client to gain a better understanding of their strengths, or to develop particular strengths more fully. Most often, strengths coaching is a combination of both of these.

Strengths coaching offers an unparalleled opportunity for the application of positive psychology. After explosive growth in the last decade, the practice of coaching is now established as one of the primary means of supporting individual and organizational development. The interests of coaching and positive psychology, as the science of optimal human functioning, overlap substantially. Focus on strengths, in particular, has been a feature of positive psychology since its inception and is attracting increasing interest among coaches and coachees. Research is linking strengths use with enhanced performance and well-being (outcomes of interest to both individuals and organizations) and strengths-focused coaching methods are being discovered (rediscovered in some cases) that seem to be effective in practice. Although scientific understanding of strengths is steadily growing, strengths coaching (like coaching more generally) has received very little attention from researchers.

Strengths can be applied to coaching in a wide variety of contexts, both within and outside organizations, and in many different ways. In some cases coaching may simply be informed by an understanding of strengths and their significance, for example, in relation to goal attainment; in others, identification and effective deployment of a coachee's strengths may be the object of coaching itself. Accordingly, strengths coaching is seen to encompass an underlying philosophy or appreciation of strengths (coaching from a strengths perspective) as well as an approach or methodology (coaching on strengths). Strengths coaching not only draws on positive psychology as a basis for practice, but also provides a potent channel for its dissemination.

Defining Strengths Coaching

The International Coach Federation have defined coaching as "a professional partnership between a qualified coach and an individual or team that supports the achievement of extraordinary results, based on goals set by the individual or team" (2007). This definition is broad enough to include team coaching (optimal strengths use is an essential aspect of teamwork), but excludes a good portion of coaching which is undertaken by people who are not qualified, including line managers, teachers and parents. Strengths coaching, as most other forms of coaching, can be undertaken by anyone, albeit with different degrees of proficiency and professionalism. Sir John Whitmore's description of coaching as "unlocking a person's potential to maximize their performance" (2002, p. 8) gets closer to the essence of strengths coaching and is broad enough to encompass the various contexts in which it takes place.

As well as the contexts in which coaching takes place (e.g., business coaching, sports coaching, life coaching), different kinds of coaching are often distinguished in terms of the approach employed (e.g., cognitive behavioral coaching, psychodynamic coaching, solution-focused coaching) or the (intended) outcome (e.g., skills coaching, performance coaching, leadership coaching). Strengths coaching does not sit easily in one box or the other, being at times the outcome (e.g., where the intention is for the coachee to gain clarity on his strengths or to develop a particular strength), at times the approach (e.g., where the intended outcome is more effective leadership and a focus on optimal deployment of strengths is a means to that end) and, most often, a combination of the two.

To define strengths coaching, first it is necessary to explain what we mean by strengths. Alex Linley at the Centre for Applied Positive Psychology (CAPP) has shed new light on strengths and their significance, defining a strength as "a pre-existing capacity for a particular way of behaving, thinking, or feeling that is authentic and energising to the user, and enables optimal functioning, development and performance" (Linley, 2008, p. 9).

In a study conducted with his colleague Reena Govindji, Linley established that strengths use is significantly associated with organismic valuing (authenticity), vitality and well-being. Using strengths enables people to be authentic because they are acting in a way that is right for them, something which is an integral part of human nature and intimately linked to our well-being and fulfillment. When people use their strengths they feel more engaged, more alive and as if they have more energy available to them. In terms of optimal development, we learn better in areas where we are already strong because these are preexisting capacities (the neural networks already exist for our strengths and it is easier for the brain to build on these pathways than it is to develop new ones). Optimal performance follows naturally from optimal functioning and development. Research involving over 19,000 employees by the Corporate Leadership Council found that focusing on performance strengths *increased* performance by 36.4%, while focusing on performance weaknesses led to a *decline* in performance of 26.8%.

In the light of this evidence, we borrow Linley's definition of a strength to offer the definition of strengths *coaching* as facilitating the identification, use and development of strengths to enable optimal functioning, performance or development.

The same research also contributes to a shift in perspective that is fundamental to strengths coaching and at the core of positive psychology itself. Essentially, the strengths perspective is concerned with what is strong and, by association, with what is working and what is right. In this respect it is similar to the perspective of Appreciative Inquiry, which has also informed approaches to coaching. The strengths perspective is in contrast – and reaction – to the deficit model which has prevailed, not only in psychology but in many corporations too, and is characterized by the treatment of illness in one context and the improvement of weakness in the other. A fundamental assumption of the strengths perspective is that the best opportunity for growth lies in improving what is already good and making strengths stronger. Another flows from our concept of human nature and our understanding, with psychologists Karen Horney and Carl Rogers, that there is an innate developmental tendency within each of us to realize our potential, or self-actualize. A significant part of that potential lies in our strengths and its realization can be facilitated by coaching. Some of the most important and enduring benefits of coaching flow from changes in the coachee's structure of interpretation; appreciation of the strengths perspective is one that many find affirming, motivating and empowering.

Standing on Shoulders

Neither the strengths perspective nor strengths-focused practices are new. Three key strengths pioneers can be identified, all recently deceased, whose work on strengths in the twentieth century has contributed significantly to the knowledge and practical effectiveness of the strengths coach today.

Management "guru" Peter Drucker (1909–2005) made his greatest contribution to the field through writing. "One cannot build on weakness," he stated in *The Effective Executive* in 1967. "To achieve results, one has to use all the available strengths . . . These strengths are the true opportunities" (1967, p. 60). His advice to the individual on how to develop him or herself is still sound today: work on improving your strengths, put yourself where your strengths can produce results, discover where your intellectual arrogance is causing disabling ignorance, remedy your bad habits, decide what not to do, and mind your manners!

Drucker was not the first to bring the question of strengths to the attention of management science, a distinction which goes to Bernard Haldane (1911–2002), who wrote an article in the *Harvard Business Review* in 1947, providing an explanation for people's lack of efficiency at work:

> One of the reasons for this neglect and waste of manpower is that very few top-management men know and recognize the varieties and number of human aptitudes. Another is general lack of information on how these aptitudes combine to form personality and work patterns. A third reason is a failure to realize the results of misapplication or neglect of talents. (Haldane, 1947, p. 652)

The same might be argued today, in spite of advances in our understanding of "human aptitudes." Working with military personnel in transitioning back to civilian life after the war, Haldane had already begun the development of the Dependable Strengths Articulation Process (see below), which would contribute to his recognition as a key innovator in the field of career management. Haldane's work was pioneering and inspirational and is perhaps best characterized by his view that, because you are unique, there is something you are better at than anyone else.

The third pioneer is Donald O. Clifton (1924–2003), formally recognized by the American Psychological Association as the "grandfather of positive psychology and the father of strengths psychology." Clifton dedicated his working life to the question of what you discover when you look at what is *right* with people. In leading development at Gallup of the Clifton StrengthsFinder assessment tool (see below) and in authoring or coauthoring several of the popular accompanying books, Clifton did more than anyone else has yet done to raise awareness of strengths and facilitate strengths use and development.

Strengths Identification

Inventories and Surveys

Clifton and colleagues at Gallup interviewed many thousands of professionals to discover the "themes of talent" associated with excellent performance. They developed a model of strengths as being the combination of these innate talents with skill and knowledge, acquired through learning and practice. The Clifton StrengthsFinder tool was developed to assess the 34 most common talent themes and accompanied by books providing details of the themes and suggestions for their development. Made available through the purchase of one of these books (which include a unique access code) the Clifton StrengthsFinder has been used by over 1 million people.

A more recent strengths classification project, under the leadership of positive psychologists Christopher Peterson and Martin Seligman, has resulted in the development of another strengths identification tool, the VIA Inventory of Strengths (VIA-IS). Freely available online (www.viastrengths.org) the VIA-IS looks set to attract an even larger number of users. Based on a combination of literature review and consultation with subject experts, this tool measures 24 character strengths that are believed to be universally valued, across time and culture. These are grouped under Wisdom and knowledge, Courage, Humanity, Justice, Temperance, and Transcendence, virtues which are thought to derive from the exercise of the relevant character strengths. Just as the Clifton StrengthsFinder reports the five most dominant themes of talent, so the VIA-IS sets out to provide its users with their five "signature strengths."

A third inventory, the Inspirational Leadership Tool (ILT), was developed in the UK by Caret Consulting on behalf of the state Department of Trade and Industry. The basis of this classification was a literature review, again, this time combined with a survey of 2,600 British workers. The ILT measures 18 attributes of leadership, clustered in four groups: Creating the future; Enthusing, growing, and appreciating others; Clarifying values; and Ideas to action. With its focus on leadership, the ILT is unsuitable for general use and fewer supporting resources are available than for either the Clifton StrengthsFinder or the VIA-IS. However, it is also distinguished from these other tools by the fact it reports the user's scores on the complete list of strengths. Limiting results to the top five strengths is likely to exclude some strengths (among those ranked 6–10, say) that are not currently "in play" and others of which the user is relatively unaware. Since some of our greatest opportunities for development are to be found in these areas, it is a significant limitation of the leading strengths assessment tools.

A limitation shared by all these tools is that the classifications themselves include only a limited number of strengths (34, 24 and 18 respectively), albeit the ones judged to be most significant in the terms of their creators. The research behind the Clifton StrengthsFinder itself identified several hundred "talent themes" and the Personality Strengths Project, which is concerned with identifying, defining, measuring and classifying strengths, has – at the time of writing – identified over 100 different strengths. The danger is that a tool based on a reduced number of strengths is likely to provide insufficiently precise assessments of some strengths and will miss others completely. The Dependable Strengths Articulation Process (DSAP) developed by Bernard Haldane avoids this problem. Through a systematic process of reviewing "good experiences" and how he or she made them happen, the user is relied upon to identify their own strengths and in their own terms. As well as avoiding artificial limitation of the strengths assessed, it is argued that the results of such an assessment are more comprehensible and meaningful to the user. It might also be argued, however, that this method of assessment is itself limited, in this case by the perception, structure of interpretation and language of the user. Indeed, many coaches invite a coachee to use a strengths assessment tool as a way of introducing or reinforcing a language of strengths that many lack.

Strengths Spotting

More often than not, assessment tools are used in coaching as a way of beginning a conversation, with equal or greater focus being placed on discussion of the results and their significance. In conversation there is the opportunity not only to engage the coachee in analysis of his or her strengths, but also for the coach to make and share their own observations about the strengths displayed. For a strengths coach in any setting, the skill of "strengths spotting" is essential. Strengths spotting involves listening for and observing the hallmarks of a strength, among which energy, appetite and a repeated pattern of successful performance are key. Based on the principles of strengths spotting, strengths coaches at the Centre for Applied Positive Psychology (CAPP) have developed a methodology called the Individual Strengths Assessment. Using a semi-structured interview, the coach works with the participant in joint construction of an appreciation of the coachee's strengths through question-led exploration and dialogue. The advantage of this approach over the strengths assessment inventories is its sensitivity to context and to a wide array of possible strengths. Other strengths assessment approaches developed and used by CAPP include the design of bespoke strengths profiles (e.g. a framework of leadership strengths) and strengths-based 360 degree feedback.

Self-Assessment

Whatever other methods may be used, an essential component of strengths identification in coaching is the coachee's own assessment. When provided with a strengths assessment, the coachee's validation of the results is essential if they are to be fully understood and internalized. In the case of strengths, there are often barriers to be overcome (see below). Self-assessment of strengths can also be used as an alternative to external assessment and usually takes the form of self-observation over a period of time. An example is provided by Marcus Buckingham in *Go Put Your Strengths to Work*. He suggests the 3-step process of: 1) capture (making a note of what you are doing when you feel powerful, confident, natural, etc., and also when you feel drained, frustrated, forced, etc); 2) clarify (in each case asking yourself where this applies, where it does not, and how far it can be generalized); and 3) confirm (testing possible strengths against a set of 12 questions which relate to what you do, the way you do it, how you feel about it and how successful you are in it). Exercises in self-observation of strengths are an important part of the coaching process, not least because, ultimately, the coachee will be the best judge of their own strengths. Critically, also, they help to equip the coachee with the understanding and technique they need in order to go on developing their strengths when the coaching is over.

Enabling Optimal Use and Development of Strengths

Barriers to Strengths Coaching

Beyond a simple resistance to change, the most significant barrier to focusing on strengths in coaching is our negativity bias. The relic of a defensive mechanism we carry with us from our evolutionary past, this makes us more attuned to the negative, the problem or the deficit. There are also a number of reasons why people can find it difficult to talk about their strengths. First there is the difficulty many people have in receiving positive feedback, whether that be out of a concern for appearing (or becoming) arrogant, the fear of raised expectations or, more fundamentally, out of an inability to see or relate to the positive. Added to that is the practical obstacle that we do not yet have a well-developed language of strengths. Many strengths remain unidentified as a result. The strengths coach often needs to introduce new language before understanding of the perspective, or of a particular strength, can be achieved. In so doing, the strengths coach needs to balance the interests of clarity with the risk of alienating or disengaging the coachee, and to use the coachee's own terminology wherever possible. Finally, there is the misconception that a strengths approach must be soft, unscientific or unbusinesslike. This view is sometimes reinforced by one-dimensional depictions of strengths as a panacea, leaving some people in no doubt that the approach is unrealistic.

Attending to Weaknesses

While it is true that the strengths perspective suggests that developing weaknesses will be less productive than developing strengths, strengths coaching is also concerned with weakness. First, it is hard to understand where we are strong without also understanding where we are weak. In practice, it appears that people who are clear (and feel good about) their strengths are more prepared to face up to and do something about their weaknesses. Second, coachees need to be aware of the time they spend on activities in which they are weak, where both their performance and well-being might be at risk. The third concern is the opportunity cost of spending time and energy unproductively. The approach towards weaknesses in strengths coaching is first to ask, does it matter? If the area of weakness is irrelevant in terms of what the coachee or their organization is trying to achieve, it can be ignored. Then, if it does matter, can it be made irrelevant by redesigning the role or the approach to the project? Then, if it cannot be made irrelevant, there may be a need to find a collaborator with complimentary strengths for support or, finally, to accept that it will be necessary to invest in developing the required level of skill.

Harnessing Strengths

It is central to the value of 1:1 coaching that support can be focused on, cognizant of and tailored to the specific circumstances of the individual. And strengths, like weaknesses, are sensitive to context. It was shown above how the coachee might be enabled (among other means) to use their *current situation* to identify and clarify strengths; having done so, they will be better able to bring their identified strengths to bear on *current challenges* and to use them as a foundation on which to build their *future*.

A key concept in enabling optimal use of strengths is the understanding that strengths can be both underplayed and overplayed, and, since this is little understood, an important objective of strengths coaching is to help the coachee see where (in the terms of Bob Kaplan and Rob Kaiser's *Versatile Leader*) they may need to turn up or turn down the volume. Alex Linley explains the idea of optimal use of strengths with reference to Aristotle's "golden mean," which is about doing the right thing, to the right amount, in the right way, at the right time.

Most often the underuse of a strength results from now knowing that we have it – it may come so naturally to us that we do not notice it, or we do not notice that others lack it. The practice of developing underused strengths, our most fertile area for development, is as simple as experimenting with using them more and in different situations. Recent research into a number of positive psychological interventions by Seligman, Steen, Park and Peterson found that using a signature strength in a new way resulted in lasting increases of happiness and decreases of depressive symptoms over a 6 month period.

Strengths can be overplayed when we are under pressure to perform, when we do not know another way of achieving a task or when we continue to use the same strength without noticing that the context has changed. The concept of the volume control (rather than an on/off switch) helps coachees to understand the workings of their strengths and realize that they are able to do something less or only in particular circumstances and thus achieve greater versatility.

Finally, the coachee can be enabled to build a future on the foundation of his strengths. If strengths are allowed to inform the process of goal-setting, which is at the center of many coaching conversations, the coachee's pursuit of those goals will benefit from the combination of capacity, motivation and well-being that flow naturally from strengths use. Also, in their achievement, the coachee will experience the fulfillment of self-actualization.

Future Directions

Alongside basic research into the general nature of strengths and the nature of particular strengths, it is hoped that applied research in the area of strengths coaching will begin to provide an empirical base for practice in due course. The question of the effectiveness of strengths coaching, when compared to other forms of coaching, would be of particular interest. In practice, the tools available to support the critical area of strengths assessment are not yet as effective and reliable as they need to be. Current provision of training and development in strengths coaching, although begun in one or two corners (including at the Centre for Applied Positive Psychology), appears to be insufficient to meet the likely demand, either from within or from outside the corporate sector.

Strengths coaching is not new but, perhaps in response to the needs of the age, its theoretical foundations are deepening and its practice becoming more widespread. Many coaches already hold the perspective of, and use approaches associated with, strengths coaching. Others may benefit from considering how and why the perspective of strengths coaching rubs against their existing assumptions about coaching, well-being and human or organizational development; and they will certainly benefit from adding some strengths-based approaches to their repertoire. All will be able to learn from the theoretical and practical developments which arise from the growing interest in this field.

SEE ALSO: ▶ Applied positive psychology   ▶ Coaching psychology
▶ Strengths-based organization   ▶ Strengths perspective (positive psychology)

References

Drucker, P. F. (1967). *The effective executive*. London: Heinemann.

Haldane, B. (1947). A pattern for executive placement. *Harvard Business Review, 25*(4a), 652–663.

International Coach Federation. (2007). Retrieved December 10, 2007, from: http://www.coachfederation.org/ICF/For+Coaching+Clients/What+is+a+Coach/FAQs/

Linley, A. (2008). *Average to A+: Realising strengths in yourself and others*. Coventry, UK: CAPP Press.

Whitmore, Sir J. (2002). *Coaching for performance*. London: Nicholas Brealey.

Strengths Perspective (Positive Psychology)

P. Alex Linley
Centre for Applied Positive Psychology, UK

The strengths perspective is fundamentally concerned with what is right, what is working, and what is strong. It is interested in prevention, strength, and appreciation. It stands in contrast to the deficit model, and its interest in treatment, weakness, and alleviation. The strengths perspective could be described as being interested in taking people from +3 to +8, that is, building on what is right, whereas traditional deficit models are more focused on taking people from −8 to −3, that is, ameliorating what is wrong. The strengths perspective represents the fundamental assumption of positive psychology at the meta-theoretical level. At the pragmatic level, positive psychology can be defined in relation to the topic areas within its remit. At the meta-theoretical level it can be defined in relation to the approach that is taken to the study of those topic areas, with reference to the nature of the research questions that are asked, and the approaches that are taken, in dealing with the topic areas of pragmatic concern. As such, the strengths perspective represents a philosophical position that defines the approach of positive psychology.

The Deficit Model and the Need for the Strengths Perspective

The deficit model prevalent in traditional psychology stands as the counterpoint to the strengths perspective, and accounts for the existence and need for the strengths perspective. The deficit model, informed by the early history of clinical psychology training within psychiatric hospitals and assumptions, became the dominant model in psychology following World War II, driven by the research and intervention dollars of the Veterans Administration (founded in 1946) and the National Institutes of Mental Health (founded in 1947), both of which were focused on the amelioration and treatment of psychopathology. Given this illness focus, the illness ideology took root within psychology, and became the dominant assumption, typically unquestioned and uncritically accepted, of many psychologists.

The illness ideology equates psychological problems with biological problems, holding that they rest in the biology of the individual, rather than being influenced by a wider social context. As such, these problems require medical intervention that is best administered by suitably qualified medical experts, with this intervention typically being delivered in medical establishments. Such was the typical model that was also applied to clinical psychology throughout the second half of the twentieth century. This negativity bias, for which substantial empirical evidence has been provided, also pervaded empirical psychology throughout the second half of the twentieth century, with social and cognitive psychologists, for example, more typically focused on errors, biases, illusions and delusions – the negative poles of their areas of inquiry – rather than more positive constructs.

In this context of the deficit model, the strengths perspective was put forward as an alternative fundamental assumption for the positive psychology approach. Rather than focusing on what is broken, the strengths perspective focuses on what works, on what is improving, on what is strong and effective. It works from the counterassumption that growth can best ensue from working on what is already effective to make it even better, that the biggest improvements come from taking something that is "average" and making it "superb," rather than taking it from "bad" to "not bad." Understood in this way, the strengths perspective is ultimately a mindset shift, a change in philosophy and assumptions, which then subsequently leads to new ways of framing old questions, and to new questions that have not been previously considered.

The Origins of the Strengths Perspective

The origins of the strengths perspective in positive psychology may be traced explicitly to Martin E. P. Seligman's presidential address in 1999 which inaugurated the field of positive psychology, but these origins are also informed by the work of Marcus Buckingham and Donald Clifton in relation to the strengths revolution. The strengths revolution described by Buckingham and Clifton was interested in shifting the focus from what is wrong with people to what is right with people, and understanding the strengths that people possess which enable them to deliver their best performances and be functioning at their most optimal level.

Almost inevitably, however, one can also trace other roots and influences of what is now recognized as the strengths perspective. In organization development, David Cooperrider's appreciative inquiry is also focused on what is working and what is best. In business, Jim Collins and Jerry Porras studied companies that could be distinguished between being good and being great. In social work, Charles Rapp and Dennis Saleebey are two of the pioneers of strengths-based social work practice. In the field of psychotherapy, Steve de Shazer's solution-focused therapy shares similar principles with a focus on the solution, rather than the problem. In community psychology, the work of Emory Cowen was typically focused on wellness and what was right with people. In the field of psychological trauma, Richard Tedeschi and Lawrence Calhoun introduced the concept of posttraumatic growth as a label for the experience of positive outcomes following trauma, in contrast to the dominant focus on posttraumatic stress disorder. In health, Aaron Antonovsky promoted the concept of salutogenesis to describe processes that contribute to healthy physical and psychological outcomes. In all cases, these approaches have challenged the predominant emphasis of the field on pathology, problem, dysfunction, and disease. The strengths perspective in positive psychology has done the same for the field of psychology, as well as providing the impetus for the establishment of new areas of focus, including positive organizational scholarship and applied positive psychology.

Empirical Evidence for the Strengths Perspective

There are, to date, a handful of studies that speak to the central premise of the strengths perspective, that is, that the strong get stronger. Perhaps the earliest demonstration of this was the doctoral work of J. W. Glock during the 1950s. The Nebraska School Study Council supported a statewide research project, involving around 6,000 10th grade students, which aimed to investigate different methods of teaching rapid reading. Upon analyzing the data, it was found that the students who were the better readers at the outset had made the greatest gains in their rapid reading ability, increasing their reading rate from around 300 words per minute to approximately 2,900 words per minute. While the poor readers had improved, their gains were insignificant by comparison.

Research by the Corporate Leadership Council in 2001 with a diverse sample of 19,187 employees found that a focus on performance strengths enhanced performance by 36.4%, and a focus on personality strengths enhanced performance by 21.3%. In contrast, a focus on performance or personality weaknesses both led to declines in performance. Clearly, focusing on strengths enabled better performance, one interpretation of which is that the best got better, as with the students learning to read more rapidly.

In a study designed to assess a goal attainment support intervention with 90 psychology undergraduates, Kennon Sheldon and colleagues found, unexpectedly, that participants who were already well-integrated benefited most from an intervention to enhance their goal attainment. They interpreted this in relation to dynamical systems models. Nonlinear dynamical systems are poised for continuous evolution and shift towards ever more highly organized and effective states. Thus, they are receptive to interventions designed to change their state, and integrate these interventions toward increasing their efficiency and effectiveness.

Understood in this way, people who are already well-functioning are likely to have existing forward momentum in their lives and therefore to be in a position to transform themselves and grow even further. The same principles can be extended to an understanding of the strengths perspective in relation to the strong getting stronger: Well-functioning individuals who are working from their strengths are already successful in their lives. This success, in turn, primes them with a readiness to adapt further to ensure future success. In contrast, people who have not attained this successful state are likely to be more static, and may not have the resources to move beyond their existing circumstances.

The same parallel applies to a focus on developing weaknesses: When people are not good at something, they struggle perennially to take it to a level of mastery. Another explanation that may be applied to this issue is that architecture of neural circuitry. It is well-established that mastering a new domain involves strengthening the neural connections in the brain that underpin the affect, behavior, or cognition that is relevant to that domain. Equally, through genetic selection and early environmental experiences, people have predispositions to particular ways of thinking, feeling or behaving. Trying to change these established neural circuits (that is, strengthening a weakness) is much harder than building on existing neural circuits (that is, enhancing a strength). Overall, the evidence points to easier and more effective momentum, whether in relation to performance or to growth, when people are working from a basis of strength. This forms one of the central tenets of the strengths perspective.

The Strengths Perspective at the Pragmatic Level

While recognizing the strengths perspective as a fundamental assumption and approach at the meta-theoretical level, it can also be understood and presented at the pragmatic level, that is, in relation to the topics of interest within its remit. In this way, the strengths perspective in positive psychology has engendered a range of research in relation to strengths as individual differences within psychology, whether from the perspective of character strengths, occupational strengths, or personality strengths, or at the individual construct level through the study of human strengths including hope, optimism, creativity, empathy, gratitude, and kindness, for example. At the individual construct level, it is recognized that many of the constructs had been investigated as individual differences prior to the advent of the strengths perspective. They were not, however, investigated as constructs with reference to a wider framework and understanding of them as human strengths, and it is this wider framework and context that the strengths perspective has enabled.

Historically, the study of human strengths was effectively defined as being outside the remit of psychology by the Harvard personality psychologist, Gordon Allport, who defined *character* (within the parameters of which strengths may have been studied) as being part of ethics and philosophy, rather than personality, and so having no further place in psychology. The effect of Allport's pronouncement was that psychologists effectively ignored the research and applications of strengths in any systematic way, until, that is, the strengths perspective was put forward within positive psychology, and systematic and extensive research into human strengths was undertaken. At the individual difference level for strengths, exemplars of the strengths perspective in positive psychology include the different strengths identified and studied in the Clifton StrengthsFinder, the VIA Inventory of Strengths, and the work of the Personality Strengths Project. While each of these approaches differs in their specific understanding of strengths and as a result in the constructs they identify as strengths, all share the common heritage of being informed by the strengths perspective in positive psychology.

Strengths and Weaknesses in Context

Taking the meta-theoretical and pragmatic levels of the strengths perspective together, a further emerging central tenet of the strengths perspective could be taken to be the advice to focus on building on strengths while ignoring weaknesses. This view has been taken by some to be the clarion call of the strengths movement, but it is a view misplaced. In practice, more practical wisdom and mature perspective is required. While it is the case that focusing on strengths leads to more positive outcomes than trying exclusively to develop weaknesses, this position should not be interpreted as an excuse for an absolute focus on strengths and an absolute ignorance of weaknesses. Such an approach simply transposes the problem of imbalance from one end of the continuum to the other. In contrast, the question of where to focus requires the application of practical wisdom to establish the right thing to do, in the right way, and at the right time.

If a weakness is identified as performance-critical, and other means of emasculating it cannot be established, then it has to be dealt with – and often through the typical development means advocated by traditional approaches, including skills training, remedial coaching, or behavioral intervention. Similarly, the mature strengths perspective recognizes that strengths are strengths only so long as they are defined as strengths by the situation and context: honesty taken too far can become cruelty; curiosity overplayed can become nosiness.

Within the leadership literature, Bob Kaplan and Rob Kaiser have identified the need for leadership versatility, that is, the need to turn up and turn down different leadership strengths according to the demands of the situation, while being mindful that taking one strength too far likely indicates a deficit in the exercise of a strength at the corresponding pole. Their empirical research indicates that leadership effectiveness is significantly and substantially predicted by leadership versatility, thereby speaking to the need to deploy strengths appropriately as the situation demands, another example of practical wisdom in practice.

Current Challenges and Future Directions

These challenges, and the need for practical wisdom to determine when, how, and to what extent strengths should be deployed, form the state of the science for the applications of the strengths perspective. Applied work in organizations is addressing these issues, and the coming years can be expected to produce significant advances as interest and applications of strengths-based organization progress. Empirically, while dislocated studies and insights exist, much work remains to systematically integrate and expand what is known about the strengths perspective in positive psychology, and the value of applications and interventions that are developed from this position. Work to date does suggest, however, that building from strengths can be one of the most significantly powerful ways in which people can be enabled to deliver their best performances at work and in life. Future investigations should bear out precisely where, how, and with whom strengths-focused interventions and applications deliver the greatest value and benefit.

SEE ALSO: ▶ Character strengths (VIA) ▶ Strengths (Gallup)
▶ Strengths (personality) ▶ Strengths perspective (social welfare)

Strengths Perspective (Social Welfare)

Dennis Saleebey
University of Kansas

The essential ideas of a strengths approach to practice are these. It is far more productive, conducive to positive change and interesting for both clients and helpers to concentrate on, and marshal individual and collective resources in our work.

It brings new energy, and can lead to inventive pathways for client change. In the past we have been far too energetic in seeking out and highlighting the deficits and troubles that people bring to us. What follows is a brief introduction to elements of the strengths perspective in social welfare.

In American culture, in its many varieties, strengths-based ideas can be traced back to the ideals of democracy, the importance of diversity, the romance of the frontier, Transcendentalism, the Social Gospel, and more currently, the empowerment literature, all marching along to the unrelenting drumbeat of positive thinking. In the history of the dominant culture, strains of optimism, hope, positive expectations, the promise of tomorrow, and the possibility of remaking the self have flourished in one form or another. Evident in philosophies, religions, as well as nostrums and panaceas peddled by a variety of gurus and evangelists, today we find the shelves of libraries, bookstores and online booksellers bursting with manifestos on self-development and improvement. This is a robust remnant of a frontier mentality – paradise is just over the next rise and the self is always conditional. The profession of social work has a long tradition of interest in building on the strengths of individuals, families, and communities as part of its repertoire.

The further articulation of the strengths-based ideas in social work began at the University of Kansas School of Social Welfare in 1982 and eventually became the strengths model of case management with people with severe and persistent mental illness. In 1982, the School was awarded $10,000 to provide case management services to those people with serious mental illness (schizophrenia, principally). Professor Charles Rapp and then doctoral student Ronna Chamberlain evaluated the standard practice of case management with this group. On the basis of their findings regarding the usual practices of case management with this population, they were convinced that with its emphasis on connecting clients only with official, institutional mental health services case management as practiced could not realize the outcomes that were most important to the people being served – living in the community, real work, constructive and enjoyable use of leisure time, and independent living. So they abandoned that conventional approach and developed another, based on the recognition and recruitment of individual and community strengths in order to achieve "normalization." A field unit of four social work students, supervised by Chamberlain, did a trial run of the model and found that, over the course of the year, 19 of 22 indicators of positive outcome were realized. The model rapidly expanded conceptually and practically so that by the middle of the 1980s it had become the bellwether of community support services in mental health in the state of Kansas. Strengths model training spread to other states, and also broadened to work with other populations – the elderly, youth in trouble with the law, community development, parents and children in the child welfare system, and TANF (Temporary Aid to Needy Families) recipients. But it was Rapp and Chamberlain and their associates at the University of Kansas who built the conceptual, ethical, and methodological framework for the launching of the model.

In 1988, a small seminar involving scholars and practitioners from around the country who had been working with ideas and tools that seemed strengths oriented was convened at the University of Kansas School of Social Welfare. Two days of paper presentations and discussions were later fashioned into a book on the strengths perspective, *The Strengths Perspective in Social Work Practice*, now in its fourth edition.

Philosophy and Principles of the Strengths Perspective

The strengths perspective in social work practice is based, in part, on the strengths model of case management. But it is applied, primarily, in direct clinical work with individuals and families, as well as community-building work, in mental health and other fields of practice as well. The values and philosophy of the strengths perspective clearly overlap with those of social work and other human service professions. At a minimum, these include the beliefs that: 1) all people, individually and collectively, no matter how dispirited, despised, or disorganized have the urge and the right to develop their human nature and capacities; 2) social groupings function well when their members ply their strengths and competencies toward the social good – such resources are a fundamental kind of social capital; 3) out of misfortune and tragedy may come despair and defeat, but also transformation, redemption, and release of potential; and 4) to become the people(s) that we hope to become, the discovery and employment of those resources that fortify optimal human development, and strengthen the ligaments of community are essential.

At the core of the strengths perspective are two philosophical/conceptual strains that reflect two undying elements of the human condition: oppression and liberation. *Liberation* refers to the boundless possibilities for choice, action, and belief, even in dire circumstances. Somewhere within, all humans have the urge to be heroic: to transcend difficult conditions, to develop their potential, to overcome hardship, to be recognized, and responsible. Too often this urge is suppressed or thoroughly crushed by a variety of institutional and interpersonal influences and circumstances. Imprisoned within the margins of such oppressive conditions, some still find the courage and cunning to liberate themselves, if only in spirit. *Oppression*, on the other hand, involves the considered impeding of human capacities and possibilities, and collective will. Oppression, like liberation, can be subtle or flagrant, and it often veils to the observer and to those who experience it, the reality of their strengths and resources, and their dreams of a better life. As the great pedagogue and practitioner of liberation, Paulo Freire (1995) put it: "There is no change without the dream as there is no dream without hope. (p. 91)" The dream is the "untested feasible" – a transformative idea if there ever was one.

These imperatives can be further reduced to a subset of three beliefs, each with some refining secondary tenets.

Empowerment

There is a saying among Caucasus mountaineers: "Heroism is endurance for one moment more!" Many of the people we seek to assist have endured situations and conditions that stagger our minds and break our hearts. This is the starting point of the work of empowerment: We must discover how people have managed to survive; how they have summoned the grit to confront or simply endure their tribulations. Tapping into the energy and imagination, the will and promise of individuals is to help them recover or command the power to change, using old skills and resources and/or discovering and developing new ones. We commonly don't know fully or very well what people, individually or collectively, are capable of. Sometimes they don't either. But the budding literature on resilience, strengths, positive psychology, health realization, solution-focused and narrative approaches to practice offers some clues about how people, collectively and individually, endure and surmount adversity. Drawing from these domains as well as its own essential principles, the strengths perspective affirms that, without exception, *every* individual, *every* family, *every* community, and *every* culture has assets, capacities, and wisdom to be used in the making of a better life. While suffering subjugation of the body, spirit, and/or environment, people inevitably learn things, acquire competencies, unearth resources, and foster personal traits and relationships that may become the devices of, and provide energy for, change. Every human being has innate wisdom, a sense of what is right for them, a capacity for self-righting that, while they might be obscured by negative expectations, labels, regrettable decisions, bad luck, nonetheless remain important resources to be tapped. The hatch marks of divergence and difference between people, whether they are drawn by culture or class, or values and beliefs, or gender and sexual orientation should be regarded as distinctive resources for meeting the challenges of facing trials and realizing one's hopes. But, in the end, people empower themselves. That notwithstanding, the crux of much of the work that we do is connecting people and resources in the service of releasing their energy and capacity, of helping them become agents on their own behalf.

Resources

A decade ago, Kretzmann and McKnight contended that, in approaching communities that are under siege or in economic and social distress, our usual predilection as professionals is to turn them into *clients* (clearly we do this with individuals and families as well). We should be mindful here of the distinction between service and care. Care involves a consent and commitment on the part of all parties involved. Such care is the manifestation of community. All too often service involves the importation of unfamiliar ideas and alien agendas, and making community members dependent on those in order to continue receiving assistance. Anyone working in the community must be attentive to the fact that every environment has unused, abundant natural resources and assets – individuals, associations, institutions, families, symbols, celebrations, heroes, heritage, rituals and tools – that can be part of the emancipation from socioeconomic and political burdens. The potential of a community is a function of the combined assets and resources of each individual and family in that community. When people are working together for common and urgent intentions an energy that can transform elements of any community is created.

In terms of individuals, the possible resources and assets any individual might possess are untold. Certainly these include talents, skills, personal traits and virtues, lessons learned from experience, connections to others, spirituality, cultural meaning systems and rituals, personal and communal beliefs and values, and hopes and dreams. It is impossible to actually know the limits and parameters of a person's talents and capabilities. Neither can we convincingly gauge the boundaries of a person's potential for development and transformation.

Possibilities

Many people who seek the help of social workers and other professionals at first seem unable to surmount the trauma and pain inflicted on them by others or by themselves. They are stuck in the past and cannot conceive a brighter future. Many of the labels we affix to them (e.g., bipolar borderline personality disorder, victim) and the approaches we take with them may aggravate that. But human beings are always in the making and full of possibilities even though this may be hidden by despair and anguish. In helping individuals, families, and communities rekindle the spark provided by their hopes and dreams, existing desires and needs should be taken seriously, elaborated as vividly and vigorously as possible. Steps toward the dream should be made explicit and the taking of them conceived as a collaborative project between the social worker and the individual or family. One often finds hope expressed in the vocabularies of promise, possibilities, and positive expectations. These become the conceptual basis for drawing blueprints for the future.

These principles and their correlates provide a way of thinking about those we help, their day-to-day lives, and the contexts in which they work, love, and play. Working from a strengths perspective does require something of a different lens and language for looking at, and naming the worlds where we do our work. A strengths approach to practice, persuades us and our clients to, in Emily Dickinson's felicitous phrase, "dwell in possibility" (1960, p. 327), to be hopeful, and to believe in the individual, family, or community – even or especially when they do not believe in themselves.

By way of summary, imagine an equilateral triangle. The left angle is fronted by the letter *C*; the angle to the right by the letter *R*. The apex of the triangle is topped with the letter *P*–CPR, as it were. *C* represents capacities, competencies, courage, and character. *R* symbolizes resources, resilience, relationships, resolve, and reserves. *P* stands for promise, positive expectations, potential, purpose, and possibility. This imaginary graphic signifies the dynamic core of a strengths-based approach to practice. All three "angles" must be a part of any kind of healing or helping. The calculating of all three dimensions and how they are played out in the contexts of people's lives becomes the essence of an assessment of strengths and assets. In the original sense of CPR, we breathe for someone until they can breathe for themselves. In this CPR, we believe in someone until they can believe in themselves.

Core Conditions of Change

In a survey of the research carried out into psychotherapy over the last couple of decades, Ted Asay and Michael Lambert concluded that, when it works, psychotherapy is driven by four common factors that reach across schools of thought, theories of psychotherapy, and clinical practice of all kinds. We can take them even further to provide some conceptual ballast for a strengths-based approach to helping.

The Environment: Strengths, Resources, and Contingencies

The matrix of clients' daily lives includes their capacities, interests, beliefs, and skills. Likewise, the socioeconomic, political, and cultural resources in the environment can make potent contributions to a change for the better. This web of resources in individuals' surroundings, such as social support networks, as well as their own assets and knowledge has a great deal to do with quality of day-to-day life. It is also true and usually overlooked, that the play of contingencies (luck) in people's lives can be a significant source of change and challenge. In the end, the interaction of these factors may matter more than the ministrations of professional helpers. Asay and Lambert claim that in their review of the research these factors accounted for 40% of the positive change. The strengths perspective encourages professionals to capitalize on these resources in a deliberate and responsive way.

The Caring Relationship

It has been a shibboleth of sorts in the social work profession that the medium of change is ultimately the helping relationship. Over half a century ago, Carl Rogers and his associates defined the core conditions of change as the vital elements of therapeutic relationships – caring, empathy, respect, unconditional positive regard, and genuineness. The palpable presence of these assured that a therapeutic alliance would develop between the helper and the helped. In his research and a review of others' research over the past 30 years or so, Hans Strupp claims that the quality of the helping relationship is the root factor underlying positive change. Practitioners of the strengths perspective add to these conditions the importance of collaboration – developing a mutually crafted project to work on, the cooperative laying out of a concrete path to dreams and hopes. Charles Rapp and Rick Goscha, drawing from the work of Deegan state that, "The relationship between service provider and participant is based on compassion, understanding, and knowing each other as unique individuals" (2006, p. 32). They further define the effective helping relationship in a strengths approach as purposeful, reciprocal, friendly, conversational, mirroring, trusting, and spirit-inducing (as opposed to spirit-breaking) as well as reflecting the core conditions – empathy, genuineness, and unconditional positive regard. Asay and Lambert posited, in their review of outcome research, that the relationship accounted for about 30% of the positive change in clients' lives.

Positive Expectations, Hope and the Placebo Effect

Of great interest to those who subscribe to a strengths-based orientation is the influence of positive expectations, hope, and the placebo effect. Consider the following: Michael Fisher reported recently that in the 1950s at the University of Kansas Medical Center, in order to test a new medical procedure for the treatment of angina, surgeons performed real operations on one group of patients with angina, and a "placebo operation" on the other group of men with angina. The placebo group was told that they were going to have heart surgery; they were given a general anesthetic, and incisions were made in the chests. But no operation was done, the surgeons just messed around a little bit and the patients had the sutures and pain to indicate that they actually had surgery (the ethics of this seems, on the face of it, distressing but in 2005 Groopman reported that over the years there have been several sham surgery studies). Of the people who had the real surgery, 70% reported long-term improvement in their angina, but *all* of the placebo group did. It is not at all uncommon, in tests of psychoactive drugs, for the placebo groups to show anywhere from 25% to 60% improvement. The extent that the real drug is better than the placebo is thought to be the extent that the drug is effective. But we cannot say, for instance, just how much of the effect of the real drug is also a placebo phenomenon. The most thorough and statistically adroit study in this area was undertaken by physicians who, using the Freedom of Information Act, were able to get results of clinical trials over the last 15 years reported by drug companies to the Food and Drug Administration for the six most popular antidepressants (Selective Serotonin Reuptake Inhibitors; SSRI). Up until then no-one had access to the results of these trials so we have had to take the drug companies' word about their efficacy. Here, Kirsch and his fellow researchers conducted several meta-analyses of these data and, no matter how generous or conservative their analysis, they found *no clinically significant differences* between the drugs and the placebos. "Whatever else this means it does, I think, bespeak the power of hope, possibility, positive expectations, and the belief in the healing power of the ministration" (Saleebey, 2006). Expectancy and the placebo effect account for 15% of desirable change according to Asay and Lambert. It would not be surprising if the effect were somewhat larger than that.

We can suggest, then, that the power of positive expectations, belief in the possibilities inherent in the individual, family, or community, and the mysterious placebo effect are truly important to the process of change. These inhere in the strengths perspective. Pat Deegan, who in spite of (and in some instances because of) the many vulnerabilities in her life triumphed over them in pursuit of her dreams (she became a professional psychologist, for example) says this:

> The Strengths Model . . . represents a powerful antidote to the high cost of the deficits approach. In this model, strength is not constructed as some superheroic state of invulnerability. Rather, we learn that even when people present with obvious vulnerabilities, they also have strengths. Their strengths are in their passions, in their skills, in their interests, in their relationships, and in their environments. (2006, p. viii)

Contrast the pictures that the strengths perspective paints with those drawn in 2000 by the authors of the *Diagnostic and Statistical Manual* (DSM-IV-TR) of the American Psychiatric Association. Although each carries heavy symbolic and linguistic freight, creating expectations and, over time, suffusing into identities of those so portrayed, the diagnostic gallery of the DSM, unleavened by the acknowledgment of positive attributes, constitutes a kind of rhetorical and symbolic whammy, a canvas of dreadful, and ominous portraits.

Related to the power of the placebo is the *plasticity of the brain*. Once thought to be as virtual monolith after adolescence, it is now known that the brain is changing constantly. It is something of a miracle that this organ, as Richard Restak observes, " never loses the power to transform itself on the basis of experience and the transformation can occur over short intervals. . . . your brain is different today than it was yesterday." (2003, p. 8) As neuroscientists know, most of these changes take place at the synapse (the space through which neurons chemically "communicate" with each other) and are the result of experience and learning or simply one's current state of mind (emotions, for example, have a profound ability to change the brain, both in the moment and, occasionally, permanently). Therefore, we have a stunning capacity to alter, extend, and reshape our behavior, feeling, motivation, and cognition. This is why talk therapies can be successful because, at one level, when we interact with each other, we are talking to our brains. As we do so, we effect minute changes in the brain's (and, thus, the mind's) landscape. And as we do that, we may be party to changes in the way people perceive and act in their environments. This is also why, individually and collectively, our brains will be different tomorrow than today because they undergo these relentless minute alterations daily.

The Technical Operations of the Theory or Perspective

These contribute about as much to "therapeutic" gain as do positive expectations and hope. They do make a difference, of course, but not as much as we might think. It is clear, for example, that interpersonal therapy and cognitive-behavior therapy are generally effective treatments for moderately severe depression. It is also likely that without the presence of the above factors, they would be less potent.

Conclusion

It should be said here that the strengths perspective is not about ignoring the real adversity and ordeals that people must confront. Cancer, abuse, abandonment, war, interpersonal violence, for example, are on the daily menu for far too many people. The strengths approach, at the least, is about restoring balance to the way that we regard people contending with such tribulations and the way that we think about work that we do – "a balance that requires that we appreciate the struggles of an individual, family, or community but more importantly that we look at those struggles for hints and intimations, or solid evidence of strengths, capacities, and competencies" (Saleebey, 2006, p. 22).

Duncan and Miller (2000, p. 216) put it well:

> If therapists are to resist the pull to steer clients automatically toward diagnosis and medication, the belief in client capacity to conquer even extreme (and often dangerous) personal circumstances must go deep. Clients can use an ally in overcoming often dramatic obstacles to personal recovery. When professionals use their inevitable positions of power to hand power back to the clients rather than block client capacities, clients can even more readily reach their goals.

On a much broader canvas, the historian Howard Zinn (1999, p. 648) paints this picture:

> To recall this [the many rebellions of the masses over the centuries] is to remind people of what the Establishment would like them to forget – the enormous capacity of apparently helpless people to resist, of apparently contented people to demand change. To uncover such history is to find a powerful human impulse to assert one's humanity. It is to hold, even in times of pessimism, the possibility of surprise.

Here's to that possibility.

SEE ALSO: ▶ Character strengths (VIA) ▶ Strengths (Gallup)
▶ Strengths (personality) ▶ Strengths coaching ▶ Strengths perspective (positive psychology)

References

Deegan, P. (2006). Foreword. In C. A. Rapp & R. J. Goscha, *The strengths model: Case management with people with psychiatric disabilities* (pp. vii–ix). New York: Oxford University Press.

Dickinson, E. (1960). *The complete poems of Emily Dickinson.* Ed. by Thomas A. Johnson. Boston: Back Bay Books/Little, Brown & Co.

Duncan, B. L., & Miller, S. D. (2000). *The heroic client: Doing client-directed, outcome-informed therapy.* San Francisco: Jossey-Bass.

Freire, P. (1995). *The pedagogy of hope.* New York: Continuum International.

Saleebey, D. (2006). Introduction: Power in the people. In D. Saleebey (Ed.), *The strengths perspective in social work practice* (4th ed., pp. 1–24). New York: Allyn & Bacon/Longman.

Strengths-Based Organization

Nicky Page and Dominic Carter
Centre for Applied Positive Psychology, UK

Strengths-based organization is a term used to describe both the process and the outcome of harnessing individual strengths for joint performance in organizations.

As Peter Drucker maintained:

> To make strength productive is the unique purpose of organization. It cannot, of course, overcome the weaknesses with which each of us is abundantly endowed. But it can make them irrelevant. Its task is to use the strength of each man as a building block for joint performance. (Drucker, 1967, p. 60)

Peter Drucker, Bernard Haldane, Donald Clifton, Marcus Buckingham, and Alex Linley have all offered significant insights into the theory and practice of strengths-based organization.

Recently Buckingham argued that it is not *people* that are an organization's greatest assets, but people's *strengths*. Among the organizations that have reached the same conclusion and are acting on it are the corporate members of the Centre for Applied Positive Psychology (CAPP). CAPP characterizes a strengths-based organization as an entity in which: *individuals* know their strengths, actively seeking to use and develop them; *managers* know the strengths of their people, also actively seeking to use and develop them; and the *organization* is equipped with the tools, processes and expertise required to support this.

There is growing evidence that significant organizational benefits accrue from this approach to cooperation and management. They include: tapping into unused talent, attracting and retaining the best people, improved individual performance, enhanced employee engagement, increased flexibility, enhanced working relations, and stronger teams. For example, a survey of over 19,000 employees by the Corporate Leadership Council in 2002 found that when manager feedback emphasized performance strengths, individual performance *improved* on average by 36.4%, whereas an emphasis on performance weaknesses had a negative impact on performance, with average *declines* in performance of -26.8%. The personal benefits associated with knowing and using one's strengths, including increased levels of happiness and well-being, combine with the organizational benefits to offer the possibility of a powerful double-win.

Despite this, few organizations have succeeded in implementing strengths-based practices throughout their whole corporate structure. Among the main challenges faced by those that try are: the absence or inconsistency of language around strengths; inexperience among employees and managers in identifying and harnessing strengths; and people management and development systems that have been designed principally to identify and eradicate weakness.

Organizations can begin to overcome these challenges by: "seeding" a consistent language of strengths; equipping managers and individuals to realize strengths; and embedding strengths-based approaches in their human resource management (HRM) strategies and systems.

A consistent language for strengths is essential to achieve a common understanding across the organization of what strengths are. CAPP's definition of a *strength* is "a pre-existing capacity for a particular way of behaving, thinking, or feeling that is authentic and energizing to the user, and enables optimal functioning, development and performance" (Linley, 2008). An organization's understanding of, and language for, strengths, can be developed simultaneously, through presentations, training, coaching and sharing written resources.

Equipping managers and individuals to identify and develop strengths starts with the activity of recognizing when strengths are being displayed, or "strengths spotting." Strengths spotting involves listening for and observing (usually over a period time) the hallmarks of a strength. Among these, energy, appetite and a repeated pattern of successful performance are key. Managers who successfully spot strengths are able to develop unique insights into what truly engages their employees. This practice is essential to the development of a strengths-oriented organizational culture and the information it provides is vital for optimal task allocation and employee development.

Developing people strategies and systems which help to embed strengths often starts with the reevaluation of current practices and procedures, and follows with the adaptation of these strategies and systems to support the identification of strengths in existing or potential employees, together with their effective deployment. Examples of organizations which have undertaken this realignment of HRM processes include Norwich Union, which has successfully introduced strengths-based recruitment, Standard Chartered Bank which has deployed a strengths-based approach to its people management, and BAE Systems, which has placed strengths at the heart of board-level leadership development in one of its major business units. In each case, the organizations associate their strengths-based initiatives with tangible business benefits.

Increasingly, organizations are coming round to the view that Drucker expressed over 30 years ago: that their best opportunity for competitive advantage lies in harnessing their employees' strengths. Although the field of strengths-based organization is emergent, it is already proving to deliver its promise of both individual and organizational benefits and performance results.

SEE ALSO: ▶ Applied positive psychology   ▶ Organizational psychology
▶ Positive organizational behavior   ▶ Positive organizational scholarship
▶ Strengths coaching

References

Drucker, P. F. (1967). *The effective executive*. London: Heinemann.
Linley, A. (2008). *Average to A+: Realising strengths in yourself and others*. Coventry, UK: CAPP
   Press.

Successful Aging

Gail M. Williamson and Juliette Christie
The University of Georgia

Aging successfully, remaining vital and actively engaged with life, is quite possible, and gerontological science focuses on finding ways to help our aging population live well in the years ahead.

History of Aging Research and Outlook for the Future

Historically, attitudes about aging have been fraught with mythical thinking, a short-sightedness we are just beginning to overcome. Traditionally, old people have been viewed as sick, cognitively inept, isolated, a financial drain on society, and depressed by their circumstances. These attitudes and the projected increase in elderly people within the next few years have seduced scholars, commentators, and policy-makers into the doomsday philosophy that our society is about to be overwhelmed by people who are disabled, requiring constant care, and not making worthwhile contributions. With fewer children per capita than previous generations, a major concern is that as the Baby Boomers age into disability, there will be fewer adult children available to provide care, creating a demand for formal (e.g., nursing home) care that may severely (if not, impossibly) tax societal resources.

Of course, as with any substantial demographic shift, there are concerns to be addressed. With these challenges, however, come opportunities, and we summarize evidence indicating that there are offsetting parallel, positive arguments to these catastrophic predictions. Many solutions revolve around actions that should be and, in some cases, already are being taken at governmental and societal levels. Fortunately, aging individuals and their immediate social networks can solve many problems without resorting to public assistance. The solution lies in changes in behavior that will enable older adults to continue to engage in valued normal activities with each advancing year. First, however, we need to take a real-istic look at today's elders and what future generations can expect as they age.

Are Old People Sick People?

An important truth is that most adults over age 65 are remarkably healthy. Rates of disability, even among the very old (i.e., those over age 95) as well as the percentage (and absolute numbers) of nursing home residents have been steadily declining since 1982. Along with increasingly widespread public know-ledge and acceptance of the behavioral aspects of chronic illness, advances in medical technology forecast an even rosier old age for Baby Boomers and sub-sequent generations. In addition, older adults are quite skilled in making gradual life-style changes to accommodate diminishing physical abilities. Also, nature is remarkably forgiving. In other words, it is never too late to begin a healthful lifestyle.

Are Old People Cognitively Deficient?

Cognitive abilities naturally slow down with increasing age. Luckily, however, the "use it or lose it" adage about sexual functioning also applies to learning and memory abilities. Short of organic disorders (e.g., Alzheimer's disease), older adults in cognitively challenging environments show minimal, if any, declines in think-ing and learning abilities. Like any other age group, when elderly people are less mentally challenged, their cognitive performance declines. Older adults typically encounter mental challenges less frequently than the college students to whom they usually are compared, but they can learn new things – and learn them quite well. Moreover, whether people *believe* they can learn and remember is crucial. The lesson here is that aging adults bear some responsibility for making sure that they engage in cognitively challenging activities.

Using current and emerging technologies can improve cognitive capacities of seniors. The first step may involve no more than learning to use an automated teller machine, but that effort can promote subsequent skills. "Neurobic exercises" both preserve and improve brain and memory functions. Routine activities that require little cognitive effort can exacerbate cognitive decline. Accordingly, researchers recommend actively seeking new and enjoyable experiences – simply because they are different.

Are Old People Isolated and Lonely?

Recent evidence does not support the stereotypical view that older individuals deplete the resources of an ever-diminishing support system. Rather, social net-works remain remarkably stable in size throughout the lifespan, with the number of close relationships among noninstitutionalized older adults equaling those of younger people. Network losses do occur over the lifespan through death, relocation, and retirement, but even among very old people, new social relationships are formed to replace lost ones.

Aging Baby Boomers will have even wider social networks than previous generations. With their computer competencies, they will routinely use email to maintain contact with family members and friends. We already have evidence that they are more likely than their younger counterparts to access Internet information and support from a wide spectrum of people who share their needs and concerns.

Do Old People Drain Society's Resources?

The benefits elders receive have been scrutinized as potentially wasted and taking away from "more needy" groups and the overall economic well-being. However, the evidence is contrary to this view. Older adults vary as widely as their younger counterparts in health, financial security, and willingness to accept public support. More important, senior citizen benefits depend on social status and past work experience, favoring high income earners with a continuous work history, i.e., white middle-class men. The truth is that, without Social Security, the percentage of people over age 65 who live in governmentally-defined poverty would increase from 12% to 50%. Thus, cuts in Social Security would hit hardest those who need them most.

Older adults do not drain societal resources. Future elders will be more educated than their predecessors and, with their higher earnings, will continue to save after retirement rather than "spend down" their assets. Even those who do not continue to work for pay make substantial contributions. "Paid" work tends to be overvalued in our society, but unpaid (e.g., in the home, volunteer efforts) and underpaid (e.g., working in fast-food restaurants and bagging groceries) activities contribute a great deal to the social enterprise. When given the opportunity, large numbers of seniors eagerly do volunteer work and take on low-paying part-time jobs. But, the most telling, and least appreciated, example of the financial contributions of older adults is the economic value of the care they provide to disabled family members, estimated in 1999 to be between $45 and $200 billion annually. Put simply, older adults contribute a great deal to society – whether or not they collect a paycheck.

Should they choose to continue to work for pay, Baby Boomers and subsequent generations will be more advantaged than previous generations. Attitudes about older workers are changing, and the attitudes of older workers themselves are changing. Because of post-Baby Boom declines in birth rates, as the Baby Boomers age, the number of employable adults will decrease relative to the number of new jobs. Following the law of supply and demand, older workers will be more valued and sought-after. Moreover, younger retirees and Baby Boomers are looking at retirement as both a lifestyle transition and a new opportunity. Nearly 70% of Boomers expect to continue working after retirement, and those who do not feel ready to retire will not be compelled to do so.

The traditional retirement age of 65 has lost much of its significance. In terms of health and life-expectancy, age 70 today is roughly the equivalent of age 65 in the 1930s when Social Security was established. Indeed, changing health status and attitudes have led to age 65 no longer being considered "old." Although most individuals who have adequate financial resources will retire at the usual time or earlier, they will be able to choose to continue working either because they want to or feel the need to supplement their retirement benefits.

The point to be made here revolves around personal choice. We have known for a long time that people who feel in control and who can make choices about the important aspects of their lives are both physically and psychologically healthier than those who perceive that they lack personal control.

Are Old People Depressed?

In certain segments of the population, clinically relevant depressive syndromes, including major and minor depression, may affect 13–15% of older adults. And, while empirical findings do indicate higher rates of "depression" among disabled older adults, the same is true in younger adults with disabilities. The truth is that, overall, clinical depression is no more, and probably is *less*, prevalent in older than younger adults. Indeed, there is evidence that elders cope more effectively with stressful life events than do younger adults. Over the life course, through life experiences and successfully coping with various stressors, the typical adult builds adaptive attitudes that generalize to coping with new stressors. A key component is personal control. Regardless of age, people are motivated to exercise control over the important aspects of their lives. Solving the problems that go along with getting older (e.g., death of a spouse) simply may not be possible. Consequently, those who adapt well will shift their focus from actively trying to change the situation to managing stress-related emotional reactions by, for example, accepting the situation and continuing to function as normally as possible. By doing so, they will maintain a sense of control.

Activity Restriction and Depressed Affect

Exemplifying the impact of loss of control, *activity restriction* has been operationalized as the inability to continue normal, valued activities (e.g., self-care, care of others, doing household chores, going shopping, visiting friends) that often follows stressful life events such as debilitating illness. Indeed, it appears that major life stressors lead to poorer mental health outcomes *because* they disrupt normal, valued activities.

Numerous factors, other than physical disability, contribute to activity restriction. For example, older adults tolerate pain better than do younger adults, a phenomenon most commonly attributed to the increased exposure to pain and disabling conditions that older people experience. Indeed, experience, rather than age, matters more in terms of predicting those who will restrict their activities in the wake of stressful events. In other words, old age need not foster either activity restriction or depression. Another potentially important contributor to coping with stress is financial resources. Inadequate income interferes with normal activities. Moreover, if financial resources are merely *perceived* as being less than adequate, activities are more restricted. Thus, when life becomes stressful, a first line of defense may be to cut back on normal activities that involve spending money, e.g., shopping, recreation, and hobbies. Personality also contributes to activity restriction. Some people cope in maladaptive ways across all situations throughout their lives. In contrast, there are those who routinely face the situation, rationally evaluate possible solutions, seek help and information as appropriate and, if all else fails, accept that the problem has occurred, deal with their emotional reactions, and make every effort to resume life as usual.

Another important factor is social support. People with stronger social support resources cope better with all types of stressful life events, and routine activities are facilitated by social support. Comparable benefits are seen in people who merely *perceive* that social support is available if it is needed, and the benefits of perceiving that one has supportive others remain after controlling for demographics (e.g., age, financial resources), illness severity, and personality variables. Social support, however, appears to be a function of personality variables that, in turn, influence activity restriction. Those with more socially desirable characteristics also have more supportive social ties and, therefore, may be less subject to activity restriction.

Summary of Current Research Findings

The forecast for our aging population is that, more than ever before, older adults will be physically, cognitively, psychologically, and socially healthy. Still, significant numbers of elders will be disabled, socially isolated, and depressed. Often people become depressed by stressful life events largely because of disruptions in their ability to go about life as usual, and illness severity, younger age (or lack of experience), inadequate income, less social support, and personality variables also play a role.

In their acclaimed book, *Successful Aging*, Rowe and Kahn proposed that there are three components of successful aging: 1) avoiding disease; 2) engagement with life; and 3) maintaining high cognitive and physical function. Other factors (e.g., personality, financial resources) also influence how well one ages.

Avoiding disease is largely a function of routine activities. Temperance in detrimental behavior (e.g., smoking) is related to better physical health, less disability, and greater longevity. People need to engage in personally meaningful activities (whether intellectual, physical, or social). Maintaining high cognitive and physical functioning is a key to aging successfully. When confronted with seemingly overwhelming life events, the telling factor may well be the extent to which at least a semblance of normal activities can continue.

Interventions to Increase Activity and Decrease Depression

Coping with the stresses of getting older is a complex, multifaceted process that is influenced by numerous factors. With age, physical and psychological stressors often become less controllable. Successful interventions may require helping elders shift from problem-focused to emotion-focused coping mechanisms. By acknowledging that psychological well-being is a function of restricted normal activities, we can design interventions to reduce both activity restriction and depression. Efforts to increase activity should focus on identifying manageable activities and available resources. Programs can be implemented to engage aging adults in pastimes that not only meet their specific interests and needs but also fit their functional capacities.

Beyond evaluating demographic characteristics such as age and financial resources, a second line of intervention involves assessing stable traits that predispose people to restrict their normal activities. For instance, people low in optimism do not cope effectively or adjust well to stress. They also have less supportive social ties, increasing their vulnerability to activity restriction. High levels of neuroticism are related to a maladaptive coping style that may include foregoing pleasurable activities. When faced with disrupting life events, individuals who are less agentically oriented and do not have a strong sense of mastery will have more difficulty finding ways to continue their rewarding activities. In addition, those who are low in the dispositional predilection to hope for positive outcomes are less likely to conceptualize ways to continue (or replace) valued activities or to persist in their efforts to do so, particularly when pathways to achieving these goals are blocked. Once individuals predisposed to restrict activities have been identified, a particularly fruitful line of intervention may be an adaptation of hope therapy.

Social support, like personality and experience, interacts with health-related variables to affect normal activities. With more supportive social support networks, activity restriction is less likely. Thus, identifying community-residing older adults with deficits in social support is another important avenue for intervention. Deficits in social support can range from instrumental (e.g., grocery shopping) to emotional (e.g., coping with life changes) support. Available resources often are underutilized because family and friends are not aware of the elder's needs. Thus, a prime point of intervention is to identify tapable resources and facilitate social network cooperation.

Directions for Future Research

Models of stress and coping typically imply that the causal path is unidirectional – e.g., that stress causes activity restriction that, in turn, causes negative affect.

However, as clinicians have long known, being depressed causes people to forego many of their previously enjoyed activities. In fact, one of the better behavioral treatments for depression is to motivate patients to become more socially and physically active. Controlled experimental studies are needed to clarify previous results by demonstrating that strategies designed to increase activity level will, in fact, improve well-being. In addition, identifying differences between people who will tolerate discomfort in order to continue engaging in meaningful activities and those who will not voluntarily make such efforts under similar levels of discomfort will bring us closer to successful intervention programs.

SEE ALSO: ▶ Locus of control   ▶ Personality   ▶ Social support
▶ Wisdom

Acknowledgment

Manuscript preparation was supported by the National Institute on Aging (AG15321, G. M. Williamson, principal investigator) and further facilitated by a fellowship from the Institute for Behavioral Research at The University of Georgia.

Suffering

Sherlyn Jimenez
University of Connecticut

Suffering, or to bear or be weighed down, is a universal human experience, central to the human condition, and in all likelihood, the primary reason why people seek psychological treatment. Historically, suffering has taken on various meanings and significance, and presently, fields from medicine to theology have conceptualized and defined suffering in several ways. Nonetheless, there seems to be a general agreement that suffering is a phenomenological experience involving not only physical, mental, and emotional pain but also existential and spiritual pain. In psychology, however, the meaning of suffering has been fundamentally altered. The language of mental pain and suffering has been primarily replaced by a vocabulary of illnesses and disorders with suffering reduced to diagnoses made from symptoms and criteria. Not surprisingly, given the phenomenological nature of suffering, psychology has largely been silent on the construct of suffering with discussion about suffering relegated to areas of pastoral psychology and occasionally, humanistic and psychoanalytic literature. Outside psychology, research on suffering has mostly been confined to the nursing and medical sciences, generally in the context of pain and palliative care, and mainly of a qualitative nature.

Historical Overview

Suffering has held various meanings over culture and time. The Stoics in Greece believed that suffering is at the core of life, and counseled detachment. In the Judeo-Christian and Western tradition, suffering is seen as something to be endured, a learning experience that provides the path for redemption. It is seen as an inescapable part of human experience valued as a way to go beyond one's self and achieve grace and salvation. The message that is reinforced within these traditions is that transcendence over suffering is possible and attainable and that pain has a positive and motivating purpose. During the Enlightenment, the possibility that suffering could and should be eradicated and that humanity can be liberated from suffering began to prevail. However, Kierkegaard and Nietzsche believed that suffering was intrinsic to the human experience and held it as a prerequisite of human achievement – that is, it challenged individuals to cultivate previously undiscovered strengths within them. Sartre and Camus held that it is our existential responsibility to accept the inevitability of suffering and the absurdities of life. However, they believed, along with existential psychologists such as Frankl, that suffering may also offer opportunities for growth, and that by finding meaning in threatening events, suffering can be transcended. Freud proposed three sources of painful experience and suffering: physical pain, the external world and our relationship with others. In Freud's view, interpersonal relationships constituted the greatest source of our suffering – the bedrock of what it means to be human.

Levinas concurred with the significance of interpersonal relationships, proposing that the primary encounter we have as humans is between our being and the being of the other. However, Levinas offered a different perspective on suffering, which he perceived as offering us a unique opportunity for surmounting the isolation that we all experience. According to Levinas, our encounter with the suffering of another allows us to rise above our own self-concern to a sense of caring and responsibility. It is this recognition of our shared suffering, our connection to the suffering of others, which provides meaning for our own suffering. In this sense of interconnectedness brought about by suffering, *compassion* and the desire to alleviate suffering may arise – provided that our own suffering is experienced in full, not avoided or denied. In Levinas' view, only if one allows oneself to fully experiences suffering can one be changed or transformed by it.

Buddhist View on Suffering

While Western tradition sees suffering as a negative which is transformed into positive once it is transcended and ascribed meaning, the Buddhist/Eastern tradition views *dukkha*, translated as suffering or unease, as a general fact of existence in which individuals themselves must take ultimate responsibility for their suffering. In Buddhism, the origins of dukkha are aversion, attachment, and delusion.

That is, suffering is caused by pain (e.g., physical, emotional and mental pain); by impermanence and change (e.g., violated expectations and loss); and by unstable and unreliable conditions (e.g., uncertainty and attachment to our mental constructs or habitual ways of thinking, feeling and acting). The fourth noble truth in Buddhism states that the path to the relief from suffering involves training and transformation of the consciousness through wisdom, conduct and meditation. Accordingly, the purpose of living is to benefit others and to avoid giving harm such that ultimately, the wish to end suffering becomes rooted in the feeling of *compassion* for both oneself and of others.

Recent Conceptualizations of Suffering

Recently, more concrete definitions of suffering have been proposed. In the health sciences, Cassell has defined suffering as a state of extreme distress or impairment associated with events that threaten the integrity of a person. Cassell's definition emphasized the role of prior experience and expectancies along with the assessment of the seriousness of the perceived or anticipated threat. For Cassell, it is the impact – the meaning or significance and value attributed to the experience – that is the essential fact, not the severity. Moreover, suffering is ultimately a personal and private matter, a phenomenological event that nonetheless has a social dimension in that it may lead to isolation. For Van Hooft, however, suffering is not necessarily a phenomenological experience. To him, people who are experiencing health-threatening conditions such as poverty are suffering even if they may not be aware of it or may not consider the adverse conditions to be a threat to their integrity. Van Hooft conceives suffering as the derailment or frustration of goals; specifically, not being able to attain and fulfill biological needs, appetitive (desires and relationships), deliberative (self-efficacy) or contemplative (sense of meaning) goals. In this way, pain is simply one form of suffering (e.g., biological). Edwards adds that suffering must be of significant duration and must have a fairly central place in the mental life of the subject but that suffering does not necessarily include a threat to the intactness of the self.

In the theology and palliative care literature, Dame Cicely Saunders defined total pain or suffering as including psychological, spiritual and interpersonal aspects along with its physical aspects. Suffering is differentiated from pain in medical terms in that pain is often associated with objective symptoms and sensations while suffering is defined as a behavioral and emotional response. Previously, Williams had defined suffering as an anguish experienced as a pressure to change and as a threat to our integrity and the fulfillment of our intentions. Millspaugh has equated suffering with spiritual pain which affects the person's body, mind and spirit, and is triggered by either our interpretation of an experience or our inability to interpret an experience. Thus, it is the spiritual and existential dimension of our existence and not only the bodily aspects of ourselves that is implicated in suffering. A crisis of meaning ensues when we come to the realization and awareness of the essential and existential facts of life: that life is fragile, that we are not in control, that we are ultimately alone and that therefore, our lives no longer have purpose. Millspaugh suggests that spiritual pain is mitigated when a person discovers a transcendent sense of purpose and sense of control, when life is once again invested with meaning. Suffering takes on redemptive qualities and may lead to spiritual growth once the necessity of suffering is accepted and meaning is found.

Social scientists take issue with the portrayal of suffering as a response to a discrete event that happens to individuals without context. Kleinman and colleagues proposed the concept of social suffering, that suffering is a social experience shaped by political, economic and institutional forces which may simultaneously create and/or exacerbate suffering and influence responses to it. Thus, suffering is a social process that is simultaneously a matter of health, politics and culture, extending beyond simply an emotional response triggered by pain and distress. This consideration of suffering reveals the moral dimension of suffering and critiques the treatment of pain and suffering which prevents it from being contextualized through a multitude of factors. The point Kleinman makes is that suffering is not only situated in the body but linked to the social world as well as to the invisible world of spirit in an interconnected web.

Thus, social scientists would be critical of the reductive nature of psychological diagnoses, of which posttraumatic stress disorder (PTSD) provides the closest equivalent to suffering. Their critique of psychology is that mental health disorders such as PTSD are addressed without context and the problem is shifted to what is wrong with the patient rather than what is wrong with what happened to the patient. According to the DSM-IV-TR criteria, PTSD involves a threat to the physical integrity of self or others resulting in intense fear, helplessness, or horror and includes the following psychological and physical symptoms: intrusions or reexperiencing; hyperarousal; and avoidance. What it leaves out is the contextual and existential significance of the event. Moreover, while PTSD might be representative or closely related to suffering, it leaves out the suffering experienced from other disorders, medical conditions or living conditions.

A recent study on suffering at end of life by Abraham and colleagues provides support for the social scientists, mainly that the source of suffering extends beyond pain to include emotional, spiritual and cultural dimensions. Moreover, the authors suggest that suffering is not just a solitary experience devoid of interpersonal context but also involves psychological and existential quality of life issues. Specifically, the study found that factors other than distress, such as diagnosis, age, and quality of life, affect perception of pain and suffering in patients. In addition, lack of distress from physical symptoms was not necessarily related to lack of suffering because of the symptoms or lack of overall suffering.

Future Research

Although varying discourses on suffering exists, presently, there is a dearth of literature on suffering in psychology, perhaps because of the challenge of doing research on a primarily phenomenological experience involving existential, spiritual and social dimensions. Nonetheless, people continue to seek out mental health workers desiring that their suffering be acknowledged, attended to, and alleviated. Yet, despite the health field's best intention to alleviate or eradicate pain and suffering, whether through pharmacological or therapeutic interventions, certain disorders appear to resist treatment. It may be that interventions focusing on the reduction of symptoms alone are not enough to alleviate suffering and that it is also important to address psychic and spiritual suffering. Additionally, it might be helpful to consider the contributions of the social, cultural and political environment on suffering and how these factors are uniquely internalized in the sufferer. Finally, it must be acknowledged that suffering is a reality of life and that certain problems may never be eradicated or cured. These unaddressed issues point to a need to reconsider the construct of suffering. Through the study of the multidimensional nature of suffering, psychology can reexamine pain, trauma and other disorders as social experiences shaped by multiple realities. Although there may be limits to operationalizing suffering, the study of suffering could be informed by the integration of the multiple definitions of suffering suggested by historical, existential, spiritual, and social perspectives. Further, current work on suffering in the fields of palliative medicine, theology, medical anthropology, and social sciences could help refine the experiential descriptions of suffering and suggest workable methods to define and measure it.

SEE ALSO: ► Buddhism ► Compassion ► Existential psychology

Taylor, Shelley

Sally S. Dickerson
University of California, Irvine

Shelley E. Taylor (1946–) is a leading positive psychology scholar whose ground-breaking research examines how positive psychological and social resources (e.g., social support, optimism) can protect one's health. She has published over 300 papers that have shaped our understanding of factors that buffer individuals from the deleterious effects of stress, and the mechanisms through which this occurs. Dr Taylor received her bachelor's degree from Connecticut College and her PhD from Yale University. After teaching at Yale and Harvard University, she joined the faculty of University of California, Los Angeles in 1979, where she is currently a Distinguished Professor.

For the past 25 years, much of Dr Taylor's research has delineated how social and psychological resources promote positive adaptation under threatening situations. For example, she has documented that holding positive beliefs about the self or expectations about the future predict enhanced psychological and physical health, even when these beliefs are overly optimistic or unrealistic (i.e., positive illusions). Dr Taylor and her colleagues have found that these health benefits are due, in part, to reduced biological responses to stressors (e.g., dampened cardiovascular, hormonal, and immune reactivity) among individuals possessing these positive beliefs. She has tested her theories not only in healthy adults, but also in individuals facing life-threatening illnesses, enabling her to demonstrate that positive resources can prevent disease progression in certain populations. Dr Taylor also has elucidated how supportive, nurturing relationships can have health-protective effects, particularly under stressful situations. Her theoretical and empirical work has identified specific biological substrates – such as oxytocin and endogenous opioids – that are implicated in these social processes, providing a potential mechanism linking positive social relationships with beneficial health outcomes.

Dr Taylor's work seamlessly integrates multiple scientific perspectives (e.g., health psychology, social neuroscience, genetics) and multiple levels of analysis (e.g., genetic contributions, neural mechanisms, emotional processes, physiological systems, cultural influences). As an illustrative example, Dr Taylor and colleagues recently found that growing up in a supportive, caring environment protected genetically "vulnerable" individuals from depressive symptoms in adulthood, demonstrating a powerful interaction between social processes, genetic predispositions, and positive health outcomes. Her unique brand of cross-cutting, interdisciplinary research has important applications for intervening to protect and optimize health and well-being.

Dr Taylor has received many prestigious research awards. In 2006, she was the inaugural recipient of the Clifton Strengths Prize, which recognizes ground-breaking theory, research and practice in positive psychology. She has received the William James Fellow Award from the Association for Psychological Science and the Distinguished Scientific Contribution Award from the American Psychological Association, the highest scientific honors bestowed by these organizations. Dr Taylor has also received Distinguished Scientist awards from numerous other organizations (e.g., Society for Experimental Social Psychology; Positive Psychology Initiative), and has been elected to membership in many selective scientific societies (e.g., American Academy of Arts and Sciences; Institute of Medicine, National Academy of Sciences). These prestigious honors attest to her seminal contributions to positive psychology as well as the broad impact of her work in the fields of psychology and medicine.

SEE ALSO: ▶ Health psychology   ▶ Positive illusions   ▶ Social support

Teaching Positive Psychology

Amy C. Fineburg
Spain Park High School/The University of Alabama

Teaching positive psychology involves communicating the core concepts of positive psychology to students. Typically, instructors choose to teach positive psychology in two distinct ways: as a separate course specifically dedicated to positive psychology in general or certain topics in particular; or infused throughout a typical course in psychology. The positive psychology concepts that would be included in a course would depend on which approach a teacher chose to follow. If a teacher chose to teach a separate course in positive psychology, he or she might choose to teach a general overview of topics typically researched in the field (e.g., happiness, flow, optimism, subjective well-being) or a course that focuses specifically on a particular topic. If a teacher chose to infuse a typical psychology course with positive psychology, the same types of topics would be addressed, but their mention would occur during the appropriate subunit in the course. For instance, when a teacher discusses depression in the psychological disorders unit, he or she might also discuss happiness and the ways in which one might "diagnose" happiness and interventions that could lead a person to greater happiness.

The teaching of positive psychology has overcome some roadblocks that inhibited its inclusion into courses and programs in psychology. In traditional psychology courses, curricular resources are populated with concepts that highlight the negative aspects of behavior. Many psychology textbooks emphasize the negative rather than the positive, encouraging teaching psychology from a negative perspective. The emphasis on negative aspects of behavior is supported by a decades of scientific research. Since World War II, psychologists have concentrated on diagnosing and curing mental illness rather than studying qualities that promote happiness or talent. Psychologists have been largely successful in identifying many major illnesses and finding successful treatments for them. Much of what is taught in psychology courses highlights these successes. Graduate programs in psychology also capitalize on the research funding available to those seeking to understand mental illness and disease. As a result, the canon of psychology includes more of the well-established concepts in negative psychology rather than positive psychology constructs. Research has shown that negative psychology terms are more prevalent than positive ones in introductory psychology textbooks. Students taking courses in psychology may leave with the impression that disease diagnosis and treatment are the only foci of psychology. Additionally, introductory psychology students most often recalled negative psychology and illness model concepts such as Phineas Gage and his brain injury, systematic desensitization, narcolepsy, Milgram's obedience study, attitudes influencing behavior (presented through a "controversial issue" debate), and two disorders – dissociative identity disorder and schizophrenia. The teaching of positive psychology became an important goal for those interested in promoting the research and dissemination of positive psychology concepts and practices.

In 2000, Martin E. P. Seligman of the University of Pennsylvania brought together high school teachers and collegiate instructors to form the Positive Psychology Teaching Task Force, a group charged with developing curricula and dissemination strategies for positive psychology. The group hoped to strengthen positive psychology's "fifth pillar" – the teaching of positive psychology. The task force, chaired by high school psychology teacher Randy Ernst of Lincoln, Nebraska, developed a unit plan for high school teachers, an essay contest for high school students, a website for posting syllabi, workshops for teachers and instructors led by task force members, and the development of textbooks for high school and collegiate audiences. The task force members worked extensively to encourage instructors to teach distinct courses in positive psychology and to infuse positive psychology concepts into traditional psychology subject areas. The two-pronged approach was designed to support the growing positive psychology movement in two ways. Teaching distinct courses in positive psychology on the advanced undergraduate and graduate levels would give the movement credibility as a research area and develop graduate students interested in exploring positive psychology for a thesis or dissertation. Infusing positive psychology into high school and undergraduate courses would develop a generation of students who did not see psychology as "negative" and "positive," and an integrated psychology including both disease and prevention models would emerge.

Separate courses in positive psychology have become popular in graduate and undergraduate programs where instructors who specialize in the field teach. Although similar programs in health psychology and other positive aspects of behavior had existed previously, the first courses to use the term *positive psychology* in the course title or course description were taught at Harvard University and the University of Pennsylvania in 1999. Robert Nozick of Harvard taught a course entitled *The Philosophy of Psychology* in which the reading list included numerous positive psychology readings. Martin E. P. Seligman, taught the first course entitled *Positive Psychology* to graduate students. Seligman has since offered courses in positive psychology to undergraduate students at Penn. Additionally, faculty at over 200 universities around the world offer positive psychology courses to advanced undergraduates and graduate students. In 2006, Harvard instructor Tal Ben-Shahar offered an undergraduate course in positive psychology which boasted the largest course enrollment (over 800) at the university that semester. Several textbooks have also been written to accommodate the growing popularity of these courses, authored by prominent positive psychologists including C. R. Snyder, Shane Lopez and Christopher Peterson. Numerous universities with cadres of faculty members dedicated to researching positive psychology offer PhD students the opportunity to conduct research in positive psychology. In 2004, Penn began a Master of Applied Positive Psychology (MAPP) program, the first of its kind.

Infusing positive psychology into existing curricula continues to be a major emphasis. According to the *National Standards for High School Psychology Curricula*, the major domains of psychology include biological bases of behavior, cognition, methodology, developmental psychology, and variations in individual and group behavior. Positive psychology concepts have been integrated into the current version of the *National Standards*. The *National Standards* are used to determine the content taught by high schools and introductory psychology teachers, and the integration of positive psychology concepts ensures the teaching of both positive and negative psychology. Several high school and introductory psychology textbooks now include positive psychology throughout, among them *Thinking About Psychology* and introductory texts by Myers.

SEE ALSO: ► Positive psychology (history) ► Seligman, Martin ► Strengths perspective (positive psychology)

Templeton Foundation, John M.

Robert Emmons
University of California, Davis

The John M. Templeton Foundation funds research projects that scientifically explore the link between religion and spirituality and the virtues and human strengths that reflect humanity's highest aspirations and noble qualities including, but not limited to: creativity; purpose; perseverance; gratitude; prayer; awe and wonder; personal responsibility; unlimited love; altruism; courage; honesty; joy; humility; talent and genius; and thrift and generosity. Cutting-edge work on these core themes is supported and encouraged by the foundation. New and generative methodological approaches that advance the science of spirituality are emphasized. The overall objective of the foundation's grant initiatives is to take research on the human spirit to new levels of scientific sophistication and significance. Beyond research on these core themes, the foundation's mission is to serve as a philanthropic catalyst for discovery in areas engaging life's biggest questions. These questions include explorations into the laws of nature and the universe such as: Do we have a soul? Is mathematics discovered or invented? Do we have free will? What is the nature of ultimate reality? What is freedom? What is the nature of divinity? These are the sorts of questions that are not usually supported by philanthropy, and are a distinguishing characteristic of the foundation.

The Templeton Foundation was established in 1987 by the internationally renowned financial investor Sir John Marks Templeton. Sir John Templeton's core vision for the foundation is to promote "enthusiasm for spiritual progress and new spiritual information" in drawing together the scientific and spiritual quests in ways that are serious, rigorous and open-minded (2000, p. 11). *Spiritual information* is a broad term that refers to knowledge generated through and by scientific research. The foundation seeks to strategically invest in research by scientists, scholars and high-level thinkers in ways that might lead to important advances in fundamental spiritual understanding via insight, blending the tools of empiricism with sophisticated conceptual analysis. Cosmology, evolutionary biology, mathematics, neuroscience, social science, and medicine are fields supported by foundation philanthropic investments. By increasing references to religious concepts in scientific journals and by moving religion into public discussion at universities, the foundation has sought to stimulate an appreciation for the importance of spiritual realities. Much of their success has resulted from the creation of transdisciplinary networks of scholars that has made it easier for previously marginalized "believers" within elite universities to form communities in a spirit of open-minded discovery. Sir John Templeton's motto is "how little we know, how eager to learn" (quoted in Harper, 2005, p. xvii).

The first programs that were sponsored by the foundation emphasized the constructive engagement of science and religion. Much of the spectrum of scholarly activity had to do with issues of current or recent scientific research as well as with a wide range of issues where the interface discussions are naturally philosophical (or theological or sociological or psychological) in nature. Course programs in science and religion in colleges and universities around the world represented a major emphasis of the foundation. Today, the Templeton Foundation funds hundreds of programs on science and religion, spirituality and health, religion and the human sciences (including positive psychology), and free enterprise. Among their most successful initiatives was the Campaign for Forgiveness Research, in which an initial $2 million investment catalyzed the emergence of an entire scientific research discipline beginning in the late 1990s. This campaign has funded over 50 research projects and has generated more than $5 million dollars in additional funding and resulted in scores of journal articles, chapters, and books on basic research and application of forgiveness principles. A number of other initiatives have funded various positive psychology programs including research on many of the core themes listed above.

The core challenge of the Templeton Foundation is to become an effective philanthropic catalyst for scientific discoveries and an influential worldwide hub for vision, creativity, and progress. To help realize this goal, six long-range strategies have recently been developed. These include: 1) working with top scientists and scholars from the world's top research institutions; 2) effectively communicating the vision of the Foundation; 3) developing signature programs in each philanthropic area (e.g., the core themes); 4) developing a solid reputation for scientific rigor and innovativeness; 5) building a culture of excellence in scientific philanthropy (in contrast to be known for doing "nice" things); and 6) encouraging opportunities for philanthropic innovation. Paraphrasing the mission of its founder, the Templeton Foundation exists to transform individuals so that they will quite naturally want to invest in whatever for them at that time will qualify as ways to use methods of science to advance "spiritual progress." The leadership of the foundation anticipates that such a transformation will lead to a greater appreciation for the infinite wonder, beauty, wisdom and creativity of the richness of an ultimate reality that surrounds them and makes life possible.

The foundation has not been immune from criticism. Some have accused it of having a religious agenda while others have been concerned that because of its considerable financial resources it is shaping the direction of science in a manner that is contrarian to traditional models of scientific advancement. In response the Foundation has argued that is not a religious organization and does not advocate or privilege a particular religious worldview. Rather, it welcomes proposals from researchers and theologians from all the major world religions, including non-Christian and non-Western perspectives.

Located in Conshohocken, Pennsylvania, outside Philadelphia, the Foundation now invests more than $60 million dollars annually to support innovative grants and research projects on a global scale. John M. Templeton, Jr., MD ("Jack") is president and chairman of the John Templeton Foundation, and directs all foundation activities.

SEE ALSO: ▶ Religiousness ▶ Spirituality

References

Harper, C. L. Jr. (Ed.) (2005). *Spiritual information: 100 perspectives on science and religion.* Radnor, PA: Templeton Foundation Press.
Templeton, J. M. (2000). *Possibilities for over one hundredfold more spiritual information.* Radnor, PA: Templeton Foundation Press.

Terman, Lewis

Jeff G. Rettew
University of Kansas

Psychologist Lewis M. Terman (1877–1956), spent most of his life studying individual differences with a focus on intelligence. Raised on an Indiana farm, Terman spent his early career as a schoolteacher and high school principal before receiving his doctorate in psychology from Clark University in 1905. After four years of teaching pedagogy at Los Angeles Normal School, he joined the education faculty at Stanford University in 1910. In 1922 he became head of Stanford's Psychology Department, where he remained until retiring in 1942.

While at Stanford, Terman published a revised and perfected Binet-Simon scale for American populations. This "Stanford Revision of the Binet-Simon Scale," became known as the "Stanford-Binet," and was the most successful English language test of intelligence. The "Intelligence Quotient" or IQ, was an index that had not been previously used in mental tests. In 1917 Terman played a key role in the development of intelligence tests for the army, group-administered tests largely based on the Stanford-Binet. Such tests enabled large numbers of individuals to be tested at one time and, after the war, Terman used this efficient form of test administration in schools. In collaboration with psychologists who had worked on the army tests, he developed the "National Intelligence Tests" for grades three to eight. Throughout the 1920s he played a leading role in establishing the use of group intelligence tests in schools to classify students into homogeneous ability groups, called *tracking*, a practice that became well established in America by the 1930s. Terman was also a leader in the development of group achievement tests, which assessed school learning. He collaborated on the construction of the Stanford Achievement Test, the first of its kind.

Terman viewed intelligence as an adaptive quality that paved the way to life success, specifically national leadership. The widespread adoption of tests in schools was how Terman conceived testing could be useful to American society, as the means of achieving his vision of a meritocracy. Consistent with the views of other leaders of the mental testing movement, Terman believed mental abilities were primarily hereditary. The highest purpose that testing could serve, according to Terman, was the identification of intellectually gifted children – the potential leaders of society. Therefore, in the 1920s, Terman began an unprecedented study of 1,500 intellectually gifted children (IQ > 140) in California. Data from the "Termites" (a participant-coined nickname), continues to be mined by psychologists today. Terman chose his participants to test the early ripe-early rot myth, whether high IQ children had intellectual success or failure as adults. Terman contended that unusually precocious children were more likely to bloom rather than wilt later in life. His findings included that the gifted were taller, healthier, physically better developed, and superior in leadership and social adaptability, dispelling the ubiquitous contrary opinion. Furthermore, most graduated from college and successfully landed professional jobs. To Terman's consternation, however, few Termites went on to positions of national leadership.

SEE ALSO: ▶ Developmental psychology   ▶ Giftedness   ▶ Successful aging

The Nun Study

Matthew W. Gallagher
University of Kansas

In 1986, members of the School Sisters of Notre Dame religious community in Mankato, Minnesota agreed to participate in a study examining disability and aging. Since that time, what began as a small pilot project has transformed into one of the most groundbreaking and enlightening longitudinal psychological studies ever conducted. Now affectionately referred to as "The Nun Study," the work conducted by David Snowdon and colleagues has helped to shape current knowledge regarding the potential for healthy aging, how the expression of positive emotions can promote longevity, and how linguistic markers such as idea density may provide early clues as to who will suffer from Alzheimer's disease.

Methods of the Nun Study

In 1990, members of the School Sisters of Notre Dame who were born before 1917 were asked to participate in a longitudinal study of healthy aging and Alzheimer's disease. From seven congregations across the United States 678 women agreed to participate. These women ranged in age from 75 to 102 years old, with an average age of 83, when they were recruited to participate in the Nun Study. Each of these women agreed to undergo annual cognitive, physical, and medical assessments including a series of tests assembled by the Consortium to Establish a Registry for Alzheimer's Disease (CERAD). Additionally, each of the 687 sisters agreed to donate their brains upon death so that the neuropathological assessments which are necessary to accurately diagnose Alzheimer's can be conducted.

Strengths of the Nun Study

The Nun Study has many distinct characteristics that make it unique among longitudinal and epidemiological research and which make the findings of the Nun Study particularly important. Specifically, the women in the study have all lived very similar adult lives. They have all resided in similar convents for many years, they have all been celibate, none of them drink or smoke excessively, they have all had similar access to medical care, and they all had similar vocational experiences. Although it is true that the sample may not be representative of the general American population, the homogeneity of environmental factors removes many of the potential confounds that often hinder epidemiological studies. Researchers can therefore more confidently conclude that the individual differences between the nuns which have been found to predict various health outcomes may, in fact, be causal factors of those outcomes.

An additional unique advantage of the Nun Study is that, as previously mentioned, all 678 Sisters participating in the study have agreed to donate their brains to researchers upon their death. Scientists do not currently have a foolproof method of diagnosing Alzheimer's disease while individuals are living. Post-mortem neuropathological examinations are necessary to identify the neurofibrillary plaques and tangles that are indicative of Alzheimer's. The sacrifice of the School Sisters of Notre Dame will therefore allow researchers to amass an unprecedented collection of brains from a population and allow researchers to understand more fully how developmental and lifestyle factors may relate to the development of cognitive decline and Alzheimer's disease.

The most significant advantage of the Nun Study comes from a fortuitous discovery that occurred shortly after the study began. In 1930, the Mother Superior of the North American Sisters of Notre Dame requested that all of the Sisters compose an autobiography. Almost 60 years later the autobiographies of many of the Sisters who joined the order between 1931 and 1943 were found by David Snowdon and colleagues at the University of Kentucky when examining the archival records of the convents. These autobiographies and the accompanying medical and archival records have provided researchers with a treasure trove of information. Although the parameters of the autobiographies were very similar across the nuns, the style in which they were written varied dramatically and provided researchers with interesting clues regarding individual differences and cognitive abilities. In particular, the autobiographies of 180 Sisters from the Baltimore and Milwaukee convents have provided the data for many of the most fascinating findings of the Nun Study to date.

Findings from the Nun Study

One of the most interesting findings of the Nun Study came from an examination of the emotional content of the autobiographies of these 180 nuns and the effects that this emotional content had on longevity. The autobiographies, written by the nuns at an average age of 22, were read and coded in terms of the raw number of positive, negative, or neutral emotional words included and the number of sentences which contained a positive, negative, or neutral emotional word. The outcome variables for this study were measures of mortality that were adjusted for the age at which the autobiography was written. What Danner, Snowdon, and Friesen found was that there was a strong association between the frequency of positive emotion expression in the autobiographies and the survival rates of these women almost 60 years later. The sisters who were in the highest quartile for number of sentences containing positive emotional content were found to have a median age of death of almost 7 years later than those sisters who were in the bottom quartile of positive emotions sentences. When examining the raw number of positive emotion words the effects were even more pronounced, a 9.4 year difference between the median age at death of individuals in the highest and lowest quartile of positive emotion words. Although the exact mechanisms mediating the apparent relationship between the expression of positive emotions and longevity are not yet clear, these findings provide one of the most powerful indicators to date that research examining the positive aspects of life may in fact lead to vital clues to how individuals can lead longer, healthier, and more productive lives. These findings have also recently been replicated in a study of the emotional content of the autobiographies of famous deceased psychologists.

Future of the Nun Study

Perhaps the most remarkable aspect of the Nun Study is that it will continue for many years to come. Each of the Sisters will receive cognitive and medical assessments annually and, as previously mentioned, each participating Sister has agreed to donate her brain upon her death. The generosity of the Sisters will lead to the collection of an extraordinary amount of data that could provide the key to unlocking some of the secrets of Alzheimer's disease and how individual differences may promote healthy aging. The Nun Study provides a great model for future positive psychology research because it demonstrates how positive psychology constructs, in this case positive emotions, can have powerful effects on important life outcomes, survival and longevity. The Nun Study also demonstrates the importance of conducting longitudinal research which can, more effectively, tease apart complex cause and effect relationships. Finally, the Nun Study provides a great example of the dramatic impact a small group of people, 678 nuns, can have when they unite behind the shared goal of improving the knowledge and well-being of our society.

SEE ALSO: ▶ Developmental psychology   ▶ Positive emotions ▶ Successful aging

Transformational Leadership

Ronald E. Riggio
Claremont McKenna College

In 1978, political scholar, James MacGregor Burns, published *Leadership*, a book that distinguished between traditional leaders who use a more transactional leadership style and transformational leaders. Transactional leaders offer social exchange – money for labor, or recognition in exchange for loyalty. Transformational leaders raise leadership to a higher level. Transformational leaders inspire followers to achieve extraordinary outcomes, and in the process, they help develop followers' own leadership qualities. Transformational leaders are often seen as *visionary* and as agents of change.

An important central element of Burns's theory is the moral quality of transformational leaders who are more concerned with the common good than achieving their own self-interests. It is this moral or ethical element that distinguishes transformational leadership from earlier notions of charismatic leadership. While both transformational leaders and charismatic leaders are able to inspire followers with a compelling vision, transformational leaders go beyond mere charisma and strive to develop meaningful interpersonal relationships with followers and are characterized by a concern for individual followers' needs. Moreover, while charismatic leaders can be both morally good or bad (e.g., Hitler), transformational leaders, by definition, are ethical and put concerns of others over their own.

Inspired by Burns's work, psychologist Bernard M. Bass developed the concept of transformational leadership further, including outlining the components of transformational leadership, measuring these leadership components, and demonstrating that transformational leaders do indeed lead groups to high levels of performance and follower commitment. As a result of both Bass's efforts and the positive nature of the theory, transformational leadership has become the most researched theory of leadership from the 1990s forward.

Components of Transformational Leadership

The four components that make up transformational leadership are: idealized influence; inspirational motivation; intellectual stimulation; and individualized consideration.

Idealized Influence

Transformational leaders serve as positive role models for their followers. They emphasize the collective mission of the group or organization and demonstrate high standards of ethical conduct. As a result, followers want to be like the leader, they believe the leader has extraordinary capabilities, and they have great admiration and respect for the leader.

Inspirational Motivation

Transformational leaders are able to inspire and motivate followers through their display of enthusiasm, optimism and the articulation of attractive future outcomes. Together, the components of idealized influence and inspirational motivation represent the transformational leader's charisma.

Intellectual Stimulation

Transformational leaders challenge followers in an effort to stimulate their creativity and innovation. They do this by questioning assumptions, reframing problems, and encouraging followers to take risks and try new approaches.

Individualized Consideration

Focusing on individual followers, transformational leaders pay particular attention to each follower's needs, concerns, and personal development and growth. The leader accepts that there are individual differences in followers and encourages the personalized development of each one through mentoring and coaching.

Although many leaders could have the qualities associated with transformational leaders, such as charisma, Burns describes truly transformational leaders as "morally uplifting." Initially, Bass did not include this moral component in his conceptualization of transformational leaders. In recent years, however, Bass has agreed with Burns about the necessity for the moral element, referring to leaders who are self-serving and only appear to be concerned about followers, as *pseudotransformational*, or *inauthentic* transformational leaders.

Together Bass and leadership scholar, Bruce Avolio, created the Multifactor Leadership Questionnaire (MLQ), which measures each of the four components, and is widely used in research on transformational leadership. This measure requires followers to rate their leaders using the MLQ items. In their full range of leadership model, Bass and Avolio view leadership as a continuum of effectiveness, with transformational leadership at the top, transactional leadership as effective, but less so than transformational leadership, and laissez-faire leadership – where the leader abdicates his or her leadership obligations – at the bottom. In addition to measuring the components of transformational leadership, the MLQ also assesses laissez-faire leadership and different forms of transactional leadership.

Research on Transformational Leadership

Research has clearly demonstrated that transformational leaders lead groups that are more committed and loyal to their leaders. The level of satisfaction of followers of transformational leaders is also quite high. As a result, groups led by transformational leaders are also more effective than groups led by nontransformational leaders, in terms of both ratings made of group performance and more objective measures of group productivity.

Transformational leaders affect followers through the building of a relationship characterized by trust and mutual respect. The transformational leader holds high expectations for follower performance, but provides the inspiration, encouragement, and stimulation to think creatively that followers need to reach and maintain high performance levels. As a result, followers of transformational leaders develop self-esteem and a sense of self-efficacy in their abilities to succeed. This then translates into more effective performance and high levels of group loyalty and job satisfaction.

Bass also asserts that transformational leaders are particularly effective in conditions of crisis and stress. He cites leaders such as Mahatma Gandhi, Franklin Roosevelt, and Winston Churchill who were effective in calming followers' fears in times of crisis. Inspiring courage and stimulating innovative thinking and solutions, transformational leaders help followers turn stressful situations into challenging ones.

Bass, Avolio, and colleagues have shown that transformational leadership training can produce leaders who do indeed enhance followers' loyalty and commitment, although developing transformational qualities requires a great deal of time and effort. Some success has also been achieved in training work groups for transformational team leadership.

The Future

Research on transformational leadership continues at a robust rate. The popularity of the theory stems in part from its positive nature. In fact, critics have suggested that transformational leadership is really just a description of an "ideal leader." In looking toward the future of work on transformational leadership, Bass suggests that women, who tend to be more transformational than men, will have much better representation in upper-level management and leadership positions. He also notes that leaders who are able to develop followers through coaching and mentoring – hallmarks of the individualized consideration characteristic of transformational leaders – will be a future leadership requirement, as will leaders with a strong ethical orientation.

In looking toward the future, James MacGregor Burns suggests that the future "test" for transformational leaders will be to address significant global problems such as world poverty and hunger. He views leadership as a moral undertaking and transformational leadership as the epitome of good leadership.

SEE ALSO: ▶ Charisma ▶ Job satisfaction ▶ Leadership ▶ Self-efficacy ▶ Self-esteem

Utilitarianism

James O. Pawelski and Maya C. Gupta
University of Pennsylvania

Utilitarianism is the view that utility (defined variously as pleasure, happiness, well-being, and the like) should be maximized. In its classical form, utilitarianism contains an element of hedonism, which equates utility with pleasure. Utilitarianism assumes that utility is measurable and that it is possible to maximize it impartially within a society. The idea that actions are good to the extent that their consequences maximize utility is one of Western philosophy's major ethical doctrines.

History of Utilitarianism

Although Jeremy Bentham (1748–1832) is usually considered to be the founder of utiliarianism, its hedonic dimensions can be traced back to the ancients. In a passage in Plato's *Protagoras*, Socrates equates the pleasant and the good – the fundamental assumption of hedonism. The classical utilitarians Bentham and John Stuart Mill (1806–1873) adopted this assumption, and can hence be characterized as hedonistic utilitarians. Utilitarianism, however, need not be a hedonistic doctrine: twentieth century philosophers such as G. E. Moore and John Dewey rejected in part or whole the hedonistic aspects of utilitarianism in favor of ideal theories of utility, which hold that some things can be inherently good or bad independent of the pleasure derived from them.

Jeremy Bentham invented a hedonic (also called "felicific") calculus as a method for quantifying utility. His hedonic calculus measured pleasure in terms of *hedons* and pain in terms of *dolors*. He divided pleasure into seven categories: intensity, duration, certainty, propinquity in time, fecundity, and extent. John Stuart Mill recognized that such a calculus, under certain circumstances, does not accord with ordinary moral perceptions (a pleasure such as attending a party might rank higher in all of Bentham's categories than a pleasure such as reading a poem). To correct this cognitive dissonance, Mill sought to rank pleasures by their quality, as well, and not just by their quantity.

It is possible to found an egoistic ethical doctrine on the basis of a hedonic calculus like Bentham's, that is, to assert that goodness consists of engaging in acts which maximize the pleasure of the person who commits them. Bentham and Mill, however, viewed utilitarianism as a universalistic, social doctrine which implies that the pleasure and pain of all affected by a given act should be considered, not just the pleasure and pain of the act's perpetrator.

Both egoistic and universalistic positions, it should be noted, indicate that an action is good or bad depending solely upon its consequences, as opposed to, for instance, the intent of the agent; in other words, they are *act consequentialist* positions. Critics have pointed out that act consequentialism, be it egoistic or universalistic, can have unpalatable implications (punishing an innocent man for a crime he did not commit, if it deters hundreds of others from committing crimes themselves, is good according to act consequentialism because it maximizes utility). This has led some utilitarians to embrace *rule consequentialism* – the view that good actions are ones that conform to a general, hypothetical rule which, if obeyed, would maximize utility. (Since punishing innocent men does not generally lead to the maximization of utility, such punishment should not be practiced.)

Several problems linger in utilitarian doctrine. First, the hedonistic view that nothing is good but pleasure excludes meaning and other elements that ordinary moral perceptions might indicate are important to human flourishing. Furthermore, under a Benthamite approach, the utilitarian must face the problem of measuring pleasure and pain. For an individual actually to perform a hedonic calculus like the one Bentham outlines is difficult enough, but when it is a matter of measuring the collective balance of pleasure over pain for a group of individuals, as universalistic utilitarianism demands, the consequences can be philosophically alarming (recommending, under certain circumstances, that a small number of lives be sacrificed in the interest of the greater pleasure of the many). Another problem with utilitarianism is that it rests on the assumption of interpersonal comparability, an assumption which, if invalid, seems as though it would undermine the foundations of utilitarianism. Finally, while universalistic utilitarianism is a lofty ideal, it is unclear just how far individuals will go in sacrificing their own private happiness in the interest of the public good.

Utilitarianism and Positive Psychology

Utilitarianism has had an important influence on some areas of positive psychology. The work of Ed Diener, Daniel Kahneman, and others on subjective well-being, for example, is utilitarian in nature. Subjective well-being (a term coined by Diener as a scientific synonym for happiness) is based on a hedonic theory of happiness and is defined in terms of high positive affect, low negative affect, and high life satisfaction. In good universalistic utilitarian fashion, researchers in this area argue that subjective well-being should be maximized not just for individuals, but for all. For this reason, they advocate the establishment of well-being indicators to measure national averages of subjective well-being. The maximization of these national averages could then be an intentional goal of public policy decisions.

It should be noted that these positive psychologists are also helping to advance utilitarianism. As mentioned previously, one of the notorious difficulties of utilitarianism has been the measurement of happiness. Operationalizing happiness in terms of affect and life satisfaction allows for much more effective measurement. Until now, economists have mainly relied on economic indicators as proxies for happiness. But increasing evidence that wealth and happiness are not correlated well enough to justify this reliance point to the need for subjective well-being indicators as complements to economic indicators. Thus, subjective well-being research is helping to provide more reliable ways of measuring happiness and its maximization.

Not all positive psychology is based on utilitarianism, however. The work of Peterson and Seligman on strengths and virtues is based on virtue ethics and a eudaimonic theory of happiness. While utilitarians argue that ethics is about choosing actions that will lead to the best consequences (the maximizing of happiness), virtue ethicists argue that the emphasis should be on becoming a good person. And while hedonic theories hold happiness to be a function of subjective mental states, eudaimonic theories emphasize the importance of objective factors including biological tendencies, environmental conditions, and the cultivation of individual character traits. Strengths-based approaches argue that the development of good character may not always be pleasant, but that it is an important part of happiness. On these approaches, pleasure may be a by-product of a good life, but not its direct aim.

While positive psychologists recognize these differences in perspectives, they also work toward their reconciliation. Subjective well-being is not a purely hedonic view, since it includes not only affect measures, but also life satisfaction. Furthermore, Diener holds that subjective well-being is a necessary but not sufficient condition for the good life. It is one important thing we desire, but not the only one. On the other side, Seligman and Csikszentmihalyi (2000) have defined positive psychology as the "science of positive subjective experience, positive individual traits, and positive institutions" (p. 5), indicating the importance of both subjective well-being approaches and strengths-based approaches. Seligman has developed this position further in terms of what he sees as three equally valuable pathways to happiness: the pleasant life (emphasizing subjective well-being), the engaged life (emphasizing strengths), and the meaningful life (emphasizing strengths used in the service of something larger than the self).

The nature of the relation between utilitarianism and positive psychology calls for further work in at least two different areas. First, positive psychologists must continue to reconcile utilitarian with nonutilitarian elements of positive psychology. Further work is needed to determine whether the utilitarian threads in positive psychology are incompatible with those from virtue ethics, whether they can simply peacefully coexist, or whether it will be possible and desirable to create a single, integrated view. Since hedonic and eudaimonic theories of happiness seem mutually incompatible, further work is also needed to determine whether they can both continue to play central roles in positive psychology.

Second, utilitarianism has passed along to subjective well-being research some thorny problems. As discussed, a key problem in utilitarianism is the measurement of happiness. Defining happiness as subjective well-being, and then resolving subjective well-being into the more easily measured factors of affect and life satisfaction, seem to be promising steps (although eudaimonic theorists will not be satisfied with this hedonistic definition of happiness). Unfortunately, affect and life-satisfaction levels are currently determined chiefly through self-report measures, and there is ongoing debate as to the reliability of such measures. For this reason, researchers are looking for other, more objective measurements of subjective well-being that may bolster the accuracy with which happiness can be measured. Another utilitarian problem subjective well-being researchers have inherited is an ethical one, going back to the distinction between egoistic and universalistic utilitarianism. If subjective well-being is to be maximized, should it be done on the individual level, or on the universal level? It seems that these two levels will often, if not always, be incompatible. This raises a larger question (with cultural implications) for positive psychology in general. Is positive psychology chiefly about individual happiness or about collective happiness? Some researchers are suggesting that a balance must be struck between these two approaches. Perhaps such a balance would be the ideal way of maximizing utility.

SEE ALSO: ▶ Hedonics   ▶ Virtue   ▶ Virtue ethics

Reference

Seligman, M. E. P., & Csikszentmihalyi, M. (2000). Positive psychology: An introduction. *American Psychologist*, *55*, 5–14.

Values

Sonia Roccas[a] and Lilach Sagiv[b]

[a]The Open University of Israel; [b]The Hebrew University of Jerusalem

What Values Are

Personal values represent transsituational desirable goals that serve as guiding principles in peoples' lives. Values express what people believe to be good or bad, desirable or objectionable and what they think should or should not be done. As guiding principles, values affect the way people perceive and interpret the world and their preferences, choices, emotions, and actions. Values are organized hierarchically: Whereas all values are desirable to most people, each person has a unique value hierarchy. Some values are of supreme importance, others are very important, and some are only moderately important. The more important a value to a person, the more it is likely to serve as a guiding principle. Consider the example of the value of independence. A person who emphasizes this value is likely to prefer an occupation that allows some autonomy in crafting her/his tasks; to vote for a political party that endorses freedom; to judge severely infractions of people's freedom; and prefer to send his/her children to schools that encourage them to express independence of thought and action.

What Values Are Not

Values differ from other personal attributes in several important ways. Values transcend specific situations: They are important across situations and over time.

This feature distinguishes values from norms, attitudes, and specific goals, which usually refer to specific actions, objects, or situations. In addition, values may serve as standards or criteria and provide social justification for choices and behaviors, distinguishing them from personal attributes like traits or interests. Whereas traits, needs and motives may be either positive or negative, values are inherently desirable. Unlike needs and motives that may be unconscious, values must be represented cognitively in ways that enable people to communicate about them. Finally, values differ from other personal attributes because they are ordered by subjective importance, forming a hierarchy of value priorities. So far, little research has empirically addressed the question of differences between values and close constructs. Examining these differences and their implications for attitudes and behavior provide directions for future research.

Content and Structure of Values

For many years, research in psychology devoted relatively little attention to the study of values. Milton Rokeach contributed more than any other researcher to creating a new momentum in value research. Rokeach suggested that personal values serve as reference points which people use to formulate attitudes and behaviors, and developed a self-report measure of personal values, distinguishing between instrumental and terminal values.

Building on Rokeach, Shalom Schwartz proposed a theory of the content and structure of personal values. Schwartz suggested that values differ in the type of motivational goal they express. Based on universal requirements of human existence, Schwartz identified ten motivationally distinct types of values: power; achievement; hedonism; stimulation; self-direction; universalism; benevolence; tradition; conformity; and security.

Actions taken in the pursuit of a certain value type carry social, psychological and practical consequences that might conflict or may be compatible with the pursuit of other value types. Thus, for example, taking a trip to the Amazons jungles may serve to fulfill stimulation values that reflect the motivation to experience change and novelty and to be daring and adventurous. It is also compatible with emphasizing self-direction values that reflect the motivation for autonomy of thought and actions. Wandering in the jungles, conflicts, however, with emphasizing security values which reflect the motivation to maintain safety and stability. The total pattern of conflict and compatibility among value priorities yields a circular structure of value systems, in which competing value types emanate in opposing directions from the center, and complementary types are adjacent going around the circle.

The circular structure of values can be summarized into two basic conflicts. The first conflict is *self-enhancement* vs. *self-transcendence*. Self-enhancement values emphasize the pursuit of self-interest by focusing on gaining control over people and resources (power) or by demonstrating ambition and competence according to social standards and attaining success (achievement). These values conflict with self-transcendence values that emphasize serving the interests of others: expressing concern and care for those with whom one has frequent contact (benevolence) or expressing acceptance, tolerance, and concern for all people regardless of group membership (universalism).

The second conflict is *openness* to *change* vs. *conservation*. Openness to change emphasizes openness to new experiences: autonomy of thought and action (self-direction); and novelty and excitement (stimulation). These values conflict with conservation values that emphasize preserving the status quo: commitment to past beliefs and customs (tradition); adhering to social norms and expectations (conformity); and preference for stability and security for self and close others (security). Hedonism values share elements of both openness and self-enhancement and are in conflict with self-transcendence and conservation values.

The Schwartz theory has been tested in cross-cultural research in more than 200 samples from over 70 countries and received strong empirical support. This research indicates that the meaning of the 10 value types is similar across most cultures. In addition, there is a considerable consensus regarding the hierarchical order of values: Comparing the value ratings of individuals in more than 50 nations revealed that benevolence, self-direction, and universalism values are consistently among the most important values, whereas power, tradition, and stimulation values among the least important. Still, there are substantial cross-cultural differences in values. Moreover, individuals within a culture vary substantially in the importance they attribute to different values.

Social Correlates of Values

Gender differences in the importance attributed to values are surprisingly small. Theses differences are, however, consistent across many cultural groups: Men tend to value slightly more than women self-enhancement and openness to change; the reverse is true for self-transcendence values. Socioeconomic status has a greater impact: In a monumental longitudinal research, Kohn and Schooler found that people whose place in the social structure leads them to jobs characterized by high complexity increase the importance they attribute to self-direction versus conformity values.

The pattern of correlations between values and religiosity is strikingly consistent across monotheistic religions: Among Catholics, Protestants, Greek-Orthodox, Muslims, and Jews, religiosity correlated positively with emphasizing conservation values and negatively with emphasizing values of openness to change. Families are powerful vehicles of value socialization. Research identified several mechanisms through which parents' values are transmitted, such as child rearing practices and the accuracy in perception of parents' values. Note, however, that much of the value similarity between parents and children can be attributed to their sharing the same culture, socioeconomic status, and immediate environment. Future research should aim to achieve a better understanding of how society shapes values of individuals.

Values and Behavior

Values and behaviors are closely linked. The same value type may lead to many different behaviors, and the same behavior may be the result of different values. Thus, for example, a student's decision whether to stay at home and study for a test or to join his/her friends and go to the cinema has implications for achievement, hedonism, benevolence and conformity values. Trying to predict the behavior based on one only of these values is likely to fail: It is the tradeoff among competing values that guides behavior, rather than the importance attributed to any single value.

Studies conducted in the last decade found that values are related to a large variety of behaviors and behavioral intentions, ranging from daily actions such as the decision how much to study for an exam, to substantial decisions such as career choice and political voting. Values were related to consumer purchases, cooperation and competition, counselee behavioral style, delinquent behavior, environmental behavior, tolerance towards outgroup members, willingness to use innovative technology and more.

Recent studies pointed out the complex ways through which values guide behavior. Values influence behavior when they are highly accessible. Moreover, reflecting about the reasons for endorsing values increases the associations between values and behavior. The strength of associations between values and behaviors depends also on the type of behavior: The correlations are relatively weak for behaviors that are socially desirable. Furthermore, people vary in the extent to which their behavior matches their values: Values are related to behavior more strongly for people who attribute low importance to conformity values, which reflect the motivation to comply with social norms, than for people who value strongly conformity.

Values and Well-Being

The links between values and well-being are of special interest because they relate to the basic issue of what makes people happy. Values are related to well-being through multiple pathways. Self-determination theory engendered a view that directly links values and well-being: Values and strivings that are intrinsic by nature (autonomy, relatedness and competence) lead to positive well-being because they reflect self-actualization needs that are inherent to human beings. A second path toward happiness is suggested by the goal-attainment perspective: According to this view, well-being results from the attainment of goals that are pursued for intrinsic reasons, irrespective of the value content of those goals. The third path, suggests that it is the fit between individuals and their environments that affects subjective well-being. According to that path, even extrinsic values may lead to a positive sense of well-being if a person holding such values operates in an environment that encourages these values.

Cultural-Level Values: Values of Social Collectives

Values of cultural groups allow for the understanding of cultural differences. Cultural values are shared, abstract ideas about what a social collectivity views as good, right, and desirable. They are the broad goals that members of the collectivity are encouraged to pursue; they serve to justify actions taken in pursuit of these goals. Consequently, cultural values play a crucial role in the way that social institutions function.

Cultural values can be inferred using a variety of methods. One possible way is asking individuals to report the values that are important in their cultures. This, however, can be problematic because individuals may have highly biased or inaccurate ideas of the values endorsed by the larger culture. An alternative approach is to infer cultural values from artifacts produced by the culture such as symbols, rituals and archival documents. The validity of this approach depends on the accuracy of the interpretation of these artifacts. The large-scale studies comparing dozens of cultures adopted a third approach: They asked people to report their own personal values and aggregated across individuals to determine what values are "shared" within the culture. This approach allows for a systematic comparison across cultures. It also has limitations, however: It can reflect only those cultural values that are translated into personal motivations and are reflected in individual-level values.

Studies of cultural values have focused most extensively on nations. Hofstede originated the first major endeavor to understand cultural differences in values. He studied more than 100,000 IBM employees from about 50 nations. He identified four value dimensions. *Individualism* vs. *collectivism* refers to the relative importance of self as opposed to community identification. In individualistic societies, ties among people are loose: Individuals are expected to take care of themselves and those close to them only. In collectivistic societies, in contrast, people are strongly integrated into groups. They feel obligated to express loyalty to the ingroup, which, in return, protects them throughout life. Power distance refers to the extent to which power inequality is accepted as legitimate: In all societies, resources are distributed somewhat unequally. When power distance is high, however, this is seen as acceptable. *Masculinity* vs. *femininity* describes the relative importance of personal accomplishments, *success and power* vs. *relatedness and nurturing*. Finally, *uncertainty avoidance* refers to the extent to which people feel threatened by uncertainty, and respond by setting up rules. To date, Hofstede's seminal work is the most influential and yielded numerous studies. The four cultural dimensions have been related to a variety of social, political and organizational indices. Individualism-collectivism is by far the most studied dimension.

Hofstede's dimensions did not originate from any explicit theory. The dimensions identified are bounded by the topics (and items) included in the questionnaire used to assess them. Researchers have pointed out that this questionnaire largely reflects Western thinking. Taking a different approach, Michel Bond developed a value measure based largely on what Chinese researchers considered important in Chinese culture. Studying student samples from 23 countries, Bond identified four factors that distinguish among cultures. Three of these factors correlated with Hofstede's dimensions (no factor correlated with Uncertainty Avoidance). The fourth, unique, factor was termed *Confucian work dynamism*. Hofstede later adopted this as a fifth cultural dimension, and labeled it *long-term orientation*. Hofstede views this dimension as opposing a dynamic future orientation to a static present and past orientation.

Another large-scale project comparing cultural values was initiated by Schwartz. After establishing a cross-cultural equivalence in the meaning of values at the individual level, Schwartz aggregated these values to create cultural-level indices. He studied both students and teacher samples and found consistent cultural differences in the two populations.

Schwartz considered three basic issues that confront all societies. He derived three bipolar cultural dimensions that reflect possible solutions to those issues or challenges. The location of each society on each cultural dimension reflects the culture of that society. The first issue considered by Schwartz was the extent to which people are *autonomous* vs. *embedded* in their groups. In embedded cultures, people are viewed as entities embedded in the collectivity who find meaning in life through identification with the group and participation in its shared way of life. In autonomous cultures, in contrast, individuals are viewed as autonomous, bounded entities who find meaning in their own uniqueness and who are encouraged to express their internal attributes. Schwartz distinguished two types of autonomy: affective and intellectual.

The second challenge that confronts all societies is how to guarantee responsible behavior to preserve the social fabric. Cultures high on hierarchy rely on hierarchical systems of ascribed roles to insure responsible behavior. People are socialized and sanctioned to comply with the obligations and rules attached to their roles. Where egalitarianism is high, people are encouraged to recognize one another as moral equals who share basic rights as human beings. People are socialized to cooperate with others and to be concerned for everyone's welfare. The third issue is how to regulate the relation of humankind to the natural world. Mastery values encourage active self-assertion in order to master, change, and exploit the natural and social environment to attain personal or group goals. Harmony values encourage individuals to accept and comprehend the world as it is, and to fit in to this world rather than to change or exploit it.

Whereas all other large-scale projects examined values of specific groups in society, the value project headed by Inglehart studied representative samples of 63 nations. He identified two main value dimensions: *survival* vs. *self-expression* values, and *traditional* vs. *secular-rational* values. Survival values emphasize giving priority to economic and physical security over self-expression and quality-of-life. Self-expression values emphasize the opposite. Traditional values emphasize conservative views, and the importance of God rather than independence and determination. Secular-rational values emphasize the opposite. Inglehart found that value emphases in the society correlate with the religion dominant in that society. For example, Protestant European countries attributed very high importance both to self-expression and to secular-rational values, whereas Catholic European countries attributed only moderate importance to both types of values.

A promising direction for future research is multilevel analyses which examine how individual values interact with cultural values in affecting behavior. Another important line of future research is achieving a better understanding of patterns of stability and change in values. At the personal level, it is of interest to investigate how values develop through the lifespan. At the cultural level, of special interest are nations that are undergoing profound sociopolitical changes.

SEE ALSO: ▶ Indigenous positive psychology ▶ Well-being

Vigor

Arie Shirom and Ofira Shraga
Tel Aviv University

Vigor is the sense of possessing physical strength, emotional energy and cognitive liveliness. In the context of work, it represents a discrete, positive affective response to one's ongoing interaction with specific elements in the work environment and with the workplace situation as a whole.

The construct of vigor goes back a long way in human history. The Taoist culture of ancient China refers to *Chi* and *Jing* as representing the feeling of having internal energy and power which can be accessed by individuals, depending on their lifestyles and personal habits, while in ancient Japanese cultural traditions the concept of *Ki* related to one's feelings of being able to mobilize mental and physical energy. Psychoanalytic thought, including the contributions of Freud, Jung, and Perls, emphasized the construct of psychic energy, mostly arguing that it could be lost (as when investing it in defenses or conflicts) or gained in various ways, depending on how it is invested.

Vigor as an Affective State

Following widely accepted views of emotions and moods, vigor combines elements of a specific emotion in that it is contextualized in the work situation, but it is closer to a mood state in that it tends to last days and even weeks. Therefore, we refer to vigor as a specific affective state that combines elements of an emotion and of a mood state. Like all other specific affective states, vigor represents a fundamental action tendency. Following Lazarus' appraisal theory, individuals' appraisals of their energetic resources are theoretically distinct from the feeling of vigor. In nature, these appraisals and the feeling of vigor probably appear conjoined, mutually affecting each other over time. The focus on vigor as an affective state follows the cognitive-motivational-relational theory developed by Lazarus and his colleagues. This theory implies a discrete-category approach to affective states, each having its own core relational themes and coping implications. It follows that understanding the antecedents and consequences of each enriches and extends our understanding of employees' attempts to survive and flourish in their work environment.

Vigor and Other Affective States

How does vigor relate to other affective states? Russell proposed that each affective state can be identified and differentiated from other affective states by where it lies on the two-dimensional space consisting of the horizontal pleasure-displeasure dimension and the vertical arousal-sleepiness dimension. In this two-dimensional space, vigor represents positive arousal or a combination of moderate amounts of arousal and pleasure, probably akin to what Thayer referred to as calm-energy. In the same space, vigor's counterpart in the displeasure-arousal quadrant is anxiety, and its mirror-image in the displeasure-sleepiness quadrant is burnout, combining displeasure with lack of arousal. In contrast to burnout and anxiety, however, vigor is a component of the approach-oriented behavior facilitation system. This system, directs organisms toward situations and experiences that may potentially yield pleasure and reward and facilitates the procuring of resources like food, shelter and sexual partners – resources that are essential for the survival of both the individual and the species.

Vigor's Conceptual Framework

Vigor is seen as a composite variable, comprised of three interrelated affective components, namely one's feelings concerning one's: 1) physical strength; 2) emotional energy; and 3) cognitive liveliness. Theoretically, this view of vigor is derived from Hobfoll's conservation of resources (COR) theory, according to which people are motivated to obtain, retain and protect their resources, which can be material, social or energetic. The concept of vigor relates to physical, emotional and cognitive energetic resources for several reasons. The first follows from the COR theory argument that personal resources are closely interrelated and that the expansion of one is associated with the others being augmented. The second reason is that these components represent the three most salient domains of energy that humans possess: physical, emotional (relating specifically to one's interpersonal interactions with others and one's feeling capable of expressing empathy and sympathy to others) and cognitive (relating to one's feelings concerning one's capability of generating ideas, his/her vital thought processes, etc).

How does vigor relate to affective states that reside on the opposite pole, representing the combination of low arousal and displeasure? Some measures of vigor as a mood state were based on the theoretical position that the vigor and burnout (or chronic fatigue) pair represented bipolar affective states on the same dimension that could not be experienced simultaneously. In contrast, we argue for the theoretical position that vigor and burnout are obliquely related and do not represent the extreme poles of the same continuum, with the exception perhaps of situations characterized by very high levels of stress. This theoretical position rests first on the fact that the underlying biological systems of approach and avoidance activations have been shown to be basically independent. Second, positive and negative affective states are physiologically represented in different systems. Third, positive and negative affective states are known to have different antecedents, and may function relatively independently. Therefore, on theoretical grounds, it could be concluded that the relationships between positive and negative affective states is not bipolar but bivariate. Considerable support for this position has been provided by studies that have found different across-time fluctuations of positive and negative affect, and that the relationship among tension and energy self-ratings is not bipolar.

Measures of Vigor as a Mood State

The Profile of Mood States

The Profile of Mood States, abbreviated as POMS and first published in 1971 by McNair and his associates, was one of the earliest measures of any positive mood. Among its six subscales of different moods, the POMS includes an eight-item subscale gauging vigor-activity, using items like feeling cheerful, lively, alert, active, carefree and vigorous, which on the face of it probably represents a combination of vitality and vigor. Results that concern the vigor subscale have often been reported in studies using the POMS. In the area of exercise psychology, a recent meta-analysis of 26 studies that used the POMS vigor scale found that chronic exercise increased feelings of energy by a mean effect size of .37. Several additional studies have used the POMS and its vigor subscale to predict physiological outcomes, like sleep quality. Different aspects of the construct validity of this scale have been extensively studied, but primarily with clinical samples such as cancer patients, drug abusers and patients undergoing brief psychotherapy. Hardly any studies have related to work organizations.

Other Measures of Vigor as a Mood State

A widely used measure of mood is the Activation-Deactivation Adjective Check List, available in short- and long-forms, described in Thayer's book. It includes a subscale that gauges energy level. Mood inventories developed by other researchers also include measures of vigor or energy levels. Additional scales, used much less frequently, were described in the recent volume on character strengths and virtues by Peterson and Seligman. The set of studies on engagement by Schaufeli and his colleagues is not covered here because these investigators defined vigor, in their conceptualization of engagement, as comprising of high levels of energy, motivation to invest effort at work, and resilience; clearly, they refer to vigor as a cluster of different evaluative or attitudinal facets and not as an affective state. In sharp contrast, vigor, as conceptualized here, is an affective state not confounded with motivational processes or with individuals' behaviors following encounters with adverse events – namely resilience. Vigor at work can be experienced with or without encounters with adverse events.

A construct that overlaps to a certain extent with vigor is that of vitality, conceptualized by Ryan and Frederick as referring to the subjective experience of being full of energy, alert, and alive or vital. It overlaps in that both vigor and vitality refer to one's feeling energetic as reflecting one's internal resources and as unrelated to specific stimuli in one's environment. Vitality includes also the components of feeling alive and vital and of feeling awake and alert. Future research on the vitality measure has yet to test the possibility that the vitality measure actually represented two different dimensions, vigor and vitality, respectively.

This review of past attempts to gauge vigor as a mood state leads to the following conclusions. First, vigor has been studied primarily as a mood state. Second, vigor has hardly been studied in the work environment; in most past studies, respondents were patients, students, or sportsmen. Third, in past research, vigor has been conceptualized as reflecting one form of energy – physical strength. This is in contrast to the current focus on vigor as an affective experience at work reflecting three interrelated forms of energetic resources. Fourth, some measures adopted the practice of reverse-scoring tiredness or fatigue items in the vigor scales to arrive at a total score representing the positive mood of vigor, while above we argued that this practice is problematic on both theoretical and methodological grounds.

SEE ALSO: ▶ Positive affectivity

Virtue Ethics

Blaine J. Fowers
University of Miami

Virtue ethics refers to the contemporary study of virtue, which has appropriated Aristotle's account of virtue and the good life in the *Nicomachean Ethics* for present-day concerns. The core idea of virtue ethics is the concept of *eudaimonia*, sometimes translated as happiness, but better rendered as flourishing. Flourishing is not an experience or steady state. Rather, it is a pattern of *activity* through which a person enacts excellence not only in extraordinary actions, but in the daily activities of life. This ethical account focuses on what it is to live a rich and meaningful life by exercising human capacities such as reason, sociality, and creativity in the service of characteristically human goods such as knowledge, democracy, and justice.

Flourishing is seen as the ultimate human good because it is the only aim that is sought only for its own sake, not for the sake of any other end. A flourishing life is characterized by actions consistently and cumulatively undertaken for the sake of worthwhile ends within meaningful social bonds. Flourishing is not an episodic experience, but a matter of the way that one's life shapes up as a whole over time.

Virtue

"The original Greek term for virtue was *arête*, best translated as excellence. Virtues are, simply put, human excellences or character strengths that make it possible for individuals to flourish as human beings" (Fowers, 2005, p. 4). Because flourishing is a matter of actively pursuing characteristically human goods such as knowledge and positive social relations, particular virtues such as honesty and friendship are called for. For example, the scientific pursuit of knowledge necessitates the virtue of honesty, because science involves one in a genuine search for the best ways to understand the phenomena of interest. Dishonesty about one's procedures or results is not merely an error. Rather, it is a kind of bad faith that is intrinsically contradictory to science because distorting or fabricating one's findings negates the very possibility of pursuing the most accurate account of a phenomenon. Scientists' honesty serves the good of expanding our knowledge and the only way to pursue this good is to be truthful about one's procedures and results.

Because the human good is seen differently in various historical cultures, there have been many different conceptions of virtue. Warrior societies favored martial virtues that promote soldierly prowess and victory, whereas religious communities have emphasized pietistic virtues that promote deeper relations with the divine. For this reason, there is no final formulation of the human good nor is there a definitive list of virtues. Although many authors have put forward various lists of virtues, no list has widespread acceptance or substantial evidence for its primacy. For this reason, virtue ethicists generally hold that part of the human good is the ongoing debate over what is best for humans.

Virtues are multidimensional characteristics that have considerable overlap with standard psychological topics. Having virtue involves a cognitive understanding of what is good and of what counts as virtuous. When individuals are drawn to particular goods (e.g., knowledge, democracy) they are spontaneously motivated to act in accordance with them. An enduring attraction to admirable aims creates a reliable disposition or habit of acting for their sake. In the best life, the dispositional, cognitive, emotional, and behavioral aspects of character strengths are integrated seamlessly. This integration of knowledge and affect regarding how to act well is a very appealing aspect of virtue ethics. Individuals who have developed good character *want* to act ethically because they are attracted by what is good. This attraction to worthwhile goals elicits a desire to pursue them wholeheartedly rather than being conflicted between duty and desire. Disharmony of will and desire is an accepted aspect of many perspectives on ethics, but it is an indicator of incomplete character development in virtue ethics. Indeed, when one acts in the service of cherished ends and in ways one sees as praiseworthy, one takes pleasure in those activities. From this point of view, pleasure is not an adventitious pursuit in life, but an integral part of living well. For these reasons, virtue generally does not involve self-sacrifice or self-denial.

Aristotle (ca 330 BCE/1999) emphasized that "virtues are implanted in us neither by nature nor contrary to nature; we are by nature equipped with the ability to receive them, and habit brings this ability to completion and fulfillment" (p. 33). In contrast to humanistic theories, we cannot count on some innate goodness to give rise to excellence given favorable conditions. Cultivating virtue is a matter of a long series of choices to develop excellence actively in oneself. Virtues are obtained through developing reliable habits of thought, affect, and behavior. This generally involves observing individuals who exercise the virtue and practicing the virtue until it becomes second nature. Good habits of thought and emotion are fostered by developing a firm and consistent attachment to important human goods, which results in the desire to pursue those goods. Virtues are known as character strengths because they become characteristic of the person through the process of making them habitual. At best, virtuous action attains a significant degree of automaticity.

Character and Character Types

Although specific virtues can be acquired and discussed independently to some extent, many virtue ethicists see character as substantially unified. The argument for unity of character is twofold. First, flourishing and excellence of character involve the ability to respond well to many situations. Situations of risk call for courage, circumstances involving human frailty call for compassion, conditions concerning distributing goods call for justice, and so forth. If an individual can only enact a subset of virtues, that individual will fall short in many situations and will be unable to act consistently in pursuit of what is good. Second, flourishing is a matter of how an individual's life shapes up as a whole. Good character cannot be episodic because enacting virtue consistently across all life situations is necessary to have a flourishing life as a whole. Just as having a good day or a good year does not constitute a flourishing life, having one or two fine characteristics or acting well episodically does not mean that one has a good character.

The virtuous character may be best understood by contrasting it with the four other character types. Virtuous individuals have a clear vision of what is good and admirable, and they pursue those goods consistently and gladly. A person of good character *wants* to act for the best, which manifests as a settled disposition to act virtuously and a harmony between desire and duty. This emotional harmony and spontaneous desire to act well are defining features of virtue.

The most common way to think about "acting morally" in both popular consciousness and in modern ethical theories is that one must follow a rationally derived course that is either contrary to one's personal inclinations and feelings or at least independent of them. From a virtue ethics perspective, the conflict between moral will and desire is a defining feature of a pair of character types known as continent and incontinent. Individuals with these character types know how to act well, but their understanding of the best kind of action and their desire to follow through with admirable action are at odds with each other. Continent individuals are those who know how to act well and decide to do so, even though this decision is contrary to their desires. Typically, continent individuals have to struggle between what seems best and what they want to do. Their understanding of what is best generally triumphs over their desire, but it requires some effort to decide to act for the best, and this ambivalence is often manifest in the action. Individuals who know what they should do but frequently cannot bring themselves to do it are called incontinent persons. When their will to act well loses the struggle with less worthy desires, it is costly to these individuals because they frequently feel guilt, regret, or shame about their inability to act in the ways they think are fitting.

The vicious character refers to those who are characteristically greedy, deceitful, exploitive, self-indulgent, etc. The term *vicious* does not necessarily connote hostility or mean-spiritedness, simply that one consistently chooses to act ignobly. A key feature of character vice is that the individual feels entirely justified in their ignoble actions. This justification is not mere rationalization, but is based on a misguided sense of what is good. This erroneous vision of what is good is one of the key features that differentiates vicious from virtuous character. Vicious individuals pursue ends such as acquisitiveness, domination of others, and self-indulgence as goods in themselves. They do this by construing themselves and the world in a way that makes their actions seem appropriate and justified to them. For example, individuals who seek to dominate others may pride themselves on their hard-headed "recognition" that human life is nothing more than a struggle for power, a dog-eat-dog affair.

Individuals with beastly characters become enslaved to desires or habits that suppress or destroy their basic human capacities to reason, make choices, and engage in good relationships with others. Perhaps the best examples of beastliness are those who become so desperately addicted to a drug that all of their actions are oriented to serving their addiction. Theft from strangers or loved ones, prostitution, and myriad forms of deception or violence are deemed acceptable means to obtain the drug. Beastliness can also take forms such as an indiscriminate gluttony, a wanton tendency toward violence, uncontrollable gambling, and so forth. The key feature is the abandonment of one's humanity.

Practical Wisdom

One intriguing feature of virtue ethics is the nearly complete absence of rules for moral behavior. There is, of course, a general injunction to act virtuously, but virtue is not a matter of following rules. Rather, it requires cultivating excellence in character, from which fine and noble action will naturally ensue. Because the circumstances individuals encounter are endlessly variable, no set of rules or guidelines could provide enough direction to know how to act, and actors have to rely on their ability to choose wisely. In practical situations, the virtues require good judgment to know which traits are appropriate for a given situation and to know how to enact them, given the circumstances. The capacity to recognize the essentials of what we encounter and to respond well and fittingly to those circumstances is known as *phronesis*, often translated as practical wisdom, or judgment. According to Aristotle (ca 330 BCE/1999), practical wisdom is central: "it is impossible to be good in the full sense of the word without practical wisdom or to be a man of practical wisdom without moral excellence or virtue" (p. 172).

"In a nutshell, practical wisdom is the ability to make wise decisions about how to act in a specific situation" to pursue what is good (Fowers, 2005, p. 13). Practical wisdom begins with the ability to see what is important in the particular circumstances, to sort out what is central and what is peripheral so that one can respond to what is essential rather than being distracted by less important concerns. Wise individuals then deliberate about how best to pursue their overall sense of what is good in this particular situation. For example, a parent who is committed to teaching their child self-responsibility will respond to the child's misbehavior in a way designed to increase responsibility rather than simply reacting angrily or punitively. Practical wisdom results in choosing an action that is appropriate to the specific situation that allows one to pursue the goods that are relevant to it.

As individuals pursue worthwhile goals in a given situation, they must decide whether their actions should be guided primarily by courage or modesty, generosity or justice or by some other virtue. In addition, they have to decide what would count as courageous or generous action in each instance. Aristotle famously describes virtue as the mean between excess and deficiency. For example, courage is the mean between rashness and cowardice. Practical wisdom is the capacity for recognizing which virtues are relevant in the circumstances and then where the mean is for each concrete situation.

SEE ALSO: ▶ Civility ▶ Eudaimonia ▶ Good life ▶ Well-being

References

Aristotle. (1999). *Nicomachean ethics.* (M. Ostwald, trans.) Upper Saddle River, NJ: Prentice Hall.

Fowers, B. J. (2005). *Virtue and psychology: Pursuing excellence in ordinary practices.* Washington, DC: APA Press.

Virtues

Blaine J. Fowers
University of Miami

There are many virtue traditions from which one can draw a concept of virtue and lists of virtues, including warrior cultures such as the Homeric Greeks, the Lakota tribe, and the Bushido code, philosophical sources such as Aristotle and Confucius, and religious traditions such as Christianity, Judaism, and Buddhism. Each of these traditions has a particular understanding of what it is to live a good life as a human, and its list of virtues are those character strengths that make it possible for a person to live in the best way as conceived by the tradition. Among warrior cultures, virtues related to martial prowess and honor will predominate, whereas in religious traditions, virtues that enhance worship of the divine are central. Although virtue catalogs and descriptions of individual virtues vary across sociohistorical settings, there is also a great deal of overlap and great potential for fruitful dialogue among virtue traditions.

It is important to distinguish between virtue and the virtues. The singular term *virtue* refers to the general concept whereas the plural *virtues* refers to specific personal strengths such as courage or honesty. It is vital to have a clear, systematic general conception of virtue within which specific virtues can be defined. Virtue can be defined as the overall constellation of virtues that make it possible to live the best kind of life. The term *character* is generally used synonymously with virtue and the term *character strength* is interchangeable with a specific virtue.

Contemporary virtue ethicists tend to follow Aristotle in conceptualizing virtue in terms of a mutually supportive composite of characteristics including an understanding of what is good, knowledge about virtue, consistent virtuous action, affective concordance with virtuous actions, and practical wisdom. Goods are valued ends such as democracy, knowledge, and good relationships. Because a virtuous individual is attracted to these goods, he or she will act spontaneously in an honest or generous manner because it will help to bring the desired goods into being. This attraction to what is good is a key part of virtue because it gives rise to a harmony between duty and desire, in contrast to the conflict between duty and desire found in other prominent Western ethical systems. Virtue ethicists emphasize that virtuous action is informed and shaped by knowledge and reason rather than simply being the result of a generous impulse, for example.

Although there is some debate on this point, this composite structure is generally taken to entail the understanding that virtue involves the demonstrable ability to enact a full range of virtues or that there is a unity to virtuous individuals' character such that they act ethically across widely varying situations. The unity of virtue argument suggests that it would be inappropriate to attribute virtue to someone who could be honest but not generous or courageous but not just.

Virtue Catalogs

In the earliest Western list of virtues, Socrates identified four virtues in Plato's *Republic*: courage; justice; temperance; and wisdom. Aristotle expanded this list and the concept of virtue dramatically in his *Nicomachean Ethics*, the first full text devoted to ethics in the Western world. Aristotle added virtues such as liberality, proper pride, honesty, ready wit, and friendship. In addition, he emphasized the necessity of *phronesis* or practical wisdom in enacting virtue: "it is impossible to be good in the full sense of the word without practical wisdom or to be a man of practical wisdom without moral excellence or virtue" (Aristotle, ca 330 BCE/1999, p. 172). Thomas Aquinas incorporated Socrates' four virtues and called them the four cardinal virtues. He added three theological virtues: faith; hope; and charity. For Aquinas, "God Himself is the very object of these [theological] virtues" (ca 1265 CE/1966). Confucian virtues include reverence (*li*), love within the family (*hsiao*), righteousness (*yi*), honesty (*xin*), benevolence (*jen*), and loyalty to the state (*chung*).

These and other catalogs of the virtues often have a good deal in common, but it is obvious that they differ substantially as well. Peterson and Seligman (2004) set out to "reclaim the study of character and virtue as legitimate psychological topics" (p. 3) by examining "dozens of inventories of virtues and strengths" (p. 15) from a wide variety of sources. These authors hoped to create a comprehensive classification system for virtue. Their system contains six virtues (courage, justice, humanity, temperance, transcendence, and wisdom) with 24 character strengths distributed within these virtues. It is impossible to pass judgment on this classification system at this time, but it has been greeted with both acclaim and criticism, rendering it just as ambiguous in its general acceptability as all the other virtue catalogs.

The lesson from these catalogs is that no system of virtue has obtained universal acceptance or finality. Each catalog represents and expresses a particular outlook on what is important in human life, and these outlooks vary across time, culture, and the standpoint of their authors. Virtue catalogs are developed and reinterpreted according to a society's need for a coherent account of good character and of how to live well. Although the domain of human life is quite variable, it is not infinitely so. For this reason, there are significant commonalities across virtue catalogs, with virtues such as courage, honesty, and justice appearing frequently. These commonalities suggest that it is possible to recognize and meaningfully discuss some virtues across cultural and historical contexts. This is not to suggest that the differences in concepts of virtue are trivial, only that dialogue about them can be quite meaningful and enlightening.

General statements about particular virtues are complex because the enactment of virtues is not only relative to a worldview, but also strongly situation dependent. Aristotle famously described virtue as the mean between deficiency and excess. For example, generosity is defined in contrast to the deficiency of miserliness and the excess of profligacy. Recognizing the proper way to be generous is not simply splitting the difference between the extremes, but attending to what generosity requires in a particular situation. Decisions about what constitutes a generous gift are entirely dependent on the nature of the occasion, the kind of relationship one has, the means at one's disposal, and other related factors. Misreading any of them can render a gift miserly or profligate. Practical wisdom is the requisite capacity for reading situations well and understanding what the circumstances call for. This key virtue is delineated first among the frequently cited virtues because contemporary virtue ethicists generally agree with Aristotle that it is a necessary element in all other virtues.

The Virtues

Practical Wisdom

Virtue ethics is based on the premise that there is far too much variability in the ethical life of human beings to ever hope to formalize ethics into a set of rules or principles of action that can provide unequivocal guidance about how to act. Therefore,

> any set of rules requires an extensive array of exceptions, caveats, and qualifications to make it flexible enough to be responsive to the endless variation of daily life. These qualifications would have to be qualified further, leading to an infinite regress. (Fowers, 2005, p. 13)

In the absence of an algorithm for life, virtue ethics recommends learning to recognize what is good, cultivating a good character, and exercising judgment or practical wisdom as the keys for deciding how best to act, and living the best kind of life.

Practical wisdom is the ability to recognize what is important or at stake in a situation, to see how one can pursue important goods in that situation, and to decide which actions will be appropriate both to the situation and to promoting what is good. In sizing up situations, individuals with practical wisdom are able to differentiate between what is central and what is peripheral. They zero in on the important features of the situation and avoid being distracted by secondary concerns.

A clear-sighted appraisal of the circumstances allows these individuals to decide which of the virtues are called for. A situation in which important goods are threatened requires courage; one in which the distribution of resources, duties, or rights are at issue demands justice. Some situations will require more than one virtue and it takes wisdom to recognize how to appropriately harmonize them in action. As noted above, practical wisdom also guides the individual in knowing what constitutes a virtue in a particular situation. That is, given a particular context, how much risk taking constitutes courage or how much giving constitutes generosity? Being able to answer these questions is vital because, for example, one can err through excess or deficiency (i.e., by risking too much or risking too little given what is at stake). The parameters of practical wisdom will be exemplified in descriptions of each virtue below, highlighting the centrality of practical wisdom for practicing virtue.

Courage

Courage is a frequently recognized virtue and it is called for when an important good is at risk. Situations that involve risk-taking for the sake of defending something important are ubiquitous in human life. Such situations might involve natural disaster, war, crime, class conflict, exploitation, among other threats. Various circumstances call for different types of risk-taking, including physical, political, social, or psychological risks. In spite of this variability of context and form, a common requirement for courage is evident, and acting courageously means taking risks that are commensurate with both the good that one wants to protect and the situation. To name a few examples, fire fighters put their physical safety on the line for public safety; attorneys take publicly reviled dependents' cases to serve the cause of justice; and individuals and groups confront powerful exploiters for the sake of human rights or the environment.

Courageously taking risks means that one is protecting an important good (e.g., public safety), but doing so in a way that is fitting for the situation. It would be foolish for a firefighter to rush into a burning building to salvage mere property, but if lives were at stake, such a risk might be appropriate. Similarly, if there were no hope of saving someone, it would be rash to risk one's life for an unrealizable rescue. In contrast, a refusal to take reasonable risks to protect something of significant value would be cowardly.

Justice

Justice is a ubiquitous concern in human society. In North Atlantic societies, there is a tendency to see justice primarily as matters of equal treatment before the law, and of following correct procedures. There is a lot to be said for general equality and procedural justice, but there is also great latitude for interpretation and action in the context of the law, leading to significant risk that justice may be miscarried through excessive attention to "the letter of the law" or misapplication or outright misuse of the law. Moreover, in the vast majority of human interactions, the law is, at most, a distant consideration. Matters of justice in everyday life are decided more on an ethical or customary basis than a legal one. All of this suggests that it is important for individuals to cultivate justice as a virtue because the just application of the law and justice in day-to-day relating require a personal commitment to justice.

The virtue of justice is the ability to properly assign resources, rewards, burdens, duties, and rights. From a virtue perspective, this proper assignment has to do with what a person or group deserves or is owed. In some cases, everyone deserves equal treatment, as in allowing equal opportunity for achievement, jobs, equal pay for equal work, and so forth. In other cases, merit will guide the just assignment of benefits and burdens, as in giving awards for outstanding achievement, giving greater responsibility to those capable of shouldering it, or giving extra resources or assistance to those who suffer through no fault of their own.

The virtue of justice is complex in many ways. Most importantly, it is one of the virtues that is most sensitive to its context because what is seen as the proper assignment of benefits and burdens depends strongly on the political and economic environment. A just distribution is seen differently in theocratic, aristocratic, and democratic political systems. Similarly, justice is cast in different terms in communist, socialist, and capitalist economies. Variations in what individuals and groups deserve will inform different accounts of justice and their appropriate actions.

In spite of these variations, the virtue of justice can be understood in contrast to the vices of excess and deficiency in the particular political and economic context. Excess occurs when one aggrandizes too much to oneself vis à vis one's desert and deficiency when one allows oneself to be disadvantaged relative to one's desert. Moreover, when individuals participate in decisions of desert regarding others, just individuals will work toward a proper assignment of benefit and burden among their fellows. Here, as elsewhere, practical wisdom is indispensable in identifying the proper distribution of resources and expectations among individuals and groups and understanding how to bring that about.

Honesty

The virtue of honesty is necessary to facilitate communication and cooperation in joint activities in the service of important goods. One of the most obvious goods that honesty facilitates is good personal relationships, but it is also central to the pursuit of justice as a good, as well as the pursuit of knowledge. Dishonesty in any of these pursuits seriously undermines the endeavor itself. For example, planting false evidence or misleading a judge or jury may lead to or avoid a conviction, but it undermines the pursuit of justice, which is devoted to assigning culpability for wrong-doing correctly.

Honesty is found in the mean between excessive candor and deficient candor. Excessive candor includes well-known instances such as telling a murderer where to find the intended victim, making overly candid and needlessly hurtful statements about others' appearance, and so forth. Deficient candor can occur through commission (e.g., lying) or omission (e.g., misleading or withholding information). In all cases, the proper level of candor is largely determined by the situation and the goods being pursued. In scientific endeavors, rather complete candor is appropriate regarding the methods, analyses, and discussion, but still limited by considerations such as redundancy and relevance. In polite conversation among acquaintances, rather less candor is called for because the goods of this kind of interchange have as much to do with social convention and amity as with truth.

Generosity

Although the term *generosity* is less commonly used than other virtue terms, it can encompass several virtues. Aristotle used the term *liberality*, Aquinas named it *charity*, and Confucius called it *benevolence*. The virtue of generosity involves situations in which one group or individual gives to another. Generous individuals give "to the right person, to the right extent, at the right time, for the right reason, and in the right way" (Aristotle, ca. 330 BCE/1999, p. 50). Generosity can involve gifts, time, disaster relief, forgiveness, kindness, and so forth.

Generosity is defined as giving that goes beyond what is required by justice or friendship and that conduces to the recipient's good. Giving fails to be generous when it does not contribute to an individual's overall flourishing. For example, some giving has the effect of maintaining the dependence of the recipient on the giver rather than helping the recipient to become more capable. In other cases, offering admission to an applicant who is ill-prepared for a degree program or offering a job to someone who is not capable of succeeding at it would not be doing those individuals a kindness.

Like the other virtues, generosity is also clarified by recognizing the excess (profligacy) and deficiency (miserliness) associated with it. Circumstances help to define what counts as generosity, including the occasion, the relationship between the giver and receiver, and social custom. A gift that would be viewed as stingy in one circumstance might be seen as excessive in another. Practical wisdom serves to guide the giver in recognizing the appropriate level and kind of gift taking all these factors into account.

Friendship

Virtue ethics differs from modern approaches to ethics in that it deals more directly with the intricacies of relational life. This is particularly evident in Aristotle, who devoted two of the 10 books in the *Nicomachean Ethics* to friendship. He saw friendship as an essential element of a flourishing life, reasoning that living well would require close, cooperative relationships with others oriented to mutually desired goods. "No one would choose to have all good things by himself. . . . It follows that the happy [flourishing] man needs friends" (Aristotle, ca 330 BCE/ 1999, p. 264). He is making the important claim that the best kind of life must include friends because humans need partners in their activities, mutual support, and well-wishing to flourish.

For Aristotle, friendship is more than an affective bond. It encompasses relationships of many types, including the peer relationships that we generally consider friendship, as well as family and business relationships. Friendship is marked by partiality toward one's friend: wanting the best for him or her and taking pleasure in his or her happiness and well-being. This partiality contrasts sharply with modern ethical theories that emphasize *impartiality* as a key element in ethical action. Friendship also involves individuals in joint activities which the friends find worthwhile and pleasant.

Aristotle described three kinds of friendship. The first is based on pleasure, and pleasure friends' relationships are a matter of enjoying one another's company and shared activities. The second is based on utility. Utility friends assist one another in various ways and the relationship is primarily devoted to assisting each other in areas like business or politics. The third is called character friendship and it is based on recognizing and valuing the quality of the friend's character and on sharing the pursuit of worthwhile ends such as justice, knowledge, art, and other goods with the friend. Aristotle thought that all three forms of friendship were valuable, but that the third form of friendship was the noblest and most enduring because character and the pursuit of worthwhile ends are more stable than pleasure or utility. Character friends spend time together doing the things they love, and affiliating with people who have good character helps one to improve oneself.

Although there is some disagreement about the degree to which character strengths can be understood and practiced independently, it is clear that the best kind of life will be one that is characterized by consistently acting well about things that matter in a wide variety of situations. It is likely that some version of the virtues described in this entry will have a place in most virtue catalogs because they deal with key aspects of human life. Nevertheless, the virtues discussed above should be seen as illustrative rather than exhaustive. The various catalogs of the virtues indicate the complexity of human life by recommending an array of virtues. Virtue ethicists emphasize that cultivating the character strengths that are necessary to pursue the goods identified by one's tradition is the best way to live well according to that tradition. Empirical research on and the conceptual development of virtues in psychology are in their infancy, but there is a growing body of evidence that virtues do contribute substantially to human flourishing, indicating that this promising area of inquiry merits ongoing study.

SEE ALSO: ▶ Virtue ethics

References

Aquinas, T. (ca 1265 CE/1966). *Summa theologica* (Vol. 33, W. J. Hill, trans.). New York: McGraw-Hill.

Aristotle. (ca 330 BCE/1999). *Nicomachean ethics* (M. Ostwald, trans.). Upper Saddle River, NJ: Prentice Hall.

Fowers, B. J. (2005). *Virtue and psychology: Pursuing excellence in ordinary practices.* Washington, DC: APA Press.

Peterson, C., & Seligman, M. E. P. (2004). *Character strengths and virtues: A handbook and classification.* Washington, DC: American Psychological Association.

Vitality

Netta Weinstein and Richard M. Ryan
University of Rochester

Vitality refers to a state of organismic well-being in which individuals feel energetic, alert, and fully alive. Various researchers have provided measures of this concept. Richard Ryan and his colleagues have assessed *subjective vitality* in terms of dynamic energy that emanates from the self and is relatively free from tenseness, jitteriness, or anger. For them, vitality represents a feeling of aliveness that is affected by both physical (e.g., health, fatigue) and psychological conditions. Robert Thayer described a similar construct, termed *calm energy*, which requires the experience of liveliness that is free of tension and pressure. As such, vitality is associated with a number of positive emotions, including feelings of joy, interest, and enthusiasm as well as physical health and improved physical functioning. Although vitality relates to positive affect, the state is differentiated from happiness or subjective well-being in that it consists of higher levels of experienced activation or energy as well as positive affect.

In philosophical and religious texts, vitality is described as essential for creativity and growth. Ancient Chinese and Japanese traditions respectively refer to vital energy as *chi* or *Ki*, and cite it as the source of life, creativity, and organismic health. Balinese healers describe *bayu* as a vital force that underlies growth and resilience. In the Western tradition, the concept of vitality was central to Freud's economic model. Freud proposed that people have a limited supply of psychic energy essential for functioning. Intrapsychic conflict depletes available resources of ego energy, leading to lower levels of perceived vitality. When an individual is self-congruent and nondefensive, he or she may experience greater feelings of aliveness and energy. In line with this idea, researchers such as Ryan, Ken Sheldon, Tim Kasser, and Robert Emmons have found that integrated, self-congruent individuals experience higher vitality. State levels of vitality may also be experienced when one acts autonomously or in a self-congruent fashion, or experiences a sense of competence. Furthermore, individuals experience greater vitality when engaging in intrinsic pursuits. Experimental data presented by Glen Nix and his colleagues show that succeeding at an activity for which one feels pressured leads to increased happiness but not vitality, but that succeeding at an activity autonomously undertaken leads to increases in both. Thayer's lab also shows that ego involvement has similar effects to those of pressure, ultimately leading to greater losses in vitality. Research by Harry Reis and colleagues provides further support for the importance of psychological well-being in freeing up vitalizing energy, showing that on days in which individuals experience greater autonomy, relatedness to others, and competence, they also experienced greater vitality. Along similar lines, Roy Baumeister and his colleagues have viewed energy as a limited resource, and emphasized the role of self-control in depleting this resource. Baumeister and his colleagues have shown that extending self-control in an effort to attain difficult goals depletes energy resources, effectively reducing levels of vitality.

Yet another view of vitality was provided by Hans Selye, who pioneered stress research. He described *adaptation energy* as a limited resource required for resilience to stress. Such energy facilitates one's ability to regulate emotions and to cope with stressful life events. Stressful life events, in turn, have the capacity to deplete individuals' levels of vitality. Stressful life events are one of a number of circumstances of behaviors that can thwart vitality.

Researchers such as Ryan and Thayer find that physical habits also have an impact; Individuals who have poor physical health and who smoke or have poor nutrition experience less vitality, while individuals who engage in physical exercise experience higher vitality. Ancient Eastern practices such as tai chi, yoga, and meditation can also lead to greater experiences of vitality. Vitality has also been associated with better psychological and cognitive functioning. Studies show that vitality contributes to enhanced problem-solving, concentration, and performance, and greater readiness for new challenges.

Presently, a number of scales measure vitality. As noted, Robert Thayer's Activation-Deactivation Adjective Check List (AD ACL) measures a state of calm energy, which in contrast to tense energy, reflects a feeling of vigor and positive energy. McNair and colleagues' Profile of Mood States (POMS) assesses a state called *vigor* that reflects positive energized mood. Also, the Emotional Vitality Scale developed by Pennix and colleagues measures an energy state comprised of personal mastery, happiness, and decreased anxious and depressive symptoms. Finally and most recently, Ryan and Frederick developed the Subjective Vitality Scale (SVS), which assesses vitality with items such as "I feel alive and vital," and "I feel energized." These measures reflect the diversity in thought and the continuing interest in vitality as a central measure of well-being. This interest arises from deep roots founding the discussion of vitality, as well as the intimate relation of this dynamic construct with choices, motivations, and adaptive functioning.

From the present research emerge a number of notable directions for future studies. A burgeoning subset of vitality research has recently focused on identifying factors that effectively enhance vitality. In particular, mindful states and contact with nature are promising to be effective vitalizing interventions. Future studies may explore these and other interventions that enhance the experience of vitality. Additionally, the body of research utilizes self-reported and behavioral indicators of vitality. To understand the nature of vitality, it will be fruitful also to examine physiological processes that contribute to vitality and their interaction with the psychological factors reviewed. Finally, the concept of vitality appears to have significance in varied cultures and contexts, but few studies have examined whether there are cultural or developmental differences in what fosters vitality. Future studies should examine cultural and age-related differences in vitality, including different subjective experience and expression.

SEE ALSO: ▶ Hedonics   ▶ Positive affectivity   ▶ Vigor   ▶ Well-being

Vocation

Christopher A. Ebberwein
Psychology Consultants, Wichita, Kansas

Vocation, which comes from the Latin word vocare, meaning "to call", is best understood as one's *calling*, or motivation, to participate meaningfully in the world. Traditionally understood as a calling from God, vocation maintains this meaning (e.g., a vocation to priesthood or religious life), but is more commonly understood today as one's particular place in the world of work. The spiritual roots of the word vocation are found in the implication that one's vocation *fits* the person's unique nature – that it presents an opportunity to implement one's meaning or purpose in life. Richard Bolles, author of a widely popular career change manual, points out that vocation is synonymous with the word *mission*. Most people, at some point in their lives, wonder about their *mission in life*. This internal pull toward an opportunity to contribute something lasting, or toward a meaning greater than the self, seems to distinguish vocation from simply performing a job. For this reason, vocation inherently includes one's calling to work that is both paid and nonpaid. For instance, a woman who works a difficult low status job for no reason other than the income might describe her vocation as mother or grandmother, with her meaning and her contribution being the love and support of family. Individuals seeking a vocation can be heard saying things like the following: "I want more than a paycheck;" "I want to create something;" "I want to make a difference." They want a vocation. A person implements his or her vocation by answering the call, which requires an understanding of both the self and the calling. Examining theories of vocational psychology illustrates important factors an individual faces in order to gain this dual understanding.

Though job placement and vocational guidance emerged along with factories during the late 1800s, the study of vocational choice took formal shape in the early 1900s when Frank Parsons defined a three-part method of choosing a vocation to include: an understanding of one's self; an understanding of the nature of work available to the individual; and the reconciling of these two groups of information into a fitting decision. Most view Parsons' model as the beginning of the field of vocational psychology, which devotes part of its research and practice to helping individuals respond to their calling in meaningful ways that allow them to be satisfied, and ideally fulfilled. His model of using information about self and occupations as the basis for vocational decision-making remains relevant today, with great advancements through the work of researchers like John L. Holland, René Dawis, Lloyd Lofquist, and Linda Gottfredson. Their theories emphasize different aspects of *vocational choice* and illustrate the many implications that can be drawn and studied from Parsons' model.

People who find their calling know their interests and find places to express them. According to Holland's theory, patterns of vocational interests demonstrate an individual's primary personality type. Along with work environments, the personality can be understood as fitting one or more of six descriptive themes (realistic, investigative, artistic, social, enterprising, and conventional). Personal satisfaction and effectiveness within this theory depend on the degree of fit, or congruence, between the personality type and the type of environment attributed to the vocation. This theory has led to widely used scales and inventories that aid with vocational decision-making.

Implementing a vocation allows an individual to meet both their personal needs and the needs of the environment in which they work. Dawis and Lofquist's important concept of correspondence reflects the ideal interaction between the needs and aspirations of an employee and the needs of an employer. The quality of the vocational decision relies on both the ability of the environment to match the individual's aspirations and the ability of the individual to contribute to the goals of the organization.

Not uncommonly, people take on undue pressure to find the *one perfect match*, with the fear that anything less will lead to disappointment or unhappiness. Vocation points to one's unique and meaningful contribution more than it points to a specific job title. Expressing one's self genuinely and authentically does not have to mean finding *the one right* vocation, but might result in a number of possible vocations. The natural born teacher might find himself at the head of a 1st grade classroom, a member of a distinguished faculty, a corporate trainer, and/or the first and best teacher of his own children. An individual might choose one of these vocations for a lifetime, might transition from one to another over time, or might implement more than one at a time, as is the case for most mothers and fathers, who see parenthood as a calling in addition to that which they pursue in their work lives.

People answer the call within a unique life context. In addition to vocational choice theory, another major line of research known as career development theory emphasizes developmental factors and attempts to understand how vocation interacts with other facets of a person's life. No one furthered this line of research more than Donald Super, whose *lifespan, life-space* theory of career development calls attention to the fact that a vocation takes place within a life. Satisfaction depends on how well the person implements his or her self-concept at different stages in life across some number of available roles, including but not limited to one's vocation.

Some period of imagining a preferred calling often ends in compromise. Linda Gottfredson's work contains important elements of both vocational choice theory and career development theory. It highlights an ongoing process of decision-making within the individual's social context. Factors such as social class and gender stereotypes contribute to and limit a person's aspirations over time. Individuals maintain some vocational options and eliminate others depending on how well the options match his or her view of self. As the person encounters the world at large, he or she gives up some of the preferred occupations due to real and perceived external factors that limit access to that type of work. This compromise can range from hardly noticeable to highly distressing, depending on the degree to which alternatives allow implementation of the self-concept. When the only accessible options result in a great mismatch between the vocation and the person's self-concept, the distress is at its worst.

Sometimes a calling is beyond reach. Importantly, the developmental theorists' emphasis on life context demonstrates some factors that limit one's vocational options. Certain factors affect whether a person ever aspires to a particular vocation and other factors force a choice that is less desired at the time of decision-making. Some limiting factors include characteristics or traits such as physical stature, intelligence, particular skill-sets, or personal values. These limiting factors are important and, though disappointing at times, aid in the choice of a realistic vocation. Every person encounters factors that make some vocations realistic and others unrealistic. Other limiting factors are not inevitable, but have been constructed by society over time and have served often to unfairly discriminate against various groups of people. Researchers such as Nancy Betz have shown that women often underestimate their ability to succeed in certain vocations compared to men, possibly due to customary role divisions between men and women. This belief in one's ability to succeed, known as self-efficacy, significantly affects one's perceived options and subsequently one's choice of vocation. Similarly, disability, membership in a particular ethnic group, religion or social class, and sexual orientation often have served to limit the aspirations of members of these groups. At times these limits have resulted from subtle, unspoken patterns among groups, and at other times they have resulted from overt discrimination. Poverty dramatically affects the pursuit of paid work as a vocation, both in the ways that it limits experiences that might otherwise contribute to vocational development, and in the simple fact that survival needs take precedence over needs for self-fulfillment.

The vocation one pursues often reflects priorities that extend beyond his work life. As with any human endeavor, people view and approach vocation differently based on a number of personal differences. Such differences might arise based on gender and cultural influences. Within groups, differences might be based on social class, level of education, values particular to a family, religious affiliation, or genetic endowment. For instance, choice of vocation for some individuals will depend heavily on the family's needs and preferences. For others, individual preferences take precedence over the family.

When answering the call, know that change is inevitable. In a study Super conceptualized the successful completion of age-appropriate vocational tasks across the life span as *vocational maturity*, but this construct fell short of explaining how individuals should adjust when unexpected change interrupts normally expected developmental tasks. This shortcoming became apparent with the rapid change in the world of work in the 1970s and 1980s, when significant change in one's vocational life became the expectation, not the exception. Super himself suggested that a greater understanding of adult transition was needed. In recent years, Mark Savickas has updated Super's theory and emphasizes *career adaptability* over vocational maturity. Adaptability, or one's readiness to cope with internal and external change in order to implement one's self-concept, applies across the lifespan. It includes an individual's degree of concern, control, confidence, and curiosity for tasks that contribute to vocational development. With an understanding that much of what contributes to a person's vocational choice is subtle and intuitive – even outside of awareness – Tom Krieshok and colleagues are studying the component of career adaptability termed *engagement*, which naturally expands the individual's fund of vocational information and subsequently his or her perceived options, through direct experiences. Such experiences can include planned activities such as observing others at work or volunteering, or they can include those encounters that John Krumboltz has coined *planned happenstance*, the kinds of enriching experiences that arise from a willingness to see unplanned events as potential opportunities for learning about oneself or the vocation. Adaptability, engagement, and openness to planned happenstance promote a ready stance toward an ever-changing world, and using these skills allows the individual to answer and find meaning in multiple callings across a lifetime.

SEE ALSO: ▶ Adaptability   ▶ Calling   ▶ Career development ▶ Self-efficacy

Watson, John B.

Janice E. Jones
Cardinal Stritch University

John Broadus Watson (1878–1958) was an American psychologist whose work greatly influenced the behaviorism movement. Behaviorism is the field of psychological study that looks at what we do rather than how we think or feel. This was far removed from the Freudian school of thought that examined the unconscious mind and that favored introspection. John B. Watson's work influenced B. F. Skinner's research on operant conditioning and also had a major influence on behavior therapy.

Early in his career, John B. Watson studied behavior using animals. He progressed to studying human behavior and began to research emotional reactions. The Little Albert experiment, which could be called one of his most famous experiments, involved his ideas that people have three emotional reactions, those of love, rage and fear. He began his Little Albert Experiment on children at Johns Hopkins University. This involved specifically one little boy called Albert. Watson used classical conditioning to create fear in the little boy by showing Albert a white rat while simultaneously creating a loud, sudden noise. This research procedure created fear in Albert by making him associate the white rat with the loud, scary noise. Watson progressed from the white rat to larger and seemingly scarier animals with the children. Archival film footage of John B. Watson himself dressed in a Santa mask with a white flowing beard shows the viewer how scared the child was as he made the connection between the fur of the animal and the beard on the mask. These findings indicate that classical conditioning had taught people to transfer the fear from the loud noise that was associated with fur to other furry or hairy things. The theory indicated that people generalize their fear and is indicative of how people react to their environment through conditioned responses.

Although John B. Watson was the president of the American Psychological Association in 1915, he did not have a lengthy career in academia. He left the field by 1920 and entered the world of advertising where he became a vice president in a large advertising firm. Although he was in a different field, he continued to publish some psychological works.

SEE ALSO: ▶ Entrepreneurial behavior   ▶ Positive organizational behavior

Well-Being

Matthew W. Gallagher
University of Kansas

Introduction

The scientific study of well-being has dramatically expanded in recent years. Although as early as 1948 the World Health Organization stated that mental health is more than the absence of mental illness, it was not until recently that psychologists began to systematically study the causes, correlates, and consequences of flourishing mental health and states of well-being. Hedonistic and eudaimonic traditions in well-being research have evolved from different philosophical and theoretical roots, yet modern day hedonistic (subjective / emotional) and eudaimonic (psychological and social) aspects of well-being appear to be closely related components of psychological functioning. Although these models have previously been presented as competing alternatives, recent theoretical and empirical work has focused on how these three theories and components of well-being complement one another and can be integrated into comprehensive models of flourishing mental health.

Hedonic Well-Being

To date, the hedonic model of well-being has been the most extensively studied. Hedonic well-being is also commonly referred to as subjective or emotional well-being or happiness. This research tradition was pioneered by Ed Diener, whose seminal review paper in 1984 on subjective well-being proposed a model of well-being focusing on an individual's cognitive and affective evaluations of his or her life. More specifically, Diener and his colleagues have defined hedonic (or subjective) well-being as the frequent experience of pleasant emotions and moods, the infrequent experience of negative emotions and moods, and high levels of self-reported life satisfaction. This model of well-being is an extension of the philosophy of hedonism, which identified the pursuit of pleasure and avoidance of pain as the primary goals in life, and is predicated on the belief that individuals are the best judges of their happiness or well-being. Decades of research provide support for hedonic well-being as a reliable and valid conceptualization of well-being.

Eudaimonic Well-Being

The eudaimonic tradition of well-being focuses on the aspects of human functioning that promote and reflect the pursuit of meaningful life goals. Exemplifying this tradition, Carol Ryff and colleagues at the University of Wisconsin have developed a model of eudaimonic well-being that is intended to provide a holistic and theoretically grounded model of positive functioning. Specifically, Ryff and colleagues have identified six related but distinct factors that are proposed to encompass the eudaimonic idea: autonomy; environmental mastery; personal growth; positive relations with others; purpose in life; and self-acceptance. Individuals high in these aspects of well-being are independent and primarily driven by their own standards (autonomy), able to effectively identify and pursue external opportunities (environmental mastery), continually looking for opportunities to grow and develop (personal growth), engaged in mutually satisfying, warm, and trusting relationships (positive relations with others), able to identify and pursue meaningful goals (purpose in life), and have a positive attitude about both their personality and self (self-acceptance). This model is an extension of the Aristotelian philosophical tradition, which identified the pursuit of one's "daemon," or true self, as the ultimate purpose in life. Recent factor analytic research supports Ryff's model of eudaimonic well-being and the proposed theoretical distinctions between the hedonic and eudaimonic aspects of well-being.

Sociologist Corey Keyes of Emory University has argued that the failure to consider the importance of an individual's social condition and relationship reflects an intrapersonal bias in psychological research and has developed a model of social well-being that draws upon classical sociology. Whereas Ryff's model of psychological well-being focuses on primarily private phenomena that reflect the challenges encountered by adults in their private lives, Keyes' model of social well-being focuses on primarily public phenomena that reflect whether individuals are flourishing in their social lives. Specifically, social well-being consists of five factors that represent the extent to which individuals are overcoming social challenges and are functioning well in their social world. The five factors include social acceptance, social actualization, social coherence, social contribution and social integration. Individuals high in these aspects of well-being are comfortable with and have favorable views of others (social acceptance), believe that other individuals and the institutions of society are helping them reach their full potential (social actualization), perceive order and meaning in their relationships and society (social coherence), believe themselves to be a valuable and appreciated member of society (social contribution), and feel as if they are united with and supported by other members of their community (social integration). Social well-being is therefore an extension of the eudaimonic tradition of well-being from the intrapersonal focus of Ryff's model to the interpersonal realm. Recent factor analytic research using nationally representative samples of American adults supported Keyes' theory of well-being, as well as the distinctions between the components of social well-being and the components of hedonic and eudaimonic well-being.

Integrated Models of Well-Being

Researchers studying well-being have recently begun to explore the potential for integrating the theories and components of hedonic, psychological, and social well-being into a comprehensive model of flourishing mental health. The potential for integrating these three models was first proposed and empirically examined by Corey Keyes. More recently, we have used confirmatory factor analysis to examine the latent structure of well-being in large samples of American adults. This empirical work provided support for the theoretical models of hedonic, psychological, and social well-being as distinct latent constructs, and demonstrated that these three models and the fourteen factors of well-being could be successfully integrated into a hierarchical structure of well-being. This integrated model of well-being maintains the theoretical distinctions of well-being, while simultaneously demonstrating that these models and components are strongly related to one another.

Categorical Models of Well-Being

In addition to exploring the various dimensions of well-being, researchers have recently begun to examine the utility of categorical models of well-being that distinguish between different levels of positive mental health. Two categorical models of well-being have been developed in recent years and found to have preliminary empirical support. The first was developed by Barbara Fredrickson and colleagues and focuses on the ratio of positive to negative emotions that individuals experience. Fredrickson's research indicates that a ratio of more than three positive emotions for each negative emotion is indicative of flourishing mental health, and therefore that these affect ratios can be used to diagnose levels of well-being. The second categorical model of well-being was developed by Corey Keyes. This model distinguishes between flourishing, moderate, and languishing levels of mental health based upon levels of the fourteen factors of well-being that comprise the hedonic, eudaimonic, and social theories of well-being. Although more research examining both of these models is needed, these theories provide promising methods to distinguish between the presence or absence of mental health in a manner similar to how the DSM-IV distinguishes between the presence or absence of mental illness.

Predicting Well-Being

One question that is often raised about well-being is to what extent do higher levels of well-being simply reflect life circumstances such as age or income. Surprisingly, these factors appear to determine only a modest amount of individuals' levels of well-being. A recent review paper by Lyubomirsky and colleagues indicated that demographic variables and life circumstances determine roughly 10 percent of the variance in individual levels of hedonic well-being. This review paper also reviewed research from twin studies, and concluded that roughly half of the variance in hedonic well-being can be explained by genetic factors. Fortunately, the remaining 40 percent of the variance in individuals' levels of well-being appears to be dependent on intentional activities, and is therefore subject to change. Psychological factors that appear to be particularly important in promoting adaptive intentional activities include hope, curiosity, optimism, and gratitude.

Benefits of Well-Being

In addition to examining important predictors of well-being, researchers have recently begun to explore the benefits of high levels of well-being. In particular, the Midlife Development in the United States (MIDUS) studies have provided an unprecedented amount of information about the psychological and social functioning of American adults. The results of the first MIDUS survey demonstrated that Americans who report having flourishing mental health miss fewer days of work, are less likely to suffer from a diagnosable mental illness, report more intimate relationships, have fewer chronic physical diseases, have less trouble sleeping, and generally have better psychosocial functioning than individuals who report moderate or low levels of mental health. A particularly noteworthy finding is that well-being and mental illness appear to be independent risk factors for the development of cardiovascular disease. Recent review papers have also demonstrated that various aspects of well-being have robust effects on important life outcomes. The most comprehensive of these reviews was conducted by Sonja Lyubomirsky, Laura King, and Ed Diener. This review demonstrated across a variety of important life domains (e.g., work, family, friendships, and health) that individuals who report higher levels of happiness or well-being report improved outcomes in each of the life domains. Together the MIDUS data and the Lyubomirsky et al., review provide promising evidence that, beyond feeling good, high levels of well-being promote positive outcomes in a variety of domains.

Future Directions

Although the scientific study of well-being has made great progress in recent years, there are many areas in which additional research is needed. First, additional research is needed to determine the validity of the hedonic, eudaimonic, social, and integrated models of well-being. These models have been supported by promising empirical work to date, but it is likely that the future research will lead to additional theoretical refinements that could help us to better articulate the latent nature of well-being. Second, these models of well-being need to be studied in more diverse samples to clarify how ethnicity, gender, age, socioeconomic status and other demographic variables influence the various aspects of well-being. Finally, perhaps the most important area of future research will be longitudinal research that could help us better understand if and when lasting gains in well-being can be achieved. Historically, well-being researchers have often concluded that individuals are stuck on a "hedonic treadmill" that inevitably causes us to revert to a primarily genetically determined level of well-being. More recently, Lyubomirsky and colleagues have challenged this theory and suggested that as much as 40 percent of individual levels of well-being can be determined by intentional activities. Unfortunately, existing empirical research has not adequately examined this hypothesis and the potential for change. Future research examining individual trajectories and pathways to well-being could therefore help us to better understand how to promote and protect well-being.

SEE ALSO: ▶ Happiness   ▶ Global well-being   ▶ Carol Ryff

Well-Being Therapy

Giovanni A. Fava and Chiara Ruini
University of Bologna, Italy

Well-being therapy (WBT) is a new psychotherapeutic strategy with the aim of enhancing psychological well-being. It was originally applied and validated in the residual phase of mood and anxiety disorders but its efficacy has also been extended to the prevention of relapse in recurrent depression; to the loss of anti-depressant efficacy during maintenance pharmacotherapy in recurrent depression; and recently to the treatment of posttraumatic stress disorder and of generalized anxiety disorder. Well-being therapy is based on Ryff's multi-dimensional model of psychological well-being, encompassing six dimensions: autonomy; personal growth; environmental mastery; purpose in life; positive relations; and self-acceptance. This model was selected on the basis of its easy applicability to clinical populations; in fact it can be used to describe specific impairments of patients with affective disorders and calls for behavioral and psychological modifications in order to reach optimal human functioning. The goal of WBT is to improve the patients' levels of psychological well-being according to these six dimensions.

Structure of Well-Being Therapy

Well-being therapy is a short-term psychotherapeutic strategy, that extends over 8 sessions, which may take place every week or every other week. The duration of each session is usually in the range of 30 to 50 minutes. It is a technique which emphasizes self-observation, with the use of a structured diary, and interaction between patient and therapist. In the initial phase (sessions 1 to 2) the therapist asks the patient to record in the diary the circumstances surrounding the episodes of well-being, rated on a 0–100 scale, with 0 being absence of well-being and 100 the most intense well-being that could be experienced. Then the patient is encouraged to identify thoughts and beliefs leading to premature interruption of well-being, and is instructed to reinterpret those thoughts viewed from an observer's standpoint (*cognitive restructuring*). The technique is aimed at changing beliefs and attitudes detrimental to well-being, stimulating personal growth, and reinforcing well-being-promoting behavior. In the final sessions, the therapist can use these reinterpretations to increase a sense of well being in any of the 6 areas which might be impaired. WBT includes:

- *cognitive restructuring*: change from negative to positive any thoughts which interrupt periods of feeling well;
- scheduling of *pleasant activities*: negotiate with patients enjoyable activities they will carry out each day, e.g., go for a walk, listen to music;
- *graded tasks*: e.g., to improve positive relations, encourage a patient to phone a friend, invite that friend out for dinner, spend further time with that friend, etc.;
- *assertiveness training*;
- *problem solving* to improve patients' autonomy and environmental mastery, e.g., help patient deal with everyday activities; ask for a promotion at work etc.; and
- increasing optimism and positive thinking.

WBT shares techniques and therapeutic ingredients similar to those of standard cognitive-behavioral therapy. It thus may be conceptualized as a specific strategy within the broad spectrum of self-therapies. However, the main point of distinction of WBT is the focus: It is not the abatement of distress (as in cognitive-behavioral therapy), but the enhancement of psychological well-being and the promotion of optimal human functioning.

Further Applications of WBT

WBT could play an important role in *preventive interventions*, for example with children or adolescents. Improving their levels of psychological well-being could be crucial in the development of their personality and could provide protection against future adversity and against health-risk behavior (e.g., smoking, alcohol or drug abuse, etc.). In a recent study WBT has been modified into a psychoeducational program performed in school with students. The results of this intervention showed that WBT was effective in improving psychological well-being and in decreasing distress.

WBT could play an important role in *psychosomatic medicine*, where increasing psychological well-being may counteract the feelings of demoralization and loss which are part of chronic disease and thus improve the individual coping.

WBT could also have an important role for the treatment of severe psychological disturbances such as obsessive-compulsive disorder (OCD) and posttraumatic stress disorder (PTSD). Clinical observation suggests that anxiety-provoking thoughts (typical of OCD) may often be preceded by feelings of well-being, suggesting that these patients may have a low threshold for well-being-related anxiety. Case reports show the potential of WBT in the treatment of OCD. Another case report documents the suitability of WBT in the treatment of PTSD, without using debriefing or other ways of dealing with the central traumatic event.

Further lines of research in the next few years could disclose new applications of WBT under the positive psychology umbrella. Engendering the positive and not just alleviating the negative may lead to more enduring results in treatment of mood and anxiety disorders.

SEE ALSO: ▶ Positive psychotherapy   ▶ Positive therapy
▶ Quality of life therapy   ▶ Well-being

Werner, Emmy

Janice E. Jones
Cardinal Stritch University

Emmy E. Werner (1929–) is a developmental psychologist whose research has focused on *resilience*, which she defined as a person's ability to recover from a traumatic event(s) and go on to live a happy, healthy life. She is currently professor emeritus at the University of California at Davis. She received her PhD in 1955 from the University of Nebraska. Dr Werner's groundbreaking longitudinal study examined the lives of Hawaiians born on the island of Kauai in 1955. The research revealed that people can bounce back or be resilient if they had the following components: a healthy body; emotional support; psychological stability; and intelligence. In this longitudinal study Dr Werner followed the participants, who were the entire birth cohort, all of the people born on this island in one year. Her study was very important in that it was one of the first longitudinal studies that examined such a large group of people. Her most significant finding was that many of the children she followed from birth through to adulthood exhibited signs of resilience despite having had significant challenges throughout their life. Dr Werner identified a number of protective factors in the lives of these people who exhibited resilience which helped them cope when faced with stressful events and helped them balance the many risk factors they faced. These participants exhibited signs of resilience and the use of protective factors at critical periods in their life and throughout their development.

Dr Werner has won numerous awards for her work including the Recipient of the Society of Human Development Award for Distinguished Career Contributions to the Scientific Study of Life Span Development in 2005 along with being the Recipient of Distinguished Scientific Contributions to Child Development Award from the Society of Research in Child Development in 1999. In addition Dr Werner has won awards from both Harvard University and Radcliffe College as they recognized the importance of her landmark study of the children on Kauai. Dr Werner's work today includes the study of risk and resilience across the lifespan and studying children in historical context.

SEE ALSO: ▶ Resilience ▶ Social support

Wisdom

Robert J. Sternberg
Yale University

Different approaches have been taking to understanding wisdom. Wisdom has been called by different names, including, in addition to wisdom, "good work," and working for the "common good." There are three major approaches to understanding the nature of wisdom: philosophical, implicit-theoretical, and explicit-theoretical approaches. They largely have in common three attributes. First, they regard wisdom as a melding of cognitive, affective, and motivational aspects of the individual's functioning. Second, they emphasize the use of skills for some kind of positive common good. Third, they view wisdom as occurring in thought and deed, not only in thought. Wisdom is at least as much about what one does as it is about what one thinks or feels. Wisdom is a critical construct in positive psychology because it is, in the end, the use of one's repertoire of skills and dispositions for a positive common good.

Philosophical Approaches

Philosophical approaches have been reviewed by Robinson, who noted that the study of wisdom has a history that long predates psychological study, with the Platonic dialogues offering the first intensive Western analysis of the concept of wisdom. Robinson pointed out that, in these dialogues, there are three different senses of wisdom: wisdom as: a) *sophia*, which is found in those who seek a contemplative life in search of truth; b) *phronesis*, which is the kind of practical wisdom shown by statesmen and legislators; and c) *episteme*, which is found in those who understand things from a scientific point of view.

Aristotle distinguished between two kinds of wisdom: *phronesis*, the kind of practical wisdom mentioned above, and *theoretikes*, or theoretical knowledge devoted to truth. Robinson noted that, according to Aristotle, a wise individual knows more than the material, efficient, or formal causes behind events. This individual also knows the final cause, or that for the sake of which the other kinds of causes apply.

Other philosophical conceptions of wisdom have followed up on the early Greek approaches. For example, an early Christian view emphasized the importance of a life lived in pursuit of divine and absolute truth. To this day, most religions aim for wisdom through an understanding not just of the material world, but also of the spiritual world and its relationship to the material world. Not all religions search for absolute truth, however. In some matters, it is not clear any such truth exists.

Implicit-Theoretical Approaches

Implicit-theoretical approaches to wisdom have in common the search for an understanding of people's folk conceptions of what wisdom is. Thus, the goal is not to provide a "psychologically true" account of wisdom, but rather an account that is true with respect to people's beliefs, whether these beliefs are right or wrong. Implicit theories have been comprehensively reviewed by Bluck and Glück.

Holliday and Chandler used an implicit-theories approach to understanding wisdom. Approximately 500 participants were studied across a series of experiments. The investigators were interested in determining whether the concept of wisdom could be understood as a prototype, or central concept. Principal-components analysis of one of their studies revealed five underlying factors: exceptional understanding; judgment and communication skills; general competence; interpersonal skills; and social unobtrusiveness.

Sternberg has reported a series of studies investigating implicit theories of wisdom. In one study, 200 professors each of art, business, philosophy, and physics were asked to rate how characteristic were the behaviors obtained in a prestudy from the corresponding population with respect to the professors' ideal conception of each of an ideally wise, intelligent, or creative individual in their occupation.

Laypersons were also asked to provide these ratings but for a hypothetical ideal individual without regard to occupation. Correlations were computed across the three ratings. In each group except philosophy, the highest correlation was between wisdom and intelligence; in philosophy, the highest correlation was between intelligence and creativity. The correlations between wisdom and intelligence ratings ranged from .42 to .78 with a median of .68. For all groups, the lowest correlation was between wisdom and creativity. Correlations between wisdom and creativity ratings ranged from −.24 to .48 with a median of .27. The only negative correlation (−.24) was for ratings of professors of business.

In a second study, 40 college students were asked to sort three sets of 40 behaviors each into as many or as few piles as they wished. The 40 behaviors in each set were the top-rated wisdom, intelligence, and creativity behaviors from the previous study. The sortings then each were subjected to nonmetric multi-dimensional scaling. For wisdom, six components emerged: *reasoning ability; sagacity; learning from ideas and environment; judgment; expeditious use of information;* and *perspicacity.*

Examples of behaviors showing high loadings under each of these six components were "has the unique ability to look at a problem or situation and solve it," "has good problem-solving ability," and "has a logical mind" for reasoning ability; "displays concern for others," "considers advice," and "understands people through dealing with a variety of people" for sagacity; "attaches importance to ideas," "is perceptive," and "learns from other people's mistakes" for learning from ideas and environment; "acts within own physical and intellectual limitations," "is sensible," and "has good judgment at all times" for judgment; "is experienced," "seeks out information, especially details," "has age, maturity, or long experience" for expeditious use of information; and "has intuition," "can offer solutions that are on the side of right and truth," "is able to see through things – read between the lines" for perspicacity.

In this same study, components for intelligence were: *practical problem-solving ability; verbal ability; intellectual balance and integration; goal orientation and attainment; contextual intelligence;* and *fluid thought.* Components for creativity were: *nonentrenchment; integration and intellectuality; aesthetic taste and imagination; decisional skill and flexibility; perspicacity; drive for accomplishment and recognition; inquisitiveness;* and *intuition.*

In a third study, 50 adults were asked to rate descriptions of hypothetical individuals for intelligence, creativity, and wisdom. Correlations were computed between pairs of ratings of the hypothetical individuals' levels of the three traits. Correlations between the ratings were .94 for wisdom and intelligence, .62 for wisdom and creativity, and .69 for intelligence and creativity, again suggesting that wisdom and intelligence are highly correlated in people's implicit theories.

Yang studied wisdom among 616 Taiwanese Chinese people. She found four factors of wisdom: competencies and knowledge; benevolence and compassion; openness and profundity; and modesty and unobtrusiveness. Similar factors were obtained by Takayama in a study of implicit theories of wisdom among Japanese men and women of widely varying ages. The four factors that emerged were knowledge and education, understanding and judgment, sociability and interpersonal relationships, and an introspective attitude.

Takahashi and Bordia compared implicit theories of wisdom in Australian, Indian, and Japanese participants. They found identical factors for American and Australian groups. For them, the adjective *wise* was semantically most similar to *experienced* and *knowledgeable*. It was least similar to *discreet*. The ideal self, among this group, was characterized as knowledgeable and wise. In contrast, being aged and discreet were seen as quite undesirable. The Indian and Japanese adults, in contrast, viewed *wise* as semantically closest to *discreet*, followed by *aged* and *experienced*. The Japanese saw being wise and discreet as most desirable, and being knowledgeable was seen as much less desirable. In all four cultural groups, being wise was seen as extremely desirable, but being aged was seen as being extremely undesirable. So none of the groups of young people wanted to be old!

Montgomery, Barber, and McKee asked six older people to characterize wisdom in their lives. Six attributes emerged from their study. These attributes were giving guidance, having knowledge, having experience, having moral principles, and engaging in compassionate relationships. In a related study, Sowarka found that narratives of wise people emphasized their ability to solve problems through the use of novel and efficacious strategies.

Explicit-Theoretical Approaches

Explicit theories are constructions of (supposedly) expert theorists and researchers rather than of laypeople. In the study of wisdom, most explicit-theoretical approaches are based on constructs from the psychology of human development.

Some scholars define wisdom in ways that suggest it is a property of increasing maturity. Birren and Fisher, for example, defined wisdom as "the integration of the affective, motivational, and cognitive aspects of human abilities in response to life's tasks and problems" (1990, p. 326). This definition reflects not only psychological approaches to wisdom, but historical approaches as well. Wisdom is a balance between the opposing valences of intense emotion and detachment, action and inaction, and knowledge and doubts. *It tends to increase with experience and therefore age but is not exclusively found in old age* (Birren & Fisher, 1990). In many views, some degree of age is, at best, a necessary but not sufficient condition for the development of wisdom.

Taranto offered another view of wisdom, based on a thorough review of the literature. She defined wisdom as the recognition and response of the individual to human limitation. A related view is that of McKee and Barber, who defined wisdom as seeing through illusion. Brugman defined it as expertise in uncertainty. On this view, wisdom involves cognitive, affective, and behavioral components.

Brugman believes that wisdom goes hand in hand with increasing doubt and uncertainty regarding the comprehensibility of reality.

Ardelt has proposed a somewhat more complex view. She has defined wisdom as involving three components: the cognitive ability to see truth or reality as it actually is; reflectivity, in becoming aware of and transcending one's subjectivity and projections; and empathy and compassion for others. Kant, in the *Critique of Pure Reason,* took a different view, stating that people could not see truth or reality as it actually is, but only as it is filtered by their senses.

The most extensive program of research has been that conducted by the late Paul Baltes and his colleagues. For example, Baltes and Smith gave adult participants life-management problems, such as "A fourteen-year-old girls is pregnant. What should she, what should one, consider and do?" and "A fifteen-year-old girl wants to marry soon. What should she, what should one, consider and do?" Baltes and Smith tested a five-component model on participants' protocols in answering these and other questions, based on a notion of wisdom as expert knowledge about fundamental life matters or of wisdom as good judgment and advice in important but uncertain matters of life. Wisdom is reflected in these five components: *rich factual knowledge* (general and specific knowledge about the conditions of life and its variations); *rich procedural knowledge* (general and specific knowledge about strategies of judgment and advice concerning matters of life); *lifespan contextualism* (knowledge about the contexts of life and their temporal [developmental] relationships); *relativism* (knowledge about differences in values, goals, and priorities); and *uncertainty* (knowledge about the relative indeterminacy and unpredictability of life and ways to manage).

Three kinds of factors – general person factors, expertise-specific factors, and facilitative experiential contexts – are proposed to facilitate wise judgments. These factors are used in life planning, life management, and life review. An expert answer should reflect more of these components, whereas a novice answer should reflect fewer of them. The data collected to date generally have been supportive of the model.

Over time, Baltes and his colleagues collected a wide range of data showing the empirical utility of the proposed theoretical and measurement approaches to wisdom. For example, Staudinger, Lopez and Baltes found that measures of intelligence and personality as well as their interface overlap with but are non-identical to measures of wisdom in terms of constructs measured. Staudinger, Smith, and Baltes showed that human-services professionals outperformed a control group on wisdom-related tasks. In a further set of studies, Staudinger and Baltes found that performance settings that were ecologically relevant to the lives of their participants and that provided for actual or "virtual" interaction of minds increased wisdom-related performance substantially.

Sternberg also proposed an explicit theory, suggesting that the development of wisdom can be traced to six antecedent components: 1) knowledge, including an understanding of its presuppositions and meaning as well as its limitations; 2) processes, including an understanding of what problems should be solved automatically and what problems should not be so solved; 3) a judicial thinking style, characterized by the desire to judge and evaluate things in an in-depth way; 4) personality, including tolerance of ambiguity and of the role of obstacles in life; 5) motivation, especially the motivation to understand what is known and what it means; and 6) environmental context, involving an appreciation of the contextual factors in the environment that lead to various kinds of thoughts and actions.

Whereas that theory specified a set of *antecedents* of wisdom, the balance theory proposed by Sternberg specified the *processes* (balancing of interests and of responses to environmental contexts) in relation to the *goal* of wisdom (achievement of a common good). This theory is incorporated into the balance theory as specifying antecedent sources of developmental and individual differences, as discussed later.

According to the balance theory, wisdom is the application of intelligence, creativity, and knowledge as mediated by values toward the achievement of a common good through a balance among intrapersonal, interpersonal, and extrapersonal interests, over the short and long terms, in order to achieve a balance among adaptation to existing environments, shaping of existing environments, and selection of new environments.

What kinds of considerations might be included under each of the three kinds of interests? Intrapersonal interests might include the desire to enhance one's popularity or prestige, to make more money, to learn more, to increase one's spiritual well-being, to increase one's power, and so forth. Interpersonal interests might be quite similar, except as they apply to other people rather than oneself. Extrapersonal interests might include contributing to the welfare of one's school, helping one's community, contributing to the well-being of one's country, or serving God, and so forth. Different people balance these interests in different ways. At one extreme, a malevolent dictator might emphasize his or her own personal power and wealth; at the other extreme, a saint might emphasize only serving others and God.

What constitutes appropriate balancing of interests, an appropriate response to the environment, and even the common good, all hinge on values. Values, therefore, are an integral part of wise thinking. The question arises as to "whose values?" Although different major religions and other widely accepted systems of values may differ in details, they seem to have in common certain universal values, such as respect for human life, honesty, sincerity, fairness, and enabling people to fulfill their potential. Of course, not every government or society has subscribed to such values. Hitler's Germany and Stalin's Russia blatantly did not, and most societies today only subscribe to them in some degree but not fully.

On this view, people may be smart but not wise. People who are smart but not wise exhibit one or more of the following fallacies in thinking: *egocentrism* – thinking that the whole world revolves around them; *omniscience* – thinking they know everything; *omnipotence* – thinking they can do whatever they want; *invulnerability* – thinking they can get away with anything; and *unrealistic optimism*.

Some theorists have viewed wisdom in terms of post-formal-operational thinking, thereby viewing wisdom as extending beyond the Piagetian stages of intelligence. Wisdom thus might be a stage of thought beyond Piagetian formal operations. For example, some authors have argued that wise individuals are those who can think reflectively or dialectically, in the latter case with the individuals' realizing that truth is not always absolute but rather evolves in an historical context of theses, antitheses, and syntheses. Consider a very brief review of some specific dialectical approaches.

Kitchener and Brenner suggested that wisdom requires a synthesis of knowledge from opposing points of view. Similarly, Labouvie-Vief has emphasized the importance of a smooth and balanced dialogue between logical forms of processing and more subjective forms of processing. Pascual-Leone has argued for the importance of the dialectical integration of all aspects of a person's affect, cognition, conation (motivation), and life experience. Similarly, Orwoll and Perlmutter have emphasized the importance to wisdom of an integration of cognition with affect. Kramer has suggested the importance of the integration of relativistic and dialectical modes of thinking, affect, and reflection. And Birren and Fisher, putting together a number of views of wisdom, have suggested as well the importance of the integration of cognitive, motivational, and affective aspects of human abilities.

Other theorists have suggested the importance of knowing the limits of one's own extant knowledge and of then trying to go beyond it. For example, Meacham has suggested that an important aspect of wisdom is an awareness of one's own fallibility and the knowledge of what one does and does not know. Kitchener and Brenner have also emphasized the importance of knowing the limitations of one's own knowledge. Arlin has linked wisdom to problem finding, the first step of which is the recognition that how one currently defines a problem may be inadequate. Arlin views problem finding as a possible stage of post-formal operational thinking. Such a view is not necessarily inconsistent with the view of dialectical thinking as such a post-formal-operational stage. Dialectical thinking and problem finding could represent distinct post-formal-operational stages, or two manifestations of the same post-formal-operational stage.

Although most developmental approaches to wisdom are ontogenetic, Csikszentmihalyi and Rathunde have taken a philogenetic or evolutionary approach, arguing that constructs such as wisdom must have been selected for over time, at least in a cultural sense. In other words, wise ideas should survive better over time than unwise ideas in a culture. The theorists define wisdom as having three basic dimensions of meaning: that of a cognitive process, or a particular way of obtaining and processing information; that of a virtue, or socially valued pattern of behavior; and that of a good, or a personally desirable state or condition.

Future research is needed especially on how we can teach children to think wisely and how theories of wisdom can be applied in important everyday life decisions, at the personal as well as the professional level. Many leaders are knowledgeable and even intelligent, but not wise. Schools might take greater responsibility for ensuring the leaders they prepare will be in a position to make decisions that reflect not only immediate concerns, but the long-term common good.

SEE ALSO: ▶ Character strengths (VIA)   ▶ Civic responsibility and virtues ▶ Moral judgment   ▶ Strengths perspective (positive psychology)   ▶ Virtues

Reference

Birren, J. E., & Fisher, L. M. (1990). Conceptualizing wisdom: The primacy of affect-cognition relations. In R. J. Sternberg (Ed.), *Wisdom: Its nature, origins, and development* (pp. 317–332). New York: Cambridge University Press.

Wrzesniewski, Amy

Paul Rozin[a] and Jane Dutton[b]
[a]*University of Pennsylvania;* [b]*University of Michigan*

Amy Wrzesniewski is a great exemplar of positive psychology. Amy was part of the first generation in her family to get a college degree. She is now an associate professor at Yale University and is one of the leading figures in the study of work from a positive psychology perspective. She has contributed to our understanding of how work, the major waking activity of human beings, can be a meaningful and positive experience.

Amy began psychological research with Paul Rozin in her sophomore year of college. This led to a three-year collaboration that generated five different published papers, on four different topics. Amy showed an incredible aptitude to study productive topics, and to mobilize the world to assist in her research. Her crowning achievement as an undergraduate was her honors thesis, on a topic that she formulated to reflect her already deep interest in the nature of work. The thesis was sponsored by three faculty members (Clark McCauley, Barry Schwartz, and Rozin), and was a major advance in understanding work: It demonstrated that individuals' conceptions of their own work (their work orientations) could be easily classified into one of jobs, careers, and callings. It also showed that even in the same jobs, done within the same organizations, work could be framed as a job, career, or calling by different individuals. This important finding became the launching pad for what is likely to become a distinguished career in the study of work.

Her dissertation work, conducted at the University of Michigan in Organizational Psychology, tested how individuals' work orientations affect how unemployed workers search for jobs and how these search behaviors affect their rates of reemployment. Her findings demonstrated that work orientation shapes both the reemployment goals and outcomes found during a period of unemployment in different ways; while job-oriented job seekers look to replace an income stream, the career-oriented aim to advance in their standing in the new job, while the calling-oriented seek to find meaningful work above all else. Her dissertation is part of a high-impact stream of work on how individuals construct meaning at work. Her unique focus has been on individuals as active crafters of their jobs and the results that follow. She has studied hospital cleaners and how they craft their work as a calling and, in the process, provide competent caring for patients and patients' families. Amy has also helped researchers understand the interpersonal bases of work meaning. She has developed a model of work meaning that is based on a process of interpersonal sensemaking. With this work she is effectively tying together ideas of interactional dynamics, sensemaking, meaning and identity. She is bringing this work to life in several empirical studies of new job incumbents, telecommuters and hospital cleaners. Amy has been a major bridge-builder between positive psychology and the more organizationally-focused positive organizational scholarship. As a pioneer and bridge-builder, her work will have lasting impact on how positive psychology builds new insights into the difference that work makes in peoples' lives.

SEE ALSO: ▶ Calling ▶ Career development ▶ Employee engagement ▶ Job satisfaction ▶ Positive organizational behavior ▶ Positive organizational scholarship

Name Index

Subject Index

Note: page numbers in **bold** indicate main entries.